Theo van Gogh

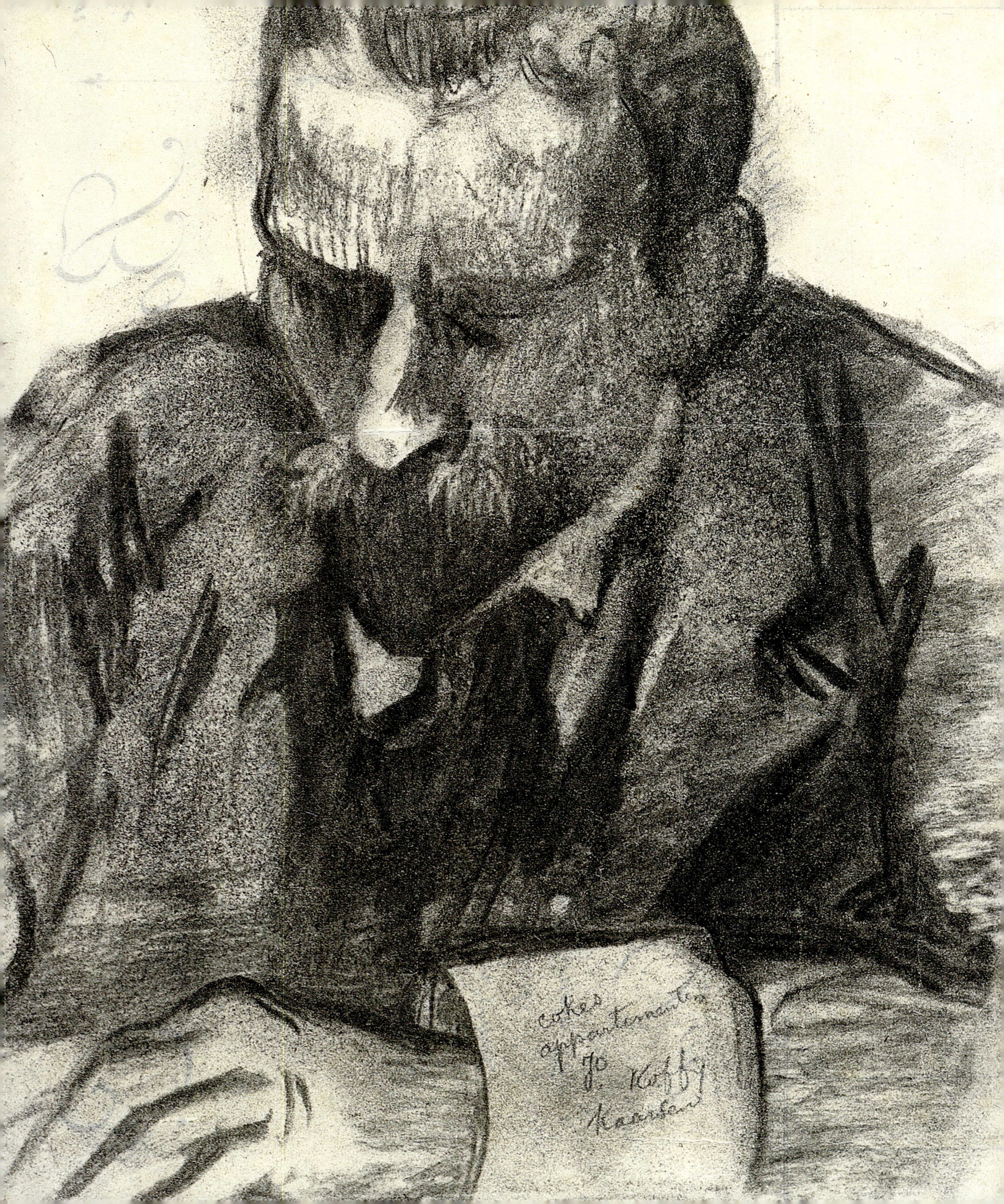
cokes
Koffy
Kaarsen

Theo van Gogh 1857–1891

Art dealer, collector and brother of Vincent

Chris Stolwijk and Richard Thomson

with a contribution by Sjraar van Heugten

Van Gogh Museum, Amsterdam
Waanders Publishers, Zwolle

Dear Theo,

'I've just posted you a package with
5 large pen and ink drawings...
Please write and let me know if they arrive safely.
They started a row with me again at the post office
because it was too big... but they took it in the end,
much to my satisfaction.'

Vincent, 13 July 1888

Sponsor's foreword

Holland is a small country: foreigners travel through it without even having to stop for petrol. I have met some who thought that Copenhagen or Brussels was the Dutch capital. The Netherlands is a boggy marshland, the gift of several large rivers, which for a large part lies below sea level. This is basically the image that outsiders have of this country: windmills and Hans Brinker with his finger in the dike.

Despite the fact that the Dutch tend to assign themselves an important role on the world stage, in reality their influence is limited. And, how could this be otherwise for a country with a population equal to that of São Paulo or Shanghai?

Yet there are areas in which the Netherlands has exerted considerable influence. One of these was art. Painters such as Rembrandt and Vermeer have become world famous, their pictures engraved in the minds of billions of people.

To the list of internationally renowned artists a third Dutch painter may certainly be added, namely Vincent van Gogh. The unique vision of the world embodied in his paintings radically altered our views of art. At the moment Van Gogh is extraordinarily popular, not only among a select group of connoisseurs, but foremost among the general public. More than a million people visited the Van Gogh Museum in 1997, a number surpassed in the Netherlands only by the Rijksmuseum.

It is striking that almost everything we know about Vincent van Gogh is derived from the correspondence between Vincent and his brother Theo. This fact alone justifies an exhibition on Theo van Gogh, an exhibition that also gains importance from the leading role he played in the European art world in the last quarter of the previous century. A more worthy opening of the new exhibition wing of the Van Gogh Museum is hardly conceivable.

The Theo van Gogh exhibition and the Van Gogh Museum with its new wing stand for allure and innovation, for daring and quality. TNT Post Group stands for these very same qualities. The central place occupied by the exchange of letters between Theo and Vincent in this exhibition made it virtually inevitable that TPG should act as a sponsor. As a business operating worldwide with roots in mail delivery, we were naturally drawn to this exhibition. I hope you enjoy it.

A.J. Scheepbouwer
Chairman of the Board of Management TPG

To the reader

The illustration numbers are given in the text in bold between square brackets: **[1]**. *The works from the Van Gogh Museum belong to the Vincent van Gogh Foundation.*
Van Gogh's letters are taken from: De brieven van Vincent van Gogh, *ed. Han Crimpen and Monique Berends-Albert, 4 vols., Amsterdam 1990. The new and old letter numbers are placed in the text between square brackets:* [744/573].
The b-numbers in the notes refer to archival *sources (largely family correspondence). These are kept in the Van Gogh Museum, Amsterdam (Vincent van Gogh Foundation).*

Contents

Theo van Gogh

Foreword

Theo van Gogh is chiefly known as the self-effacing yet amiable younger brother of Vincent van Gogh. But Theo was more than simply the brother who provided Vincent with the means to develop as an artist: he supported other painters, collected art and tirelessly devoted himself to promoting other artists in his capacity as an art dealer.

While working for the Parisian art dealers Goupil & Cie. – from 1884 Boussod, Valadon & Cie. – Theo found himself at the heart of the French art world in the 1880s. He dealt on a daily basis in best-selling art, by artists such as members of the Barbizon School, and works by innovative painters such as Edgar Degas, Paul Gauguin, Claude Monet and Camille Pissarro. Artists and collectors respected the young Dutch art dealer for his insight and integrity. Paul Gauguin described Theo's death in 1891 as an irretrievable loss.

Although Theo was not an artist himself, his legacy is highly visible. Without Theo's efforts as an art dealer and collector the Van Gogh Museum would not exist; other collections – both public and private – would also be considerably leaner. The Van Gogh Museum therefore decided that the time was ripe to honour his life and work with an exhibition.

The exhibition *Theo van Gogh* (1857-1891)*: art dealer, collector and brother of Vincent* is a homage to the man whose activities meant so much to the propagation of modern art, to his brother Vincent and the Van Gogh Museum. With the opening of the exhibition the museum will inaugurate its new exhibition wing, the 'little brother' to Gerrit Rietveld's renovated building.

Using works in various media by a range of artists, and documentation never previously displayed, the *Theo van Gogh* exhibition will provide a unique survey of Theo's life, and a lively portrait of European painting in the second half of the 19th century.

The exhibition was prepared by a team that was initially led by the museum's former director Ronald de Leeuw, and, from spring 1997, his successor John Leighton. The organisational side was handled by Andreas Blühm, with the support of Martine Kilburn, Aly Noordermeer, Sandra Sihan, Sara Verboven and Roelie Zwikker.

Researcher Chris Stolwijk was responsible for the bulk of the research. It is largely thanks to his tremendous dedication that we now have so much information available, enabling us to form a picture of Theo van Gogh's life and work. Valuable contributions were made by trainees Thomas Macsotay Bunt and Melissande Lips; as well as Monique Hageman, Leo Jansen, Hans Luijten, Fieke Pabst, Benno Tempel and Louis van Tilborgh. Richard Thomson, Watson Gordon Professor of Fine Art at the University of Edinburgh and a major authority on 19th-century French art, assisted in the preparation of the exhibition as an outside expert. His knowledge and experience proved indispensable.

The Van Gogh Museum is particularly delighted to have the Réunion des Musées Nationaux/Musée d'Orsay, Paris, as partners in the exhibition's organisation. This collaboration was highly constructive and will allow the French public to be introduced to Theo in the Musée d'Orsay. Irène Bizot, Anne Fréling, Anne de Margerie, Ute Collinet and Bénédicte Boissonas organised the exhibition in Paris for the Réunion des Musées Nationaux. Monique Nonne, of the Musée d'Orsay, compiled the French exhibition.

On behalf of the authors we would like to thank the following people for their cooperation: Alexander Apsis, Richard Armstrong, Joseph Baillio, Damien Bartoli, Edwin Becker, Michael Bing, Monique A. Bodmer, Aimee Brown Price, Anne Bury, Elly Cassee, Robert Clémentz, Stephane Cosman Connery, Amanda Corriero, Tim Craven, Jean-Pierre Cuzin, Götz Czymmek, Chris Dercon, Anne Distel, Miranda and Robert Donneley, Bianca Doria, Christopher Drake, Douglas Druick, Ann Mara Dugourd, Caroline Durand-Ruel Godfroy, Philippe Durey, Sarah Faunce, Jan Piet Filedt Kok, Walter Feilchenfeldt, Michael Findlay, Frances Fowle, Claire Fons, Carol Forman Tabler, Ann Friedman, Mario Garibaldi, Kate Garmeson, Thomas H. Gibson, Franck Giraud, George R. Goldner, J.M. de Groot, Beth Ann Guynn, Marcus Halliwel, Anne d'Harnoncourt, Colin Harrison, Ernst Haverkamp, Freek Heijbroek, William J. Hennessey, Sarah Herring, Ay-Whang Hsia, Naoya Inoue, Catherine Johnston, Richard Kendall, Gillian M. Kinloch, Dorothy Kosinski, Peter Kort Zegers, Ling Ling Kuo, Geneviève Lacambre, Hélène Lafont-Couturier, Jean-Marc Léri, Marie-Josée Linou, Irvin M. Lippman, Stephanie Maison, Melissa De Medeiros, Pierre Miquel, Philippe de Montebello, Michael Pantazzi, Julee Pearson, Nicholas Penny, Claude Pétry, Joachim Pissarro, Lionel Pissarro, Sandrine Pissarro, Griselda Pollock, Earl A. Powell III, Jussi Pylkkänen, Alain Richarme, Joseph Rishel, Michael Schlossberg, Robert Schmit, Michel Schulman, George T.M. Schackelford, Karin Siden, Marianne S. Simpson, Anne-Berit Skaug, Annette Stabell, Theodore E. Stebbins Jr., Susan Alyson Stein, Evert van Straaten, Anna Swinbourne, Virginia Tandy, Belinda Thomson, Gary Tinterow, Diane Upright, Roxanna Vélásquez Martinez del Campo, Marije Vellekoop, Aukje Vergeest, Anita Vriend, Martha Ward, Neil Watson, Bogomila Welsh-Ovcharov, Gabriel P. Weisberg, Eliane de Wilde, Edward Wilson, Juliet Wilson-Bareau, Wim de Wit, B. Woelderink, Scott Wolff, James N. Wood, Johannes van der Wolk, Gerhard Wurzer and Eric M. Zafran. Pierre-Lin Renié deserves a special word of thanks for helping to research works in the Musée Goupil in Bordeaux.

The following organisations offered assistance during research into the life and work of Theo van Gogh: Archives de la Ville de Bruxelles (Brussels), Archives Générales du Royaume (Brussels), Bibliothèque Nationale de France (Paris), Bibliothèque Royale Albert I (Brussels), Christie's London, Christie's New York, Gemeentearchief Dordrecht, Gemeentearchief Tilburg, The Getty Research Institute for the History of Art and the Humanities (Los Angeles), M. Knoedler & Co. (New York), Musée Goupil (Bordeaux), The National Gallery (London), The National Gallery of Scotland (Edinburgh), The National Library of Scotland (Edinburgh), Phillips (London), Regionaal Archief West-Brabant (Zevenbergen), Rijksbureau voor Kunsthistorische Documentatie (The Hague), Rijksprentenkabinet (Amsterdam), Service de Documentation du Musée d'Orsay (Paris), Sotheby's London, Sotheby's New York, and the Streekarchief Langs Aa en Dommel (Den Bosch).

The Van Gogh Museum would like to thank its sponsor TNT Post Group N.V., whose generous donation helped make this exhibition possible.

The Dutch ministry of Education, Culture and Science provided the indemnity for the exhibition in Amsterdam.

Without the enthusiastic cooperation of many museums and private collections this exhibition could not have been arranged. We are therefore particularly grateful to everyone who loaned works for their willingness to contribute to this homage to Theo van Gogh.

John Leighton
Director, Van Gogh Museum

Henri Loyrette
Director, Musée d'Orsay

Introduction

Theo van Gogh shares the lot of many a relative of famous figures. For more than a century he has been overshadowed by his brother, Vincent. He is known only as the painter's brother. Yet Theo had a noteworthy life and career. As an art dealer, collector and as Vincent's brother he made an important contribution to art history. This book, published together with the exhibition *Theo van Gogh* (1857-1891)*: art dealer, collector and brother of Vincent*, highlights for the first time the life and work of Theo van Gogh.

The Van Gogh Museum thus directs attention to an influential connoisseur of art, who, as dealer and collector, played a not insignificant part in Europe's cultural capital during one of the most turbulent periods in the history of art – Paris in the 1880s. From 1881 Theo was manager of the Paris branch Boussod, Valadon & Cie. (formerly Goupil & Cie.) at 19, Boulevard Montmartre.

The Van Gogh Museum, which exists thanks to Theo, is happy to have this opportunity of paying him its respects. After all, the core of the museum's collection, which includes the largest number of Vincent's works in the world, was made by Theo van Gogh. After considerable travels, this collection, via Theo's widow, Johanna van Gogh-Bonger and their son Vincent Willem van Gogh, reached its final destination in Amsterdam. In this sense, the Van Gogh Museum has been remembering the work of Theo van Gogh as a collector, with its permanent exhibition since 1973.

An exhibition dedicated to an art dealer (and collector) is no everyday occurrence. However, this show in honour of Theo van Gogh fits into a series of exhibitions held over the past few years that have taken the business of art dealing and collecting as their topic. There was the show entitled *Daniel-Henry Kahnweiler: marchand, éditeur, écrivain*, held at Paris's Centre Pompidou in 1984-85, and there was the show exploring the art dealer J.H. de Bois (1878–1946) at the Rijksmuseum in Amsterdam in 1993. Running more or less simultaneously with the show in the Van Gogh Museum, the Rijksmuseum will present an overview of the business activities of Elbert Jan van Wisselingh (1848-1912), a former colleague of Theo van Gogh's.

Theo died on 25 January 1891 at the early age of 33. He was deeply mourned by a small circle of friends, acquaintances and colleagues. The artist Paul Gauguin recalled the Dutch art dealer as the one person who had made an effort to build up a group of clients for his (Gauguin's) as yet little-known or regarded paintings. The artist Camille Pissarro described Theo as a 'devoted friend,' while the avant-garde critic Albert Aurier spoke of him as a 'sympathetic and intelligent expert,' who had been a significant figure for modern art.

Theo's reputation as an art dealer was soon forgotten. Not until 1973 did John Rewald publish the first study dealing with Theo van Gogh's activities. In the spirit of the time, he limited himself in his important article, entitled 'Theo van Gogh, Goupil and the impressionists,' to a discussion of Theo's dealings in modern artworks from the 1880s. As Rewald saw it, Theo refrained from dealing with the more popular contemporary art by famous figures such as William-Adolphe Bougereau or Jean-Léon Gérôme, or by the masters of the Barbizon School. Consciously acting against the wishes of his superiors at Boussod, Valadon & Cie., Theo made every effort to promote the work of artists who at that time were considered (too) avant-garde and were therefore underrated. Interestingly, these very artists have turned out to be pioneer figures in modern art. In Rewald's view, Theo, like his brother Vincent, was far ahead of his time.

Such an opinion is understandable but misleading. A balanced picture of the art of the day in general, and the contribution made by Theo van Gogh as a member of the staff of a prestigious French art dealer's in particular, can only be given when both traditional and more avant-garde types of art production are valued in the same way. After all, both existed side by side. As such, they both form part of the history of 19th-century art.

In this book we sought to give a fuller picture of the life and work of Theo van Gogh, and so have departed from the relatively narrowly defined paths of modern art (read: impressionism). The book presents the life and work of Theo van Gogh, seen in the context of the French art market. The emphasis lies on the years 1881–90, when Theo was in charge of the branch on the Boulevard Montmartre. Naturally, his formative years as a young dealer in Brussels and The Hague are also discussed.

Using the records of sales from Goupil & Cie. (The Getty Reserach Institute for the History of Art and the Humanities, Los Angeles) an effort was made to trace *all* the works of art Theo van Gogh bought and sold – in contrast to the research carried out by Rewald. Next, in preparation for the exhibition, those artworks were selected that could be described as representative for Theo's efforts as an art dealer. An important criterion when making this primary selection was that the pieces had either been exhibited or handled by Theo himself. We have also tried to include work by artists who played an important part in Theo's day-to-day business. Thus we have included paintings and drawings by less well-known figures, beside the work of famous modern artists.

Every effort has been made to present the complete breadth of Theo's activities as an art dealer. He dealt not only with contemporary paintings. Visitors to his shop on the Boulevard Montmartre had plenty to choose from: there were paintings and drawings, watercolours, pastels, graphic works and sculptures. The artworks included in this exhibition were never exhibited by Theo as one group. Nevertheless, as different as they are, and originating in all corners of the globe, they create a picture of Theo's work which is authentic, lively and panoramic. They reflect the many aspects of art production in the 1880s.

Diversity is also the hallmark of Theo's collection. Despite limited means he managed to build up a large collection of contemporary art of varying quality. He owned several works by impressionists, an important group of paintings, drawings and etchings by notable avant-garde artists, and various pieces by artists whose names are now forgotten. Works from Theo's collection by artists other than Vincent were on view to the Dutch public for the first time in 1953 (and in 1960) in an exhibition entitled *De verzameling van Theo van Gogh*. The present exhibition is a clear sequel to these. However, here a prominent place has also been given to works by Vincent that held a special significance for his brother Theo.

Among both artists and art connoisseurs Theo van Gogh was known as a sensitive and honourable art dealer, and a professional in his business. Friends and family speak warmly of his 'loving nature.' Shortly before his death in July 1890 Vincent wrote to Theo that he was not a 'run-of-the-mill Corot dealer,' and rather than being a calculating businessman, he let his heart rule his judgment. The exhibition and this book honour the life and work of Theo van Gogh: an influential art dealer, a passionate collector, and loving brother of the famous Vincent.

Chris Stolwijk and Andreas Blühm

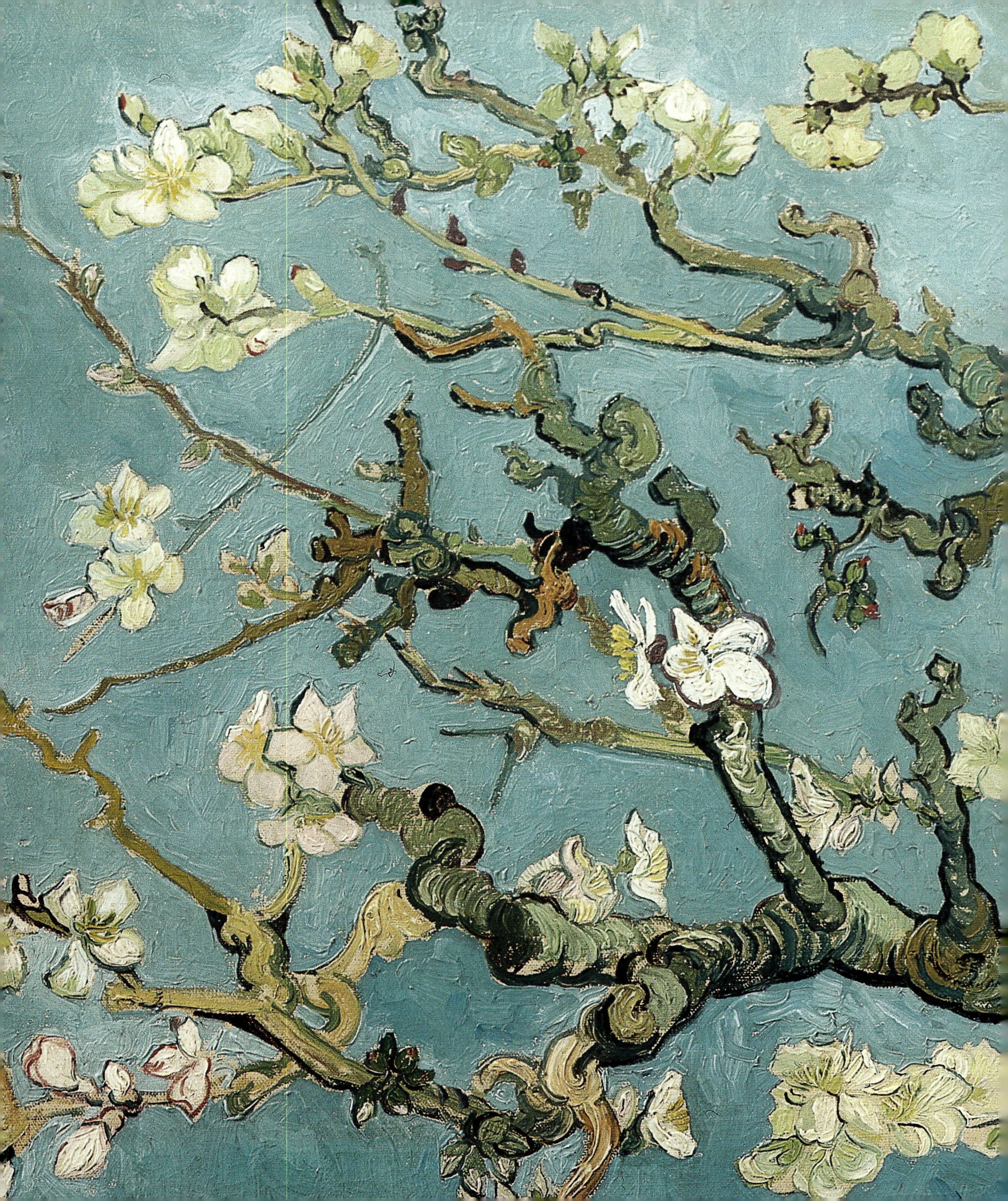

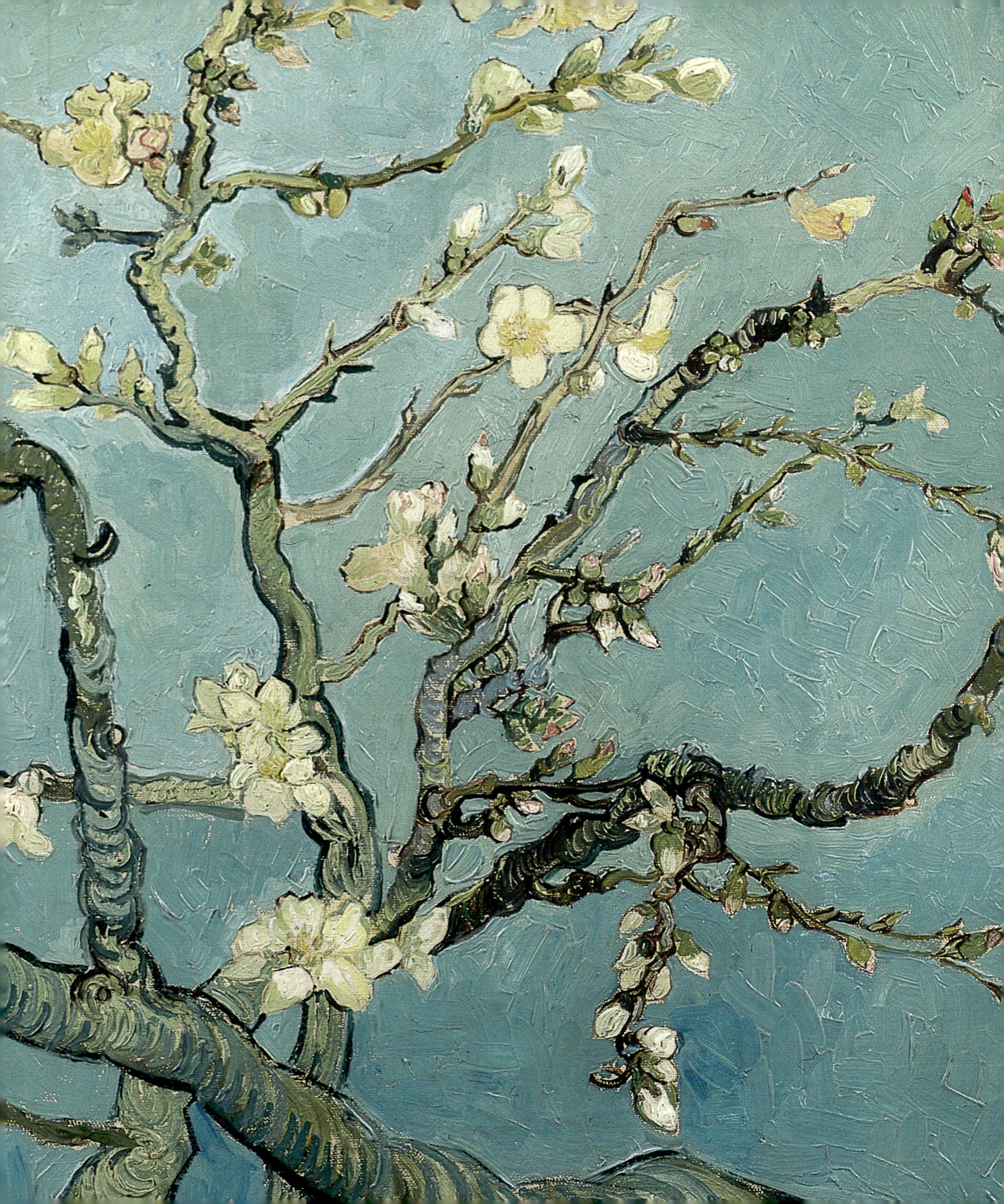

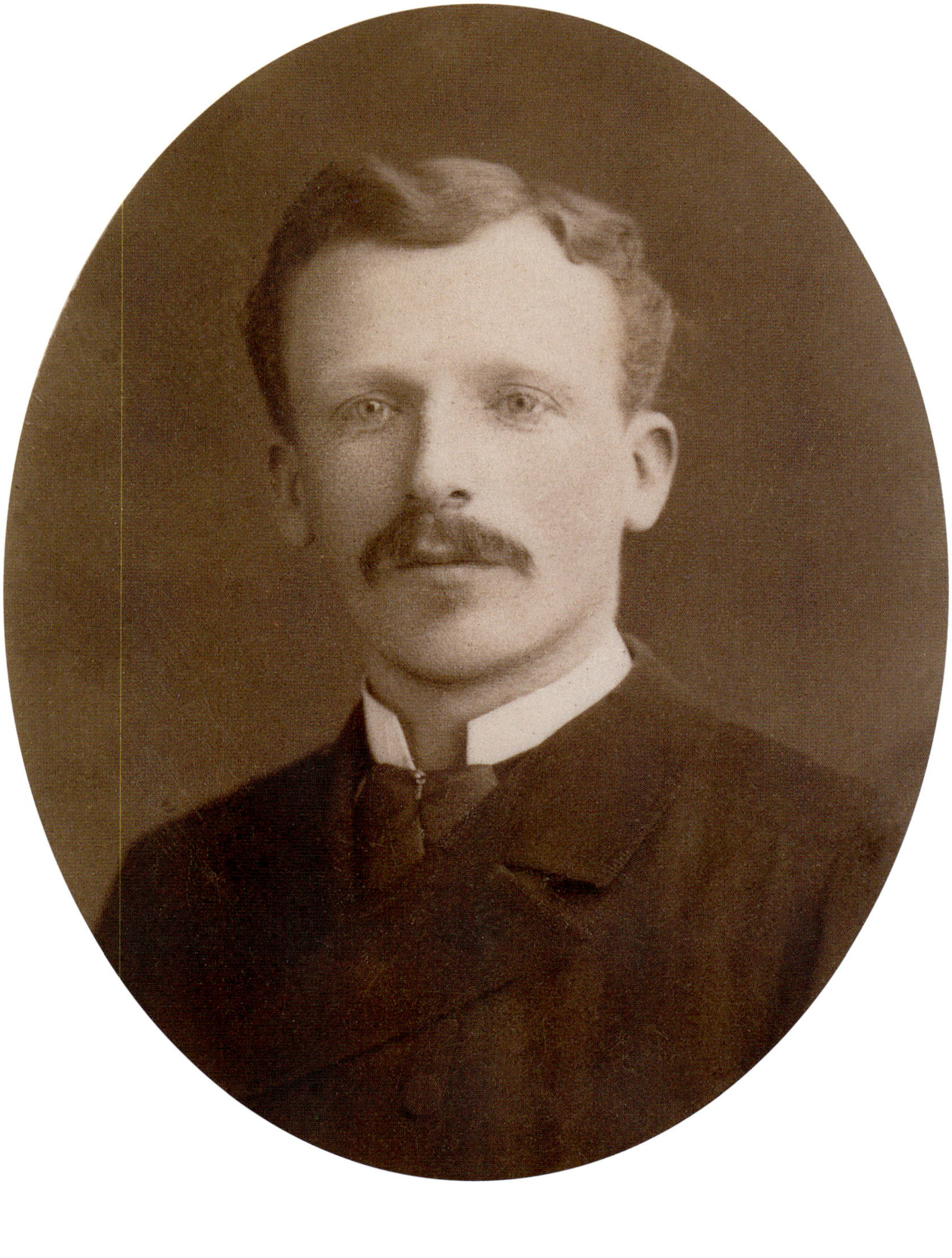

1
Theo van Gogh in 1889

A life

Theo van Gogh

Chris Stolwijk

Ossip Zadkine's impressive monument, entitled *De gebroeders Van Gogh*,[1] was officially unveiled in Zundert's main square by her majesty Queen Juliana of the Netherlands on 28 May 1964. The bronze statue shows the brothers in a fond embrace, the two bodies melting into one. [2] It depicts their symbiotic relationship, expressing unconditional love and self-sacrifice. Their lives, and their sudden deaths within six months of one another – Vincent on 29 July 1890 and Theo on 25 January 1891 – provided the perfect breeding ground for this symbolism.

This interpretation of Theo and Vincent has a long history. The key to its meaning lies in the reception of modern art, and more specifically in the reception of Van Gogh's work in the late 19th and early 20th centuries.[2] At that time artists and critics were fighting for the cause of modern art and therefore felt the need to express their views in bellicose terms. Armed with literary weapons derived from the language of warfare, the 'moderns' attacked traditional ideas of art and art forms, giving metaphors like 'battle,' 'heroism,' 'sacrifice,' 'tragedy' and 'immortality' a prominent place in contemporary art criticism. These were the terms used to describe modernism's arduous crusade. In his description of Van Gogh, the critic Boele van Hensbroek went so far as to compare him to a knight, 'sans peur et sans reproche,' killed in action while fighting for the good cause (impressionism). Theo, who had been

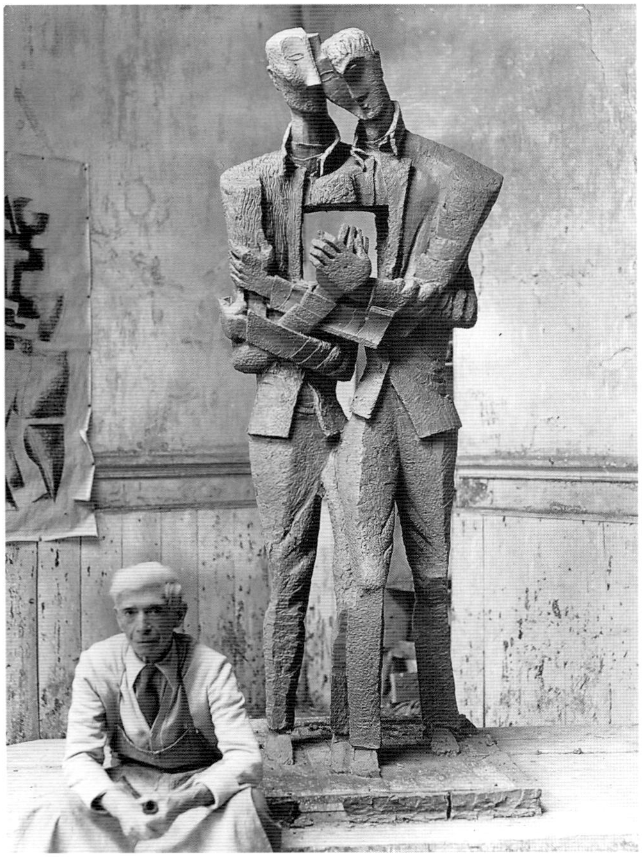

2
Ossip Zadkine in his atelier, with De gebroeders Van Gogh c. 1964

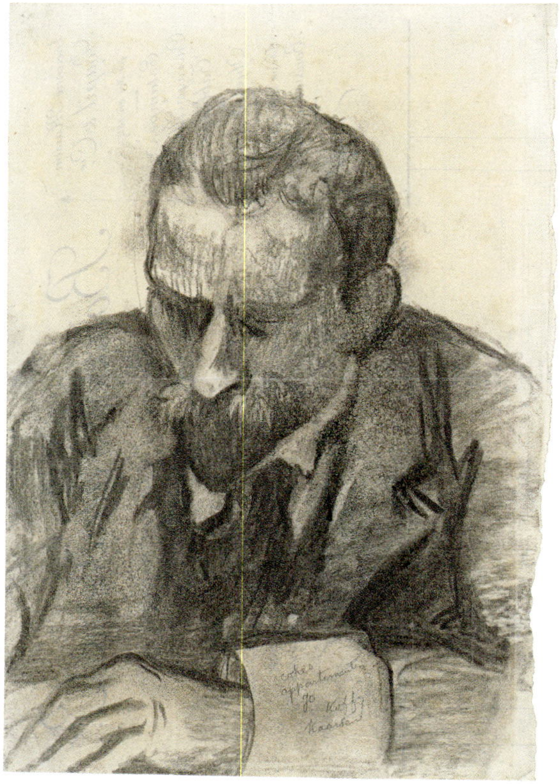

3
Meijer de Haan 1852–1895
Theo van Gogh 1889
Van Gogh Museum, Amsterdam

his brother-in-arms, was forced to pay for his collaboration with his life.[3]

Once upon a time, however, Theo had been judged on his own merits – that is, before critics gratefully deployed him in their aggressive championing of Vincent's art. This made him into little more than a (vital) link in his brother's biography. During his lifetime, though, the work Theo carried out for Boussod, Valadon & Cie at their branch at 19, Boulevard Montmartre was discussed and commented on in several Parisian periodicals by critics such as Albert Aurier and Felix Fénéon. After his sudden death, his Dutch associates, the painter-critics Jan Veth and Jozef Isaacson, too, focused on his excellence as a dealer. In these *in memoria*, Theo's labours on behalf of Vincent are barely given a mention;[4] instead, these writers saw him as an important protagonist in their hypothetical pantheon of modern art. Isaacson believed Theo had fought, suffered and made the ultimate sacrifice in defending the cause of several modern painters.

Theo's skills as a dealer were soon eclipsed by the image of his unfailing support of his brother's artistic calling. At the turn of the century, Van Gogh's work – which loomed large in the reviews and exhibition halls – was admitted into the canon of modern art, and has remained there ever since.[5] In this process many reviewers focused on Vincent's life as well as his unique oeuvre, and so Theo's love and support for his brother became intricatly woven into the tale. In her reminiscences of Vincent, published in 1910, their sister, Elisabeth du Quesne-Van Gogh, confirmed Theo's intense devotion to his brother. She described it as part of 'every breath, every heartbeat, and every thought.'[6]

The first 'complete' edition of Vincent's letters to Theo, which was edited by Theo's widow Jo van Gogh-Bonger, played a decisive role in creating the now-popular image of the two brothers.[7] For the first time, the general public was introduced to the life of this remarkable Dutch painter who, far from home, developed into one of the major figures of modern art. Between the lines of Vincent's letters, an image of Theo emerges as the brother who supported him through thick and thin. Publication of the letters led to a stream of new interpretations of Van Gogh's life and work, especially in the Netherlands and Germany – where the letters appeared in translation in 1914. Attention focused on the theme of brotherly love. In his biography of Vincent, published in 1919, the German writer and critic Julius Meier-Graefe even

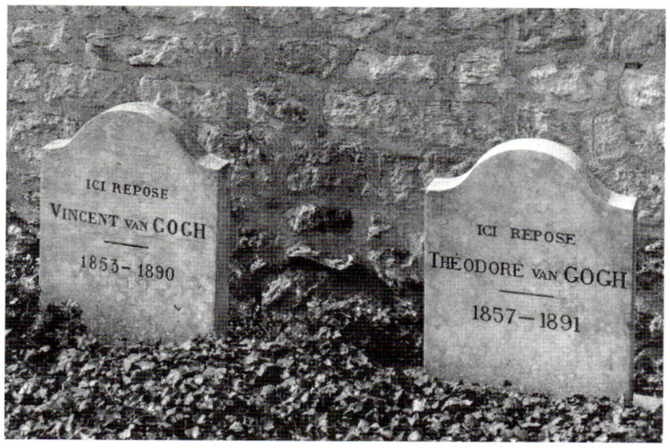

4
The graves of Vincent and Theo van Gogh in Auvers-sur-Oise

intimated that he was keen to foster this legend of brotherly fidelity.[8]

Jo van Gogh-Bonger, who had known Theo so intimately towards the end of his life, must have been saddened by the way the public exaggerated the Vincent and Theo saga. In her introduction to the 1914 edition of the letters, she stated that she had opted for a biographical approach precisely in order to avoid their lives and work becoming entangled.[9] Nevertheless, she realised that the legend growing up around the two brothers could no longer be stopped. Already the following year she wrote that by reuniting Theo with Vincent in the cemetery at Auvers-sur-Oise, and by furnishing their graves with identical headstones, she had relinquished her husband's memory in favour of a combined memorial which was dominated by Vincent.[10] [4]

As the years went by the alleged brotherly bond did indeed take on a legendary character, changing only in its form and in the diversity of its aims.[11] No matter how hard one searched for Theo, it was always Vincent one would find. In 1929 the Dutch art historian Just Havelaar wrote: 'Those two can no longer be separated: the social outcast, down-at-heel painter, and the well turned-out art dealer, forced to live right at the centre of the impenetrable vortex of Parisian snobbism, to consider art as merchandise at work, yet who still remained an idealist and an artist, even in his official role; in fact he went further than the call of duty: though faced with genteel impoverishment, he gave as much as he could to support his outstanding, hard-working brother.'[12]

In recent years this image has been somewhat modified, but it is striking that art historians still relegate Theo to the rank of 'brother of,' or a mere dealer in avant-garde art. In 1985, Jan Hulsker, who has devoted himself to critical research on Van Gogh's life and work for some decades, published a weighty tome entitled *Vincent and Theo van Gogh: a dual biography*. In this work he gave body to the brothers' lives together, supported by numerous extracts from letters and source material never before published. Vincent played the lead and, as of old, Theo played the understudy. Following in the tradition of Veth and Isaacson, John Rewald focused once again on Theo's efforts as an impressionist art dealer.[13] The result is that Theo van Gogh's life has yet to be studied exhaustively. Naturally, whoever undertakes this task is bound to encounter Vincent. However, it is the choice of perspective which determines whether Theo is consigned to the shade. And, even if he is, there are many reasons why he cannot be completely overshadowed by Vincent's genius.

This biographical sketch presents a portrait of Theo van Gogh based on an extensive study of the source materials.[14] Nonetheless, it is inevitable that many questions will be left unanswered. This is because Theo's life must be reconstructed mainly through the eyes of his contemporaries – Vincent's in particular – owing to the loss of a great deal of his own correspondence. Be that as it may, if more light can be thrown on Theo's life using this method, there is a great deal to be gained. It may also be useful in research on Vincent, whose life and work continues to pose problems.

The family

On 1 April 1849, a passer-by could have heard the notes of the Dutch Reformed Church's organ in Zundert's main square. There was cause for celebration, in particular for Vincent and Theo's father, Theodorus van Gogh [6]. His family and congregation were witnessing his confirmation into the ministry by his own father, Vincent van Gogh [5], 'an intellectually gifted man with an exceptional devotion to duty.'[15] Before taking up this position, Theodorus had studied theology in Utrecht (1840-1846), then spent some time preaching in Breda, and finally worked for six months as a curate in Middelburg. The young, still unmarried, and from all reports, handsome minister, subsequently moved to the adjoining village parsonage, where he set up house with his younger sister, Maria Johanna.

Theodorus's bachelor days were numbered; barely a year later he became engaged to Anna Cornelia Carbentus.[16] [7] The couple were married on 21 May 1851 in The Hague, and it was not long before children's voices filled the air of the old rectory. Vincent Willem, named after his grandfather, was born on 30 March 1853, exactly a year after the loss of their first son, Vincent, who was stillborn. Father's namesake,

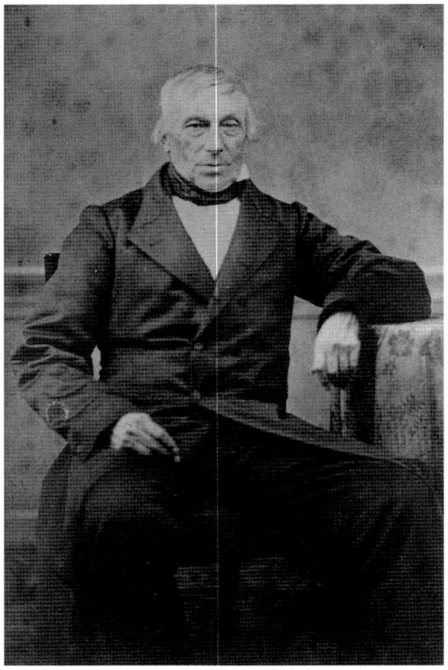

5
Vincent van Gogh 1789–1874

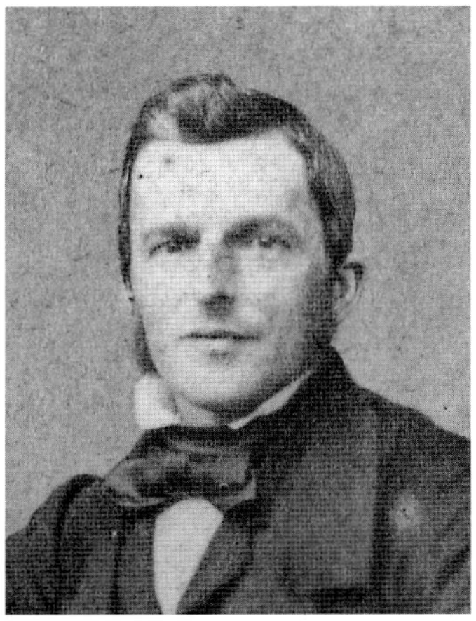

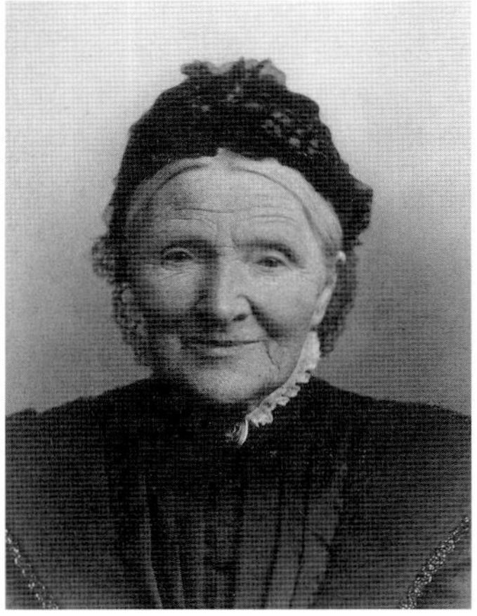

6
Theodorus van Gogh 1822–1885, *at c. age 30*

7
Anna Cornelia van Gogh-Carbentus 1819–1907

Theodorus, was third in line, after Anna Cornelia (Anna) **[8]**. Theo was born on 1 May 1857, at half past three on a 'pleasingly bright, magnificent May morning' after a 'turbulent night.'[17] On 21 May, Theo was christened by his father, in a robe decorated with 'the first May rose to bloom in Zundert,' a symbol of future prosperity.[18] In the years that followed the Van Goghs were blessed with the arrival of Elizabeth Huberta (Lies) **[9]**, Willemina Jacoba (Wil) **[10]** and last-born Cornelis Vincent (Cor) **[11]**.

Their father was to continue to climb the pulpit of his intimate, early-19th century church for another 22 years. Unlike his own father, who had enjoyed great prestige as a minister and governor of several charities, he was not a great speaker. His lack of rhetorical skills apparently prevented him from obtaining a more ambitious, better paid position, but he compensated for this deficiency with his unselfish affability and genuine social conscience. He was greatly respected, as can be gleaned from the obituary that appeared in the Kerkelijke Courant after his sudden death in March 1885. He was described as a man who 'won the hearts of all those who knew him with his piety, integrity, love and forbearance,' and who was 'respected and loved' by both Protestants and Catholics.[19] This was no mean feat in Dutch society of the period, when life and work were strictly segregated along denominational lines.

Their mother, who was later described by her daughter-in-law, Jo van Gogh-Bonger, as a remarkably amiable woman with an 'innate love of nature,'[20] also won the esteem and sympathy of her rural community. She did her best to help her husband in the daily running of the parish. After his father's death, Theo wrote to her: 'How often he asked you for your advice and how much you contributed to his work.'[21] For Vincent his parents' marriage was exemplary [744/573].

Van Gogh's salary was far from generous, but living cheaply in the Brabant countryside they managed, with a little juggling, to give their children a sound education. They were also able to maintain their respectable position, keeping a carriage and servants – essential trappings for a minister's family.[22] In February 1873 Anna gave a laconic résumé of the family's social standing: 'We have no money but we still have a good name.'[23]

When describing his parents in November 1881, Vincent referred to them as 'amiable, quiet people, so friendly and good,' who had gone to great lengths to ensure that their children enjoyed a carefree childhood [184/159]. 'You all love one another so much,' his

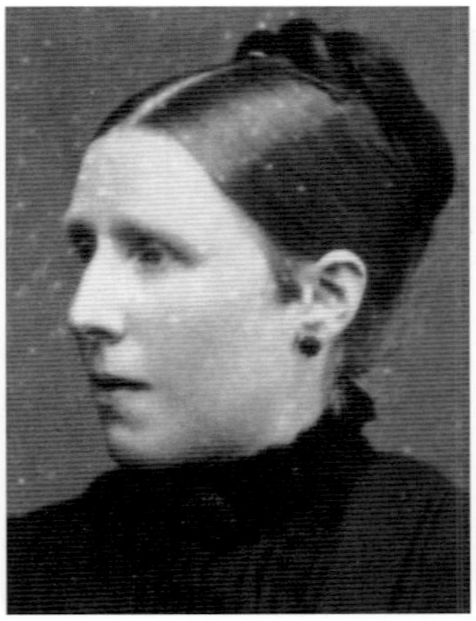
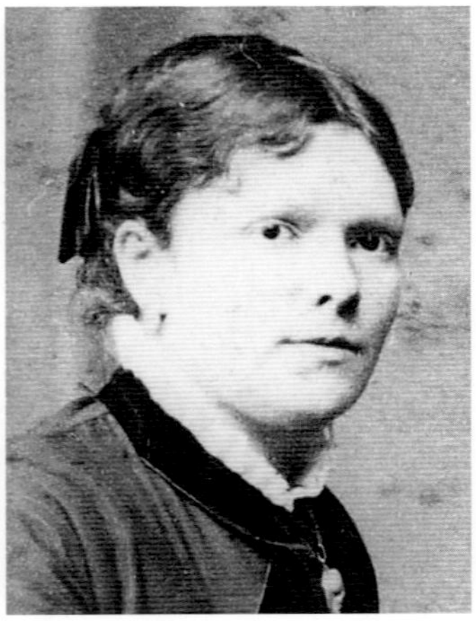
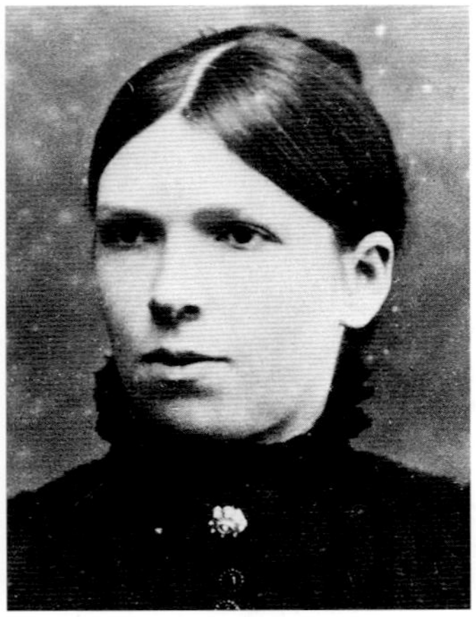
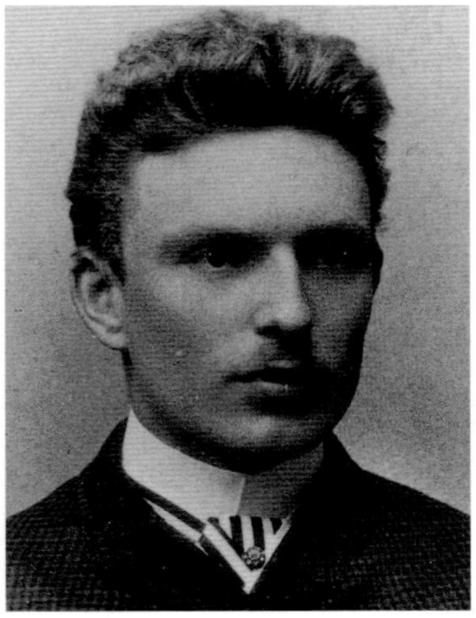

8
Anna Cornelia (Anna) van Gogh 1855–1930

9
Elisabeth Huberta (Lies) van Gogh 1859–1936

10
Willemina Jacoba (Wil) van Gogh 1862–1941

11
Cornelis Vincent (Cor) van Gogh 1867–1900

parents noted with joy.[24] Using gentle coercion they taught their children the virtues they considered important – dutifulness, politeness, honesty and charity. Their cultural education consisted of Christian literature, dominated of course by the Bible – deemed to be absolutely 'the best book.'[25] [12] Most of their offspring left home at a young age, but the elder Van Goghs continued to be greatly concerned about their welfare long after they had gone. A steady stream of letters reminded them constantly of their parents' cherished ideals. When Theo left for Brussels in January 1873 they impressed upon him to make the most of his time abroad and secure his independence, 'in all respectability and true piety.'[26]

This loving care could be suffocating at times, and attempting to live up to their lofty notions proved to be a fertile breeding ground for feelings of guilt and inadequacy. The constant threat of failure hung over all the children like a cloud. In January 1876 Lies expressed her concern in a letter to her brother: 'Oh Theo, we shall have to love father and mother so much to repay them for what they have sacrificed for us. I reproach myself all the time, as if I am nowhere near good enough for them.'[27] Theo must have understood exactly what she meant, for he knew the feeling all too well.

Although, as an adult, Theo tried to avoid his parents' overbearing solicitude, and Vincent was eventually quite blunt in his opposition of their views, they still shared fond childhood memories of Sundays spent at home in Zundert [13], particularly 'the delightful twilight hour after dinner.' In 1876 Theo wrote to his sister Lies that she would never again experience a setting that was so 'calm and peaceful.'[28]

The poetry of country life

Theo's younger years were spent mostly in the company of Vincent, Anna and Lies, as they were his nearest contemporaries. He only became close to Wil, who was five years his junior, long after leaving home. The age gap between him and his youngest brother Cor was too large for there to have been much of a bond between them. He was only five years old when Theo left the rectory for good, and they rarely met after that. Theo and Vincent were a different story: they must have been good friends from a very young age, even though they could not have been at home together for more than eight and a half years. Theo did not go to the village school in Zundert like Vincent, but was taught privately by governesses: Anke Maria Schuil and, in all probability, Jeanne Struick. In 1864 Vincent

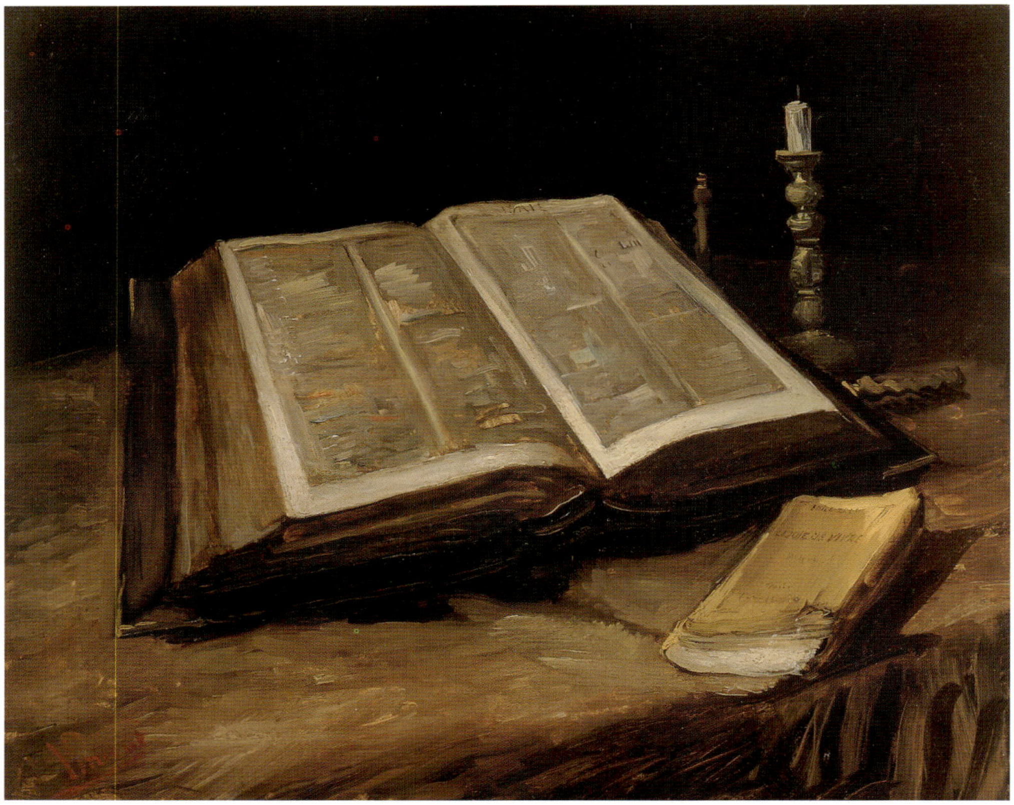

12

Vincent van Gogh 1853–1890
Still life with Bible 1885
Van Gogh Museum, Amsterdam

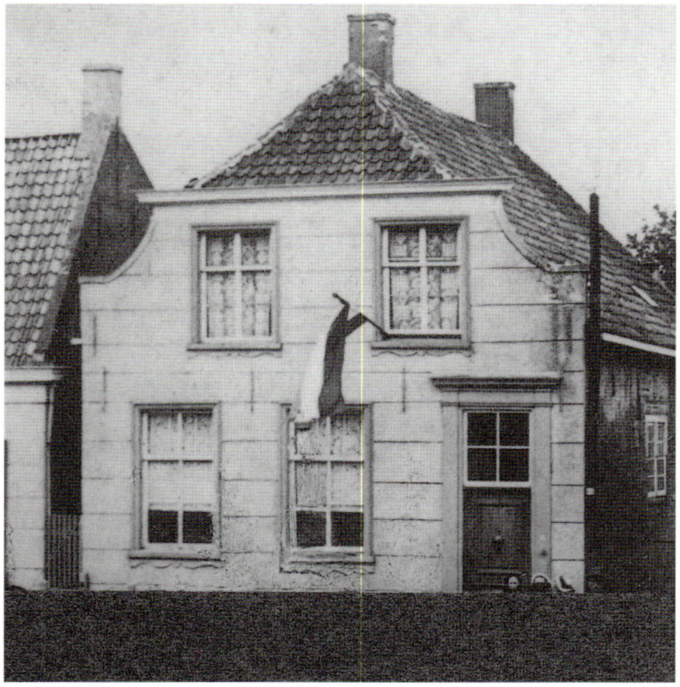

13
The vicarage at Zundert

left for boarding school in Zevenbergen, after which the boys met only during the school holidays. However, in 1868-69, after two years at the Tilburg grammar school, Vincent returned to his parents' house for 18 months before moving to The Hague.

Theo's character and physical make-up were very different from Vincent's, who Jo van Gogh-Bonger described as sturdy, solid and broad shouldered. In looks they were both 'equally reddish-blond [...] with the same pale-blue eyes that sometimes changed to a deeper shade of greenish-blue.'[29] Theo did not have Vincent's strong constitution. [14, 15] Suffering terribly from the cold as a child, he would always 'hug' the stovepipe in the early morning; as an adolescent he was regularly ill – in 1876 very seriously – and throughout his adult life he was plagued by ailments like a chronic cough.[30] Whereas Vincent was reported to have been a difficult child, Theo seems to have been just the opposite.[31] His sister Lies was convinced that

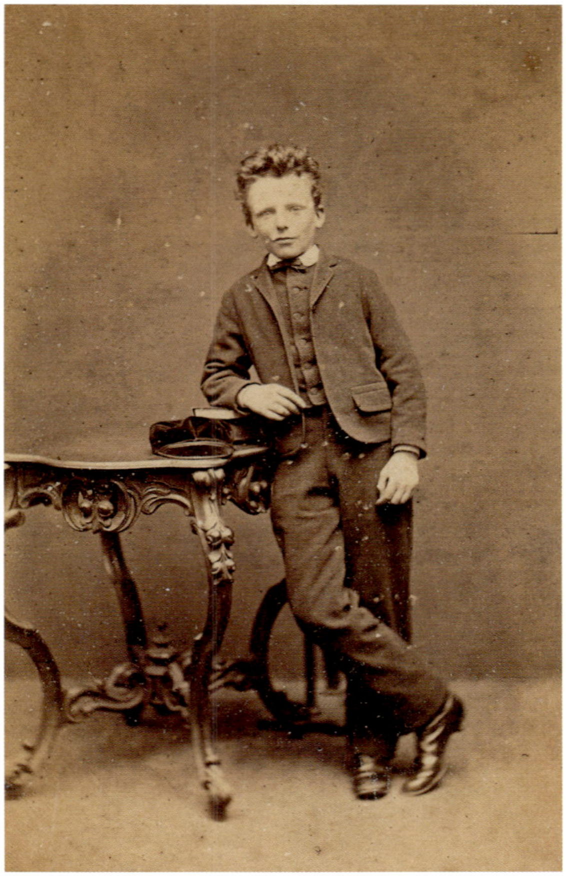

14
Theo van Gogh, age 13

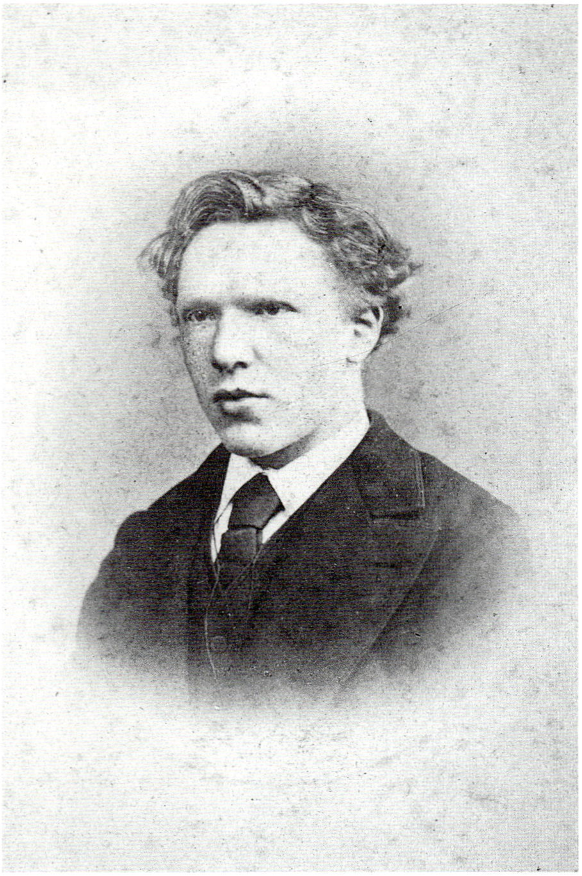

15
Vincent van Gogh, age 16

he had assumed his father's 'warm-heartedness,' whereas Anna's view was that he had been a friendly soul from the moment he was born.[32]

The image of Theo that emerges from the known correspondence is that of a good-natured, friendly, sympathetic, unassuming person who was extremely loyal to his family. And no matter how one may judge what he did for Vincent, he continued to support his brother – albeit sometimes reluctantly – even after he had been branded the black sheep of the family. After Vincent's death, his mother even went so far to suggest that Theo's 'loving care' had 'brought [Vincent] to life.'[33] At times his talent for caring was a major drawback: he was so often busy offering sustenance to others that his own needs were given little room to surface. If, on occasions, he did give his own interests priority, he soon ran into trouble: his parents' strict morality, Vincent's constant demands, unforeseen mishaps and a strongly developed sense of guilt all conspired to thwart him. With all this constantly on his mind, he found it virtually impossible to make clear decisions for himself.

Vincent, being the oldest son, was a role model, and Theo's parents advised him to follow in his brother's footsteps – that is until Vincent's career took a dramatic turn at the end of 1875. Lies tells us that when they were young Theo had looked up to Vincent, had even worshipped him for quite some time, and considered him to have been 'more than just a normal human being.'[34] Despite their differences, Vincent considered that, as brothers, they had a lot in common: 'not just memories of the past, but that you are in the same line of business as I have been in up to now, and that you know so many people and places that I know, and your great love of art and nature' [77/43]. These memories were of the lush rectory garden and its views of Zundert's broad heathlands and sandy moors – a unique playground where the broth-

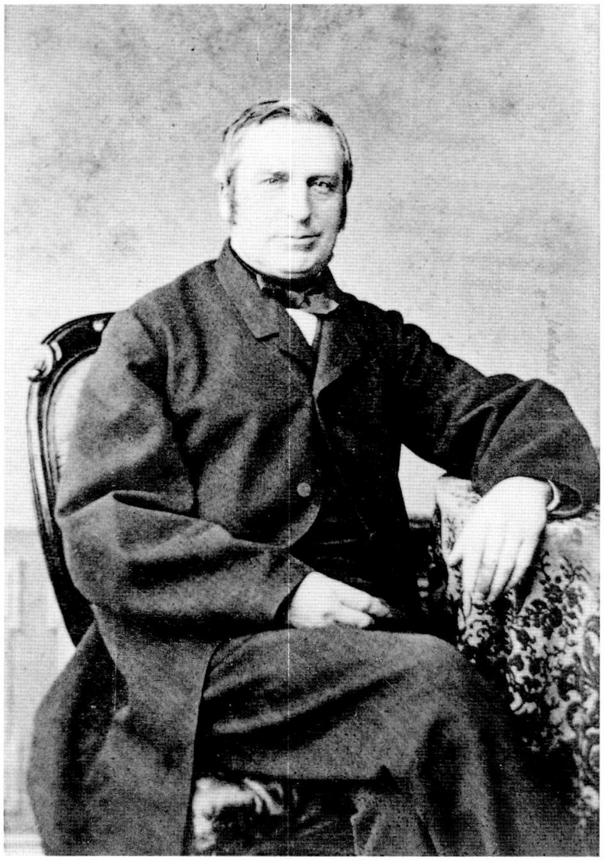

16
Hendrik Vincent (Uncle Hein) van Gogh 1815–1877

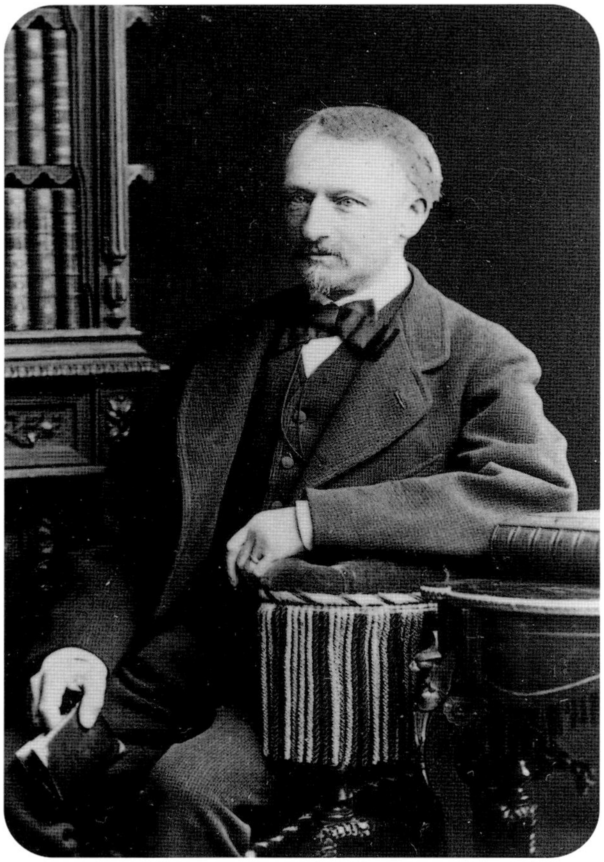

17
Vincent (Uncle Cent) van Gogh 1820–1888

ers built sandcastles and played games invented by Vincent [76/62].[35] Their love of nature sprang from this childhood paradise. In 1877 Vincent looked back with nostalgia on those carefree days: 'how often we walked to Zundert together past the black fields sprouting fresh green wheat, where, if we went out with father, we could hear the lark at this time of year' [109/89]. Theo lived in towns from the age of 15, but out of sheer necessity; he never really felt at home there. He remained an outdoor type, and whenever the occasion arose he went off into the countryside.[36]

In January 1871 the Van Gogh family moved to Father's new benefice in Helvoirt. This was the start of a new life for Theo. Every day he left the sheltered environment of his parents' house and walked six kilometres to school in Oisterwijk, officially called the 'non-subsidised Special School for more advanced education,' where the headmaster, Cornelis Adriaan Heintz, taught him French, German, English and Maths.[37] For unknown reasons, Theo's brief school career came to an end in December 1872. It might have been that his results were so disappointing that his parents decided not to allow him continue.[38] Whatever the case, it was a godsend for his future career that three of his father's bothers were art dealers.[39] [**16, 17, 18**]

After deliberations with Uncle Cent, who had arranged Vincent's appointment to Goupil's in The Hague, and with the assistance of his Uncle Hein, Theo was able to start work in January 1873 as the youngest assistant at the latter's old firm, the Brussels branch of Goupil & Cie at 58, Rue Montagne de la Cour. [**19**] It pleased Theo's parents that his time was to be put to good use and that he would be more financially independent; Vincent was delighted, too, because Theo and he were now working for the same company. On 13 December 1872 he congratulated Theo warmly: 'That was good news that I read in

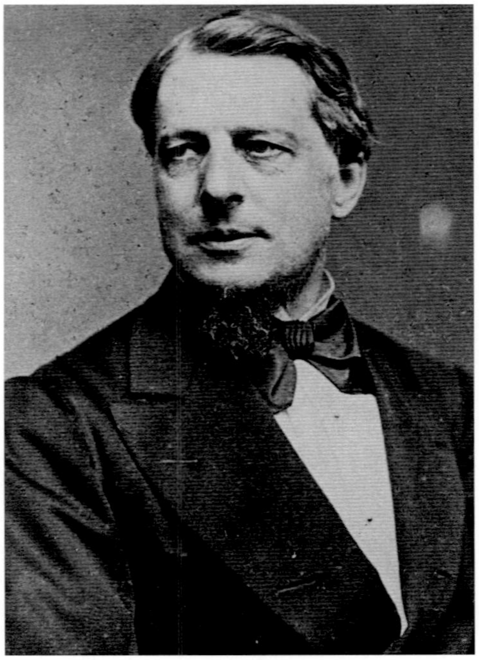

18
Cornelis Marinus (Uncle Cor) van Gogh 1824–1908

father's letter. I wish you all the luck in the world. I have no doubt that you will enjoy yourself, it is such a superb business. It will make quite a change for you. I am so pleased that we are now both in the same profession and in the same firm; we must write to one another often' [2/2].

Independence

At the beginning of January 1873, Theo's father took him to the house of Reverend Hendrik van den Brink on the Place Saint Catherine, where he was to board.[40] There is no record of Theo's early days in Brussels, but he must have felt very lonely after his father left. His mother tried to cheer him up by reminding him of Christ's consoling words: 'Still I am not alone, our Father in Heaven is with me.'[41] For the first time in his life he was far away from home, and for an indefinite period of time; the contrast between the rustic environment in Helvoirt, with its intimate community, and the Belgian metropolis could not have been greater.

Theo's leaving home was difficult for his parents, too, and their words of encouragement in their first letter to him at his new home were thus also directed at themselves.[42] After this move, the Van Gogh family was only complete on religious holidays, which they all greatly looked forward to – Theo considering that it made life 'a real pleasure [...] to have a home which you so longed for.'[43] Letters had to compensate for his loss,[44] and much to his parents' joy, Theo was a faithful writer.

He adapted to his new surroundings surprisingly quickly. The fact that he was now able to earn part of his keep pleased his parents even more than it pleased him.[45] As the youngest assistant, Theo's apprenticeship involved carrying out all manner of stockroom work, such as packing and unpacking paintings, and sending reproductions from the publisher's catalogue list. A whole new world opened up for him. In contrast to home, where his knowledge of contemporary art had probably been confined to conversations with Vincent, leafing through his print album, and the odd visit to Uncle Cent's art collection in Princehage,[46] in Brussels he was in daily contact with work produced by the important artists of his time.

Vincent, who had been working in London from June 1873, was delighted that in future he would be able to share his interest and love of contemporary art with Theo. As the more experienced of the two, he tried to show his brother the ropes, and in his letters he often urged Theo to pass on his views about the work he saw and handled.[47] Theo appreciated Vincent's encouragement and proved a keen pupil. He regularly wrote about pictures that caught his eye and, on Vincent's initiative, became an ardent collector of prints. Eventually, this compilation was to form the basis of his art collection, purchases often being finalised in consultation with Vincent. Brussels offered sufficient scope for putting his elder brother's counsel into practice. In those years the city was one of Europe's most important cultural centres, with an extensive network of art dealers, museums and exhibition locales.[48] Theo spent the little spare time he had taking long walks, which reminded him of life back home.[49] Later on, in Paris,

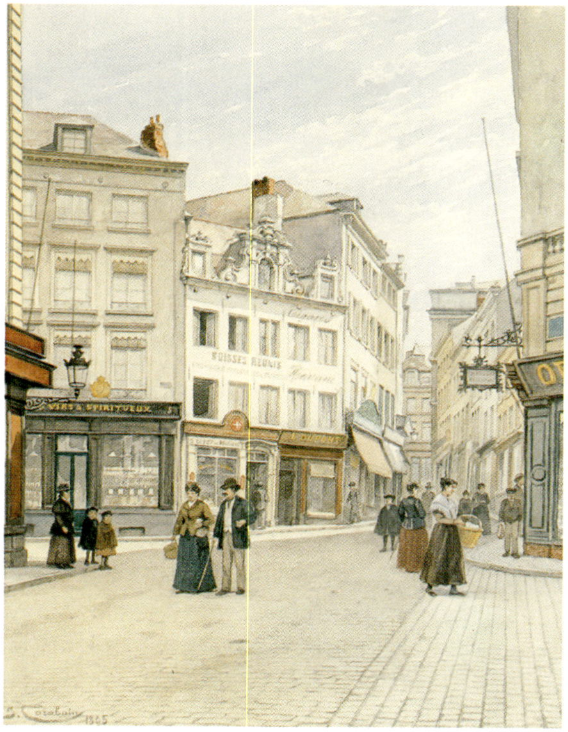

19
Corabain
The junction of the Rue Cantersteen, the Rue Montagne-de-la-Cour and the Rue de l'Empereur in Brussels 1895
Stadsmuseum, Brussels

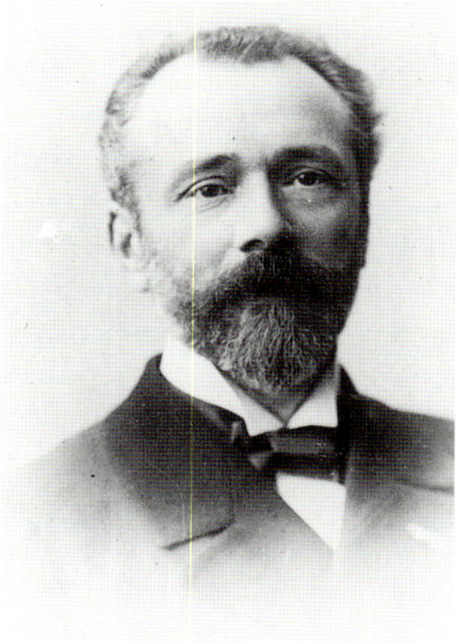

20
Hermanus Gijsbertus Tersteeg 1845–1927

he was to dearly miss these hours spent in the countryside.

Theo was extremely devoted to his profession. His parents were glad to see that he had taken their advice and was dedicating himself to the business.[50] His supervisor, Tobias Victor Schmidt, was pleased with his progress, and in the summer of 1873 he was given more responsible tasks. Around 25 June he probably sold his first painting independently, and in the period from 25 August to 6 September he was given the opportunity to cover for Mr Schmidt while he was in the Netherlands on business. Theo was only 16, but as his mother remarked, 'he had grown up fast.'[51]

Uncle Cent was also extremely content with his nephew. In September 1873, after consulting Theo's parents and his future employer, Hermanus Gijsbert Tersteeg [20], he decided to transfer him to the more prestigious branch of Goupil's in The Hague, starting in November of that same year. Theo was unhappy about leaving Brussels, but he had no say in the matter. His father was at the train station in Tilburg to welcome him home when he arrived on 5 November. Theo must have been proud to show his parents Mr Schmidt's letter of reference extolling his many virtues.[52]

The Hague

'I think you will enjoy working in the Hague branch once you get used to it. I have no doubt that your lodgings with the Roos family will suit you, too. You must go out for walks if you can find the time' [15/12]. These words, written by Vincent from London, welcomed Theo to the city where he himself had enjoyed working from 1869-73. Theo arrived on 12 November and moved in with the Roos family at the Lange Beestenmarkt 32, in the house Vincent had once made his home.

For the second time within a year Theo had to make a new start. It was probably less difficult the second time, as he had already shown that he could stand on his own two feet. His parents were convinced it would work out well: 'Of course in the beginning it will seem a little strange in such an unfamiliar, new house, but at least you have had to adjust once before.'[53] In fact, it was not such an unfa-

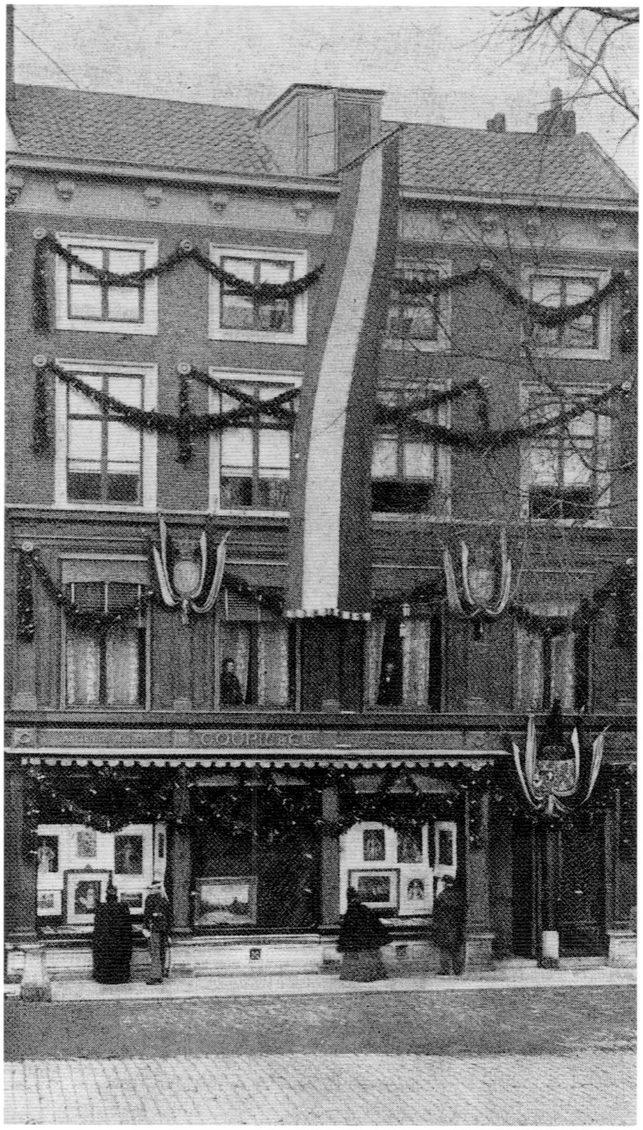

21

Boussod, Valadon & Cie.'s (Goupil & Cie.) gallery in The Hague in 1898

miliar house at all: he had been introduced to the Roos family in September 1872, when he had stayed with Vincent for a few days. In addition, Theo could visit several members of his own family who lived in the city. Its country setting, between the sea and open Dutch polders, once again provided him with the opportunity for his much-loved walks. As expected, Theo settled in quickly, and his parents found that he looked happy and well.[54]

For someone starting out as an art dealer, The Hague, and this branch of Goupil's in particular, were ideal. [**21**] In the early 1870s, in the wake of the Hague School movement, the royal capital had developed into the country's cultural centre. There were numerous exhibitions where Theo could become acquainted with recent developments in contemporary art, while he could admire the work of Dutch masters of the Golden Age in the Mauritshuis. Goupil's Hague gallery profited from the booming economy and from a growing public interest in modern art. Consequently, the gallery was able to negotiate worldwide sales of works by both popular French masters and by local luminaries, such as *The mill* by Jacob Maris [**22**] and *The kitchen princess* by Thijs Maris [**23**].[55]

Theo dealt with customers on his own in the firm's busy salon at Plaats 14; he was also responsible for shipping purchases and helped with the annual stock-taking and auctions.[56] In the spring of 1876 he took over the so-called 'spring circuit,' travelling around the country to show clients the firm's *nouveautés*. This responsibility was proof that Tersteeg had the greatest confidence in him. His success meant that Theo was soon able to alleviate some of his parents' financial burdens. In the spring of 1876 they were very pleased when he offered to contribute part of his New Year's bonus to the education of his younger sister, Wil.[57]

For the first 18 months Theo, too, was happy with the way things were going. He was quite content living with the Roos family, made new acquaintances, and regularly went round to see his parents' friends and relations. The volume of letters to Vincent increased; they kept one another up to date on the daily running of their respective shops, and on the painters and writers they most admired.[58] In the evolution of their taste, it was Vincent who took the lead.[59] Both had a preference for work dealt by Goupil's, including Cézar de Cock, Emile Jacque, Jean-François Millet and Dutch masters like Jozef Israëls, Jacob Maris, Thijs Maris [**25**], Anton Mauve and Ary Scheffer, whose *Christ in Gethsemane* [**24**] Theo and Vincent had seen in Dordrecht.

One of the books Vincent supplied him with in 1874, *L'amour* by Jules Michelet, was one of his brother's favourites and it also made a deep impression on Theo.[60] He could identify with the work because, that spring, he had fallen in love with Annet Haanebeek, daughter of Carl Adolph Haanebeek and Cornelia

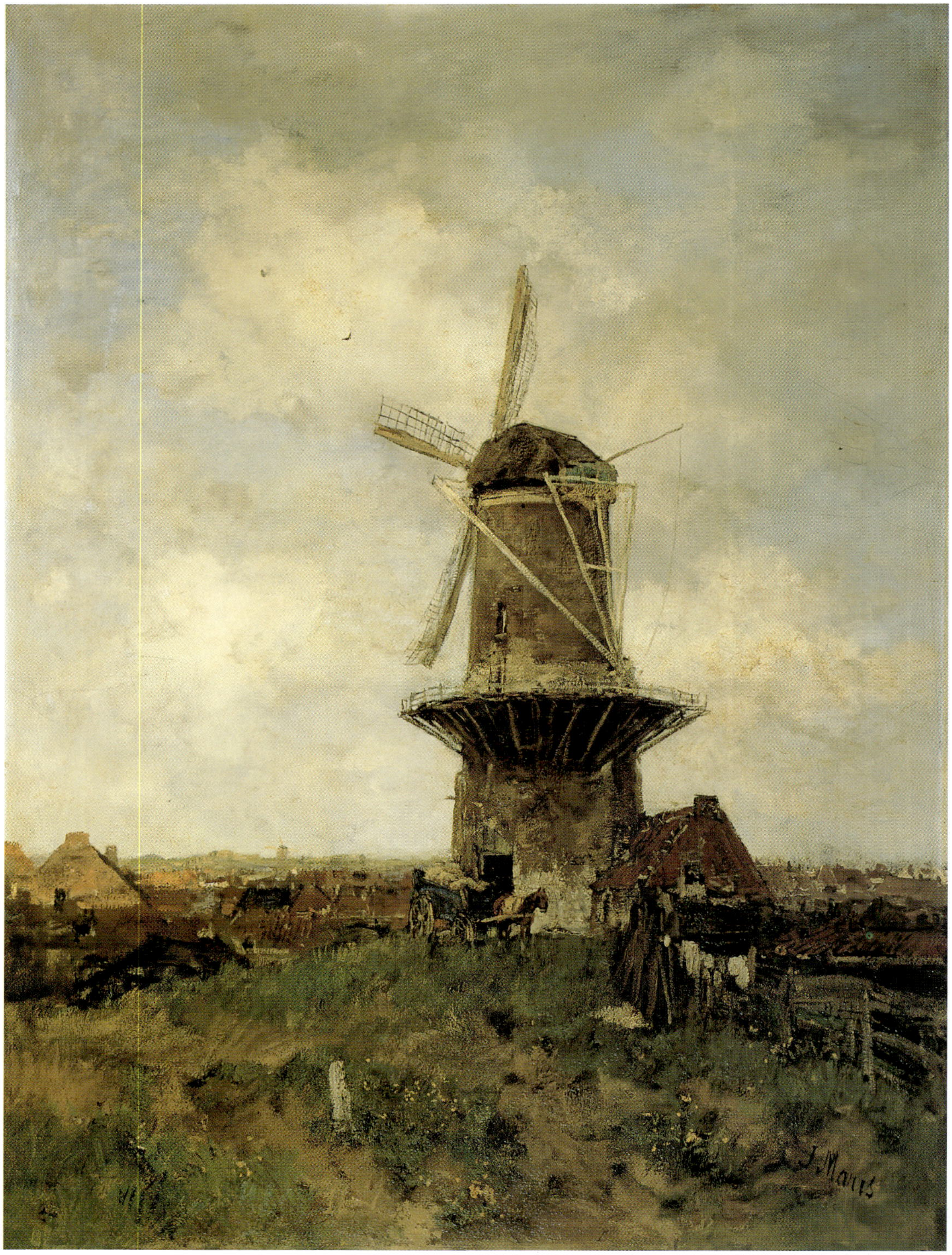

22
Jacob Maris 1837–1899
The mill 1879
Museum Mesdag, The Hague

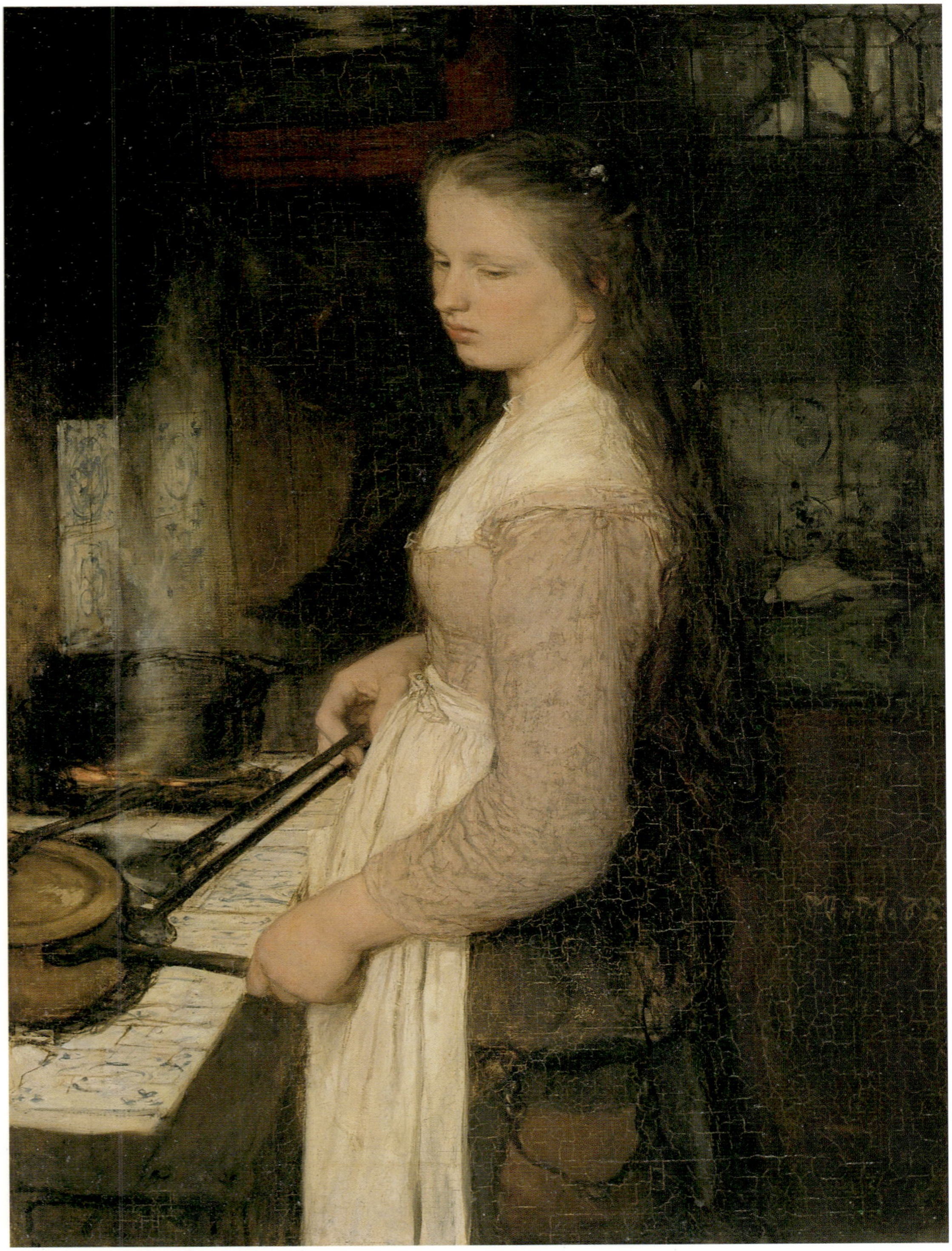

23
Matthijs Maris 1839–1917
The kitchen princess 1872
Museum Mesdag, The Hague

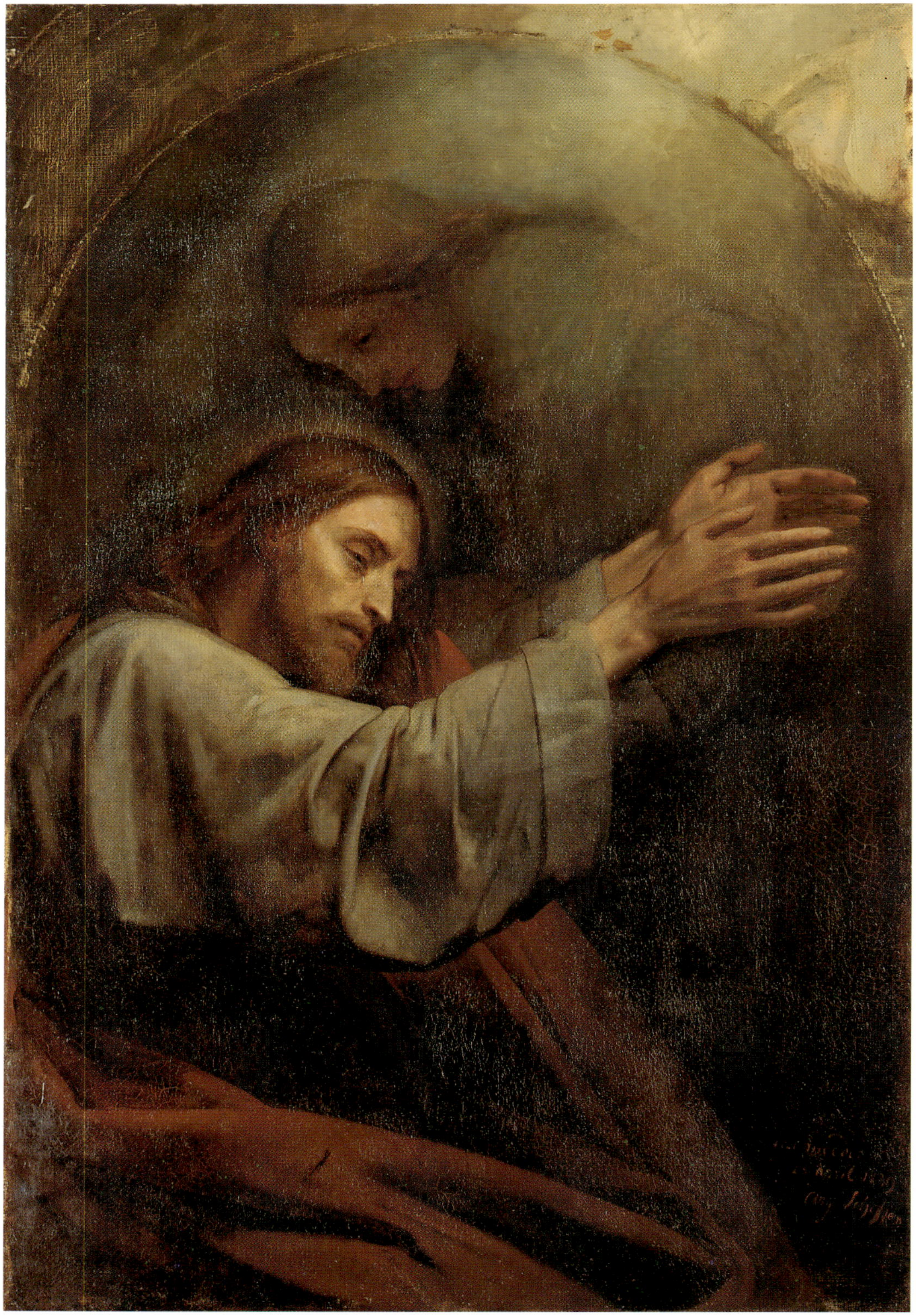

24
Ary Scheffer 1795–1858
Christ in Gethsemane 1839
Dordrechts Museum, Dordrecht

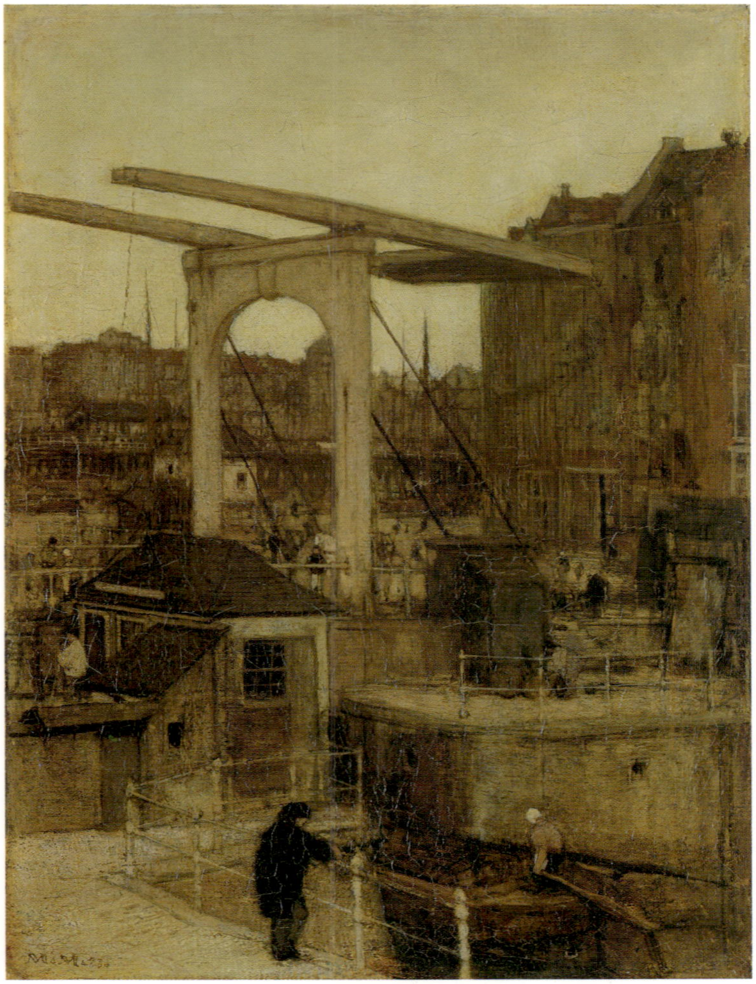

25
Matthijs Maris 1839–1917
Souvenir d'Amsterdam n.d.
Rijksmuseum, Amsterdam

Jacoba van Zuylen. Annet's mother had died young, and Annet's father had remarried, the second time to Leonarda Catherina Adriana Stricker. In his parents' view, they were 'good, respectable people' and could play an important role in their son's education. Theo contacted them in April 1874, and his interest for Annet must have grown during the weekly visits that followed.[61] After reading Michelet's book, Theo was moved to discuss his amorous feelings with Vincent. His brother replied on 31 July 1874: 'That a woman is "quite a different mortal" from a man, and a mortal that we do not yet know, at least, as you say, that we only know superficially, yes, I certainly believe you are right. And that a woman and a man can become one, that is, one whole rather than two halves, I believe that too' [27/20].[62] Theo's longing for symbiosis was tragically disrupted when Annet died, after a serious illness, on 14 June 1875.

This was not the only loss Theo had to bear in this ill-fated year. On 4 March he had to cope with the sudden death of his friend and housemate Johannes Wilhelmus Weehuizen; this was followed on 22 September by the demise of yet another housemate, Willem Laurens Kiehl. The death of these three young friends came as a great shock to Theo. He could find no relief in his father's words of consolation, which reminded him of the inevitable 'trials and tribulations of life,'[63] and none in Vincent's sympathy either. Reading Friedrich Rückert's melancholy poetry only made things worse. Theo's good humour and lightheartedness were lost, and he remained dejected for quite a long time.[64] In November 1875 he told Lies that from then on he would have to fight 'to be good.'[65] He hinted to Vincent for the first time that he wanted to leave The Hague.

While Theo hovered between relinquishing his carefree childhood and acceding to early maturity, his inner struggle was exacerbated by his parents' urgent appeal for help. In late October 1874 his father took him into his confidence: they had not heard from Vincent since he had left for Paris three weeks earlier. His parents were very worried about their eldest son's black moods, and tried to exert their influence on him through Theo, in the hope that he could stop him straying from the straight and narrow. They urged Theo to continue writing to Vincent and to keep them informed as to how he was getting on.[66] In January 1876, when it became clear that Vincent was to leave Goupil's, his parents were at their wit's end.[67] Now that Vincent's chances of making a career as an art dealer were gone for good, Theo had to shoulder the heavy burden of atoning for the disgrace and ignominy of his dismissal: 'Now [that] the oldest has rocked the boat, we hope all the more that the second will steer a steady course.'[68] Theo was faced with a conflict of loyalties. Who should he support? The demanding Vincent, his brother he had so looked up to and with whom he was in frequent contact? Or his parents, who had put all their trust in him? He was faced with a hopeless dilemma.

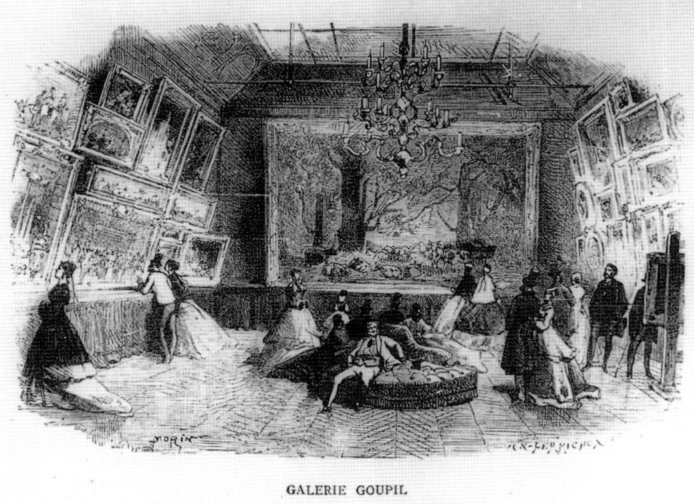

26
Goupil & Cie's gallery in Paris, c. 1850

To Paris

But Theo, too, brought his parents 'grief and sorrow' by starting a relationship with a lower-class woman. They were unable to give their blessing to a liason with someone who, in their view, came from an inferior background.[69] Theo was pressed into continuing to set a good example: 'You shall and must be our joy and honour! We cannot do without it';[70] Theo's feelings on the matter were of little interest to them, but in actual fact he felt extremely guilty, and in May 1877 he wrote to tell Vincent that he knew he was causing his parents a great deal of pain [117/98].

As in the summer of 1875, Theo could only see one solution to his problems: to leave The Hague as soon as possible, preferably for London or Paris [118/99]. His father was not against the idea, but convinced him that he should wait for the right moment to start work at a foreign branch of Goupil's. **[26]** If he were to go to the Paris branch immediately it would mean a demotion; but the most important reason was that 'after what had happened to Vincent' he would do better to stay where he was.[71] This came as a blow, but by then Theo had learned to take it like a man, and he resigned himself to carrying on as best he could. In 1878 his parents confirmed that he was doing well again, enjoying his work and seeing things 'in a clear[er] light.'[72] Quite unexpectedly, he was offered a temporary job at Goupil's in Paris in March of that same year.[73]

In the French capital, Theo helped with the firm's stand at the Exposition Universelle. His stay was a unique opportunity to gain international experience, as the show attracted people from far and wide. The change had clearly done him good.[74] Upon completeing his job, he very much wanted to continue working in Paris, but, as so often was the case, his hopes were dashed. Uncle Cent, who had arranged for his temporary transfer to Paris, thought Theo ought to return to The Hague, 'as long as there is nothing better for you to do [in France].'[75] On 15 November Theo travelled back to Holland, more determined than ever to return to Paris at the first possible moment.

It was not easy for him to get used to The Hague again. He found life there 'anything but fun.' After living in an impressive city like Paris, it required a great deal of patience to get through what was to be his last year in this Dutch city.[76] After discussions between his parents, Tersteeg and Uncle Cent, the case was settled: Theo was transferred permanently to Paris in July 1879. In barely seven years, Theo had developed from a shy, amicable boy, loyally trying to fulfill his par-

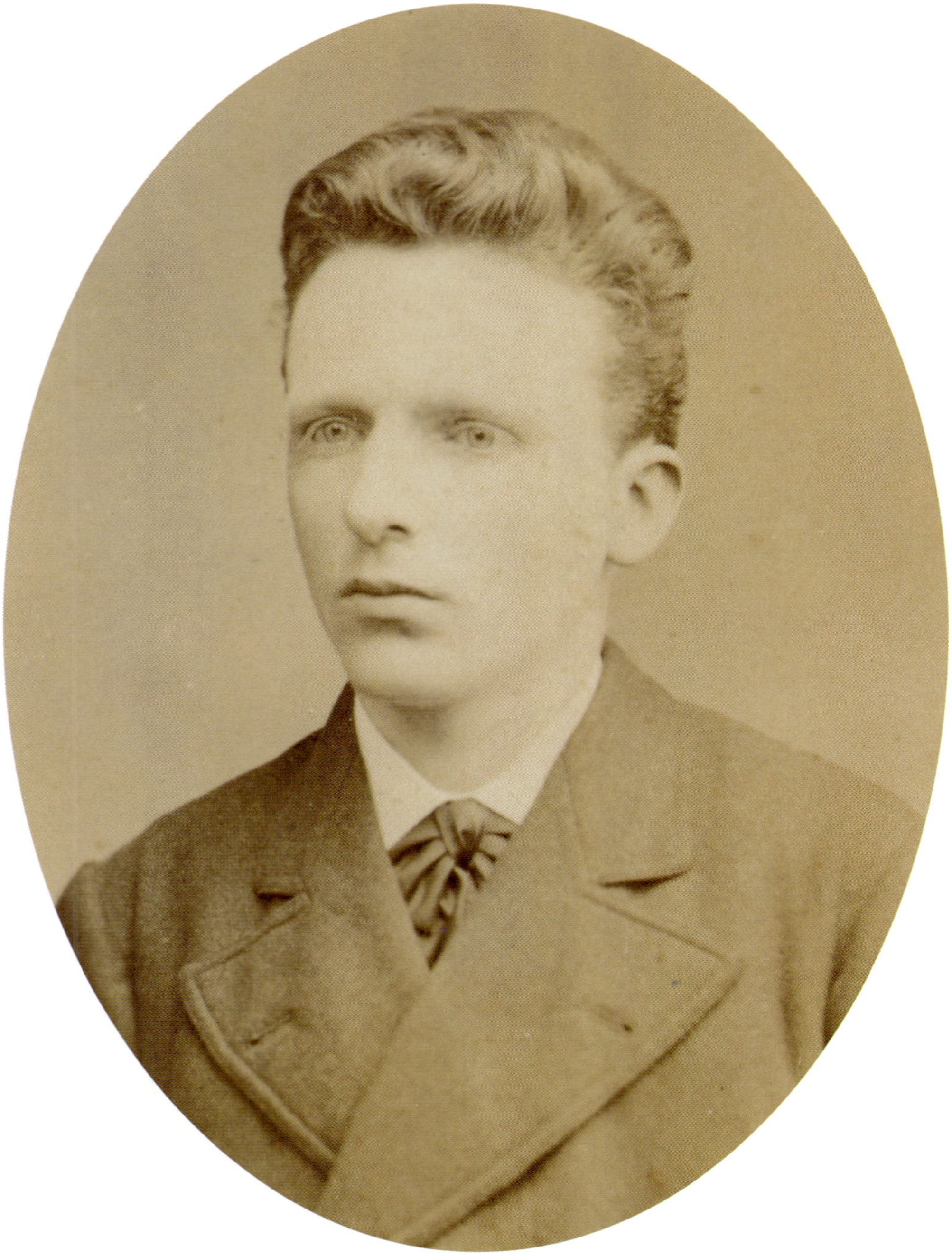

27
Theo van Gogh at c. age 21

ents' expectations, into a mature, financially independent man with a respectable job. Although still very young, he not been spared life's trials. Paris offered him the opportunity to make a new start.

Originally, Vincent had been the one to take the lead, offering his advice to Theo; but as the years went by, their roles were gradually reversed. On the few occasions on which they met – in Amsterdam, Brussels, Dordrecht and The Hague – they talked at great length about personal matters, which are either not mentioned in the letters at all or only casually or in guarded terms.[77] After Vincent's dismissal from Goupil's in April 1876, worries about his future

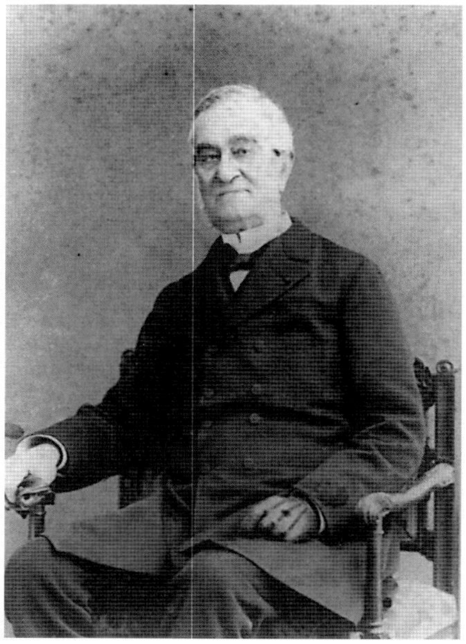

28
Adolphe Goupil 1803–1889

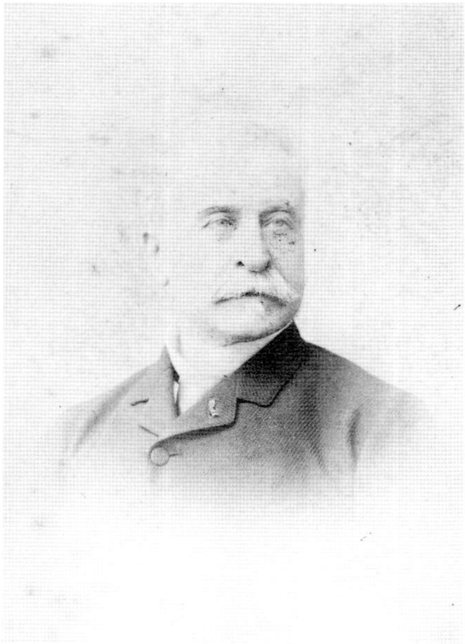

29
Léon Boussod 1826–1896

prospects became more pronounced. Theo was saddled with the difficult job of mediating between his parents and Vincent. He tried to defend his brother's actions to his parents, but with no success.[78] In their eyes, Vincent had fallen from the social ladder, while Theo continued a steady ascent. Vincent became increasingly isolated within the Van Gogh family. He clung to Theo and was adept at manipulating his feelings: 'How little we see of one another, [...]. And yet so strong is our sense of family and brotherly love that my heart is sometimes lifted and my eyes raised to God to beg: "Let me not stray too far away from them, not for too long, Oh Lord!"' [94/78].[79] Theo, who was caught between the demands of his parents and those of Vincent, could not remain entirely impartial, and – initially – he seems to have been more inclined to take his parents' side. On 15 August 1879 he visited his brother in the Borinage. During a walk near the abandoned mine shaft, La Sorcière, he had a serious talk with Vincent about the future [154/133]. Theo suggested 'plans for self-improvement, change and action,' but his remark that his brother should stop leading a life of leisure at his parents' expense infuriated Vincent. Theo's visit had done him some good, but its main effect had been to make him more depressed and dismal, as he could not fail but notice that Theo had become estranged from him [153/132].

For the first time Theo had told Vincent the plain truth, and the latter's response was both swift and painful: they had no contact for a whole year. It was not until July 1880 that Vincent, somewhat reluctantly, resumed their correspondence, remarking again that to a certain extent Theo had become a stranger to him, 'and I am perhaps even more of a stranger to you than you think' [154/133].[80]

In Paris

Theo had lived in Paris since the beginning of November 1879. He had moved into a room at 46, Rue de la Tour d'Auvergne, a house he already knew from his earlier stay the year before. As an assistant at Goupil's oldest Parisian branch, at 19, Boulevard Montmartre, strategically situated between the opera house and the stock exchange, Theo had arrived at the very hub of modern art. At this period Paris was *the* place for artists, where thousands tried their luck and

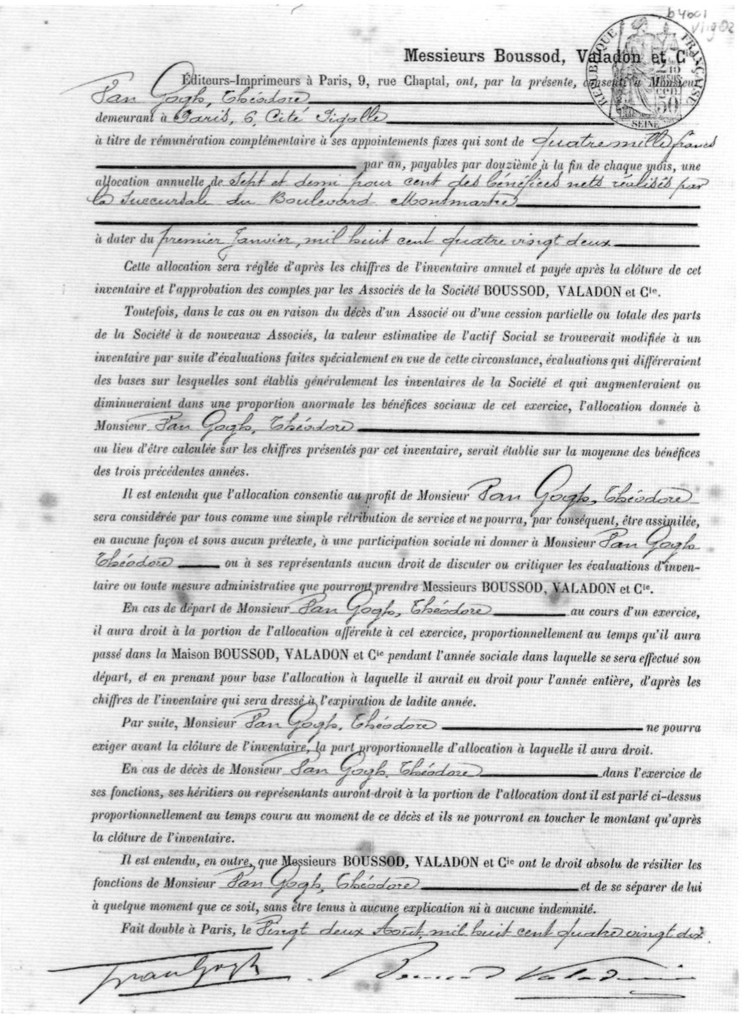

Messieurs Boussod, Valadon et Cie

Éditeurs-Imprimeurs à Paris, 9, rue Chaptal, *ont, par la présente, consenti à Monsieur* Van Gogh, Théodore

demeurant à Paris, 6, Cité Pigalle

à titre de rémunération complémentaire à ses appointements fixes qui sont de Quatre mille francs *par an, payables par douzième à la fin de chaque mois, une allocation annuelle de* Sept et demi pour cent des bénéfices nets réalisés par la Succursale du Boulevard Montmartre

à dater du premier Janvier, mil huit cent quatre vingt deux

Cette allocation sera réglée d'après les chiffres de l'inventaire annuel et payée après la clôture de cet inventaire et l'approbation des comptes par les Associés de la Société BOUSSOD, VALADON et Cie.

Toutefois, dans le cas ou en raison du décès d'un Associé ou d'une cession partielle ou totale des parts de la Société à de nouveaux Associés, la valeur estimative de l'actif Social se trouverait modifiée à un inventaire par suite d'évaluations faites spécialement en vue de cette circonstance, évaluations qui différeraient des bases sur lesquelles sont établis généralement les inventaires de la Société et qui augmenteraient ou diminueraient dans une proportion anormale les bénéfices sociaux de cet exercice, l'allocation donnée à Monsieur Van Gogh, Théodore *au lieu d'être calculée sur les chiffres présentés par cet inventaire, serait établie sur la moyenne des bénéfices des trois précédentes années.*

Il est entendu que l'allocation consentie au profit de Monsieur Van Gogh, Théodore *sera considérée par tous comme une simple rétribution de service et ne pourra, par conséquent, être assimilée, en aucune façon et sous aucun prétexte, à une participation sociale ni donner à Monsieur* Van Gogh Théodore *ou à ses représentants aucun droit de discuter ou critiquer les évaluations d'inventaire ou toute mesure administrative que pourront prendre* Messieurs BOUSSOD, VALADON et Cie.

En cas de départ de Monsieur Van Gogh, Théodore *au cours d'un exercice, il aura droit à la portion de l'allocation afférente à cet exercice, proportionnellement au temps qu'il aura passé dans la* Maison BOUSSOD, VALADON et Cie *pendant l'année sociale dans laquelle se sera effectué son départ, et en prenant pour base l'allocation à laquelle il aurait eu droit pour l'année entière, d'après les chiffres de l'inventaire qui sera dressé à l'expiration de ladite année.*

Par suite, Monsieur Van Gogh, Théodore *ne pourra exiger avant la clôture de l'inventaire, la part proportionnelle d'allocation à laquelle il aura droit.*

En cas de décès de Monsieur Van Gogh, Théodore *dans l'exercice de ses fonctions, ses héritiers ou représentants auront droit à la portion de l'allocation dont il est parlé ci-dessus proportionnellement au temps couru au moment de ce décès et ils ne pourront en toucher le montant qu'après la clôture de l'inventaire.*

Il est entendu, en outre, que Messieurs BOUSSOD, VALADON et Cie *ont le droit absolu de résilier les fonctions de Monsieur* Van Gogh, Théodore *et de se séparer de lui à quelque moment que ce soit, sans être tenus à aucune explication ni à aucune indemnité.*

Fait double à Paris, le Vingt deux Août, mil huit cent quatre vingt dix

30

Theo van Gogh's contract with Boussod, Valadon & Cie., Paris 22 August 1890

developments in art could be followed at first hand. Theo thus came to participate in the enormous expansion of the French art market, which had been growing steadily since the early 19th century.[81] Traditionally, the Salon was where living artists showed their work to the public.[82] However, in the 1870s and 80s, new channels began play a more prominent role in the circulation of contemporary art. Art dealers, and Goupil's in particular, benefited from this development. **[28, 29]** Using new sales techniques and market strategies they were able to present the oeuvre of a select number of modern masters to a group of prosperous enthusiasts, usually hailing from the world of industry and commerce.[83]

Theo must have viewed his new job and surroundings with astonishment. In the summer of 1880 his father remarked: 'Your life is truly extraordinary and you certainly have every opportunity to study people and characters. Not to mention the great variety of bustling activity all around you. I expect the days will just fly by.'[84] He soon made himself useful at the branch on the Boulevard Montmartre. After a reorganisation at the beginning of July 1880, he became one of the youngest assistants to be given a supervisory function.[85] Six months later, probably from 1 February 1881, he became manager, at the young age of 23. His father was overjoyed at his promotion; his prayers for a solid social position for his son seemed to have been answered.[86]

Theo's father had another reason to be pleased. In a letter now lost, written somewhere around January or February, Theo offered to assist him with Vincent's allowance. In the autumn of 1880, after trying his hand at several jobs, Vincent had taken Theo's advice and decided to pursue a career as an artist; since October 1880 he had been studying in Brussels.[87] Whether Theo's financial sacrifice was an expression of his faith in his brother's artistic ability is questionable: Vincent had as yet barely shown what he was capable of. It was rather that Theo and his parents sought to ensure that Vincent would not slip any further down the social ladder. Theo's relationship with Vincent must have been difficult at the time; in January 1881 he had not written to him for more than two months [160/139]. Confidence was restored as the year continued, however – on Vincent's initiative. But the roles were now reversed, and from then on it was Theo who gave Vincent advice.[88]

By January 1882 Vincent was not only dependent on his younger sibling for advice, but for total financial support as well. After a violent row with his father, Vincent had left his parents' home in Neunen and gone to The Hague, making it clear that he no longer wished to accept their money [194/166].[89] From then on Theo supplied Vincent with 100 French francs a month, but not before making it quite clear that he did not understand why he had treated their parents in such a deplorable way. Theo could not comprehend Vincent's childish behaviour and thought it was disgraceful of him to make life so difficult for their elders [198/169].

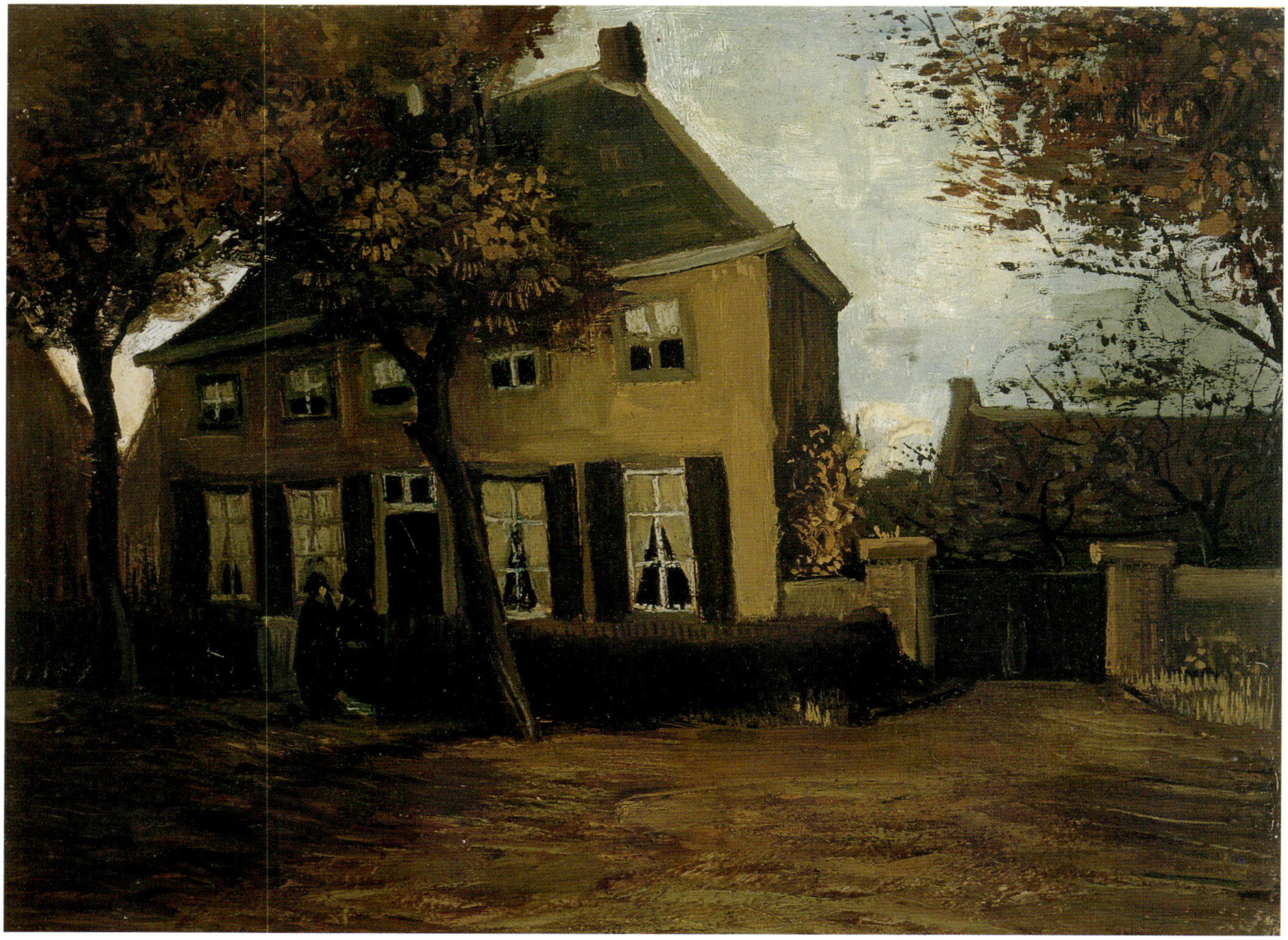

31
Vincent van Gogh 1853–1890
The vicarage at Nuenen 1885
Van Gogh Museum, Amsterdam

He was probably even more puzzled and annoyed when Vincent urged him in March and April of that year to relinquish his career as an art dealer and become a painter [210/181].[90] Vincent's proposal was certainly not very realistic, since, as far as anyone knows, Theo had no interest in changing jobs. On the contrary, his employment in Paris had given him a new lease on life.[91] In May 1882 their bond was further endangered when Theo criticised Vincent's relationship with Sien Hoornik, a prostitute. Vincent described Theo's reactions to his marriage plans as shallow, biased and very wrong.[92] Bitter words were exchanged and Vincent threatened to break with his brother on a number of occasions, although nothing ever came of it. Eventually he was to thank Theo in his New Year's letter for the 'faithful friendship' from which he had 'benefitted all year' [297/255].

Experiencing difficulties

At the beginning of January 1883, Theo confided in Vincent for the first time in quite a while, telling him that he had met a woman from Brittany, called 'Marie,' who had been deserted by her husband, was suffering from poor health and had gotten herself into financial trouble. Given the circumstances, Theo had offered to help her [308/263].[93] His relationship with this woman had obvious parallels with Vincent's recent experience with Sien. At the end of January Vincent gave a moving account of the brothers' dilemma: 'Broadly speaking [...] a solemn, sorrowful figure of a woman has appeared on a cold, unmerciful pavement, and neither you nor I have passed on by, instead we stopped and followed the dictates of our hearts' [307/262].

This love affair was to put Theo in a awkward predicament – as it had in 1877. Marie was lower class, too, and his parents were bound to disapprove; he was thus not sure how long he could continue to support her. Vincent's reply, 'From here to eternity,' was quite definite [338/279]; he was even keen on Theo getting married, 'because life becomes so very different with a woman' [318/267]. This was probably exactly what Theo wanted to hear because for a short time from the end of April he was indeed contemplating marriage. He told his parents of his plans in May, and what he had feared happened: his father refused to entertain the idea of such a match.[94] Strictly speaking, Theo no longer needed permission to marry, as he had reached the age of consent; all the same he bowed to his parents' judgment. He was probably unsure of his feelings for Marie, and Vincent made him even more ambivalent. He thought Theo's love was founded not on 'passion' but on 'fathomless pity,' which he considered a poor basis for marriage [301/259]. Although critical, his parents could not prevent him seeing Marie, and they continued to meet during the spring of 1884. Doubts about whether he had done the right thing continued to trouble him.[95]

In the second half of September 1883 Theo had a difference of opinion with his superiors, probably due to the disappointing sales results he had booked in August and the beginning of September.[96] Up to that point he had worked to everyone's satisfaction, but once his employers started to make what – in Vincent's opinion – were unreasonable demands, he wanted to flee the city and work for someone else. Yet again he sought to solve his problems by dodging them, this time by spiriting himself away or by leaving the firm altogether [301/259].

Vincent was sympathetic to Theo's difficult situation. He wrote to him around 12 October 1883 that he understood what he was going through, 'because I had a period when I was tense and suffering from nervous exhaustion, days in which the most beautiful things outside did not seem beautiful to me at all because I had lost the power to react to them in a normal way. That was caused by the bustle of life on the streets and the office – and cares – and nerves' [397/332]. Vincent claimed Theo was suffering from the same problem and that he would have to do his best to recover. He would never recuperate if he remained an art dealer: the trade would eventually get the better of him [408/341]. Vincent, who had been having a hard time in Drenthe since September 1883, had a better idea. He had made the same suggestion to his brother 18 months earlier, so Theo must have been amazed at his bringing it up again: 'Go on old chap, come and paint with me out on the heath, out in the potato fields, come and walk behind the plough for a change, and follow the shepherd – come and gaze into the fire in the hearth with me – breath the fresh air as the storm breaks over the moors, do something unusual [...] Change your life – look for inspiration out on the heath' [404/339]. But while Vincent continued to urge him to make a radical change, business at Goupil's began to pick up in October and November, with the result that Theo was only too delighted to stay on after all. Not that he had a great deal of choice, as various members of his family – his parents, Vincent and Wil – depended on his income.

Once Theo's business interests had taken a turn for the better, he again began to treat his brother with more reserve. After the unsuccessful sojourn in Drenthe, Vincent had once more moved in with his parents in Neunen and was making life difficult – particularly for his father [415/346]. He frequently denounced Theo for being aloof and siding with their father. In December he questioned their friendship a number of times [416/347]. He accused Theo of not being honest with himself; although he must have known better, he still continued to pursue his career as an art dealer: 'And I believe that even though you are now so sure that you must remain a dealer, your true nature will continue to torment you, and you may regret this decision more than you think' [416/347]. Once again Theo was caught between a rock and a hard place, for while Vincent inveighed against his decision to remain with the firm, his father impressed upon him not to be too much influenced by Vincent, and exhorted him to 'be wise enough not to be talked into things which are impractical. For that, unfortunately, is his trouble!'[97]

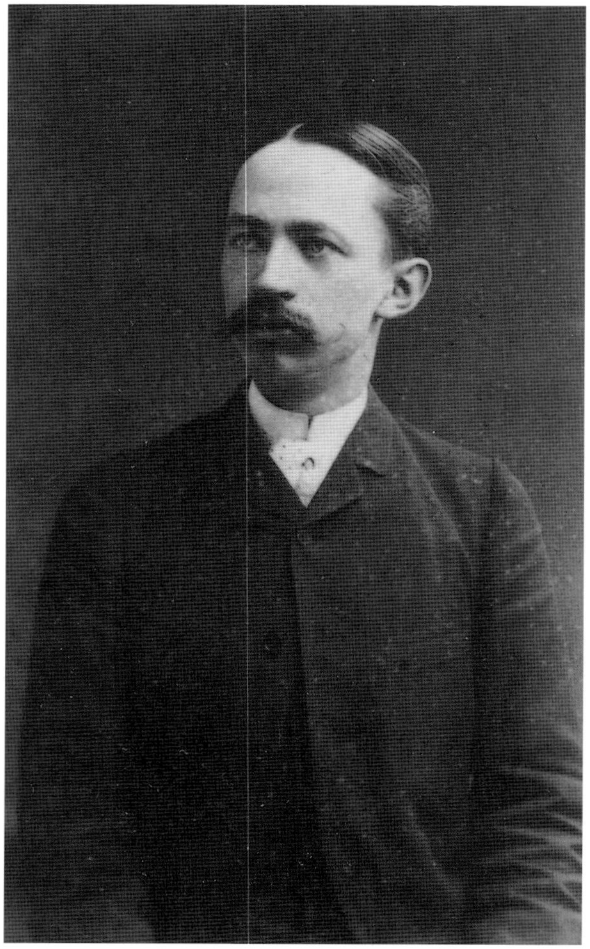

32
Andries Bonger 1861–1936

In the months that followed relations were tense. It was thus only logical that Vincent should propose their dealings become more business-like. His suggestion – made in February 1884 – was that his monthly allowance be considered as earnings, paid in exchange for works of art. He hastened to add that he hoped Theo would not ruin this agreement by behaving like a dealer, but would instead act more like someone 'with a heart,' who wanted to help a novice painter [430/360]. When, later that month, Theo remarked that Vincent's work would have to become a lot better before it could be offered to potential buyers, his brother – although agreeing in principle – nonetheless accused him of not trying hard enough. If Theo was not going to make more of an effort then he no longer wanted his protection [434/358]. What this effort entailed was to became clear later on. In April Vincent explained that the proposed arrangement did not mean that Theo had control of his work; it was meant as an unconditional vote of confidence in Vincent's future as an artist – that, and nothing more [444/363a].

Theo ignored his brother's bitter criticisms and remained detached. Sometime between the end of October and the beginning of November 1884 he wrote that Vincent would do better to spend his time making good paintings than discussing all sorts of business matters. Theo's attitude was unacceptable to Vincent: either one was for him or against him. In December he wrote that he was certain they should part ways if they could not become closer: 'You, like many others, have always got something to criticize about my person, whether it be my clothes and manners or what I say [...] and [...], thanks to this, after years of wear and tear, our intimate brotherly feelings [...] are about to succumb. My past is always dragged in to the discussion, too, you the real gentleman at G. & Cie. and me the "bête noire" and "mauvais coucheur"' [476/386a].

Friendship with Andries Bonger

After the conflict with his superiors in the autumn of 1883, business went well in 1884, leaving Theo content with his position. So much so that in January 1885 he refused an offer to go and work at one of his client's offices.[98] As *gérant* at Goupil's he was responsible for buying and selling works of contemporary art and for doing the annual stock-taking. He was also in close contact with collectors, other dealers and artists.[99]

The pressure of a six-day working week left Theo little time for a private life. His appears to have been a solitary existence, without many friends.[100] The Hollandsche Club offered some amusement and it was there that he met Andries Bonger [32] in August 1881. However, it took until the end of 1884 or the beginning of 1885 before he became close with this Amsterdam insurance broker's son, and before Dries became for Theo 'the most likeable person I have been out with in Paris up to now': 'He is a charming fellow. One could not wish for more entertaining company.'[101]

Theo and Bonger were in the same boat. Both had demanding jobs, were outsiders in the metropolis, had a shared interest in culture, and both enjoyed going on long walks. Dries Bonger – who had been in Paris

at the offices of the insurance brokers Geo Wehry since 1879 – was an avid reader and kept up with French literature. It was, however, Theo who introduced him to the world of art. These were interests he had once shared with his brother, but Vincent was far away and their relationship had become fraught over the years. Bonger proved the ideal replacement.

The sudden death of Theodorus van Gogh on 26 March 1885 brought Theo and Dries closer to one another.[102] The death of his much-loved father came as a hard blow. Thoroughly dejected, he left for Neunen on Friday, 27 March to attend the funeral. Dries accompanied him to the station: 'I have never taken a friend to the northbound train terminal under such sad circumstances as I did last Friday. That morning my friend Van Gogh had received the news that his father had suffered a stroke and died. [...] Van Gogh himself is not very strong. You can imagine the state he was in when he left.'[103]

When Theo returned to Paris at the beginning of April Bonger took good care of him. Sharing his grief with Vincent was not a real option since his brother had recently done nothing but quarrel with his father, and had in effect already taken leave of him. Around 1 April Vincent wrote that, like Theo, he found that his 'first days back at work did not run as smoothly as usual.' That was all he said about how the event had affected him. It must have been painful for Theo to realise that Vincent could be so unmoved by their father's passing. He was chillingly rational, reminding Theo simply that life was short and then proceeding to discuss at great length various artistic matters that were currently occupying his thoughts [492/397].[104] Theo did not reply for two whole weeks; his silence spoke volumes.

For Theo, his father's death meant an irrevocable break with the past. He was now the *pater familias*, who set himself the task of keeping the family together. Although understandable, his attempts to reconcile Vincent with his mother and sister proved to be a waste of time. Vincent was convinced of 'the incompatibility of people who had their position in society to think of and a farmer-painter not in the least bit interested in either' [496/400].[105] Perhaps Theo's mother might give him a helping hand? In May he asked her to show some understanding for Vincent's situation: 'Even very famous painters are having a hard time selling at the moment, so it is even more difficult for an unknown, novice painter to sell his work. His time will come, just you wait and see.' There was to be no rapprochement, however. After he left for Antwerp in November 1885 Vincent never saw his mother again, and she was only to have the odd letter from him passed on to her.

The death of his father drew Theo's attention to former times but also to the future, which until now had been entirely determined by his father.[106] During this period of mourning, he seems to have decided that from now on he would commit himself more firmly to painters he truly admired. A telling sign was his first purchase of three works by Claude Monet in April, and his repeatedly expressed praise for painters like Albert Besnard **[33]** and Jean-François Raffaëlli in the months that followed.[107]

In the summer of 1885 Theo spent part of his holidays with Dries Bonger. The two of them travelled to museums in Lille, Bruges, Ghent and Antwerp to study Flemish art. Theo went on afterwards to stay in Nuenen from about 28 July to 7 August. There was a glaring contrast between home and his isolated existence in Paris. On 6 August he wrote to Bonger, who had gone on to visit his own parents in Amsterdam: 'How different it is here from where we are, such unaffected pleasure, such a zest for living and such sincerity.'[108] While in Nuenen, the brothers discussed Vincent's financial situation, which had not improved since the death of their father. They ended up wrangling about money, with Vincent feeling that his livelihood was under threat. Theo's stay in Amsterdam was a happier affair. On 7 August he visited the Bonger family, where he met his future wife, Jo, for the very first time.

After this pleasant, nostalgic visit to the Netherlands it was not easy to return to Paris. The city depressed Theo and made him listless. In Bonger's view their travelling together had made them 'much more intimate friends': '[Theo] is someone who grows on you and whose talents I am slowly learning to value with all my heart and soul.'[109] After this they spent as much of their spare time as they could in one another's company. Every evening after dinner they read and studied art and art history. On Sundays they

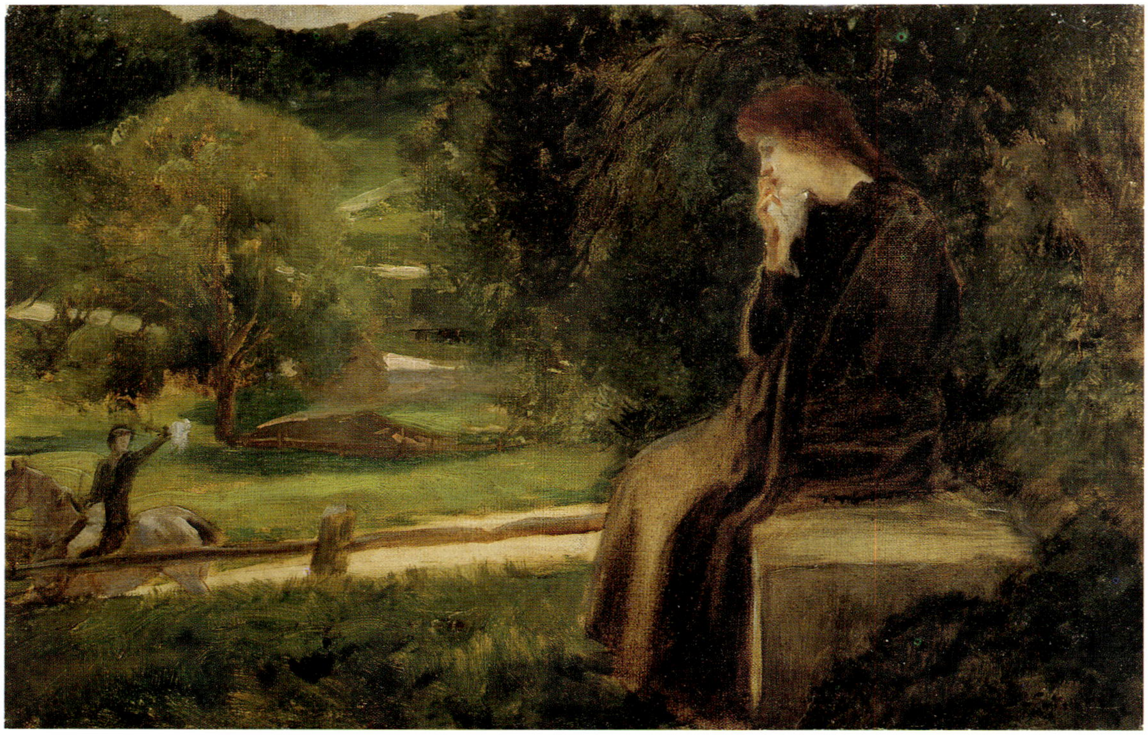

33
Albert Besnard 1849–1934
The parting n.d.
Van Gogh Museum, Amsterdam

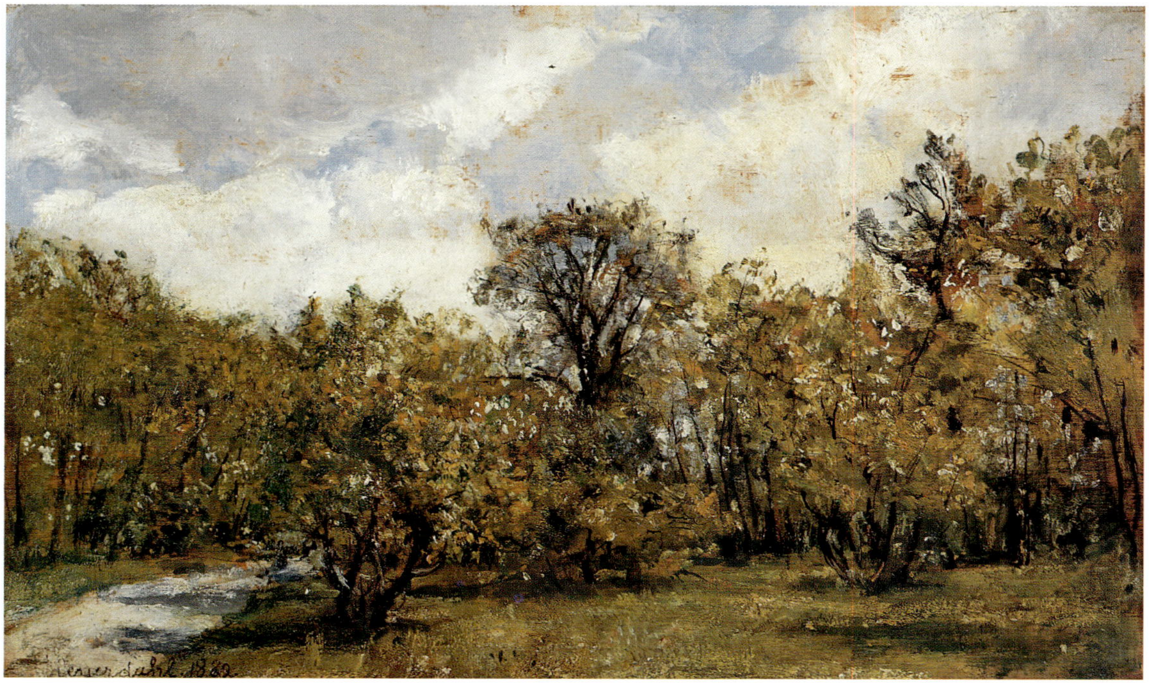

34
Hans Olaf Heijerdahl 1857–1913
The park 1882
Van Gogh Museum, Amsterdam

visited the Louvre and walked in the woods at Meudon, just outside Paris.[110]

Paris made Theo feel lonlier than ever, despite these pleasant hours spent with Bonger. Particularly at holiday time, in December, he missed 'the intimacy of Dutch society.'[111] It was not just homesickness for the conviviality of Holland that got the better of him; at this point he also began to rebel against the middle-class values that had been pumped into him at home. As he wrote to Lies on 13 October: 'The more people one meets, the more one sees that they are hiding behind the accepted language of convention; what they really mean when they say they are sincere is so often trivial and malicious.' For the first time, Theo took Vincent's side, albeit cautiously: 'He is one of those people who has seen the world up close and has withdrawn from it. Now we shall have to wait and see whether he proves to be a genius. I believe he is, and I am not the only one, Bonger agrees with me too. Once his work is good he will be a great man. As far as success is concerned, he will probably suffer the same fate as Heijerdahl [34], appreciated by a few, but not understood by the public at large.'[112] For Vincent, Theo's tentative move in his direction did not go far enough, that is, if he heard about it at all. As had become the tradition, he accused his younger brother around New Year's of 'severity and callous disregard,' and of being 'remote' [554/443].[113]

Living with Vincent

In February, Theo finally proved that he was ready to make more of an effort on his brother's behalf. He suggested Vincent come to live with him in Paris and take lessons from the famous history painter, Fernand Cormon. How soon Vincent could join him was uncertain, as Theo first wanted to find a new, more spacious apartment. Vincent's unexpected arrival around 1 March [35] must therefore have come as quite a shock. The two brothers had to share Theo's cramped apartment on the Rue de Laval – a side-street off the Rue Pigalle, near Theo's gallery and Cormon's studio on the Boulevard Clichy. [36] This was not a great success. Bonger related that Vincent, whom he found guilty of flagrantly abusing convention, was soon quarrelling with everyone in sight, including Theo, who found it difficult to cope with him.[114]

In June 1886 Theo and Vincent moved to a larger,

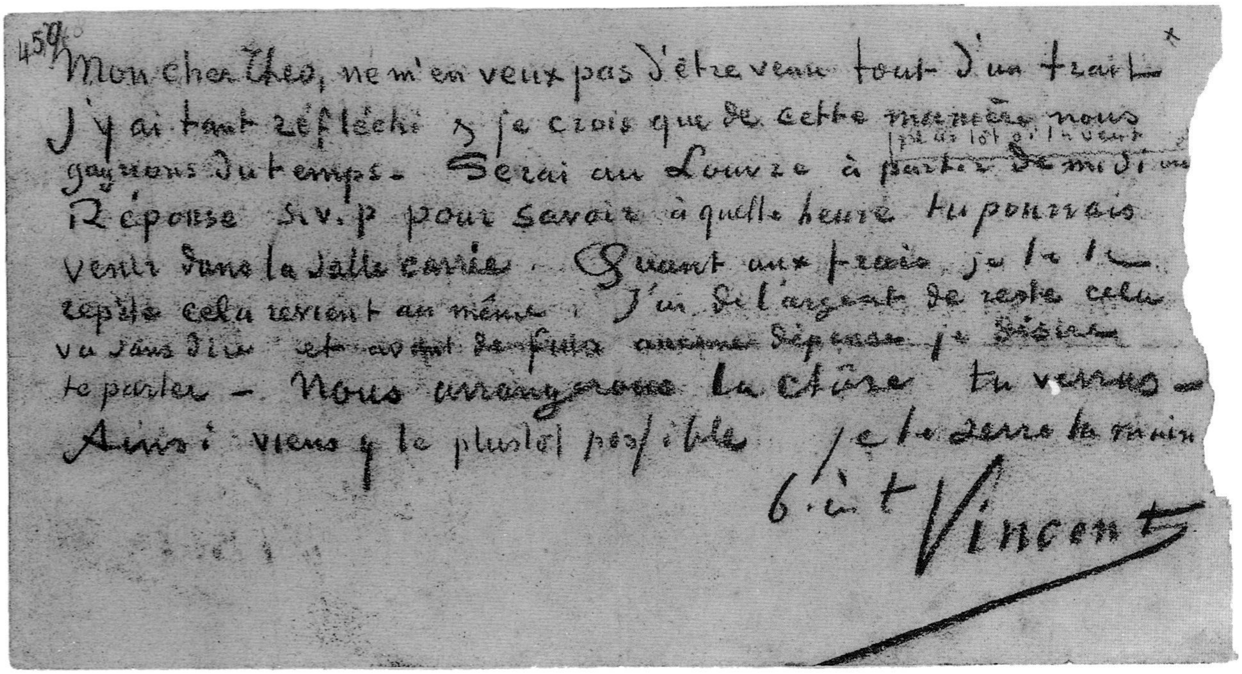
459

Mon cher Theo, ne m'en veux pas d'être venu tout d'un trait
J'y ai tant réfléchi & je crois que de cette manière nous
gagnerons du temps. Serai au Louvre à partir de midi ou plus tôt si tu veux
Réponse s.v.p. pour savoir à quelle heure tu pourrais
venir dans la salle carrée. Quant aux frais je te le
répète cela revient au même. J'ai de l'argent de reste cela
va sans dire et avant de faire aucune dépense je désire
te parler. Nous arrangerons la chose tu verras.
Ainsi viens y le plustôt possible. je te serre la main
t. à t. Vincent

35

Letter announcing Vincent's arrival in Paris c. 1 March 1886
[570/459]

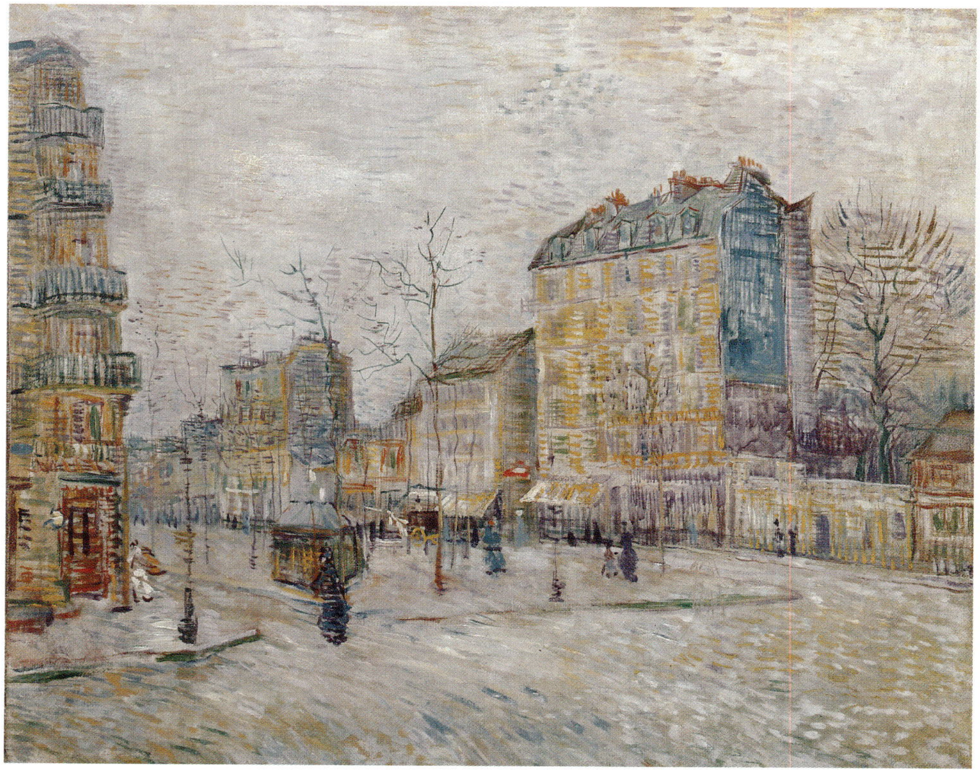

36
Vincent van Gogh 1853–1890
Boulevard de Clichy, Paris 1887
Van Gogh Museum, Amsterdam

self-contained, three-room apartment at 54, Rue Lepic [**37**], at the foot of the Butte Montmartre, which at that time had yet to be developed. Nevertheless, living together remained a struggle. Bonger recounts that Vincent constantly accused Theo of all kinds of things he was innocent of. To make matters worse, Theo was also suffering from poor health, not just physical but psychosomatic complaints as well. He looked, or so Bonger reports, terribly swollen up: 'his face has literally disappeared.'[115] Theo, on the other hand, gave his mother glowing reports: their accommodations were fine, and Vincent was making definite progress as an artist; his brother was far more cheerful than he had been before, which had made him quite popular in artistic circles.[116] Theo did not utter a single word about the difficulties he was really experiencing in the summer of 1886 – not only living with the overly demanding Vincent, but also maintaining an affair that had been dragging on for a year with a woman referred to only as 'S.' According to Bonger, this relationship had finally led to nothing because she was 'morally very ill' and Theo had been too hard on her. Both Dries and Vincent were quite firm in their conviction that she was not a suitable match [571/460].[117]

In the summer of 1886 Theo also made plans to establish himself as an independent art dealer, with the help of Vincent and Dries. He wanted to be the master of his own fortune. The death of his father, regardless of how much he might miss him, had given Theo his freedom. Unfortunately, he lacked the finances to actually exploit his new-found liberty He needed capital to establish his own firm, and was thus still dependent on his wealthy Uncle Cent, who had offered to help out once before. At the beginning of August Theo went back to the Netherlands to ask him for financial backing. Unimpressed, Uncle Cent dismissed his ideas.[118] To Vincent, this was a sign that Theo was destined to be a wage-slave at Goupil's for evermore.

Theo returned to Paris on 26 August a disillusioned man. His health had clearly suffered from the events of the recent past. Around New Year's he had a bad attack of nerves, which literally paralysed him. He still felt weak in February and looked sickly and

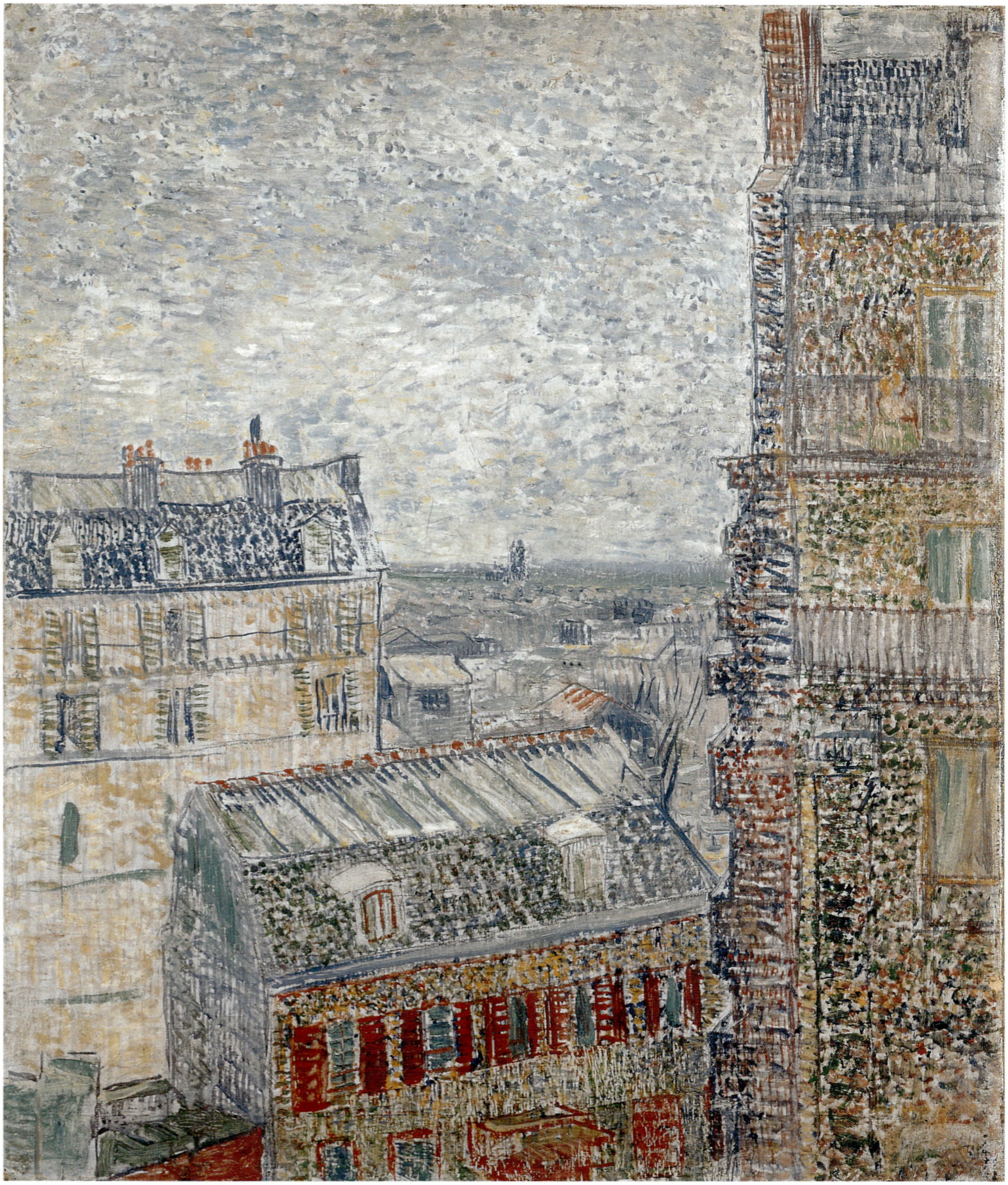

37
Vincent van Gogh 1853–1890
View from Vincent's room in the Rue Lepic 1887
Van Gogh Museum, Amsterdam

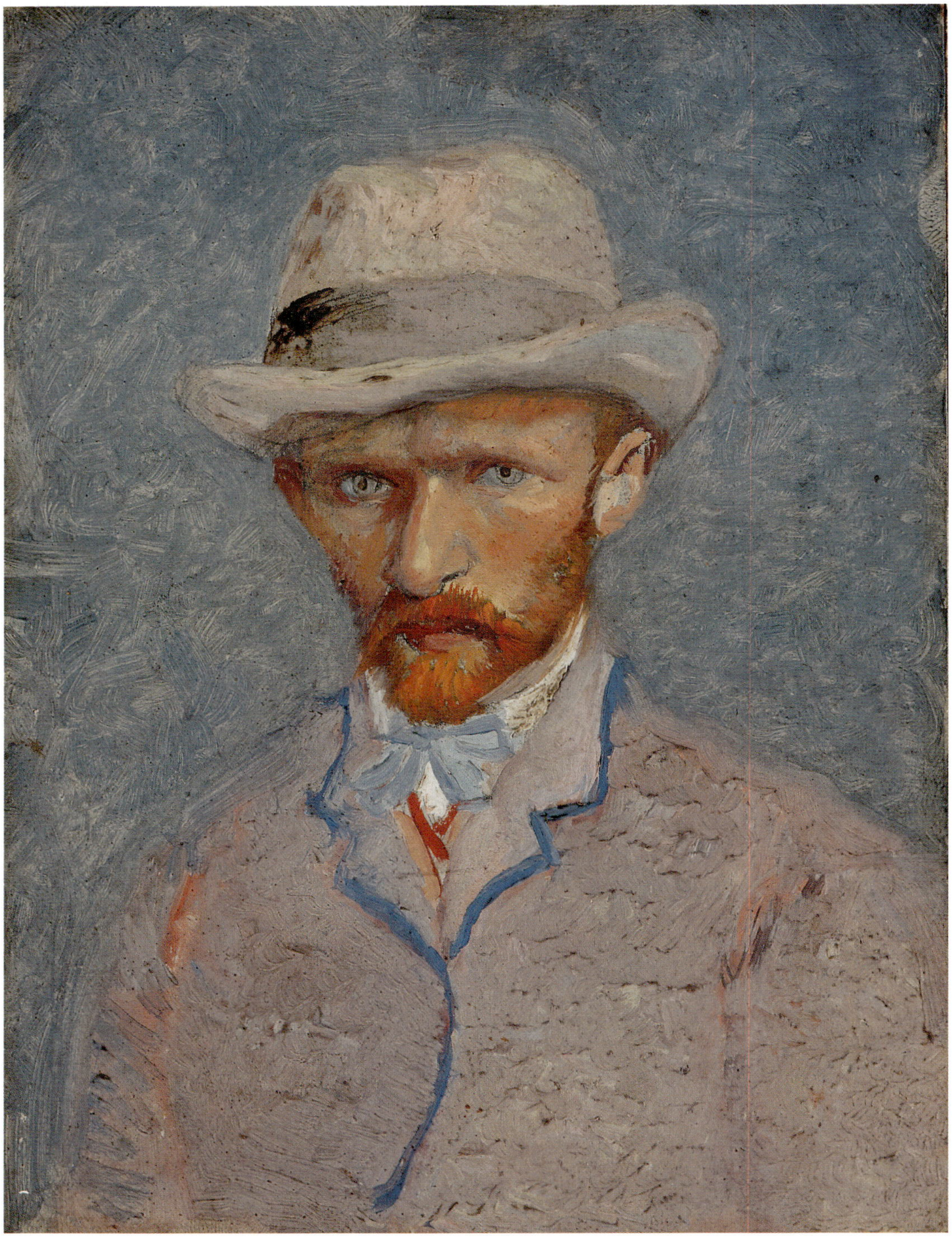

38
Vincent van Gogh 1853–1890
Self-portrait with a grey felt hat 1887
Van Gogh Museum, Amsterdam

gaunt.[119] Three months later he confided to Lies that his mental and physical health were so abysmal that he did not think he would live to see 30; his ailments were the early symptoms of *dementia paralytica*, a neurological complaint caused by syphillis, from which Theo was to die in January 1891.[120]

Theo had manoeuvred himself into a tight corner; even his relationship with Vincent was deteriorating. On 11 March he wrote to his brother Cor that he thought it was a shame that Vincent was so obstinate, and that they could not possibly continue to live together: there was simply 'no reasoning with him.'[121] Three days later he told Wil that he would have stopped supporting Vincent long ago were it not for the fact that he was a true artist. Theo thought Vincent was two people rolled into one: the first 'marvellously gifted, friendly and gentle,' the second 'self-centred and callous.' Vincent never missed an opportunity to show his contempt for Theo, which nearly led to Theo's giving up on him: 'There was a time when I loved Vincent dearly, and he was my best friend, but that is over now.'[122]

But Theo had barely given vent to his feelings before relenting once again. He was frightened of causing a permanent rift between himself and his brother, who probably knew and understood him better than anyone else in the world. About a month after complaining to Wil, he wrote to her that he had patched up things up: 'Nothing is going to change and I am glad. It would have been strange for me to live on my own again and it would not have made things any better for him either. I have asked him to stay.'[123]

La vie de bohème

Theo's curious change of heart may have been related to the new opportunities now opening up at Boussod, Valadon & Cie. following a change of management around May 1887. After Uncle Cent had refused to back him, Theo had begun to search for different ways of realising his plans to help the little known painters he admired – just as Vincent wanted him to.[124] Theo was given more freedom to transact business his own way when, in 1886, at the venerable age of 80, the founder of the firm, Adolphe Goupil retired for good and the two sons of the joint-proprietor, Léon Boussod, joined the management of the Société Boussod, Valadon & Cie. – Etienne in 1886 and Jean in 1887. From spring 1887 onwards,[125] Theo transformed the branch on the Boulevard Montmartre into a gallery which not only traded in works of the Barbizon School and popular Salon painters, but exhibited works by 'modern' artists, too.

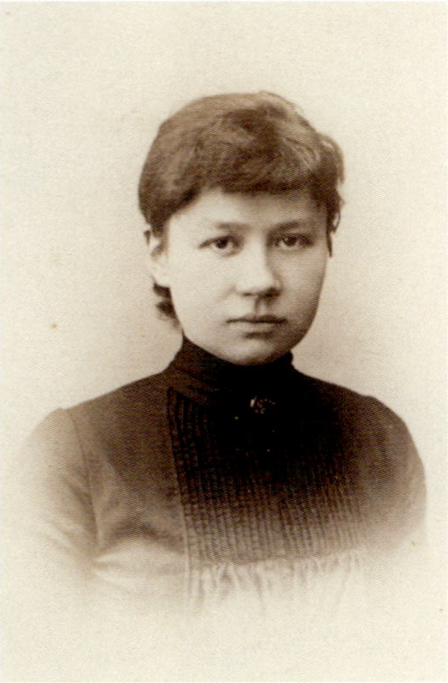
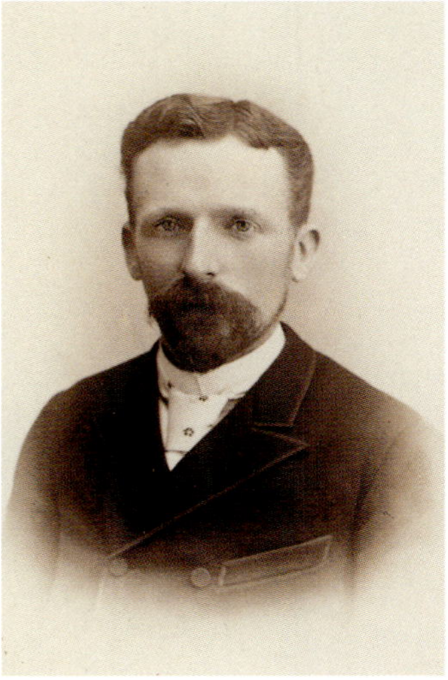

39
Johanna Gezina (Jo) van Gogh-Bonger 1862–1925
40
Theo van Gogh

The crises in 1885 and 1886 had served to highlight Theo's lonely existence. He was almost 30, had been through several unsuccessful love affairs, and must have felt that time was running out if he wanted to set up a home of his own. In 1887 he wrote to Lies that in the summer, once his position in the firm was more secure, he was planning to ask Jo Bonger, Dries's younger sister, to marry him.[126] **[39, 40]** When he was given this security a month later, he told Lies that 'the big business' would indeed be settled in July, even though he could hardly believe that he would make a suitable husband, or that a woman would want to share his 'busy life.'[127] It is unclear what Theo's hopes of marrying Jo Bonger were founded on. They barely knew one another, and his marriage proposal on 25 July completely overwhelmed her: she believed Theo had taken her aside to talk about art and literature, and instead he proposed to her quite out of the blue.[128] That she refused was understandable; besides, she was in love with someone else.

Theo's wish for a family life was not to be granted for some time to come. Theo explained his behaviour

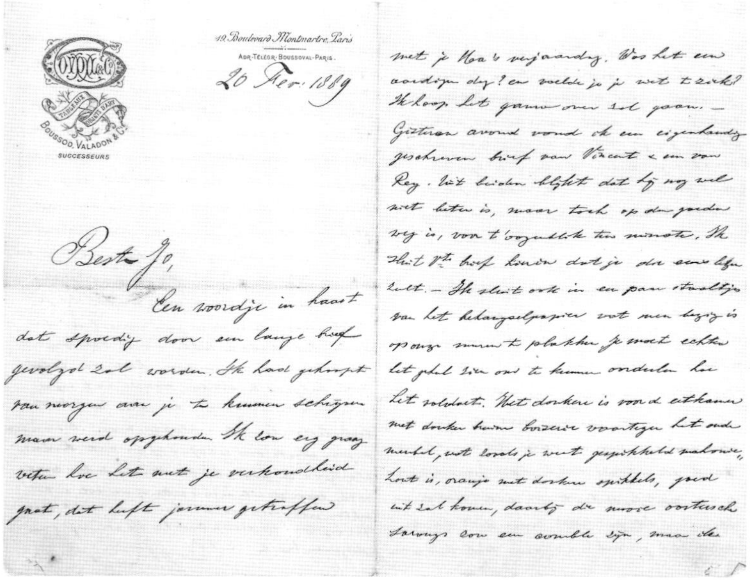

19 Boulevard Montmartre, Paris
ADR. TÉLÉGR. BOUSSOVAL-PARIS.
GOUPIL & Cie
TABLEAUX OBJETS D'ART
BOUSSOD, VALADON & Cie SUCCESSEURS

20 Feb: 1889

Beste Jo,

Een woordje in haast dat spoedig door een lange brief gevolgd zal worden. Ik had gehoopt van morgen aan je te kunnen schrijven maar werd opgehouden. Ik zou erg graag weten hoe het met je verkoudheid gaat, dat heeft jammer getroffen met je Moa's verjaardag. Was het een aardige dag? en voelde je je niet te ziek? Ik hoop het gauw over zal gaan. – Gisteren avond vond ik een eigenhandig geschreven brief van Vincent & een van Rey. Uit beiden blijkt dat hij nog wel niet beter is, maar toch op den goeden weg is, voor t'oogenblik ten minste. Ik sluit Vs brief hierin dat je dien eens lezen zult. – Ik sluit ook in een paar staaltjes van het behangselpapier wat men bezig is op onze muren te plakken. Je moet echter het geheel zien om te kunnen oordeelen hoe het voldoet. Het donkere is voor de eetkamer met donker bruin boiserie voor tegen het oude meubel, wat zooals je weet geschilderd mahonie hout is, oranje met donkere spikkels, goed uit zal komen, daarbij de mooie oostersche tapijt zou een ensemble zijn, maar dat

41
Letter from Theo van Gogh to Jo Bonger, Paris, 26 July 1887

to Jo in a poignant letter [**41**], written the day after his emotional outburst: 'Oh Jo! My actions have so often been the result of the frame of mind I was in at the time, and my life would certainly have been very different, and of course much better, if I had come across the love and support my heart so longed for, but I roamed alone for years, thought I had found the right person, but it seems I was mistaken. It is not surprising that my heart, which has been hurt so often, has become hardened, and that for a long time art was the only thing in which I took an interest – it has filled my entire life.'[129]

Art was to remain the governing factor for another 18 months. After Jo turned him down, he threw himself into his work. Within a short period he purchased work by Degas, Guillaumin, Monet, Pissarro, Renoir and Sisley. On Vincent's urging, he became involved with the circle of artists his brother had dubbed the 'painters of the Petit Boulevard.' He came into contact with Anquetin, Bernard [**42**], Seurat and Signac, whose studios he visited with Vincent, and in November 1887 he visited an exhibition of their works in the Restaurant du Chalet on the Avenue de Clichy, where Vincent's work was also shown. In the rehearsal rooms of the Théâtre Libre d'Antoine on the Rue Blanche[130] he viewed works by Seurat, Signac and, once again, Vincent. In December he met Paul Gauguin at Emile Schuffenecker's house on the Boulevard Montparnasse, and that same month he exhibited three paintings and five ceramics of his at his gallery.[131] A month later, he exhibited recent work by Degas and, for a second time, Gauguin.[132] In the evenings, after work, Theo and Vincent were often to be found in the many cafés in Montmartre, talking to artists like Guillaumin, Camille and Lucien Pissarro and Seurat. Vincent later wrote to Gauguin that they discussed 'the measures which should be taken to safeguard the livelihood of painters and the materials they need for production (paint and canvas), and how the artists [can] be guaranteed a direct percentage of the price paid for their paintings when they [are] no longer in [his] possession' [705/548].

According to Jo, who was kept up to date by her brother, this was when Theo became part of the Parisian 'young painters' bohemia.'[133] In desperation, she wondered whether she was perhaps to blame for Theo's extremely unhealthy lifestyle. Healthy or not, this was the period when Theo's life and work took a turn for the better. With great enthusiasm, he put all his energy into selling the work of painters whom he and Vincent considered to have a future. He enriched his own art collection with works by painters like Gauguin [**43**], Toulouse-Lautrec and Seurat, bought with Vincent's advice.

Despite his busy life, Theo had not become less lonely. Quite the contrary. His friendship with Dries

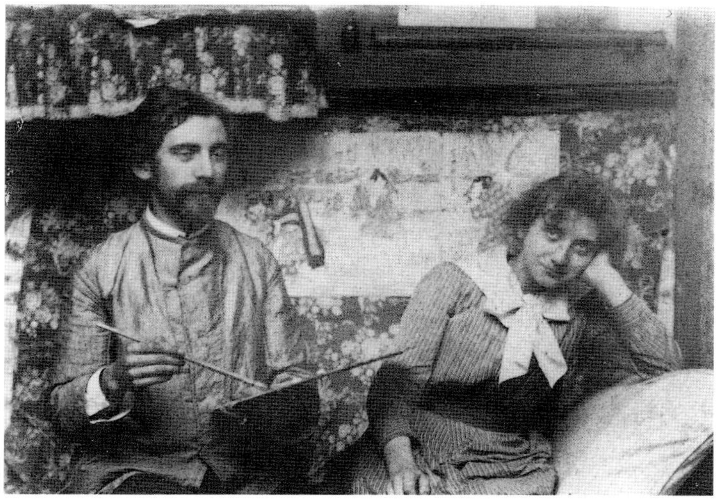

42
Emile Bernard and his wife in 1887

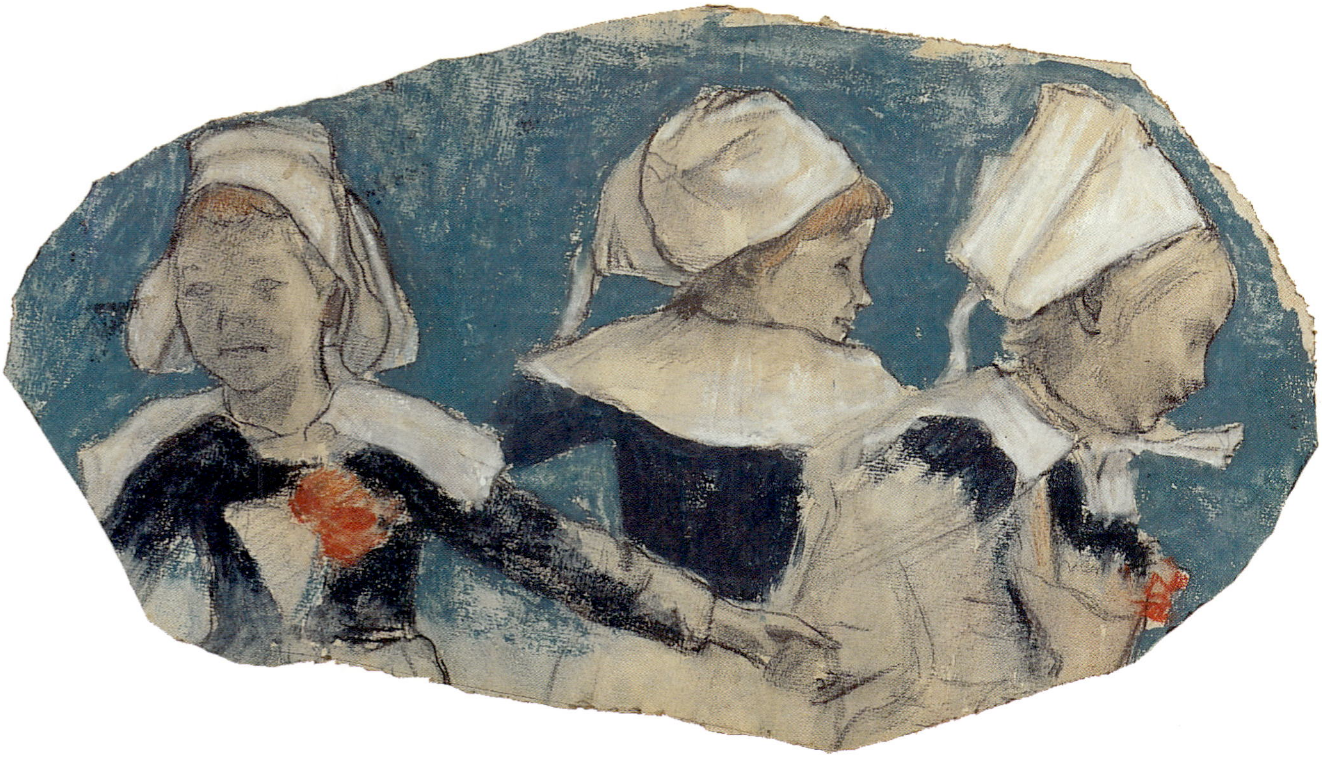

43
Paul Gauguin 1848–1903
Study of Breton girls dancing, Ronde Breton 1887
Van Gogh Museum, Amsterdam

Bonger was flagging, probably due to Theo's awkward relationship with his friend's favourite sister Jo, his less than respectable lifestyle, and Dries's forthcoming marriage to Annie van der Linden. Then, on 19 February, Vincent could stand Paris no longer and departed for Arles [698/544].[134] As a token of his affection, he decorated his brother's apartment with Japanese prints and objects and paintings the day before he left. As loving a gesture as this might have been, these silent testimonies were a constant reminder of his brother's absence. Theo had to manage on his own once again. On 24 February he wrote to Lies that he missed Vincent: 'When [Vincent] came here two years ago, I never thought we would become so attached to one another, and now I am alone again in the apartment. If I can, I shall find someone to share my house with, but someone like Vincent is not easy to replace. It is amazing the number of things he knows and what a clear view he has of the world, this is why I am sure that if he still has a few years to live, he will make a name for himself. I have gotten to know many painters through him as he is very well thought of in their circles. He is one of the champions of new ideas, but since there is nothing new under the sun, it is more accurate to say: of old ideas which have been revived, which went into a decline and almost expired after becoming commonplace.'[135]

Art dealers

Living together in Paris had cemented the bond between Theo and Vincent. In their letters the habitual reproaches of the past gave way to affection, confidentiality and concern. Vincent expressed his admiration for Theo's efforts as an art dealer on a number of occasions. He wrote to Wil around 22 June 1888: 'Theo has worked himself up to such a position that the branch he controls nowadays always has an exhibition of impressionists [...] Theo works for the impressionists, he has done something for them all, and sold their work, and he will certainly continue to do so. What I have written to you about this will show you that he is no ordinary dealer who rarely spares a thought for the painters' [633/W4].[136] Theo responded by putting his faith in Vincent and providing him with

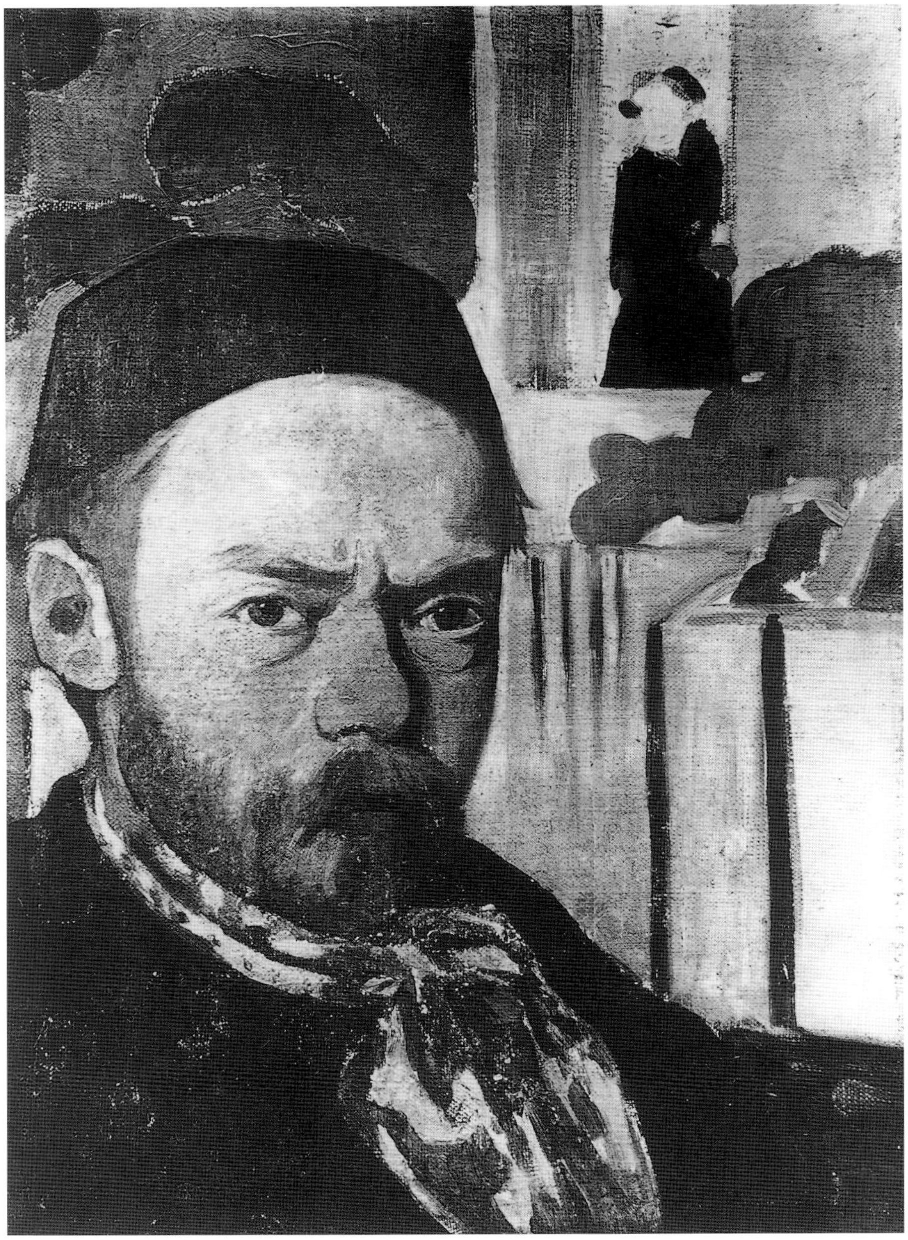

44
Meijer de Haan 1852–1895
Self-portrait 1889–91
Art Gallery of Ontario, Toronto

the financial means to carry on as an artist. He was insistent that Vincent should establish and widen his circle of artistic friends, and that he should continue to work for both their sakes [718/T3].

A recurring subject in their letters from 1888 onwards is how the two of them together could promote the work of the impressionists and improve their standard of living. They had discussed this at some length in Paris, and had probably also entertained the idea of establishing their own dealership. In his letters, Vincent frequently refers to 'our' art collection, 'our store' and 'we' when writing about matters such as fostering young artists.[137] Vincent also toyed with the idea of establishing a club or association to guarantee artists' incomes. The painters he had in mind would have to hand over their work to the association in exchange for a commensurate share of the proceeds after an eventual sale. The impressionists of the Grand Boulevard – Degas, Monet, Pissarro, Sisley and

Renoir – were to set a good example by donating somewhere in the region of ten works. Theo and Tersteeg could be taken on as member-assessors of the association, and were also to inject capital in the form of paintings [586/468]. The idea was as radical as it was impracticable. Theo, realistic as ever, did not take it very seriously. He did, however, commit himself to assisting a few artists he respected, and one of the ways he did this was to convince his former employer, Tersteeg, to exhibit works by, among others, Degas, Gauguin, Monet and Vincent at the branch in The Hague. The consignment finally returned unsold, except for one work by Monticelli.

Theo and Vincent persuaded Gauguin to leave Pont-Aven for Arles in the south of France to live and work with Vincent.[138] Gauguin's arrival on 23 October was followed by an intense period in 'the studio of the south.' [**45**] On 6 December Theo wrote to Wil that Gauguin's company meant a great deal to Vincent 'and for the time being he is quite engrossed.'[139] Their collaboration came to an abrupt end on 23 December when, in a fit of madness, Vincent threatened Gauguin with a knife, and finally cut off a piece of his own left ear. Gauguin could not leave Arles quickly enough. Theo, who had arrived by night-train on 24 December, travelled back to Paris with him on the evening of the next day, leaving Vincent in the care of the Dr Felix Rey, *chef interne* of the hospital in Arles.

Joy and sorrow

For Theo, Vincent's attack could not have come at a worse moment. After his brother had left Paris he had felt abandoned. The company of the painters Arnold Koning, Christian Mourier-Petersen, Meijer de Haan [**44**] and Jozef Isaacson, who all stayed at Theo's apartment for shorter or longer periods between March 1888 and March 1889,[140] were a welcome diversion, but he yearned, possibly more than ever, for the love of a woman.

His wish was granted, quite unexpectedly, in December 1888 when, somewhere round the tenth of the month, Jo Bonger paid him a visit. She had been staying in Paris since 8 November with her brother, Dries, and her sister-in-law, Annie. Theo and Jo had not seen each other for about a year and a half, yet within a few days they had confessed their love for one another and decided to get married. Theo could hardly believe his life was finally taking a turn for the better. On 21 December he asked his mother for her blessing. At the same time, panicking a little, he wondered if his fiancée was not making a mistake: how could he ever give Jo what she longed for? He wrote: 'Guess who I met a couple of days ago, Jo Bonger, what was to be done? [...] One thing led to another, and we were so used to one another's company that I thought I could treat her amiably, and that I would be able to be good friends with her and her brother once again. But Mother, that was impossible. I loved her too much and now that we have seen one another a lot the last few days she has told me she loves me too and that she will take me the way I am. I am actually very worried that she is making a mistake and that she will be disappointed in me, but I am so happy, and I shall try my best to understand her and make her happy, if I can.'[141]

However, just as things were looking up and everyone was so happy, Vincent became seriously ill. Theo travelled to Arles as soon as he could. He was not able to say goodbye to Jo, whom he had wanted to escort to Holland to announce their engagement. Full of remorse about the way events had overtaken them, for which he was, of course, in no way to blame, he wrote to her on the evening of his departure: 'It gives me such pain to cause you sadness when I would so much have liked to bring you joy.'[142] His happiness had lasted barely a fortnight.

At the turn of the year Theo oscillated between hope and fear. He did not have much faith in his brother's eventual recovery, as can be deduced from a letter written to Jo on 28 December: 'The possible loss of my brother, who has meant so much to me, and has grown so much in my esteem, has made me think of the enormous emptiness that would overcome me should he no longer be with us. [...] Our poor old warrior has taken a beating and nobody can do anything to alleviate the pain, yet he really feels it quite acutely.'[143] Three days later, he even went so far as to ask her to join him in cherishing Vincent's memory: 'Even if we [Theo and Jo] had been living together I would have been happy for him to have continued being my brother and mentor, in the truest sense of the word, for us, for a long time to come; that hope has now disappeared and both our lives have suffered a loss, but it is once again proof that one must stand on one's own two feet. We shall honour his memory, shall we not, my love?'[144]

Vincent's insanity vanished as unexpectedly as it had appeared. He had barely had time to recover before asking Theo not to worry any more about his health, 'because I cannot cope with that on top of everything else' [733/567]. This was probably why Theo did not tell him about his engagement. Theo left for Amsterdam on 6 January in order to arrive on time for the engagement party, to be held on 9 January. Vincent only received notification of the event on the actual day; in response he sent his best wishes to the future couple [738/570].[145]

On 14 January Theo returned to Paris alone; Jo was to stay with her parents in Amsterdam until the wedding on 18 April. They had a long wait ahead. In the three months before their marriage, Theo and Jo wrote to one another frequently, going in to great detail about their daily activities, one of which was trying to find an apartment to suit them both – no easy task. Primarily they wrote about their feelings for one another, about their expectations and doubts in relation to their future life together. Theo desperately wanted to make Jo happy, but he wondered whether he had it in him. He wanted to do his best, but sometimes he felt so empty 'that I forget all my good intentions and I am like an oyster in its shell.'[146] Nevertheless, Jo's love had made him less solitary and he hoped fervently that his loneliness would become a thing of the past.[147] With renewed energy, he studied the Paris housing market for a suitable place to live. Yet again he wanted to put the past behind him and make a fresh start.

Theo was granted precious little time or opportunity to entertain these illusions. On 7 February he received news that Vincent had once again been admitted to the hospital in Arles with symptoms of madness. This was a great blow. He was quite downcast when he wrote to Jo that he feared Vincent might never recover; the social forces his brother was forced to contend with were simply too strong. In this letter he compared Vincent's 'tormented expression' to Rodin's marble statue of *John the Baptist* **[46]**, which – along with works by Monet and pastels by Degas – he was currently exhibiting on the Boulevard Montmartre. He also expressed his admiration for Vincent's art. With foresight, he predicted that one day his brother's work would be given the place it deserved: 'That head of his has been occupied with contemporary society's insoluble problems for so long, and he is still battling on with his good-heartedness and boundless energy. His efforts have not been in vain, but he will probably not live to see them come to fruition, for by the time people understand what he is saying in his paintings it will be too late. He is one of the most advanced painters and it is difficult to understand him, even for me who knows him so intimately. His ideas cover so much ground, examining what is humane and how one should look at the world, that one must first free oneself from anything remotely linked to convention to understand what he was trying to say, but I am sure he will be understood later on. It is just hard to say when'[148]

This uncertainty about Vincent's state of mind weighed heavily on Theo's conscience. He considered having him admitted to a psychiatric clinic in Marseille or Aix-en-Provence, but this was a terrible decision to have to make on his own. Theo found the whole idea of 'him seeing spring arrive while incarcerated in an institution with high walls all round it, and no other company but madmen' atrocious.[149] He could no longer feel happy without feeling guilty, as demonstrated by a letter written on 16 March 1889: 'You have done so much for me that I am sorry to hear that you are suffering while my beloved Jo and I are likely to enjoy ourselves' [753/T4]. His feelings as he set off for the Netherlands on 30 March – Vincent's 36th birthday – must have been a mixture of joy and sorrow.

Theo and Jo were married at in Amsterdam's town hall on 18 April 1889. **[47]** The following day they travelled from Brussels to Paris where, on 20 April, they moved into their new flat on the third floor of an apartment block at 8, Cité Pigalle.[150] The honeymoon gave Theo the opportunity to forget his worries for a while. Jo reports that they spent the first week playing around like children, enjoying each another's company from the very start. Theo wrote to Vincent on 24 April that they were perfectly blissful and that he 'felt happier than I can express' [764/T5]. Vincent had made some progress since being admitted to the

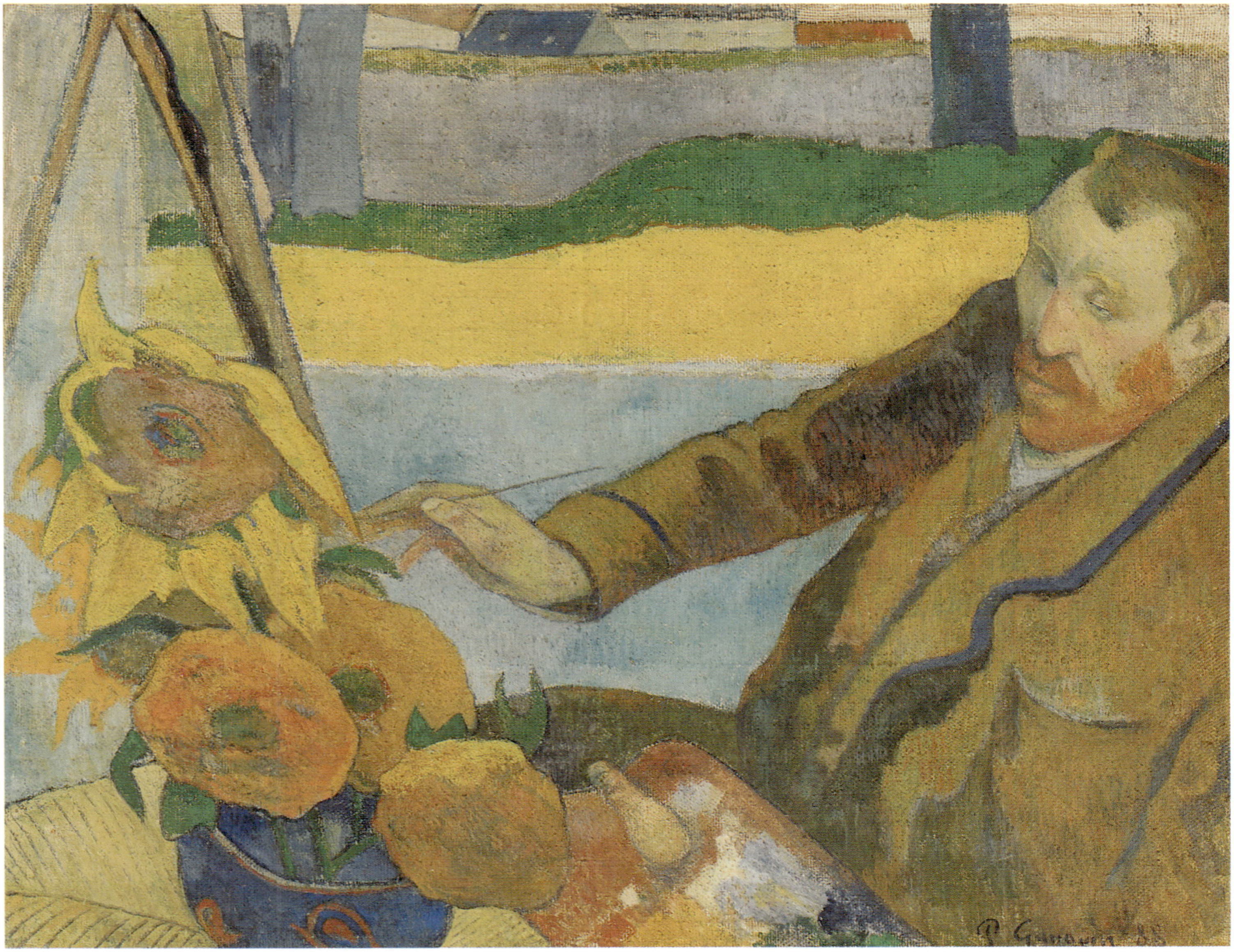

45
Paul Gauguin 1848–1903
Vincent van Gogh painting sunflowers 1888
Van Gogh Museum, Amsterdam

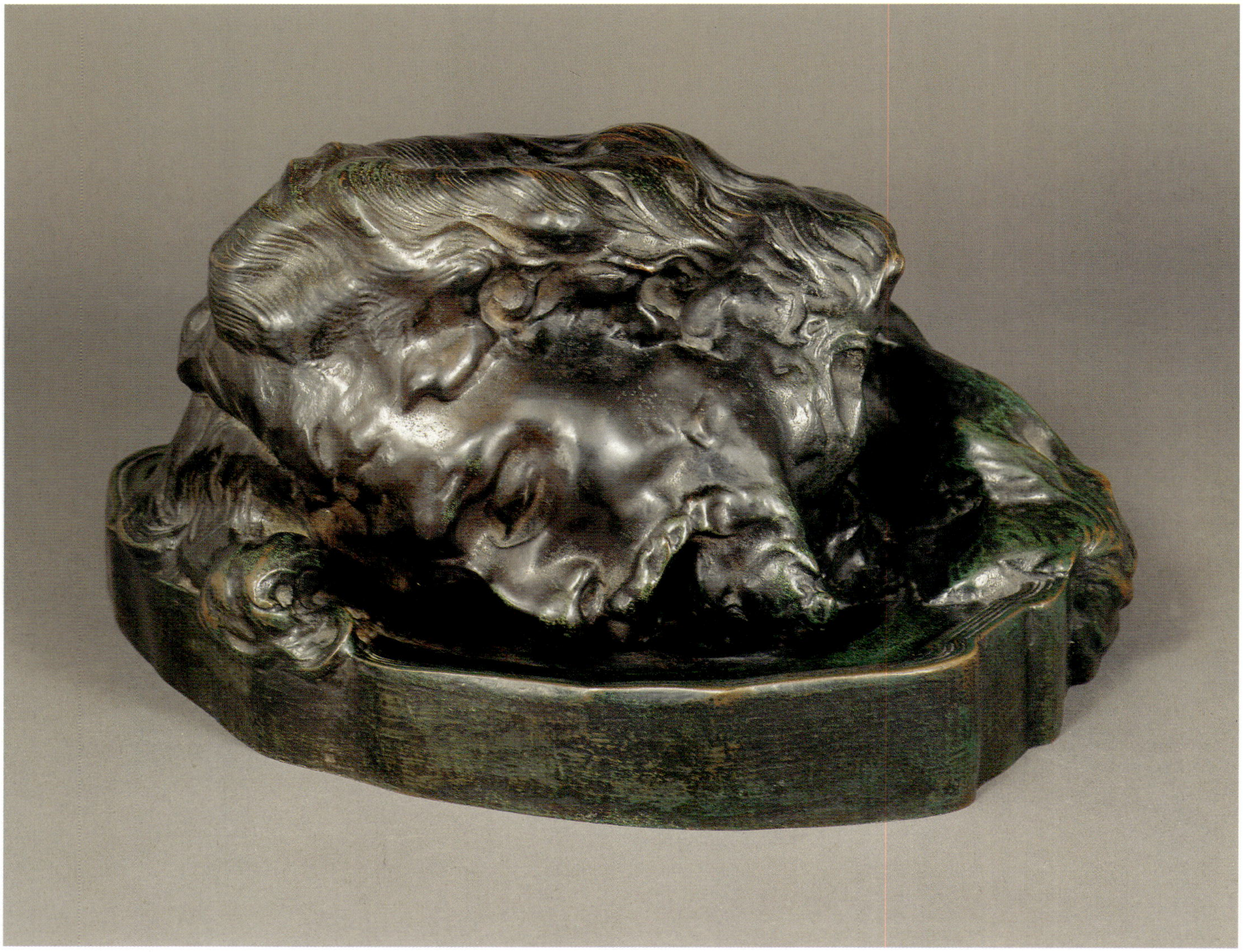

46
Auguste Rodin 1840–1917
Head of St John the Baptist 1887
Musée Rodin, Paris

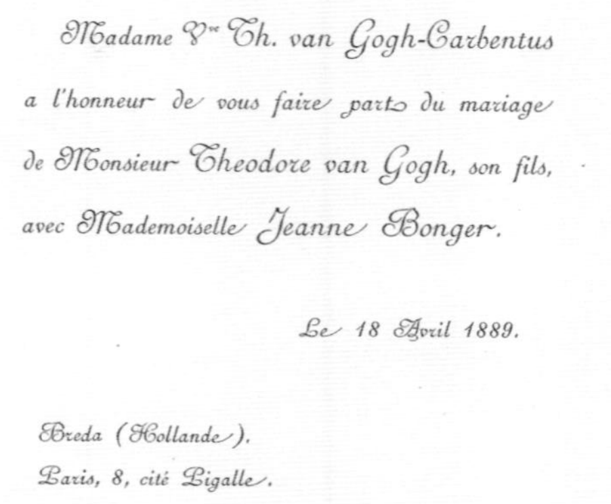

Madame Vve Th. van Gogh-Carbentus
a l'honneur de vous faire part du mariage
de Monsieur Theodore van Gogh, son fils,
avec Mademoiselle Jeanne Bonger.

Le 18 Avril 1889.

Breda (Hollande).
Paris, 8, cité Pigalle.

47
Announcement of the wedding of Theo van Gogh and Jo Bonger on 18 April 1889

psychiatric clinic Saint Paule-de-Mausole in St-Rémy-de-Provence at the beginning of May. It was there, on 5 July, that he received Jo's letter announcing her pregnancy. Vincent wrote to Theo in reply: 'I presume your thoughts are occupied by the child you are expecting and I am very happy for you. I dare say that in this way you will find greater inner peace' [792/600]. He was quite right: apart from his poor health, which was further undermined by a chronic cough, and the occasional nagging problems at work, Theo was more optimistic throughout 1889 than he had ever been before. However, this proved to be a lull before the storm.

1890 began hopefully. On 31 January Jo had a son, Vincent Willem, according to Theo's description 'a handsome boy, who cries a lot but looks healthy' [848/T27]. [**48**] Theo's happiness was, however, once again overshadowed by concern for Vincent, who suffered a new attack at the end of January. Theo's letter to Vincent announcing the birth of his son and simultaneously encouraging his brother to muster his spirits, is one of the most harrowing documents in their entire correspondence.

Theo's difficulties grew in March. Jo had had to stay in bed due to recurring blood loss. Vincent had another attack at the end of February, which made him feel more sombre and sick than Theo would ever realise. And, to add to the misfortune, Theo became embroiled in a conflict with his superiors as a result of his disappointing sales figures.[151] As so often in the past, his health suffered a noticeable decline. He was constantly plagued by a hacking cough, trembling limbs and eating disorders. His guiding principle was perseverance. He had little choice: his obligations at home and at work continued to weigh him down.

Theo was given some respite when Vincent, having been declared cured, left St Rémy for Auvers-sur-Oise, 30 kilometres northwest of Paris.[152] Following his brother's advice, he was treated by Dr Paul Gachet from 21 May 1890. On his journey up north he stayed

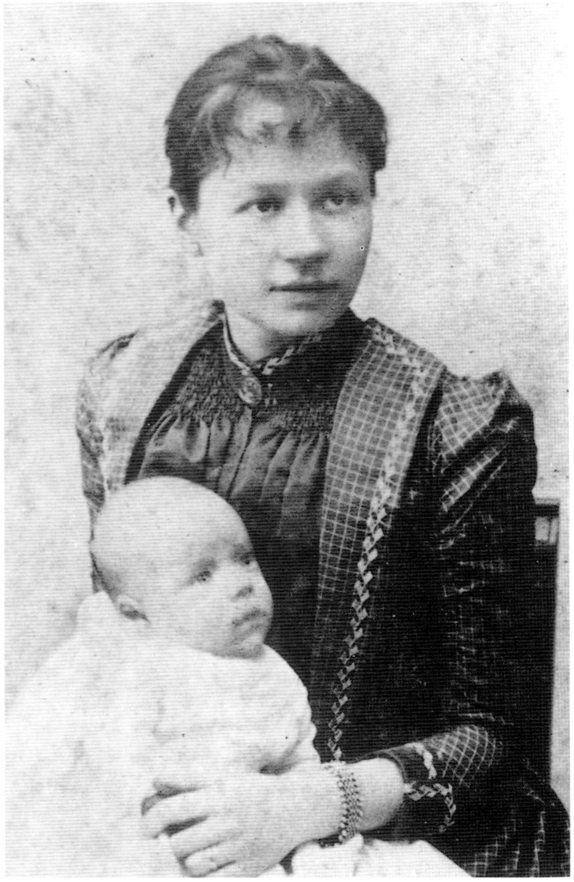

48
Jo van Gogh-Bonger and Vincent Willem van Gogh,
c. July 1890

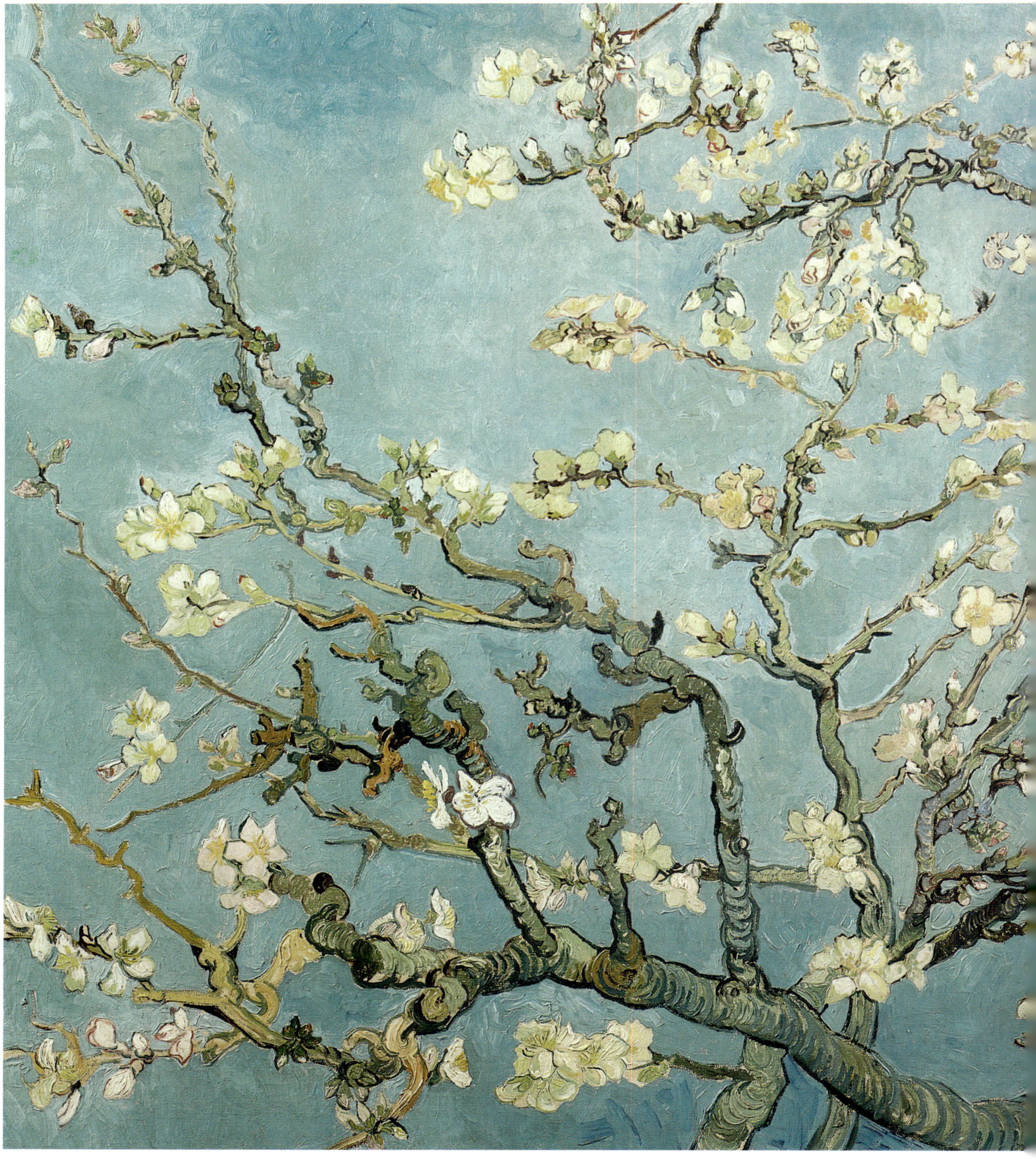

49
Vincent van Gogh 1853–1890
Branches of an almond tree in blossom 1890
Van Gogh Museum, Amsterdam

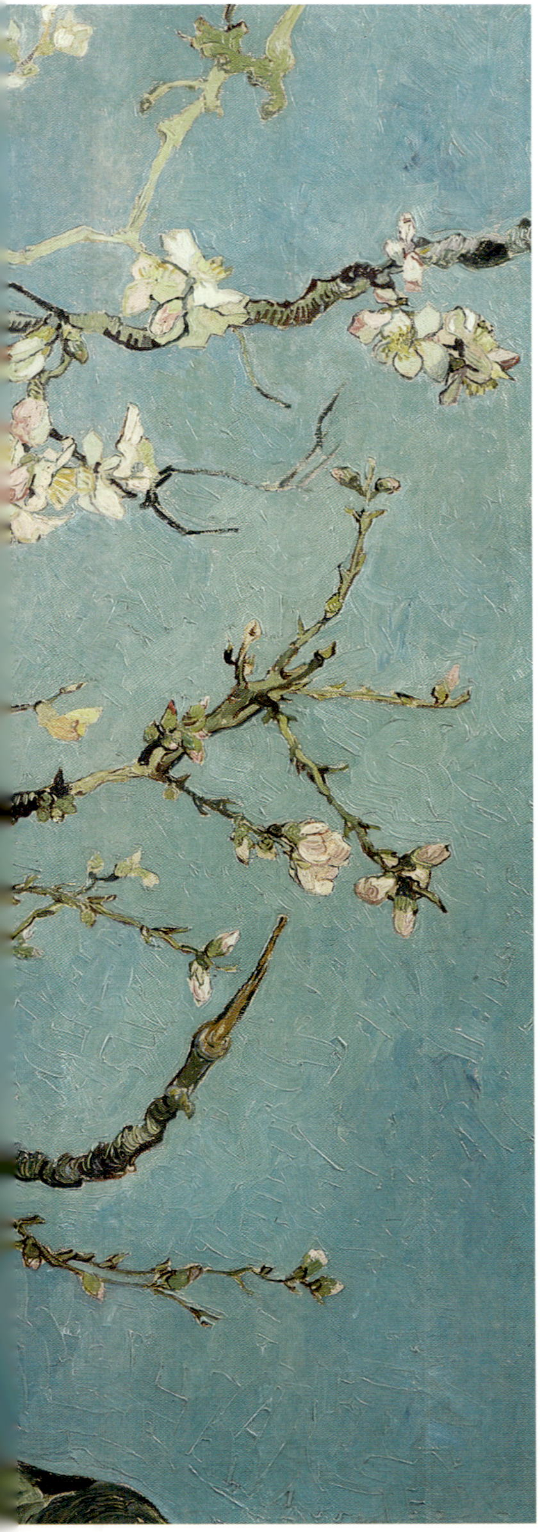

with Theo and Jo for several days, where he was introduced to his sister-in-law, whom he described to Wil in June as 'all common sense and goodwill' [833/T22]. The brothers had not seen one another since the dramatic events in Arles in December 1888. Vincent noticed that Theo was coughing more than ever, but, he wrote to his mother, thanks to family life, 'he will gradually grow stronger rather than weaker' [882/639]. Almost a quarter of a century later Jo still remembered Vincent's visit as lively and happy. Meeting his namesake had made a deep impression on him: 'He enticed Theo to the bedroom where our small boy's cot was, who was named after Vincent; without saying a word the two brothers looked at the child who was sleeping peacefully – both with tears in their eyes. Then Vincent turned to me laughing and said pointing at the plain, crocheted bedspread on the cot: "You must not coset him with too much lace, sister."'[153]

Having settled in Auvers, Vincent resumed work with renewed vigour. [50] For both brothers it was reassuring to live close to one another. Their luck seemed to have taken a turn for the better. On Sunday, 8 June Theo, Vincent, Jo and Vincent Willem were invited by Gachet to spend a day in the country village where he lived. Their time together, Jo relates, was 'so peaceful and quiet, so happy, that nobody would have dreamt how tragically our happiness was to be wrecked only a few weeks later.'[154]

Theo, however, was close to exhaustion. In late May he was busy organising a Raffaëlli exhibition, which involved working until 10 o' clock at night. At the beginning of June he felt drained and was yearning for a long holiday [880/T35].[155] In the middle of the month, Jo had to stay in bed for a week; a fortnight later Vincent Willem became seriously ill. The child's wailing was heart rending and kept Theo from sleeping for almost a week.[156] On 29 June, after a few anxious days and nights, the doctor reassured the couple that they would not lose their son.

Theo was more perturbed about his position at work. He had already clashed with his employers on a number of occasions about how the branch should be run; this time it was money that caused the conflict. Jo and he could barely manage on his annual salary, which was about 7,500 francs: they now had Vincent Willem, Vincent and Theo's mother to support. On 30 June Theo posed the following rhetorical question to his brother: 'Must I continue to live without making provision for the future, and work all day, without even being able to spare Jo the worry of making ends meet, and all that just because the old hands at Boussod & Valadon treat me as if I had just joined the firm and keep me short of money? Seeing as I am not appreciated, earn no extras, and am hard up, should I not tell them what my demands are and if they dare to reject them, finally play my trump card: Gentlemen, I shall risk my luck and establish myself as an independent art dealer?' [899/T39]. In order to carry this out, he returned to the plan the brothers had worked out a few years earlier. At the beginning of July he asked Dries Bonger if he would go in to business with him.[157]

On Sunday, 6 July Vincent arrived in Paris. It was an emotional visit and he returned to Auvers the very same day, badly shaken. The discussion about setting up the new firm had apparently become heated. Dries Bonger had been there as well, and even though he assured Theo that he could count on him, Theo and Jo had disagreed on the matter. For her, setting up in business must have seemed too risky. Nonetheless, Theo went ahead with his plans. On Monday, 7 July he gave his superiors an ultimatum: within eight days they would have to grant his demands for an increase in salary, or he would establish himself as an independent art dealer.[158] Vincent felt responsible for the financial problems that had arisen, and for Theo and Jo's quarrel. Back in Auvers he wrote on 7 July: 'I am somewhat surprised that you want to rush things through without first agreeing with one another. And if there is anything I can do to help... ? Probably not, but have I done anything wrong or can I help the two of you in some way?' [902/647]. The reply reassured him, although Theo was frightened that things would end up with Vincent suffering a new attack.

Vincent's death

Theo's ultimatum backfired. On 14 July he had not heard a word from his employers. By not sticking to his promise to provide financial backing, Dries also proved to be an unreliable partner.[159] Left in the lurch by Bonger and uncertain about his livelihood, Theo left Paris on 15 July to escort his tired wife Jo and a barely recovered Vincent Willem to Leiden, where they were to spend a long holiday at his mother's. Although he was completely worn out, there was no question of Theo taking any leave; he departed again two days later to attend to business in Antwerp. On 19 July he was back in his apartment in Paris, which seemed quiet and empty. He missed Jo and Vincent Willem 'desperately' and he hoped that he would be able to join them as soon as possible.[160]

There was no word from Theo's superiors, so on Monday, 21 July he went to see them. Instead of repeating his earlier threat, he asked them simply to consider his request for a raise, but not to dismiss him, fearful as he was of losing his job and jeopardising his family's financial position. He was allowed to stay on, but for the time being there could be no question of a higher salary.[161] Theo had gambled, the stakes had been raised and, ultimately, he had lost. He was left with nothing but continuing money worries, his quarrel with Jo, disillusionment with Bonger and anxiety about Vincent.

The stress and strain took its toll. Theo wrote to Jo that he was extremely nervous and easily shaken. On 26 July he panicked when he heard a rumour that the management of Boussod, Valadon & Cie. was planning to close down two of their galleries and channel all their business through the main branch at the Rue Chaptal. Whether Theo was stating the truth, or merely showing signs of a latent persecution complex, will remain a mystery. He told his wife that the only thing that would bring him inner rest and peace was being with her and taking a long holiday.[162] But rest and peace were in short supply.

On 28 July Theo received the message from Gachet that Vincent had shot himself in the chest the evening before. Theo dropped everything and left for Auvers straight away. When he found his brother at the Auberge Ravoux Vincent was in better condition than he had expected, although Theo realised that his life was in danger. That evening he informed Jo. He wrote that he had felt subconsciously that climactic events were about to occur, and even before Vincent had died, he was comforting Jo (and himself) for the possible loss: 'It was strange, was it not, that last week I was so nervous and anxious, it was as if I had a premonition

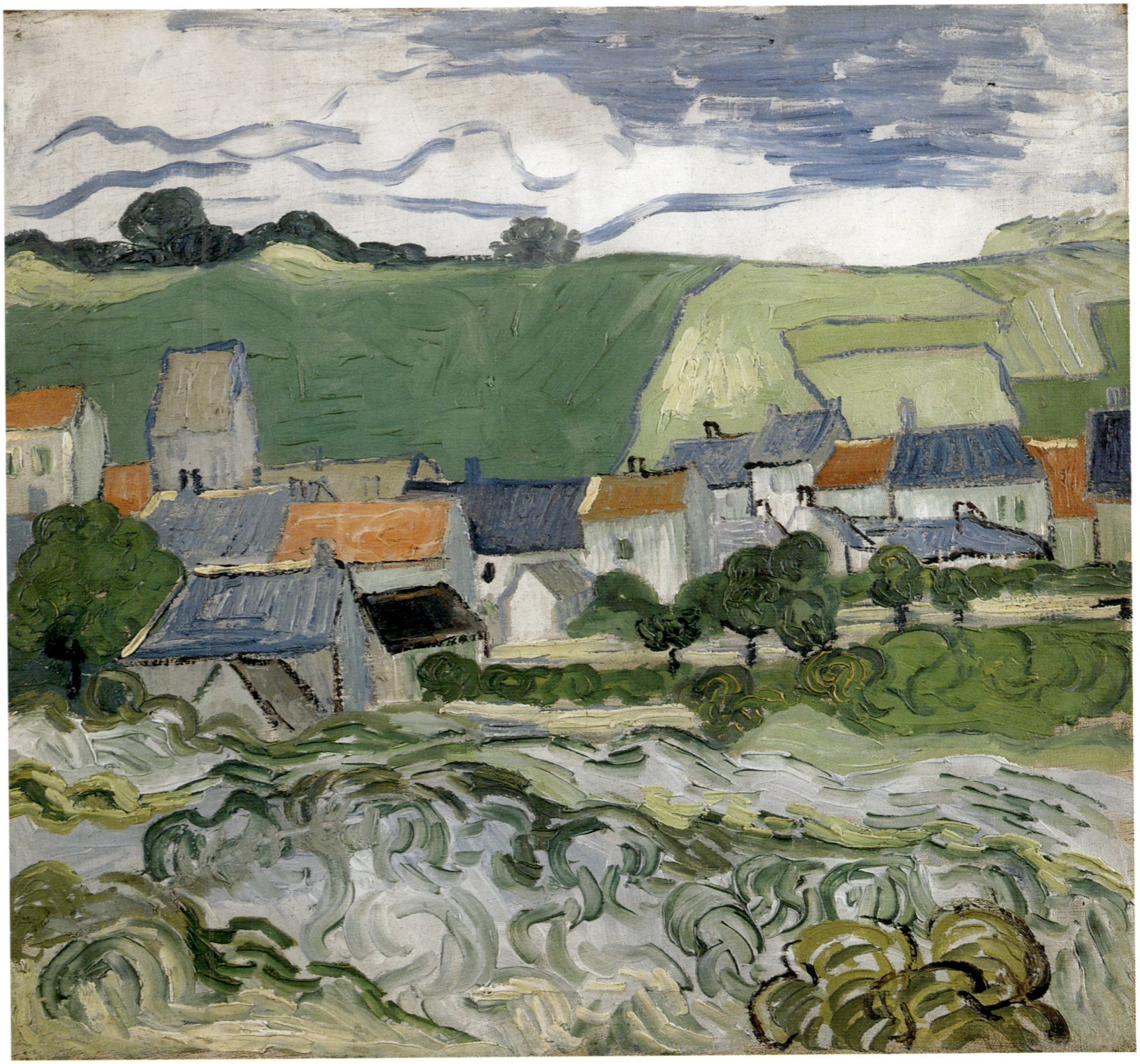

50
Vincent van Gogh 1853–1890
View at Auvers 1890
Van Gogh Museum, Amsterdam

that something was about to happen. He was able to talk to me and was so kind; he asked after you and said that you had no inkling of the sorrow life may hold in store, and that we could give him more fortitude to face life. [...] Just remember, whatever happens I shall be brave because I have you to live for; I shall not be left alone, I have my wife and my young boy. We may be sad but we shall not lose courage.'[163] Vincent died the same night, with Theo nearby: 'one of his last words was that he wished he could go quickly, and within a few moments he had passed away, thus finding the rest and peace he could never find on earth.'[164] **[51]**

Vincent was buried a day later, attended by a number of friends from Auvers. Gachet said a few words at the graveside and Theo thanked those present for coming. And 'that was it. [...] I miss him so, it is as if everything reminds me of him.'[165] Theo was already back in Paris on the evening of 30 July. He tried to express his grief to his mother on 1 August: 'It is a grief which will long weigh me down and will not leave my thoughts for the rest of my life, but there is one consolation, he has the rest he so longed for. [...] Life was such a heavy burden to him, but as is often the case, everyone is now highly complementary about his talent. [...] Oh mother, he was my very own brother.'[166]

Theo's end

The idea that Vincent had been given the rest he so longed for was scant consolation. It did nothing to soften the blow of Theo's loss. In his letter to his mother, Theo vented his anger at those who suddenly appreciated Vincent's work now that he was dead. The question of whether Theo, with his profound sense of guilt, could perhaps have seen his brother's suicide coming, must have tormented him, as in years gone by he had always been able to help him.

He was not granted much time to come to terms with his grief or to recuperate from his fatigue. He did take a holiday in the Netherlands from 3 to 16 August, but the moment he returned to Paris he did everything he could to bring Vincent's artistic legacy to public attention. He would never have been able to forgive himself if he had not done his best, as he explained to Gachet in a letter of 12 September.[167] By now it had become clear that his efforts to have the work exhibited at the Durand-Ruel's were doomed to failure, as the dealer's initial enthusiasm had waned.

Theo had lost all resistance to illness, and his health quickly deteriorated. The toilsome move to a new apartment around 16 September, the organisation of the exhibition of Vincent's paintings, and his daily work, all conspired to ruin his wellbeing.[168] On 27 September Theo wrote to Wil that his health problems were a thing of the past, while in fact they were plaguing him at that very moment: 'I was so ill after taking the drops prescribed by Dr Ter Mate that I thought I was going mad. They helped to numb the irritation at night, so I coughed less, but they gave me hallucinations day and night, and nightmares too, had I not stopped taking them I would have jumped out of a window or killed myself some other way. I was literally going insane. When I stopped taking them my cough was worse than it had been before, and I also had a bad cold and was quite hoarse; the only good thing about so much sneezing and snuffling was that it cleared my head a little. Everyone told me to go to bed and take better care of myself, but that was impossible because I still had important work to finish.'[169]

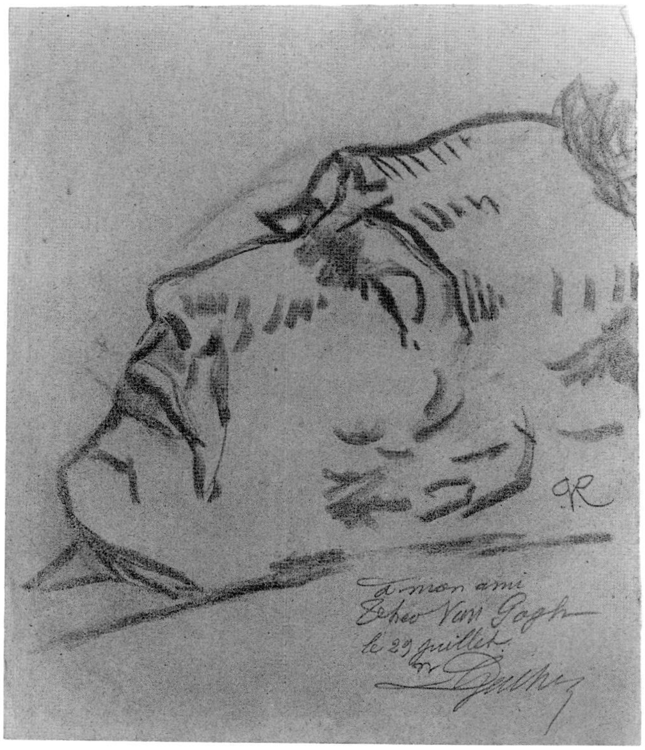

51
Paul-Ferdinand Gachet 1828–1909
Vincent van Gogh on his deathbed 1890
Van Gogh Museum, Amsterdam

On 4 October, Jo's birthday, Theo showed signs of extreme nervous exhaustion. Five days later he suffered a complete mental and physical collapse. According to Dries Bonger, the reason was again a row with his superiors: Theo had resigned on the spot and was going to establish himself as an independent dealer.[170] Others – and perhaps they saw matters more lucidly – claimed that Theo's sorrow at Vincent's death and the fatigue of the past summer were to blame for his condition.[171]

On Dries's advice, Theo was admitted to La Maison Dubois, a hospital in the Fauborg Saint-Denis on 12 October. Two days later he was transferred to Dr

Blanche's clinic on the Rue Berton in Passy. His condition was extremely alarming: he had symptoms of paralysis and was completely out of his mind. In contrast to Jo and other members of the family, Dries saw no cause for optimism: 'As far as I am concerned, I believe there is little hope. Rivet has said that the case is much more serious than Vincent's and that he did not have a shadow of a chance. It is deeply discouraging.'[172] The diagnosis made in Passy confirmed Dries's worst expectations: Theo was suffering from *dementia paralytica*, the terminal stage of syphilis.

After consultations with the writer and doctor Frederik van Eeden, an acquaintance of Jo's friend Anna Veth-Dirks, Jo decided to have Theo moved to the Willem-Arntzkliniek in Utrecht. He was admitted there on 18 November. The doctor in attendance reported that when he arrived Theo had no idea where he was and could only speak incoherently. He concluded: 'His whole appearance resembles that of a paralytic who is gravely ill and frail.'[173] In Utrecht Theo declined to such an extent that he no longer recognised his wife. Despite his condition, his death on 25 January was unexpected, and the circumstances remain mysterious.[174] He was buried three days later at the Algemene Begraafplaats in Utrecht.[175] **[52]**

Jo noted in her diary on 28 January 1892: 'On the [anniversary of his death] I went back to the spot where he rests – a ray of sunshine caught the roses I had left, the same sort of rose he gave me when we had been married for just one day.'[176] The circle was complete. The rose that had once decorated his christening robe had become a symbol of Theo's life: a fleeting bloom which, in flower, is inspiring and elegant, but never without its thorns.

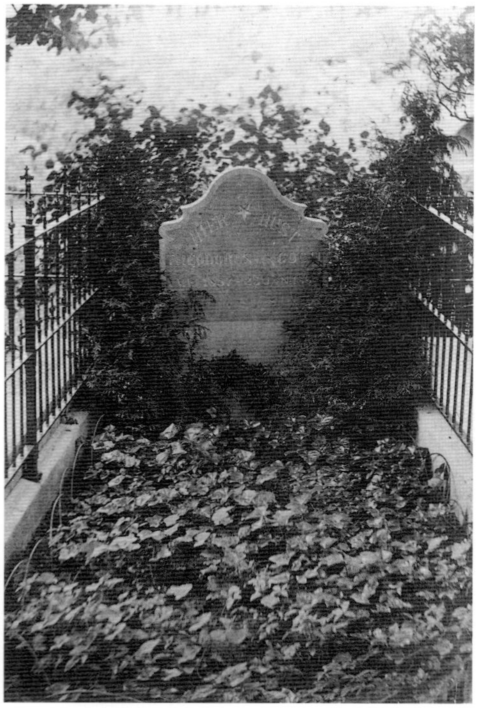

52
Theo van Gogh's grave in Utrecht 1891–1914

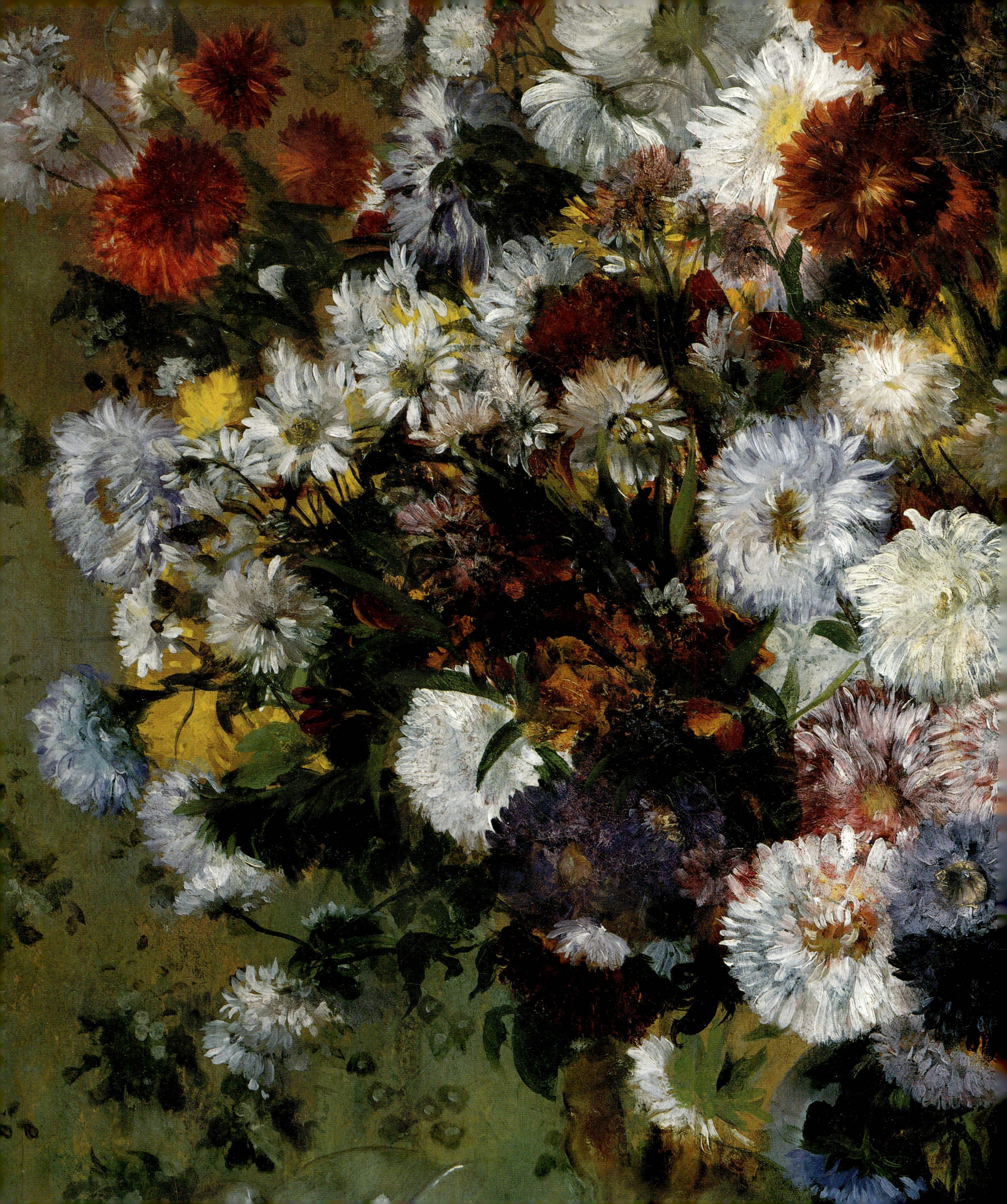

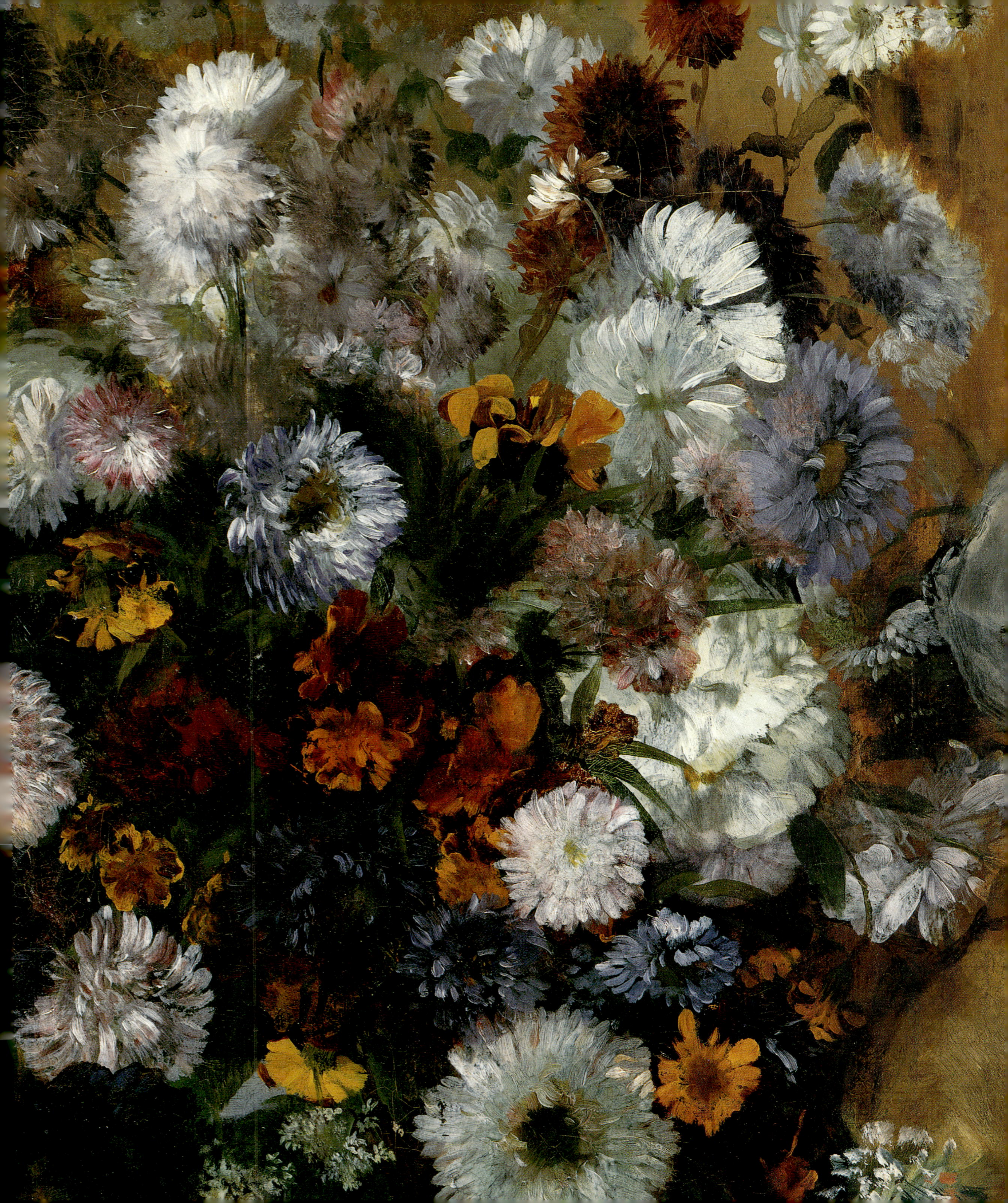

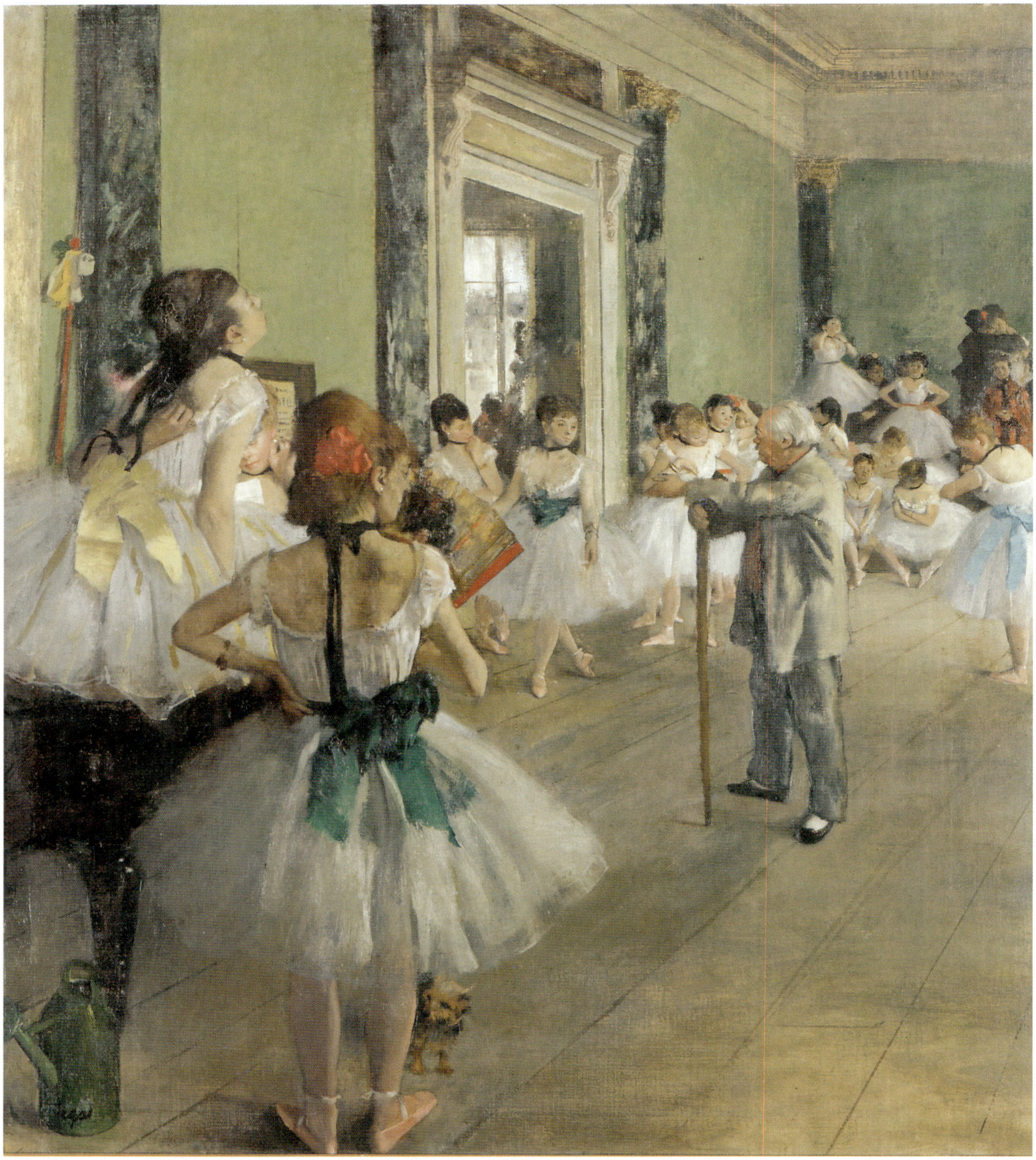

53
Edgar Degas 1834–1911
The dance school 1873–76
Musée d'Orsay, Paris

Theo van Gogh

An honest broker

Richard Thomson

When news of Theo van Gogh's death in January 1891 filtered through the myriad channels of the art world in France and the Low Countries it was met with dismay, particularly among the artists and journalists who supported new initiatives and styles. The young Parisian critic Albert Aurier, who had eloquently defended the art of both Paul Gauguin and Vincent van Gogh, referred to Theo as 'the sympathetic and intelligent expert who [had] worked so hard to make known to the public the work of the most audacious of today's independent painters.'[1] In *De Amsterdammer* of 29 January, the painter and critic Jan Veth published a lengthy appreciation of Theo's activities. Veth made substantial claims for Theo: although a dealer, he was 'in reality more artistic in his aspirations and actions than many so-called artists with famous names, who in point of fact seek only to produce a marketable commodity by the speculative manufacturing of their skilful hands.' By this account, Theo was a man of such sensibility that he transcended the rank commercialism of the art market, more artist than businessman.

Veth described his death as an 'irreparable loss' to 'a wide circle of militant French artists.' It was to Theo's branch of Boussod, Valadon & Cie. that one had to go for Degas, 'who no longer exhibited anywhere else.' This was where you went to see pictures by artists such as Monet, 'Raffaëlli and Pissarro, Redon and Sisley, Signac and Seurat,' painters who were 'fighting against the routine and middle-class mentality.'[2] The response of Camille Pissarro was less high-flown and more practical. Pissarro, who at 60 was still finding it hard to sell his work, had been substantially helped by Theo, and worried about who might replace him. 'The death of Van Gogh has really darkened [my] hopes,' he wrote to Mette Gauguin: 'That devoted friend had succeeded in digging out collectors and it was at Boussod and Valadon that I could see and admire you husband's beautiful things.'[3]

These reactions, full of praise for Theo van Gogh's achievements as both a man of integrity and a perspicacious dealer, are, however, problematic in themselves. How correct, how useful, are these immediate assessments? Several of Veth's statements are simply incorrect. Neither Monet nor Degas exhibited exclusively with Theo. Although he had staged a successful show of Monet's new paintings of Antibes in the early summer of 1888, a year later the painter had a far larger and more prestigious exhibition at the Galerie Georges Petit, which he shared with Rodin. During the time Theo bought from Degas, starting in mid-1887, the artist continued to sell to Durand-Ruel and probably to other dealers as well. And indeed, there is no evidence that Theo ever displayed, let alone bought or sold, the work of either Seurat or Signac. It seems, then, that from the very moment of his tragically early death Theo's activities and achievements were subject to a certain degree of heroicisation and obfuscation, a problem we also encounter in dealing with the career of his brother Vincent. How successful was Theo van Gogh in winning a wider public for adventurous art in the 1880s? Was he really responsible for finding new purchasers and raising prices to help progressive painters? To what extent is it true – as Veth claimed – that Theo's support for modern painting was sustained in opposition to the mainstream economy in works of art, which, as a dealer, he himself had served?

Since the immediate assessments following his death, Theo van Gogh's career has been the subject of only one major extended study, published by the late John Rewald in the *Gazette des Beaux-Arts* in 1973.[4] In this important and scrupulously documented text, Rewald used his enormous experience as a scholar of impressionism to give a detailed and vivid account of his topic, an account on which this and future studies will necessarily build. However, for all the wealth of detail about dates and prices, which Rewald sifted and deployed so effectively, in essence his judgment of Theo did not differ fundamentally from Aurier's or Veth's. To Rewald, Theo was a hero because he had supported painters such as Degas, Monet, Pissarro and Gauguin in the years after the eighth and last impressionist exhibition (1886), diligently trying to sell their work. They were the 'militant French artists' Veth listed in 1891, and whom Rewald – and, indeed, we ourselves – recognise as among the most creative, 'modern' artists of a century ago.

However, late-19th century taste would not necessarily have concurred, and Rewald's exclusive concern with Theo as an 'impressionist' dealer, and the distaste he alleges the Dutchman had for much of the other art he handled, raises questions crucial to any further appraisal of his role in the art market of the 1880s. Rewald claimed that Theo 'formed an independent taste only rarely in agreement with that of his employers.'[5] This constructs an image consistent with Veth's: Theo was a dealer who operated within but against the market, working with the then 'militant,' 'independent' artists whom posterity has proven to be the finest of their generation.[6] This essay will attempt to probe the validity of these claims. It will also explore Theo's handling of and attitudes towards the wide variety of artists with whom a prosperous business such as Boussod, Valadon & Cie. had to deal, and whom Rewald simply ignored.

On another score, and by omission, Rewald's study inadvertently points to another aspect of Theo's dealings. Rewald concentrates more or less exclusively not only on impressionist artists, but also on their paintings; he was not much concerned with works on paper or in other media, whether by impressionists or other artists. By broadening the scope of our analysis of Theo's career, by moving beyond the comparatively narrow confines of impressionism and works on canvas, and by placing his activities within the broader context of the Parisian art market, this essay hopes to come closer to the real Theo van Gogh, art dealer.

The Parisian art world

Before proceeding to a closer analysis of Theo van Gogh's role in the Paris art market, it is essential to delineate the main features of the world in which he worked. A decade ago, the late Nicholas Green convincingly demonstrated that entrepreneurial, capitalist speculation on the art market in France did not, in fact, develop during the 1870s and 1880s in harness with the culture of 'modern' art – its production, reception and consumption. By the mid-19th century, Paris already had a flourishing art market, with both established and emerging systems.

If Parisian commercial almanacs in 1821 listed only 37 art dealers, by 1850 the total was 67. These businesses offered a variety of services: selling pictures, prints, drawings, and sculptures (these could also be hired), as well as works in the new medium of photography.[7] The opening of the Hôtel Drouot in the early 1850s, located only a few paces north of the central Boulevard des Italiens and the fashionable *passages*, coincided with the booming economy of the Second Empire and speculation in Haussmann's rebuilding projects. Artists seized the opportunity to sell their work via auctions.[8] These differed little from the one-man shows dealers were undertaking in their galleries.[9] Theo van Gogh, who first entered the Paris art world in 1878, operated in a modern city whose economy was geared to speculation, and where the work of art was well understood as a unit of capital.

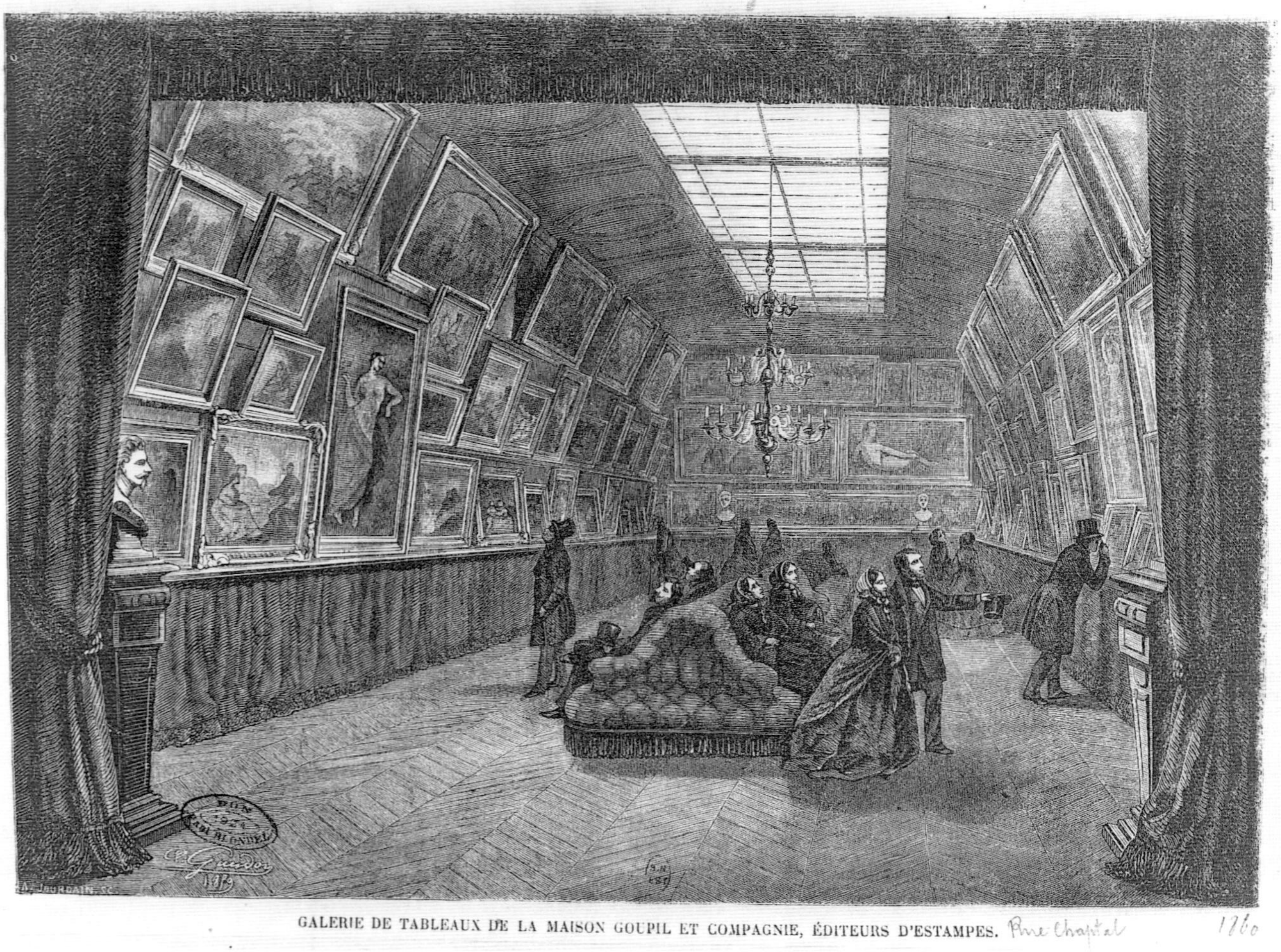

54

Goupil & Cie.'s gallery in the Rue Chaptal in Paris 1860

Within the dense patterns of Parisian capitalism, the art market was a micro-economy with multiple links. The art market of the 1880s was made up of a number of layers, and in trying to describe it one is inclined to think in geological or archaeological terms. But these metaphors are fundamentally static, and the art market was quintessentially fluid; everything – reputations, prices, taste, modernity – was in constant flux.

The annual Salon, held in the spring, remained the largest and most visible manifestation of French art. It had always been a marketplace, where duly elected artists were able to display their work to a large public of potential patrons and, by winning a medal from the jury or approbation from the critics, could raise the value of their stock and thus their prices. In the course of Theo's career, the Salon underwent two fundamental changes. In 1881 the state withdrew its support, handing over control to the artists themselves, under the aegis of the Société des Artistes Français. This 'privatisation,' as we would call it today, put considerable pressure on artists. In particular, the growing number of works exhibited – there were 4,942 entries to the Salon in 1881, rising to 5,810 in 1889 – meant that individual artists' work became less differentiated, less visible in the marketplace.[10] As *La Paix* put it in 1883: 'the quantity of works shown [...] is such that the majority of them pass unnoticed.'[11] One consequence was an increase in small-scale exhibitions at galleries and clubs.

The second change came in 1890 when, as a result of antipathetic disagreements between senior artists (ironically Meissonier and Bouguereau, the twin

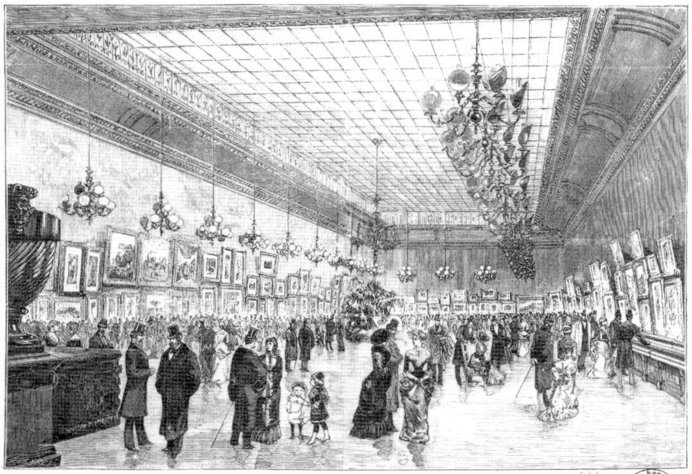

55
Exhibition at the Sociéte des Aquarellistes at the Galerie Georges Petit, Rue de Sèze in 1882
Bibliothèque Nationale, Paris

demons of Rewald's article), a schismatic group – the Société Nationale des Beaux-Arts – was established.[12] The new Salon distinguished itself from its rival by hanging the works in rooms decorated in red fabric and furnished with divans and flowers, a tactic so obviously drawn from the Galerie Georges Petit that one critic complained that 'the Société Nationale des Beaux-Arts is not and never will be anything but an inflated Rue de Sèze.'[13] Whether pushing trade the dealers' way or emulating their innovations, during Theo's career the Salon always intersected with an increasingly dominant market.

The next layer in this micro-economy was formed by the galleries. In the 1880s there were enormous variations between dealers: differences of status, taste, and price. There were highly capitalised, fashionably located operations such as the Galerie Georges Petit, the Galerie Durand-Ruel, and the business for which Theo worked: Boussod, Valadon & Cie., formerly Goupil & Cie. [**54**] Between these, too, there were differences; Petit, for instance, ran auctions, Goupil did not; and Durand-Ruel suffered capitalisation problems (notably after the collapse of the Union Générale bank in 1882), while Petit seems to have flourished steadily. There were dealers quietly fading away – like Haro, who had been closely associated with Ingres at mid-century – and dealers on the way up – such as the Bernheim firm, destined to be a force after 1900.

If such businesses represented various aspects of the market's upper crust, towards the bottom were the small operators, offering outlets to (unknown or riskily modern) artists struggling to make modest sales. Alphonse Portier, who had no shop but operated from 54, Rue Lepic, the same apartment building occupied by Theo, was one of these. Even at this level, there was some gradation, because small-time traders such as Portier or Pierre-Firmin Martin had consistent stock and a regular clientele, whereas a back-street colour-merchant like Vincent's friend, Julien Tanguy, seems to have sold pictures on an *ad hoc* basis.[14] As the manager of a major branch of a well-established house with an eye for new developments, Theo van Gogh undoubtedly had contacts throughout these layers.

His company's immediate rivals would have been at the top of the market. The Durand-Ruel firm had established itself as a leading player in the Parisian art world during the July Monarchy. Paul Durand-Ruel, son of the founder, took the reins in 1865. Although he almost immediately lost Bouguereau to Goupil, he purchased a substantial stock of small works from Théodore Rousseau. The artist died the following year, leaving Durand-Ruel in a strong position as a dealer in the landscapes of the so-called Ecole de 1830: Rousseau, Corot, Millet, Daubigny and others. In 1871, he met Monet and Pissarro in London, entering into business relations with them that lasted, despite periods of friction, until the painters' deaths. The following January, he purchased 24 important works from Manet's studio, including several Salon pictures. During the 1870s and 80s, working off a mixed stock of mid-century landscapes, Romantic masters such as Delacroix, and works in the bucolic Bouguereau vein, Durand-Ruel gave significant support to the impressionists, culminating in the cluster of one-man exhibitions he staged for Monet, Renoir, Pissarro and Sisley in 1883. The dealer had, however, been crippled by the crash of the Union Générale bank the previous year. He was only able to re-establish his position at the end of the decade by carefully managing his funds, avoiding risks (such as Pissarro's neo-impressionist canvases) and building up a market in New York, with the aid of his son.[15] As we will see, Durand-Ruel's difficulties in the mid- and late 1880s provided a window of opportunity for Theo van Gogh.

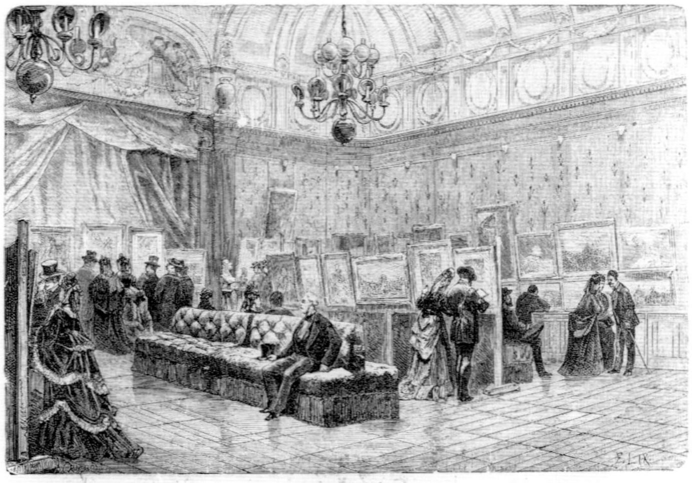

56
Exhibition at the Cercle de l'Union Artistique n.d.
Bibliothèque Nationale, Paris

Georges Petit, himself the son of an established dealer, opened his new gallery at 8, Rue de Sèze in 1882. Petit's exhibition space was deluxe, as was the market for which he aimed: the vestibule was hung with tapestries and decorated with marble busts; the exhibition space was large and draped in crimson plush, with comfortable furniture, carpets and gas-lamps. It was, as one author noted, 'unique in Paris.'[16] Petit's luxury establishment displayed a wide variety of art. The gallery opened with the chic Société d'Aquarellistes [55] and in the same year organised the first of an annual series of exhibitions by the Société Internationale de la Peinture. Their early shows included works by French and foreign academicians such as Paul Baudry, John Everett Millais and Lawrence Alma-Tadema, and were considered so prestigious that in 1883 the committee of honour included a multinational array of ambassadors, museum directors and plutocrats.

Petit adjusted the character of the Internationale throughout the decade. 1884 saw the academicians dropped and the introduction of 'modern' artists – both French and foreign – who had emerged in the last five years: Jules Bastien Lepage, Jean-Charles Cazin, Alfred Roll, Jean Béraud, and the German Max Liebermann. This trend continued the following year, when, among others, Petit also invited Monet and Jean-François Raffaëlli, coexhibitors at the impressionist shows of 1880 and 1881. By 1887 the group included the Swede Carl Larsson and a cluster of impressionists (Sisley, Pissarro and Berthe Morisot).[17] This continual shift in personnel exemplifies the way in which the market constantly recast both itself and the notion of 'modernity' – 19th-century capital being associated with progress as well as security. Petit also staged a major Meissonier retrospective in 1884, displays of faiences by Lachenal, sales for charities such as the Orphelinat des Arts, and Christmas *fêtes*. In sum, Petit ran a flexible luxury-goods business, operating across a wide range of products in a variety of media to maximise publicity and lucrative returns, and gradually colonising the more progressive areas of the market. There is a tacit assumption in Rewald's study that Durand-Ruel was Theo's main competitor, but in the 1880s Durand was in difficulties; it was Petit who set the pace.

Another layer – or, perhaps better, fault line running through the strata – was formed by the artistic clubs and societies. A few Parisian clubs for the social elite ran annual art exhibitions, notably the Cercle de l'Union Artistique (or Mirlitons) [56], established in the 1850s, and the Cercle Volney. These shows, held in the early months of the year, allowed senior and fashionable artists to display modestly scaled or informal work that they would not normally exhibit at the Salon. Additionally, the comfortable, quasi-domestic spaces of the club implicitly sited the works in the spectator's home environment in a way that the Salon or the standard dealer's gallery could not.[18]

Many of the same artists who showed in the clubs were also members of the art societies that flourished in the 1880s. The earliest of these was the Société d'Aquarellistes, established in 1879; its aim was to promote the use of watercolour in France. In alleging that this initiative was supported by 'some ingenious dealers,' critics demonstrated their awareness of the marketability of small-scale, vividly handled watercolours; this is also borne out by Petit's mounting of the Aquarellistes' shows from 1882.[19] 1885 saw the foundation of the Société des Pastellistes Français, once again a fashionable medium, rapid for the artist to produce and convenient for the dealer to sell, given pastel's association with sensual femininity and the luxury of the *ancien régime*. Its members included such rising stars of 'modern' breadth and colour as Gervex, Besnard and Ernest-Ange Duez.

Such clubs and societies were not dealerships, but, like the Salon, they operated in dialogue with the commercial market. They presented art to the upper-class, male echelon of society – prime purchasers – within a gentlemen's social ambience.[20] Petit's plush décor was evidently designed to emulate the atmosphere of the Cercles. These clubs and societies also competed with the galleries, for although their shows were only annual, they were quasi-commercial and might well cream off choice items which a dealer would otherwise have been delighted to have in his stock. More specifically, they commonly charged a mere ten percent commission on sales, whereas Theo van Gogh, following his firm's policy, charged 25 percent.[21] Dealers risked being undercut by such outlets, which perhaps explains why Petit was so keen to house the Aquarellistes and later the Pastellistes, binding them to his business.

Another way of describing the Parisian art market is from the point of view of artistic style and status. Again, several tiers can be distinguished. The market encompassed outlets for the senior, bemedalled and academic – the Cercle de l'Union Artistique, or the Aquarellistes; for the established mid-career artist with 'modern' tendencies – the Internationales, the Pastellistes; and for the impressionists – their own group exhibitions, four of which were held in the 1880s, and the one-man shows staged by Durand-Ruel and, later, Theo van Gogh. Even the newest avant-garde found its spaces. From 1888 the neo-impressionists Seurat, Signac and Dubois-Pillet took over their own room at the Salon des Indépendants, a non-juried alternative Salon founded four years earlier, while Gauguin and his colleagues seized the opportunity to display work at the Café Volpini during the Exposition Universelle of 1889. There was also traffic between these layers, of course, creating an overall picture of immense, even confusing vitality and variety as dealers and artists competed for visibility and success on the market.

What lay behind this plethora of exhibitions, this appetite for display and consumption? Armand Silvestre was one of a number of critics arguing that there were too many small shows; these did nothing but encourage artists to produce 'work purely for sale' and risked 'saturating the public with painting to the point of giving it indigestion.'[22] Critics of different ideological and aesthetic persuasions recognised that there was powerful social pressure to spend vast sums on often trifling objects as signs of chic or status. Writing in the moderate republican *Le Temps* in 1880, Jules Claretie fulminated against young painters, 'with their passion for the *bibelot*, for *Japonisme*, for boulevard success,' who made 'surplus art [...], accessible, smiling, easy to sell.' 'The art object is replacing the work of art,' he feared.[23] Five years later, in the radical *La France*, Octave Mirbeau condemned the Aquarellistes, from whom one could order a picture like 'shirts from Doucet, dresses from Félix, boots from Hazard.'[24]

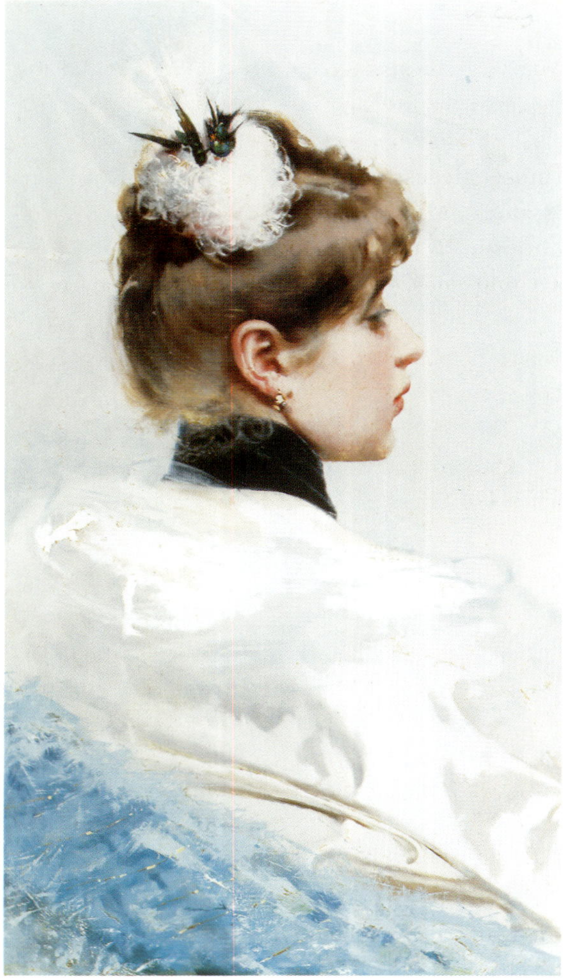

57
Vittorio Corcos 1859–1933
Lady with a hat c. 1881
Present location unknown

Artists of all kinds were inexorably swept into this spiral of production and consumption. Vittorio Corcos, whose canvases of pretty ladies formed one of the most successful staples of Boussod, Valadon & Cie.'s stock [57], wrote to Theo in 1890 that he was nothing but 'a poor plodder, condemned to produce an art that goes against my feelings, an art of rouge and powder that I feel no love for and which I will have to go on producing for God knows how long!'[25] Degas apparently felt similarly, complaining to Ludovic Halévy a decade earlier that the ballet picture was 'the only thing that people want from your unfortunate friend.'[26] Artists ran the risk of being trapped into creating fripperies or specialities because the modern city, with its obsession with the visible, the new, and the purchasable, demanded it. To buy something of value, to own something identifiable and accredited, to accumulate *bibelots*, was linked, as Rémy Saisselin proposes, to 'the bourgeois love of inheritance and passion for selling and buying and finding a bargain.'[27] As a consumer item, art was comprehensible to the bourgeoisie, and owning something tangible and valuable gave it a grasp on both the certain and the modern in an uncertain, urban world. Catering for and participating in these economic-cum-ideological systems, the art dealer functioned somewhere between the department store and the museum, a small version of former with the hope or pretension of furnishing a domestic variant of the latter.

The dealer doing business

As we have seen, dealers had to respond to the eager speculative appetites of the Third Republic. When, in 1884, on the eve of her brother-in-law Manet's posthumous sale, Berthe Morisot encouraged her sister to buy, she did so not in terms of taste or family loyalty but of speculation. 'In the old days it would never have occurred to mother or father to use a thousand or even a five-hundred franc note for a purchase of this kind,' she prompted, but a 'good speculator' like Faure (the opera singer) was waiting for prices to go up and 'everything would sell at extremely high prices if we were not in the midst of a depression.'[28] Theo van Gogh's own transactions bear out the profitability of speculative buying and selling. Take his dealings with Henri Poidatz, later director of *Le Matin*, who auctioned part of his collection in March 1888. A landscape by Chintreuil, purchased from Theo on 30 March 1886 for 1,282 francs, fetched only 1,850, a modest increase. Daubigny's *Bridge at Mantes*, on the other hand, which Boussod, Valadon & Cie. had bought in London for 2,000 francs on 12 April 1886, and which Theo swiftly sold to Poidatz on 22 May for 6,000, reached 13,000 at his sale.

Judicious buying of the right artists could reap dividends, and it was the dealer's task to find work which would increase in value. Speculation in the work of deceased painters of accepted quality such as Chintreuil and Daubigny, even Manet, was less risky than investment in living artists whose reputations were still contested, notably the impressionists. Nonetheless, Mary Cassatt's correspondence with her family about buying Monets was once again frankly commercial. She regarded his canvases as stock market futures. 'Monet is coming up,' she wrote to her brother in 1883: 'Petit, the man you bought your Raffaëlli from, has gone to Monet's pictures with a will, bought forty of them from Durand [...]; so hold on to your Monets, I am only sorry I did not urge you to buy more.'[29] Three years later she talked about 'laying in' Monets, as if his pictures were consumables like wine![30] If prices rose on the back of such speculation, this had a knock-on effect in the lower layers of the market, as Gauguin, a former businessman, was quick to realise. He wrote to a friend in June 1888, during Theo's exhibition of Monet's Antibes canvases: 'I'm not angry if Claude Monets are becoming expensive; that will always be another example for the speculator who compares the prices of yesterday with those of today – and from that point of view it's not too much to ask 400 francs for a Gauguin if Monets are going for 3,000.'[31]

In which artists would speculative collectors have invested in the 1880s? There is no doubt that taste in painting was shifting. The stock of the academic artists, with their finely brushed surfaces and classical subjects, was tumbling.[32] Another sign of change was Petit's regular recasting of the Exposition Internationale, which, as we have seen, manifested a distinct shift towards 'modern' art. So, too, did his gallery's hosting of another grouping, the Trente-Trois. Formed in 1887, this association's heterodox and international personnel – Jacques-Emile Blanche, Emile Friant, Odilon Redon, Fernand Khnopff, Louise Breslau, Fritz von Uhde and René Ménard among them – were thought to represent 'the contemporary school of grey and violet who have more delicacy than depth'; in other words, their works exhibited all the traits of recent painting: bravura handling, peinture claire, or emergent symbolist imagery.[33]

Groups such as these, not to mention radical coteries such as the neo-impressionists, exhibiting as a phalanx at the Salon des Indépendants, raised the problem of how to identify 'modern' art, how to define its characteristics and pick out its leading figures. The 'modern' – a category which would have included but not necessarily been dominated by the impressionists – was an increasingly active force on the market. In 1882 Claretie joked about the progress of the more advanced artists: now that Manet had been decorated and Degas was being collected, whatever would happen if the impressionists became 'embourgeoised to the point of being courted by the dealers?'[34] Five years later his irony was market reality. Renoir, pleased that both he and Monet had made some impact at Petit's Exposition Internationale, wrote to Durand-Ruel that popular taste was coming round to their kind of work.[35] The proof was more and more to be found in public sales. These indicate that impressionist work was increasingly valued on the market, if only within a broadly defined framework of 'modern' art and against an ebb in academic stock.[36]

With the market constantly in flux, it was crucial for dealers to have a stock of artists who were commercially viable, either lucrative or steady sellers – the safe investment – or, alternatively, ones who could be bought low and later sold high – the speculation in artistic futures. To this second category belonged the impressionists, who did not, of course, paint in a homogenous style: a tightly drawn Renoir portrait or nude, a cunning composition by Degas, a rugged Monet or a pointillist Pissarro landscape between them offered a range of stylistic, commercial and subject choices to the potential buyer.

And dealers certainly competed for their work. In a letter of 1885, which demonstrates how adept he was at playing off rival dealers, Monet informed Durand-Ruel of schemes by 'your hostile colleagues' to ruin the dealer's business by buying up all Petit's impressionist stock and selling it, unframed, at a low-grade auction. Furthermore, Petit intended to show Monet's canvases at next year's Internationale, but without having to borrow from Durand, and with the artist contracted out of the impressionist group show; this would leave Petit in a monopoly position.[37] Monet's manipulative self-promotion, combined with his very identifiable work, helped improve his market position. A colleague without the former – like Sisley, or the latter – like Renoir, were less well placed. Equally, dealers who were taking risks by investing in such speculative territory had to protect their interests. Durand-Ruel could be very aggressive on this front, instructing Pissarro in 1884 not to deal with 'that animal Heymann, who hawks your pictures without frames in grubby shops.'[38] In 1888 Durand made a concerted effort to persuade Pissarro to sell to him and not to Theo, but the artist, aware of 'these devilish picture dealings,' saw that if he allowed the former a monopoly he would be 'imprisoned in the citadel, at Durand's mercy.'[39]

Rivalry over impressionist stock was, however, only a minor aspect of the competitive art economy of the 1880s. The fact that amateurs were building up such sweeping collections is perhaps evidence not simply of eclectic taste, but also of a need for a wide range of investments as a safeguard against shifting values in different areas of the market. Both Charles Leroux and Ernest May owned not only paintings but a significant number of works on paper.[40] A collector such as Albert Hecht, who purchased his first Monet in 1873 and owned paintings by Manet, Renoir and Pissarro, assembled an Aladdin's cave of Barye bronzes, Chapu reliefs, faiences from Italy and Delft, oriental carpets, and medieval and Japanese objects: a magpie taste consistent with his business in fancy goods and symptomatic of the possessive lust for the *bibelot*.[41] Hecht also owned several Old Masters, as did a collector with somewhat more capital, Charles Deudon, whose investments in the South Wales coalfields allowed him to purchase important canvases by Manet and Renoir, but who had begun with a landscape attributed to Hobbema.[42]

As we have mentioned, a dealer like Petit made it his business to offer a substantial variety of art in order to reach the widest possible audience. Who steered the market – the dealer with a gallery full of diverse and enticing pictures and objects, or the collector with a catholic aesthetic and speculative eye – we cannot tell. Probably neither led, for both were geared into the interlocking spiral of the art economy. So, too, was the contemporary artist, who hoped to make work which would be shown, purchased, and eventually rise in value. This was the world in which Theo van Gogh made his living.

Theo's employers: an entrepreneurial paradigm

Theo van Gogh's employer was one of the longest established and most powerful players on the Parisian art market. Indeed, the Van Gogh family had been closely linked to the success and development of the firm over two generations.[43] The company's history is an intriguing case study in 19th-century capitalism and its adaptability. The business was founded in 1827 by Henri Rittner, who opened a shop in his own name at 12, Boulevard Montmartre, selling printed reproductions of works of art. In 1830 the designation changed to Rittner & Goupil, marking his partnership with Adolphe Goupil; and to Goupil & Vibert with a new partnership in 1841; finally settling on Goupil & Cie. in 1850, the year the firm moved to its new premises at 19, Boulevard Montmartre.[44] The company diversified and thrived. Branches were opened selling reproductions in London in 1841, Berlin in 1852, and, as early as 1846, Goupil's agent Michael Knoedler started up in New York. In 1853, Goupil's made its first foray into mass-produced photography, and in 1858 the company began publishing photographic reproductions after the paintings of Paul Delaroche.[45]

A major change came when Goupil joined forces with Vincent and Theo's uncle, Vincent van Gogh, or 'Uncle Cent.' He had set up as an art dealer in The Hague in 1839, and had travelled to Paris in 1846, making initial contact with both Adolphe Goupil and Francis Petit, Georges's father. From 1 January 1861 Goupil & Cie. was recast. Adolphe Goupil kept a controlling interest with 40 percent, while Vincent van Gogh and Léon Boussod, who had entered into a partnership with Goupil in 1856, each had a stake of 30 percent.[46] This was an effective business arrangement. Van Gogh added the trade in works of art – paintings, drawings, etc. – to the firm's base in art reproductions, using the established international network of galleries, to which he added a branch in The Hague.[47] Boussod, who had begun his career in the burgeoning railway business, used his industrial expertise to manage the manufacturing of printed and photographic reproductions.[48]

In 1857, during the Haussmann property boom, Goupil had purchased land, at 9/11, Rue Chaptal, north of the Eglise de la Trinité. There he built a lavish private *hôtel*, including studios for the artists linked to the business, a printing shop and a gallery: the hub of his empire. In 1863, the marriage of his daughter, Marie, to the painter Jean-Léon Gérôme, then at the height of his fame and appointed Professor at the Ecole des Beaux-Arts that same year, linked Goupil with the upper echelons of the French artistic establishment.[49] Goupil's powerful presence on the Parisian art market was manifest in his three outlets: at 9, Rue Chaptal, in a smart artist's quarter, but off the main thoroughfares; at number 19 on the busy Boulevard Montmartre; and at the prestigious central gallery at 2, Place de l'Opéra.

As the years passed the firm changed. In 1872, Uncle Cent resigned from active work, and in 1878 gave up his partnership, retiring to Princenhage, near Breda.[50] His share was purchased by René Valadon, who had married Léon Boussod's daughter in 1875. The elderly Adolphe Goupil handed over the direction of the firm to Boussod and Valadon in 1884, surrendering his partnership in 1887. 1884 was a crucial year. The firm changed its name to 'Boussod, Valadon & Cie., successeurs de Goupil & Cie.,' and the premises on the Place de l'Opéra were relinquished. A sense of dynastic continuity was established by the marriage of Boussod's son, Etienne, to Jeanne, Gérôme's daughter and granddaughter of Goupil, in 1882.[51]

The company's core business never ceased to adapt. From 1860, some 30 photogravure reproductions of popular paintings, chiefly from the Salon, were published every six months. By 1884 the catalogue listed some 1,759 items, though only 43 were added in the next twenty years.[52] Goupil gradually

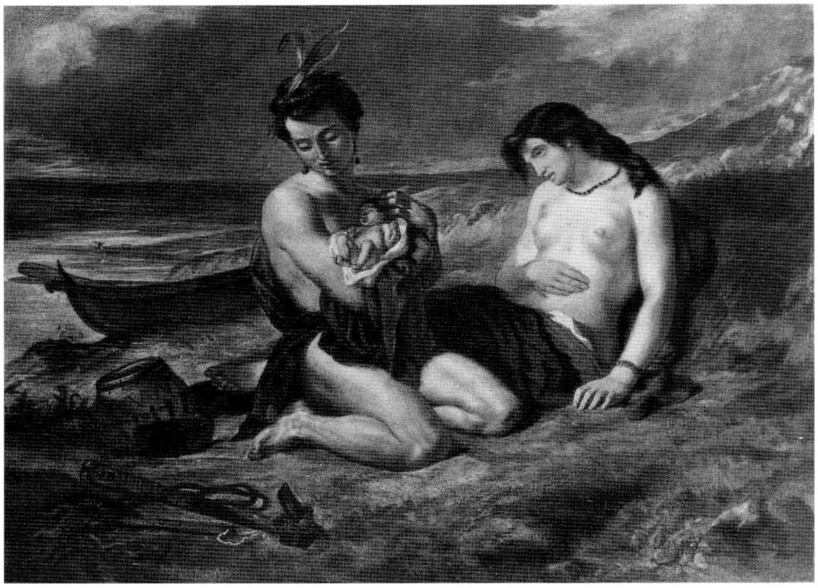

58
After **Eugène Delacroix** 1798–1863
The Natchez 1823–c.1835
Musée Goupil, Bordeaux
Original painting now in The Metropolitan Museum of Art, New York

branched out into the book and magazine market. In 1868, for example, Gérôme and Charles Bargue collaborated under his auspices on a series of books of artistic exercises.[53] This side of the business expanded when the firm became Boussod, Valadon & Cie. in 1884. The development was aided both by the introduction of new processes such as typogravure, and by the technical skills of Michel Manzi, who had joined the firm two years earlier. In 1885 the reproductions for the Salon reviews in the popular weekly *L'Illustration* were provided by 'Boussod & Valadon, gravures photographiques,' and by the next year, the company was using its technical expertise for its own publications, notably the grand folio *Figaro-Salon*. Between 1886 and 1889, Boussod, Valadon & Cie. published the up-market cultural review *Les Lettres et les Arts*, and, in 1888, it took over *Paris Illustré*, a chic middlebrow magazine.[54] Books were also published, including, in 1887, an edition of Halévy's *L'Abbé Constantin*.[55] Others treated more wholesome topics, consistent with the firm's reproductions and gallery stock, which favoured military, religious, and sentimental subjects.[56] By these various means Boussod, Valadon & Cie. kept its business up to date, linking art and artists with a broad public by means of reproductive technology.

The company also diversified in accordance with changing taste in the fine arts market. Second-guessing the Parisian scene in 1872, the American collector Samuel P. Avery wrote to John Taylor Johnston, Chairman of the Trustees of The Metropolitan Museum, New York, that '"high art" – Millet, Diaz, Daubigny, Delacroix, Decamps, Fromentin, Dupré, & & – are to put Bouguereau, Merle, and the others of "The School of Goupil," as the dealers call it, out of fashion.'[57] The suggestion was that the painters of the Ecole de 1830, whose early careers had been controversial, but who were now established figures and mostly dead, would replace the academic artists that Goupil had hitherto favoured. If some such transition did come about, it was neither as simplistic nor as soon as Avery thought it would be. In 1881, for example, Goupil purchased Delacroix's *The Natchez* [58], an important canvas that had featured at the Salon of 1835, from Prince Demidoff for 6,000 francs, but it was slow to move, and only finally left their hands on the last day of 1888, for the moderate price of 8,400 francs.[58] The Ecole de 1830 was thus not necessarily a surefire investment.

At the time of Avery's observation the company had, however, already been promoting a relatively new kind of genre painting for some years – small scale,

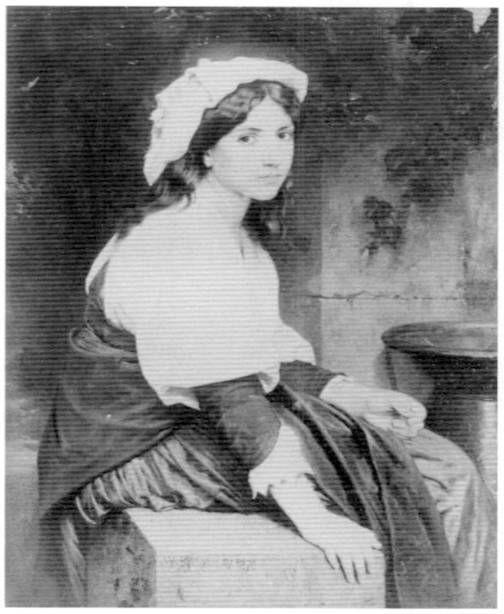

59
William-Adolphe Bouguereau 1825–1905
Italienne assise 1870
Present location unknown

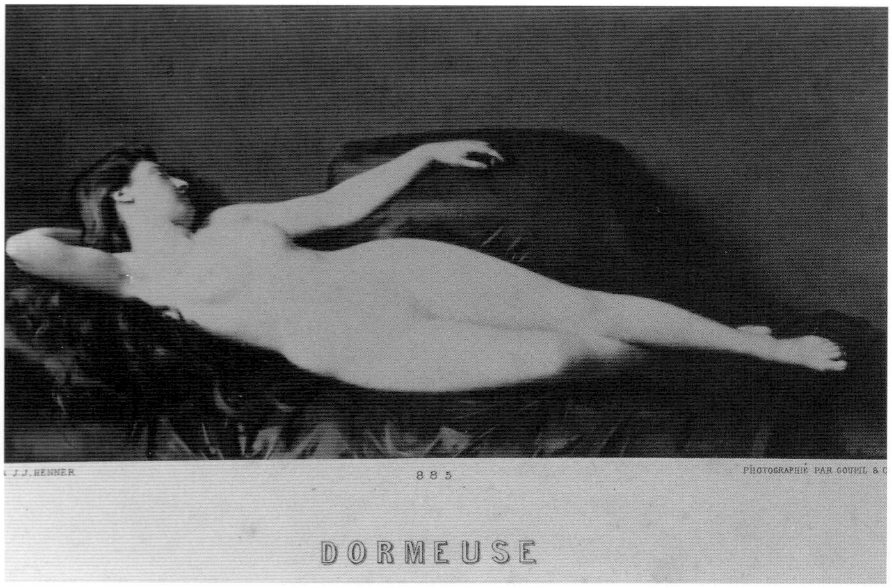

60
After **Jean-Jacques Henner** 1829–1905
Dormeuse c. 1880
Musée Goupil, Bordeaux
Present location of the original painting unknown

highly finished costume pieces that were clearly designed to build on the success of Meissonier. In 1866, Adolphe Goupil had offered an initial advance of 24,000 francs to the Spanish painter Marià Fortuny, who worked in this manner, setting him up two years later in one of the studios in the Rue Chaptal.[59] These costume pictures sold well enough in the 1870s and into the 1880s, contradicting Avery's rather absolute prophecy of the demise of the 'School of Goupil.' There does, though, seem to have been a gradual reduction in trade in the work of heavyweight Salon academics. For example, although he was under contract, only a handful of paintings by Bouguereau are entered under 19, Boulevard Montmartre, and it may be that his commitments were registered at one of the other branches. According to the lists, only four of his paintings were bought and sold between 1879 and 1884, the last being disposed of the year the firm became Boussod, Valadon & Cie.: these were probably works that did not come under the contractual arrangements. **[59]** Again, only six Gérômes appear in the stockbooks in the decade after 1876. The most important was the *Excursion of the harem* **[61]**, which had been shown at the Salon of 1869. Bought in May 1882, it was not sold for over three years, indicating perhaps that the market for such pictures was not as strong as it had been. On the other hand, the work of Jean-Jacques Henner, an academically-trained artist of a younger generation whose critical reputation remained consistently high, sold steadily throughout the 1880s, the stockbooks registering 16 pictures handled by Theo. **[60]**

Changes of taste and market forces – those slippery twins – had their effect on other artists in whose work the firm traded during the 1880s. Bargue, who had been linked to Goupil since the 1860s and was celebrated for his scrupulously wrought little costume and Orientalist pictures **[62]**, was still purchased in the 1880s; the stockbooks itemise 24. Although Bargue's pictures moved easily – by the end of 1885 only two remained in stock – after 1885 the firm purchased only a single painting. A similar case was that of Emile Pierre Metzmacher, who specialised in flirtatious scenes in 18th-century costume. The stockbooks show four pictures bought between 1879 and 1881, including the *Saut de loup* **[63]**, from the Salon of 1879. Only one of these sold quickly

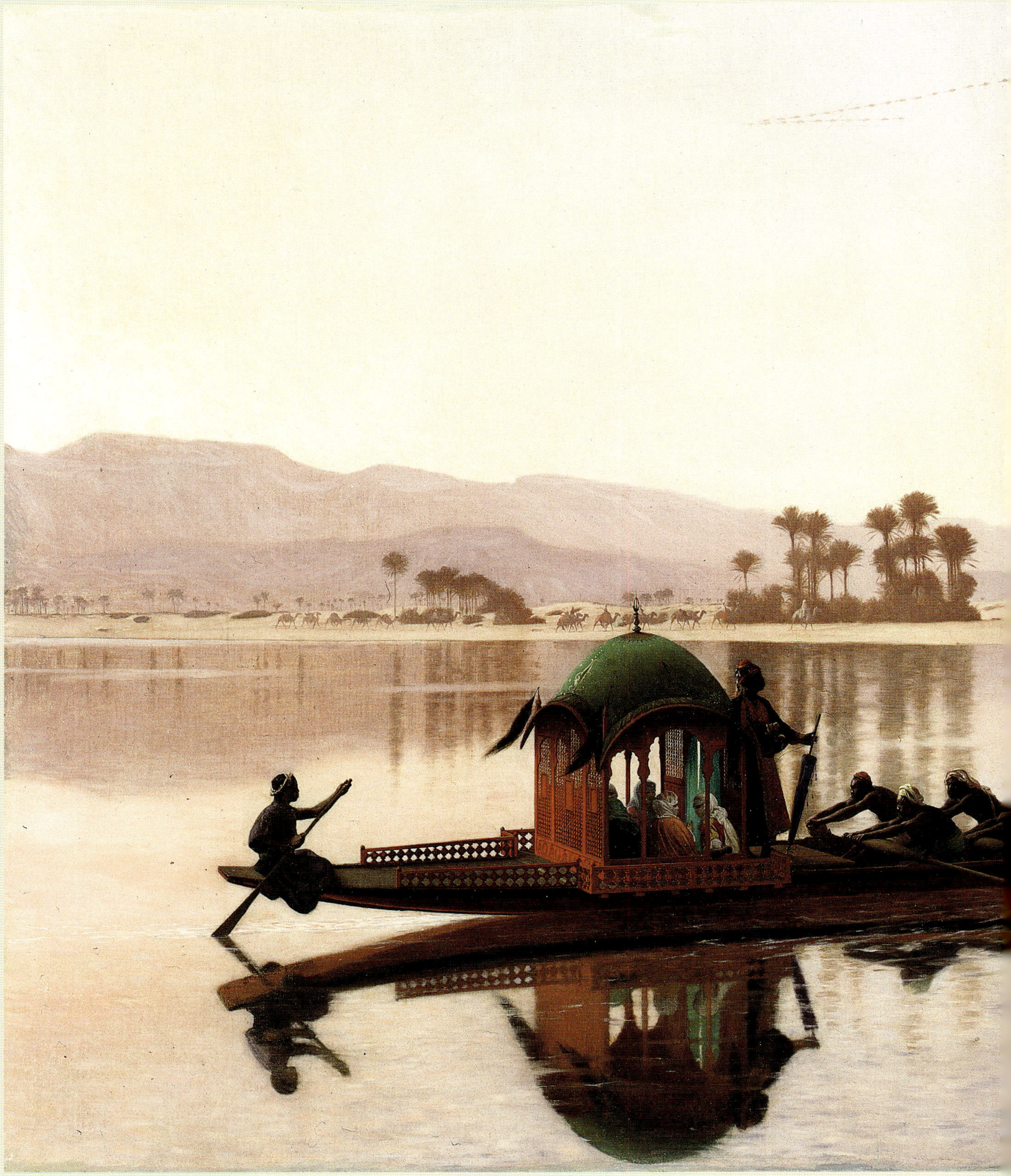

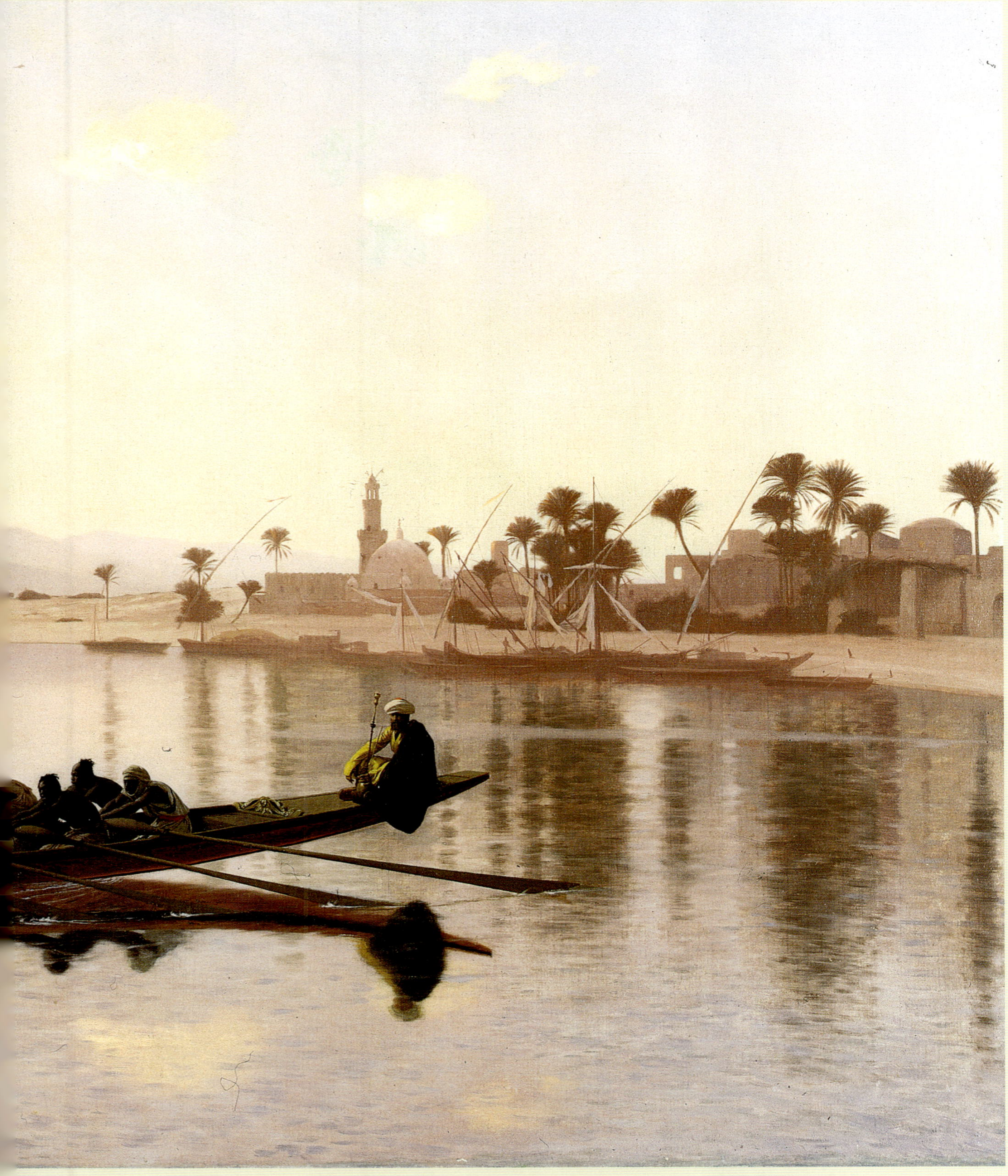

61
Jean-Léon Gérôme 1824–1904
The excursion of the harem 1869
The Chrysler Museum of Art, Norfolk, VA
Gift of Walter P. Chrysler

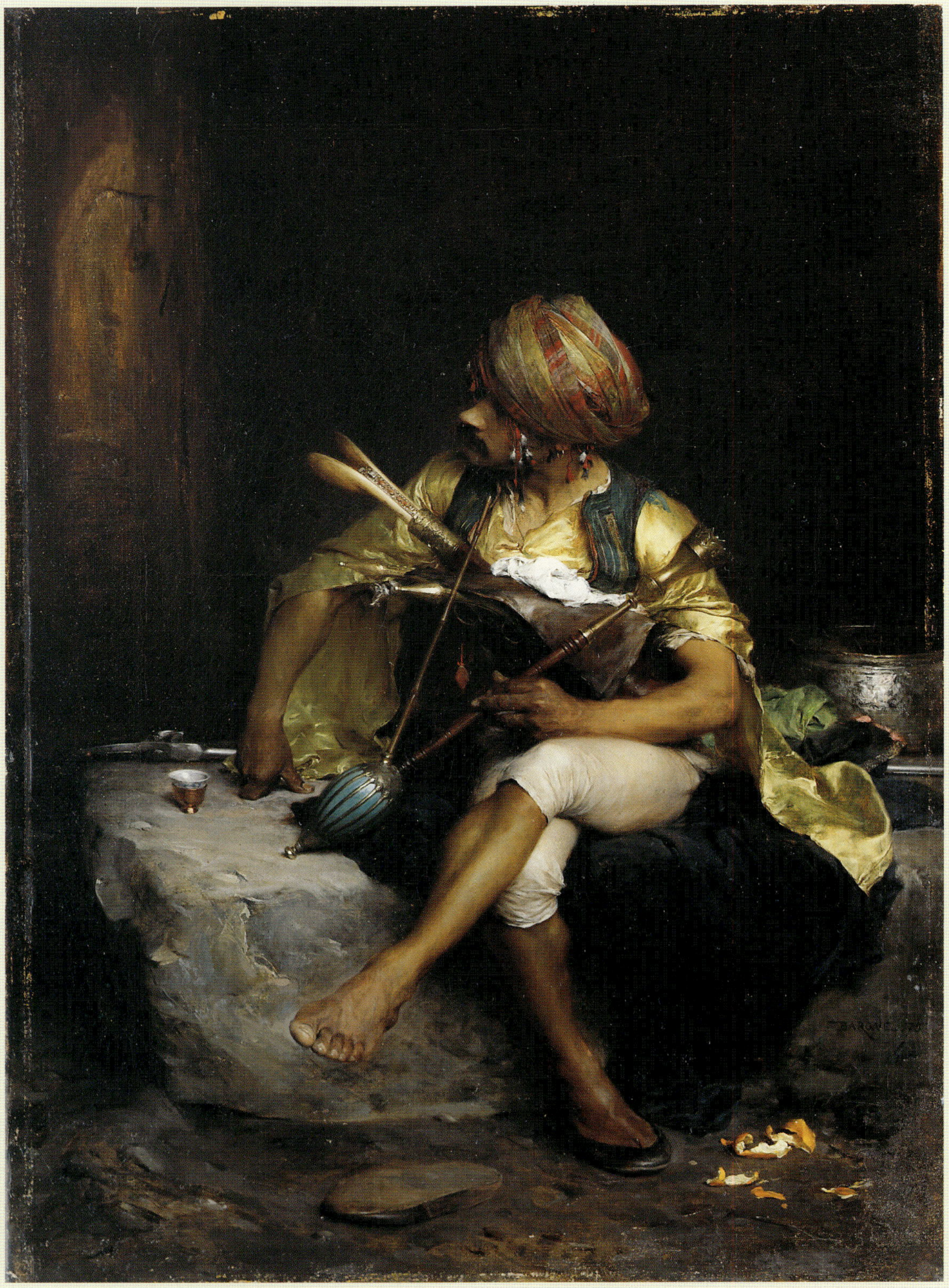

62
Charles Bargue c. 1825–1883
A bashi-bazouk c. 1875
The Metropolitan Museum of Art, New York
Catharine Lorillard Wolfe Collection

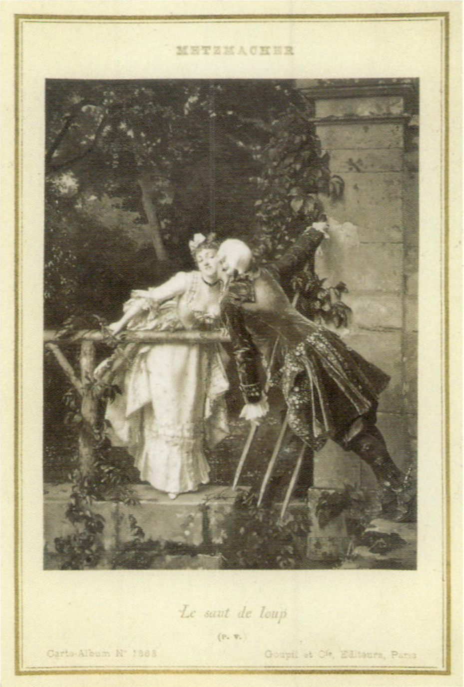

63
After **Émile-Pierre Metzmacher** 1842–1916
Le saut de loup Salon of 1879
Musée Goupil, Bordeaux
Present location of the original painting unknown

(within a month); the remaining three took two to five years to sell. No more of his paintings were listed under 19, Boulevard Montmartre until one each was bought in 1889 and 1890; their rapid turnover in the stockbooks suggests they found ready buyers. Such patterns hint that the firm was not unswervingly loyal to artists associated with so-called 'Goupil' taste; as the demand shifted away from costume, precision and sentiment such works were only handled when sales were assured.

In general Boussod, Valadon & Cie. traded in the safe stock of the period. The 1880s saw the second decade and firm establishment of the Third Republic. The regime's ideology set much store by rationality and so in art that was frank, descriptive and legible to its wide political constituency.[60] Naturalism was appropriately enough the dominant style, and imagery which reinforced national certainties and Republican values was promoted. These undercurrents are reflected in the firm's stockbooks as well. Jules Breton's *Evening in the hamlets of Finistère* [**64**], shown at the Salon of 1882 and swiftly bought by the Paris-based American agent George A. Lucas for Samuel Avery, is a case in point; so, too, is Julien Dupré's *Feeding time* [**65**]. Both represent the timeless surety of rural life in *la France profonde*, reassuring icons of continuity in an age of rapid change. To the city-based collector, they offered an image of natural rhythms and a stable society. Another favoured subject was the Franco-Prussian War of 1870-71, which the French had ignominiously lost. Pictures which recovered a degree of national dignity and, by showing heroic resistance, restored faith in French arms enjoyed enormous popularity.[61] The stockbooks of 19, Boulevard Montmartre indicate that the nine works by the military painter Alphonse de Neuville that Goupil purchased between 1879 and 1884 all sold in a month or less [**66**]. Perhaps, too, the paintings of Corcos [**67**] – 70 of which were handled by Theo between 1881 and 1890 – should also be seen in ideological terms. Neither nationalist nor Republican, Corcos's canvases present an image of womanhood which shores up twofold the (sexual) ideologies of the late 19th century. On the one hand, they show women as possessible, as objects of desire; on the other, they picture them as consumers. For whatever their implicit moral status, Corcos's women, are definitely purchasers of costumes, furs and cosmetics; they are part of the culture of capital.

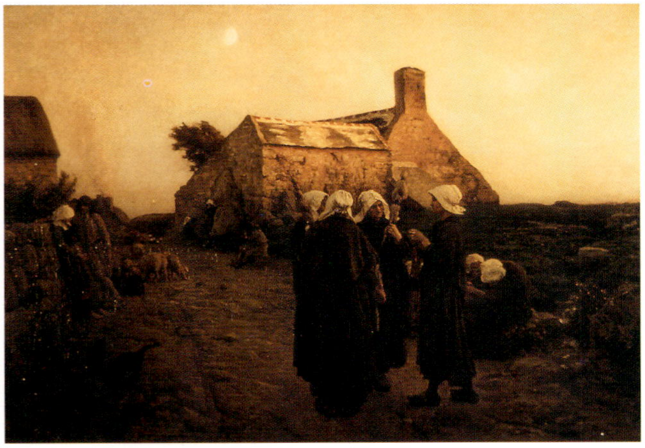

64
Jules Breton 1827–1906
Evening in the hamlets of Finistère 1881
Paine Art Center and Arboretum, Oshkosh, WI

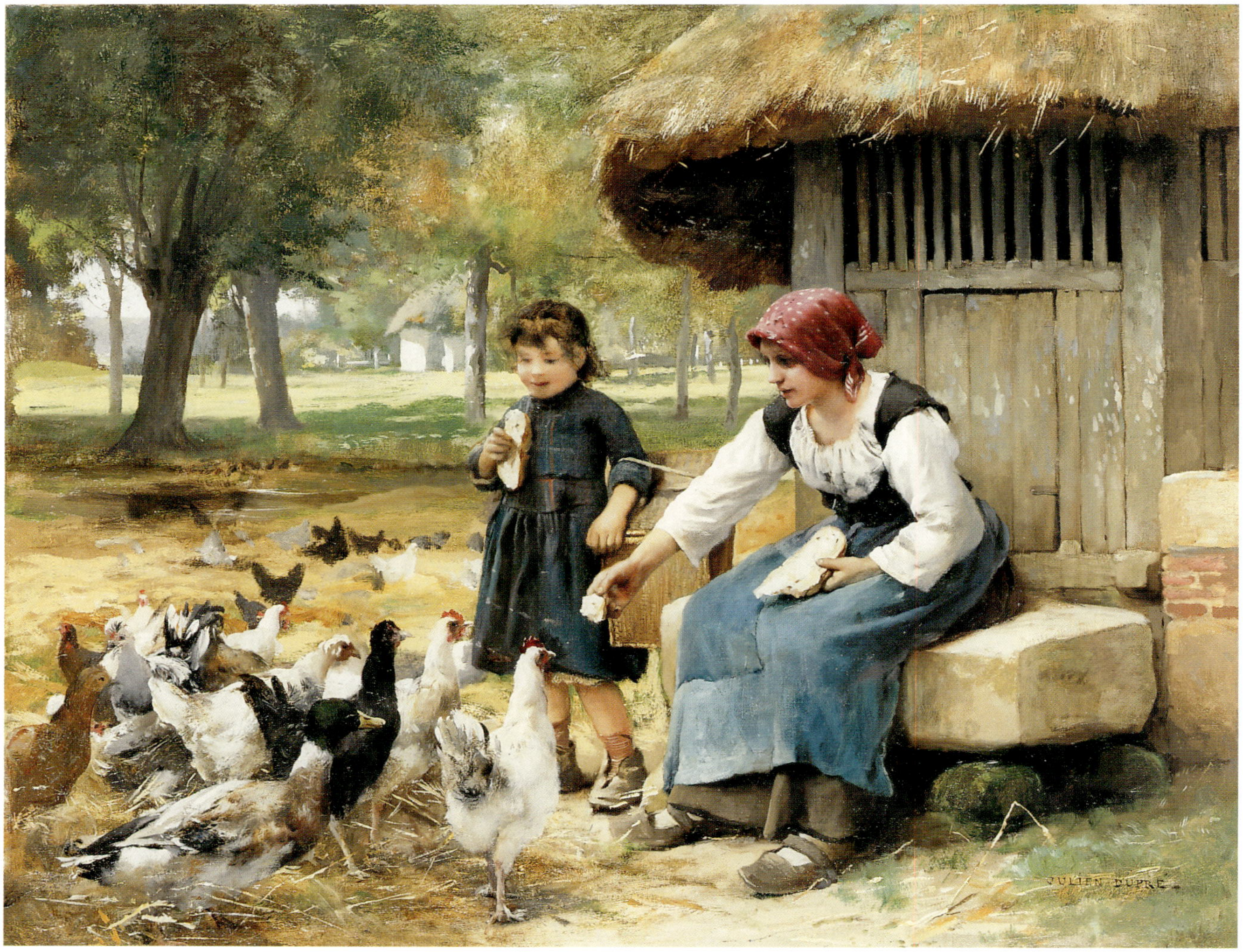

65
Julien Dupré 1851–1910
Feeding time c. 1881
Chi-Mei Fine Art Museum, Jen-te-Village, Taiwan

In the wake of the 1884 restructuring of the firm, and marking the final retirement of Adolphe Goupil, a sale was held in May 1887.[62] It was clearly an exercise in dropping stock that had proved slow to sell, and in so doing to raise capital for new purchases; it also signalled the company's transformation from Goupil's into Boussod, Valadon & Cie. Lucien Pissarro judged it harshly, but correctly, when he described it to his father as the disposal of 'a considerable lot of the foul painting which generally fuels the business – they rightly sense that it's dangerous to have in stock a pile of awful things which will certainly become obsolete at any minute.'[63] There were 546 lots, of which 216 were paintings and the rest watercolours and drawings. The range cut across the firm's holdings.[64] This heterogeneous clear-out was not a success. Works fell below estimates. Delacroix's *Natchez*, valued at 10,000 francs, was bought for half that; Boulanger's *Via Appia* fetched 6,650 rather than 10,000; and Gérôme's *Memnon and Sesostris*, from the Salon of 1857, did not quite reach its estimate of 20,000. The military pictures by Neuville and Eduard Detaille, from their collaborative *Panorama of Champigny*, did well, six large watercolour studies totalling 33,900 francs.[65]

The company took other restructuring decisions in 1887. The contract with Bouguereau – signed in 1866 – was allowed to expire.[66] An agreement was made with Léon Lhermitte, a painter of the peasants and landscapes of the Marne, for all his canvases and pastels.[67]

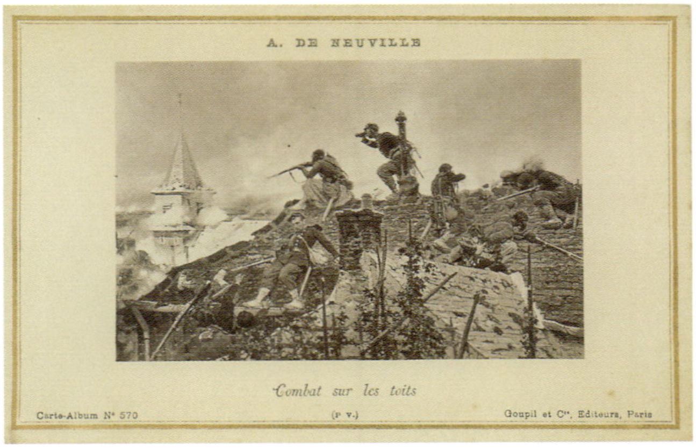

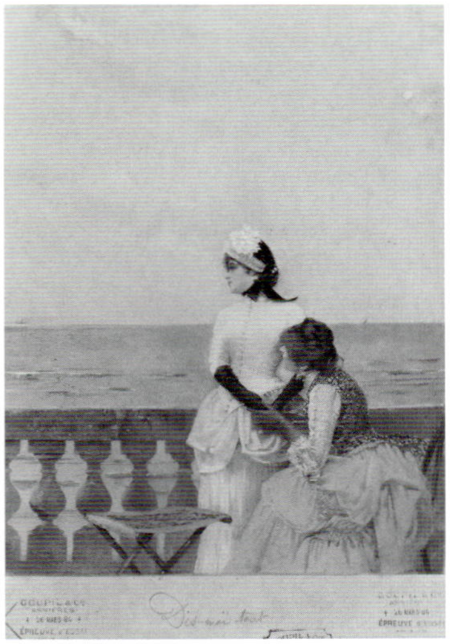

66
After **Alphonse de Neuville** 1835–1885
Combat sur les toits n.d.
Musée Goupil, Bordeaux
Present location of the original painting unknown

67
After **Vittorio Corcos** 1859–1933
Dis-moi-tout 1883
Musée Goupil, Bordeaux
Original painting now in a private collection

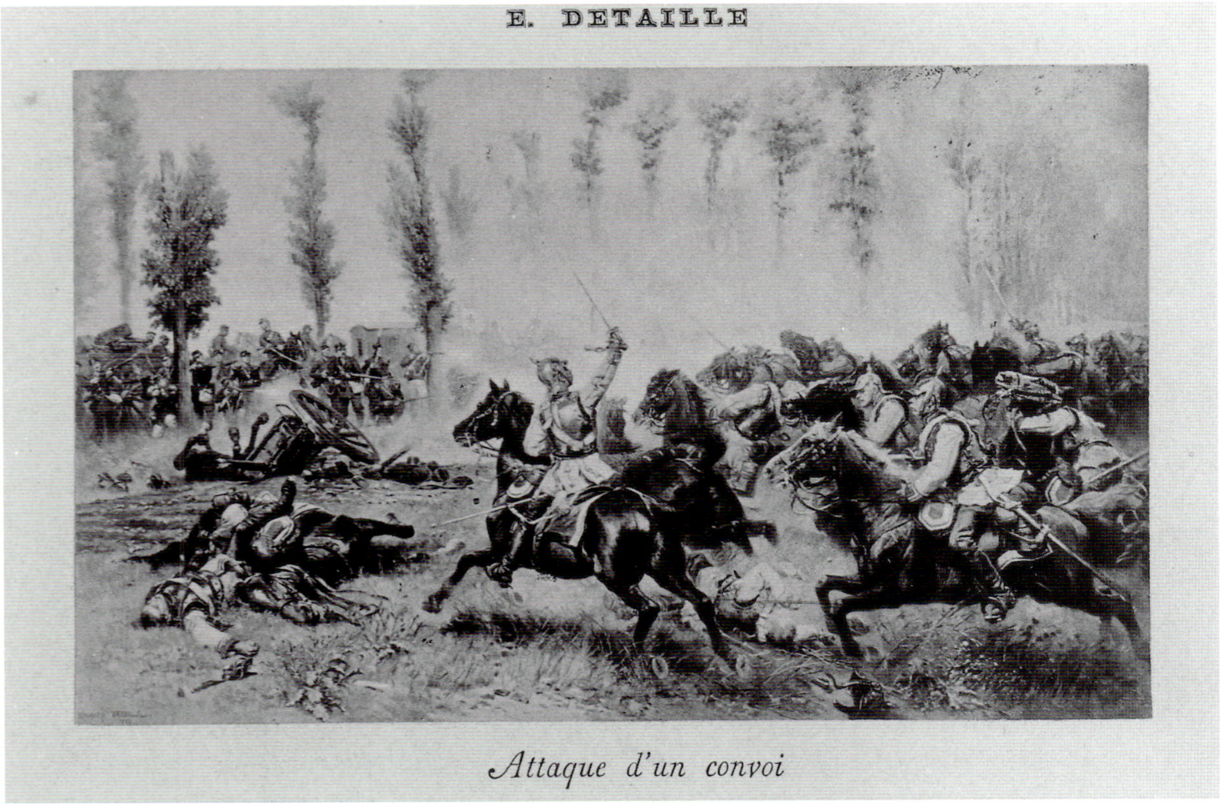

68
After **Edouard Detaille** 1848–1912
Attacking the convoy 1880
Musée Goupil, Bordeaux
Original painting now in The Forbes Magazine Collection, New York

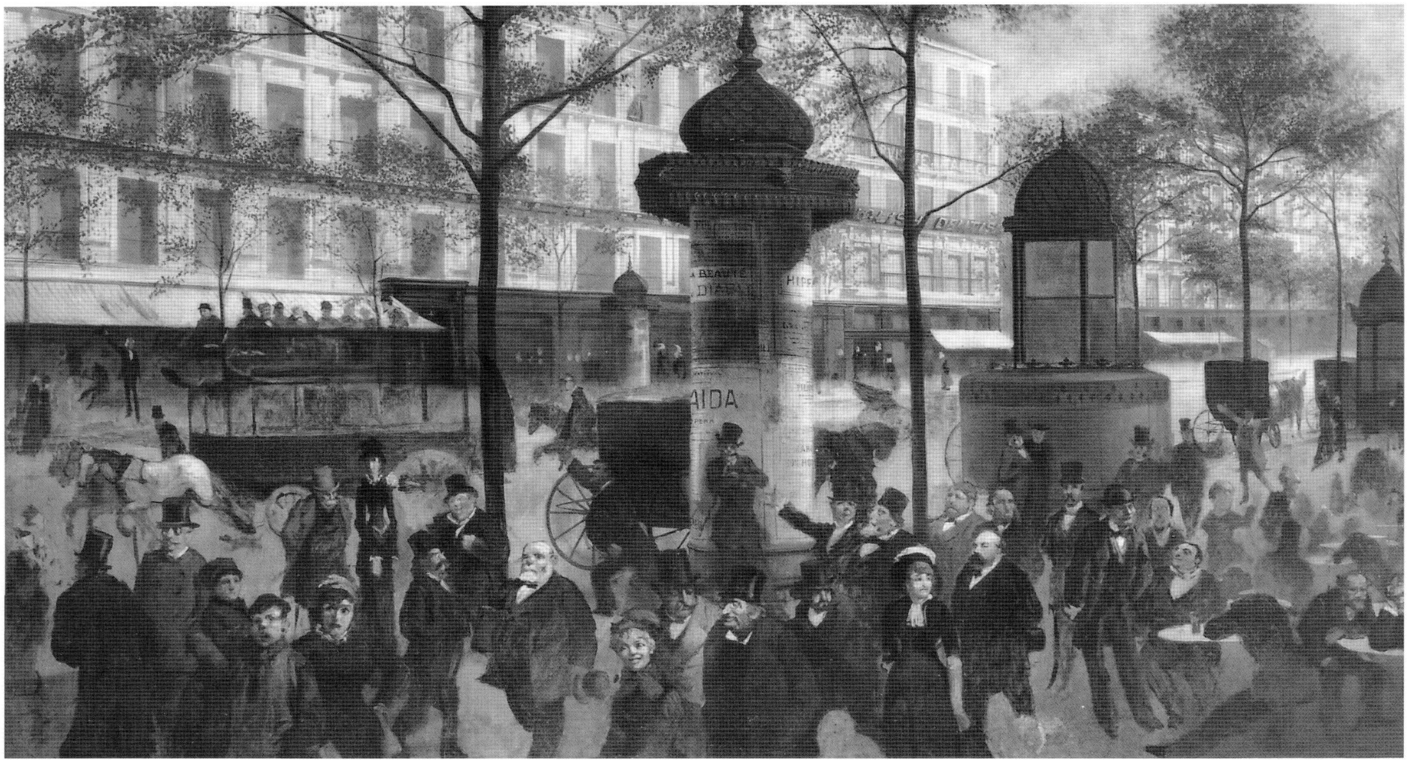

69
André Gill 1840–1885
Study for a panorama of the Boulevard Montmartre in 1877
Musée Carnavalet, Paris

This made good sense: Lhermitte had emerged as a major artist during the early 1880s, and his work was both naturalist and national. Although contracted to Boussod, Valadon & Cie. and listed in Theo van Gogh's address-book, Lhermitte's name does not appear in the Boulevard Montmartre stockbooks; apparently Theo was not responsible for selling his work. As a jewel in the company's crown, Lhermitte was handled from the premises on the Rue Chaptal, along with the prestigious and established names such as Gustave Moreau and Detaille [**68**], who were given one-man shows at just the same time Theo was promoting Monet, Raffaëlli and others at his gallery.

In sum, Boussod, Valadon & Cie. was consistently typical of 19th-century entrepreneurial capitalism. The business changed its stock and contracts as markets shifted: engaging Fortuny, Boldini and others when the Meissonier costume genre was at its peak around 1870; dropping Bouguereau in 1887, and taking on Lhermitte. It adapted its trade in reproductions to new technologies – photography in the 1850s and new colour printing methods for mass circulation magazines in the 1880s. Its outreach was international, with lucrative connections in the United States as well as other European capitals; the evidence of both the Van Gogh brothers's careers – Dutchmen employed by a French firm not just in Paris and The Hague, but also in London and Brussels – illustrates this perfectly. In other words, the notion of Theo struggling against a monolithic company wedded to obsolete tastes and conservative practices is untenable. He may at times have gone faster or farther than his employers expected in his exploration of new markets, but in general he operated within the commercial ethos of a remarkably successful, and above all, flexible organisation.

Theo van Gogh at 19, Boulevard Montmartre

In 1878, Theo was called in to help man the firm's stall at the Exposition Universelle.[68] He then moved permanently to Paris in November 1879. He must have impressed his employers, for in early 1881 he was appointed *gérant* (manager) of the gallery at 19, Boulevard Montmartre. The premises were situated at the hub of the financial quarter and the art market. Durand-Ruel relates how he would far rather have had his gallery here – 'on the path of foreigners and all the wealthy of Paris' – than on the Rue Laffitte, a side street.[69] The Boulevard Montmartre was a vibrant thoroughfare by day and night. In 1877, just before it became Theo's place of work, André Gill painted a caricatural sketch **[69]** of the celebrities likely to be seen there, among them the actresses Sarah Bernhardt and Hortense Schneider, the politicians Gambetta and Clemenceau, and the ubiquitous Claretie.[70]

19, Boulevard Montmartre is on the south side of the street. Theo's gallery occupied the ground floor, opening out on to the sidewalk (now the Café des Princes), with an *entresol* above and a basement space below.[71] **[70]** Overall, these were adequate commercial accommodations, but by no means as lavish as the galleries of Theo's chief competitors. Gustave Geffroy made a positive point of this in his review of the 1888 Monet exhibition. Although the rooms on the *entresol* were small and without artificial illumination, the walls not draped with plush or the cornices gilded, he did not miss the 'high-class décor.'[72] Theo's employers clearly though it unnecessary to invest in such things; Theo ran a shop selling art works, with no pretence of being a gentleman's club.

How did he go about his daily business? There is little evidence, and we must rely on the contemporary art world's letters, diaries, and press to piece together the patterns. An important source are the company's stockbooks **[71]**, now in The Getty Research Institute for the History of Art and the Humanities. These, however, are the company's overall ledgers.[73] Unfortunately, the stockbooks for the individual Paris branches, which might have contained more details, have been lost. In general, only paintings are registered; works on paper or in other media are noted only sporadically. These are an invaluable resource, but flaws and omissions limit their usefulness. For example, only concluded transactions were recorded: there is thus no evidence of works left on consignment. We know from their correspondence that this was common practise for Pissarro and Gauguin, and it was not necessarily only impressionist artists who did so. Another problem is that it is not always possible to decipher which branch of the firm handled the transaction.[74] Theo certainly also allowed himself a degree of latitude with his entries. As Rewald points out, in July 1890 he made a payment of 500 francs to Pissarro, but did not enter it, perhaps because he did not want to be seen speculating with the firm's money by fostering an artist who was still not a market certainty.[75]

Theo's status seems to have risen with that of his branch, the ideal business combination of effective management and burgeoning market profile. The diary of George A. Lucas, the American art agent, gives us a glimpse of Theo's early activities. On 21 March 1882 he noted: 'At Goupil's & saw Breton Salon picture, [...] At van Goghs to see Jacque [...].'[76] He is here referring to the Place de l'Opéra branch, where he went to see Breton's *Evening in the hamlets of Finistère*, an important Salon picture, and to 19, Boulevard Montmartre, where he looked at work by the more peripheral Charles Jacque, probably his etchings. Clearly, Lucas identified this branch with Theo, alluding in his diary later that year to 'Montmartre Goupils (van Gogh),' but he also seems to have implicitly acknowledged a layering in Goupil's

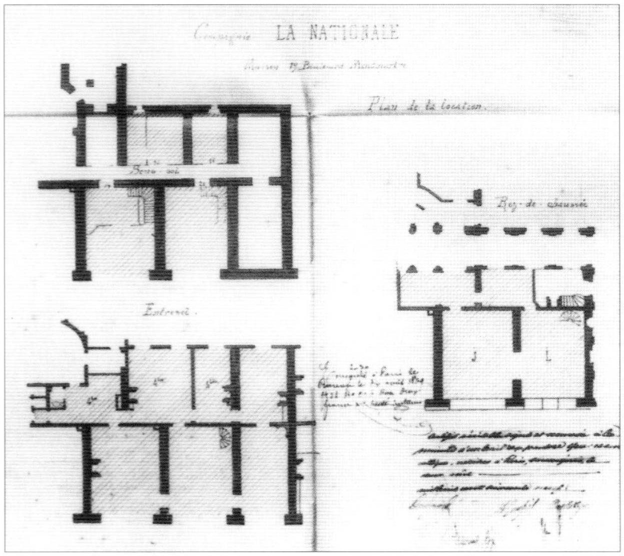

70
Ground plan of the Boulevard Montmartre branch of Boussod, Valadon & Cie. c. 1881-90
Archives Nationales, Paris

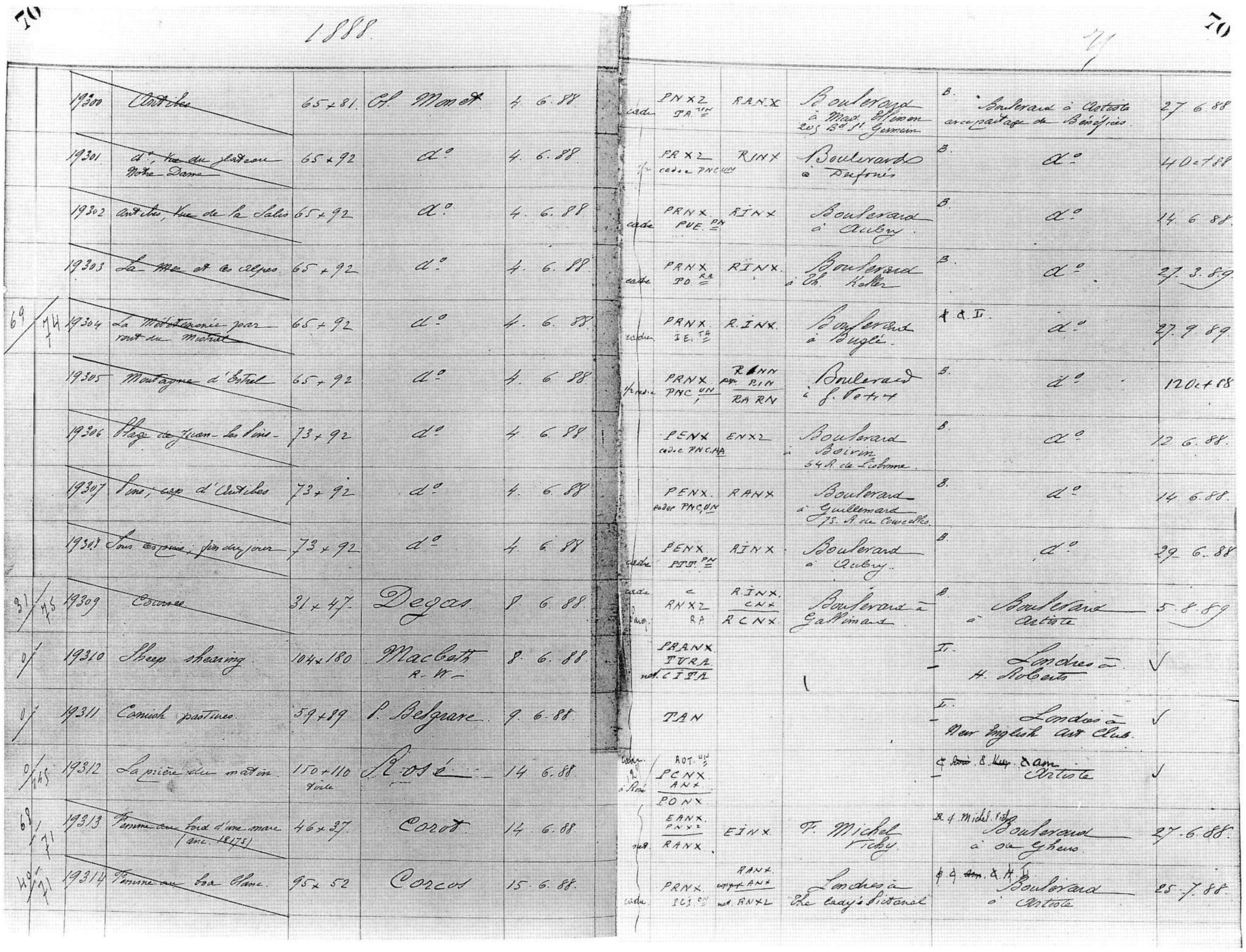

19300	Antibes	65+81	Cl. Monet	4.6.88
19301	d°, vue du plateau Notre Dame	65+92	d°	4.6.88
19302	Antibes, vue de la Salis	65+92	d°	4.6.88
19303	La mer et les Alpes	65+92	d°	4.6.88
19304	La Méditerranée par vent du Mistral	65+92	d°	4.6.88
19305	Montagne d'Estérel	65+92	d°	4.6.88
19306	Plage de Juan-les-Pins	73+92	d°	4.6.88
19307	Pins, cap d'Antibes	73+92	d°	4.6.88
19308	Sous les pins, fin du jour	73+92	d°	4.6.88
19309	Courses	31+47	Degas	8.6.88
19310	Sheep shearing	104+180	Macbeth R.W.	8.6.88
19311	Cornish pastures	59+89	P. Belgrave	9.6.88
19312	La prière du matin	150+110 toile	Rosé	14.6.88
19313	Femme au bord d'une mare	46+37	Corot	14.6.88
19314	Femme au boa blanc	95+52	Corcos	15.6.88

71
Page from the ledgers of Boussod, Valadon & Cie. June 1888

market hierarchy, which ranked the Place de l'Opéra above the Boulevard Montmartre.[77] Over the course of his tenure as *gérant*, however, Theo appears to have successfully improved the position of his gallery. Baedeker's 1881 guide to Paris merely listed Goupil's at 19, Boulevard Montmartre (and indeed 2, Place de l'Opéra) for 'estampes, gravures,' whereas by 1889 a leading art-world almanac registered it under 'Marchands de Tableaux et Curiosités' – dealers in painting.[78] By the turn of the decade, after he had been using the *entresol* for showing new and challenging work for several years, Theo's premises had become a magnet for those interested in adventurous modern painting, 'one of the surest artistic rendez-vous in Paris,' as Geffroy put it.[79]

There can be no doubt that Theo was industrious. As expected, he worked on Saturdays, and even used Sundays to network with art world acquaintances, for example, taking his Scottish colleague Alexander Reid to breakfast with Lucas one Sunday in December 1887.[80] When business was going well, he worked late, staying on until ten o'clock during the Raffaëlli one-man show in the summer of 1890 [880/T35]. Theo visited the busy annual round of Salons, Cercles and Sociétés; kept an eye on the other dealers and exhibition spaces; and maintained relations with business contacts such as Lucas, whom he saw only five times in 1885 but 14 in 1888.[81]

Above all, however, his task was to purchase works of art – either for stock or particular clients – and to sell them. He often purchased directly from artists, but also from sales and auctions, and he bought from

– and sold to – other dealers: Petit, Durand-Ruel, Brame, Arnold & Tripp, Bernheim, Heymann and others all crop up in the lists. In the to-ing and for-ing of the market, he took work from collectors as they cashed in on speculations or recast their holdings, and sold them new items. Thus, on 19 June 1889, he bought Daubigny's *Beach at low tide* [72] from Desfossés, followed by another, *Village on the banks of the Oise*, on 4 November. At the same time, he was also selling Pissarros to Desfossés: on 18 March the important *Apple picking* [74] and on 26 July *Meadow at Eragny*.[82] Desfossés was an experienced collector and would have been transferring his investments purposefully; it is to Theo's credit that such an amateur should both sell to and buy from him.

Consistent with Goupil's long-standing practice, Theo also dealt with the foreign market. During the 1880s Scandinavian painters were becoming increasingly popular in Paris, and this trend is reflected in the stockbooks.[83] The stockbook for 1888 includes entries for several very different British painters: a *Lock on the Stour* by the long-dead John Constable, *Sheep-shearing* by Robert Macbeth, and a *Woodcutter* by George Clausen, a follower of Bastien-Lepage.[84] Via the firm's London branch, Theo was provided with pickings from the local auction houses.[85] Theo also sold to the trade abroad, in the Netherlands, the United States and, once more, London.[86] [73]

Another of his tasks would have been to open up new markets, or at least to keep abreast of new developments. On this score it is not easy to make out a case for Theo as an innovator. Rewald noted that his first impressionist sale was probably a Pissarro landscape, bought and sold on the same day, 29 March 1884, for a 25 franc profit on an outlay of 125 francs.[87] However, a receipt in the archives of the Van Gogh Museum registers Theo's purchase of a landscape painting by Victor Vignon from the printmaker Henri Guérard on 24 January 1883, the price being 200 francs.[88] We do not know whether this picture was destined for Goupil's stock or his own private collection. Vignon, although a minor talent, had exhibited at the impressionist exhibitions of 1880, 1881 and 1882, and this receipt proves that Theo's interest in this kind of painting began not long after his appointment as *gérant*, and well before his brother Vincent – sometimes thought to have led him to deal in impressionism – had any knowledge of such work.

We have seen, however, that the impressionists were already attracting dealers, collectors and press support in the early 1880s, and the fact that Theo only began to trade in their work with any conviction after 1887 suggests that he or his firm – perhaps both – were unwilling to invest in them until the market was quite well developed. Once he did begin to buy their pictures competitively in 1887 – and the quantity in which he bought them strongly suggests his company's backing – he did so with a will, taking on 15 Monets and seven Sisleys in the first year.[89] The rapidity with which Theo entered the impressionist market indicates that this was part of Boussod, Valadon & Cie.'s new strategy, an effort to catch up with other dealers; indeed, the bulk of these 1887 purchases were made after the May clear-out of Goupil's old stock. Theo also sought to promote this new stock abroad. In March 1888 he sent a mixed batch of 'modern' paintings to his former colleague Tersteeg at the branch in The Hague. There was a single painting each by several former exhibitors at the impressionist shows – Degas, Monet, Sisley, Pissarro, Guillaumin and Gauguin (with his *Harbour at Dieppe* [75]) – with one each by Theo's brother and Toulouse-Lautrec, and two by Monticelli.[90] Such shipments were not unusual, frequently being used to open up new markets. This was thus not a heroic initiative but a standard business gambit. Theo was simply doing his job, trying to open up a particular market – his native Dutch one – to a new product: progressive French painting. Nonetheless, this was the first time impressionist paintings had been shown in the Netherlands – an event of no little importance.

Something of the character of what Theo displayed at his gallery can be gleaned from the brief critical notes written by Félix Fénéon in the monthly *Revue Indépendante* in late 1887 and 1888. It seems likely that Theo used the ground floor for his more standard stock, which would have been of little interest to an avant-garde critic writing for an avant-garde readership. Indeed, Fénéon only mentioned what caught his eye among the more adventurous items, which were probably shown on the *entresol*. Nevertheless, his observations give us a picture of what Theo chose to

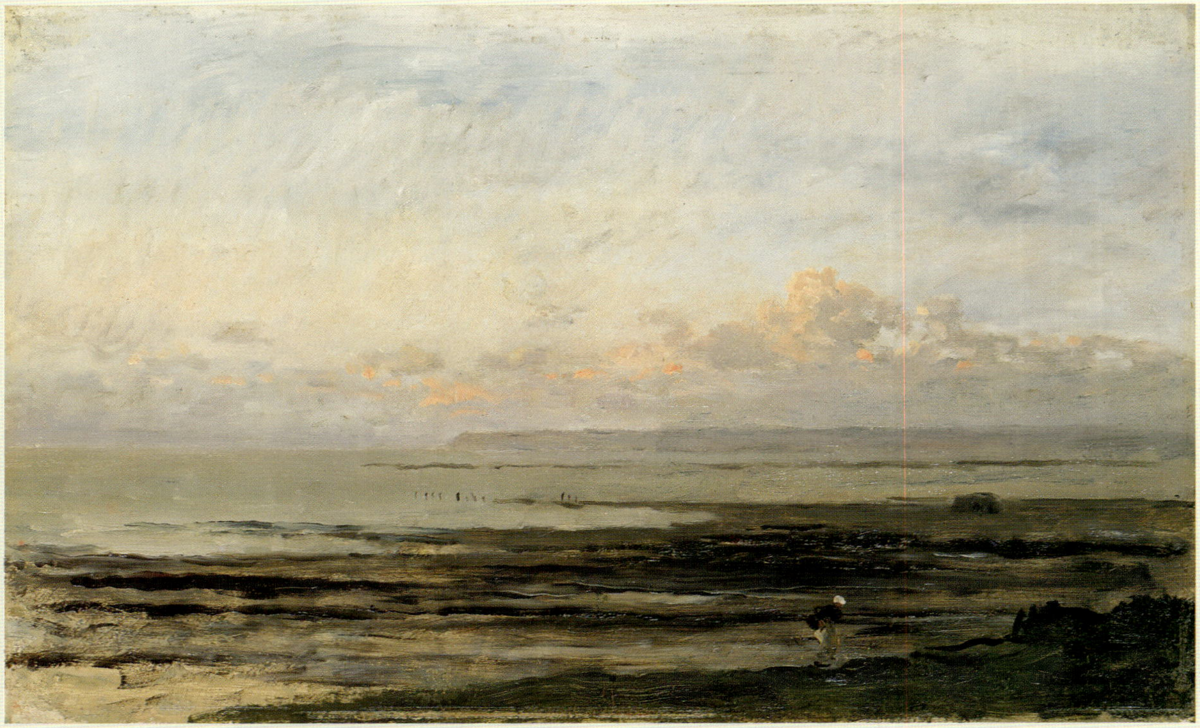

72
Charles-François Daubigny 1817–1878
Beach at low tide 1876
Rijksmuseum, Amsterdam

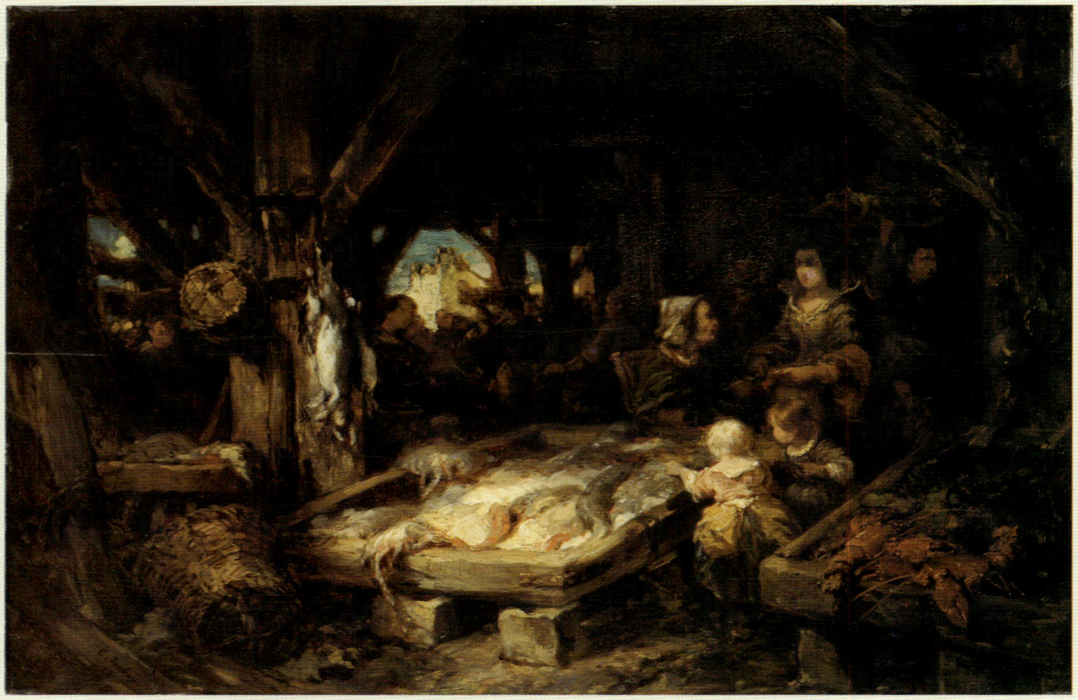

73
Eugène Isabey 1803–1886
The fish market, Dieppe 1845
The National Gallery, London

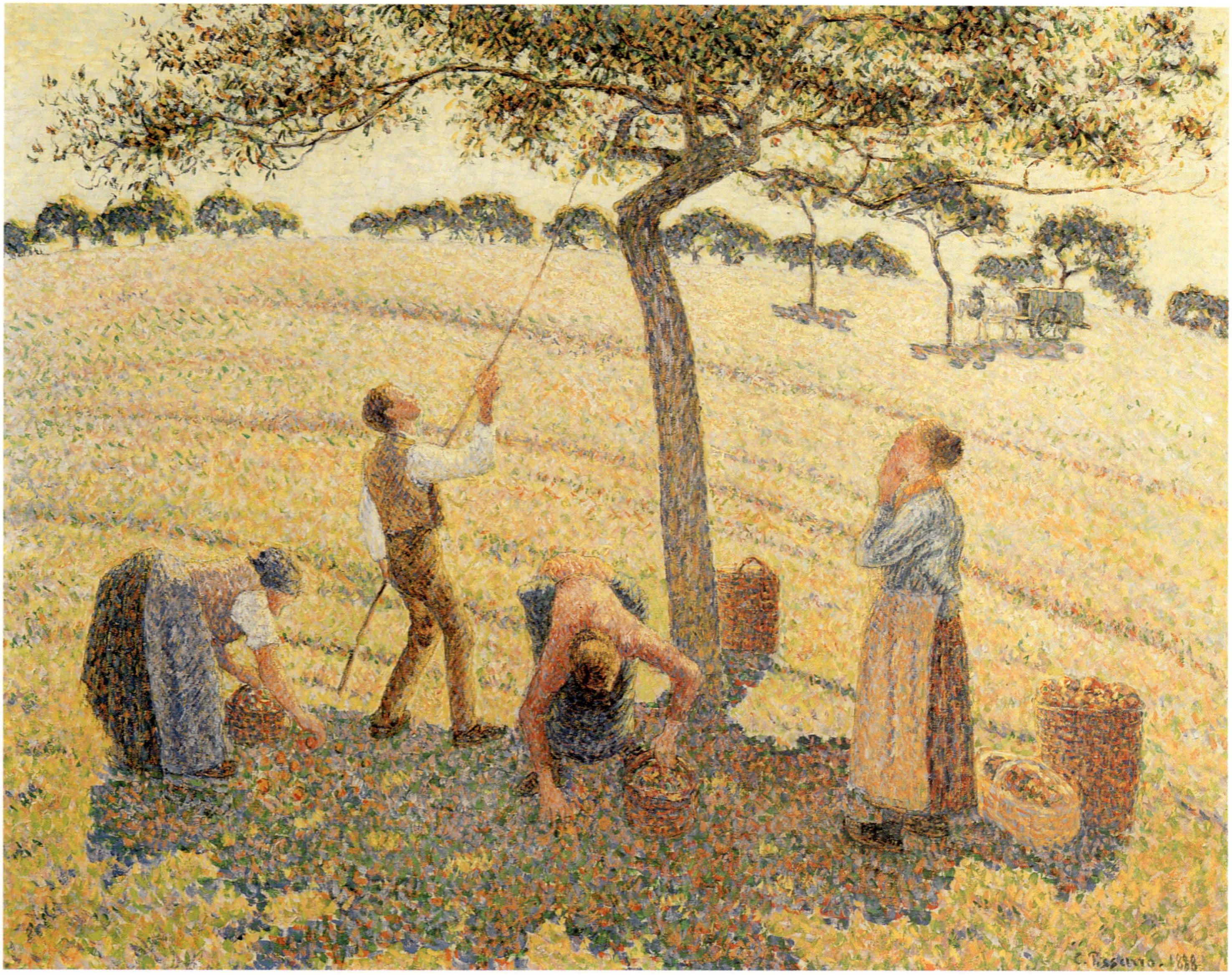

74
Camille Pissarro 1830–1903
Apple picking, Eragny 1888
Dallas Museum of Art
Munger Fund

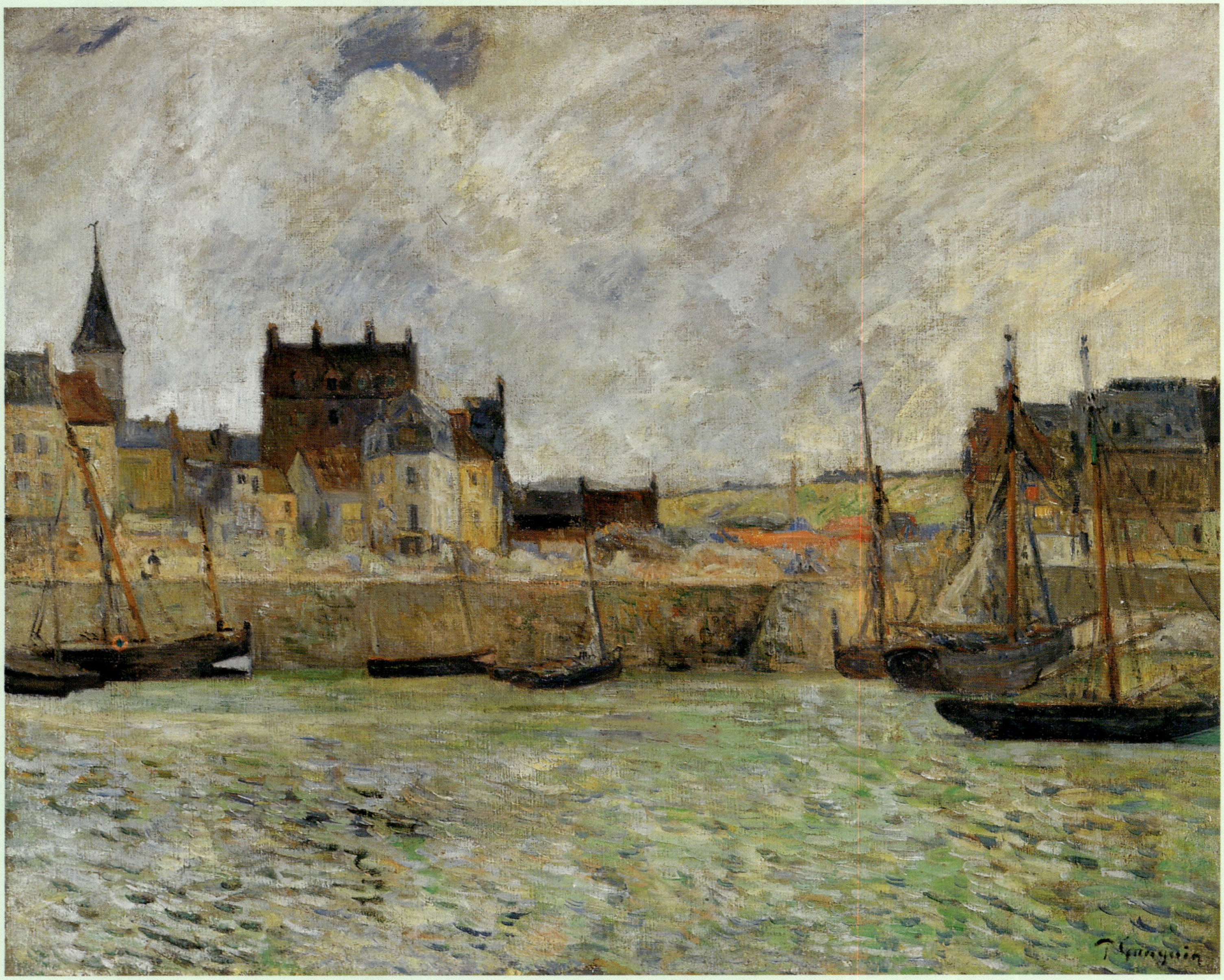

75
Paul Gauguin 1848–1903
The harbour at Dieppe 1885
Manchester City Art Galleries

exhibit, and also hint at a slight shift in his attitudes and stock between December 1887 and September 1888. In the earliest pieces, Fénéon mentions artists whose work he would have seen at the eighth impressionist exhibition in May 1886: Degas, Pissarro, Gauguin, Guillaumin. His 'Calendrier d'Avril,' however, notes a wider selection of personnel and media: pictures by Zandomeneghi and Schuffenecker, both of whom had also exhibited in 1886 but had not previously been mentioned; Thornley's lithographic reproductions after Degas; three posters by Jules Chéret; and a figure of a woman from Rodin's ongoing *Gates of Hell.* The September article praises Thornley and Pissarro again, takes Zandomeneghi to task for dabbling in the neo-impressionist manner, and notes a Manet oil sketch, which suggests that Theo was happy to display unfinished work to a discriminating public.[91] He was gradually moving beyond the impressionist stalwarts, and introducing his clientele to work in diverse media by artists outsitde the mainstream.

What of Theo's professional and personal dealings with artists? It seems likely that in these he operated within the firm's established business practice, which left limited room for the display of personal preferences or taste. On 4 June 1888 he signed a contract with Monet on behalf of Boussod, Valadon & Cie. It was based on the proven marketability of the painter's work: of the 24 canvases previously purchased, 16 had already been sold. The agreement gave Theo first refusal on Monet's work, and arranged for the purchase of ten of his recent Antibes paintings, for a total of 11,900 francs; the profits from the sale any of these were to be divided 50/50 between dealer and artist.[92] This was the standard arrangement, precisely the same terms under which Bouguereau had been contracted from 1866 to 1887.[93] Nor does Theo seem to have been particularly innovative in his use of marketing gambits. The purchase of Monet's Antibes paintings gave him the chance to stage a one-man show. But most of the artists for whom he eventually organised such exhibitions – Raffaëlli and Pissarro, in addition to Monet – had already received such treatment (in 1883-84), and one-man shows had long been a regular part of the firm's market strategy.

In personal terms, various painters' writings support the obituaries in recognising Theo as a man of sincerity and prudence, genuinely interested in art and artists, and able to give wise business advice based on sound experience. If a hot-headed young neo-impressionist like Lucien Pissarro called him 'chien' – miserly, in Parisian argot – it would have been due to the frustrations in selling his father's paintings, frustrations which Theo shared.[94] Artists trusted the Dutchman with their work. As the brother of a painter, he understood practical problems – as Pissarro recognised when he left two incompletely dry oils at the Boulevard Montmartre: 'I regret that he [Theo] wasn't there because the other employees of the gallery are quite capable of leaving my canvases encased.'[95] How trusted he was in his day-to-day dealings with a wide network of artists, critics and collectors is also demonstrated in his own surviving business correspondence.[96]

Were there any failings in Theo's professional life? Some significant artists appear not to have passed through his hands – among them Boudin, Harpignies and Fantin-Latour – but then they were contracted to other dealers: Durand-Ruel, Arnold & Tripp, and Tempelaere respectively.[97] Publicity also seems not to have been his forte, as one may gather from the fact that his activities are rarely mentioned in the press.[98] Starting with the Pissarro show in January 1890, however, Theo did produce catalogues of the one-man exhibitions he staged, and employed Gustave Geffroy, the experienced art critic of the daily *La Justice* and a man sympathetic to new styles of naturalist painting, to write the introductions. This suggests that by this stage he was increasingly aware of the need to mark his gallery's major events with publications. This was a prudent move, but in terms of other galleries' practice it was hardly new. The novelty was to devote a catalogue to what might still be considered difficult work, and to get a critic whose politics and aesthetics were left-of-centre to write for them.[99] This demonstrates once more that he knew his market, and by the turn of the decade was learning to present his exhibitions to the appropriate public.

If the 'gallery taste' of a business like Boussod, Valadon & Cie. was necessarily eclectic, what, then, was Theo's own taste in art? When he wrote dismissively of shows like the Aquarellistes, commenting in 1890 that 'there is nothing good,' he was hardly voicing a radical opinion; even the solid *Chronique des Arts* dismissed the group that year as '[that] customary little procession of bourgeois production.'[100] In a letter to Vincent of September 1889, on the other hand, he admired the 'qualities of rusticity' in Pissarro's work, and how in Gauguin's recently arrived *La belle Angèle* **[76]** 'the woman is somewhat like a young cow, but there is something fresh in it, and then again something so countrified that it is very pleasant' [800/T16]. He contrasted favourably the 'vigour' he found in pictures by Pissarro, Gauguin, Renoir, Guillaumin and his brother to the highly finished, anecdotal pictures at the Salon [777/T9]. But Theo did not dislike all the art on view at the annual exhibition. Writing to Vincent about the Salon of 1889, he mentioned approvingly Raffaëlli's *Absinthe drinkers*, Fritz Uhde's *Birth of Christ*, and Anders Zorn's nude bathers, examples of different kinds of naturalism [773/T7]. Intriguingly, he did not mention the work of other Salon exhibitors he handled, notably Carrière, but also Besnard. Perhaps he felt Vincent might not approve, which suggests that Theo – ever the dealer – tailored his talk and taste to different interlocutors.

Another crucial problem is Theo's interest in impressionist and other new painting in relation to the attitudes of his employers. I have already argued that both were evolving: Theo had shown some interest in impressionism in 1883-84, but had not begun – or wanted, or been able? – to develop it until 1887, and that it was in that year that Boussod, Valadon & Cie. also began to change direction. The real nature of Theo's relationship with the firm's proprietors in the late 1880s is difficult to decipher. We do not know why, for example, he purchased no work by Manet, Sisley or Renoir in 1889. Was it because their pictures were unavailable (unlikely, particularly in the case of Sisley), because they were slow to move on the market (true of Sisley, but surely less so of Manet), or because his superiors blocked his plans?

Theo had certainly had difficulties with them earlier in the decade. In late 1883, for example, he wrote to Vincent that they 'make the situation impossible for me' – although this hardly surprising, given that in August he had sold only a single work and acquired none. But relations improved, and by December he had a 'renewed pleasure' in his work [410/343]. At this date, it is unlikely that problems arose because of Theo's interest in avant-garde art. He seems to have become a contented employee. In 1884 he evidently spoke up for Goupil's, citing their support of Millet and Daumier – to which Vincent retorted that it was quite the opposite, ending: 'You belong to Goupil & Cie.' [465/380]. Theo's value to the restructured company is suggested by the idea mooted in the summer of 1888 that he might run their business in New York, but the idea came to nothing.[101]

By the end of the decade it seems that Theo's employers themselves were involved in business arrangements with impressionist artists. At the end of December 1888, Monet wrote to Theo to tell him that he was 'finishing off the two paintings chosen by M. Valadon,' while in March 1890 Etienne Boussod bought himself a Degas.[102] The difficulties that grew up at this time seem less due to Boussod's or Valadon's supposed distaste for impressionism, but rather to the way they behaved with artists and showed their ignorance of the market. By March 1889 Monet was writing to an embarrassed Theo that Valadon no longer seemed so keen on his work, and that Boussod's son Jean had been interfering with arrangements by taking only some the pictures the painter had brought in.[103] Three months later, Theo complained to Vincent: 'Do you know that I sold that fine picture by Corot, and that those duffers Boussod and Valadon said that it could not be sold? Well, Tersteeg sold it to Mesdag at a profit of 5,000, and Mesdag is so pleased with it that he wants to buy others like it, and he has written to Arnold and Tripp asking them to look out for similar pictures' [899/T39]. Theo knew what his bosses apparently did not – that there was a market for large, sketchily executed pictures – and feared that their ignorance would lose the firm custom. In the same letter, he called Boussod and Valadon 'rats,' concluding that the only solution would be to set up business for himself. That relations were strained during the summer of 1890 is certain, but the reasons are perhaps more complicated than has generally been assumed.

In early July, Theo was to visit Monet at Giverny with Valadon, but the visit was cancelled. Rewald suggests that Valadon wanted to keep an eye on Theo, and prevent him making 'undesirable commitments.'[104]

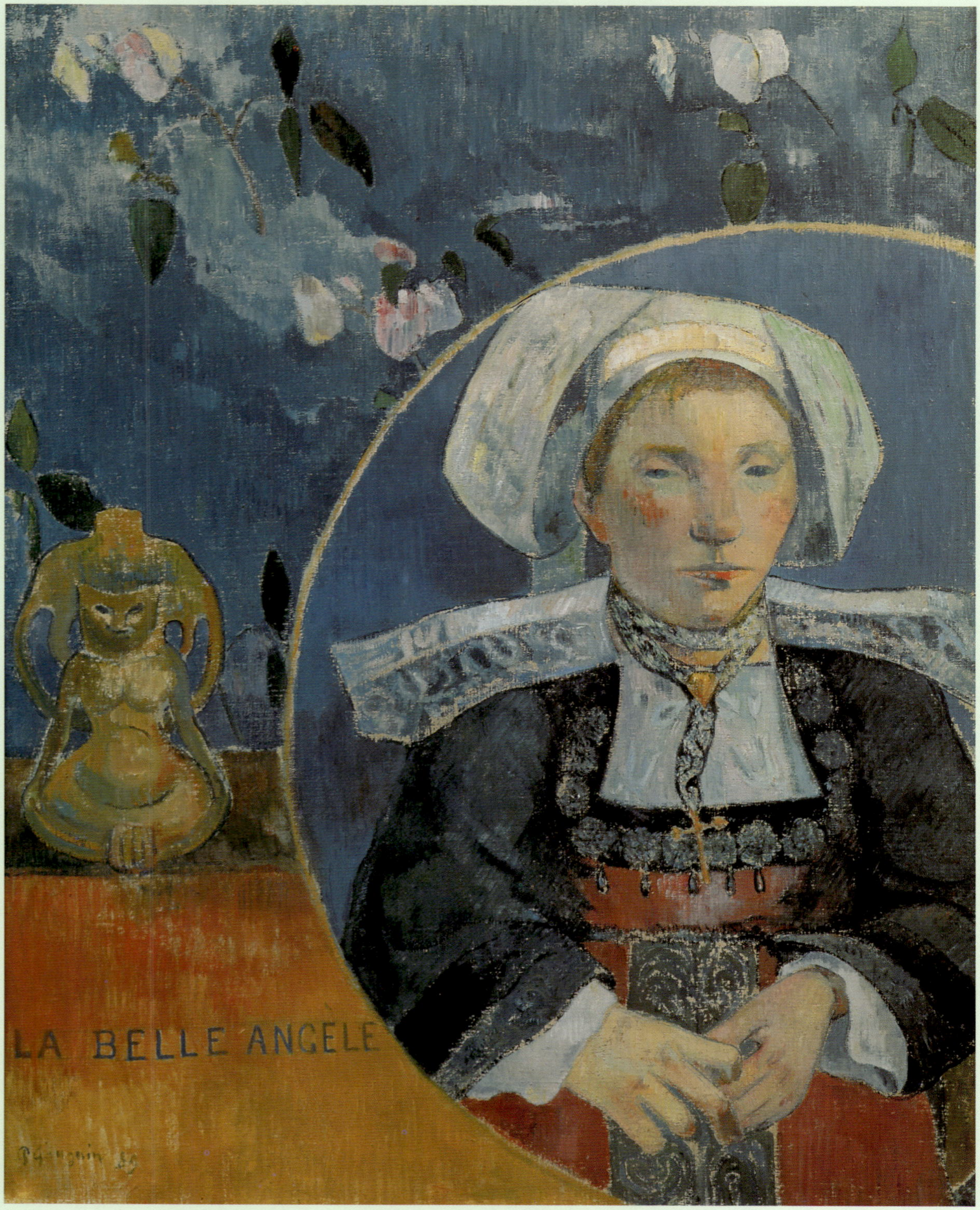

76
Paul Gauguin 1848–1903
La belle Angèle 1889
Musée d'Orsay, Paris

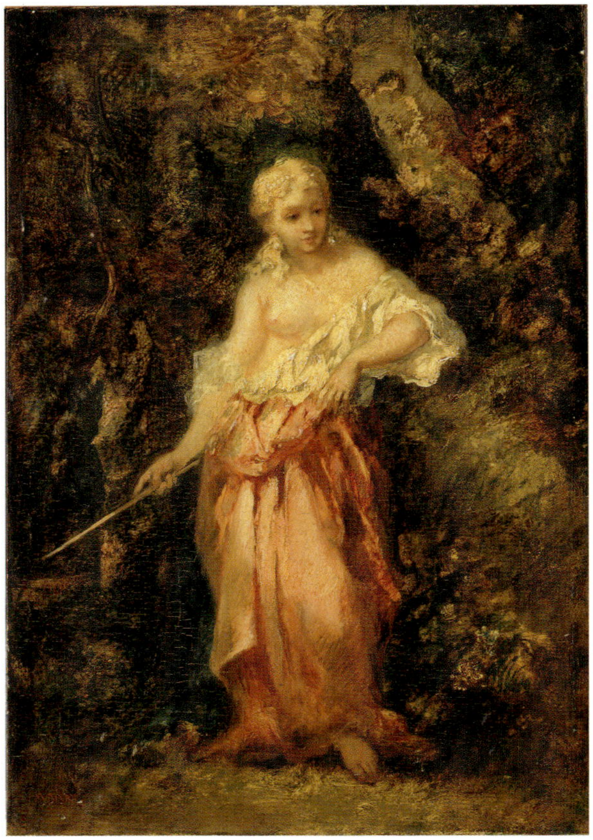

77
Narcisse Diaz de la Peña 1807–1876
The magician n.d.
Musée d'Orsay, Paris

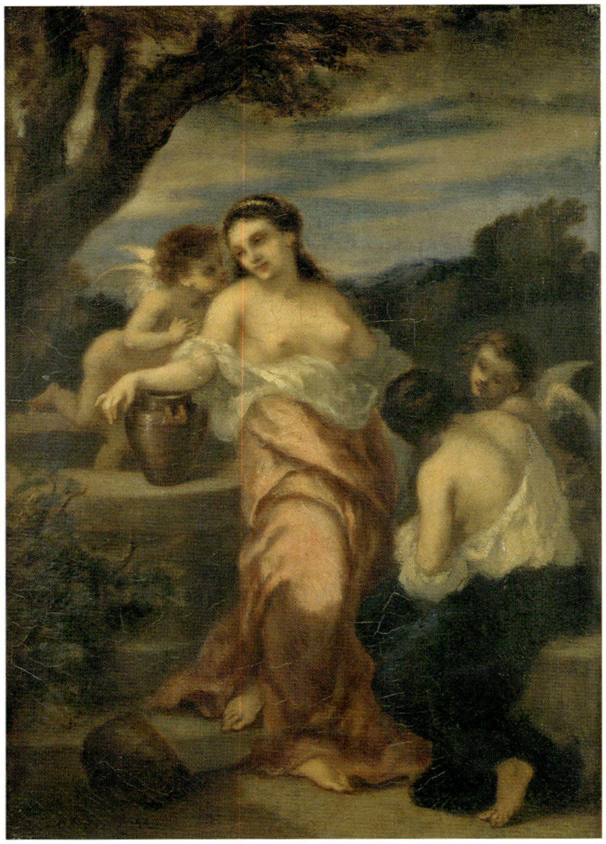

78
Narcisse Diaz de la Peña 1807–1876
At the well 1850
Musée d'Orsay, Paris

However, a letter from the artist to Theo – playing off the dealers as usual – gives more prosaic reasons for calling off the trip – bad weather, and a lack of finished works due to recent sales to Durand-Ruel. He also invited them to come in August.[105] Thus, Manichean distinctions between the firm's entrenched hostility to, and Theo's heroic enthusiasm for, impressionist painting cannot be sustained. Rewald exaggerated when he claimed that Theo had 'an independent taste only rarely in agreement with that of his employers.'[106] It is too simplistic to attribute his disputes with them to Theo's promotion of impressionism in the face of their monolithic support for 'Goupil'-type pictures. Fundamentally, there may only have been a difference over business practice. Boussod and Valadon would probably have looked for an immediate profit on any year's bottom line. Theo, on the other hand, seems to have been interested in long-term investments and in opening up new markets; had he been able to set up his own business, he might well have pursued such a policy.

Theo's strategy was not only financially defensible, it was also justified in terms of the way taste was understood to change. It was an absolute commonplace of contemporary art criticism that the painters of the Ecole de 1830 – Delacroix, Corot, Millet, Diaz [**77, 78**] etc. – had once been *contestés*, but where now considered *maîtres*. Vincent used this very cliché in his 1884 letter accusing Theo of being a mere creature of Goupil. Such recognition of how taste changed could be rationally converted in financial terms. Theo seems to have understood this, while his employers did not.

Theo van Gogh: art dealer

Some 250 artists were on the stockbooks during Theo's tenure at 19, Boulevard Montmartre. However, the

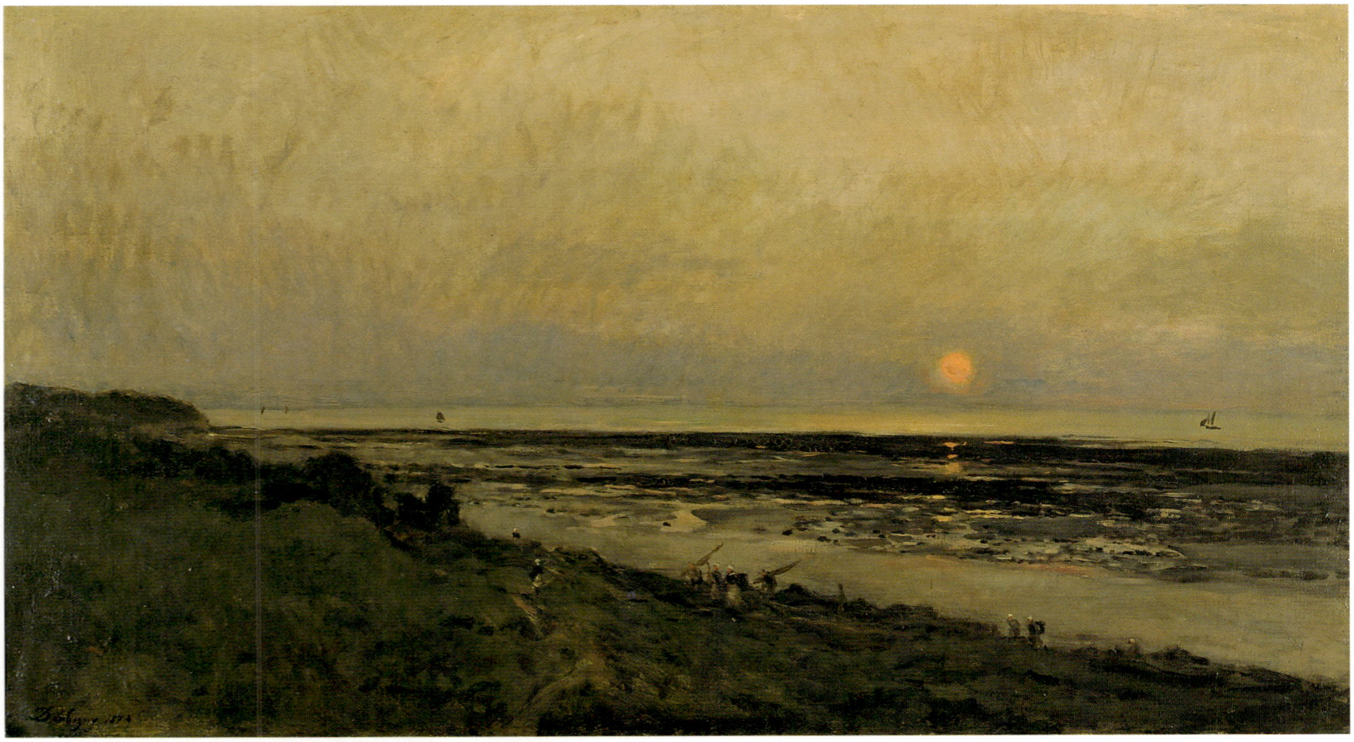

79
Charles-François Daubigny 1817–1878
Sunset near Villerville 1874
Museum Mesdag, The Hague

gallery handled only a single work by half of them, and two pictures by another forty-odd. This broad but attenuated pattern was balanced by the heaviness of trade in a few individual artists. 70 paintings each are registered by Corcos and Monet, and Corot just topped them with 75; Daubigny [79] and Monticelli follow with 46 and 43 apiece; and next in the company's ratings come two score or more by seven very different living artists: the costume painter Bargue, the elderly survivor of the Ecole de 1830 Jules Dupré, the Italian and Dutch landscapists Pasini and Jongkind, Raffaëlli, and the impressionists Degas and Pissarro. Theo's commerce was thus characterised by a combination of range and weight, and it is this complex variety one should bear in mind when assessing the configuration of trade in his business.

Trading in posthumous reputations

As it was prime stock on the market, the work of Camille Corot, who had died in 1875, was of particular importance for Theo. At the Vente Saulnier, in June 1886, Corots had fetched 250,000 francs in a sale which included good pictures by Delacroix, Millet, Bonnat, Manet and Moreau.[107] Of the 72 Corots listed in the stockbooks, 53 were bought by, and 52 sold by, 19, Boulevard Montmartre (only 30 of these were the same). Theo's gallery was the hub of the firm's Corot trade,[108] and he seems to have covered a broad scope of the artist's work.[109] [80, 82, 83, 84] Theo knew his Corot market, as we saw when he bested his superiors' prejudices with the sale to Mesdag, a collector who also bought works by Michel [85] and Troyon [86]. Theo seems to have placed Corots among his clientele according to their known tastes, the large *Toilette* [81] going to the ambitious Desfossés, and a small study of an Italian peasant going to the discriminating artist/connoisseur Etienne Moreau-Nélaton.[110]

Trade in the work of other deceased mid-century artists yielded more mixed results. Paintings by Daubigny, including important ones such as the *House of Mère Bazot* (Salon of 1874) **[87]**, passed through his stock in numbers, but generally did not reach Corot prices. Elsewhere he was not so fortunate. Only half-a-dozen Courbet's, all of them landscapes, came his way. More might have been expected, including figure paintings, and it is difficult to account for this dearth.[111] Nevertheless, with quality landscapes by one of the period's major painters available at reasonable prices – the *Châtel-St-Denis, Scey-en-Varais* **[88]** sold for 3,500 francs in 1881 – it is curious that the firm did not handle more.

A similarly perplexing case is Millet. According to the stockbooks, 19, Boulevard Montmartre handled only three works, all in the later 1880s, and one of these twice; more Millets may have been sold by other branches, however. Nonetheless, those Theo traded did extraordinarily well, among them *At sea* and *Shearing sheep* **[89]**.[112] This can probably be accounted for by the fact that the art market was increasingly international; a work could be shuffled around until it found its highest value. Factors not immediately related to the market also seem to have played a role. In 1887 the Ecole des Beaux-Arts held a major Millet retrospective, giving the artist establishment accreditation; Theo's clients profited from this.

Analogous external pressures seem to have affected Theo's dealing in a fourth dead mid-century *maître*: Daumier. Prior to 1888, Theo handled only one of his paintings, *The strong man* **[90]**, bought and sold within days in December 1887. This seems very curious, because a major exhibition staged by Durand-Ruel in 1878 had revealed that Daumier was not just a great caricaturist and draughtsman, but also a remarkable painter.[113] (Of course, Theo may not have seen the show.) However, starting in late 1888, he rapidly accelerated his trade in Daumier paintings, buying ten in two years, among them seven in a lot from Bernheim in March 1890. **[91]** Why this sudden new emphasis? Outside factors once again, it seems: the publication of an extensive monograph by Arsène Alexandre in 1888; the success of the Ecole des Beaux-Arts's exhibition of caricature that spring; and the praise for Daumier's paintings at the Exposition Universelle (the following year), where one critic called him 'a painter in the highest understanding of the word.'[114]

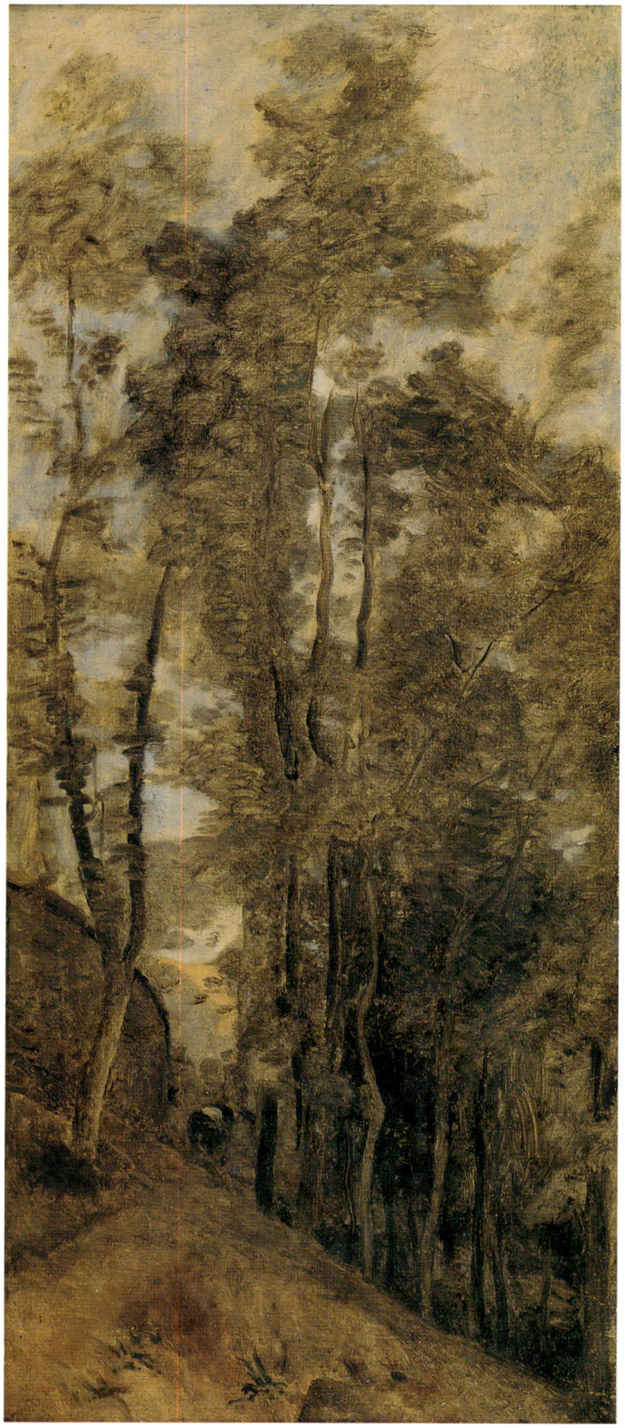

80
Camille Corot 1796–1875
Souvenir of the fortifications of Arras c. 1865–70
Museum Mesdag, The Hague

Dealing in contemporary art / defining the modern

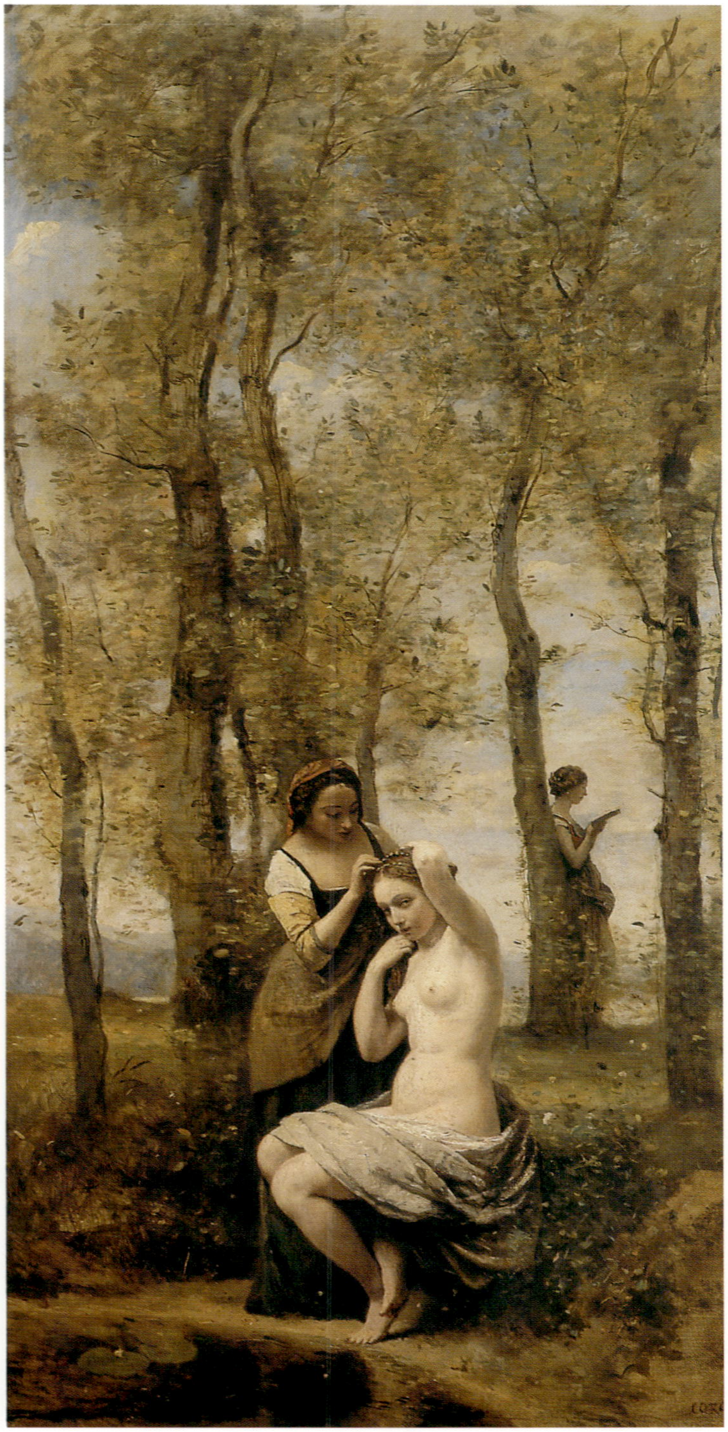

81
Camille Corot 1796–1875
La toilette 1859
Private collection

Dealing in work by living artists, whose production was continuous and on whom posterity had not yet begun to pass judgment, was a much more fraught business. Profit margins were lower, critical responses could veer alarmingly, and it required the dealer to make taxing decisions about the nature and quality of a bewildering array of styles and subjects. Landscapes and rural scenes were a staple for contemporary painters. Pissarro, Monet and Gauguin, to whom we will come later, worked in this genre; first, however, it is useful to look at several other artists, all of whom showed annually at the Salon and whose relationships with Theo make interesting points of contrast.

Julien Dupré, who made his Salon debut in 1876, was a rising star in the popular category of harvest and farmyard scenes. [**95**] Five of his works appear in the stockbooks in the early 1880s; all were sold within three months. We do not know why no more were purchased; possibly the contracting of Lhermitte, a stronger artist, obviated the need to deal in Dupré, who may himself have signed a contract with a different dealer. Another instance was Cazin, who had established a significant reputation at the beginning of the decade with large 'modern' religious subjects, and by the mid-1880s was producing moody and much admired landscapes of his native Pas-de-Calais in substantial numbers. Theo handled only four of his paintings, two of which did remarkably well.[115] Cazin was another artist whom Theo would probably have liked to handle more frequently, but he was closely linked to Petit.

A foreigner in Paris himself and working for a company which was, as we have seen, a thoroughly international operation, Theo naturally handled some non-French artists: Jongkind, Pasini and, of course, Corcos. Jongkind's landscapes of France and the Netherlands [**96**] were steady sellers. Theo had a consistent and profitable arrangement with his countryman Kaemmerer, a 'Goupil'-style painter of precise costume pieces who had connections to Uncle Cent.[116] Although nothing Theo handled could match the success of *The balloon* [**92**], he continued to buy Kaemmerer's 18th-century scenes until 1888.[117]

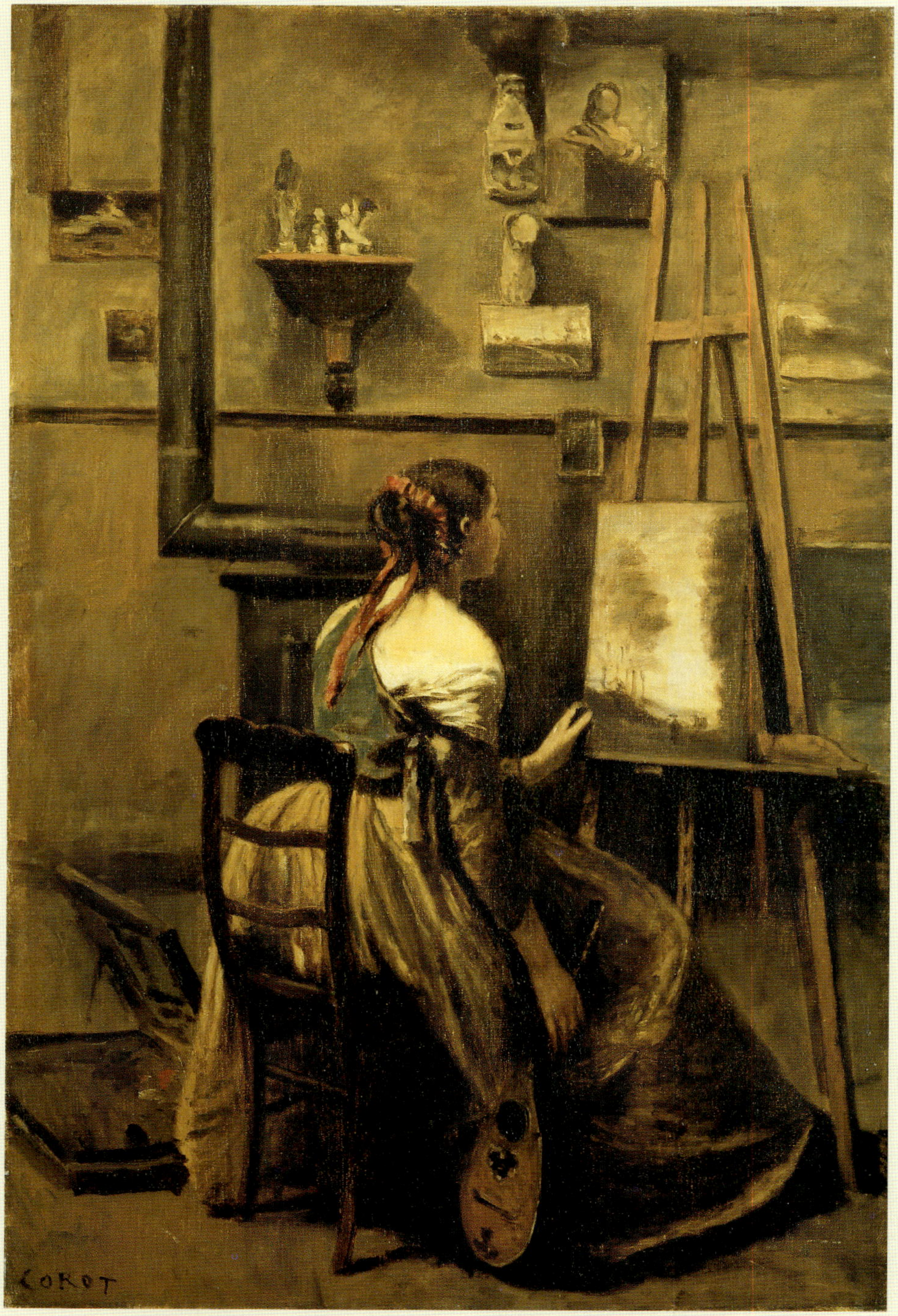

82
Camille Corot 1796–1875
Corot's studio n.d.
Musée du Louvre, Paris

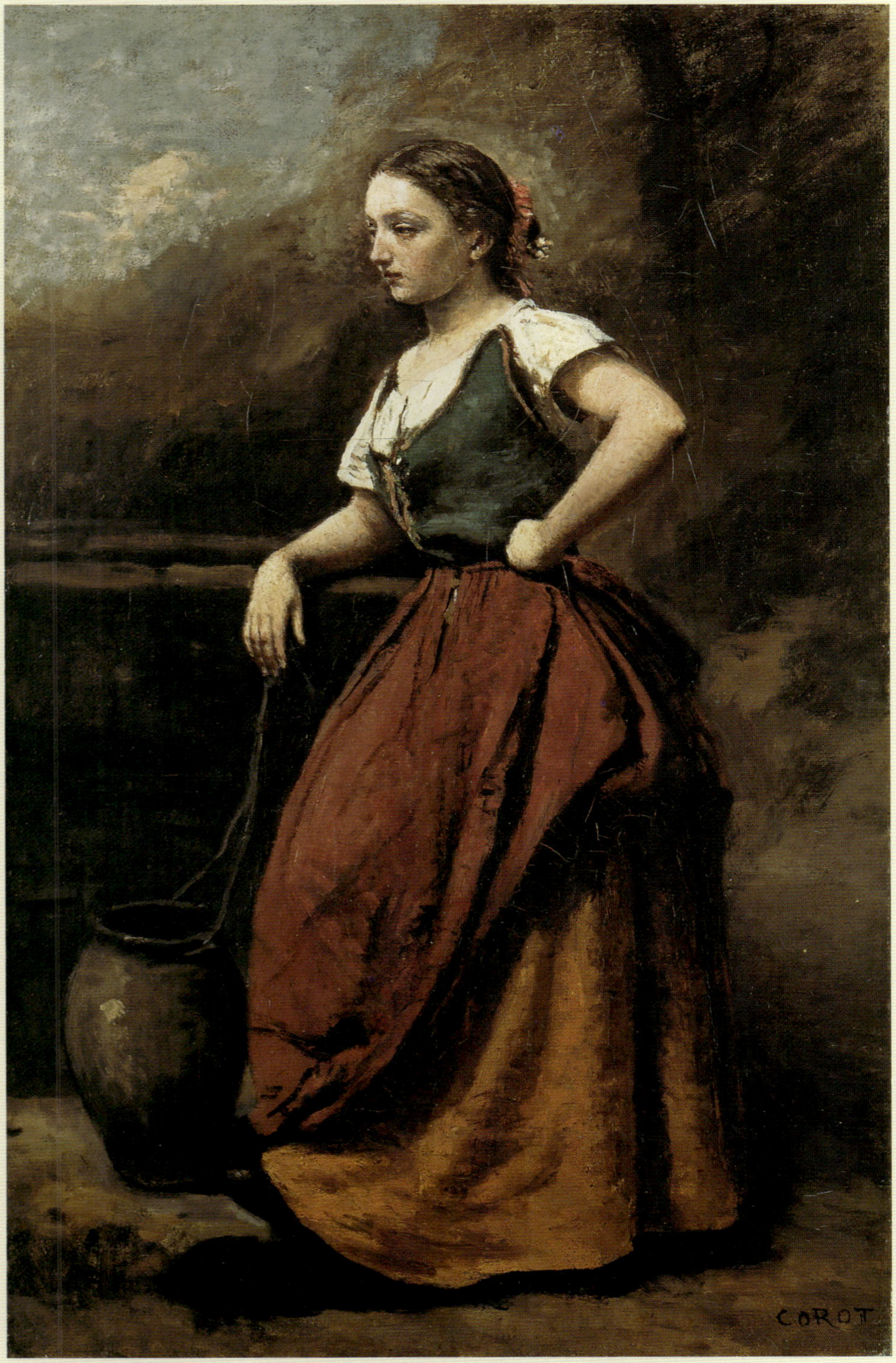

83
Camille Corot 1796–1875
A young woman near a well c. 1865–70
Kröller-Müller Museum, Otterlo

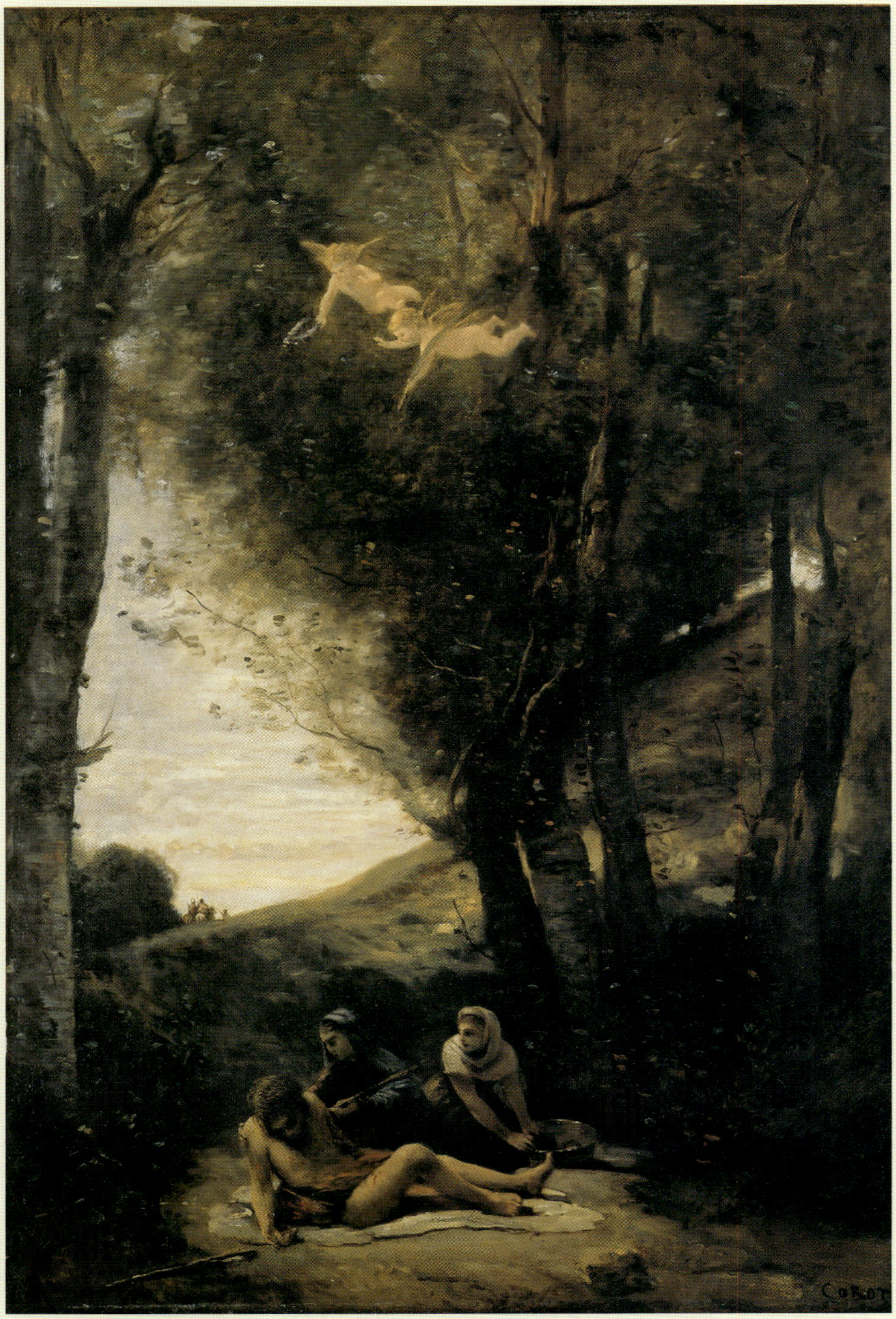

84
Camille Corot 1796–1875
St Sebastian c. 1874
National Gallery of Art, Washington, DC
Timken Collection

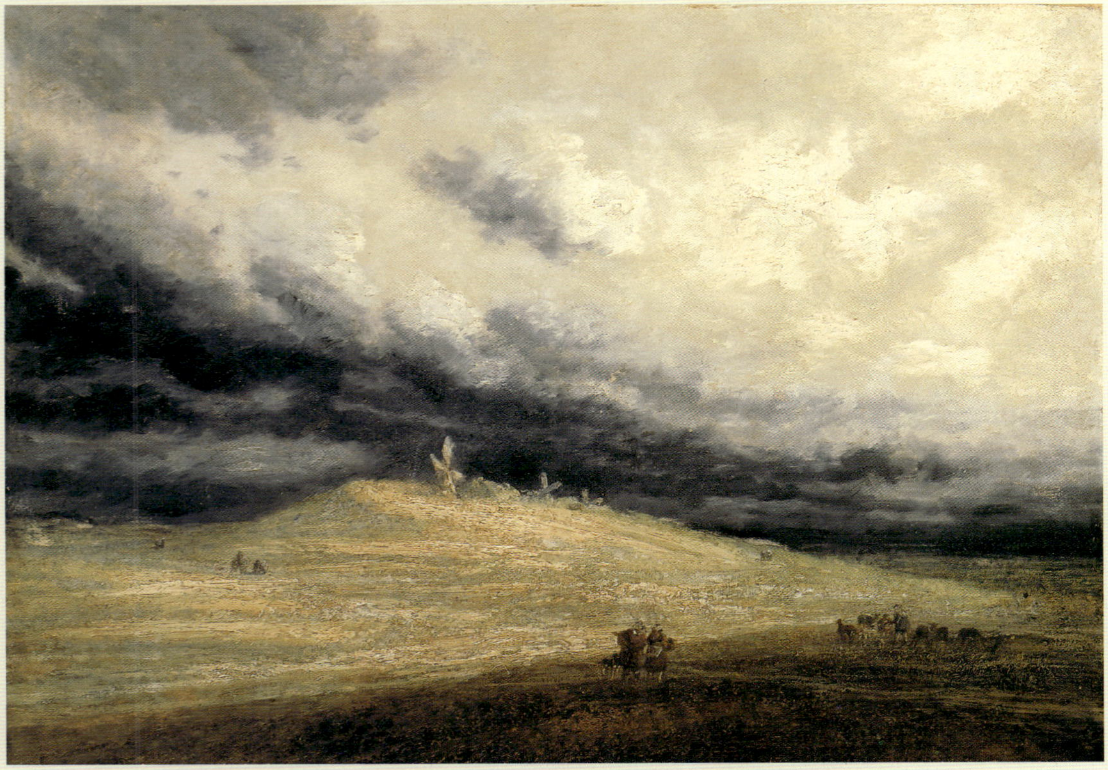

85
Georges Michel 1763–1843
Three windmills n.d.
Museum Mesdag, The Hague

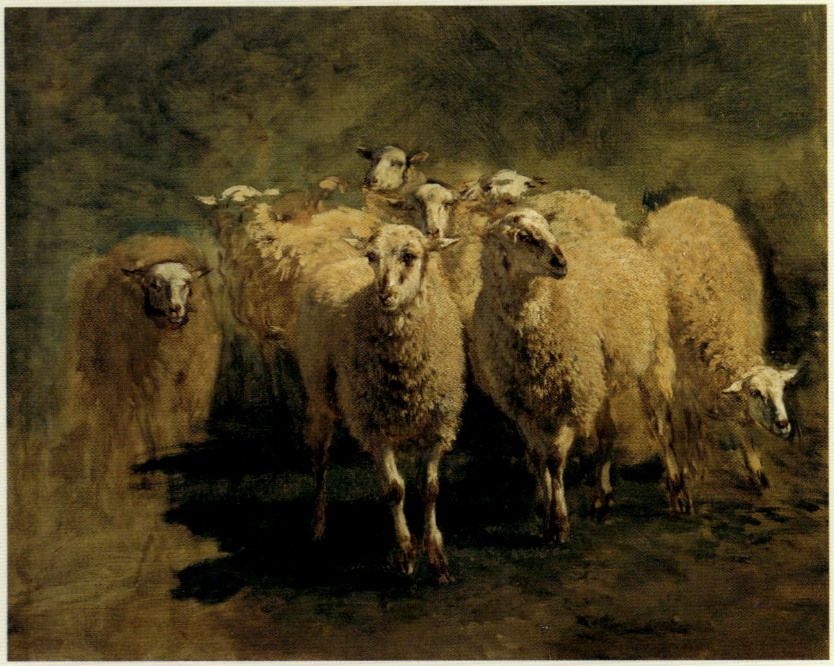

86
Constant Troyon 1810–1865
Sheep n.d.
Museum Mesdag, The Hague

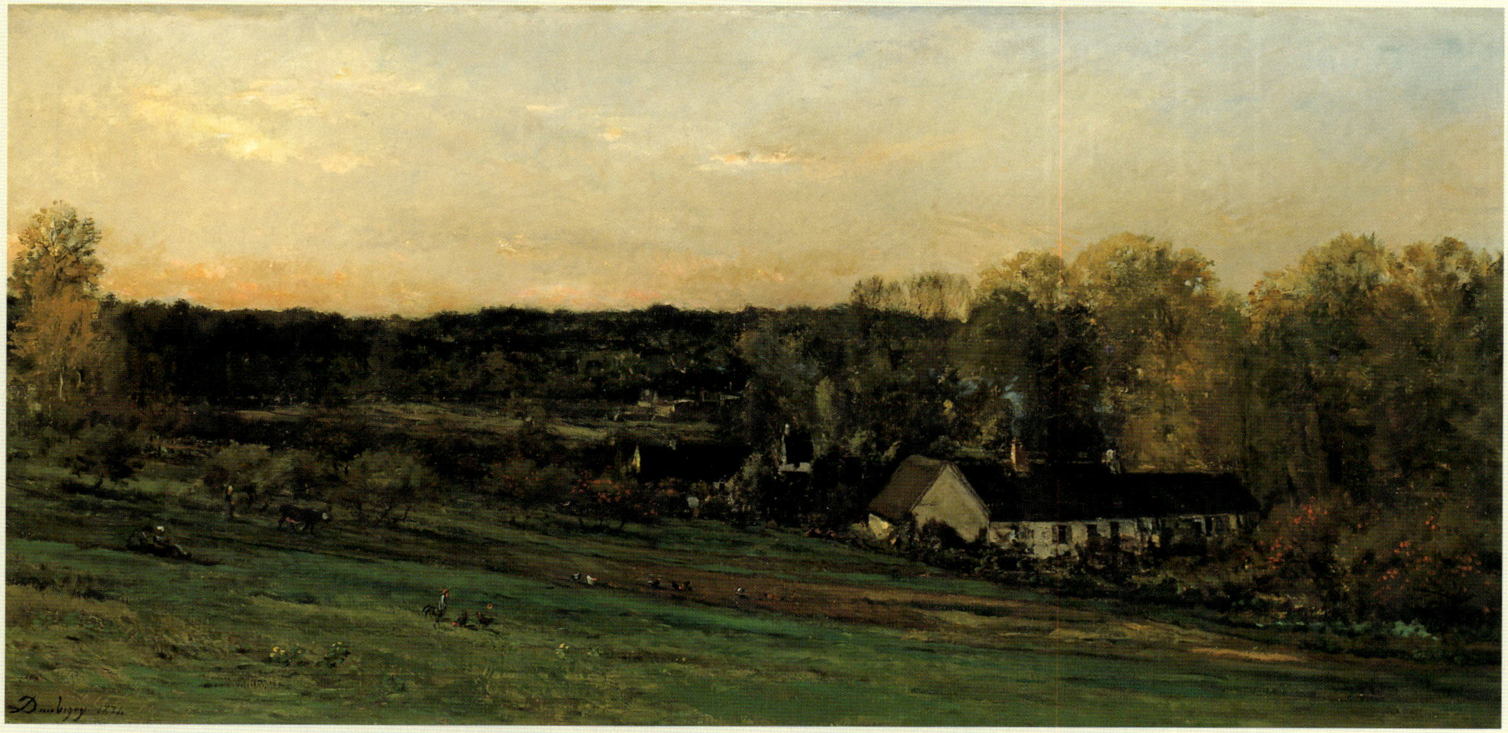

87

Charles-François Daubigny 1817–1878
The house of Mère Bazot 1874
The Art Institute of Chicago
Mr and Mrs Potter Palmer Collection

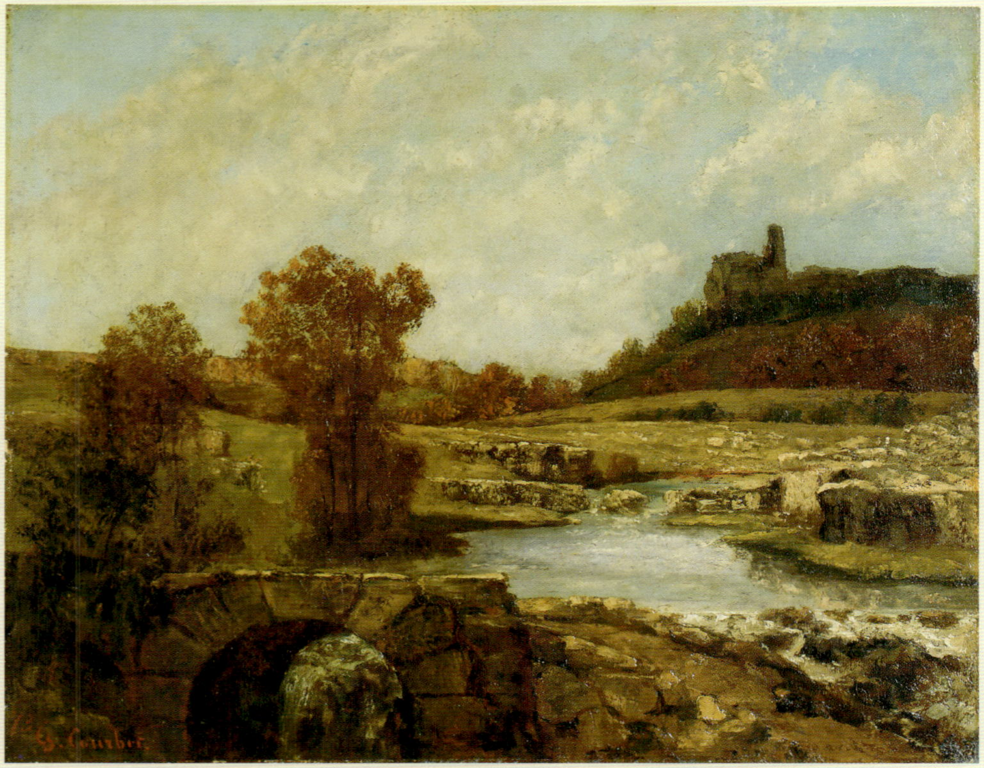

88
Gustave Courbet 1819–1877
Châtel-St-Denis, Scey-en-Varais 1873
Victoria and Albert Museum, London

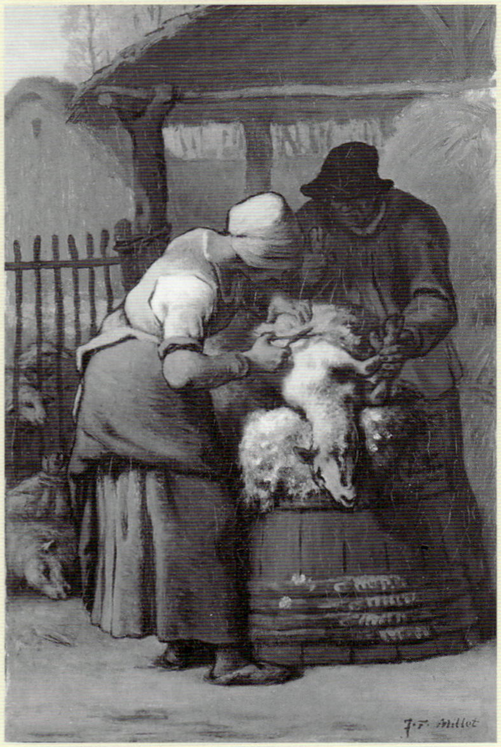

89
Jean-François Millet 1814–1875
Shearing sheep c. 1857-61
The Art Institute of Chicago
Mr and Mrs Potter Palmer Collection

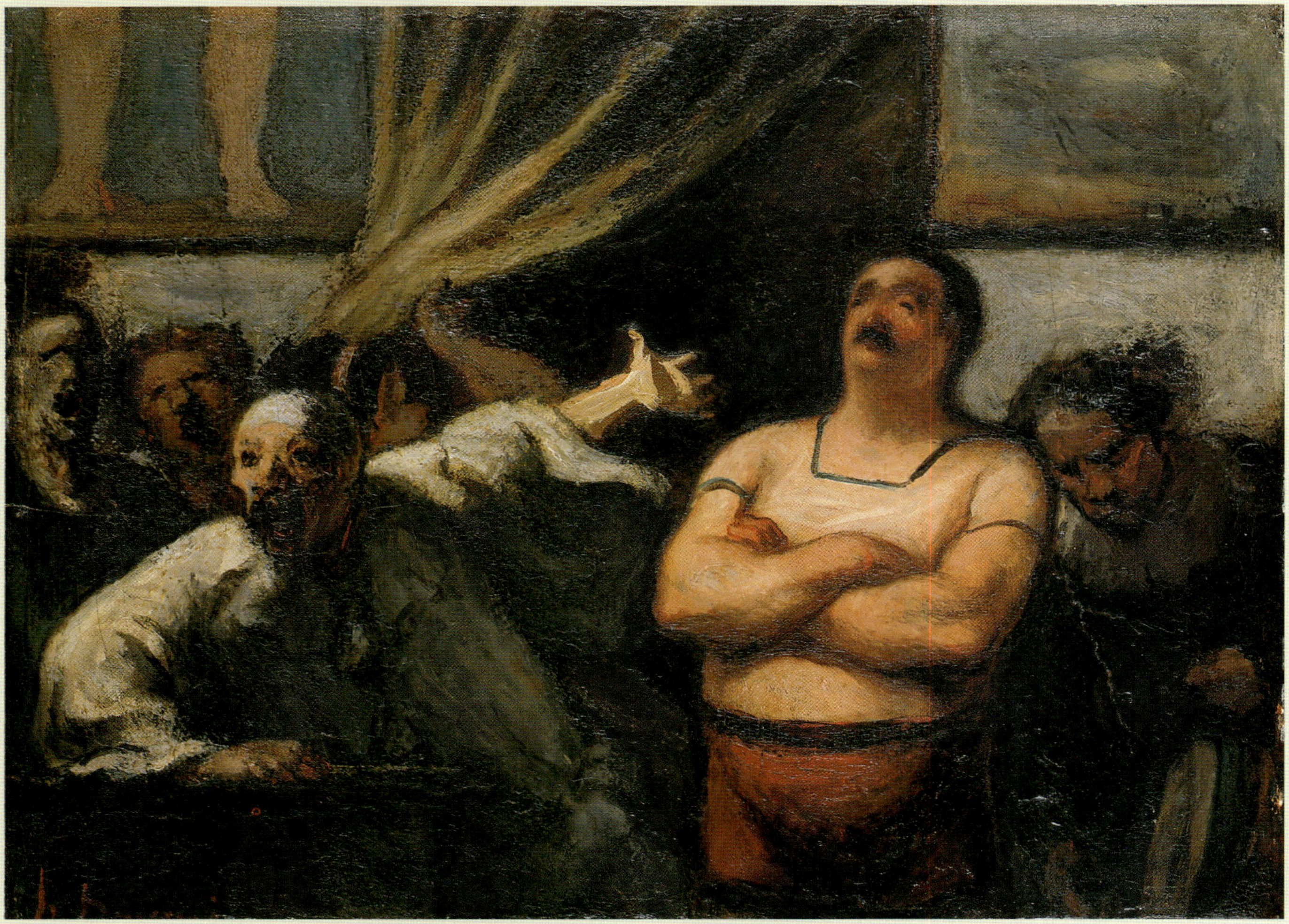

90
Honoré Daumier 1810–1879
The strong man c. 1865
The Phillips Collection, Washington, DC

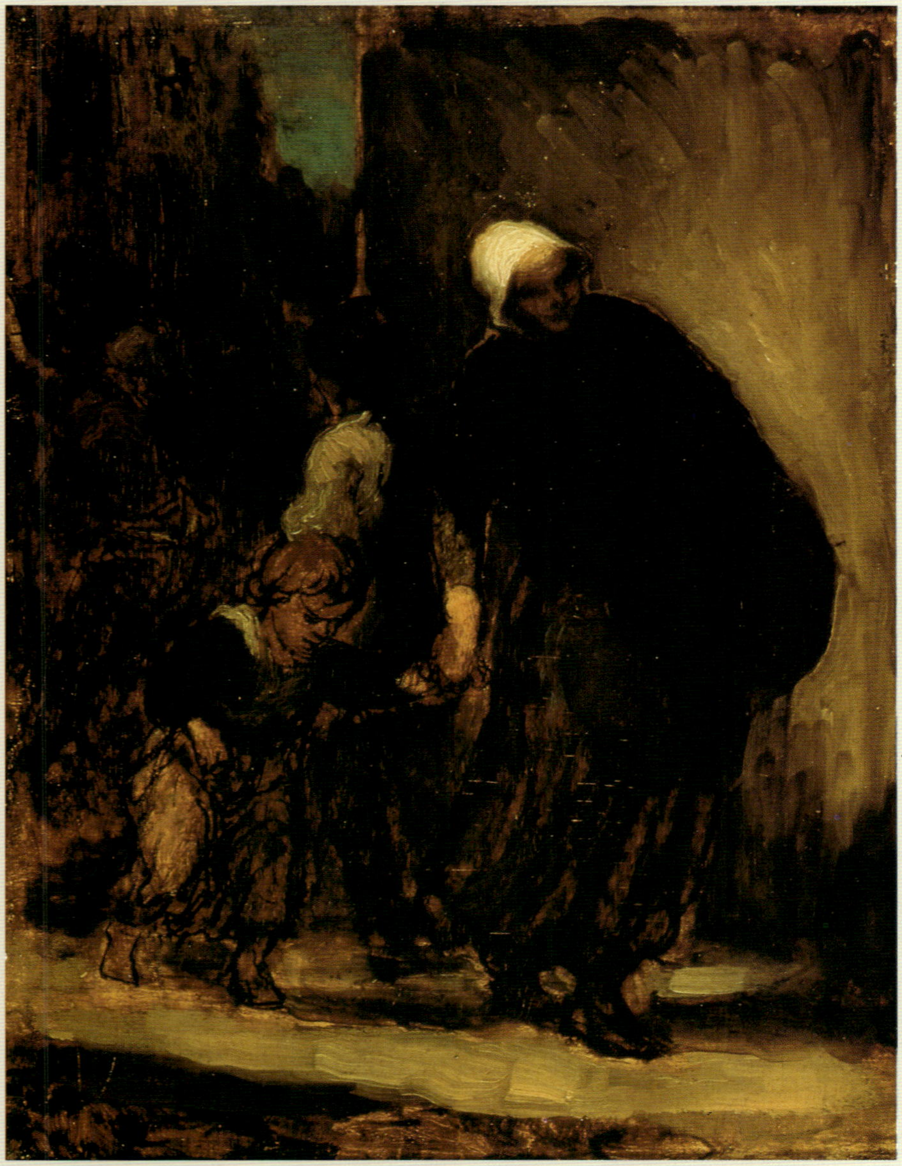

91
Honoré Daumier 1810–1879
A street scene c. 1852
Museum Boijmans Van Beuningen, Rotterdam

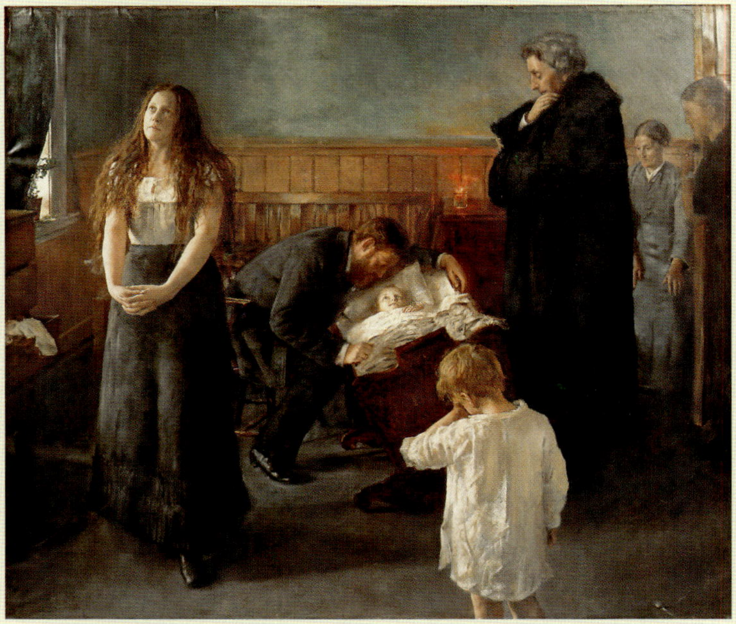

93
Hans Olaf Heijerdahl 1857–1913
The sick child 1881
Musée Regional d'Auvergne, Riom

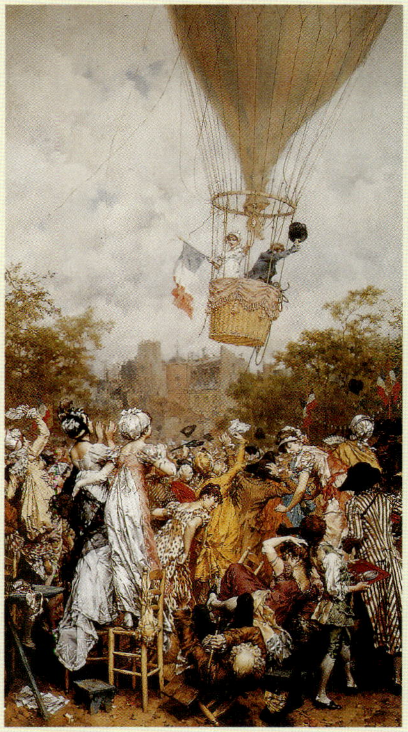

92
Frederik Hendrik Kaemmerer 1839–1902
The balloon 1880
Present location unknown

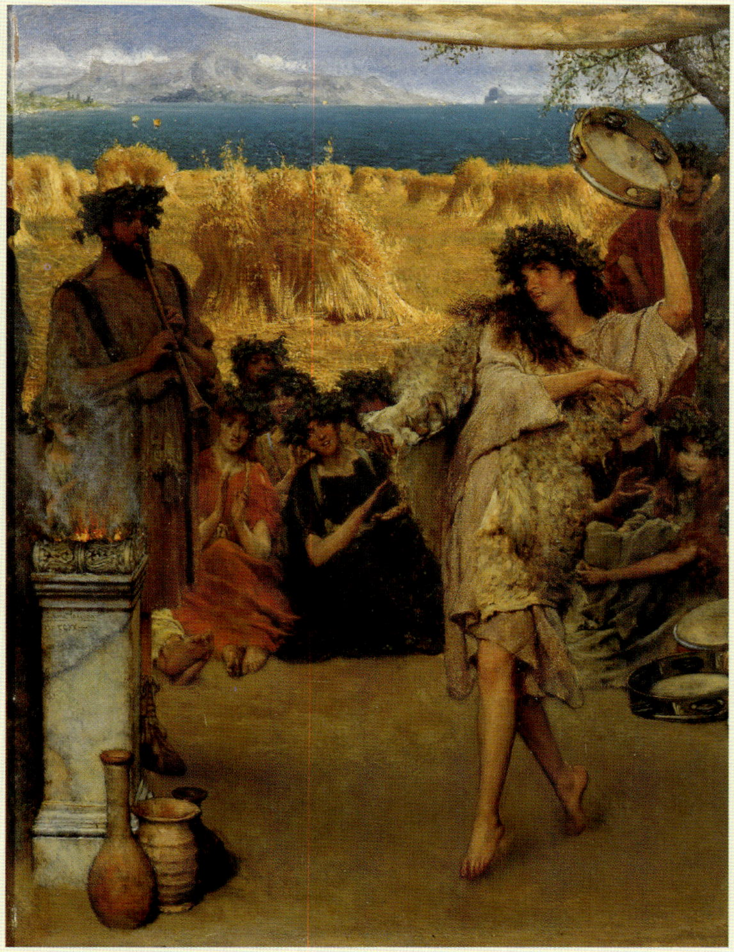

94
Sir Lawrence Alma-Tadema 1936–1912
A harvest festival. Opus CCXX 1880
The Forbes Magazine Collection, New York

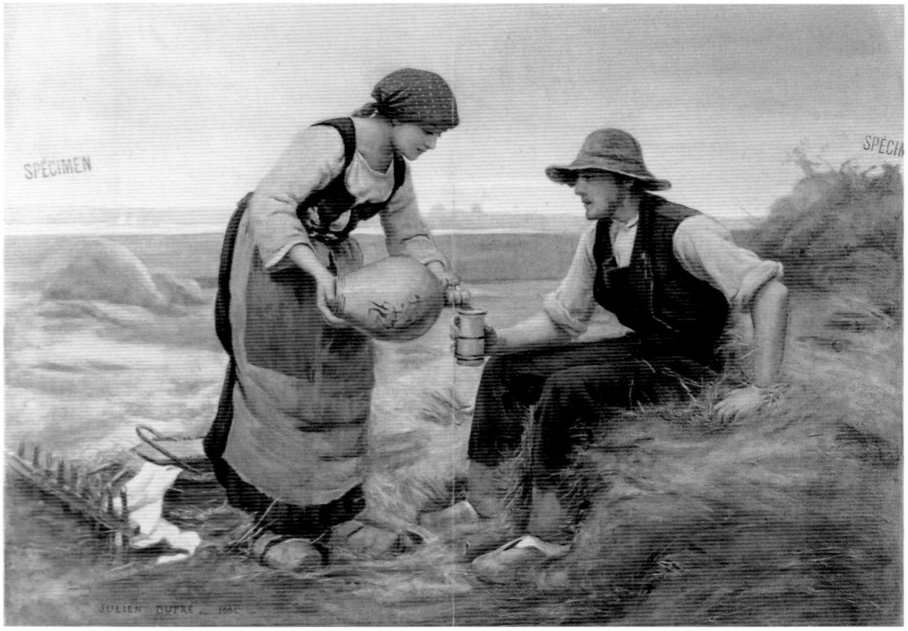

95
After **Julien Dupré** 1851–1910
The midday repast 1882
Musée Goupil, Bordeaux
Present location of the original painting unknown

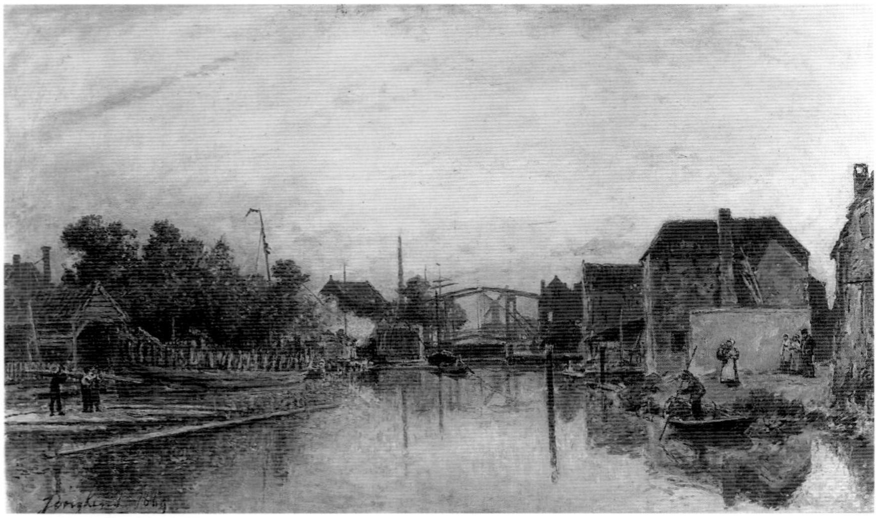

96
Johan Barthold Jongkind 1819–1891
Canal 1869
Philadelphia Museum of Art
The John G. Johnson Collection

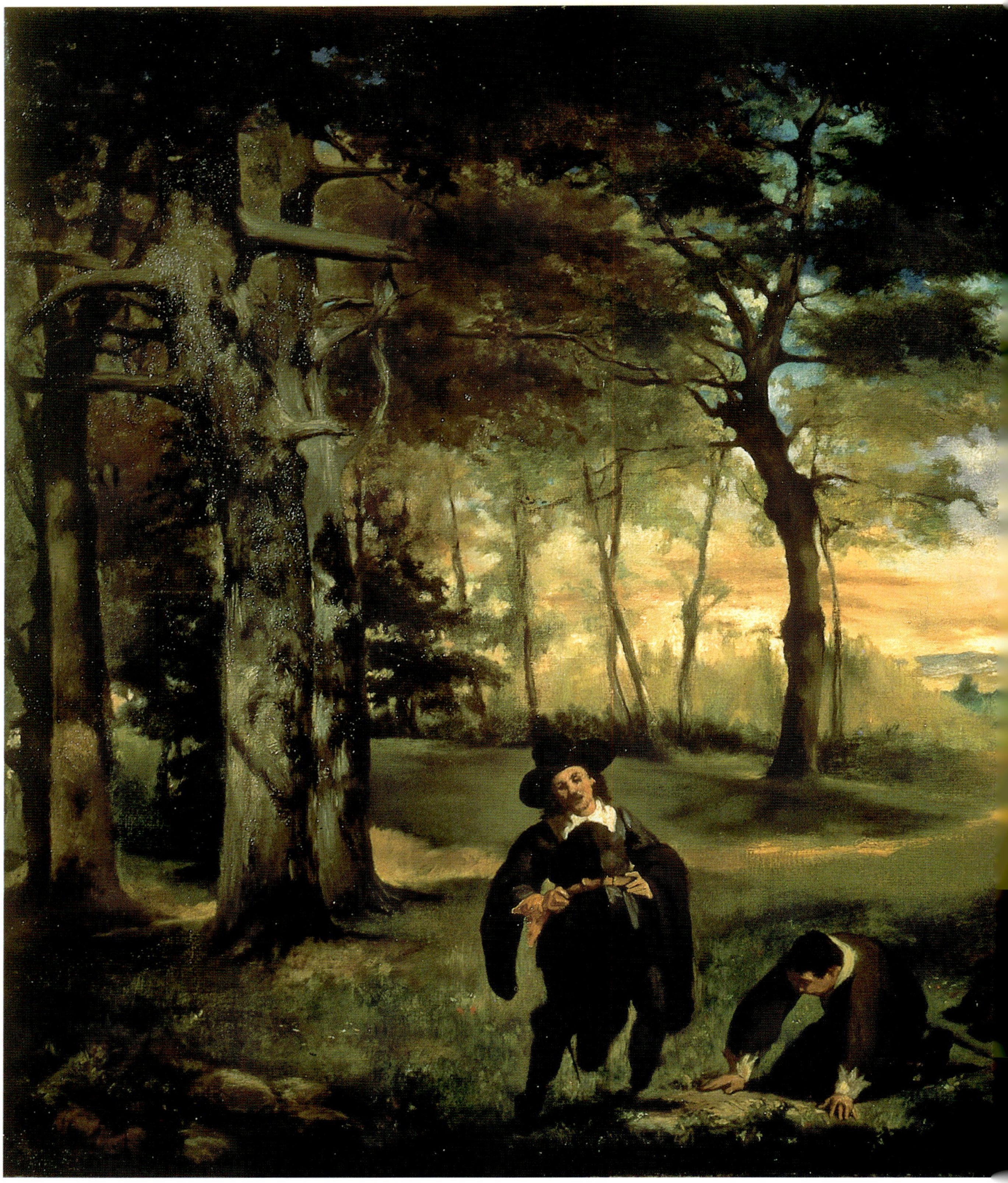

Theo van Gogh

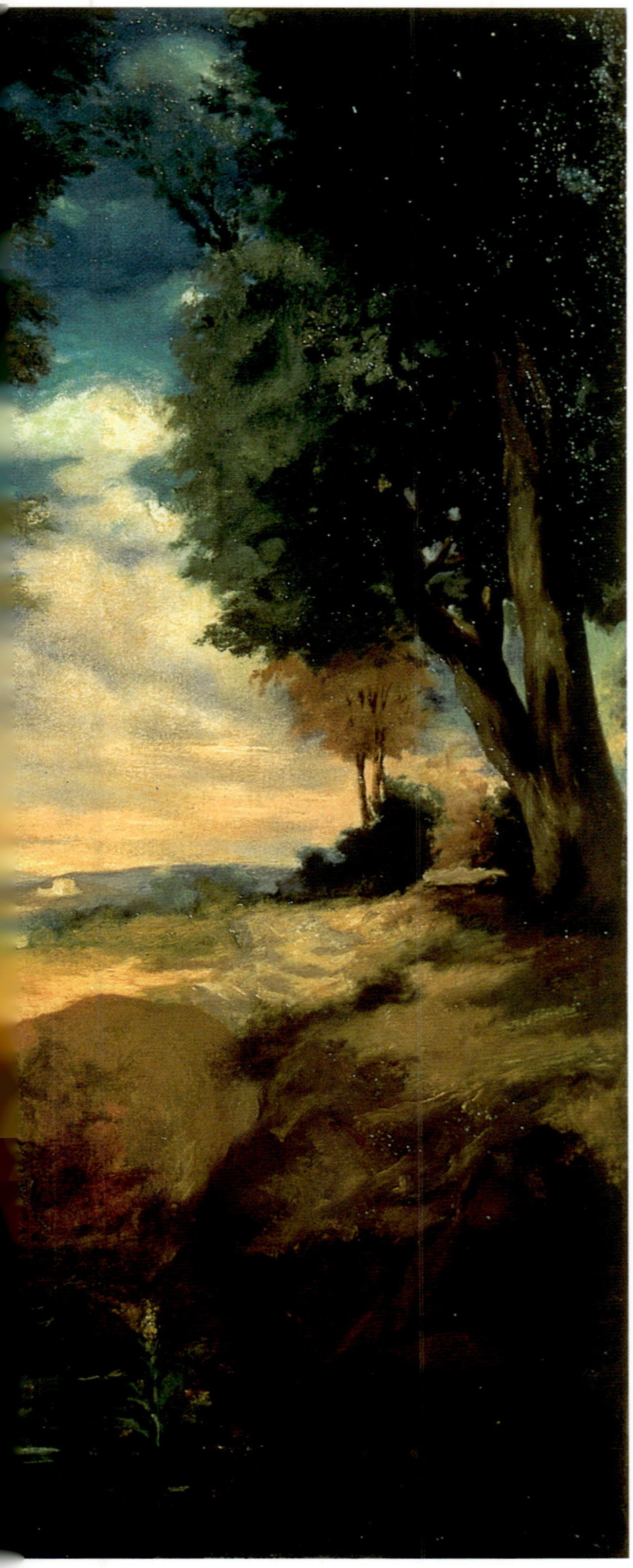

This continuity stands in contrast to Theo's relations with the Norwegian Heijerdahl. [93] In this case the pattern is like that of Dupré: a short period of intensive buying that suddenly fell away. The company purchased 12 works between 1881-83. Two of the earliest pictures bought were probably sold to Theo's Uncle Cor, who also delivered Goupil Alma-Tadema's *A harvest festival* [94]. Uncle Cor may have been responsible for introducing the artist to the business. For reasons yet unknown, Heijerdahl seems to have been dropped in the wake of the 1884 restructuring.

What modern painting might be: Besnard, Carrière, Raffaëlli

Although he traded in the work of dead mid-century artists, and although, like other dealers, he made some effort to satisfy his clients' desire for Old Masters (such as Jan van Goyen and Teniers), Theo's essential business was in contemporary art. As a dealer, he played a part in the larger debate about the character and direction of modern art. By actively promoting the work of certain painters, Theo adumbrated a certain definition of 'modern' art, particularly in the years after 1887. This has already been touched upon in discussing his personal taste and which artists he might have wished to handle more; it remains to consider more closely his dealings in those painters around whom his implicit account of the 'modern' revolved.

Two key figures in modern painting – Manet and De Nittis – died early in Theo's mature career. He had little success dealing either artist. He handled five Manets, four of them in 1890. Coming to the market so late, the pictures he could get hold of were minor works, with the exception of the early *Students of Salamanca* [97], an uncharacteristic literary painting based on Lesage's novel *Gil Blas.*[118] The trawl of De Nittis, who by 1873 had given up 'Goupilesque' historic costume pieces to become one of the most successful painters of modern Paris, was similarly slight. Theo dealt only three after the painter's early death in 1884, two of which were bought in 1888 and 1889. De Nittis, of course, had been closely associated with Petit prior to his death, which may have been to Theo's disadvantage.

97
Edouard Manet 1832–1883
The students of Salamanca 1860
Private collection, Japan

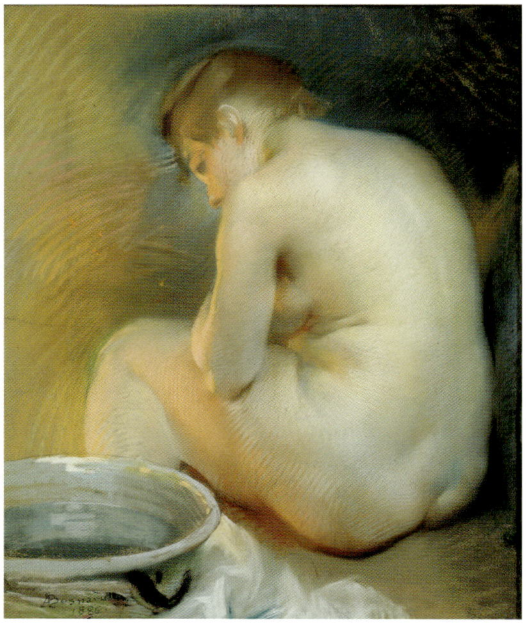

98
Albert Besnard 1849–1934
Naked woman warming herself 1886
Musée d'Orsay, Paris

A painter who made a meteoric and not uncontroversial rise to the forefront of modern French painting in the mid-1880s was Albert Besnard. Theo seems to have written admiringly to Vincent about the painter's submission to the Salon of 1885, *Paris*, an allegorical composition for a mural project [503/406, 505/408]. Theo was subsequently to handle several of his works. The first was in 1886, *Evening at Hampton Court*, a canvas from his sojourn in London (1879-83).[119] It was sold to Desfossés. The only other work mentioned in the stockbooks is *Eve*, bought in August 1888. Like the English picture it sold quickly, and Theo, who had good personal relations with Besnard, may well have been prevented from developing their business connection by the fact that the latter was busy with two major mural commissions.[120] Besnard was able to sell him smaller works, notably pastels, such as the study for his 1886 Salon painting, *Nude woman warming herself* **[98]**.[121]

If Besnard's growing reputation in the late 1880s was based on bravura brushwork, colourful compositions and often allegorical subjects, Eugène Carrière was admired for his treatment of naturalistic family themes, often seen close-up but veiled in a brown haze of paint. In their different ways, both artists were reaching beyond naturalism towards the pictorial evocation of states of mind, in parallel with the literary symbolist movement. With a growing family, no public commissions and no dealer, Carrière was in need of regular support when Theo began buying his paintings in 1889. They had been in contact since at least the year before, when the painter gave Theo a copy of his friend Jean Dolent's aphorisms on contemporary art, *Amoureux d'art*.[122] 11 of the 16 Carrière paintings Theo bought in 1889-90 came from the artist himself, allowing him to secure something of a monopoly. It is possible that the connection came via Boussod, Valadon & Cie.'s reproduction business.[123] Carrière moved well, Theo selling a dozen of the 16 he had bought between April 1889 and September 1890. **[99]** The collectors were Paul Gallimard and a M. Grünebaum, and the Americans Alfred A. Pope and John G. Johnson, who purchased the *Mother and child* **[100]**. With Carrière, Theo built himself into a strong position as the prime dealer of a leading and original voice in modern painting. No doubt he was working towards staging a one-man show, which his successor Joyant finally put on in April 1891. With a catalogue introduction by Geffroy and the inclusion of a number of paintings Theo had sold, this successful exhibition was a tribute to the recently deceased dealer's perspicacious ability to develop the reputation of a leading 'modern' painter.

The case of Raffaëlli was similar. After an ineffectual start in the Salons of the 1870s, Raffaëlli had thrown in his lot with the impressionists, exhibiting with them in 1880 and 1881. By this time he was already producing images of *petit bourgeois* and proletarian life in the Parisian suburbs, small pictures, more drawn than painted, depicting the *caractère* – the artist's term – of these marginal existences. Ambitious and enterprising, Raffaëlli was adept at self-publicity, as evidenced by the successful large one-man show he staged for himself in rented premises on the avenue de l'Opéra in 1884. Following this, he returned to the Salon the next year with a painting of Clemenceau making a speech and, in 1886, with another of a master-founder installing Dalou's relief sculpture *Mirabeau and Dreux-Brézé* at the Chambre des Deputés. This was a calculated strategy to upgrade his subject-matter and court the patronage of the

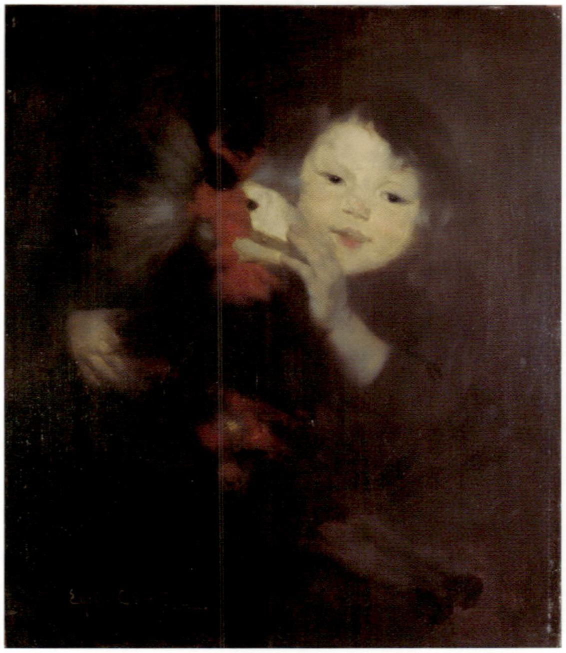

99
Eugène Carrière 1849–1906
The favorite toy c. 1887
Norton Museum of Art, West Palm Beach

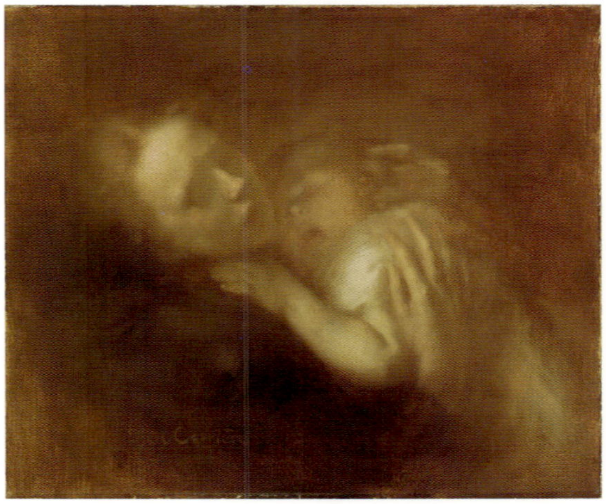

100
Eugène Carrière 1849–1906
Mother and child c. 1889
Philadelphia Museum of Art
The John G. Johnson Collection

Third Republic by celebrating its leaders, skills, artists, and antecedents. These efforts improved Raffaëlli's position enormously, but he remained an artist about whom opinions were divided.[124]

Recognised as an individual voice in modern painting, but still somewhat controversial and – although he had shown at Petit's Expositions Internationales – lacking a regular dealer, Raffaëlli was another ideal artist for Theo. We do not know how the two came into contact. In the summer of 1885 Theo sent Vincent the catalogue of Raffaëlli's 1884 one-man show, which suggests he had visited it [519/416]. However, his first purchase, from Charles Leroux, was not made until November 1886, and the picture was sold the same day. Despite this success, Theo bought no more until 1888. At the end of 1889 he began to rapidly build up stock.[125] The pictures bought for Boussod, Valadon & Cie. typified the work with which Raffaëlli had made his name, and which the market now expected. **[101]** The paintings sold steadily, but not briskly; of the 11 bought in 1889 five had sold within a year.

Perhaps to accelerate the pace, and to mark himself as Raffaëlli's main handler, Theo staged the artist's second one-man show in May-June 1890. Prefaced by an introduction by Geffroy, the catalogue lists 20 paintings and worked-up drawings of suburban low-life; a couple of decorative floral panels; and a considerable number of drawings – portraits, types and landscapes – as well as illustrations and sculpture (see below). The exhibition was announced on the front page of *Le Figaro*, although the paper, like other important dailies, did not review it, probably because the recently divided Salons had just opened, with Raffaëlli showing at the Nationale.[126] But the show, surprising in its diversity of media, was generally well received by reviewers, from the middle-of-the-road Alfred de Lostalot to the progressive Albert Aurier.[127] Sales seem to have gone satisfactorily. Although most of the exhibited work must have been on consignment, and thus remained unregistered, of the five pictures bought from the artist for the show three sold immediately; another picture, *Races at Jersey*, appears to have been purchased by Claretie.[128] Once more, Theo had brought an artist to Boussod, Valadon & Cie. whose profile – individual and identifiable, 'modern' in style and subject, well known but still slightly con-

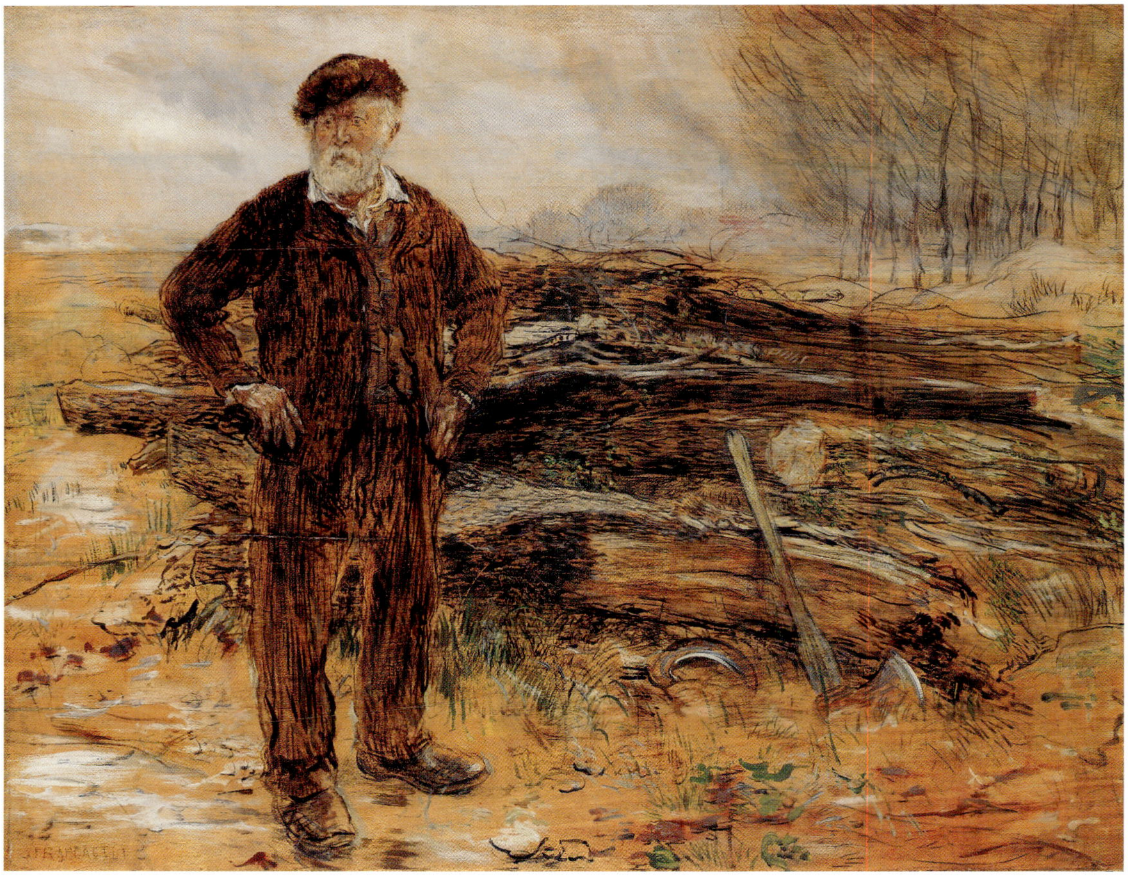

101
Jean-François Raffaëlli 1850–1924
The woodcutter 1888
Collection of Meadow Brook Hall, Oakland University, Rochester, MI

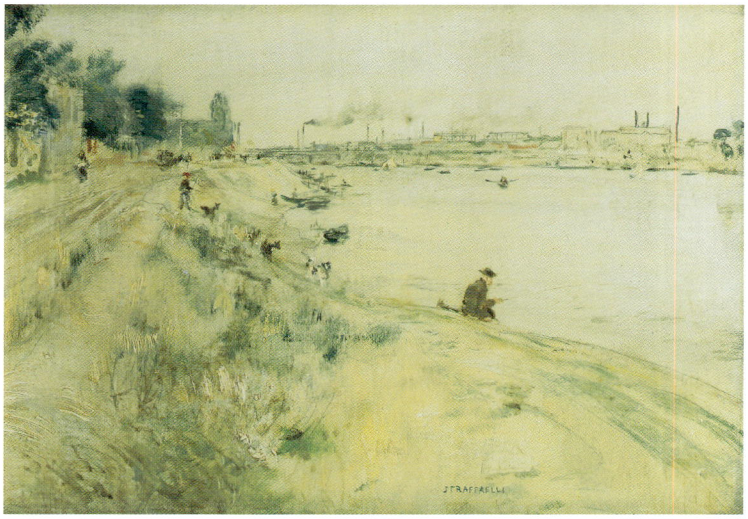

102
Jean-François Raffaëlli 1850–1924
Fisherman on the banks of the Seine n.d.
Private collection, London

troversial – made him an interesting yet sound investment for clients and a substantial name to have under the gallery's wing. [**102**]

Investing in impressionism: Edgar Degas

Theo made a concerted effort to handle work by Degas, the artist associated with the impressionists who had the highest reputation. Degas had not exhibited with the group at their seventh show in 1882, and – unlike Pissarro, Monet, Renoir and Sisley – had not had a one-man show at Durand-Ruel's in 1883. He acted with increasing independence, and to judge from the number of works on a variety of subjects he signed and dated between 1884 and 1886, it seems that he was working towards a solo exhibition of some kind.[129] When the eighth impressionist exhibition materialised in May 1886 he showed part of this accumulated work, notably seven pastels of the female nude. Degas had no regular dealer in the 1880s, although in an article of 1884 Octave Mirbeau mentioned that Durand-Ruel was well stocked with his pictures.[130] Degas did not get involved with Petit's Expositions Internationales; his relationship with Durand-Ruel was non-contractual, and he no doubt did business with other dealers.[131] Despite having a reputation for being inaccessible and difficult, Degas was much respected as an artist; and his growing 'circle of fervent admirers' was always ready to buy.[132] To handle Degas's work would have been a challenging venture for Theo.

How and when Theo and Degas came into contact we do not know. As with Carrière, it may have been through their mutual acquaintance Manzi. By October 1886 Theo had in the gallery 'a very fine de Gas,' as Vincent described it in a letter to the painter Angrand.[133] This is the first evidence of any connection, and, as it was not entered in the stockbooks, the picture was probably on consignment. The same was true of the Degas drawing Theo sold to Lhermitte, and the pastels of nudes he displayed in 1888. We cannot tell how many 'articles' – as Degas liked to call his pictures – Theo actually handled: the stockbooks list 23, over half of them purchased directly from the artist, the others chiefly from other dealers, although not from Durand-Ruel. Theo was evidently seeking to establish himself as a Degas dealer, which Durand may have resisted. A number of quick notes Degas sent to Theo show that they were in regular communication. One of these mentions 'the drawing I have done for you,' which suggests that Degas was producing work specifically for Boussod, Valadon & Cie., if not even that Theo was informally commissioning it.[134] We also know that Theo visited the artist's studio to select items or bring payments, and was trusted to frame work and ensure it dried properly.[135]

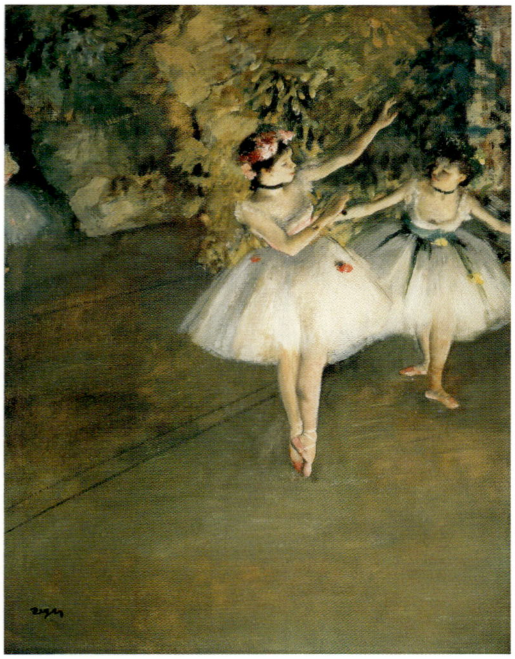

103
Edgar Degas 1834–1911
Two dancers on stage 1874
The Courtauld Collection, London

The 23 works listed in the stockbooks show a broad range of subject matter and media. There were 11 ballet pictures – such as *Two dancers on stage* [**103**] and the impressive *Dance school* [**53**] – which Degas ruefully knew the public expected; three horse race pictures; and nine portraits or studies of heads such as *Ruelle* [**105**]. Among these were some important paintings from his earlier career – *Woman seated beside a vase of flowers (Madame Paul Valpiçon?)* [**104**], all of which made a good profit.[136] These were balanced by new work, the paint not yet dry, and some quite small studies, such as two dance motifs measuring a mere

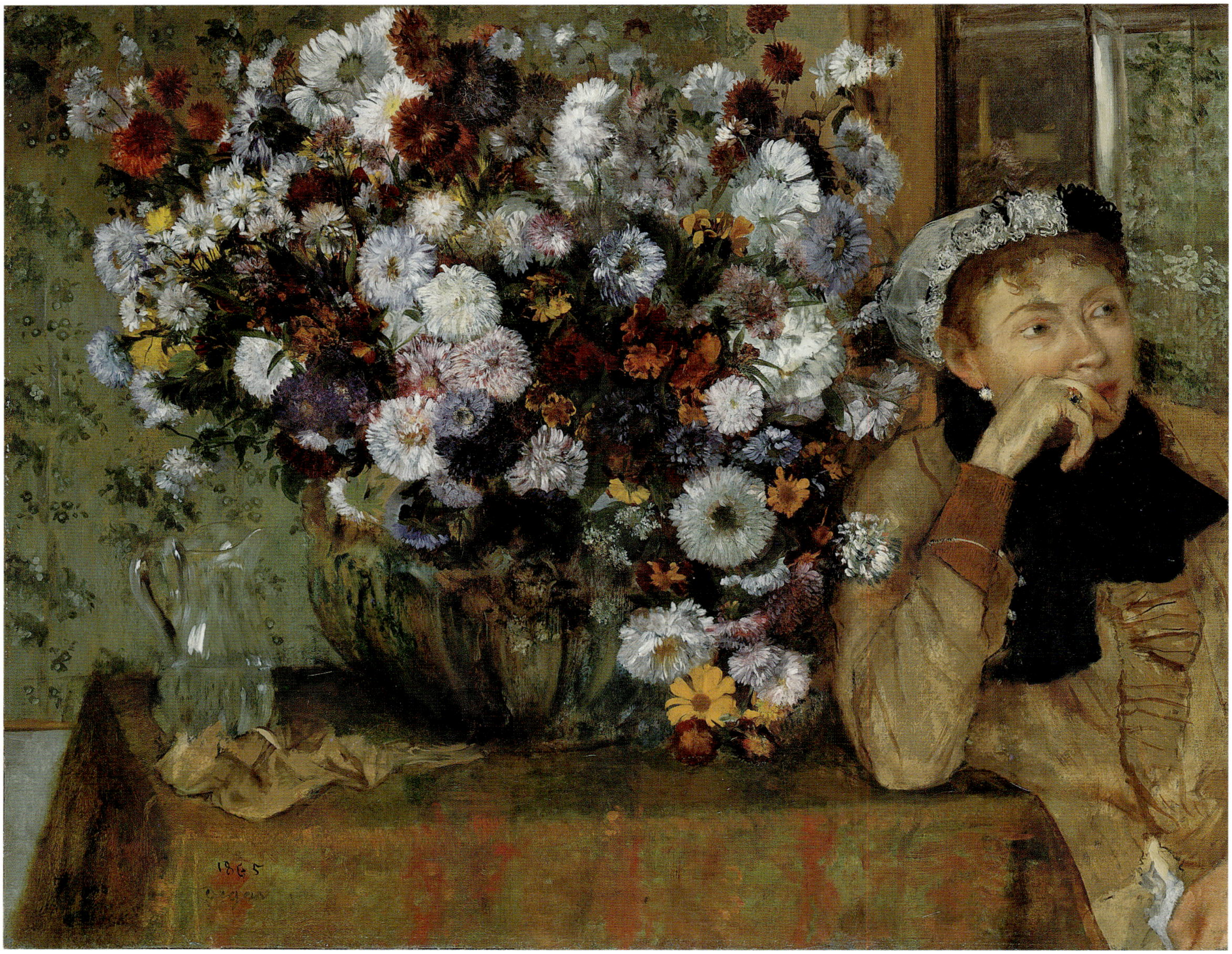

104
Edgar Degas 1834–1911
Woman seated beside a vase of flowers (Madame Paul Valpiçon?) 1865
The Metropolitan Museum of Art, New York
H.O. Havemeyer Collection

22 x 16 centimetres. One of Degas's communiqués asks 2,000 francs for 'this terrible article, which I ought to start again.'[137] The note refers to a recently completed race-course painting, a picture with which Degas was apparently dissatisfied but was nonetheless willing to put on the market.[138]

Why did Degas, a bachelor without the pressing family commitments of Monet or Pissarro, need to sell such a steady stream of work, including the old and slight? The answer seems to be to fuel his growing obsession with collecting.[139] He also needed to sustain his reputation, and seems to have considered that this could be achieved by the occasional showing of work in a focused group which he himself selected and controlled. In one such venture, a cluster of pastel nudes were shown at 19, Boulevard Montmartre in January 1888. None of these appear in the stockbooks, and were probably provided by Degas, to his own satisfaction. There was no catalogue and little critical response, due perhaps to Theo's indifferent promotion or the artist's cultivated reticence. At least nine 'articles' can be identified. Five were mentioned in Fénéon's glowing review in the Revue Indépendante: *The thorn*, a nude woman sitting on the edge of a bed removing a splinter from her foot; a woman standing in a tub and stretching her left hand to her feet; a

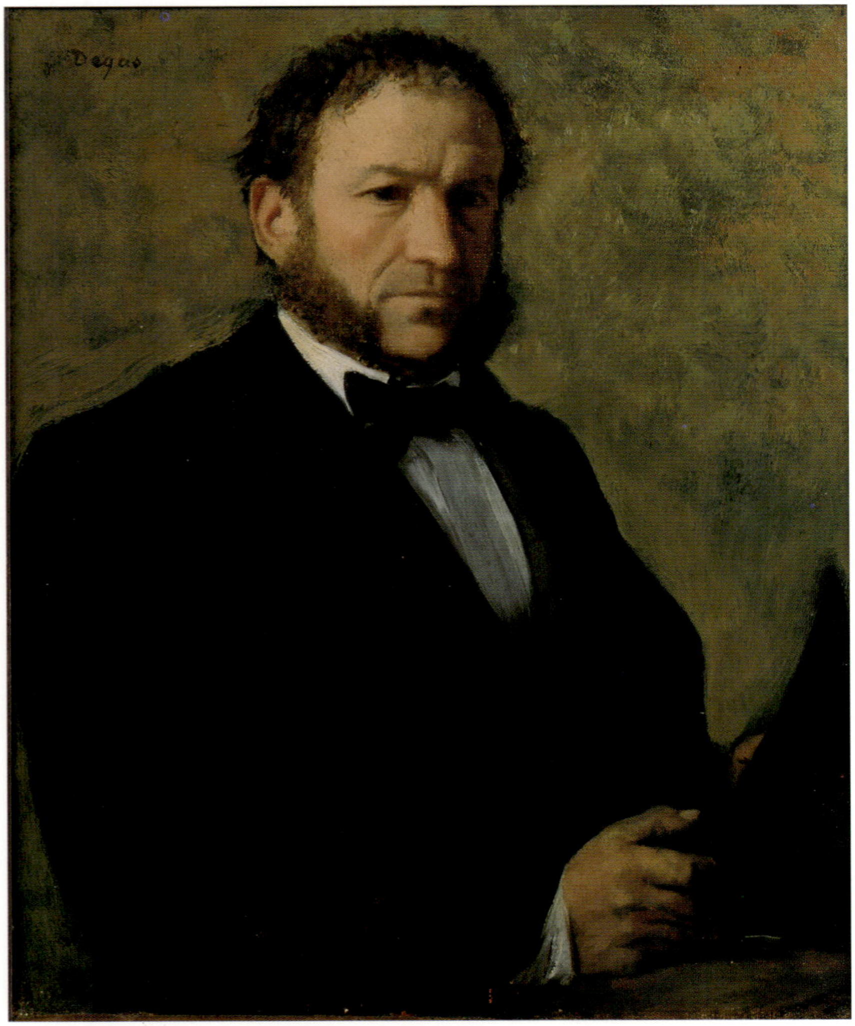

105
Edgar Degas 1834–1911
Mr Ruelle c. 1862
Musée des Beaux-Arts, Lyon

woman seated in a bath; a kneeling figure, buttocks raised; and a woman reaching out from a bath to clasp a dressing gown [**106**].[140] The last two were drawn by an enthusiastic visitor to the show, Gauguin, together with four others which have not yet been traced. The pastels seem to have sold, judging by the disappearance of the four from Gauguin's sketchbook.

Claude Monet

Like Degas, Monet had emerged from the controversial years of the impressionist exhibitions to substantial, if not unanimous, critical acclaim.[141] However, his prices were still quite low: the first painting Theo bought – *The church at Vétheuil* [**107**] – from Bernheim in April 1885, cost a mere 680 francs. For Monet, who had both his own two sons and the children of his common-law wife Alice Hoschédé to support, increasing his income was vital, and – as we have seen – he was adept at playing off dealers to his advantage. For someone like Theo, having Monet in his stock, especially alongside the contrasting work of Degas, meant the chance to benefit from a rising reputation with minimum risk.

Theo began to do business seriously with Monet in the spring of 1887, simultaneous with the recapitalisation of Boussod, Valadon & Cie. He dealt directly with the artist, in the main buying canvases Monet had painted the previous year on Belle-Isle [**108, 109**]. Contact quickly became regular and his purchases more numerous. In 1887 Theo bought at total of 14 paintings costing 19,300 francs.[142] This substantial investment paid off. Eleven were sold within a year; having cost the company 15,500 francs they realised 21,700, a profit of some 25 per cent. It is difficult to see how Theo's employers could have disapproved.

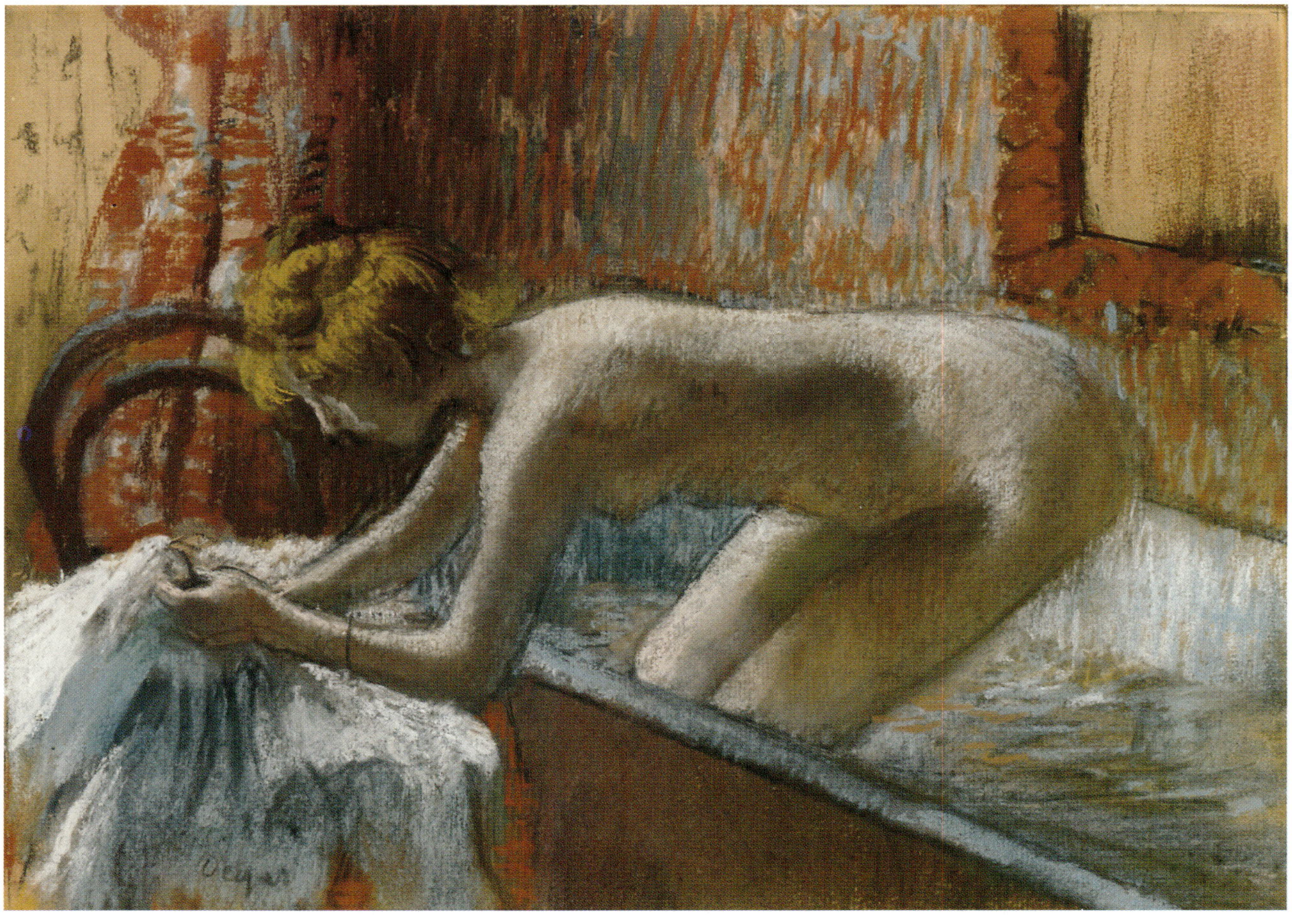

106
Edgar Degas 1834–1911
Woman leaving her bath 1886–88
Private collection

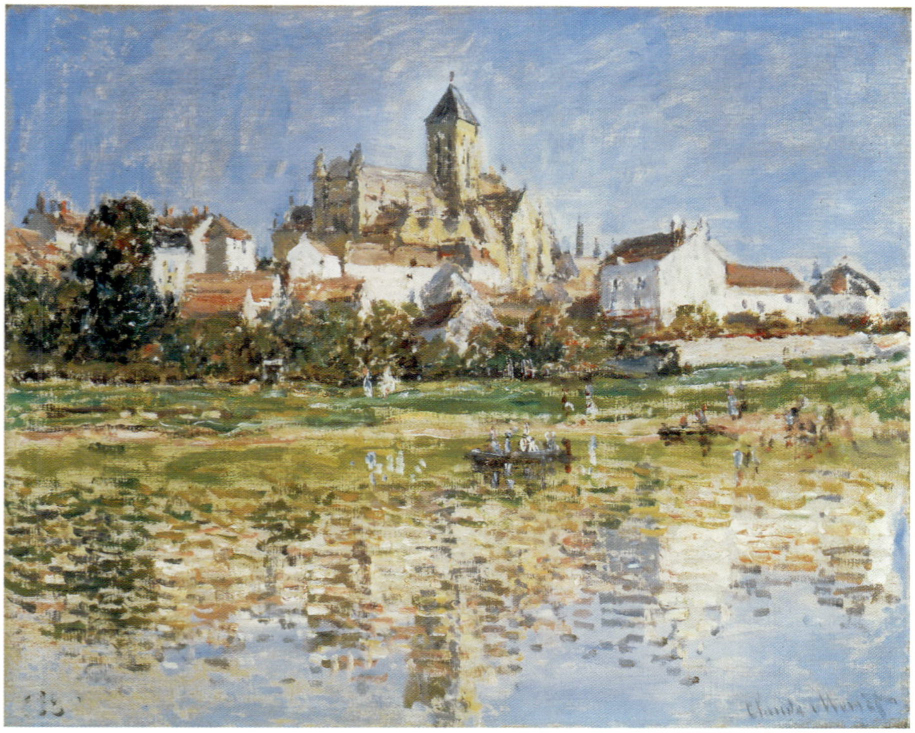

107
Claude Monet 1840–1926
The church at Vétheuil 1880
Southampton City Art Gallery

Thus encouraged, he began to buy more. [**110**] Monet, who was painting at Antibes in the first half of 1888, was difficult to reach, so Theo resorted to other expedients. In February and March he picked up four paintings at the Hôtel Drouot, none costing more than 1,200 francs, and on 9 April bought three for that sum each, remarkably enough from Durand-Ruel. These were all Argenteuil pictures from the early 1870s.[143] Unfortunately, however this gambit did not work out as planned; not one of these older canvases sold until the early 1890s, after Theo's death.

While at Antibes, Monet worried about his business arrangements, and it is clear from his correspondence with Alice that Theo was courting him. In the climate of commercial rivalry, Theo's attentions were welcome. For various reasons, at the time Monet was uncomfortable with the other dealers.[144] He thus allowed Theo to take ten of his Antibes canvases [**111, 112, 113**], now, as we have seen, under generous Goupil arrangements. The paintings were shown in June on the *entresol* of 19, Boulevard Montmartre. For Monet this was a chance to exhibit his most recent work as an ensemble, and it was his first solo show for half a decade. For Theo it was the second group of pictures he had shown by a leading impressionist within six months. Berthe Morisot wrote to Monet that the show had conquered the 'recalcitrant public,'[145] but like Theo's other exhibitions it was not widely reviewed. The critic for *Le Journal des Arts* was ambivalent, finding the Mediterranean shore in one canvas 'like a bloody wound, [...] a heavy carcass of an amphibian,' but in others he could see 'a gracious effect.'[146] Writing in the *Revue Indépendante*, Fénéon found them all shallow, vulgar and geared to New York taste.[147]

According to Pissarro, Monet had told Theo that such a response was 'to be expected,' showing his awareness of the gulf that was opening up between avant-garde critics such as Fénéon, a supporter of Seurat and Signac, and artists of the impressionist group who were increasingly accepted and marketable.[148] But painters of Monet's own generation also had similar reactions, including Pissarro, Renoir and Degas, who caustically referred to the Antibes paintings as 'an art for the market.'[149] And indeed, the

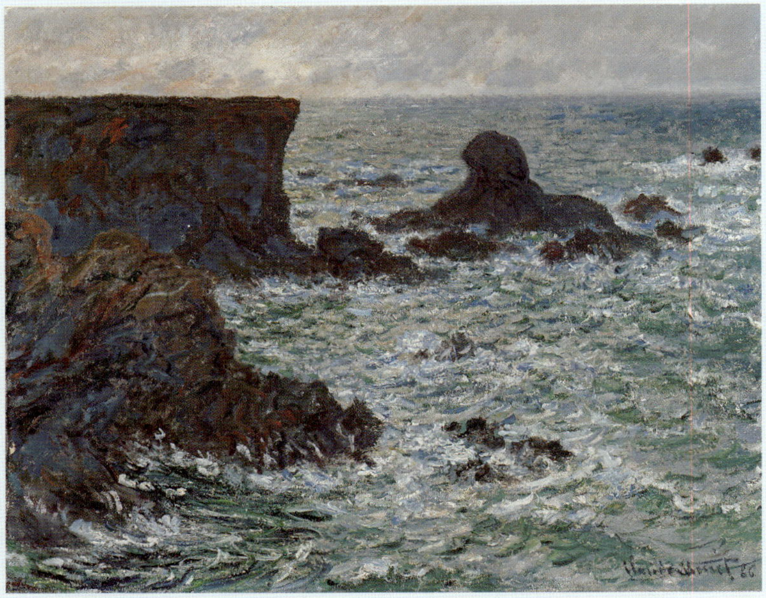

108
Claude Monet 1840–1926
Rocks near Port-Coton, Le Lion 1886
Fitzwilliam Museum, Cambridge

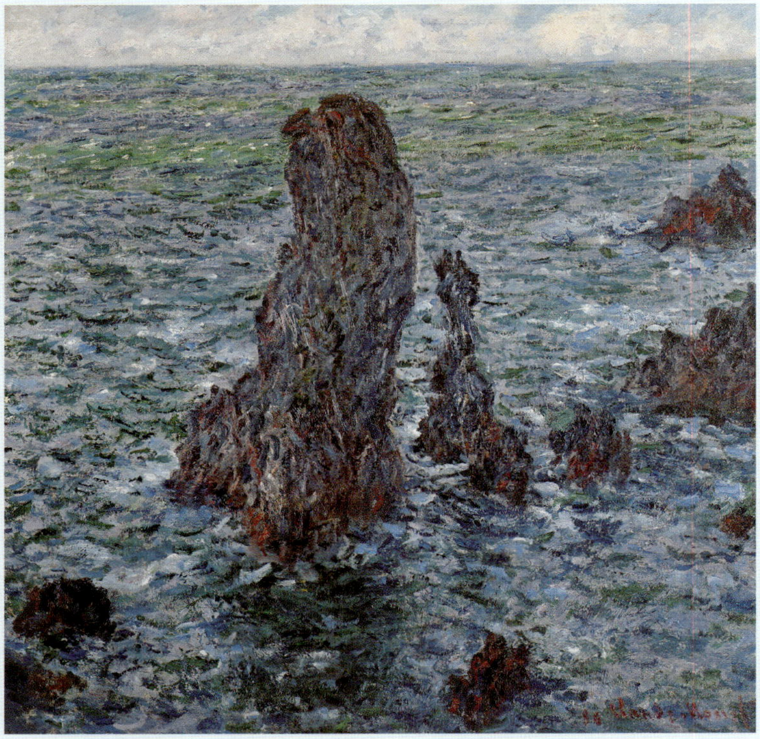

109
Claude Monet 1840–1926
Rocks near Port-Coton 1886
Fondation Rau pour le Tiers-Monde, Embraport, Switzerland

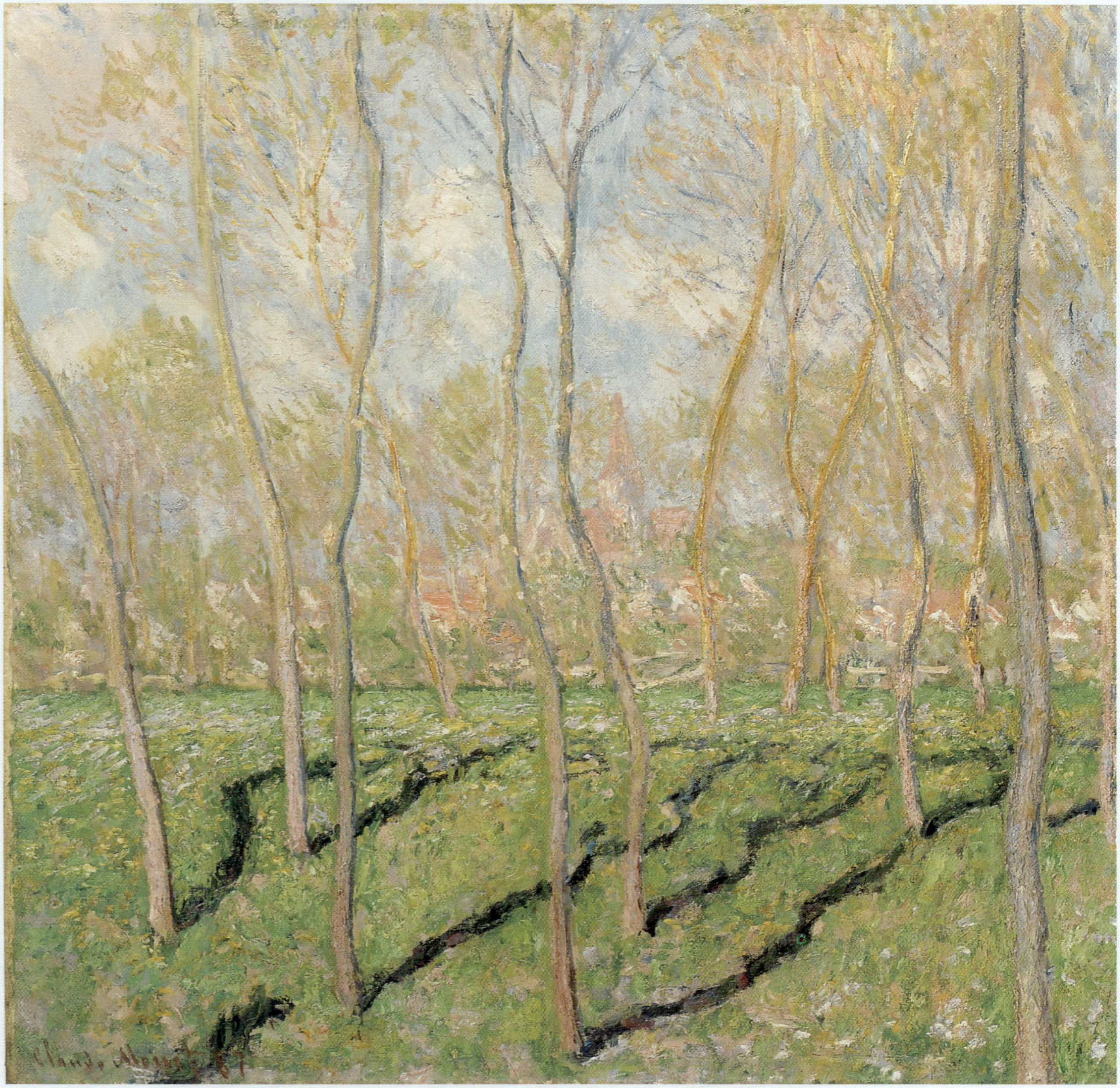

110
Claude Monet 1840–1926
Trees in winter: view of Bennecourt 1887
The Columbus Museum of Art, Columbus, OH

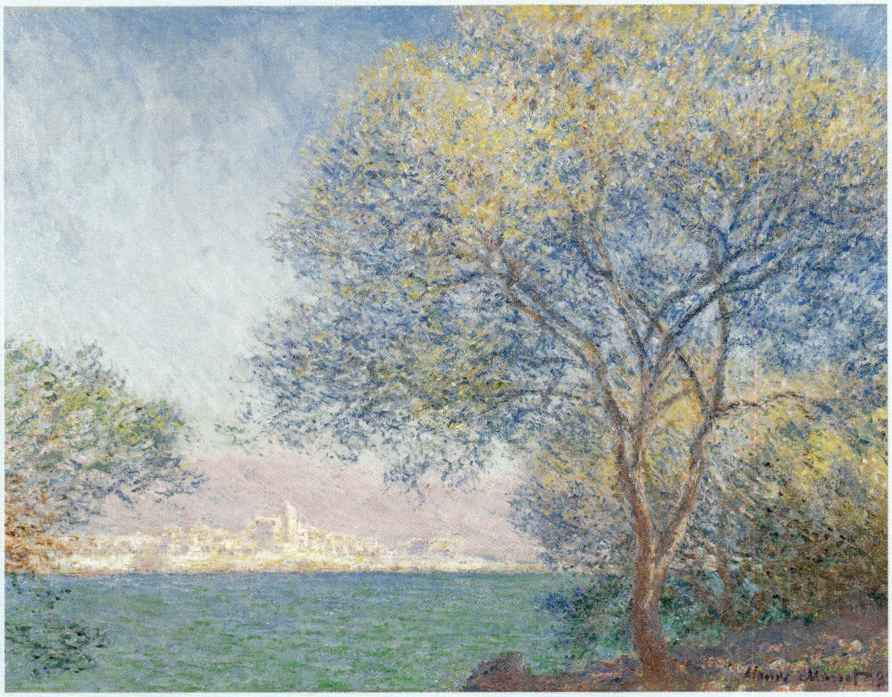

111
Claude Monet 1840–1926
Antibes in the morning 1888
Philadelphia Museum of Art
The John G. Johnson Collection

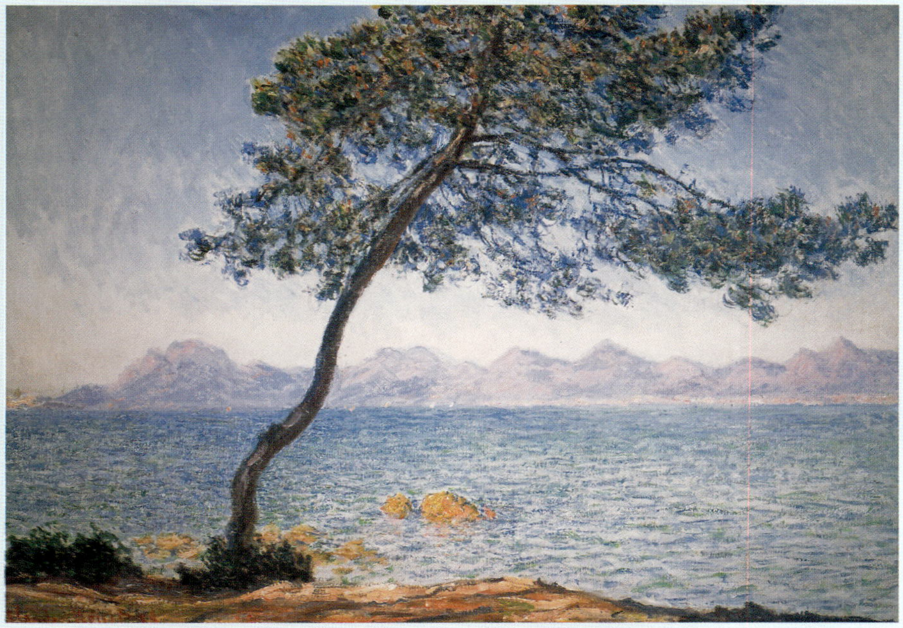

112
Claude Monet 1840–1926
Antibes 1888
The Courtauld Collection, London

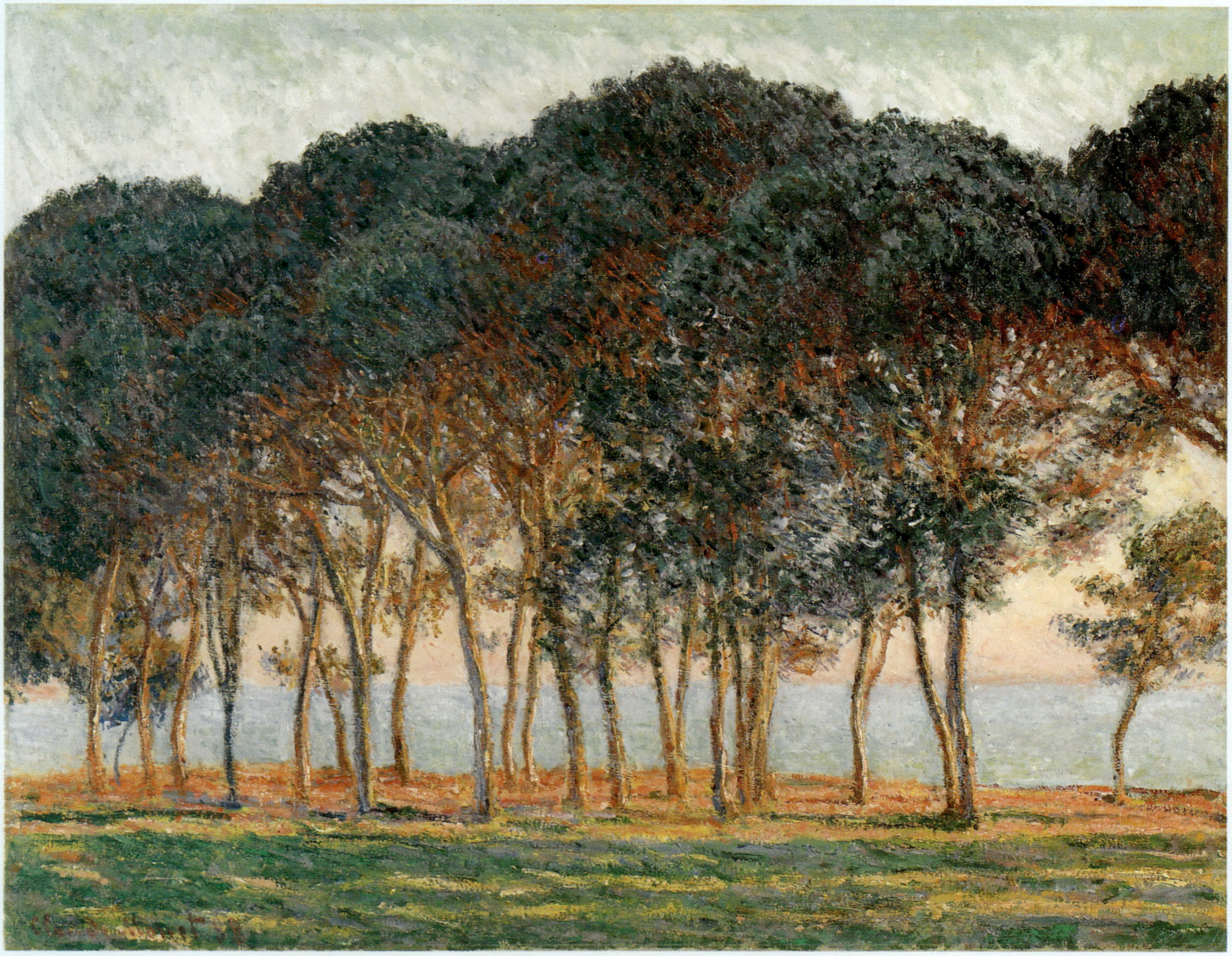

113
Claude Monet 1840–1926
Under the pine trees at the end of the day 1888
Philadelphia Museum of Art
Gift of Otto F. Haas

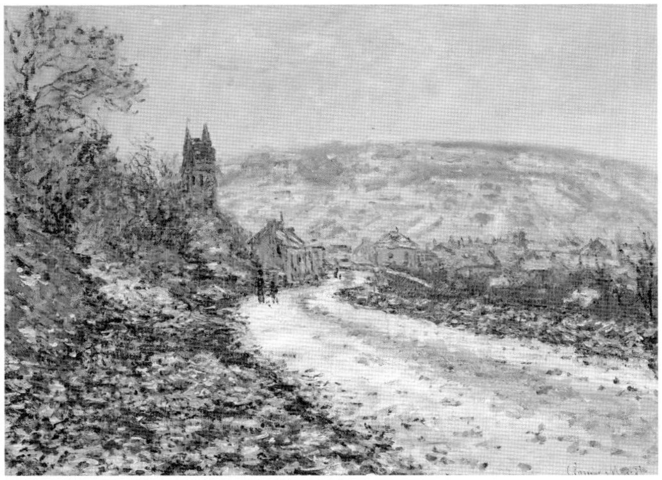

114
Claude Monet 1840–1926
Vétheuil, winter 1881
Museum of Fine Arts, Boston
Gift of Julia C. Prendergast

pictures were a commercial success. The ten canvases had cost Boussod, Valadon & Cie. 11,900 francs; seven were sold in 1888 – among them *Under the pine-trees at the end of the day* [113] – and the rest the next year, totalling 27,750.[150] Both Monet and Theo were vindicated by the market. All the Antibes paintings appear to have been sold to French buyers, but the following year six of the Monets Theo sold went to Americans, among them John G. Johnson, Alfred A. Pope and the painter John Singer Sargent [115].[151] Prices were spiralling, with Monet's reputation undoubtedly strengthened by the rapid turnover of the Antibes group; Pope paid 10,350 francs for *Haystacks in the snow* just fifteen months later.

The reason why Monet's painting began to take off commercially at this time was probably twofold. On the one hand, he was seen to be successful on the market, with rapid sales and swiftly rising prices, and he was the subject of dealers' attentions: Theo staged a second show for him in March 1889 and sent 20 pictures for show at the London branch the next month.[152] For the speculative buyer, Monet was thus a reliable investment, as Cassatt had predicted. On the other hand, since 1880, Monet's paintings of different areas of France – the Channel Coast [116], Belle Isle, the Mediterranean, and elsewhere – had given the landscape precedence over the figure, often insignificant or absent. [114] Charting his native country but denying his countrymen, he depicted France as essential, asocial, apolitical – thus appealing both to foreigners who wanted their France as pure 'art' and to Frenchmen yearning for a changeless national image at a time of considerable political unrest.

Theo's business relations with Monet began to fall off in 1889. Having sold 30 of his paintings in 1888, he managed only 20 the following year. [117, 118] Monet was now in a position to set his sights higher than Theo's ill-lit *entresol*. In July and August 1889, at the height of the Exposition Universelle, Monet shared an exhibition with his friend the sculptor August Rodin at the splendid Galerie Georges Petit.[153] Monet himself sold only five paintings to Theo in 1889, although, ironically, there were canvases at the Petit joint show lent by collectors to whom Theo had sold: Dupuis, Aubry, Boivin; the other 15 came from diverse sources.[154] In 1890 Theo was only able to buy seven Monets for stock, three from the Hôtel Drouot. The hapless visit to Giverny with Valadon in July 1890 was a determined effort to stay in touch with a painter who was slipping out of reach. Thanks to Theo's support in 1888, he had now reached the next level in the art world.

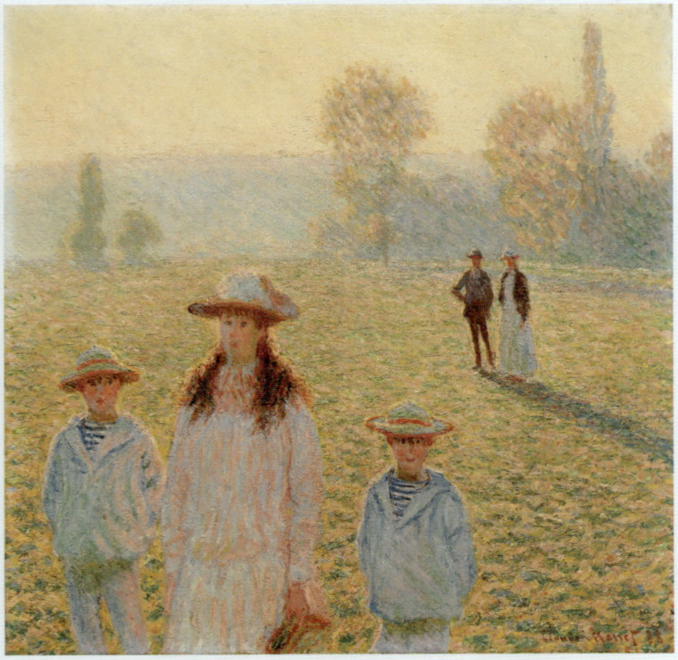

115
Claude Monet 1840–1926
Landscape with figures, Giverny 1888
The Art Institute of Chicago

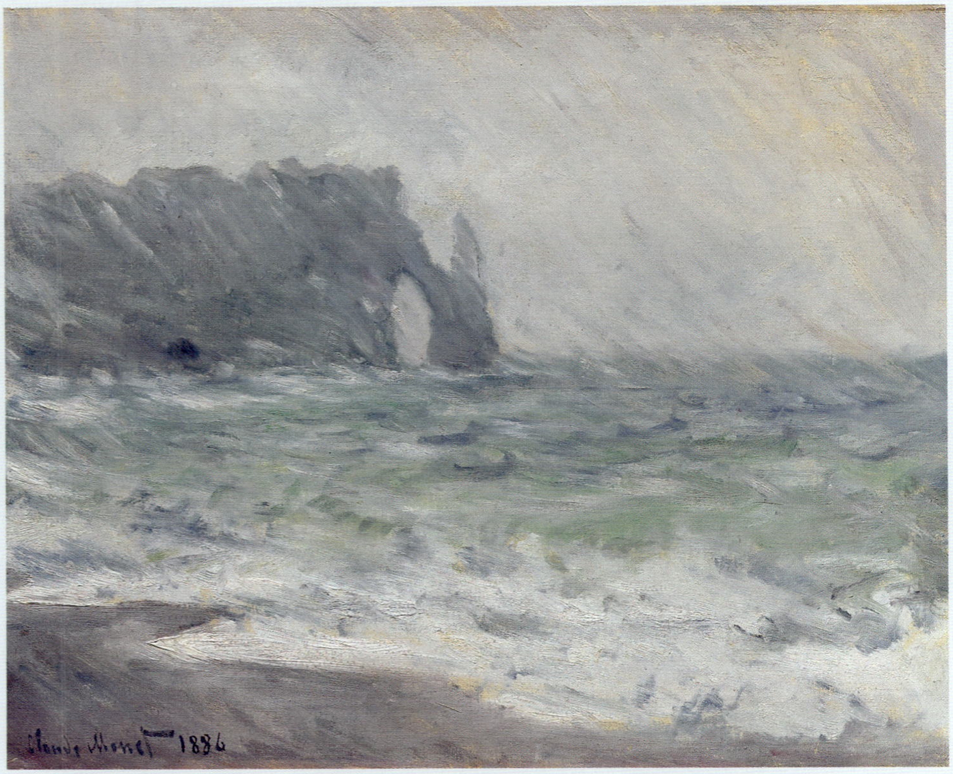

116
Claude Monet 1840–1926
Rain, Etretat 1886
Nasjonalgalleriet, Oslo

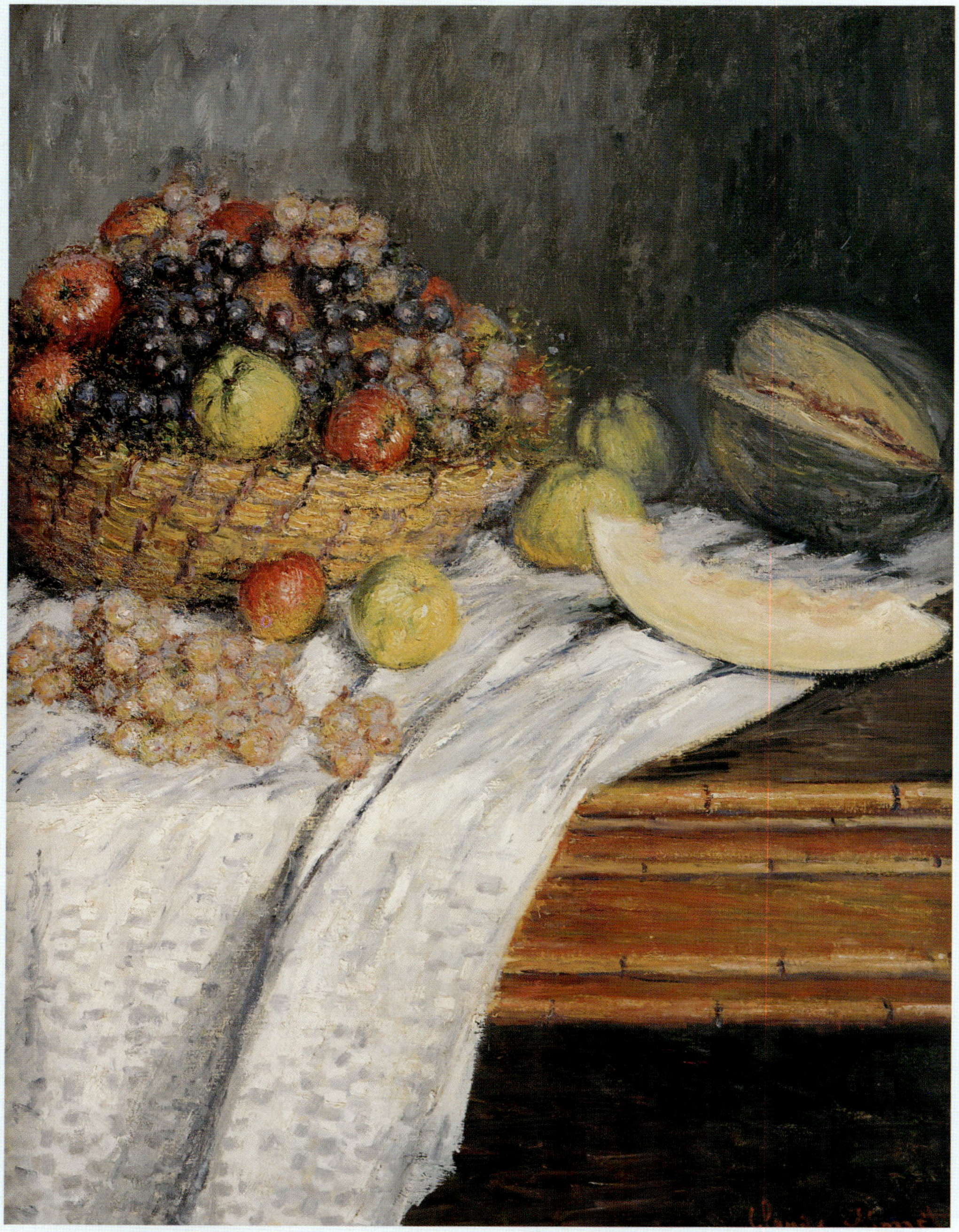

117
Claude Monet 1840–1926
Still life with a honeydew melon 1879
Private collection

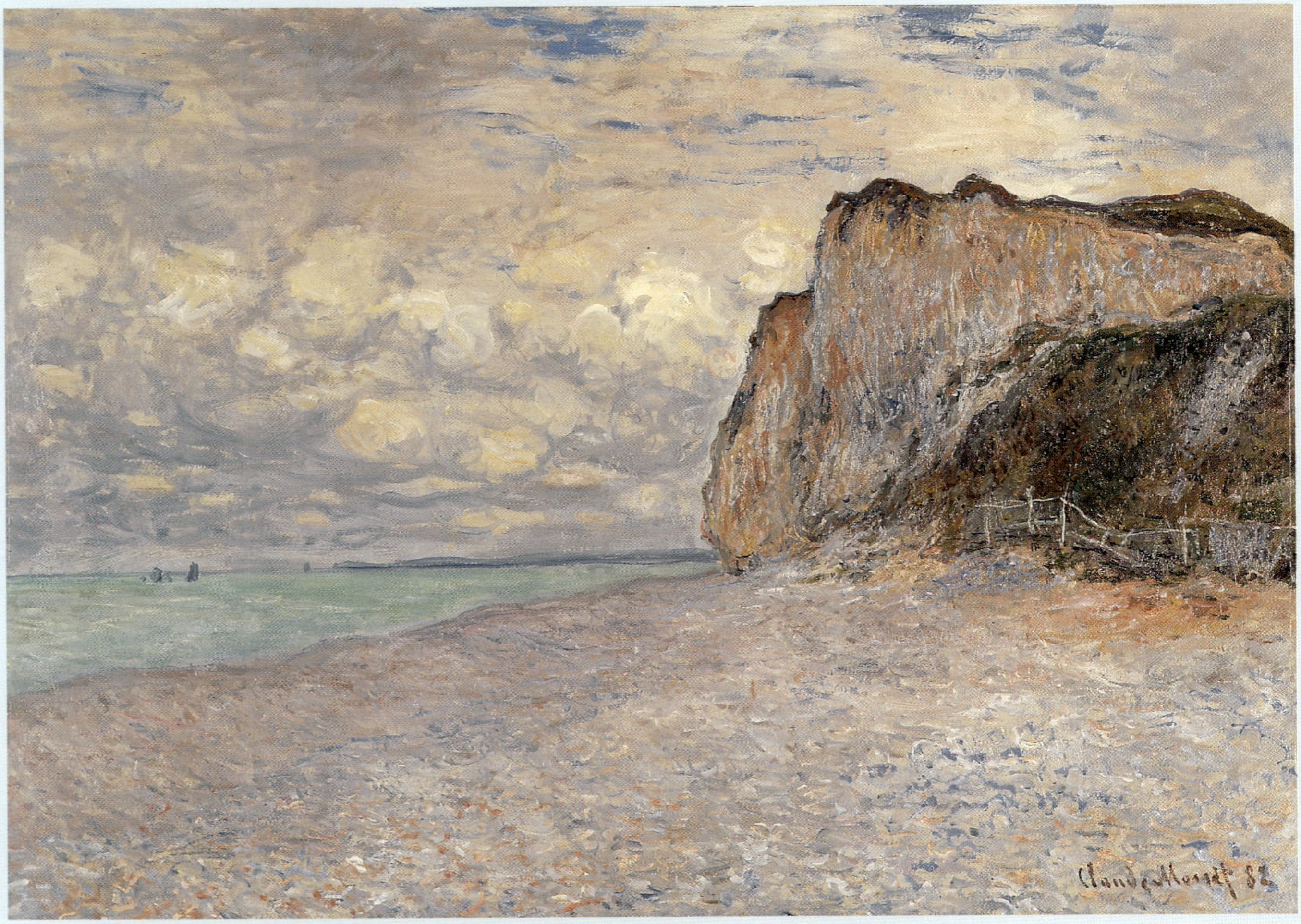

118
Claude Monet 1840–1926
Cliffs near Dieppe 1882
The Carnegie Museum of Art, Pittsburgh
Acquired through the generosity of the Sarah Mellon Scaife family

Camille Pissarro

Pissarro's market situation in the later 1880s was precarious. With a substantial family to support, and income from sales uncertain and inconsistent, Pissarro's correspondence is shot through with anxieties about money. Reaching his 60th birthday in 1890, he had struggled for a place in the art world, winning some reputation in the last Salons of the Second Empire and determinedly exhibiting at all eight impressionist exhibitions. Since 1871 Durand-Ruel had been his main commercial stay, giving him a solo show in 1883, but the dealer's recent financial difficulties had significantly lessened this support. In addition, Durand's business sense often led him to disagree with Pissarro's artistic direction.[155] For Theo, on the other hand, whose letters to the artist evince a genuine concern for his plight as well as admiration for his work, it would have been worth handling Pissarro because he was a senior member of a group whose work was attracting public and market attention. But he cannot have had any doubt that promoting Pissarro would be a longer term business than Degas or Monet.[156]

Following his conversion to neo-impressionism in 1885-86, and having no regular gallery, Pissarro increasingly relied on sales of small works like gouaches, often to minor dealers such as Beugniet, Closet or Heymann.[157] There were opportunities to move up the layers of the market, as in 1887 when Monet voted for him to join Petit's Exposition Internationale. But the machinations involved in this chance only served to highlight Pissarro's marginal position.[158] Theo van Gogh offered an alternative.

A small Pissarro painting is noted in the stockbooks on 29 March 1884, bought and sold the same day to the dealer Guyotin for 150 francs. This was one of Theo's earliest forays into impressionist pictures, though the instant sale suggests a prearrangement and the 25 francs more a handling fee than a 'profit.'

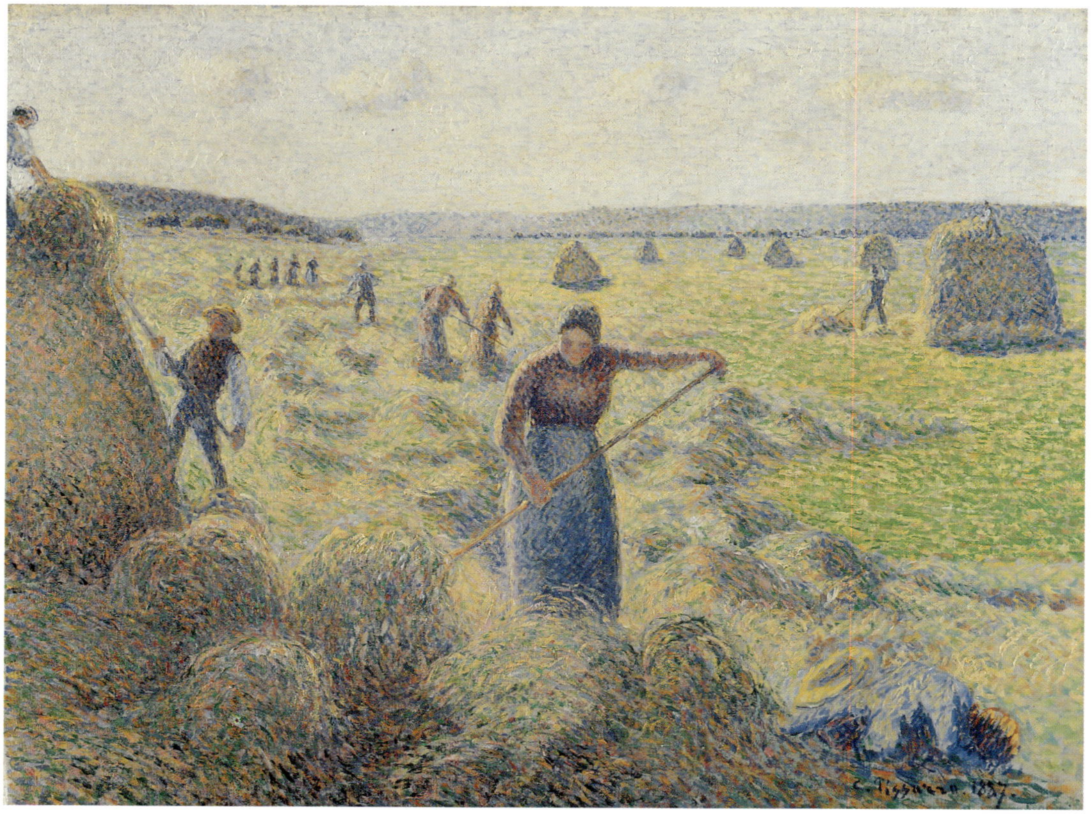

119
Camille Pissarro 1830–1903
The hay harvest, Eragny 1887
Private collection

Relations really began in mid-1887. In April, Pissarro apparently heard that Theo was not yet prepared to buy anything, but in August he bought a recent harvest motif, *The hay harvest, Eragny* [119] and in December an 1882 market scene.[159] Once more, both of these were assured immediate sales. Theo thus took up Pissarro soon after he began buying Monet and Degas, and again Manzi, whom Pissarro said he knew 'perfectly' well, may have been a link.[160] By the end of the year Theo was taking work on consignment, no doubt because he could not risk too many purchases; Fénéon noted three fans on display at the gallery in his round-up of the dealers in December.[161]

The pace barely quickened in 1888. Four paintings were bought from Pissarro, three in March [120] and one in December. The delay was probably due to the fact that only two of the March group had found buyers by the end of the year. Both these canvases moderated their 'difficult' neo-impressionist handling with the 'easy,' timeless subject of peasant gardens and cottages.[162] Theo wanted to help Pissarro as much as he could: the very day in November he sold one of these paintings he bought another, *L'Ile Lacroix* [121], which he sold to the same buyer. This was a young businessman named Dupuis, who also purchased a fan.[163] Dupuis paid only 400 francs for the Rouen picture, for which Theo had paid Pissarro 300. On the other hand, Theo's cultivation of Dupuis's interest in Pissarro (the same collector bought Degas, Monet, and others, too) is an example of how he played a long game with certain clients. Dupuis purchased two more Pissarros at about yearly intervals: *Flock of sheep: sunset* in June 1889, and *Fields at Eragny* in September 1890.[164]

In the autumn of 1888 Theo mounted an informal show of Pissarro's recent work, as he had for Degas that January. Durand-Ruel, competitively watching these goings-on, started to buy more himself.[165] The following year, Theo bought half-a-dozen paintings – among them *A street in Auvers* [no ill.]–, and they went

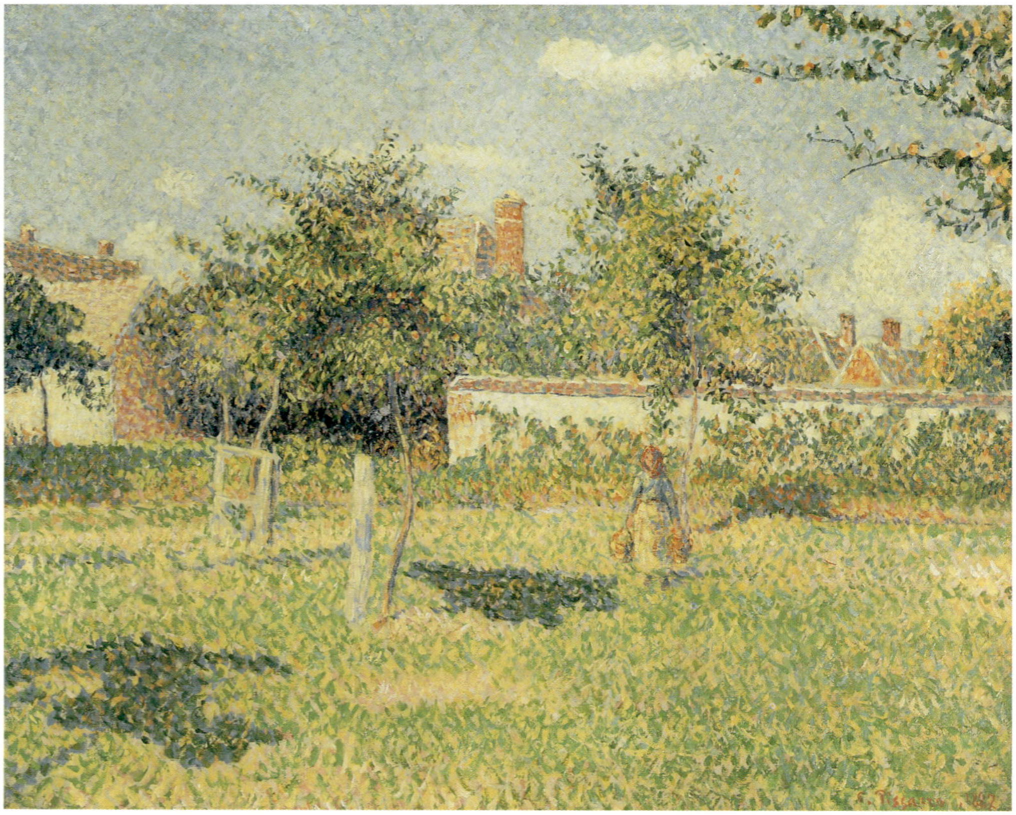

120
Camille Pissarro 1830–1903
Woman in a garden, Eragny 1887
Musée d'Orsay, Paris

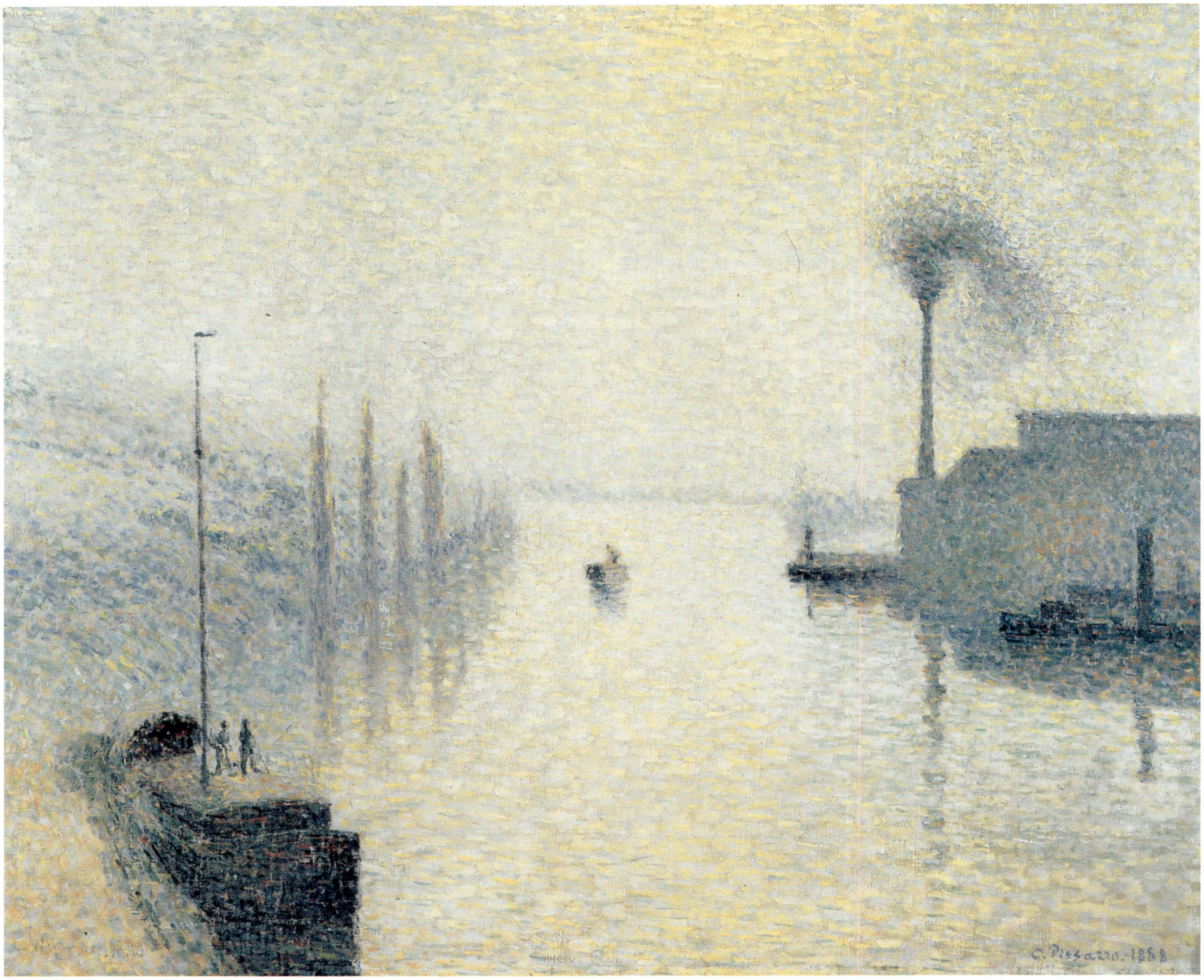

121
Camille Pissarro 1830–1903
L'Ile Lacroix, Rouen: effect of fog 1888
The Philadelphia Museum of Art
The John G. Johnson Collection

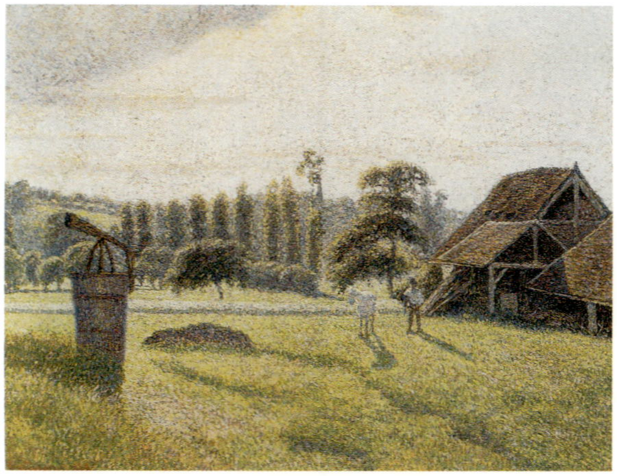

122
Camille Pissarro 1830–1903
Brick-field at Eragny 1888
Private collection

for slowly mounting prices to known clients such as Desfossés, who bought the *Brick-field at Eragny* [122], and Gallimard, men who were building up broad-based 'modern' collections. In February 1890 he staged a true one-man show, with 17 canvases, seven distempers and four gouaches. Having lost Monet, Theo needed to promote Pissarro if he was to stay in the forefront of impressionist dealership. The exhibition included both canvases Theo had bought especially for it and work he had previously sold, such as *The gleaners.*[166] On the wall, this show was a frank display of Pissarro's avant-garde credentials. Geffroy again wrote the catalogue introduction, praising Pissarro in mollifyingly pantheistic terms.[167] His writings, which referred to the works as 'an apotheosis of nature penetrated by light, trembling with sap and delicately gilded by the sun,'[168] placed Pissarro's work conveniently at a cross-roads; it could be seen as conventionally changeless, like Breton or Jules Dupré slightly brought up-to-date with dots; as consistent with the new symbolist aesthetic – allusive and emotive; or as visions of the anarchist ideal Pissarro shared with young intellectuals. Such multiple interpretative possibilities – appealing to the bourgeois amateur as well as the avant-garde intellectual – suited market requirements.

Four paintings sold for a total of 4,800 francs, all to French collectors. Pissarro was still far from Monet's status, but the exhibition was a critical success.[169] By gradually accruing clientele and judiciously waiting with the solo exhibition until the critical climate was right, Theo relaunched Pissarro as an artist with a viable future. He had never invested more than 900 francs in a single painting, which certainly would have stood him in good stead had he lived to reap the profit. Indeed, after Theo died, Durand-Ruel returned avidly to Pissarro, hosting a one-man show almost annually until the painter's death.

Impressionism and market forces

However much Theo admired the work of Degas and Raffaëlli, Monet and Pissarro, whatever steps he took to increase their incomes and raise their profits, he always had his company and the market in mind. He had not worked, as the myth would have it, out of heroic support for 'impressionism' as such. This becomes apparent when one considers his relationship with the other exhibitors at the impressionist shows.

Theo bought a Sisley as early as March 1885, but only, it seems, because he already had a buyer; Desfossés took it the same day. In 1887 four other paintings were handled in the same rapid way. Three others – *La maison abandonée* [123] among them – he purchased from the artist that year were not sold until long after his death. There was scarcely any market for Sisley, and with purchase prices as low as 145 francs it was simply not worth the effort of developing it. In both 1885 and 1887 Theo purchased a canvas by Renoir, in each case for immediate sale. The only speculative purchase he made – *Lunch at the Restaurant Fournaise* [125] in 1888 – again sold only after his death. The diversity of these pictures in both style and subject – a garden, a recreational boating scene, a view of Naples – hint at what made selling Renoir so difficult in the late 1880s: his work had no clear market identity.

Theo's relations with two very different, lesser known 'impressionists,' the landscapists Stanislas Lépine [124], a Corotesque tonal painter who had shown at four impressionist exhibitions, and Armand Guillaumin, who by the 1886 show was working in bright hues and in a style close to Gauguin, show very similar patterns. From both he purchased only a handful of canvases, spread over several years; he

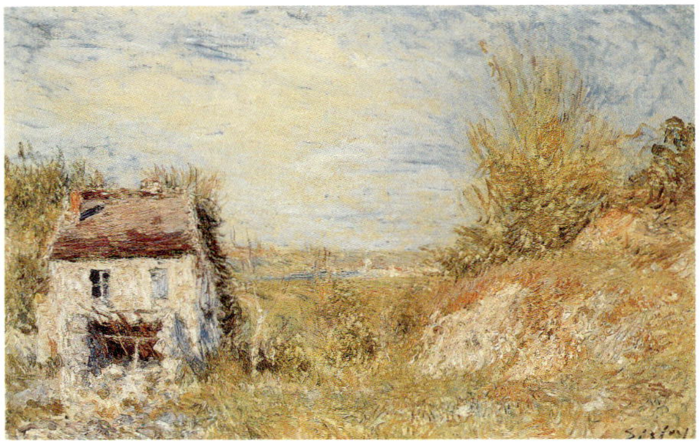

123
Alfred Sisley 1839–1899
La maison abandonnée c. 1886
Private collection

bought direct from the artists, at prices of about 200 francs; and he chose stock subjects: city views or pastoral landscapes. A letter from Guillaumin, written in the spring of 1887 to thank Theo for going to see the display of his work at the offices of the *Revue Indépendante*, gives us a flavour of their relationship.[170] By visiting a fringe exhibition linked to an avant-garde periodical, Theo, then very much in a learning phase, was reconnoitring a 'lower' layer in the art world hierarchy. But interest did not mean investment. He purchased his first Guillaumin only six months later, for immediate sale to Dupuis, and the next not for another year. All this reveals Theo as a hard-headed businessman unwilling to take reckless risks with his company's money, not as a warrior for modern art.

Trading across the range of media

Theo van Gogh was originally employed by a company, Goupil's, which had made its reputation with reproductive prints; it was later transformed into another firm, Boussod, Valadon & Cie., which diversified into high quality illustration. The gallery operated, as we have seen, in a market catering for collectors who frequently chose to spread their investments and interests wide, so dealers necessarily handled stock in a broad range of media. Theo naturally did the same, and on a larger scale than has hitherto been recognised. He was more than just a dealer of paintings.

Given the history of the company, it should be no surprise that 19, Boulevard Montmartre carried work that falls broadly under the heading of illustration. Just as Goupil had sold paintings after which photogravures had been printed in the thousands, Boussod, Valadon & Cie. sold pictures that had been reproduced in mass circulation magazines. The connection between illus-

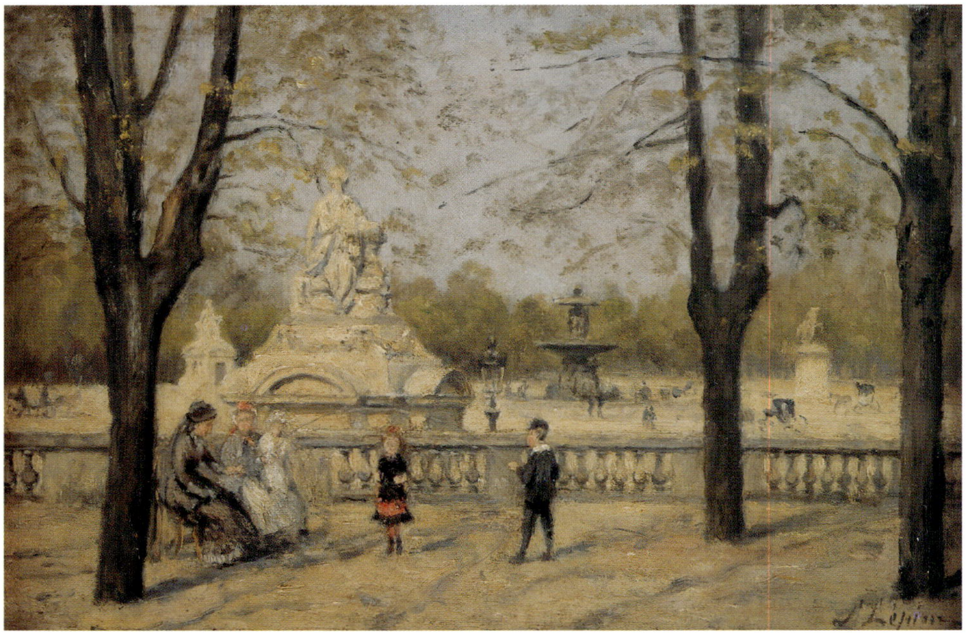

124
Stanislas Lépine 1835–1892
Place de la Concorde c. 1877–82
Musée Carnavalet, Paris

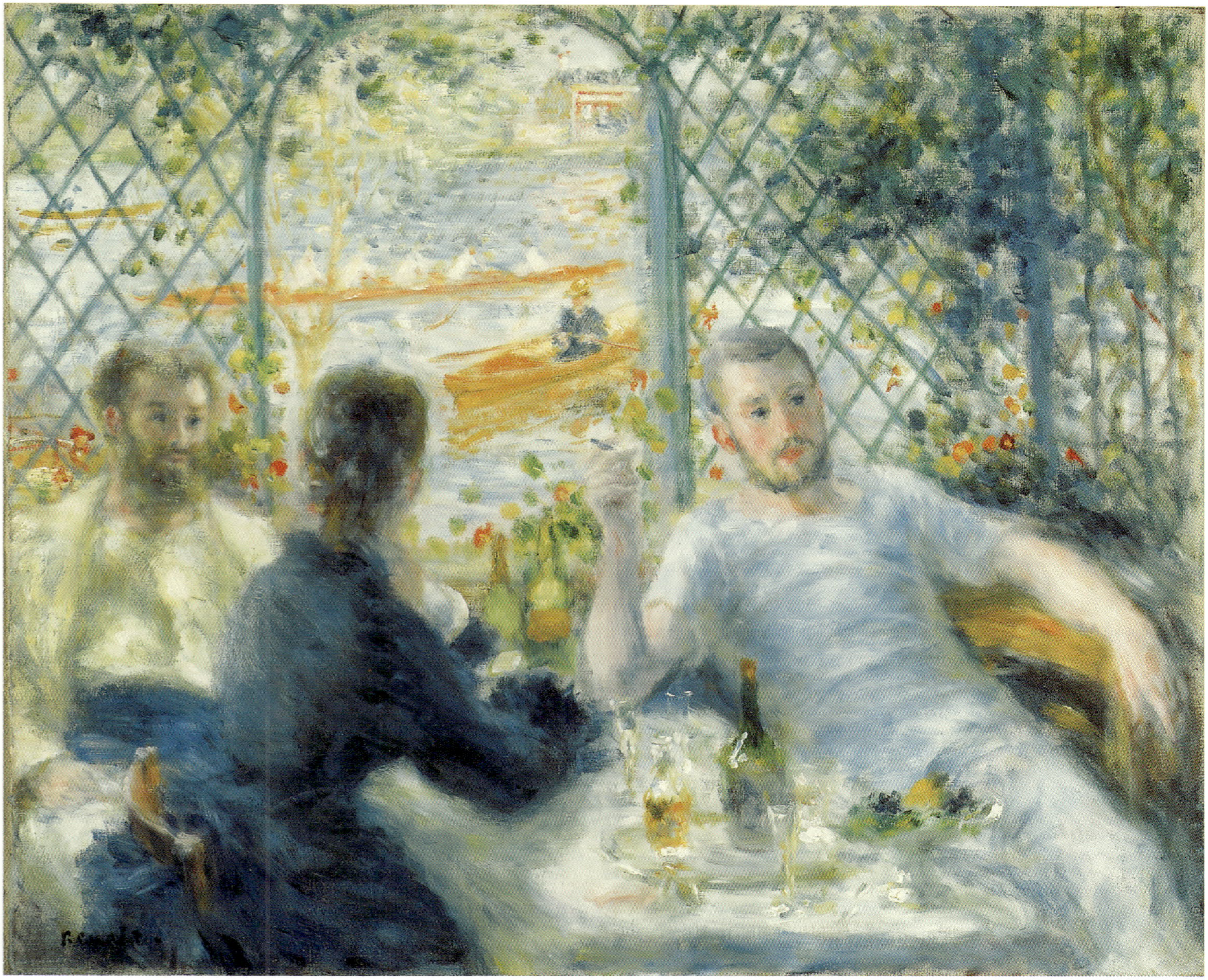

125
Auguste Renoir 1841–1919
Lunch at the Restaurant Fournaise c. 1879
The Art Institute of Chicago
Mr and Mrs Potter Palmer Collection

tration and the art trade would have been reinforced by Manzi, since 1882 the director of the company's printing works at Asnières. Manzi's interest in giving magazines like *Paris Illustré* a 'modern' look usefully coincided with Theo's need to open up new markets. In the consumerist climate of the 1880s a picture that had been given public exposure through illustration in a smart periodical might have added cachet, or at least give reassurance to the collector. For an artist, it was always advantageous for work to have more than one outlet. Thus, when Theo included in Raffaëlli's one-man show a group of 15 drawings that had appeared in an article on the Hôtel Drouot in *Harper's New Monthly Magazine* [**126, 127**], he was both showing accredited work and perhaps enabling the artist to earn twice, from reproduction fees and from the sale of the works.[171]

Theo dealt in works on paper of all kinds: pastels, watercolours, gouaches, and different kinds of drawings. With specialist societies exhibiting and selling such objects, it was clearly a market a dealer had to be in. Because the stockbooks rarely register works on paper, it is virtually impossible to know the true extent of this business. It can, however, be traced across the spectrum of Theo's trading. In May 1888, Boussod, Valadon & Cie. bought two Millet pastels from the Goldschmidt sale; the same year the stockbooks list a Millet purchased and sold to a certain 'Cahen' – perhaps Albert Cahen d'Anvers, who had a good collection of Millet pastels.[172] Handling works on paper by this rapidly appreciating artist was likely to be good business: for the collector buying a work on paper was cheaper than purchasing an oil; moreover, in some quarters Millet was more esteemed as a draughtsman than a painter.[173]

Pastel was much written about during the 1880s as a 'modern' medium, and Theo managed to sell them by a range of his 'modern' artists. One example was the large study for Besnard's *Naked woman warming herself*, sold to Antonin Personnaz, which was designated a major work by critics of various stripes when it was shown at the Pastellistes in 1888.[174] The first letter Theo received from Monet concerned a Degas pastel-over-monotype [**128**] which Monet seems to have exchanged for a canvas of Belle-Isle, reminding us how much the informal and experimental character of work on paper was admired amongst artists themselves.[175] Both Raffaëlli and Pissarro showed work in 'mixed media' at 19, Boulevard Montmartre. The former's one-man show included drawings heightened in watercolour and even oil, as well as pen-and-ink drawings. In 1889, Pissarro not only offered Theo straightforward watercolours at 250 francs each, but also sold him *Two women in a garden* [**129**], a gouache on silk, for 800 francs, prices which indicate that there was a hierarchy of value for different media.[176]

Another area in which Theo seems to have been very active was in the market for original prints. This becomes clear from George Lucas's diary. In 1884 he mentions ten contacts with Theo, most of them in relation to etchings.[177] This was not a particularly lucrative sector of the market – on 29 December 1883 Lucas 'bought a lot of Buhots for 270 fs'[178] – but it was a busy one, with a sale of 'modern etchings and engravings' like the Léon Gaucherel collection raising over 20,000 francs for some 250 lots.[179] For artist-printmakers it was certainly worth fostering relations with dealers. Both Henri Guérard and Félix Buhot gave Theo signed etchings in 1884. [**130**] With their interest in *Japonisme* and their scenes from the city, such printmakers could be counted as 'modern' artists, and they may well have contributed to Theo's developing interest in new art.

Typically, Theo's activities in the print field were consistent with the company's long-standing business practice. He used the international network: in 1888 he sent etchings by Pissarro, woodcuts by his son Lucien, and lithographs by George Thornley, as well as drawings by Degas and Seurat, to the Nederlandsche Etsclub in Amsterdam.[180] True to the Goupil ethos, he was also interested in reproductions, notably of modern pictures he admired. He exhibited four of Thornley's lithographs after Degas in April 1888, and the following year an album of 15 was published by Boussod, Valadon & Cie.[181] Theo followed up this initiative by publishing an album by the lithographer Lauzet after paintings by Monticelli, a project he had long discussed with Vincent, himself committed to the print medium and a great admirer of Monticelli's

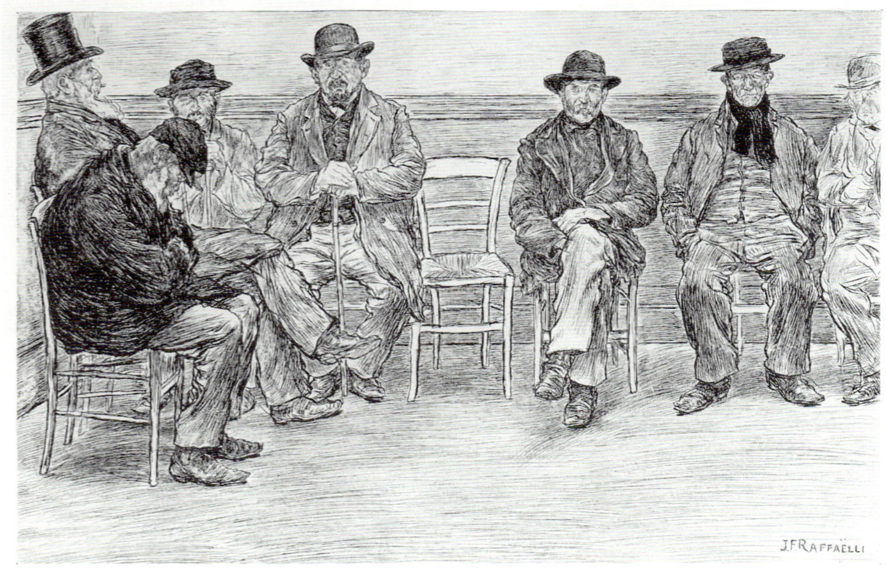

126
Jean-François Raffaëlli 1850–1924
Seedy lilies and shabby wall-flowers c. 1888
Collection of Dr and Mrs Michael Schlossberg, Eastpoint, GA

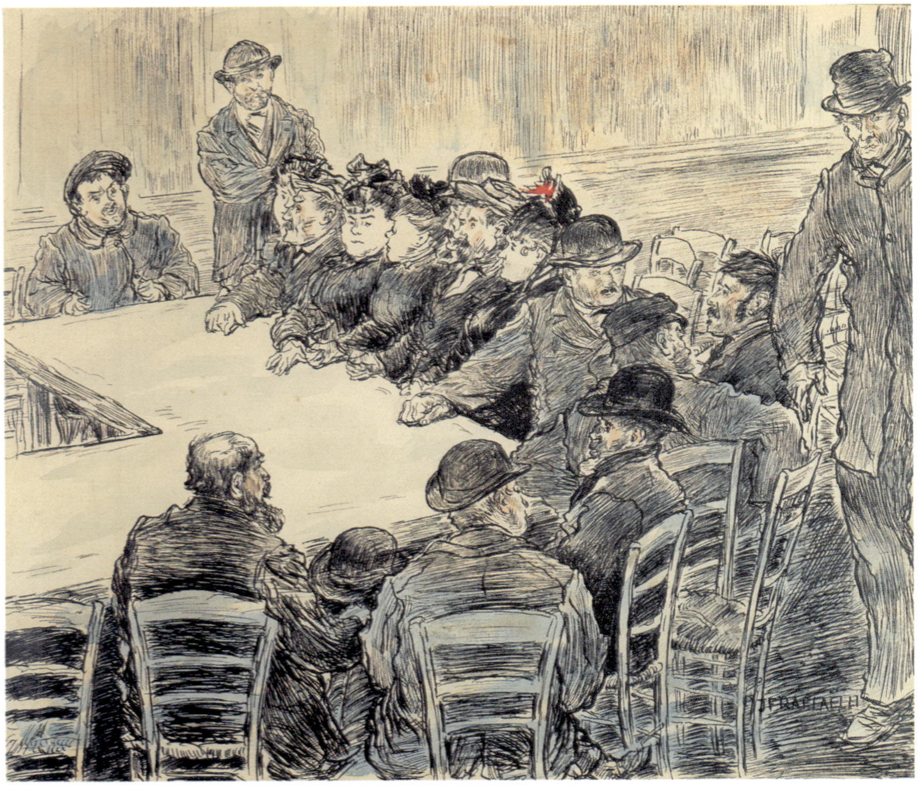

127
Jean-François Raffaëlli 1850–1924
Brokers in the Mazas, Hôtel Drouot c. 1888
Collection of Dr and Mrs Michael Schlossberg, Eastpoint, GA

work [827/T21]. Such projects served both commercial and artistic purposes. By reproducing a work of art, the print promotes it and encourages purchase of the original; at the same time, the reproductive print is an art object valuable in its own right and can be purchased as such.

In some respects Theo was more adventurous in his handling of prints than he was of paintings. This was undoubtedly because prices were much lower, but he may well also have used them for tactical purposes, i.e. as a means of introducing an artist to a potential collector. In 1889 he purchased a set of Gauguin's recent zincographs. While some of these were original compositions, others were variants of paintings such as the *Arlesian women, mistral* [**132**], which Theo had also bought. Indeed, it was Theo himself who had counselled Gauguin to produce the zincographs in order to promote his work.[182] Theo had begun to buy woodcuts by Lucien Pissarro in 1888, continuing the following year with the purchase of *The sower* [**131**], a print after an 1875 canvas by his father.[183] If some of Gauguin's or Lucien's prints were interpretative rather than transcriptive, they also used the strong 'synthetic' contour typical of radical draughtsmanship in the later 1880s, thus bringing avant-garde style to 19, Boulevard Montmartre's stock.

This use of the print medium to introduce difficult or newly fashionable artists to potential clients occurred in at least two other instances. Theo stocked both Jules Chéret's colourful lithographic posters and Odilon Redon's sombre albums of lithographs.[184] These were not such very radical choices – Redon's work had been gradually gathering support throughout the decade and Chéret was unquestionably the most celebrated poster designer in Paris. As far as we know, however, Theo handled only very few other works by Redon and no pastels by Chéret or paintings by Lucien Pissarro. Theo dealt with these artists essentially as printmakers, a modest, but forward-looking and busy, aspect of his professional practice.

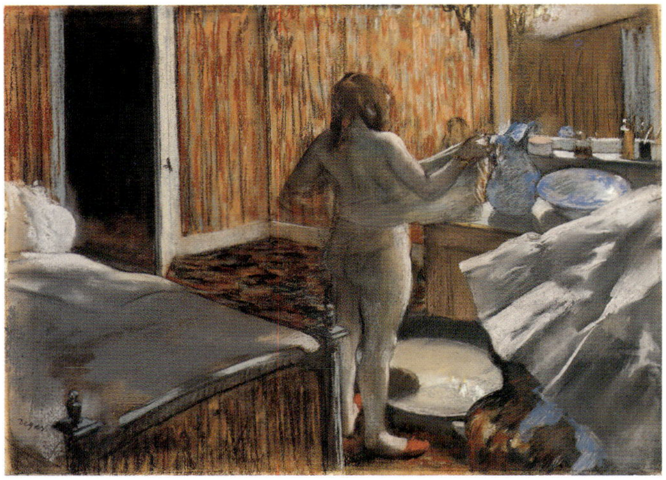

128
Edgar Degas 1834–1911
Woman at her toilette 1886-90
The Norton Simon Museum, Pasadena

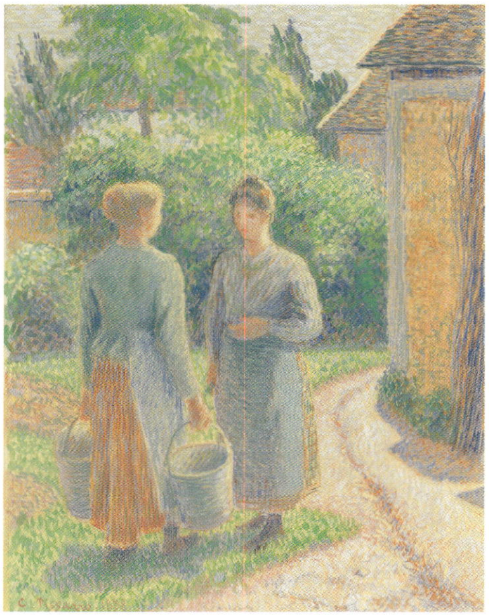

129
Camille Pissarro 1830–1903
Two women in a garden 1888
The Metropolitan Museum of Art, New York

One further field of activity which has been overlooked is Theo's trade in sculpture. Once more, Lucas's diary is revealing. His references to 'Goupils (van Gogh)' frequently concern the sculpture of Antoine-Louis Barye [**133**], who had died in 1875. Lucas, who was looking for Barye pieces for the Baltimore collector William Walters and the painter Léon Bonnat, saw Theo on this business no less than ten times in 1888.[185] Barye's reputation was on the rise.[186] In the late 1880s, while Theo was building up

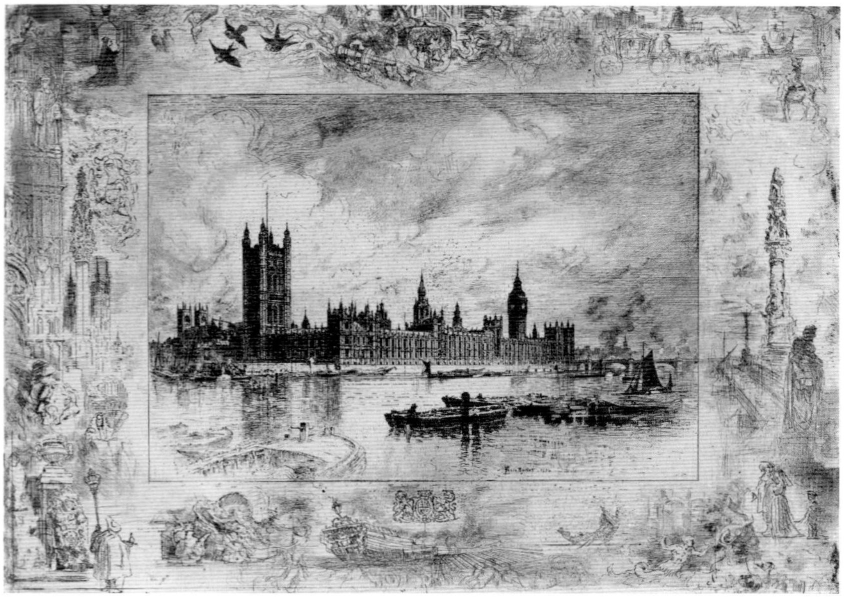

130
Félix Buhot 1847–1898
Westminster palace 1884
Van Gogh Museum, Amsterdam

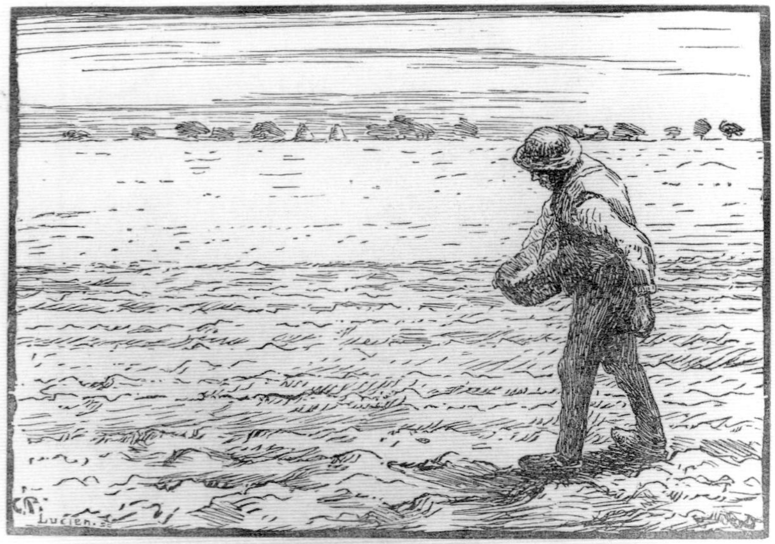

131
Lucien Pissarro 1863–1944
The sower 1887–88
The Ashmolean Museum, Oxford

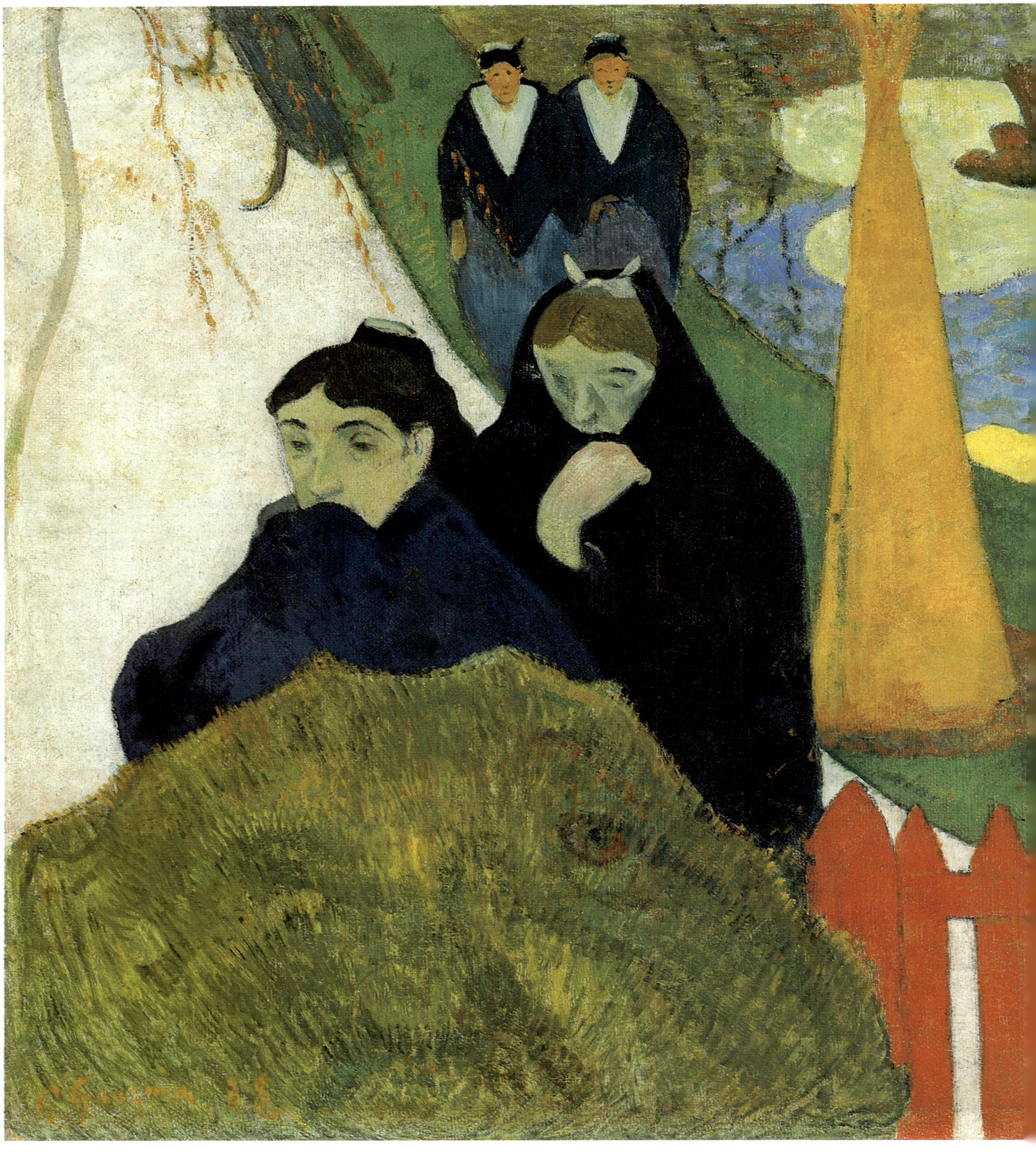

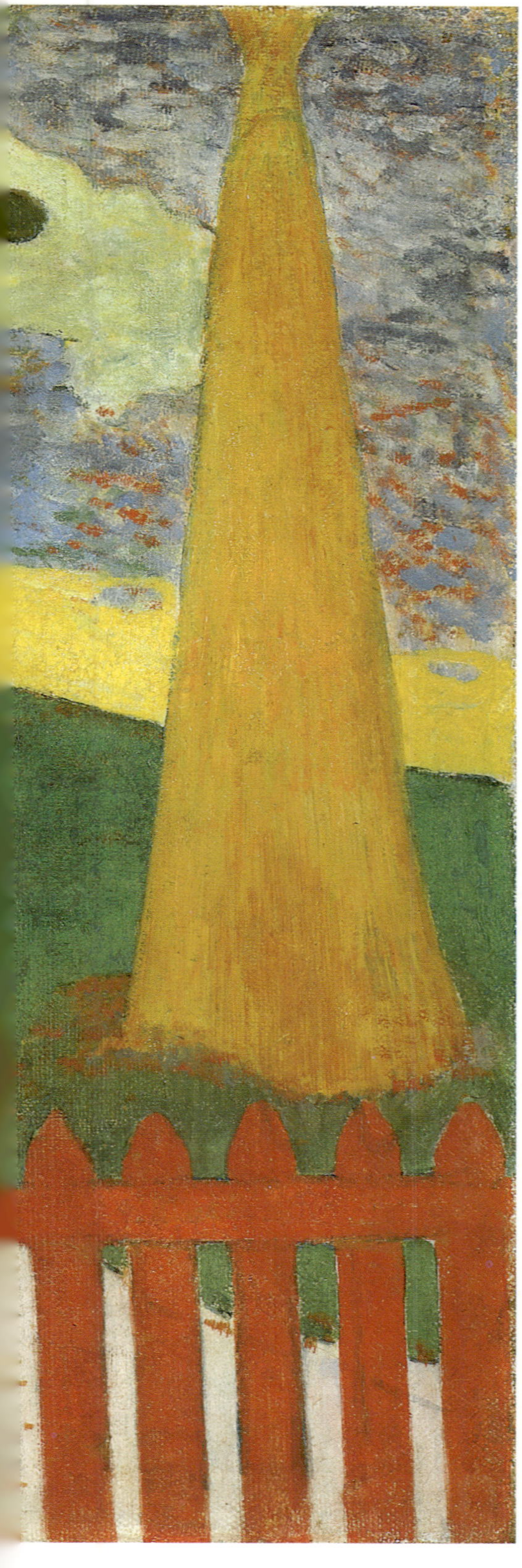

his reputation as a dealer of 'modern' pictures, his gallery was seriously committed to *animalier* bronzes. This was a market opportunity he could ill afford to miss. Barye sold well.[187] Theo also had some pieces by Rodin. In 1888 Fénéon mentions seeing a female figure – a study for the *Gates of Hell* – and in an undated note (probably from the following year) Rodin wrote that he was sending Theo a cast of his *Victor Hugo* [**135**].[188]

Theo was on more adventurous ground in handling the three-dimensional work of Raffaëlli and Gauguin. At his show in May-June 1890, Raffaëlli exhibited eight bronzes. Several of them were extremely unconventional, and drew much enthusiastic critical attention. Borrowing somewhat from oriental silhouettes, these sculptures were designed to hang on the wall like pictures and featured Raffaëlli's stock subjects of figures from the lower classes, modelled in fairly flat, open relief. [**136**] Geffroy's catalogue introduction notes that these 'sculpture[s] for apartments' were one of the main attractions of the show, and his opinion was echoed by critics such as Lostalot and Aurier, the latter sure that he would have 'a lucrative success' with them.[189] This was clearly also Raffaëlli's intention, and he showed a piece at the Nationale the following year.[190]

Gauguin had been making ceramics [**134**] and sculpted pottery since the winter of 1886-87, and these curious objects – clumsy and 'Peruvian' to match the the artistic persona Gauguin was developing – could be found at 19, Boulevard Montmartre from late 1887, when Fénéon noticed three pieces.[191] In October the following year, Theo, apparently confident that he could sell them, bought 300 francs worth.[192] Theo's interest in Gauguin's three-dimensional work was consistent if low key; for example, Pissarro's solo show in February 1890 was complemented by an important recent sculpted relief by Gauguin [**137**] and several of his ceramics. The exhibition thus recalled the pairing of painting and sculpture at Petit's Monet-Rodin show of the previous year, but in a more radical vein. Like Raffaëlli, Gauguin took advantage of the breakaway Nationale's welcome to the decorative arts, writing delightedly to his wife in

132
Paul Gauguin 1848–1903
Arlesian women, mistral 1890
The Art Institute of Chicago
Mr and Mrs Lewis Larned Coburn Memorial Collection

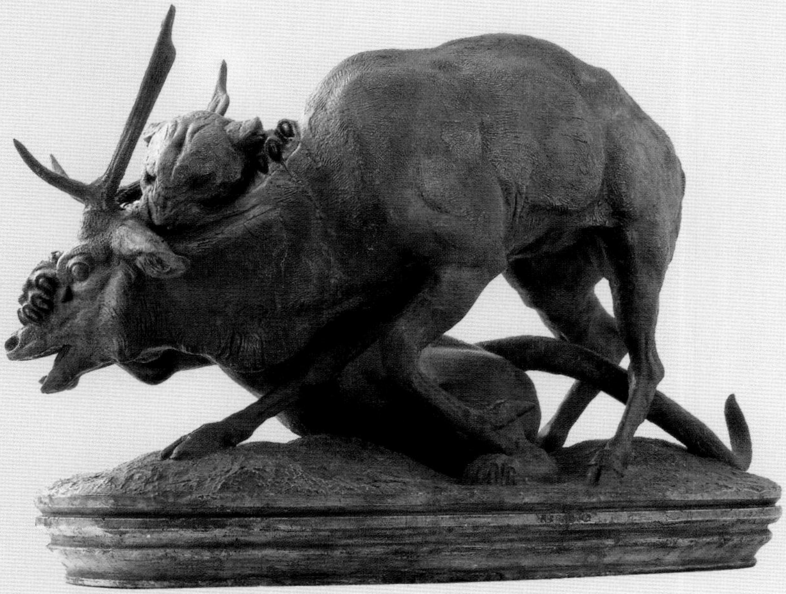

133
Antoine-Louis Barye 1795–1875
Panther attacking a stag n.d.
Musée du Louvre, Paris

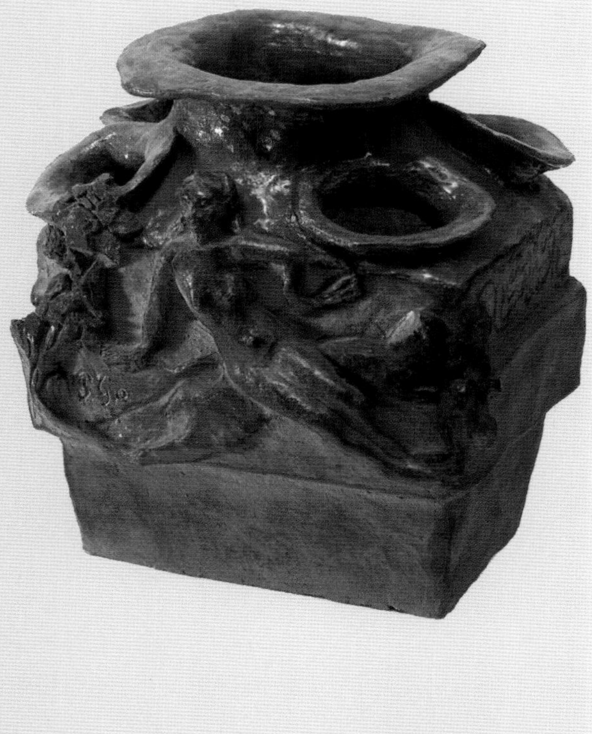

134
Paul Gauguin 1848–1903
Vase 1886–87
Van Gogh Museum, Amsterdam

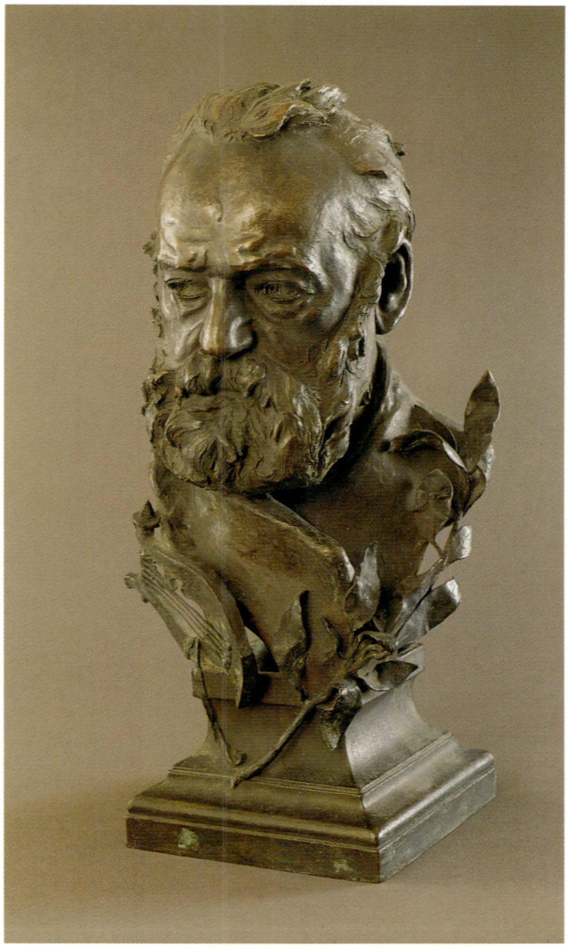

135
Auguste Rodin 1840–1917
Victor Hugo 1883
Musée Rodin, Paris

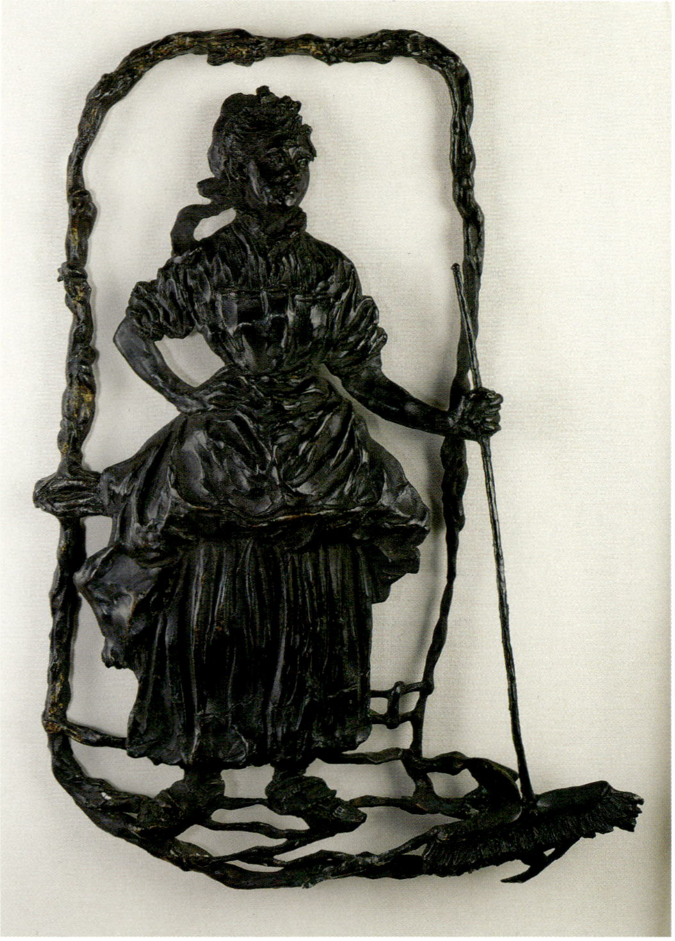

136
Jean-François Raffaëlli 1850–1924
The young housemaid c. 1890
Gerhard Wurzer Gallery/Christopher Drake, Houston

early 1891 that he had been invited to show ceramics there.[193] Here again we see a shift in art world structures. By opening its doors to objects, the new Salon was emulating what had been many dealers' practice for decades. The invitation to Gauguin also posthumously vindicated Theo's support of this avant-garde artist.

So Theo van Gogh was far from just a dealer in paintings. Typical of the art market principle – the wider the range of goods, the greater the chance of sale, and the higher the profits – he stocked and sold works on paper, prints, and sculpture. But apart from this straightforward, market-led policy, which was shared by his rivals, Theo's dealings suggest more than mere trade in *bibelots* for the bourgeois consumer: the notion of an art object that was pleasing, decorative, even quasi-ephemeral rather than ruthlessly speculative was current in his circle – for example, when Pissarro wanted to convey his thanks to Theo for the forthcoming one-man show he gave Johanna a fan. By handling not just four overdoors Pissarro had painted in 1872 for his friend Gustave Arosa, but also Chéret's vivacious posters, Raffaëlli's 'mural' relief sculpture and Gauguin's consciously exotic ceramics, Theo evinced an interest in combining art and decoration in the domestic space. This implicit elision of the experiences of art and life was at the core of the burgeoning Art Nouveau movement, and in anticipating this Theo was ahead of many of his commercial rivals.

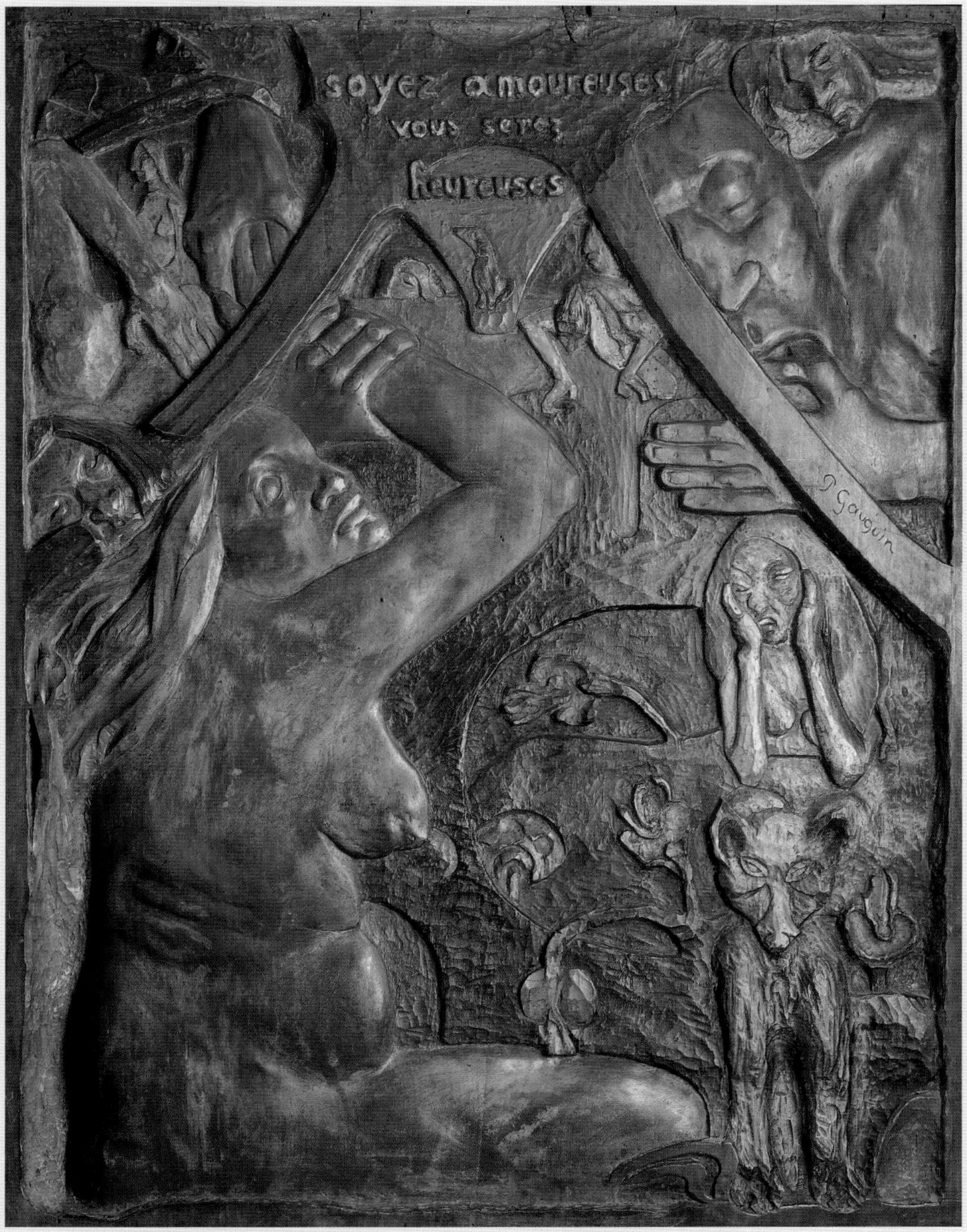

137
Paul Gauguin 1848–1903
Soyez amoureuses 1890
The Museum of Fine Arts, Boston
Arthur Tracy Cabot Fund

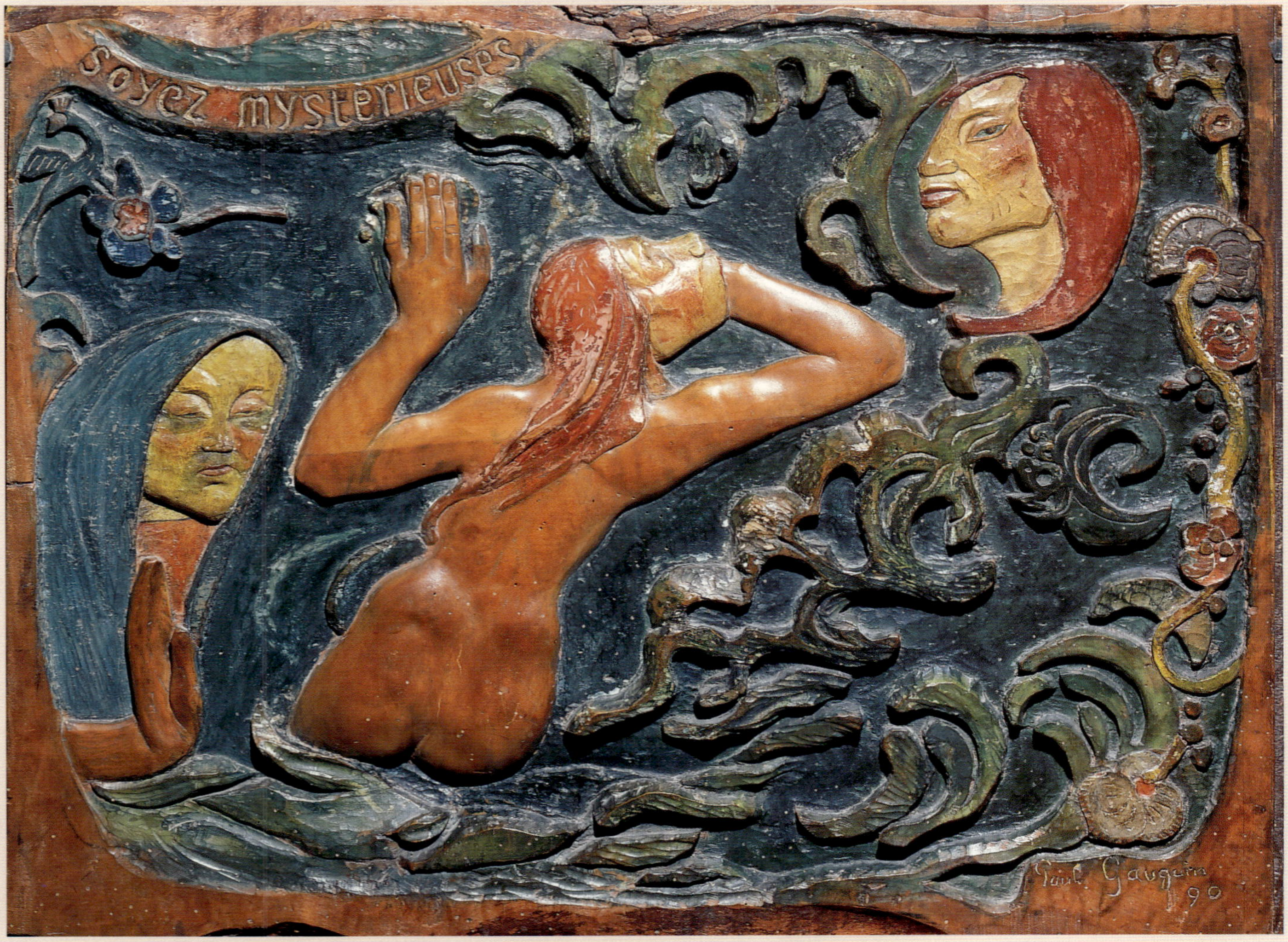

138
Paul Gauguin 1848–1903
Soyez mysterieuses 1890
Musée d'Orsay, Paris

Theo and the avant-garde

Theo's relationship to the more radical painting that emerged during the late 1880s poses an interesting problem. His brother's work constantly exposed him to new art in the making. Theo was the closest witness to Vincent's development, regularly receiving deposits of pictures, as well as letters about his aims and progress. Yet how – as a dealer, as someone whose instincts had been trained by the market, who was 'with the Goupils,' as Vincent put it in late November 1888 [726/563] – was he to come to terms with the avant-garde? Theo's ideas about art had been formed during the 1870s and early 1880s, when stylistic progress was considered a gradual evolution. This was very different from the later 1880s, when competitive avant-gardism began to agitate around the edges of the art market. By that time, many artists were confirming their identity by taking an oppositional stance to the older generation. Most of the 'modern' artists with whom Theo had extensive dealings – Degas, Monet, Raffaëlli, Pissarro, Carrière – had built up their reputations prior to his involvement with them and had (with the exception of Carrière) exhibited at the impressionist shows. However, during the late 1880s, rival groups and alliances began to form and reform, polarising, broadly, around the stylistic alternatives offered by Seurat and, later, Gauguin. Increasingly, it was possible to draw distinctions between the 'modern' and the 'avant-garde.'

These tensions were also felt at 19, Boulevard Montmartre, whether in the neo-impressionist Angrand complaining that Monet's 1889 display demonstrated 'no progress, too much lyricism and too little logic,' or Gauguin suspecting Degas of influencing Theo against his recent work.[194] Avant-garde painters did not have a gallery base in the late 1880s and were forced to show their work where they could: at the Salon des Indépendants, with marginal dealers such as Tanguy, at 'allied' premises like the offices of the *Revue Indépendante*, or improvised locales, most famously the Café Volpini. If an adventurous dealer had emerged, he would have found a stable of artists waiting.

Theo, however, seems to have been wary of moving in this direction, despite Vincent's urging. Consistent with his essentially naturalist taste, the painting that struck him most at the 1889 Exposition Universelle was a Manet representing a couple with a pram. (Jo was pregnant at the time and Theo's response to art was keenly emotive.) He used this very example to convey his anxieties about recent developments: 'I am of the opinion that the researches of symbolism need go no farther than that picture, and besides, the symbol is not premeditated forcedly' [827/T21].[195]

Theo was cautious about much of the new work he encountered, writing of Seurat's *Chahut* (1889-90, Kröller-Müller Museum, Otterlo), shown at the 1890 Indépendants, that it: 'certainly gives the impression of motion, but it has a very queer appearance, and doesn't have much in the way of ideas' [858/T29]. The previous year he had written to Vincent about Gauguin's carved relief *Soyez amoureuses* **[137]**: 'It is obviously bizarre, and does not express a very sharply defined idea, but it is like a piece of Japanese work, whose meaning, at least for a European, is equally difficult to grasp, but in which one cannot but admire the combination of the lines and the beautiful parts' [821/T20]. This sample of reactions over a roughly six month period encapsulates Theo's attitude to new art. Well aware of his brother's interest in pictorial innovation, he worked at understanding it, but found it uncomfortably difficult.

Theo's doubts extended even to the avant-garde's methods of outreach. As a professional, he visited the Indépendants and the displays at the *Revue Indépendante*, and was happy for an artist like his brother to exhibit at such venues, although they were implicitly very low in the art world hierarchy [680/534]. On the other hand, he strongly disapproved of the Gauguin group's Café Volpini initiative, which 'gave one somewhat the impression of going to the Exposition Universelle by the back stairs' [783/T10]. This was an establishment position; Theo disliked disruption to the art trade's systems. Moreover, the exclusion of Toulouse-Lautrec on the grounds that he had shown with the Cercle ran counter to both Theo's naturalist taste and his feeling that, for the best results, the 'modern' should be construed broadly.

Just how Theo was perceived as a dealer can be gleaned from a report by the Belgian artist Theo van Rysselberghe from the autumn of 1889, made while scouting Paris for the radical Brussels exhibition society Les XX. He contacted Theo about Sisley, Degas and Gauguin, but knew he had to go elsewhere for Toulouse-Lautrec, the neo-impressionists Gausson, Hayet and Dubois-Pillet, and to the Volpini for Filiger.[196] By this account, it was essentially impressionist work that could be expected at 19, Boulevard Montmartre; the avant-garde was apparently considered outside Theo's expertise.

Henri de Toulouse-Lautrec

There were, of course, exceptions. Toulouse-Lautrec, with his economical contours and penchant for quasi-caricature, was gradually extending the boundaries of naturalism in the later 1880s. He established his reputation by publishing illustrations and exhibiting substantial canvases at the Indépendants in 1889 and 1890. Theo probably became acquainted with him through Vincent, for the two artists had been fellow pupils at the *atelier* Cormon in 1886. This meant that the inexperienced Lautrec was among the first 'modern' artists with whom Theo had regular dealings.

In early 1887 the painter asked him for advice about a friend's work, and later that year his aristocratic family, although distasteful of his low-life naturalism, were nevertheless proud that he had four pictures on view 'at the big art dealer, Goupil's.'[197] In January 1888 Theo purchased the *Poudre de riz* [**177**] for his and Vincent's own collection, and at the same time Manzi bought a couple of paintings, probably ones that had been on display.[198] Later that year *Paris Illustré* published some of Lautrec's work as illustrations.[199]

Despite this support, only one Lautrec sale is registered in the stockbooks. Listed only as *Study of a head*, the picture – probably *Woman in the garden of Père Forest* [**139**] – was sold to Dupuis for 350 francs. There may have been other sales that remained unregistered, but the evidence suggests that Theo did little to promote Lautrec's work. His mixed response to the artist's *Training the new girls at the Moulin Rouge* at the 1890 Indépendants – he found it had 'great distinction' despite its 'scabrous theme' – seems to suggest that Lautrec's louche subject matter troubled him [858/T29].

Paul Gauguin

Theo's dealings with Gauguin brought him up against a leading and combative figure of the avant-garde. Their association was greatly complicated by Gauguin's fractious relationship with Vincent, and by his somewhat arrogant belief that his own earlier business experience gave him a greater understanding of how the art market worked than most artists. These personal connections are not for consideration here, but it is perhaps worth pointing out that, had they not existed, Gauguin's dealings with Theo would probably have differed little from, for example, Guillaumin's. Given his financial difficulties, it was certainly to the artist's advantage to cultivate Theo's newly found interest in former impressionist exhibitors from mid-1887. His initial contact with 19, Boulevard Montmartre was both as a seller – he planned to trade in a Manet canvas that December – and an artist: Theo took *Boys bathing* on consignment, an innocuous subject picture which he sold to Dupuis on Boxing Day.[200]

Theo probably considered his relations with Gauguin as simply another part of his phased business strategy. Just as the shift in taste and the release of capital from the 1887 Goupil sale freed him to move more purposefully into the established impressionist market, so with the success of Monet's Antibes paintings a year later he was in a position to try to open new areas in the same field. At this stage, Gauguin was still an 'impressionist' painter, and the five canvases Theo took from him on consignment between October and December 1888 were landscapes or unexceptional Breton figure subjects that were not particularly adventurous in style.[201] Again, all were sold quickly in what look like pre-arranged sales.[202]

In late summer 1888 Theo came into a small inheritance from Uncle Cent, using it to set up a deal with Gauguin, whom he would pay 150 francs a month in return for 12 canvases a year.[203] This was not visionary charity, the selfless sponsoring of an avant-garde artist. Undoubtedly the arrangement was at least partly intended to bribe Gauguin into keeping Vincent company, thus taking some pressure off Theo. From a business point of view, it represented the reinvestment of capital for future profit: the half-dozen paint-

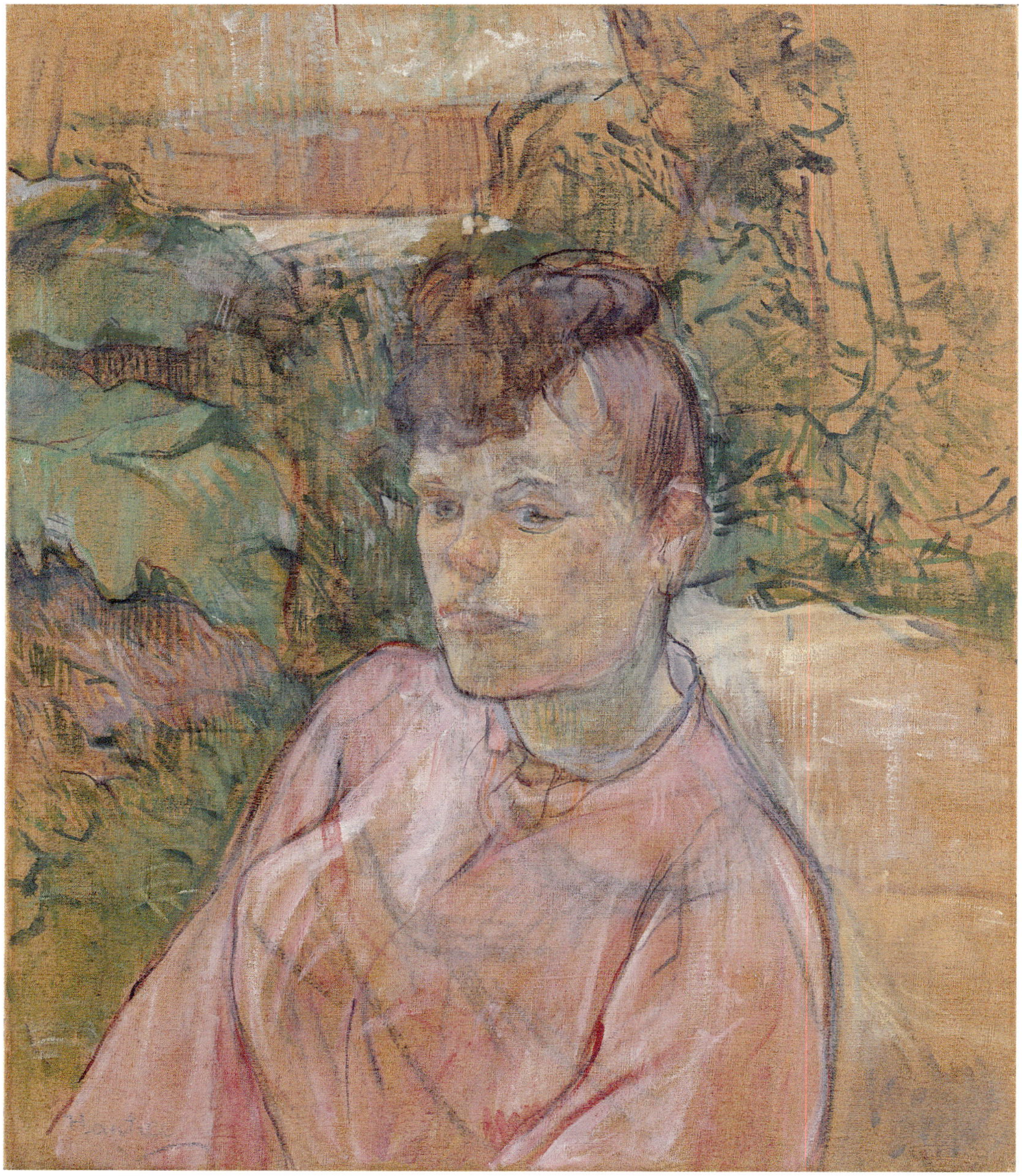

139
Henri de Toulouse-Lautrec 1864–1901
Woman in the garden of Père Forest c. 1887-88
The Metropolitan Museum of Art, New York
Bequest of Joan Whitney Payson

ings Theo bought before the end of 1888 cost an average of 320 francs, so his monthly stipend was to bring in work with a reasonable prospect of return at a very competitive rate.

Although the scheme collapsed following the crisis with Vincent at Christmas Gauguin and Theo maintained their business relations. [142, 143] This certainly indicates an absence of hard feelings on both sides, but it also suggests that Theo was concerned to preserve the link with an eye to the future. Gauguin's 1889 *carnet* reveals that Theo bought drawings, including two pastels that he kept for the brothers' collection, an album of zincographs, and both a canvas of negresses painted in Martinique in 1887 and an Arles scene.[204]

Gauguin's work was now distinctly different from the impressionist canvases he had earlier sold to Theo. This was not unproblematic. In November 1888 Theo found it necessary to ask the artist to retouch the hands in *The dance of the Breton girls* [140] because a potential buyer had asked him to; in the event, the picture did not sell until the following September.[205] Gauguin's paintings were difficult to sell: if the *Danc*e went to a collector it was artists who bought the only other two canvases.[206] [141] Gauguin himself sensed that his work was becoming less marketable, writing to Emile Bernard in November that he was going to hold on to his recent *Christ in the Garden of Olives*: 'useless to show it to Van Gogh; it will be even less understood than the rest.'[207] *La belle Angèle*, sent to Theo at the end of the summer, found no purchaser.

The first time Boussod, Valadon & Cie. actually bought a painting from Gauguin, rather than taking it on consignment, was in April 1890. This was a still-life with oranges, hardly representative of Gauguin the radical leader of the symbolist avant-garde, but something that appealed to the composer Ernest Chausson enough for him to buy it four months later. Theo was able to sell the paintings of Degas and Monet not only because they had reputations but because their work was a recognisable commodity; even Pissarro's canvases, which he had taken on after the artist had begun his neo-impressionist phase, had a stylistic consistency. Under pressure to generate an individual avant-garde identity, Gauguin kept changing the way his art looked, making it more difficult for the market to grasp. The further Gauguin moved from impressionism, a market 'brand,' the harder it became to sell his paintings. It is to Theo's credit that he was consistent with his gradualist market policy and kept Gauguin's work before the public eye, thus earning the artist's respect and gratitude.

Theo's other excursions into fields which were then considered difficult or radical were few and far between. In December 1889 he bought a painting, *In Heaven*, and a *Profile of a woman*, probably a work on paper, from Odilon Redon, whose strange imaginative world appealed to a rather elitist taste; these do not appear in the stockbooks. The following May, another Redon oil, *Virgin of the dawn* [144], was listed, being an arranged sale to Chausson; the *Mystic head* Redon sold to Theo on 7 June, however, went unrecorded.[208] Theo showed no interest in Cézanne's work,[209] but then, there was no reason why he should have: Cézanne was not exhibiting in Paris at the time, had no substantive critical support, and practically no collectors. For the radical young artists who emerged in the late 1880s, Theo did next to nothing. We have seen that he purchased some woodcuts from Lucien Pissarro but, despite his connection to the printing works, nothing else.[210] Fénéon noticed that Theo put a still-life by Emile Schuffenecker [145] on display, though this is the only evidence of any commercial contact between dealer and painter. There is even evidence of Theo purposefully not supporting the avant-garde: Vincent suggested he include a head of a Breton woman by Emile Bernard with the paintings going to Tersteeg, but he did not [591/471]. Not surprisingly, the only 'radical' artist he seems to have really tried to help was his own brother. In March 1888 one of Vincent's canvases was among the batch sent to The Hague; it was returned unsold. A recently published letter, apparently in Theo's hand, mentions a self-portrait by 'V. van Gogh' sent to the London firm of Laurie & Co. with a Corot, but neither of these paintings have been traced, leaving the arrangement mysterious.[211]

Theo might easily have made himself the dealer of several leading lights of the Parisian avant-garde, among them Seurat, Signac, Anquetin and Toulouse-Lautrec. But all these artists had some degree of private means; they did not need to push for sales as Gauguin did, and Theo did not pursue them. On the other hand, he does seem to have realised that han-

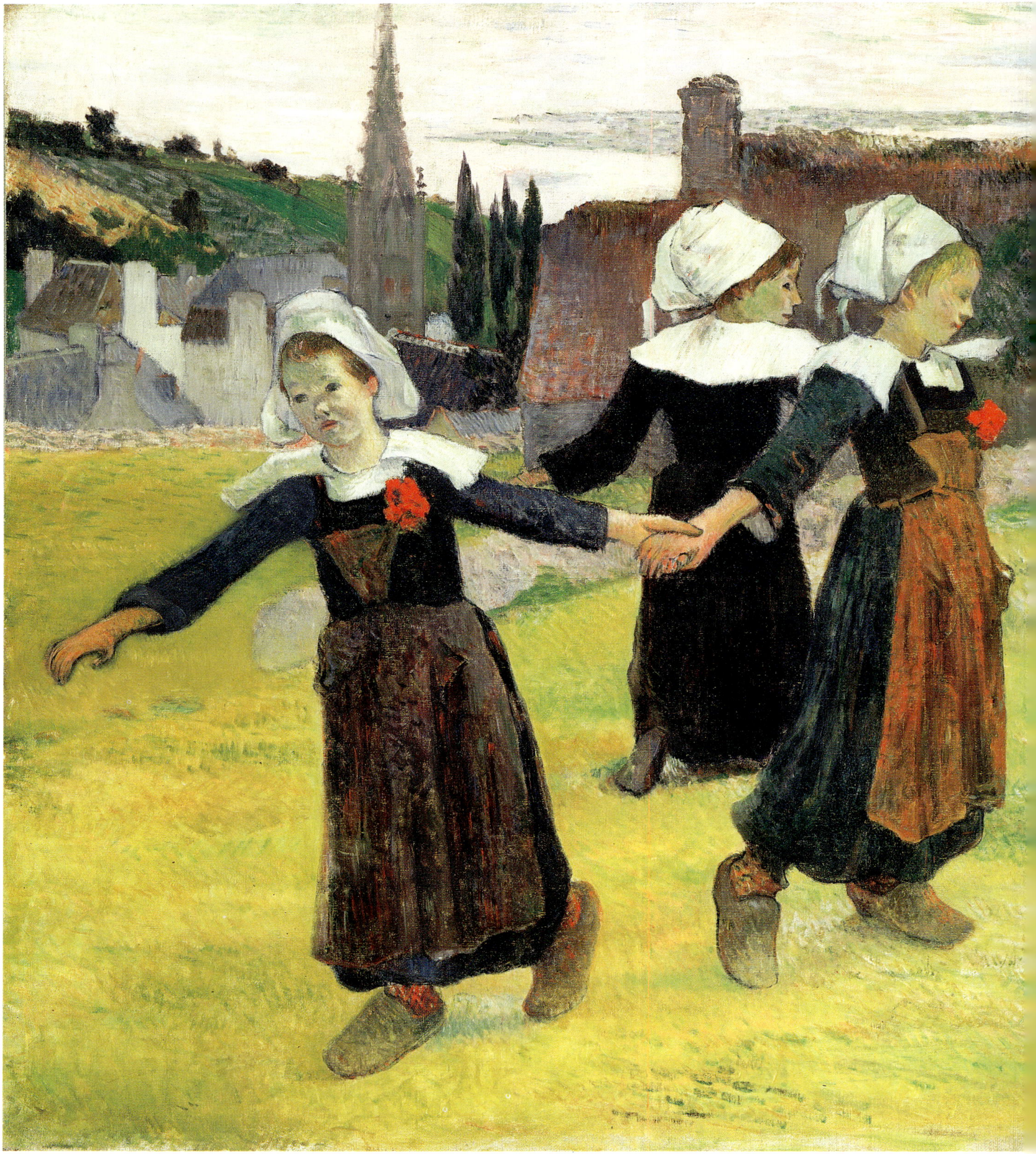

dling some challenging new work could be fruitful. It made pictures that had once looked difficult seem more acceptable, and for a collector to be a step behind the most radical work encouraged speculation. It may be that Theo had this in mind when he showed Gauguin at 19, Boulevard Montmartre: by contrast Monet or Pissarro looked more conventional. And, in turn, it pushed Gauguin's work up another layer in the market. In the end, Theo was not as thoroughgoing a dealer of the avant-garde as he might have been, or as we might assume given his relations with Gauguin and, above all, Vincent. His professional instinct told him that the market for the avant-garde, such as it was, did not yet warrant indiscreet investment. In the 1890s that market began to expand, and dealers such as Le Barc de Boutteville and Vollard emerged, but that was after Theo van Gogh's death.

Theo van Gogh in retrospect

Theo's mental and physical collapse in October 1890, and his death the following January, removed him from the Paris art world both tragically young and too early for him to have reaped the benefits of his venturesome dealing policy. The immediate impact of his disappearance from the scene on the artists with whom he had had dealings was varied. The well-placed Raffaëlli could afford to be wise after the fact, claiming he had seen Theo's breakdown coming.[212] But for Gauguin, much more dependent upon Theo's support, it was 'a real disaster': Boussod, Valadon & Cie. stopped taking his work, forcing him to try and set up little deals for himself.[213] For the practical Pissarro, whose market position was somewhere between the desperation of Gauguin and the relative security of Raffaëlli, it was a question of building on the success of Theo's one-man show and finding a supportive successor.

Durand-Ruel was quick to take commercial advantage of Theo's demise. In late 1890 he wrote to Pissarro claiming to always have been a 'warm supporter' of even his recent work, and stating that 'the sole obstacle to our business has been that wretched Van Gogh, who has finished so miserably. He had put spokes in the wheels and I never really understood your liking for him. Now that he's gone, count on me absolutely.'[214]

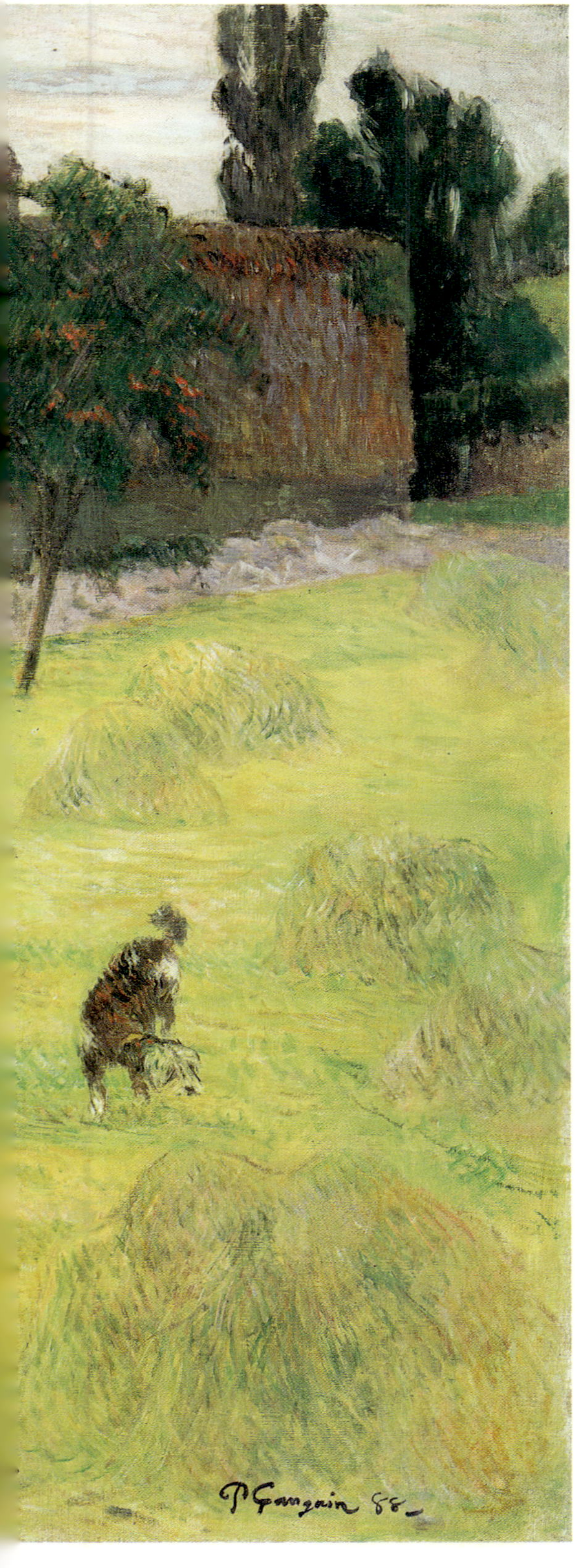

140
Paul Gauguin 1848–1903
The dance of the Breton girls 1888
National Gallery of Art, Washington, DC
Collection of Mr and Mrs Paul Mellon

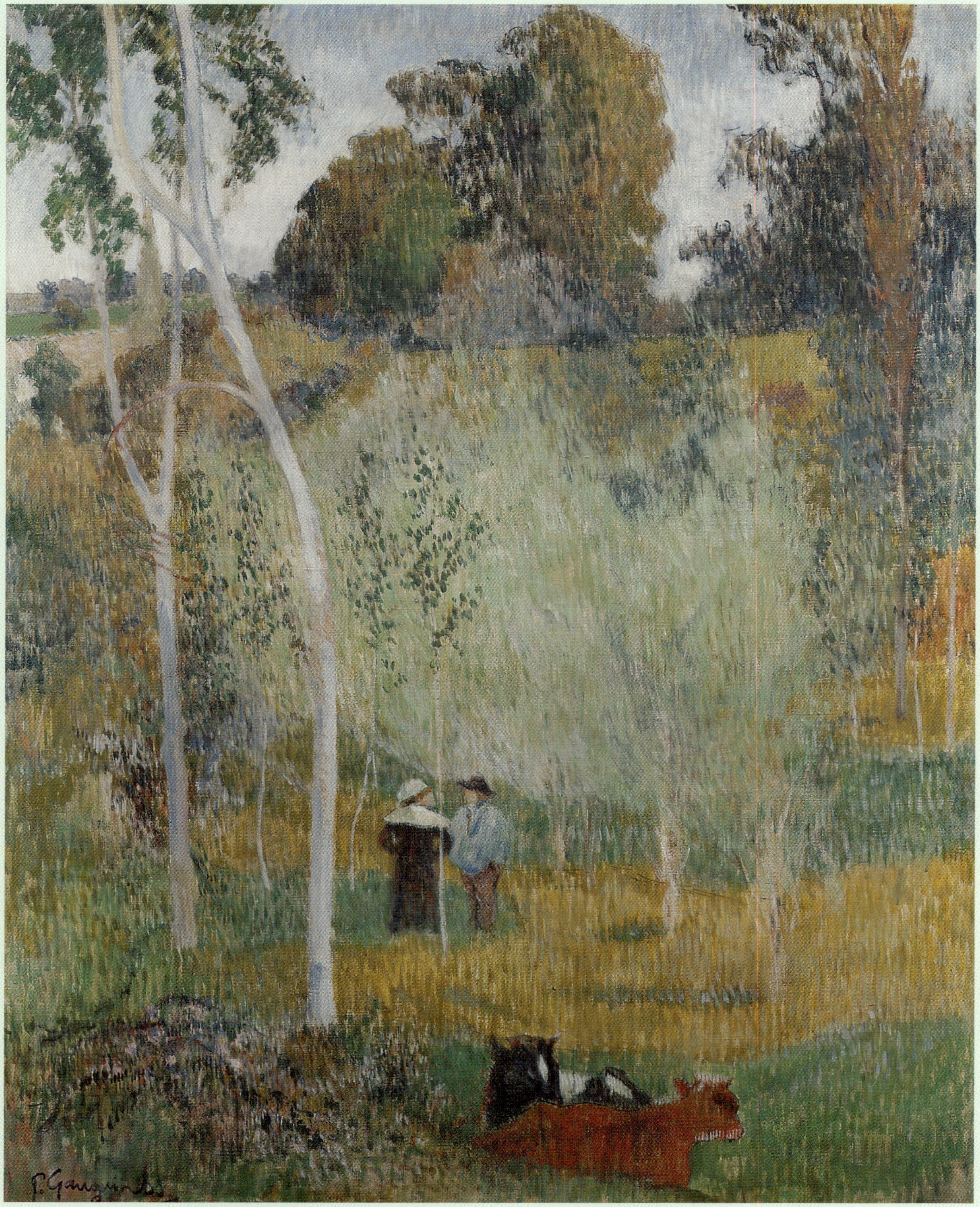

141
Paul Gauguin 1848–1903
Conversation: Bretagne 1888
Koninklijke Musea voor Schone Kunsten van België, Brussels

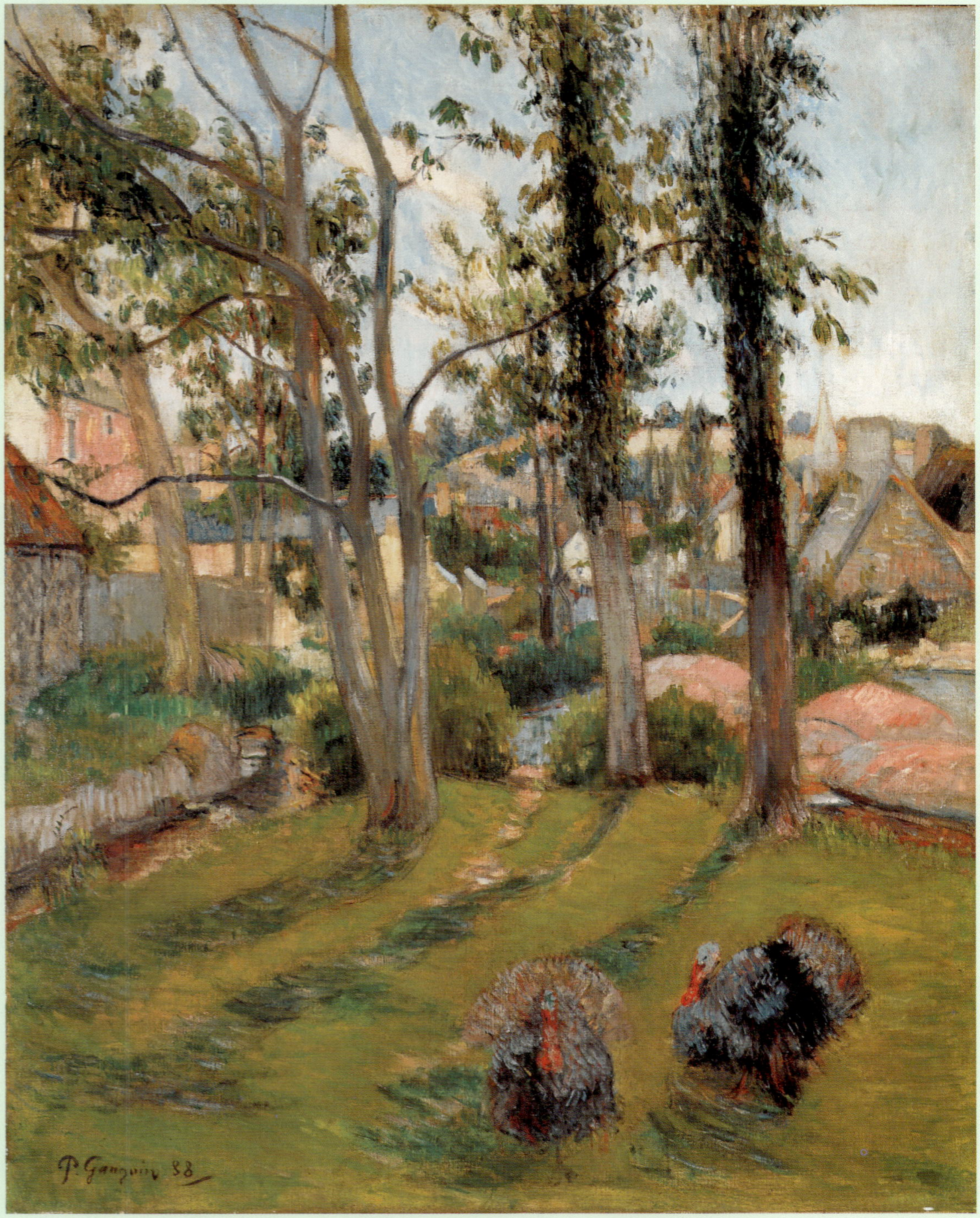

142

Paul Gauguin 1848–1903

Les dindons 1888

The Mr and Mrs C. Foundation

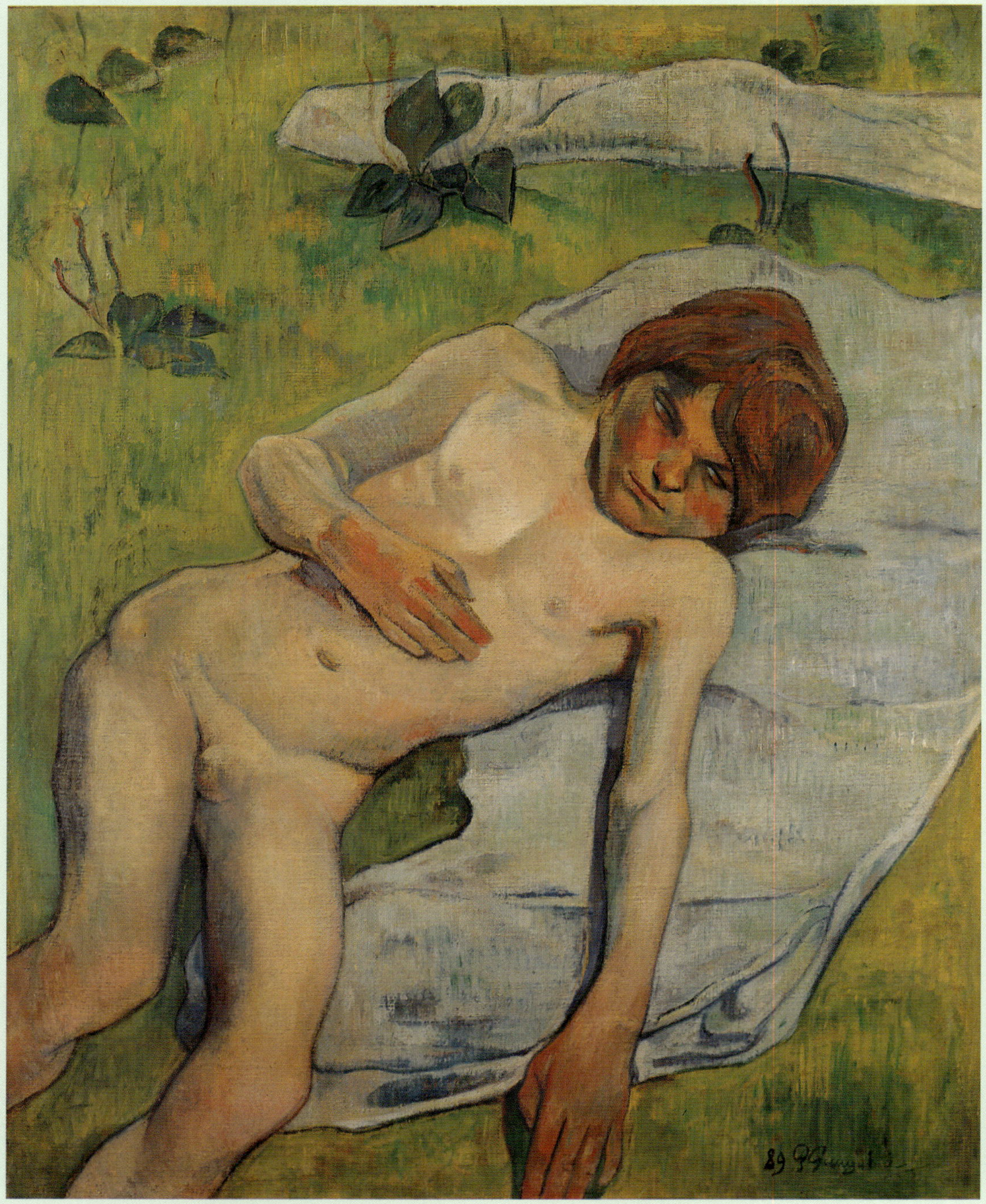

143
Paul Gauguin 1848–1903
Naked Breton boy 1889
Wallraf-Richartz Museum, Cologne

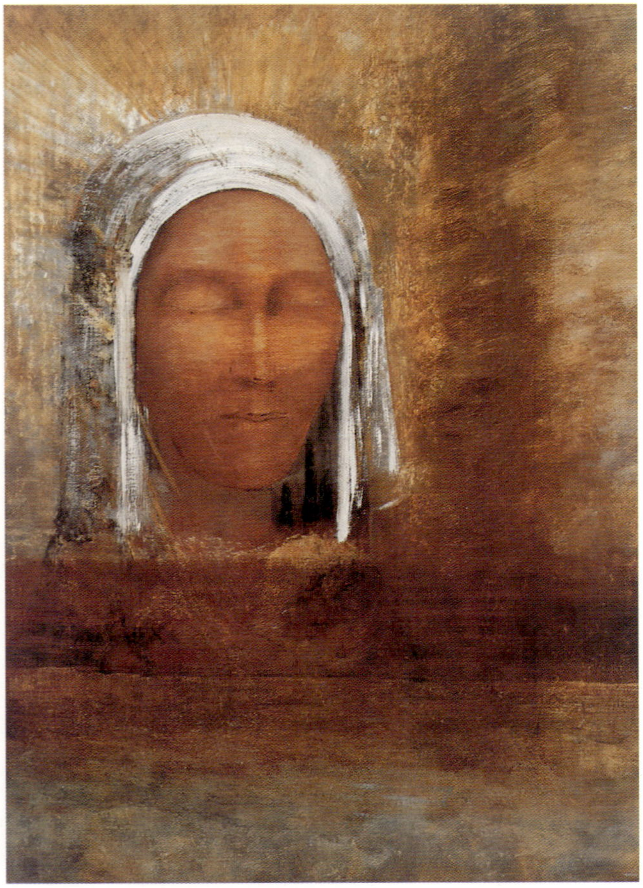

144
Odilon Redon 1840–1916
Virgin of the dawn 1890
Collection of Miranda and Robert Donneley, Chicago

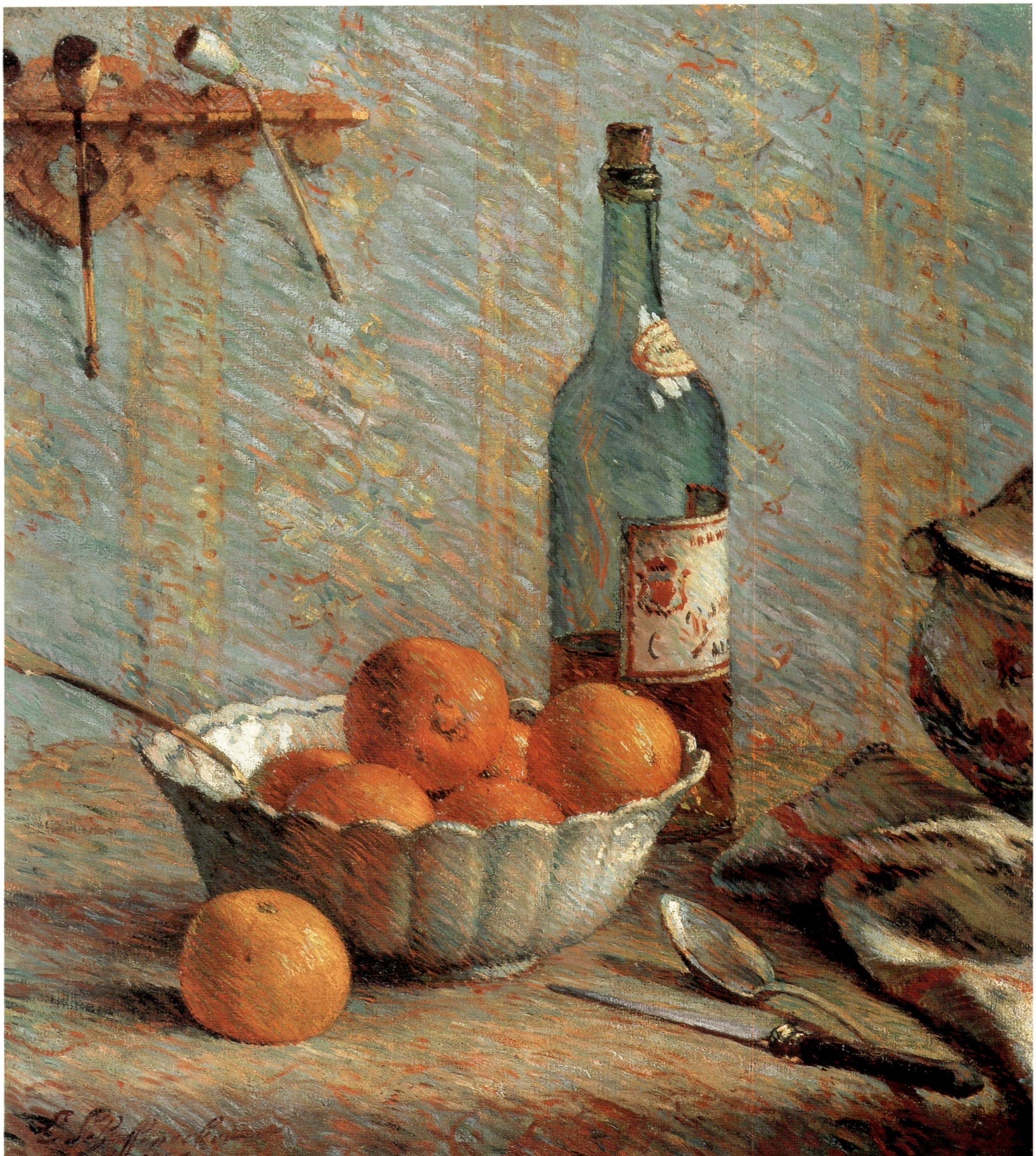

145
Emile Schuffenecker 1851–1934
Still life with a bowl of fruit 1886
Kröller-Müller Museum, Otterlo

Durand did not immediately help the artist as much as he promised, however, and Pissarro was forced to turn to lesser dealers such as Portier. There can be no doubt that Theo's exit from the scene caused considerable worry to independent and less commercially viable artists; those in better positions could afford to take a more sanguine view.

However, whatever stir Theo's death caused among the visitors to his *entresol* and the fringe community of independent artists, the larger Parisian art world took no notice of the passing of the *gérant* of 19, Boulevard Montmartre.[215] Maurice Joyant was appointed to take his place. His slightly self-serving recollection of the takeover, written 35 years later, hints that while Theo had some adventurous stock in place, he, Joyant, was able to prevent the branch from closing with the help, above all, of Carrière.[216] However, as we have seen, Carrière had been cultivated by Theo for some time, and the one-man show Joyant staged in April 1891 was essentially a continuation of Theo's policy.[217] Theo's purchasing practices were also more or less continued: Boussod, Valadon & Cie. bought 16 Monets in 1891, half of them selling the same year for profits of 50 percent or above, the only lesser profit being on a canvas Valadon marked down for himself! Here was vindication of Theo's future-oriented planning and evidence of the support he had won from his employers. Like Theo, Joyant continued to exploit the company's international network, so when David Croal Thomson of the firm's London branch passed on the news that Whistler wanted to sell *Arrangement in grey and black no.1: the artist's mother* (1871, Musée d'Orsay, Paris) it was Joyant who sounded out the French authorities prior to the State's purchase of the picture.[218]

What, then, was Theo van Gogh's achievement? He had proven himself a good employee, loyally and busily fulfilling his daily functions as a gallery manager. Although there is much that we will probably never know about his business practice, it is probably best to beware of the Manichean division, suggested by interpreters from Veth to Rewald, between the 'bad' art Theo sold to court a tasteless market and the 'good' art he bought to support the heroic impressionist or avant-garde painters. This account is too simplistic. We have heard Corcos complain about having to produce work to satisfy the market, arguing that he would rather paint less commercial pictures. On the other hand, Monet had to face Fénéon's charge that his landscapes were increasingly geared to market success. Both Corcos and Monet, however different their work and distinct their artistic calibre, were nevertheless similarly driven by commercial imperatives to deliver pictures which would find ready buyers. And, besides, it was Theo's task to sell his stock, not to have preferences about it. The fact that he continually bought and sold work by painters as different as Corcos, Kaemmerer, Henner and Monet was simply disinterested good business, working for the company.

Theo played his part in the modernisation of the firm that had taken place in mid-decade. While we will likely never know the extent to which he was responsible for Boussod, Valadon & Cie.'s active entry into the impressionist and 'modern' market in 1887, or was merely an instrument of his superiors, he undoubtedly pursued the new direction with prudence and success. His support for Carrière and Raffaëlli shows not only that his search for 'modern' artists for the gallery's stable was broad-based – itself good business policy – but also well directed, for both men developed major reputations during the 1890s.

Among the impressionists, Theo built up profitable connections with the most commercially viable, Degas and Monet, while nurturing the relationship with Pissarro and taking care to avoid over-commitment or misplaced confidence, as in the case of Sisley. Theo and his employers were neither the first nor the only dealers pushing impressionism; they were part of a current which, as the decade passed, swept its leading figures from controversial exhibitors at marginal group shows to the status of profitable celebrities with an international cachet. Theo deserves considerable credit for his part in this process. In developing the impressionist market for Boussod, Valadon & Cie. with a view to his clients' mid-to-long term investments, Theo's commercial counsel was efficacious. This became evident posthumously, with the sale of the Aubry collection on 12 May 1897. Aubry had bought two of Monet's Antibes canvases from the one-man show in June 1888 for 2,800 francs each; nine years later they made 6,300 and 7,500, respectively. A Sisley bought in August 1887 for a paltry 150 francs did even better, increasing its value eightfold to 2,350.[219] Theo van Gogh's investment advice was clearly worth its weight in gold.

Artists trusted Theo van Gogh because he was a man of principle. This is demonstrated in Pissarro's letters, which show how much he valued Theo's commercial counsel and his gratitude for the intelligent way the sympathetic dealer could talk about modern painting.[220] Gauguin's letters, while at times aggressively avant-gardist and antimarket – the artist works 'more for art than his business deals,' he insisted in 1889 – nevertheless evince a genuine need for constructive dialogue.[221] What emerges most clearly in the thinking of independent painters in the later 1880s, still uncertain of their market position, is their pressing need for support. When Pissarro craved 'a man confident enough in my talent to furnish me with enough to live on,'[222] or Gauguin dreamt of finding the capital to 'set up a dealer in impressionist pictures' [626/496], they were asking for surety to sustain their work. This is what Theo was remarkably successful in providing. He offered steadiness: he bought work, found clients, and increased purchases when he could.

Working within the market as he necessarily did, Theo could hardly have been expected to have given more support to the fractured and still-nascent avant-garde. As *gérant* of 19, Boulevard Montmartre he helped move his company's business towards more up-to-date markets; made sound profits with staples such as Corot, while either moving away from or not risking commercial uncertainties. He gave his clientele a wide range of choice across the spectrum of contemporary art, including sculpture, prints and other works on paper, so building on the bourgeois appetite for the *bibelot*. He developed the marketability of modern artists with different tendencies, from Degas to Jongkind, Monet to Carrière, Pissarro to Raffaëlli; and, by giving Gauguin all the help he could, backed one of the most difficult but significant avant-garde artists of the period. This is a very substantial roster of achievement. Although Theo died young, his policy of gradual investment in new and difficult art, with a view to long-term rather than immediate results, established a blueprint business strategy for trading modern work, which Joyant, Vollard and others in the 1890s would emulate. When we place his activities and accomplishments in the complex context of the Parisian art world of the 1880s it becomes clear that, in his undemonstrative way, Theo van Gogh was an art dealer of integrity, vision and determination, truly an honest broker.

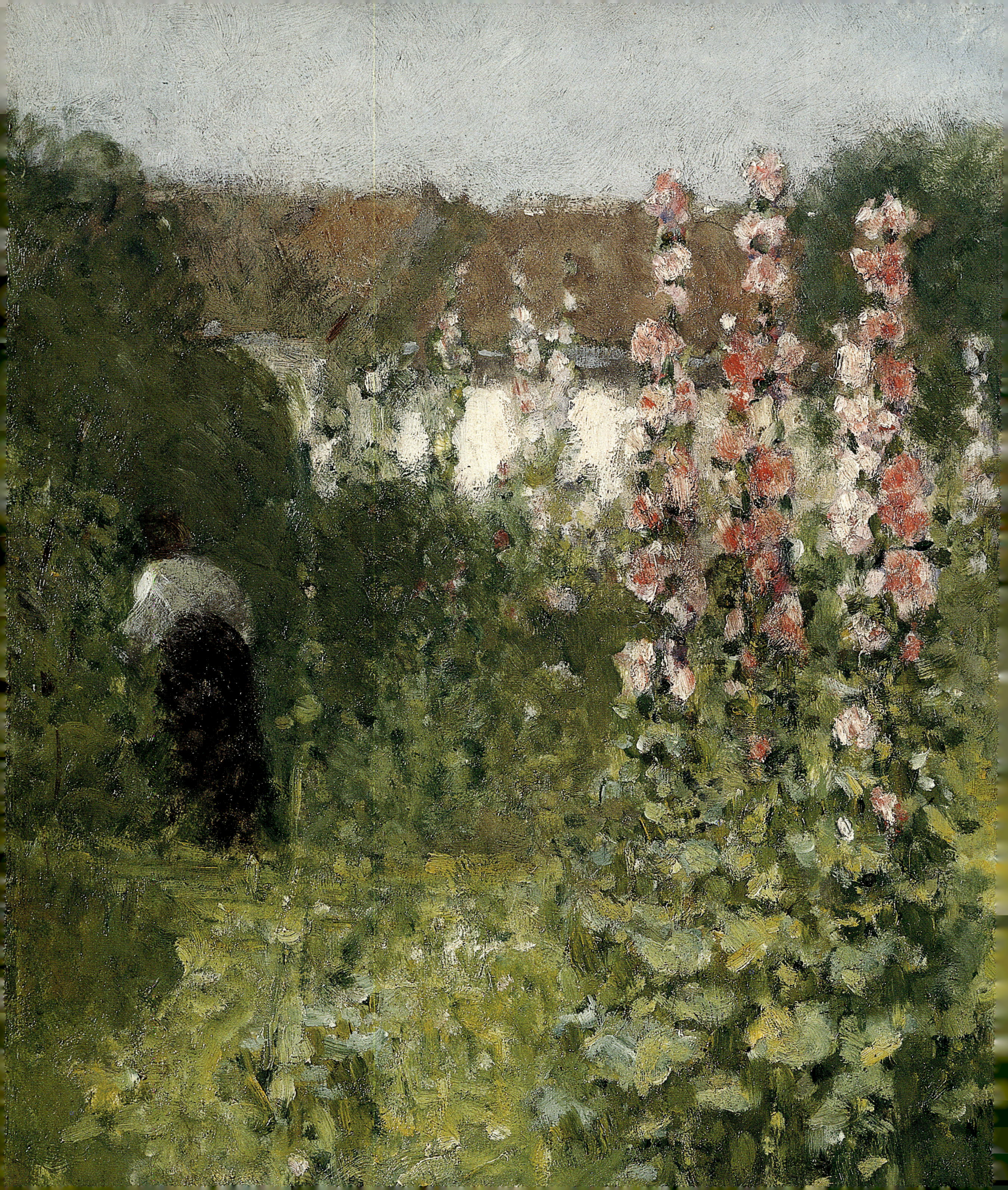

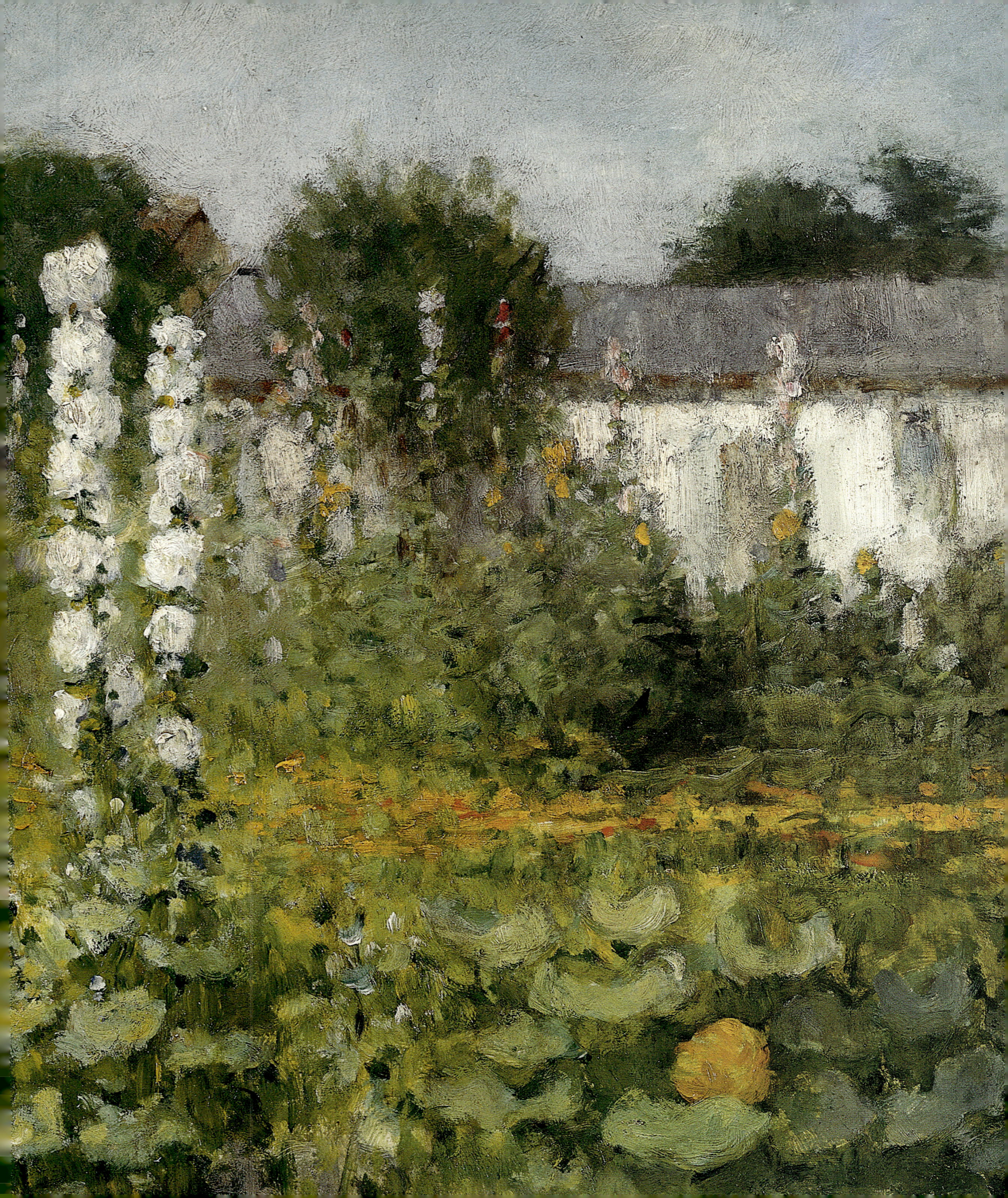

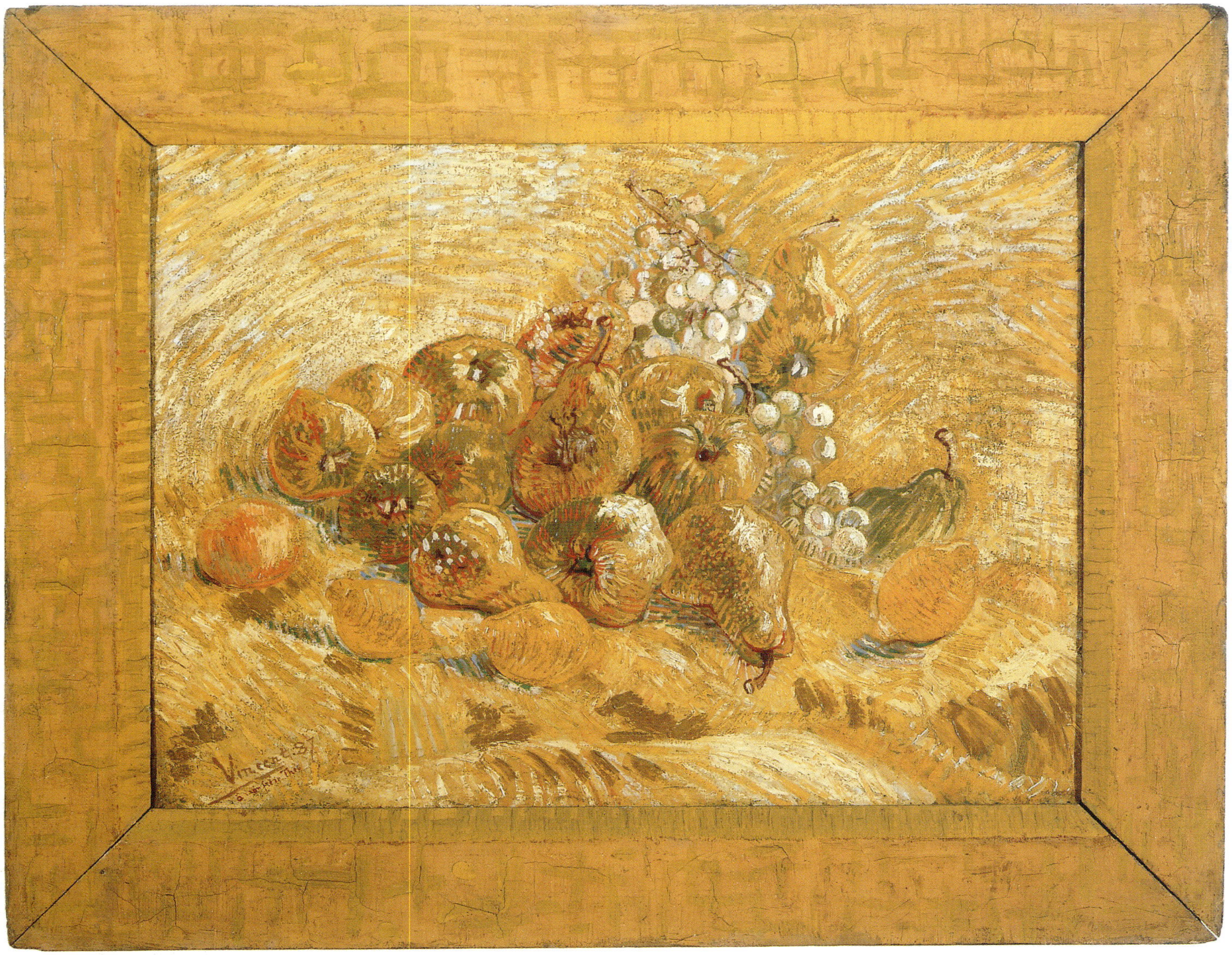

146
Vincent van Gogh 1853–1890
Lemons, pears, apples, grapes and an orange 1887
Van Gogh Museum, Amsterdam

The collector

Theo van Gogh

Sjaar van Heugten and Chris Stolwijk

Theo van Gogh regarded works of art as 'good friends to live with.'[1] In a relatively short period of time, and with a modest budget, he managed to assemble a collection of works in various media by many more or less leading modern artists. This article considers Theo van Gogh's development and activity as a collector. Since little is known of the provenances of the works in Theo's collection, now in the Van Gogh Museum, this contribution will be largely exploratory in nature. The emphasis will be on works by painters other than Theo's brother, who is, of course, well represented in the collection.[2]

Theo's collection did not remain intact over the years. His wife and heir Johanna van Gogh-Bonger (Jo) regularly sold paintings following her return to the Netherlands; she had single-handedly managed their affairs since Theo's nervous breakdown in October 1890. The works she sold were often by Vincent; these provided her with an income and could enhance her brother-in-law's reputation if displayed in leading museums. Financial considerations played a primary role when she sold paintings by Vincent's contemporaries. Presumably she selected works which were less to her taste and could command a reasonable price.

It is impossible to be sure exactly how many works from Theo van Gogh's collection were ultimately sold. Although (Theo and) Jo's accounts do list several sales, the identity of the works in question is sometimes unclear.[3] Nor were all transactions recorded: for example, there is no mention of the 1897 sale of a Renoir and a Pissarro to the art dealer Ambroise Vollard. Over the years some 12 works disappeared from the collection: two paintings by Théophile de Bock, one by George Breitner, one by Hans Olaf Heijerdahl, one by Ernst Josephson, one by Ernest Quost, one by Odilon Redon, two by Auguste Renoir, one by Camille Pissarro, one or two by Armand Guillaumin,[4] and a watercolour by Hendrik Willem Mesdag.

It is equally difficult to identify which works from the present collection belonged to Theo, to Vincent, or to both – 'our stock' [644/510] as Vincent called it – which the brothers had gathered with a view to starting their own gallery. Moreover, in many instances it is no longer possible to tell which works (by Vincent or other artists) were intended to remain in the collection, and which Vincent and Theo regarded simply as merchandise. Vincent gave Theo several works that we know had a special place in his brother's collection. These include the remarkable *Lemons, pears, apples, grapes and an orange* [**146**]. In his letters, Vincent sometimes mentioned which works might eventually be sold, but this was always his own opinion and Theo did not necessarily agree.

Prints and woodcuts

Theo van Gogh became interested in collecting art at an early age. Later in life he made no secret of the fact

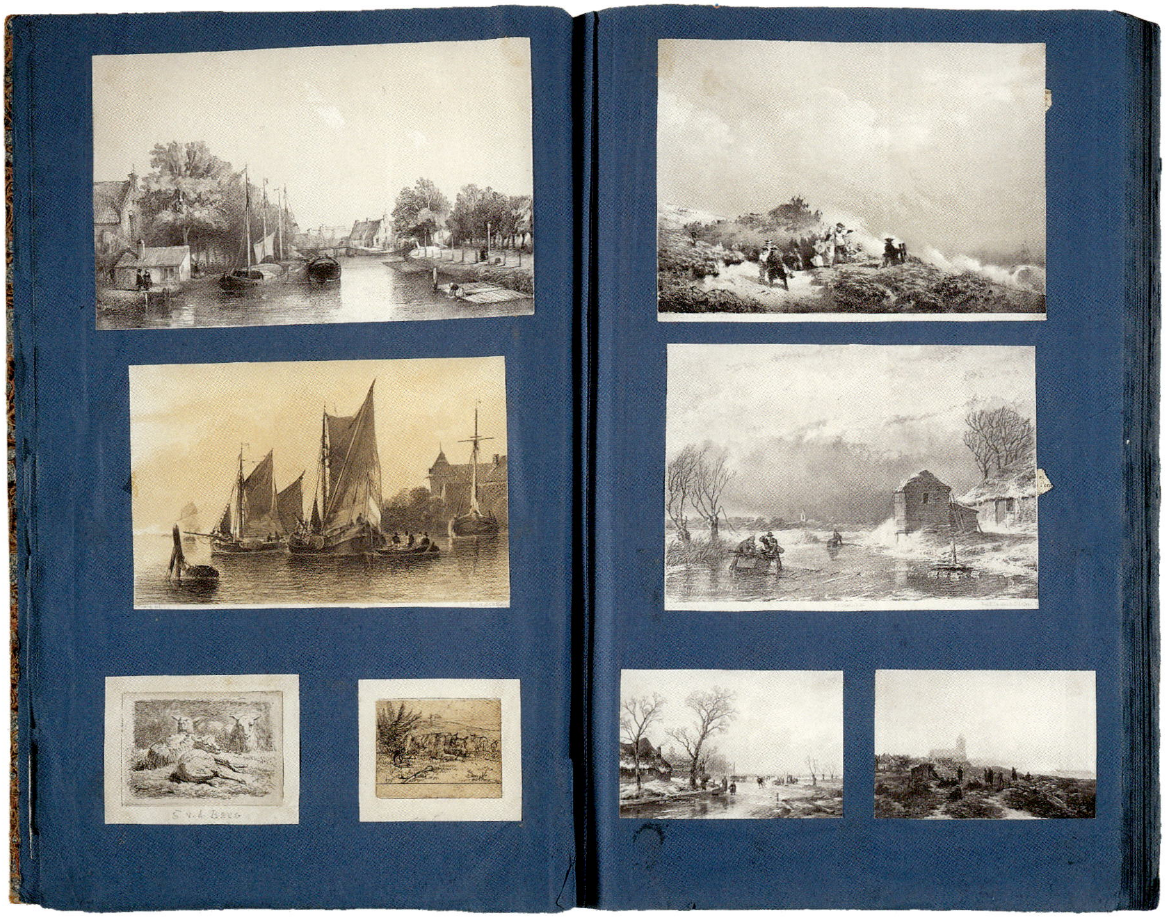

147
Theo van Gogh's scrapbook c. 1870s
Van Gogh Museum, Amsterdam

that his artistic sensibility had been largely formed by Vincent.[5] The brothers' tastes in art overlapped to a great extent, and Theo's ideas were fed by Vincent's careful theorising in his letters and conversations.

Vincent had become an enthusiastic collector of cheap prints in the 1870s, while still working for Goupil & Cie. He was mainly interested in reproductions of (contemporary) paintings. From 1873 Theo was periodically inspired by his brother's example to make similar purchases. These works eventually formed the basis for the modest art collection Theo developed in later years, often in collaboration with Vincent, sometimes at his instigation. The major portion of this collection – paintings, drawings and prints – is now housed in the Van Gogh Museum. If anything from Theo's own print collection has survived, the works in question have been incorporated into the hundreds of sheets collected by his brother.

Vincent's role in his brother's (earliest) collecting activities should not be underestimated, particularly during Theo's formative years in the art trade. Once Theo began working for Goupil & Cie. in January 1873, Vincent encouraged him to form his own opinions on (contemporary) art. On 19 November 1873 he wrote: 'I also look forward to a good talk on art with you; start thinking if you have anything to ask me' [15/12]. He also urged Theo to make lists of the works he saw in order to develop his eye and his memory [137/116a]. It must have given Theo great pleasure to read Vincent's comments on his budding activities as a collector: 'But write and tell me if you have added anything good to your collection, carry on as you have been doing, for it will certainly turn out well the way you have set about things' [140/119].

While working for Goupil & Cie. Theo and Vincent regularly exchanged prints and swapped double copies, as in August 1875 when Vincent wrote to Theo from Paris: 'I'm doing my best to find another Rembrandt engraving, *Lecture de la Bible*, for you [...] Have I sent you a Troyon litho[graph], *Effet de matin*? Français['s], *Derniers beaux jours*? If not, write and tell me; I have them double' [40/33].

Although more is known about Vincent's print collection than Theo's,[6] they were presumably quite similar.[7] [**147**] As employees of one of the major print dealers of the age, the Van Gogh brothers were in a position to survey the market and acquire examples of relatively inexpensive work with comparative ease. During this period both young men collected prints after paintings by Dutch 17th-century masters, and reproductions of work by popular, contemporary artists: painters of the Barbizon School – Charles Daubigny, Jean-François Millet and others – and the Hague School, such as Jozef Israëls and Philip Sadée. Goupil & Cie. published unprecedented numbers of such prints.[8] Vincent and Theo also had a passion for popular prints from illustrated magazines and books, another Goupil speciality.[9]

Theo and Vincent were particularly interested in woodcuts after works by artists who were moderately well known or even famous, and one-off works by the same artists. Vincent proved an avid collector of such prints, as we know from his letters from The Hague. Theo probably collected such work on a more modest scale [**148**]; they were not a source of inspiration for him as they were for Vincent.

Later in life the brothers continued to be beguiled by prints. While staying with Theo in Paris in 1886-88, Vincent built up a collection of Japanese prints from the stock of Siegfried Bing, their art-dealer friend.[10] This collection served a double purpose, providing a source of inspiration for the artist and as potential merchandise, an investment for the future.

Theo seems to have been less enthusiastic about Japanese woodcuts. Vincent's letters from Arles suggest that in July 1888 Theo was seriously considering breaking off their association with Bing and disposing of a substantial portion of the prints. Vincent, however, fiercely opposed such a move and implored his brother to acquire even more woodcuts: 'He [Bing] will give you some very fine ones for stock, of that I'm sure. Well, it's not my business, but our own stock, that's what I value' [644/510]. In Vincent's opinion, Theo's apartment would look very different 'if you didn't have those Japanese objects' [644/510].

Bing only charged Vincent three sous (about 15 centimes) for each woodcut. Vincent expected the work would greatly increase in value over the short term; he suggested to Theo that they might become an attractive asset to exchange for paintings, perhaps even a means of acquiring a painting by Claude Monet. Vincent had good reason to mention this artist, for both brothers admired Monet but lacked the funds to purchase his works. Apparently Vincent knew that Monet collected Japanese prints and fans, and regarded this as a potential avenue for adding one of his paintings to their collection. Vincent's arguments in favour of Japanese prints, however, clearly suggest that Theo felt little enthusiasm for systematically collecting this kind of art.

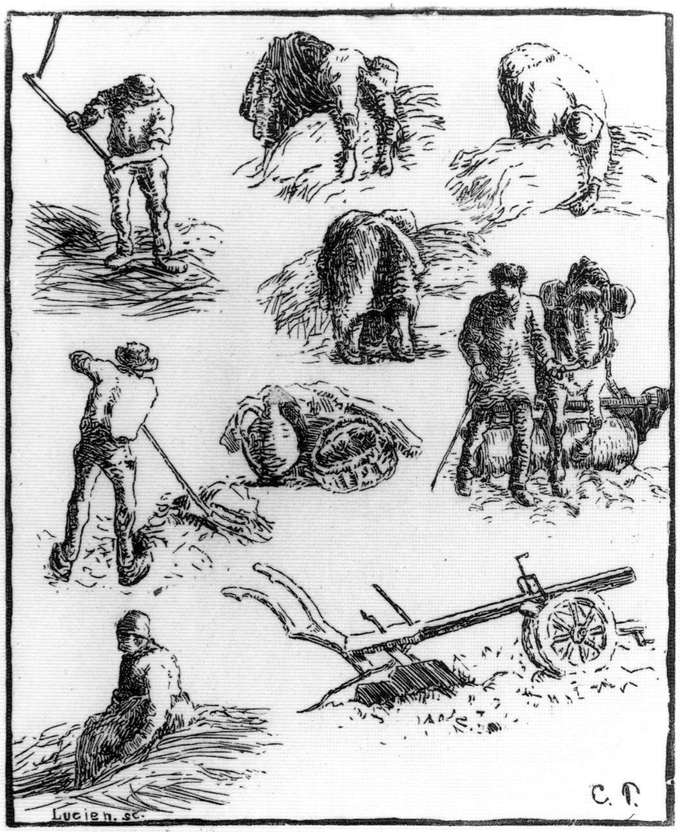

148
Lucien Pissarro 1863–1944
Studies of peasants n.d.
Van Gogh Museum, Amsterdam

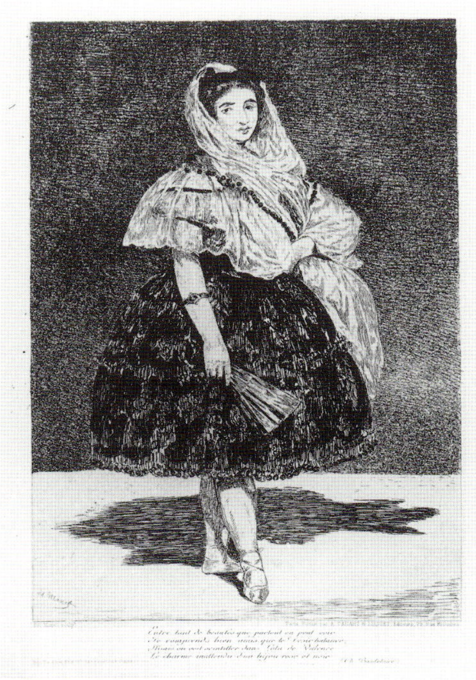

149
Edouard Manet 1832–1883
Lola de Valence n.d
Van Gogh Museum, Amsterdam

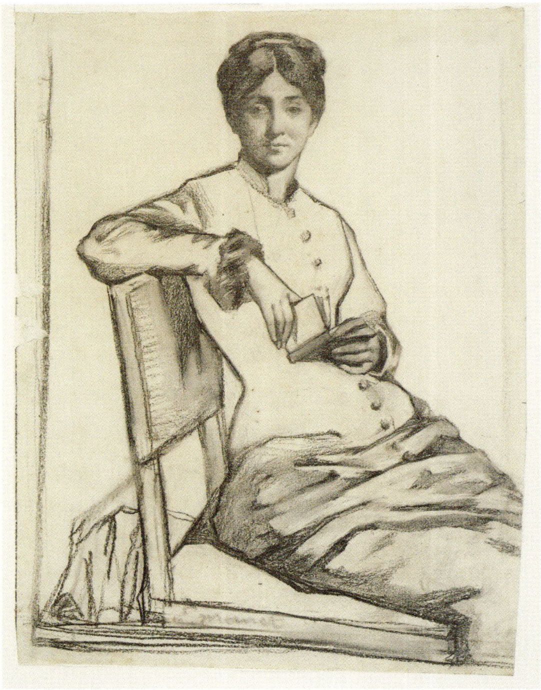

150
Edouard Manet 1832–1883
Portrait of a woman n.d.
Van Gogh Museum, Amsterdam

Aspirations and practicalities

In the early 1880s, when he was appointed *gérant* of the Boulevard Montmartre branch of Boussod, Valadon & Cie., Theo was able to a begin a modest collection of contemporary paintings and drawings. Although his position afforded him greater financial scope, his budget remained restricted in comparison to the major players on the art market. At the end of the decade Theo's monthly salary was around 900 to 1,000 francs, depending on the branch's annual results.[11] Although this was a reasonably good income, he had to support Vincent; moreover, following the death of his father in 1885, he regularly helped his mother and sisters as well. At the end of 1888 the cost of sharing a home in fashionable Paris with Jo Bonger, whom he married in April 1889, was added to his financial responsibilities.

As Theo could spend only a few hundred francs on a work of art, he was obliged to concentrate on the lower end of the market. He was thus hardly in a position to collect works by the two groups of artists whom he and Vincent particularly admired, artists who had largely determined the face of painting in the second half of the 19th century: the Barbizon School and the impressionists. Paintings by Camille Corot, Charles Daubigny, Jean-François Millet, Théodore Rousseau and other Barbizon masters, which Theo himself traded, already fetched many thousands of francs. In the mid-1880s canvases by Claude Monet and Edgar Degas also commanded considerable sums, often more than 1,000 francs.

Of the major impressionists Theo could afford only the work of Alfred Sisley and Camille Pissarro. However, it seems unlikely that he was especially interested in Sisley or wished to include the artist's work in his collection, given his negligible efforts to support this artist in his capacity as an art dealer. Works by Pissarro, on the other hand, entered 'Theo's' collection in various ways, even after the art dealer's death.

Given Theo's tight budget, his choice of inexpensive works on paper is logical. This category of 'alternative' acquisitions has a wide compass, and includes an etching **[149]** and drawing **[150]** by Edouard Manet, a pen drawing by Honoré Daumier, two small drawings by Charles Daubigny **[151]** and etchings by

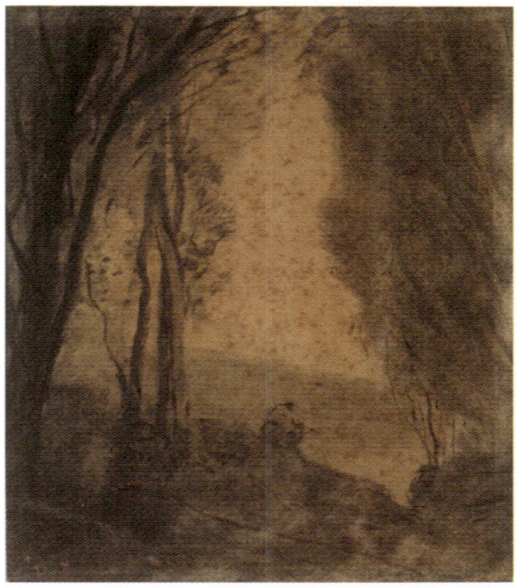

151
Charles-François Daubigny 1817–1878
Figure in a landscape n.d.
Van Gogh Museum, Amsterdam

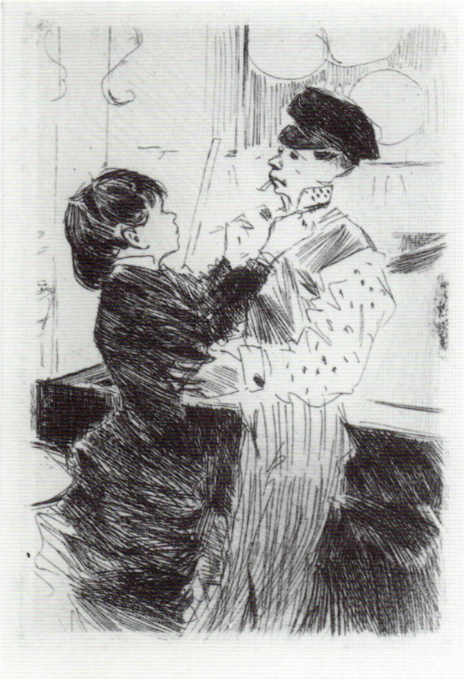

152
Jean-Louis Forain 1852–1931
Le noeud de cravate n.d
Van Gogh Museum, Amsterdam

masters whom both brothers admired: Camille Corot, Emile Jacque, Jean-François Raffaëlli and Jean-Louis Forain [**152**]. Theo must have been delighted to acquire pieces by artists whose work he also sold as a dealer.

In some instances, thanks to his good contacts, Theo also managed to obtain some fairly valuable paintings. This may have been the case with the works he owned by Théophile de Bock. Paintings by this artist of the Hague School, whom knew Theo personally and who had visited him in Paris in the summer of 1880, commanded more than 2,000 francs on the open market in the 1880s. Nevertheless, Theo managed to acquire *Lake with a boat* [**153**].[12]

In close collaboration with his Scottish colleague Alexander Reid and his brother Vincent, Theo collected a substantial group of paintings by Adolphe Monticelli. Vincent, who was a great admirer of this Marseilles painter, wrote in February 1888 that he and Theo now owned five of his works [580/464]. These were actually intended for sale but remained in the collection owing to the early death of the brothers.[13] [**154, 155, 156**]

Gifts

Theo enjoyed close contact with artists in his capacity as an art dealer. Some of them gave him work in acknowledgement of services rendered, or as a token of their appreciation for his efforts. In December 1884, for example, the Swedish painter Ernst Josephson gave him a preliminary study for *The water nymph*;[14] he had probably worked in the French capital for some time under Theo's aegis. Heijerdahl's *Portrait of a girl with a bunch of flowers* [**157**] and *Park* [**34**] may also have been gifts from the artist, although there is no specific evidence to support this theory. Theo greatly admired this Norwegian artist, who had used Theo as his dealer when he was in Paris from 1881-84.

Gifts by former house mates and friends, such as *House in a garden* [**185**] by Christian Mourier-Petersen, form an important category in Theo's collection.[15] After Vincent left Paris in February 1888, Theo provided accommodation to various artists at a low rent. In September 1888 the Dutch painter Arnold Hendrik Koning sent Theo, 'with much affection,' the 'best of my studies or paintings,' including *Windmill*

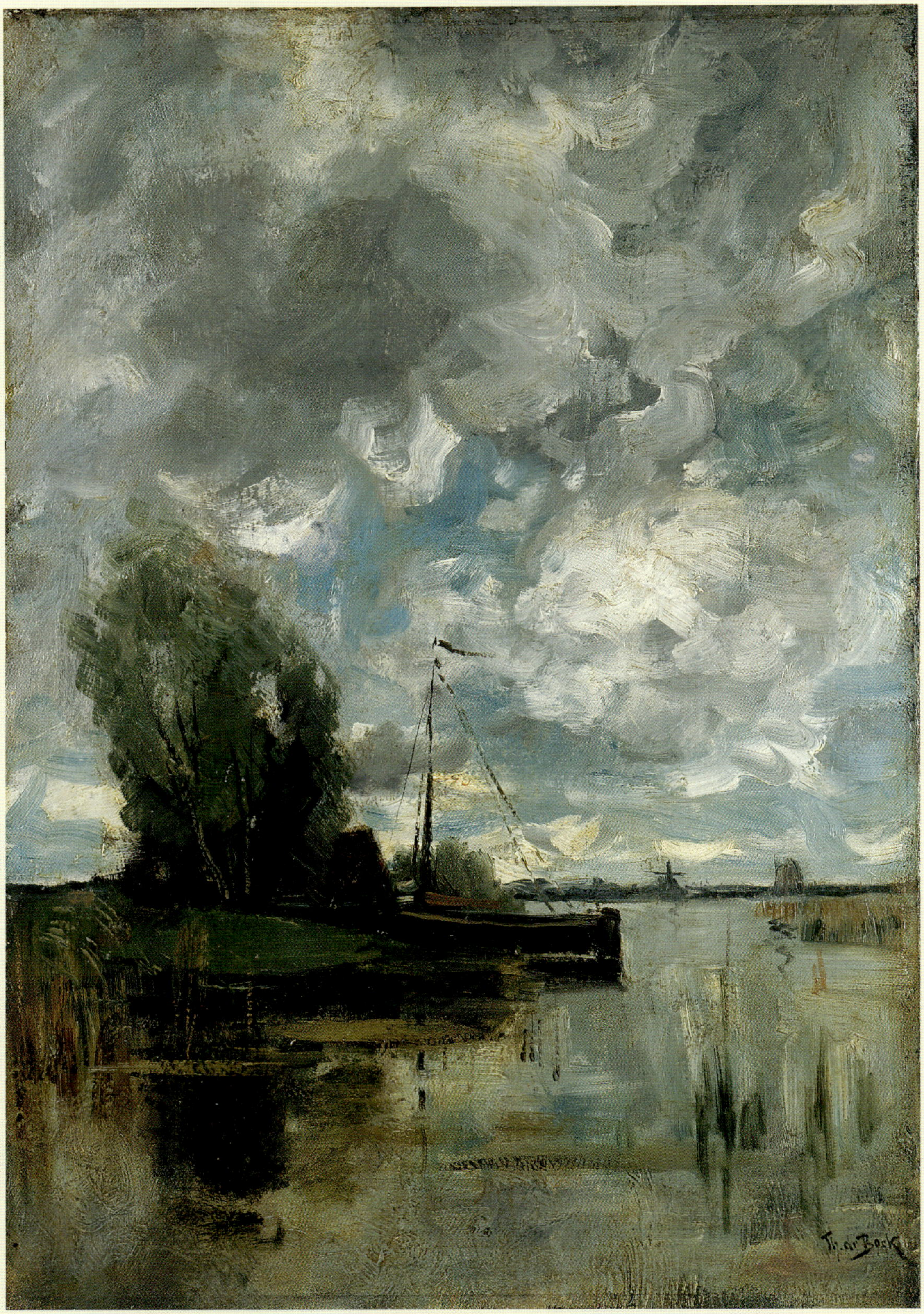

153
Théophile de Bock 1851–1904
Lake with a boat n.d.
Van Gogh Museum, Amsterdam

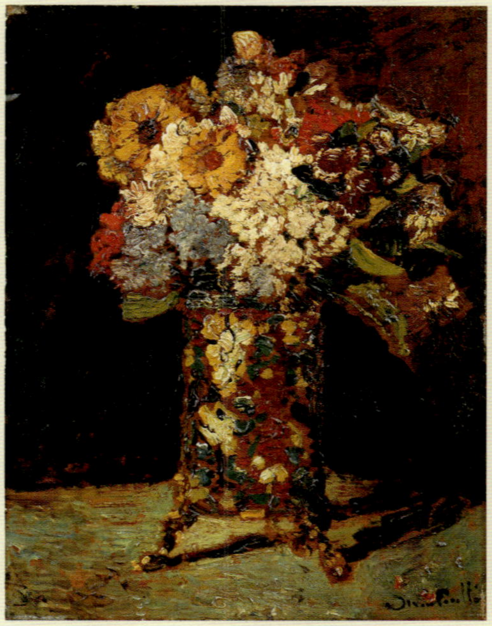

154
Adolphe Monticelli 1824–1886
Vase with flowers c. 1875
Van Gogh Museum, Amsterdam

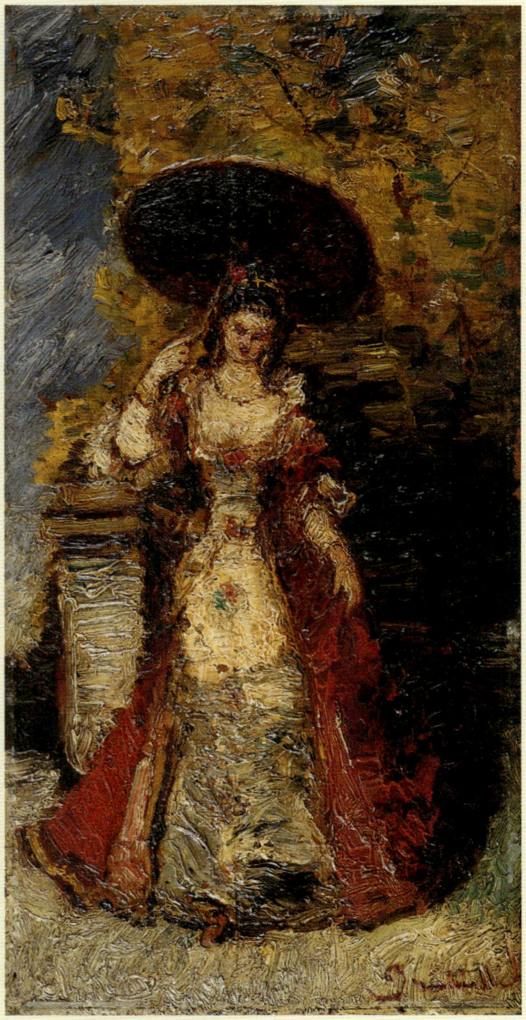

156
Adolphe Monticelli 1824–1886
Woman with a parasol c. 1879
Van Gogh Museum, Amsterdam

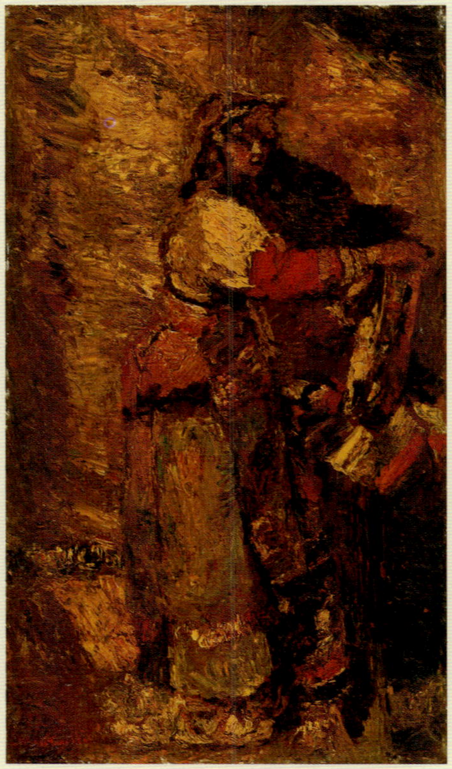

155
Adolphe Monticelli 1824–1886
Italian girl c. 1879
Van Gogh Museum, Amsterdam

on Montmartre [**158**]; these were to thank Theo for letting him stay at the Rue Lepic apartment from March to May 1888.[16]

One of the few portraits of Theo van Gogh also joined the collection in the form of a gift. On the evening of 20 January 1889, Meijer de Haan, who stayed with Theo from October 1888 to April 1889, produced a portrait – a 'scribble' – of his host.[17] Simple drawings by Jozef Isaacson, who spent many evenings with De Haan and Theo in the Rue Lepic, and by Charles Serret, were also presented to Theo as gifts. Naturally, such pieces occupied a different place in his collection than that of more ambitious works.

Curiously, Theo owned hardly any work by Meijer de Haan, although he had every confidence in his friend's abilities. His collection may once have contained several De Haan drawings and perhaps even a painting. In November 1888 Vincent wrote to Theo that the drawings by De Haan that Theo had sent him were 'very fine' [722/559]. A letter from De Haan to Theo dated 22 October 1889 has also been preserved, in which he writes that for a long time he had intended to send a particular work to Theo – 'an apple tree in full bloom against a sunny landscape, very dreamy.'[18]

Some inscriptions on works in the collection reveal that these pieces, too, were given to Theo by various artists. These include a work by Vittorio Corcos [**159**], a staple of Theo's stock at the Boulevard Montmartre.[19] Another canvas that had once belonged to Theo was traced in 1996 thanks to just such an inscription. Theo had probably received it as a memento after Vincent's death. The verso of the painting *Garden with hollyhock* [**160**], by Ernest Quost, an artist Vincent greatly admired, bears the inscription: 'A Theo van Gogh / Ce tableau qu'aime tant mon ami Vincent / Bien amicalement / E. Quost.' Little is known of Theo's relationship with this painter other than that he positively assessed Quost's submission to the 1890 Salon and had also met the artist in June of the same year [895/T38].[20]

One of the most important paintings to join Theo's collection in the form of a gift is undoubtedly Paul Gauguin's *Vincent van Gogh painting sunflowers* [**45**]. Theo regarded this as 'a great work of art' and 'the best portrait made of him as regards its likeness to the inner man.'[21] Gauguin also presented Theo with a charming little vase and perhaps several drawings. [**161**]

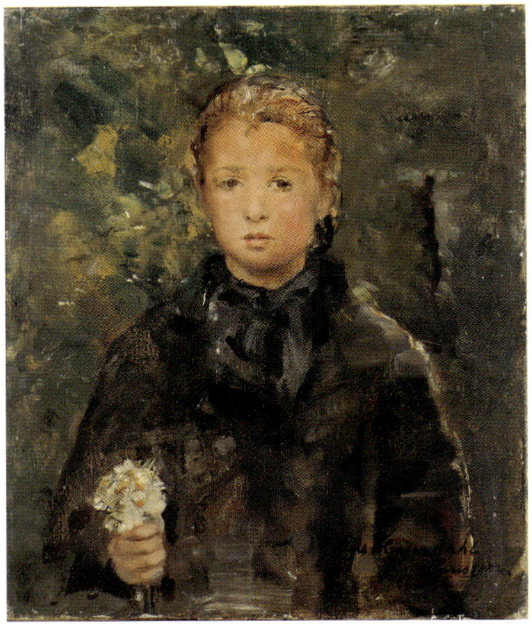

157
Hans Olaf Heijerdahl 1857–1913
Portrait of a girl with a bunch of flowers 1882
Van Gogh Museum, Amsterdam

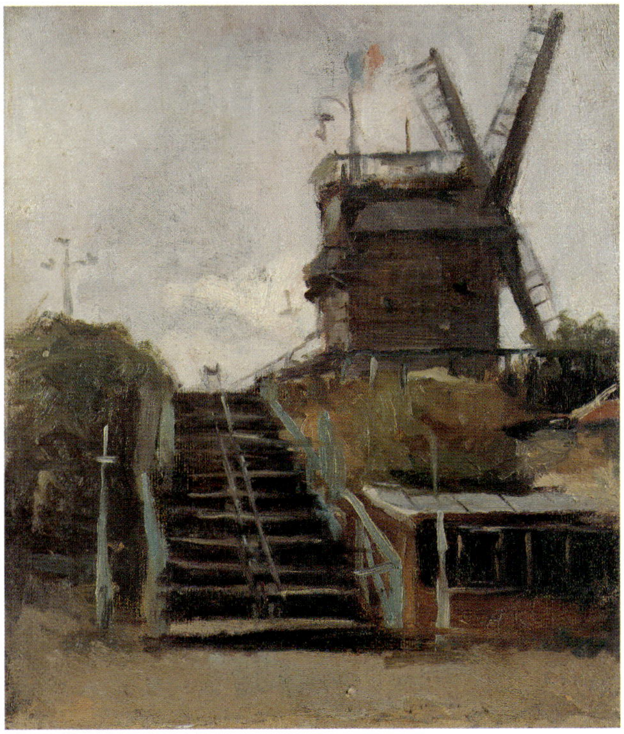

158
Arnold Hendrik Koning 1860–1945
Windmill on Montmartre c. 1887–88
Van Gogh Museum, Amsterdam

For many works in the collection, however, it is impossible to ascertain whether they were gifts or purchases. It seems very likely that the portraits of Vincent van Gogh by his friends and colleagues John Russell and Henri de Toulouse-Lautrec [**162**], however, were gifts to Theo.

Exchanges

Theo could also expand his collection actively and cheaply by exchanging Vincent's paintings for work by artists whom the brothers both knew. Their correspondence gives the impression that Vincent was the chief instigator of such exchanges, although Theo concurred with them. The brothers had begun this practice while living together in Paris (1886-88). Auguste Lepère's *Montmartre in the snow* [**163**] probably entered the collection as an exchange. As early as July 1886 Theo wrote to their mother: 'He [Vincent] has not sold any paintings for money yet, but he has exchanged his works for others. In this way we are building up a fine collection, which is naturally worth something, too.'[22] Offers to exchange works did not always meet with success, however. In August 1886 two watercolours by Eugène Isabey remained beyond the brothers' reach [571/460]; two months later Vincent also approached Charles Angrand in vain [573/-]. However, in November 1887 Vincent did manage to obtain Gauguin's *On the shore of the lake at Martinique* [**164**] by this method.[23]

From the moment he settled in Arles, Vincent endeavoured to enhance the collection via exchanges, urging Theo in dozens of letters to organise such transactions. Theo in turn asked Vincent to establish a circle of artist-friends for them [718/T3]. Vincent sometimes approached his colleagues directly with a specific offer. Although John Russell may have assented to Vincent's proposal to exchange one of his Sicilian works, it is uncertain whether the deal ever took place.[24]

Successful exchanges substantially enriched the collection. Works by progressive painters such as Emile Bernard [**165**], Armand Guillaumin [**166**], Leo Gausson [**167**] and Frank Myers Boggs [**168**] were all acquired in this manner. In June 1890 Theo exchanged one of Vincent's works for Eugène Boch's *The Crachet-*

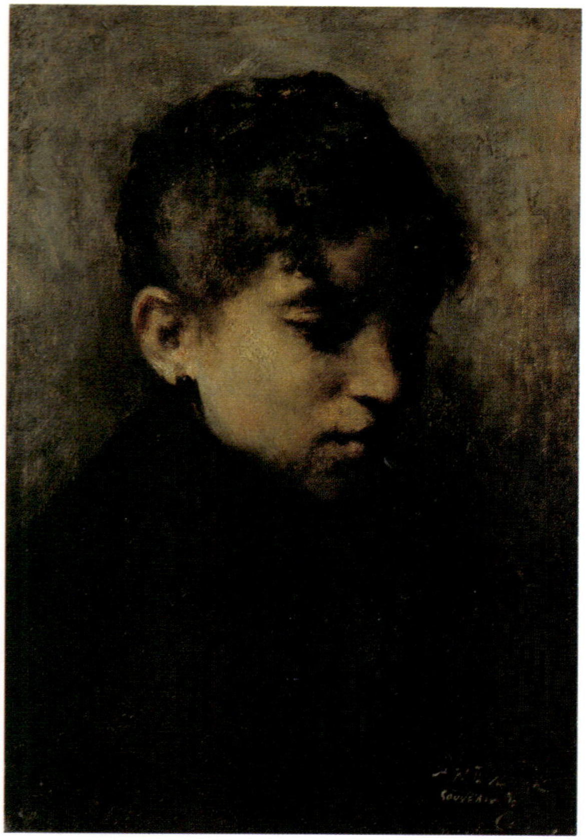

159
Vittorio Corcos 1859–1933
Portrait of young woman 1882
Van Gogh Museum, Amsterdam

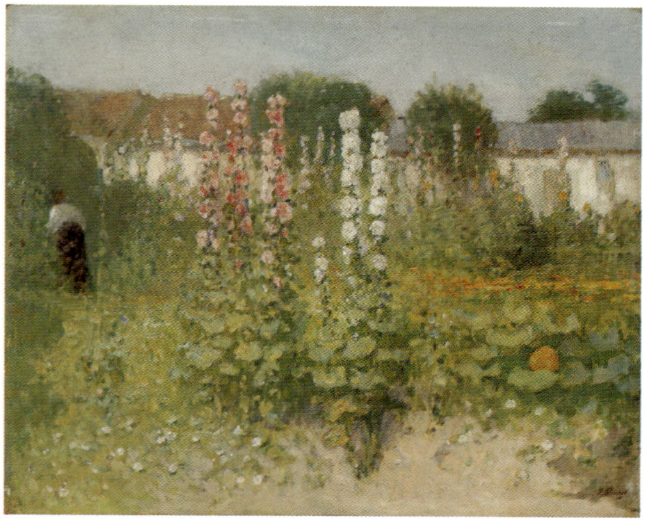

160
Ernest Quost 1844–1931
Garden with hollyhock c. 1881–90
Van Gogh Museum, Amsterdam

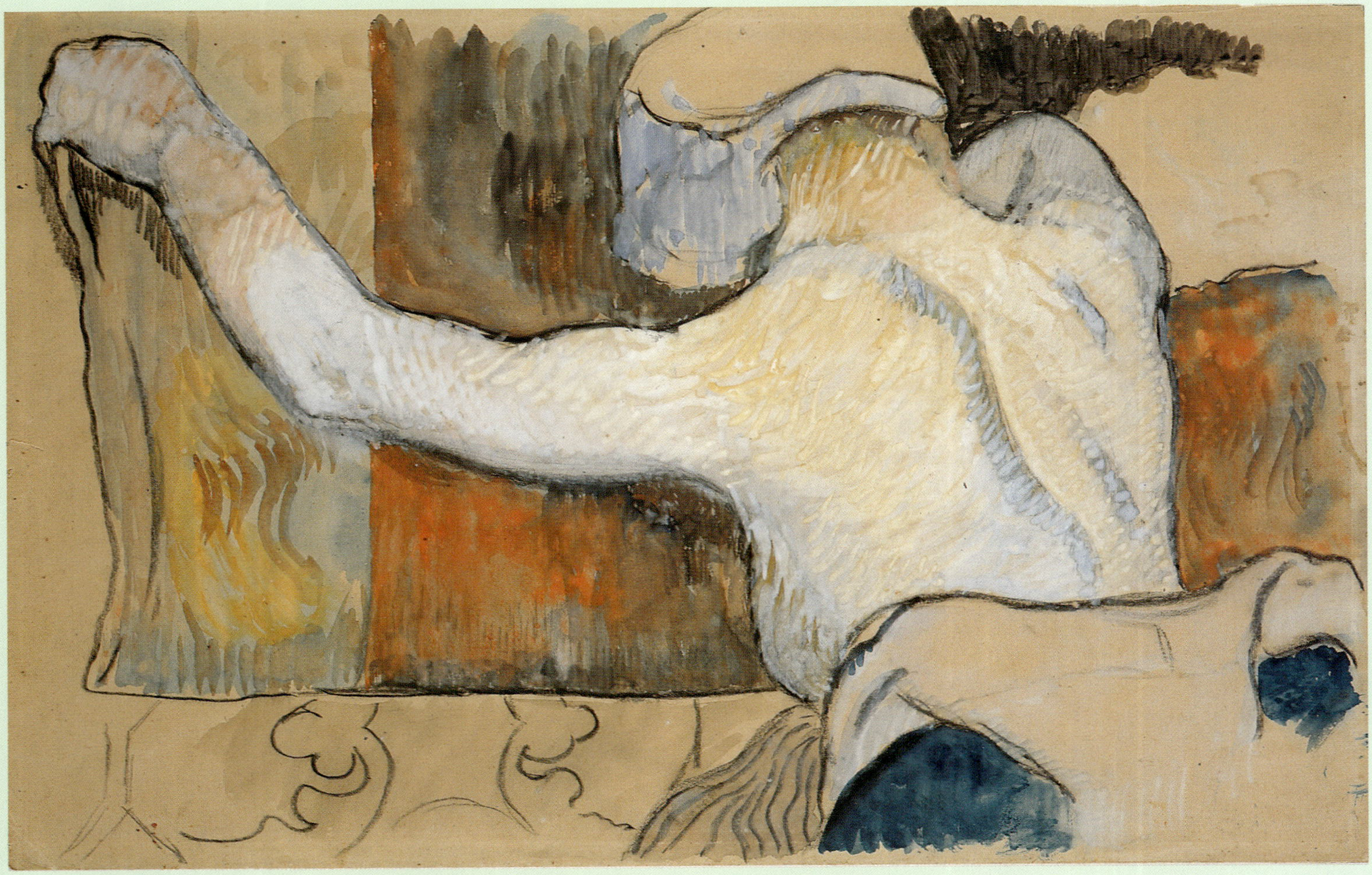

161
Paul Gauguin 1848–1903
Study for Woman in the hay 1889
Van Gogh Museum, Amsterdam

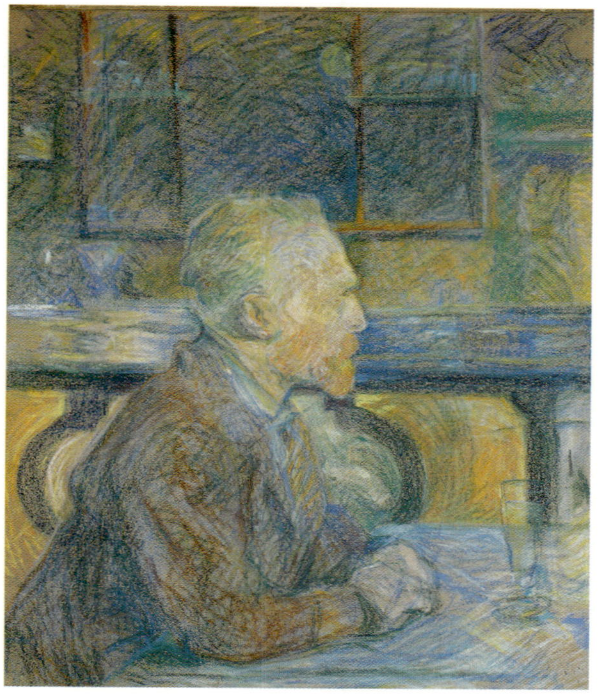

162
Henri de Toulouse-Lautrec 1864–1901
Portrait of Vincent van Gogh 1887
Van Gogh Museum, Amsterdam

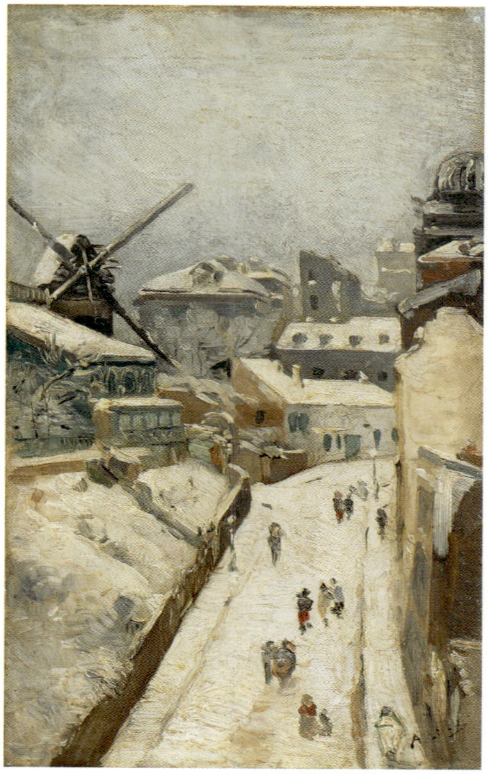

163
Auguste Lepère 1849–1918
Montmartre in the snow n.d.
Van Gogh Museum, Amsterdam

Pecry mine, Borinage [**169**], which he deemed neither 'handsome' nor 'powerful,' although it was 'sincere': 'I consider it remarkable, particularly the subject and his intention with this work' [895/T38]. The three impressive 'friendship' portraits by Bernard [**170**], Gauguin [**171**] and Charles Laval [**172**] were all acquired as a result of one of Vincent's initiatives. In 1888 he suggested that the friends exchange self-portraits. These works still form a unique group, one of the highlights of the Van Gogh Museum's collection.

Impressionists

In their early years Theo and Vincent's tastes were determined by the work they saw every day as employees of Goupil & Cie. By around the mid-1880s their interest was increasingly shifting to more 'modern' art. As an art dealer in Paris Theo soon became acquainted with the latest trends. In January 1885, for example, he bought a landscape by Victor Vignon [**173**] for 200 francs.[25] This was one of two landscapes by this painter that would later adorn the walls of Theo and Jo's dining room.[26]

At the beginning of 1889 Theo explained his idea of the most progressive art of the day in two letters to Jo Bonger. These testify to his warm sympathy for modernism and the change in his taste.[27] On 1 February he wrote that there was a tendency in contemporary art to forsake the classic ideal of beauty 'for the symbol of what is human.' Theo contended that the 'finest' art was art that which touched 'the soul.' This could be achieved even by 'the most thankless subject.'[28] In March 1889 he subsequently told his fiancée that he particularly admired a group of painters who, instead of following the traditional rules of aesthetics, based their work on the premise 'that to receive every impression from nature and render this in whatever fashion can be art.' Theo believed that a work of art should relate to life; he attached little importance to 'the manner of execution, if it comes from the soul. The form of art is not art itself.'[29]

Theo's opinions were influenced by the concepts of painters such as his brother, Gauguin and Degas, and by the naturalist French novelists, above all Emile Zola. Such ideas determined the direction of Theo's collecting activities in his final years and introduced a modern quality to his collection.

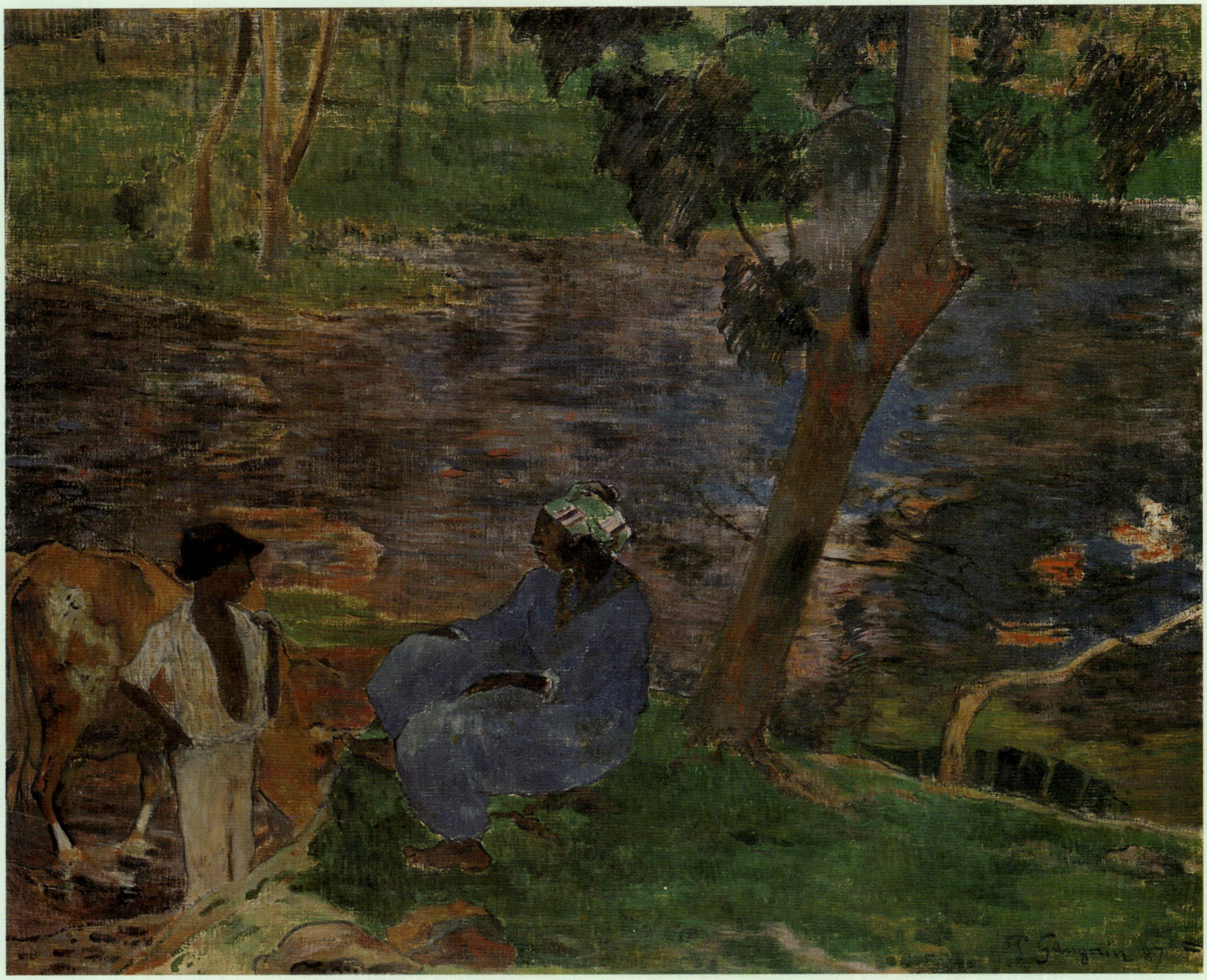

164
Paul Gauguin 1848–1903
On the shore of the lake at Martinique 1887
Van Gogh Museum, Amsterdam

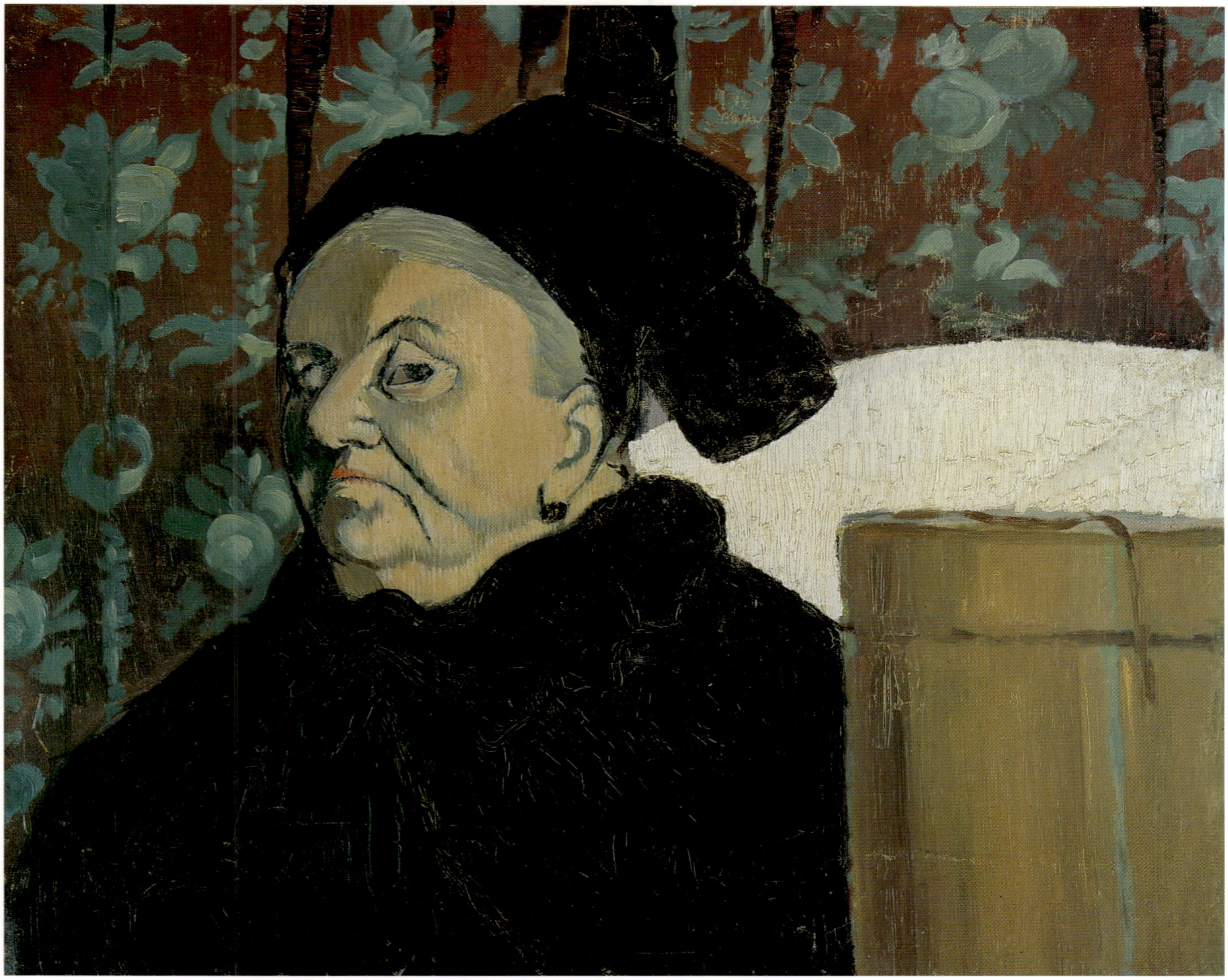

165
Emile Bernard 1868–1941
Portrait of the artist's grandmother 1887
Van Gogh Museum, Amsterdam

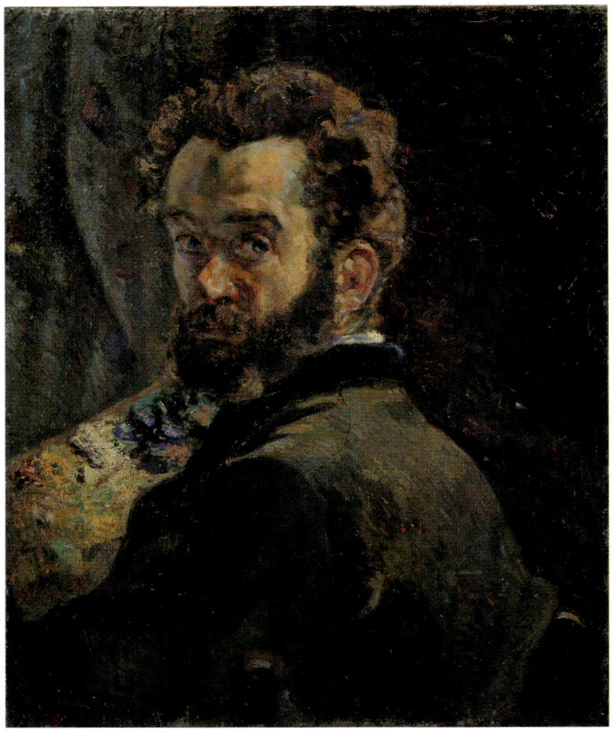

166
Armand Guillaumin 1841–1927
Self-portrait 1878
Van Gogh Museum, Amsterdam

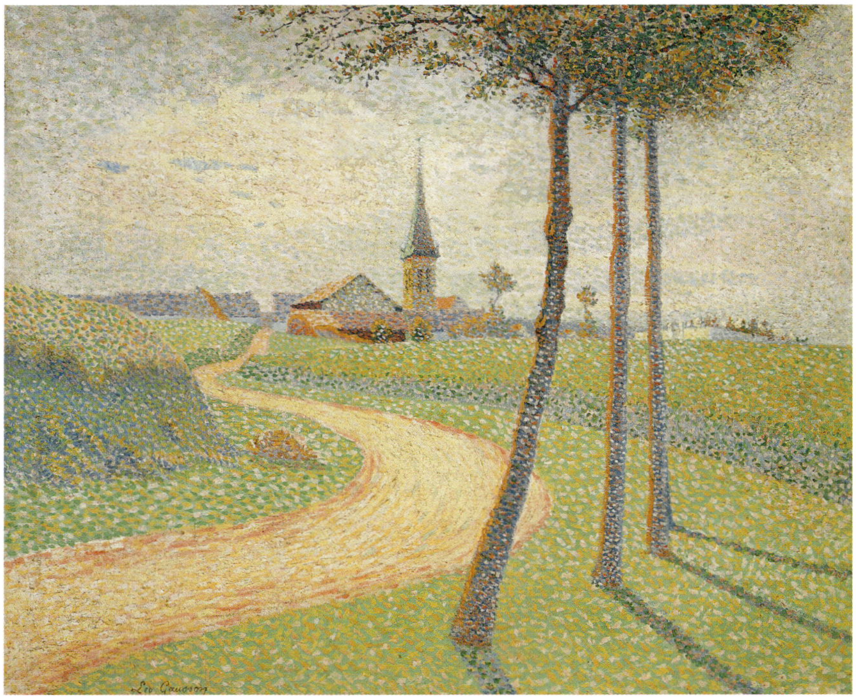

167
Leo Gausson 1860–1944
The church tower at Bussy-St-Georges, Seine-et-Marne 1887–88
Van Gogh Museum, Amsterdam

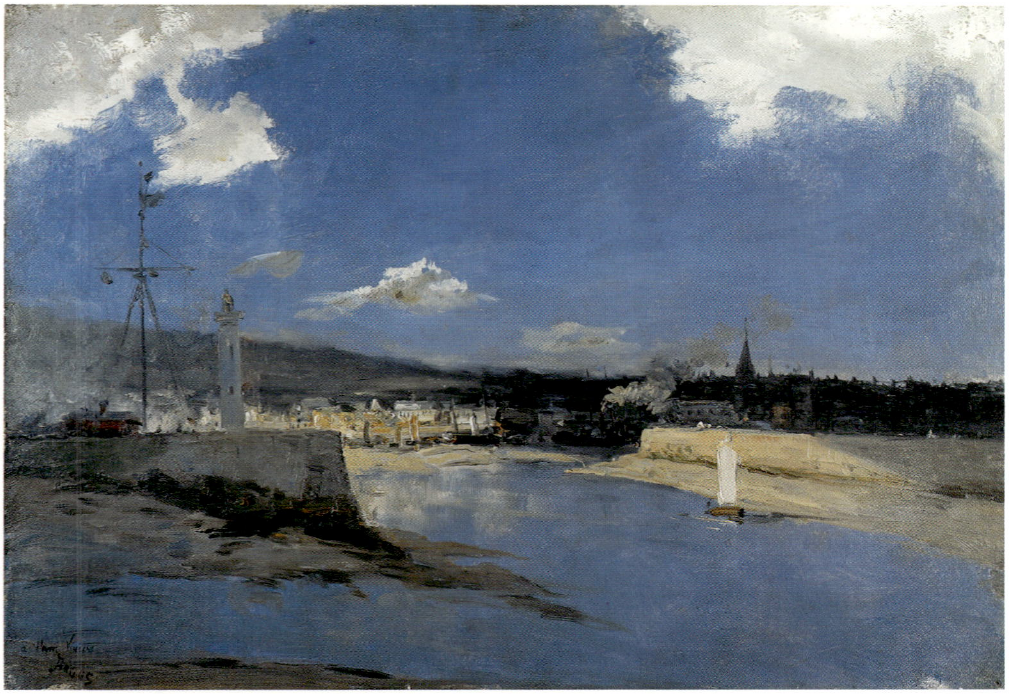

168
Frank Myers Boggs 1855–1926
The harbour at Honfleur n.d.
Van Gogh Museum, Amsterdam

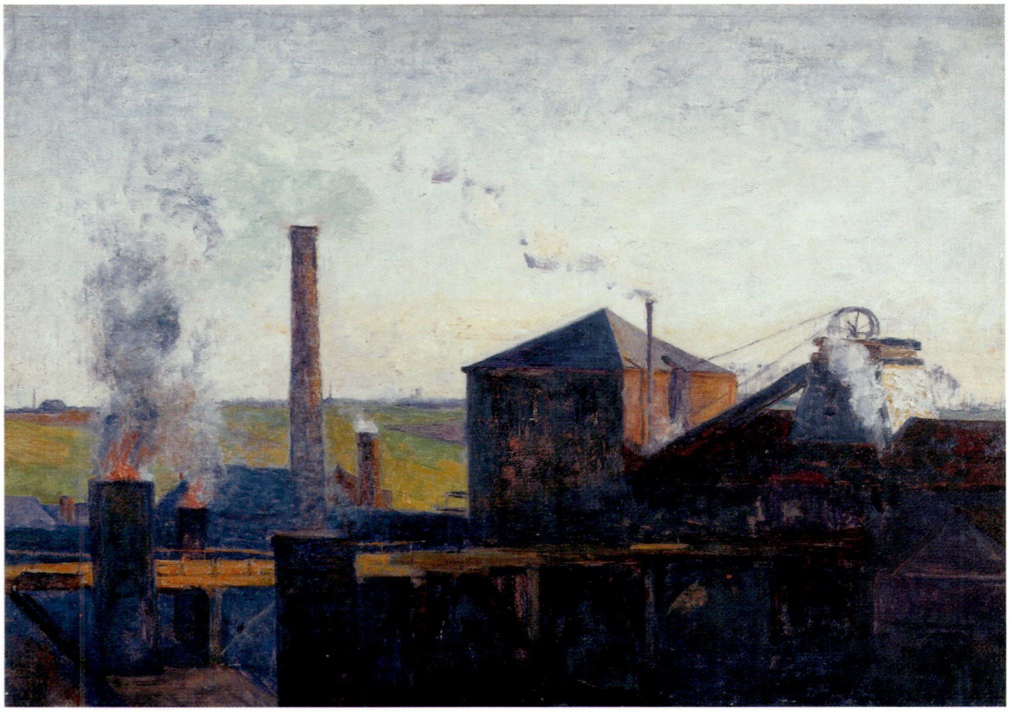

169
Eugène Boch 1855–1941
The Crachet-Pecry mine, Borinage 1888–90
Van Gogh Museum, Amsterdam

Undoubtedly Theo would have liked to embellish his collection with major impressionist canvases. In letters to Jo and his sister Wil he openly expressed his admiration for one painter in particular: Edgar Degas. He regarded Degas as a genius who was as important to painting as Zola was to literature. Theo thought Degas was 'always in charge' with his work; he described him as a 'great poet [...] no less than Millet, because his figures live and are truly of their time, they have much to say, and the thoughts which they occasion are not necessarily confined to the picture.'[30] However, Theo was never to acquire a work by this impressionist master. He could only manage a few lithographs after subjects by Degas, and even these were the gift of the lithographer, George William Thornley. Apparently, despite Theo's efforts on his behalf, Degas did not feel obliged to favour him with an original work, however modest.

Theo was also a great admirer of Monet, producer of 'magnificent' landscapes. Although he contended that Monet's paintings lacked the emotional depth of Gauguin or Degas, he thought they did possess 'the gift of casting a ray of sunshine in these pessimistic times, one which will bring clarity and give encouragement to many people.'[31] Despite Theo's admiration for Monet – whom, like Degas, he also knew quite well – and his efforts to promote his art, Monet's work remained beyond his reach. Monet was another artist who saw no reason to give his Dutch dealer a token of his appreciation.

However, Theo was in a position to purchase paintings and drawings by Pissarro: their average price – around 300 francs for a finished painting – was well within his budget. As a close acquaintance of the painter, he could probably have counted on a discount as well. Nevertheless, he did not acquire any of Pissarro's paintings. He may have been taking his time, waiting for the right moment to purchase. But his time ran out. It is highly probable, however, that he did buy a Pissarro watercolour of a market scene. In December 1889 Pissarro gave Jo a splendid fan – *Figures in a meadow* **[175]** – possibly to thank Theo for organising an exhibition of his work. On 17 December Theo thanked the artist 'mille fois' for the 'magnifique cadeau': 'Je suis vraiment touché de lui voir dedié une de vos oeuvres.'[32]

Only after Theo's death was a small, unidentified landscape added to the collection,[33] in exchange for Vincent's *Mulberry tree* (Norton Simon Museum, Pasadena). Pissarro had seen this work in August 1890, shortly after Vincent's death, and expressed his admiration for it. There is evidence that Theo took the opportunity to suggest an exchange, which was not completed, however, until 17 November 1892.[34]

Although Theo did not manage to enrich his collection with paintings by several of the impressionists he admired, in 1888 he did acquire Guillaumin's colourful pastel *Farmhouses at Janville*. Vincent considered it 'assuredly a good undertaking' [599/477]. In all likelihood Theo also expanded the collection with two, unidentified, canvases by Renoir. Both paintings – about which Theo said little more in his surviving correspondence than that Renoir's work was difficult to sell – disappeared from the collection at the end of the 19th century, reappearing in the hands of the Paris dealer Ambroise Vollard. In 1897 Jo sold a small Renoir for 200 francs, as well as the Pissarro landscape mentioned above (400 francs). According to Jo's accounts these were followed in 1899 by the second Renoir, which left the collection together with a painting by Guillaumin; these works brought in a total of 1,200 francs (577 guilders).

It is not inconceivable that, had Theo lived longer, he would have built up a considerable collection of Gauguin's work. As an art dealer he supported the artist as much as he could. He regarded Gauguin as an innovator: his works were like 'words of consolation,' as 'nature herself' spoke from them.[35] This was precisely what Theo was seeking in a work of art at the end of the 1880s, as demonstrated by the letter to Jo cited above. Following his first meeting with Gauguin in December 1887, Theo bought *Among the mangoes at Martinique* **[176]** for 400 francs at the beginning of January 1888.[36] He was proud of this purchase, which occupied a place of honour in the salon of his Cité Pigalle apartment; in 1889 he loaned it to two exhibitions.[37] According to his accounts, Theo also bought Gauguin's *Arlesian women, mistral* **[132]** for 300 francs on 25 May 1889.[38]

These accounts also list the purchase on 8 July 1889 of Odilon Redon's *Yeux clos* **[174]** for 200 francs; this work would later come into the hands of Andries

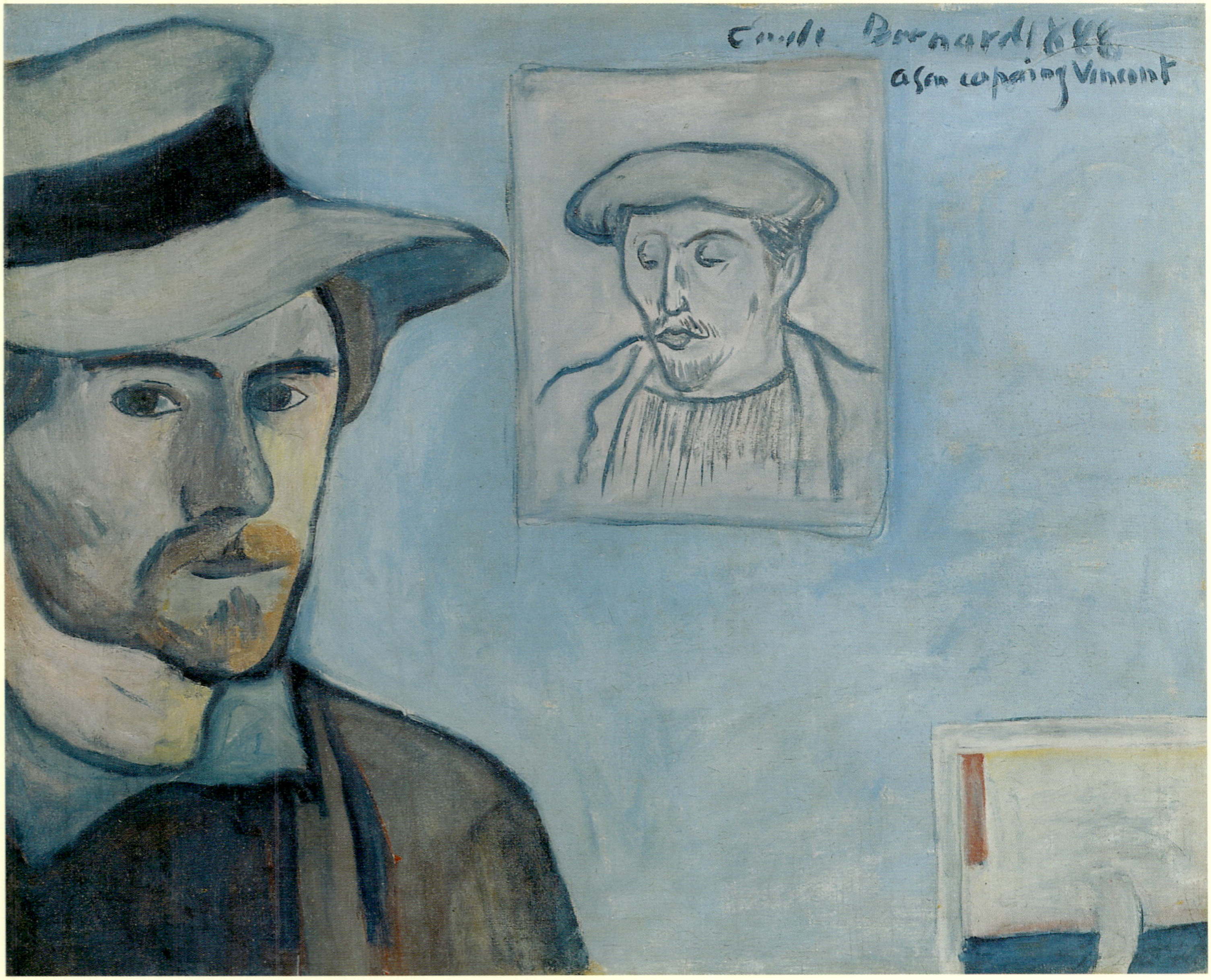

170

Emile Bernard 1868–1941

Self-portrait with a portrait of Gauguin 1888

Van Gogh Museum, Amsterdam

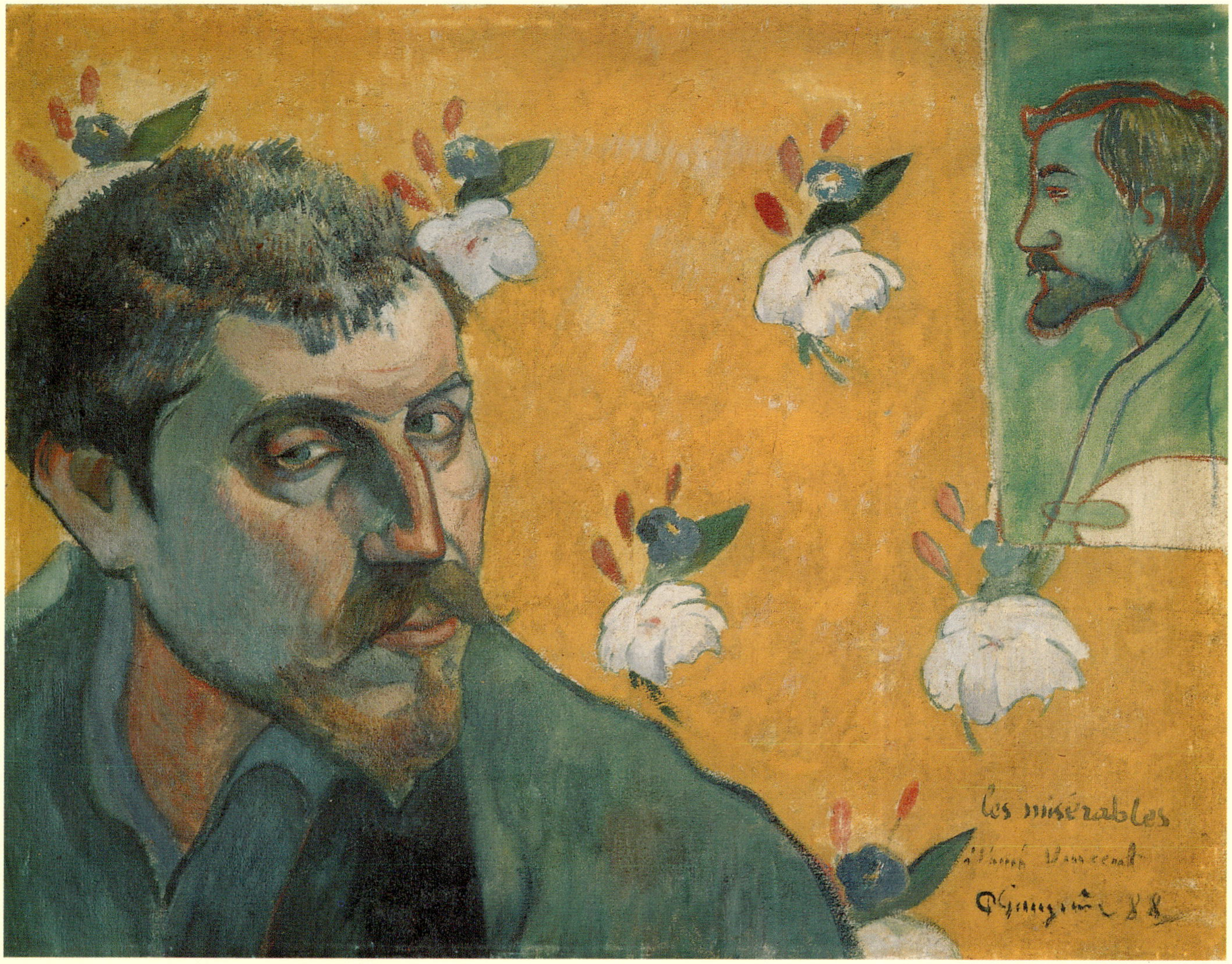

171
Paul Gauguin 1848–1903
Self-portrait with a portrait of Bernard, Les misérables 1888
Van Gogh Museum, Amsterdam

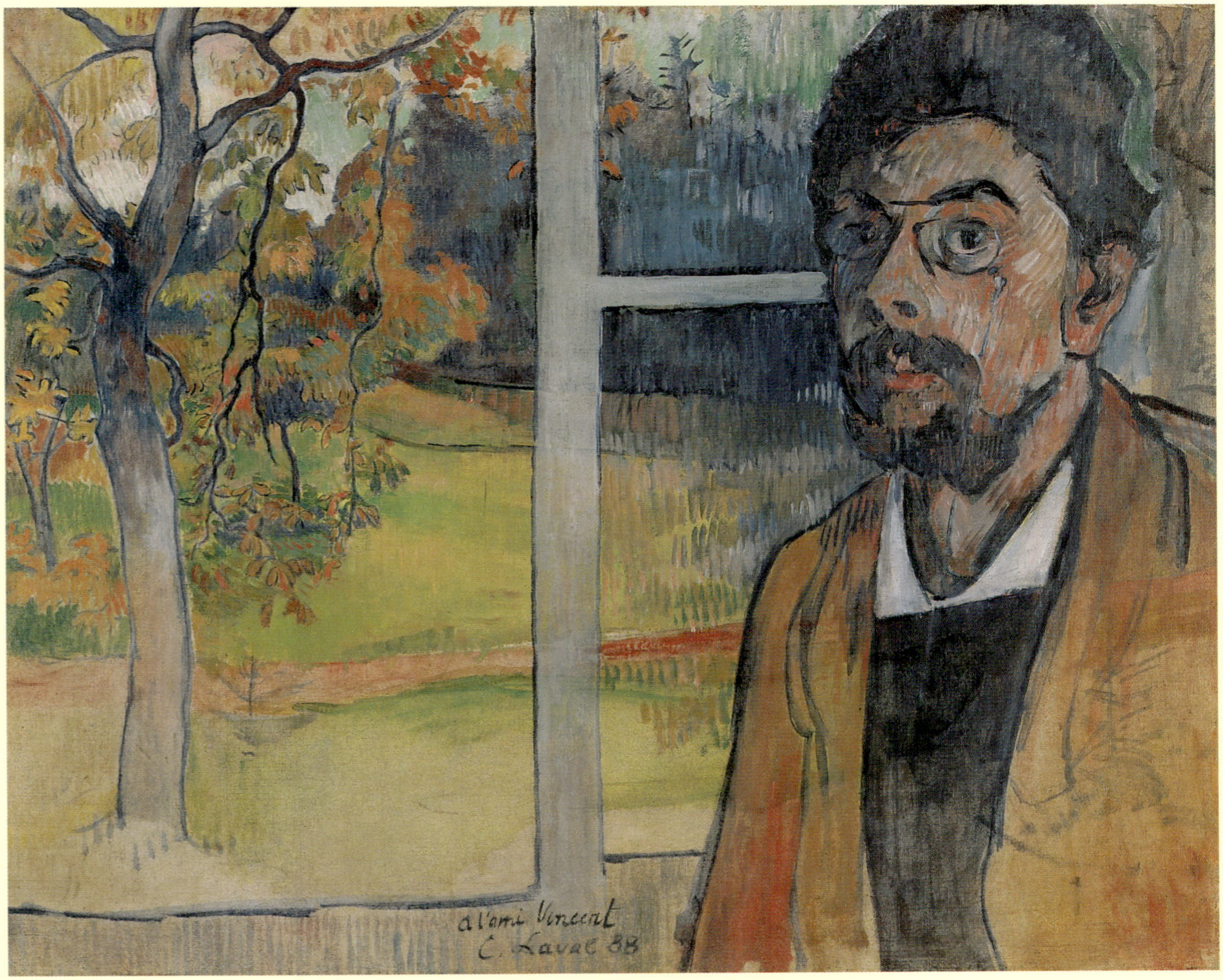

172
Charles Laval 1862–1894
Self-portrait 1888
Van Gogh Museum, Amsterdam

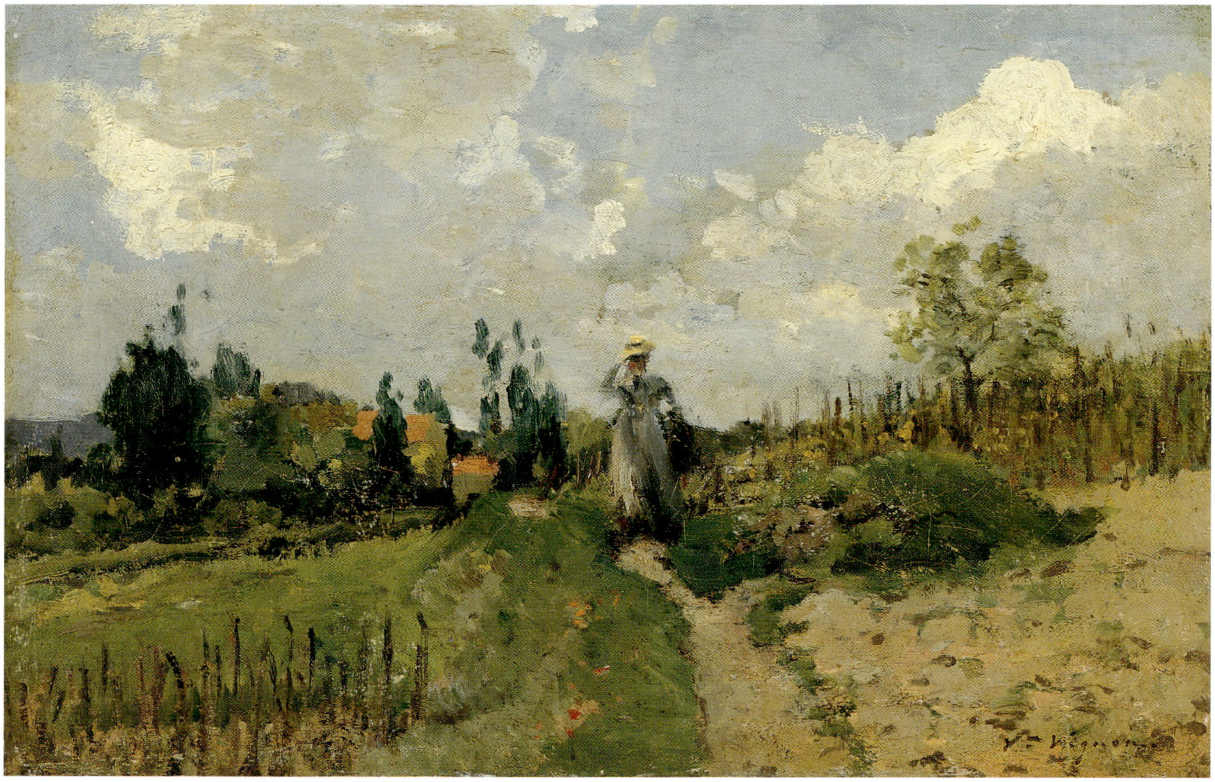

173

Victor Vignon 1847–1909
Woman in a vineyard c. 1883
Van Gogh Museum, Amsterdam

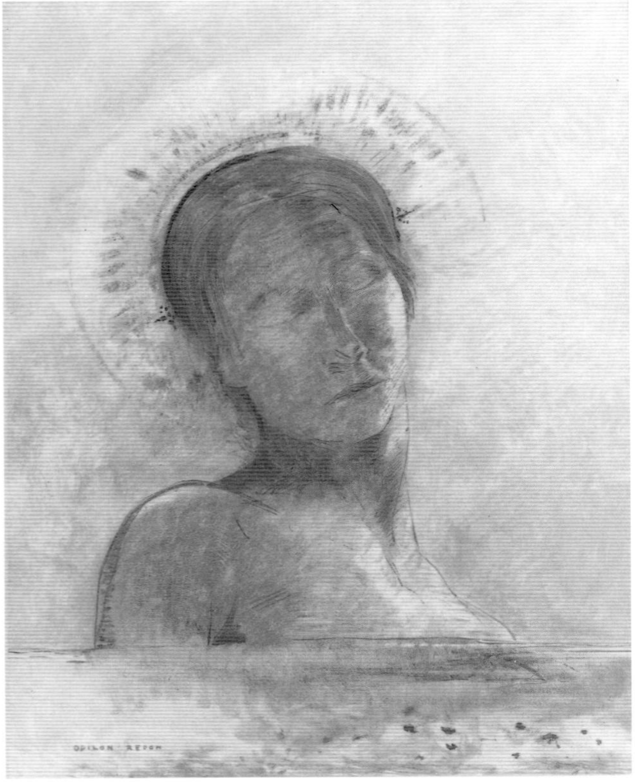

174
Odilon Redon 1840–1916
Yeux clos 1890
Private collection

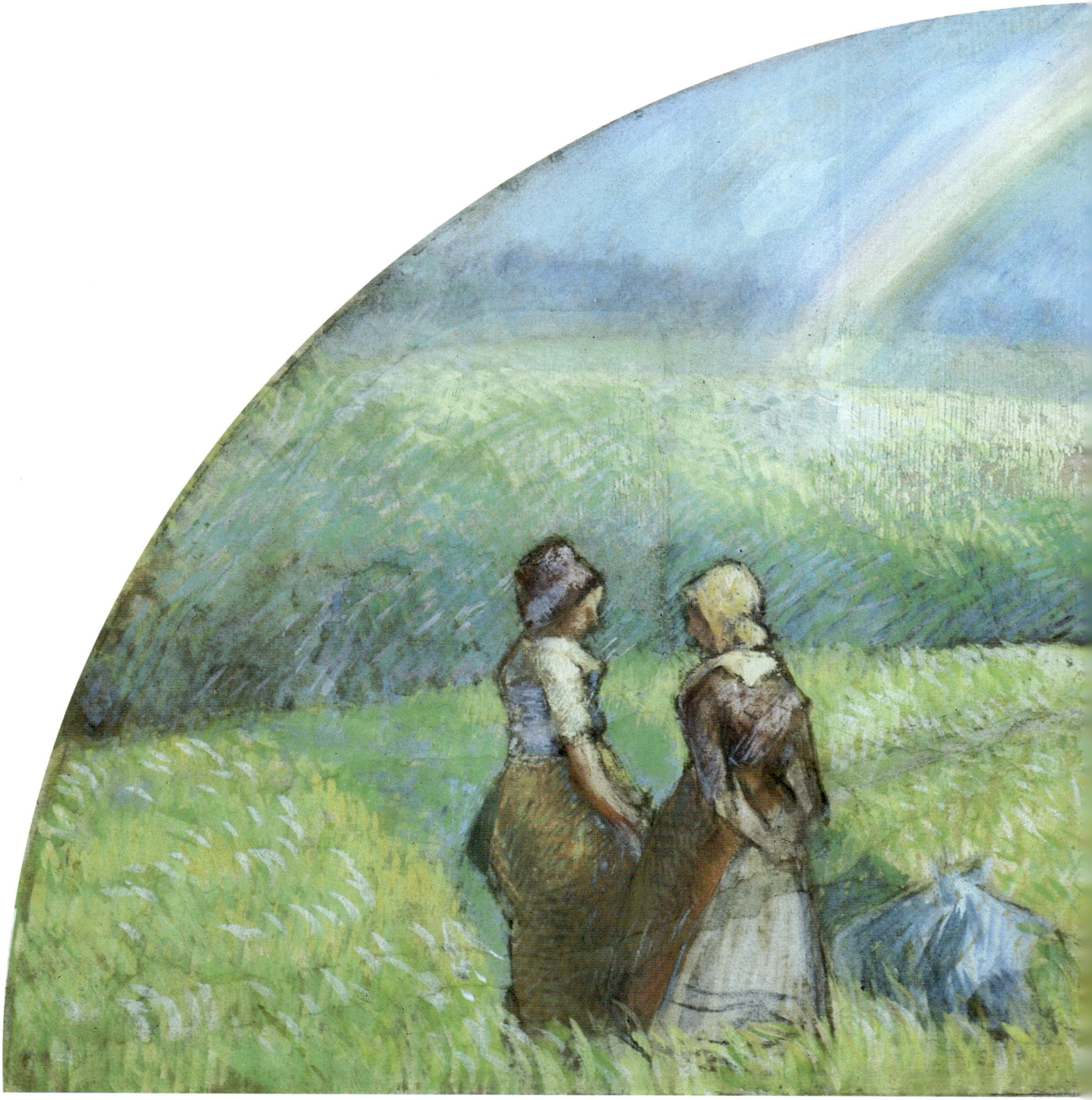

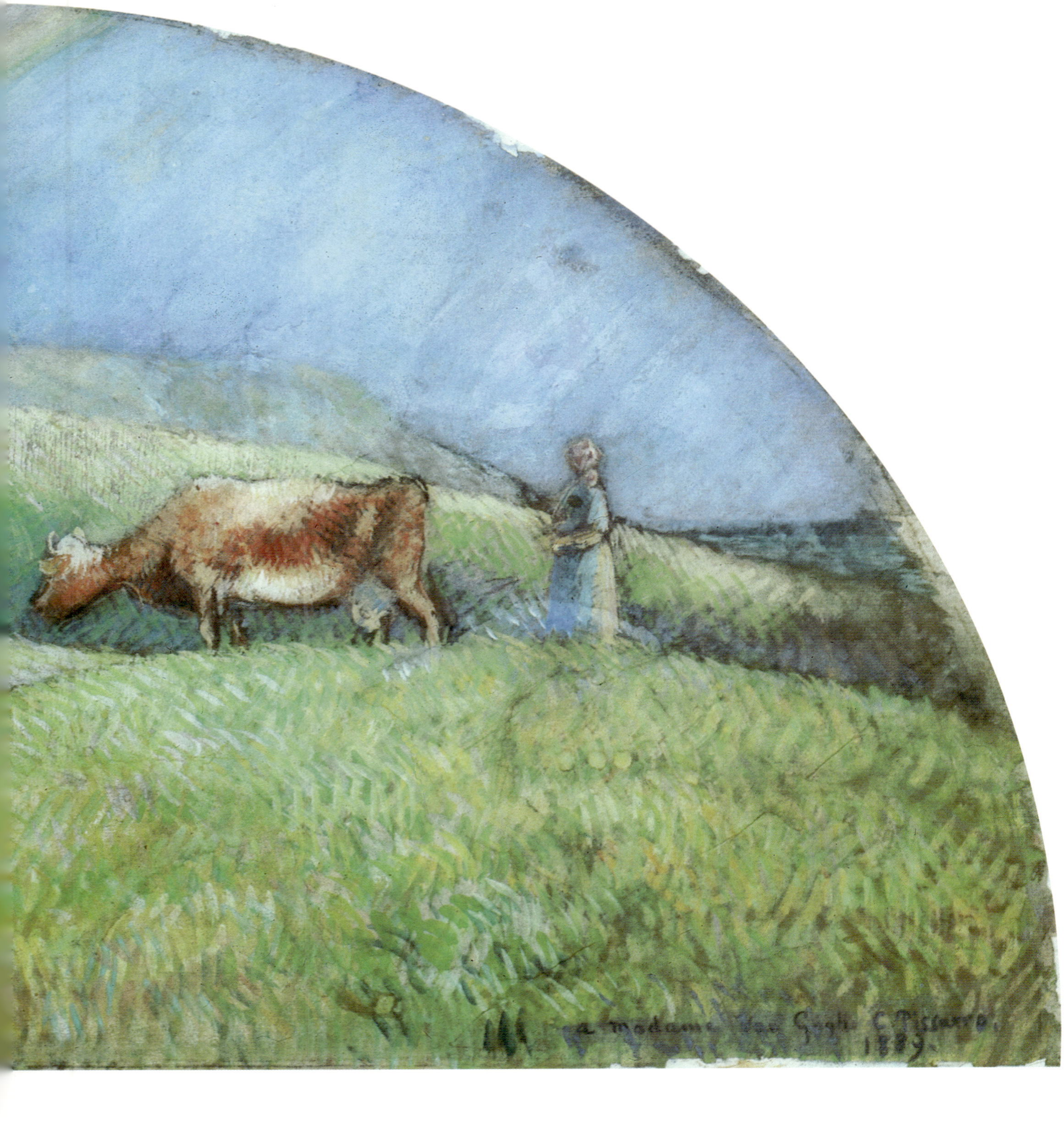

175

Camille Pissarro 1830–1903
Figures in a meadow 1889
Van Gogh Museum, Amsterdam

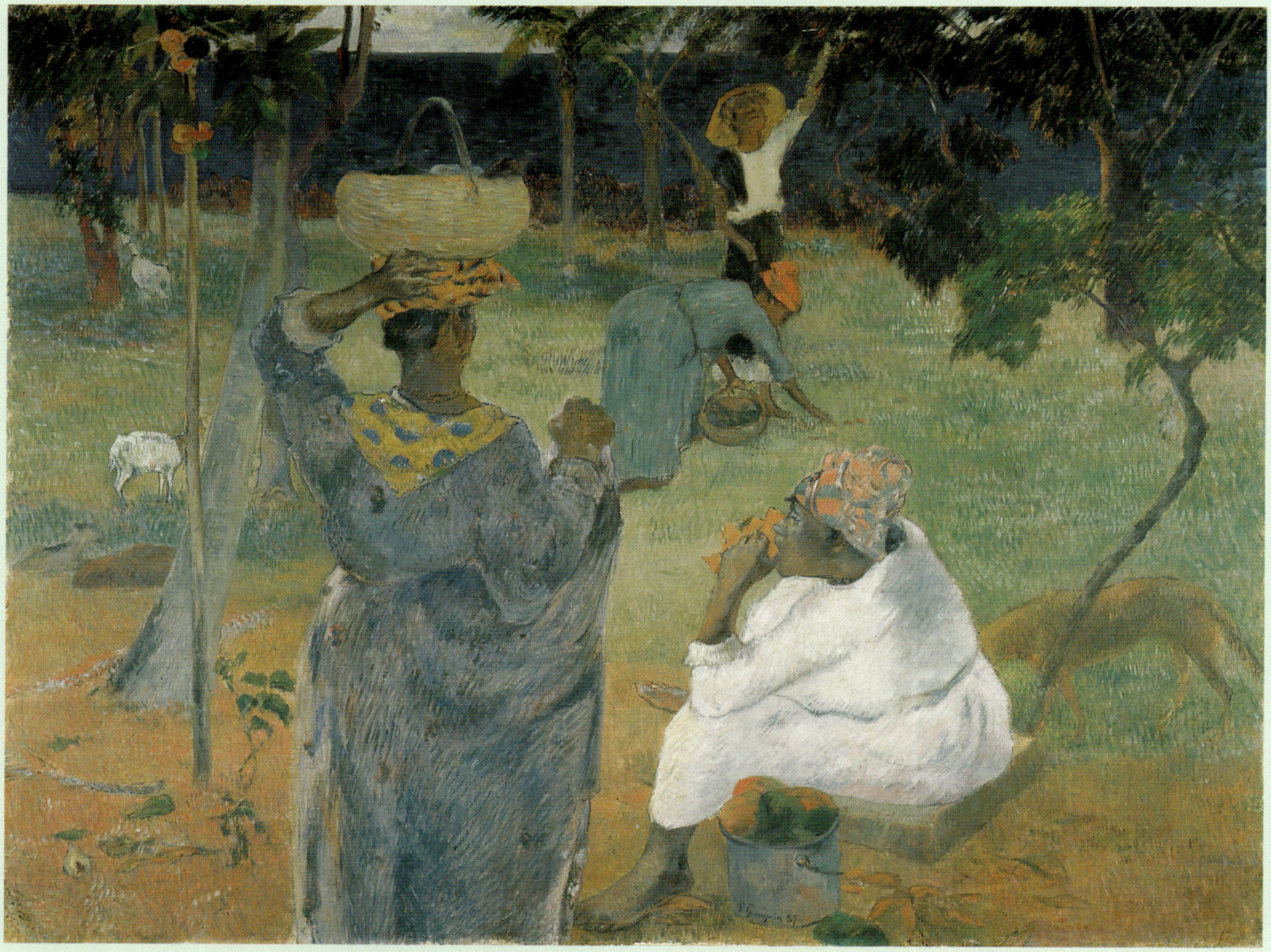

176
Paul Gauguin 1848–1903
Among the mangoes at Martinique 1887
Van Gogh Museum, Amsterdam

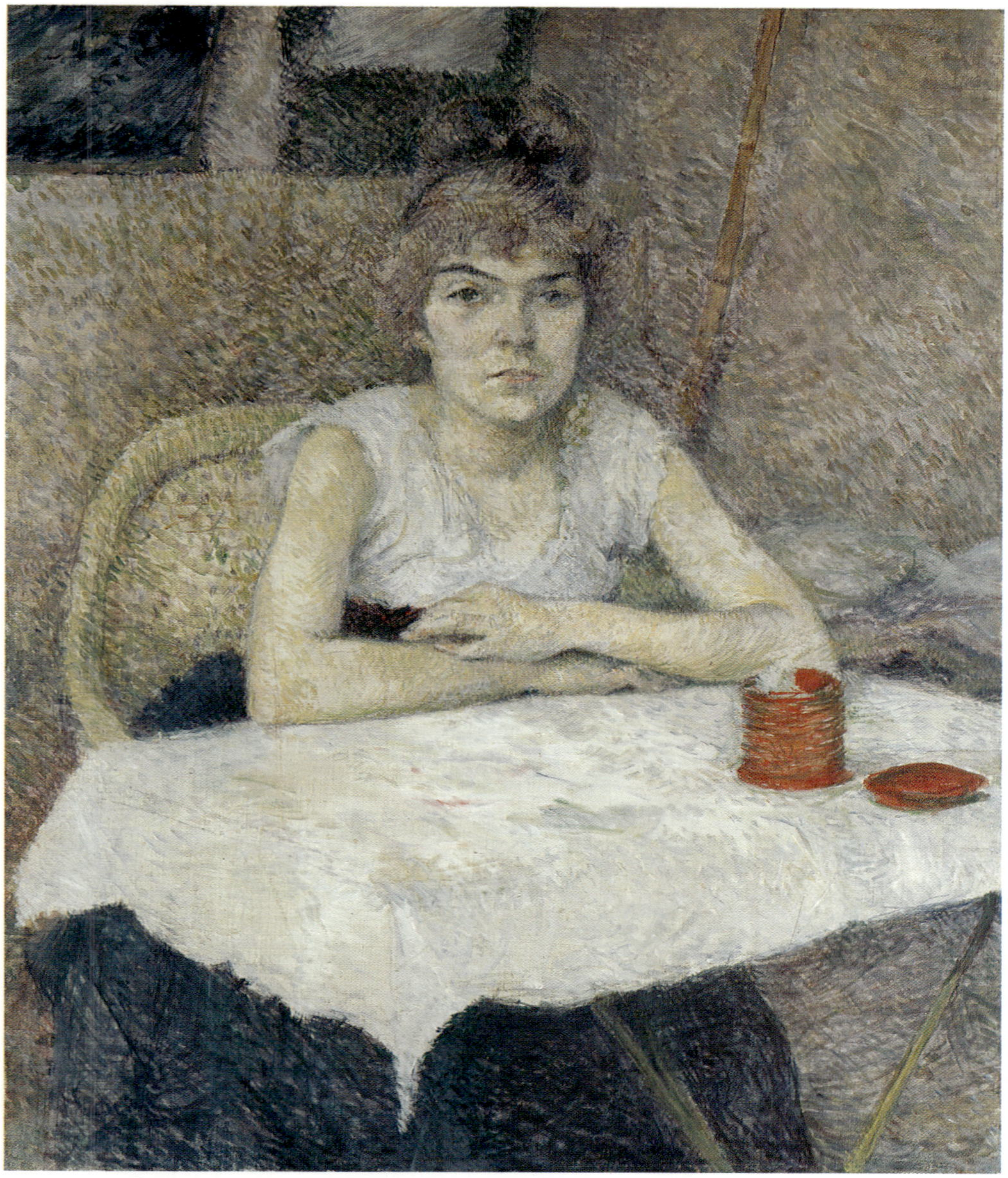

177
Henri de Toulouse-Lautrec 1864–1901
Woman at a table, Poudre de riz 1887
Van Gogh Museum, Amsterdam

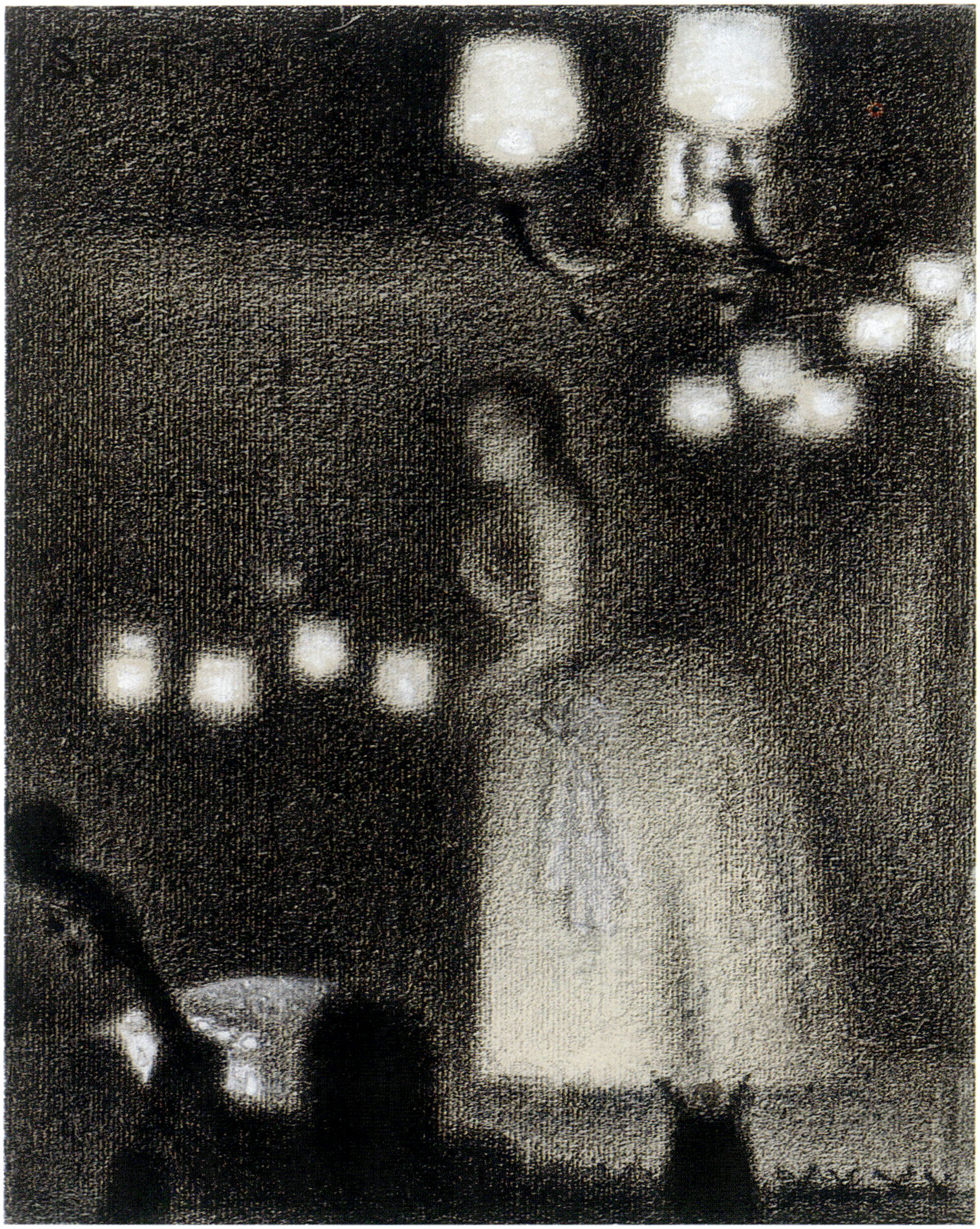

178

Georges Seurat 1859–1891

Woman singing in a café chantant, Eden concert 1887

Van Gogh Museum, Amsterdam

Bonger. In January 1888 Theo acquired Toulouse-Lautrec's *Woman at a table, Poudre de riz* [**177**] for 150 francs.[39] Two months later – on 2 or 3 March – he managed to obtain Seurat's *Woman singing at a café chantant, Eden concert* [**178**] for just 16 francs at the Pillet auction at the Hôtel Drouot.

Theo's collection cannot be regarded as a comprehensive overview of the modern art of the last quarter of the 19th century: the work of too many artists is missing. The tone of the collection in its present state is set by the works of the second generation Parisian avant-garde: Bernard, Gauguin and Toulouse-Lautrec. Thanks to his long residence in the French capital, Theo had a good understanding of the developments of modern art. He already had a penchant for the work of several impressionists – Degas, Monet and Pissarro – before even Vincent became acquainted with them. Vincent's arrival in Paris in March 1886 balanced their roles. There can be no doubt, however, that it was Vincent who mainly introduced his brother to the young artists mentioned above.

The formation of Theo's collection was not based solely on well-considered aesthetic preferences and choices. He regularly received works as gifts from artists, or in exchange for paintings by Vincent. His limited finances obliged him to restrict his purchases to the work of artists on the lower rungs of the art market. However, as *gérant* of the Boussod, Valadon & Cie. branch at the Boulevard Montmartre, and as the brother of an artist who was active in avant-garde circles, he knew his way around this layer of the art world. Without capital, but with patience, business acumen, an eye to the future and a little luck, Theo managed to assemble a collection which still captivates many a viewer.

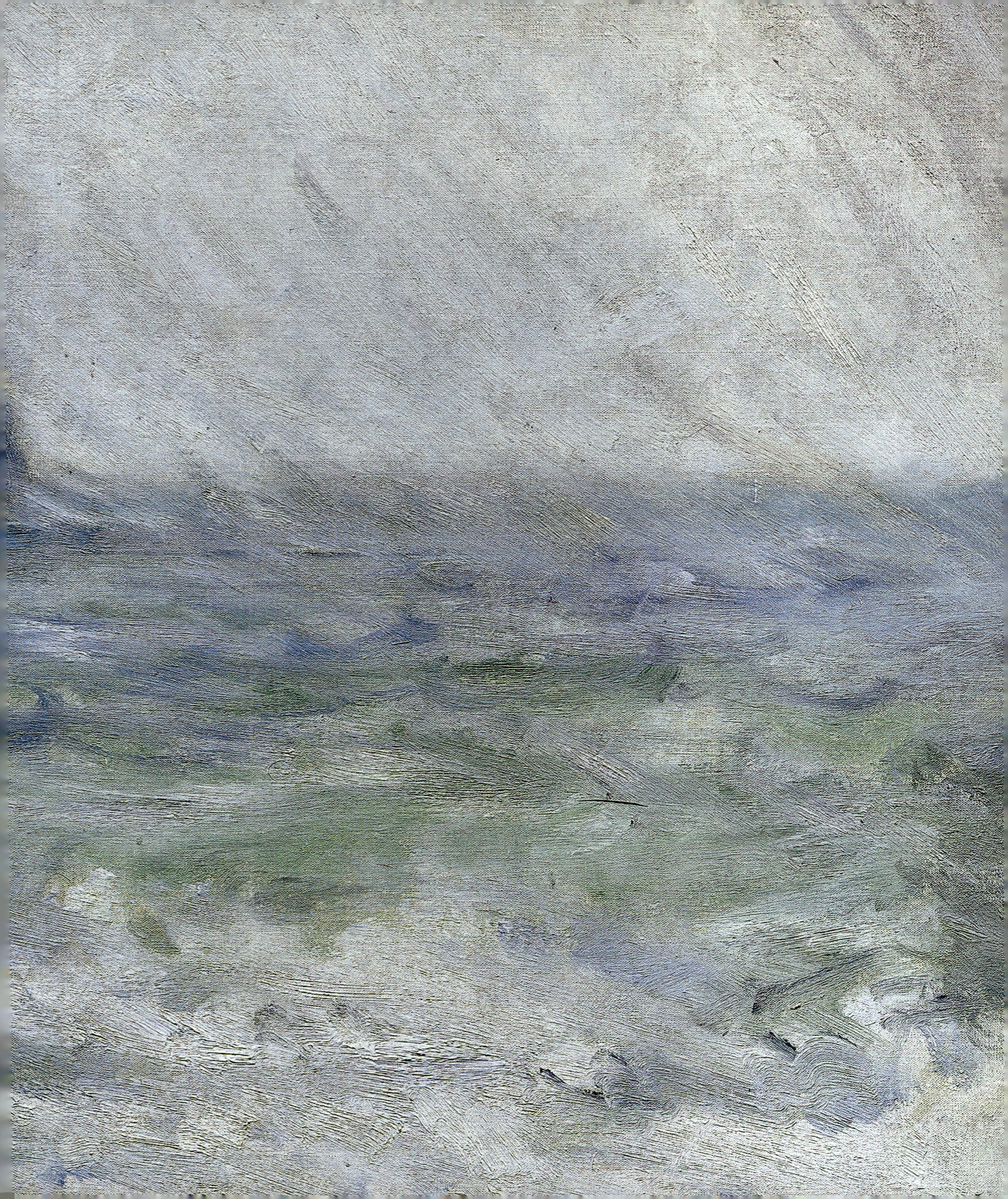

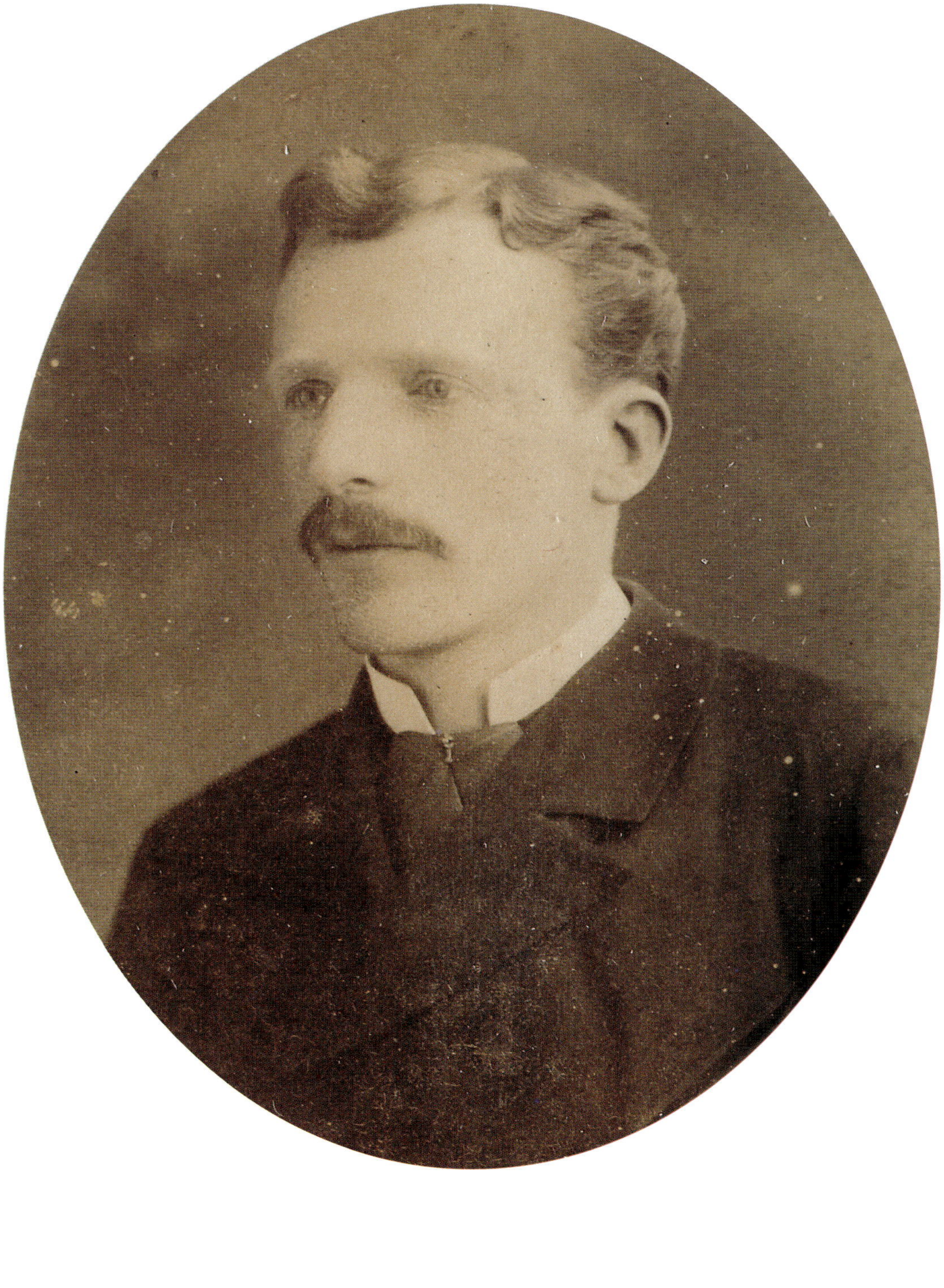

179
Theo van Gogh in 1889

Chronology

Theo van Gogh

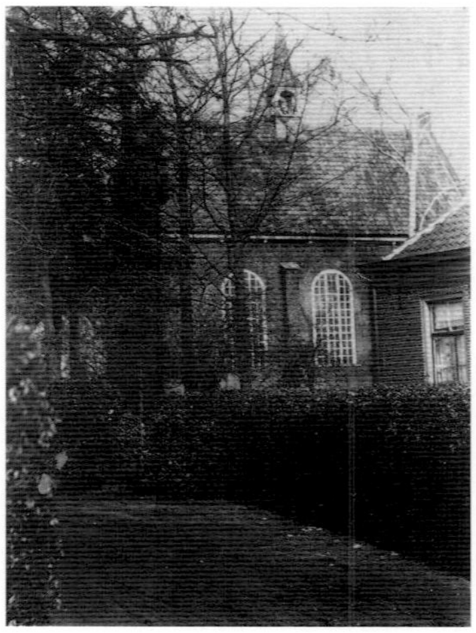

180

The Reformed church in Zundert

1857

1 May

Born in Groot-Zundert, son of Theodorus van Gogh and Anna Cornelia van Gogh-Carbentus.

1864–1871

Privately educated at home.

1871

Moves to Helvoirt. From January goes to school in Oisterwijk.

1872

September

Visits Vincent in The Hague. Start of their correspondence.

1873

January

Takes a job at Goupil & Cie., 58, Rue Montagne de la Cour in Brussels, the gallery that used to belong to his uncle, Hendrik van Gogh. Until March lodges at the home of Reverend Hendrik van den Brink at the Place Catherine and subsequently moves to the Rue St Catherine.

June

Moves to 58, Rue Montagne de la Cour.

circa 12 November

Transferred to Goupil & Cie., Plaats 14, in The Hague. Lodges with the Roos family at the Lange Beestenmarkt 32.

1875

14 June

Death of Annet Haanebeek.

1876

31 March - mid-April

Does the first spring tour for Goupil & Cie. promoting the new print bargains.

1 April

Vincent dismissed from Goupil & Cie. in Paris.

8 April

Meets Vincent in Etten before the latter leaves for Ramsgate.

October - mid-November

Seriously ill.

1877

January - April

Theo has an affair with an unidentified woman.

18 March

Travels to Amsterdam with Vincent, where they call on Cornelis Marinus van Gogh and visit the Museum van der Hoop.

19 May

Meets Vincent again in Amsterdam.

25 - 26 December

Meets Vincent during the Christmas holidays in Etten.

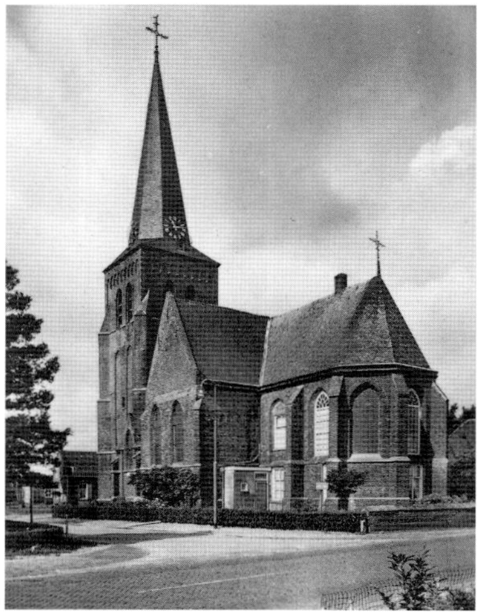

181
The Reformed church in Helvoirt

1878
1 May - I November
Temporarily transferred to the main branch of Goupil & Cie. in Paris. Works at the Exposition Universelle.
15 November
On his way back to the Netherlands visits Vincent in Laeken (Brussels).

1879
January
Comes to a financial agreement with Goupil & Cie.
14 August
Meets Vincent in the Borinage. They have no more contact until July 1880.
circa 1 November
Transferred permanently to Paris

1880
July
Given a more responsible position.
August
On Theo's advice, Vincent opts for life as an artist.
24 September
Asks Vincent to join him in Paris.

1881
January / February
Appointed *gérant* at Goupil's branch at 19, Boulevard Montmartre. Begins helping Vincent with his expenses.

1882
1 January
From 1 January 1882 earns 4,000 francs a year, in addition to a bonus of 7.5% of the net annual turnover of the branch on the Boulevard Montmartre. Supports Vincent monthly with an allowance of 100 francs.
circa 11 March
Vincent advises Theo to become a painter.
April
Moves to the 25, Rue de Laval.
4 August
Visits Vincent in The Hague.
3 December
Vincent describes Theo as `one of the best informed art dealers.`

1883
January
Has an affair with a certain `Marie` which lasts until the beginning of March 1884.
May
Theo's parents entirely disapprove of his plans to marry Marie in October 1883.
22 July
Financial difficulties; fears he will no longer be able to support Vincent.
25 - 26 July
Vincent writes to Theo that his artistic production is now Theo's property.
14 - circa 28 August
Spends his holidays with his parents in Nuenen.
October - November
Has a conflict with his superiors. Considers resigning.
December
Vincent criticises their relationship.

1884
circa 1 April
Vincent promises to send Theo work on a monthly basis; the pictures will become Theo's property.
circa 9 December
Vincent is convinced that the brothers must part ways.
circa 15 December
Financial difficulties.

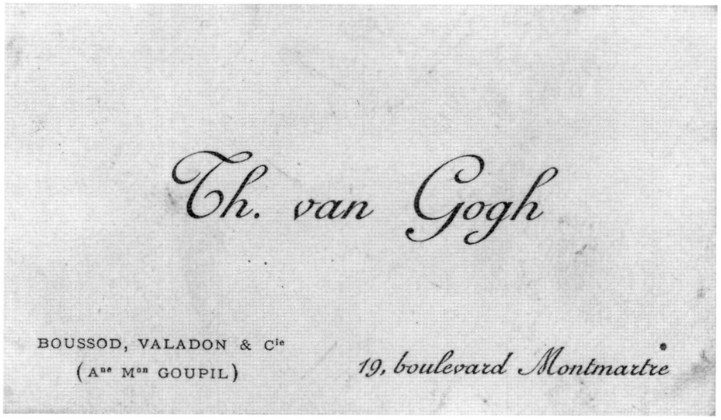

182
Theo van Gogh's visiting card c. 1881–90

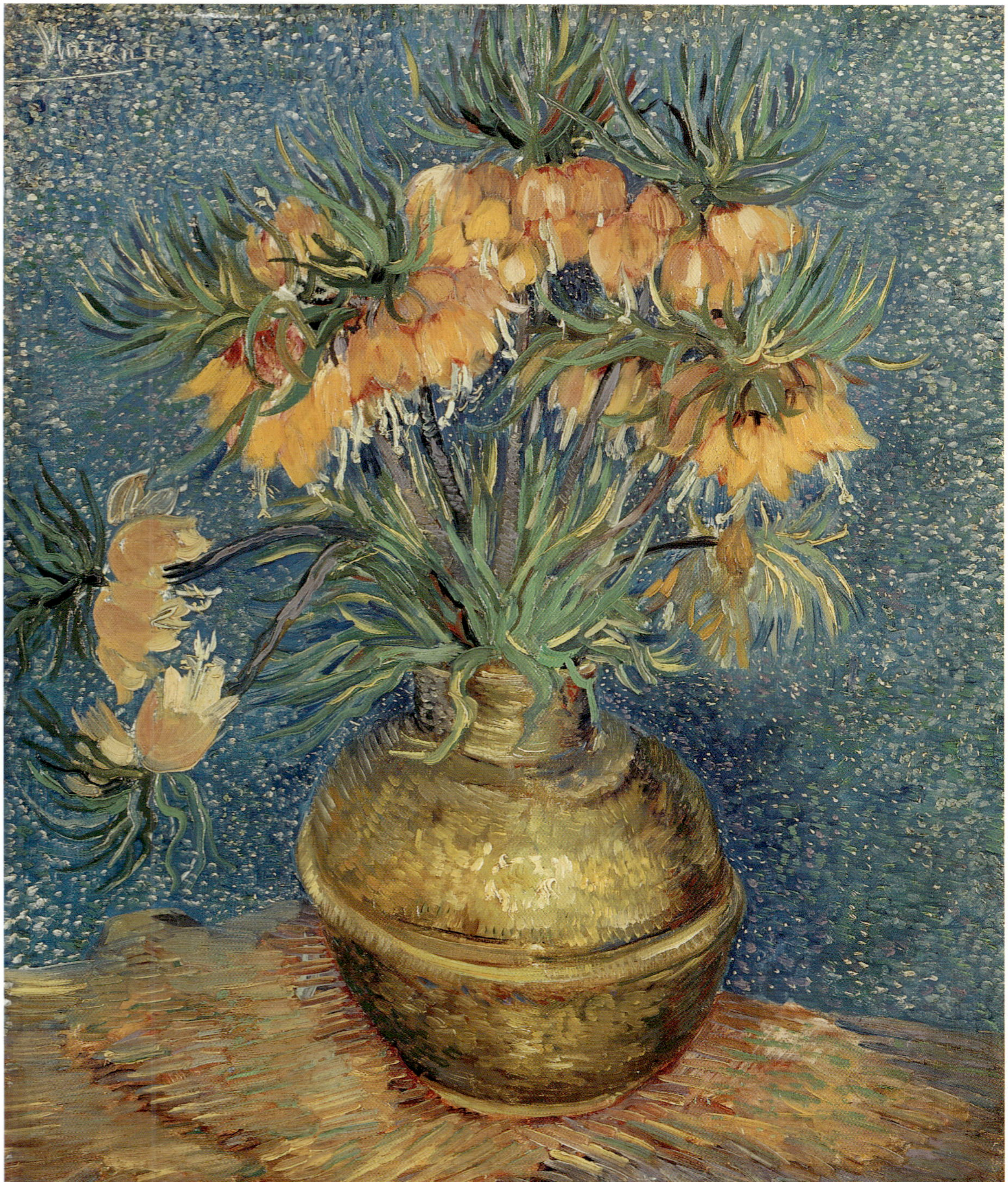

183
Vincent van Gogh 1853–1890
Imperial crown fritillaria in a copper vase 1887
Musée d'Orsay, Paris

1885

Early January

Proposes Vincent's monthly allowance be increased to 150 francs. One of his clients offers him a job at his office at a salary of 1,000 francs a month.

26 March

Theodorus van Gogh dies at the age of 63. Theo travels to the Netherlands on 27 March for his father's funeral (30 March).

5 May

Vincent remarks on the fact that Theo sees so many `Daubignys, Corots, Millets Duprés, Israëls, Herkomers, Bretons, &c.`

25 July

Travels to Nuenen with Andries Bonger.

6 August

Visits Vincent in his studio in Nuenen.

7 August

Visits the Bonger family in Amsterdam. Meets Jo Bonger for the first time.

Late August

In financial difficulties. Vincent advises Theo to choose another profession.

Early February

Suggests that Vincent study at Fernand Cormon's studio in Paris.

1 March

Vincent arrives in Paris.

Beginning of June

Theo and Vincent move to the 54, Rue Lepic

23 June

According to Dries Bonger, Vincent and Theo are not getting along. Theo has health problems.

July

Theo writes to his mother that Vincent and he are doing fine. Theo and Vincent build up `a good collection` with exchanges.

August

Has already had a relationship with a certain `S` for a year. Visits the Netherlands to see he can establish a gallery with Dries Bonger. His Uncle Cent is, however, refuses to back them financially.

October - November

Alexander Reid comes to live with Theo and Vincent, probably invited by Theo.

30 and 31 December

Has a serious nervous complaint. According to Dries Bonger, Theo has decided to break with Vincent.

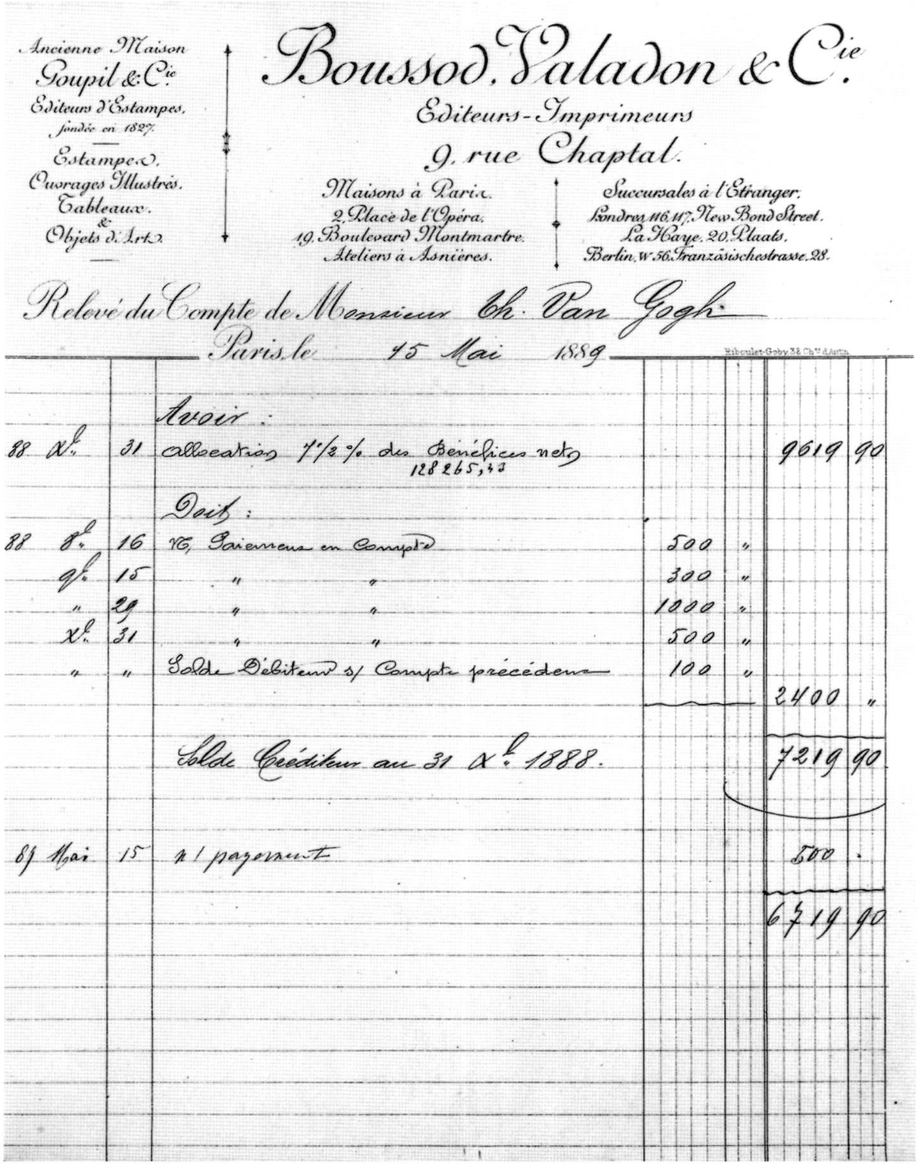

Ancienne Maison Goupil & Cie
Éditeurs d'Estampes, fondée en 1827.
Estampes, Ouvrages Illustrés, Tableaux & Objets d'Art.

Boussod, Valadon & Cie
Éditeurs-Imprimeurs
9, rue Chaptal.

Maisons à Paris. 2, Place de l'Opéra. 19, Boulevard Montmartre. Ateliers à Asnières.

Succursales à l'Étranger. Londres 116, 117, New Bond Street. La Haye, 20, Plaats. Berlin, W. 56, Französischestrasse, 28.

Relevé du Compte de Monsieur Th. Van Gogh

Paris le 15 Mai 1889

Riboulet-Goby, 38 Ch. d'Antin

			Avoir:		
88 Xbre		31	Allocation 7 1/2 % des Bénéfices nets 128265,43		9619 90
			Doit:		
88	8bre	16	N/ Paiements en Compte	500 "	
	9bre	15	" "	300 "	
	"	29	" "	1000 "	
	Xbre	31	" "	500 "	
	"	"	Solde Débiteur s/ Compte précédent	100 "	
					2400 "
			Solde Créditeur au 31 Xbre 1888.		7219 90
89 Mai		15	n/ payement		500 .
					6719 90

184

Theo van Gogh's account for Boussod, Valadon & Cie.'s main branch in the Rue Chaptal (1888) 1889

1887

10 May

Visits Monet at Giverney

14 May

Sisley visits the gallery on the Boulevard Montmartre.

6 July

Visits Degas

22 July

Visits the Bonger family in Amsterdam. Asks Jo Bonger to marry him and is refused.

1 October

Alphonse Portier and Armand Guillaumin visit Theo to see Vincent's work.

November

Vincent organises an exhibition in the Grand Bouillon, Restaurant du Châlet, 43, Avenue de Clichy, Montmartre, with work by the painters of the so-called *petit boulevard*. Theo is introduced to Gauguin, Guillaumin, Pissarro and Seurat.

December

Meets Gaugin at Schuffenecker's on the Boulevard Montparnasse. Decides to take Gauguin's work on commission. Organises an exhibition with works by Pissarro, Gauguin and Guillaumin. Is in contact with Toulouse-Lautrec.

1888

January

Exhibits pastels by Degas and work by Gauguin.

19 February

Vincent leaves for Arles.

Late February

Vincent advises Theo to tell H.G. Tersteeg of the Hague branch of Boussod, Valadon & Cie. of their plans to promote the impressionists in England.

March

Exhibits work by Pissarro.

circa 3 March

Arnold Hendrik Koning moves in with Theo.

10 March

Vincent advises Theo to deal Seurat.

circa 14 March

Visits Signac. Alexander Reid is on bad terms with both Vincent and Theo.

April

Theo exhibits work by Gauguin, Schuffenecker and Zandomenghi.

2 April

Theo sends a group of impressionist works to Tersteeg in The Hague.

9 April

Visits Emile Bernard.

circa 24 April

Conflict with his superiors because, in their view, the impressionists are not selling well enough.

May

Theo exhibits lithographs by Thornley after Degas, and work by Schuffenecker, Zandomeneghi, Rodin, Gauguin and posters by Jules Chéret.

circa 20 May

Troubled by extreme fatigue. Consults Dr Gruby, a specialist in herbal medicine. Takes iodine.

31 May

Visits Degas

4 June

Purchases ten Antibes pictures by Monet and exhibits them at the Boulevard Montmartre gallery.

circa 15 June

Meets Guy de Maupassant.

15 July

Vincent advises Theo to exhibit Japanese art.

August

Exhibits work by Pissarro.

circa 4 August

Stays in the Netherlands for the funeral of Uncle Cent, who died on 28 July.

29 September

Gauguin considers Theo his sole agent.

October

Theo exhibits works by Pissarro, lithographs by Thornley after Degas, one work by Manet and one by Zandomenghi.

23 October

Gauguin arrives in Arles.

28 October

Meijer de Haan moves in with Theo. In return for his financial support Theo gets Vincent's work and one painting by Gauguin.

November

Exhibits work by Gauguin.

Early December

Meets Jo Bonger in Paris. They decide to get married.

24 December

Theo leaves on the night train for Arles, where Vincent has cut off a piece of his ear.

25 December

Travels to Paris with Gauguin. Jo goes to Amsterdam.

28 December

Writes to Jo that he is frightened he will have to say farewell to Vincent for good.

1889

2 January

Vincent writes a few reassuring words to Theo from Arles.

3 January

Gauguin gives Theo *Vincent van Gogh painting sunflowers* as a present. [**45**]

5 January

Leaves for Amsterdam.

7 January

Vincent is discharged from the hospital in Arles.

9 January

Announces engagement to Jo Bonger.

15 January

Visited by Camille and Lucien Pissarro.

22 January

Visited by Ferdinand Hart Nibbrig and Arthur Henri Christiaan Briët.

27 January

Writes to Jo that he had been plagued by bouts of coughing for the previous two years, but since meeting her they had disappeared.

1 February

Monet visits his branch on the Boulevard Montmartre.

3 February

Visits Gauguin where he sees some `very good things.`

7 February

Opening of an exhibition of work by Monet, pastels by Degas and a Rodin sculpture. In the evening visited by Pissarro and two of his sons.

9 February

Considers having Vincent committed to a mental institution in Marseille or Aix-en-Provence.

18 February

Visited by Pissarro.

6 March
Monet again visits the branch on the Boulevard Montmartre.
10 March
Aided by Meijer de Haan, moves Vincent's paintings to the new apartment on the third floor of 8, Cité Pigalle.
16 March
Theo tells Vincent of Signac's plans to visit him in Arles.
18 April
Marries Jo Bonger
2 May
Vincent admitted to the hospital at St Rémy.
7 May
Visited by Camille and Lucien Pissarro, Jozef Isaacson, Ferdinand Hart Nibbrig and Dries Bonger.
11 May
Exhibits work by Degas.
21 May
Writes to Vincent that he is finding it difficult to sell work by Renoir, Guillaumin, Pissarro and Gauguin.
27 September
Exhibits work by Degas and a painting by Toulouse-Lautrec.
27 November
Exhibits work by Monet from the summer of 1888. For Theo, Degas is the most important painter of the age.
8 December
Albert Aurier visits Theo.
17 December
Pissarro gives *Figures in a meadow* to Jo as a present. **[175]**
22 December
Writes to Vincent that it is impossible to sell Gauguin's work.

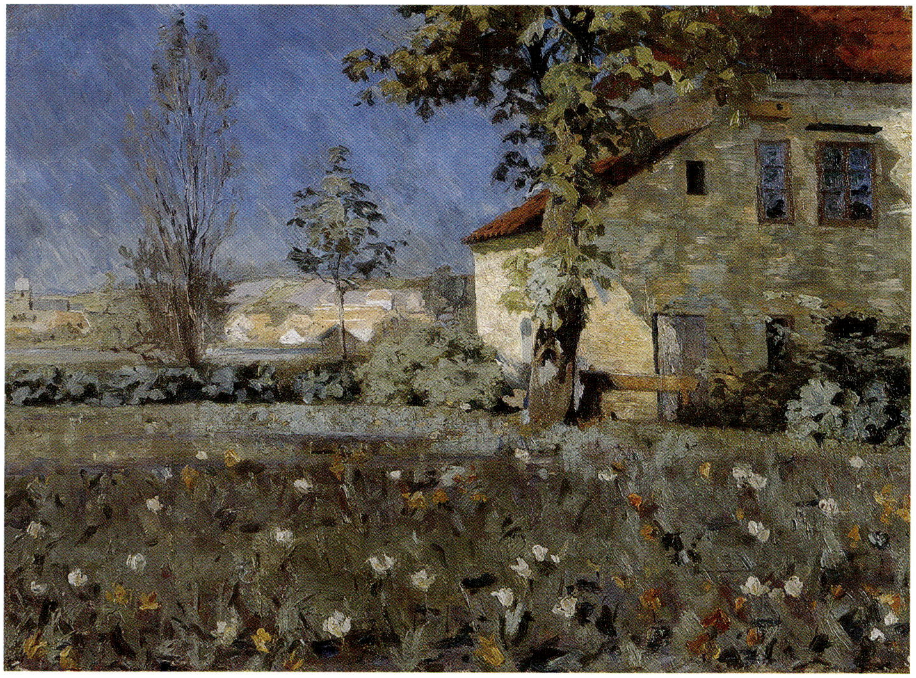

185
Christian Mourier-Petersen 1858–1945
House in a garden c. 1890
Van Gogh Museum, Amsterdam

1890
29 January
Vincent has another attack.
31 January
Birth of Vincent Willem van Gogh.
February
Exhibits a sculpture by Gauguin and recent work by Pissarro.
25 February
Mourier-Petersen gives Theo *House in a garden* (Van Gogh Museum, Amsterdam). **[185]**
9 March
Opening of the Indépendant's exhibition, where Vincent exhibits ten works selected by Theo.
3 April
He writes to Tersteeg that he has quarrelled badly with his employers.
26 April
Visits Puvis de Chavannes.
16 May
Vincent leaves St Rémy. Visits Theo and Jo in Paris.
20 May
Vincent arrives in Auvers-sur-Oise.
End May - circa 23 June
Organises a Raffaëlli exhibition.
8 June
Visits Paul Gachet **[186]** and Vincent in Auvers with Jo and Vincent-Willem.
30 June
Vincent Willem is seriously ill. Theo is worried about his position at work.
7 July
Receives a visit from Vincent.
8 July
Gives his superiors an ultimatum for a raise.
14 July
Accompanies Jo and Vincent Willem to Leiden.
16 July
Stays in Antwerp.
18 July
Stays in Brussels
19 July
Vists Rodin with Manzi.
21 July
Decides to stay in the employment of Boussod, Valadon & Cie.
28 July
Receives the news that Vincent has shot

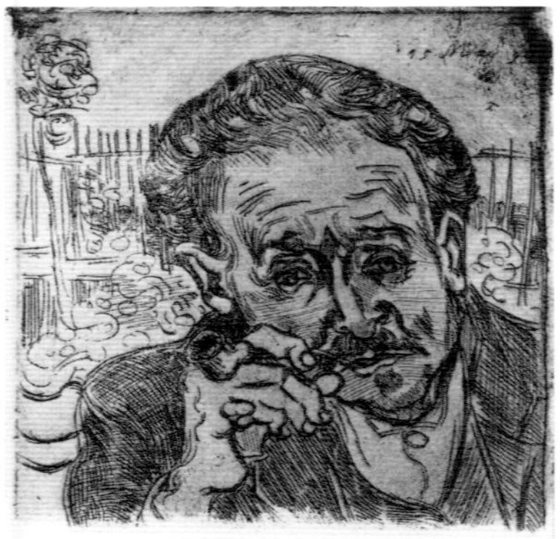

186
Vincent van Gogh 1853–1890
Portrait of Dr Gachet 1890
Van Gogh Museum, Amsterdam

himself on 27 July. Travels to Auvers.

29 July
Vincent dies.

31 July
Vincent is buried in Auvers-sur-Oise.

August
Travels to his mother in Leiden on 3 August, where Jo and Vincent Willem are staying. The family leaves on 9 August to go to the Bonger family in Amsterdam.

2 September
Theo's health deteriorates rapidly.

circa 16 September
Moves to a new apartment on the first floor of 8, Cité Pigalle. There, he organises an exhibition of Vincent's work. Emile Bernard helps Theo with the interior decorations (22-24 September).

27 September
Writes to Wil that he had been `crazy` for a while.

4 October
Appears to be suffering from extreme nervous exhaustion.

6 October
Wants to organise an exhibition of Pissarro's work.

9 October
Mental and physical collapse.

12 October
Moved to the hospital La Maison Dubois in the Fauborg St Denis.

14 October
Transferred to Dr Blanche's clinic in Passy.

18 November
Admitted to the Willem Arntszkliniek in Utrecht.

25 January
Dies at the age of 33.

29 January
Buried in Utrecht.

1914

April
Theo's remains are transferred to Auvers-sur-Oise, where he is buried next to Vincent

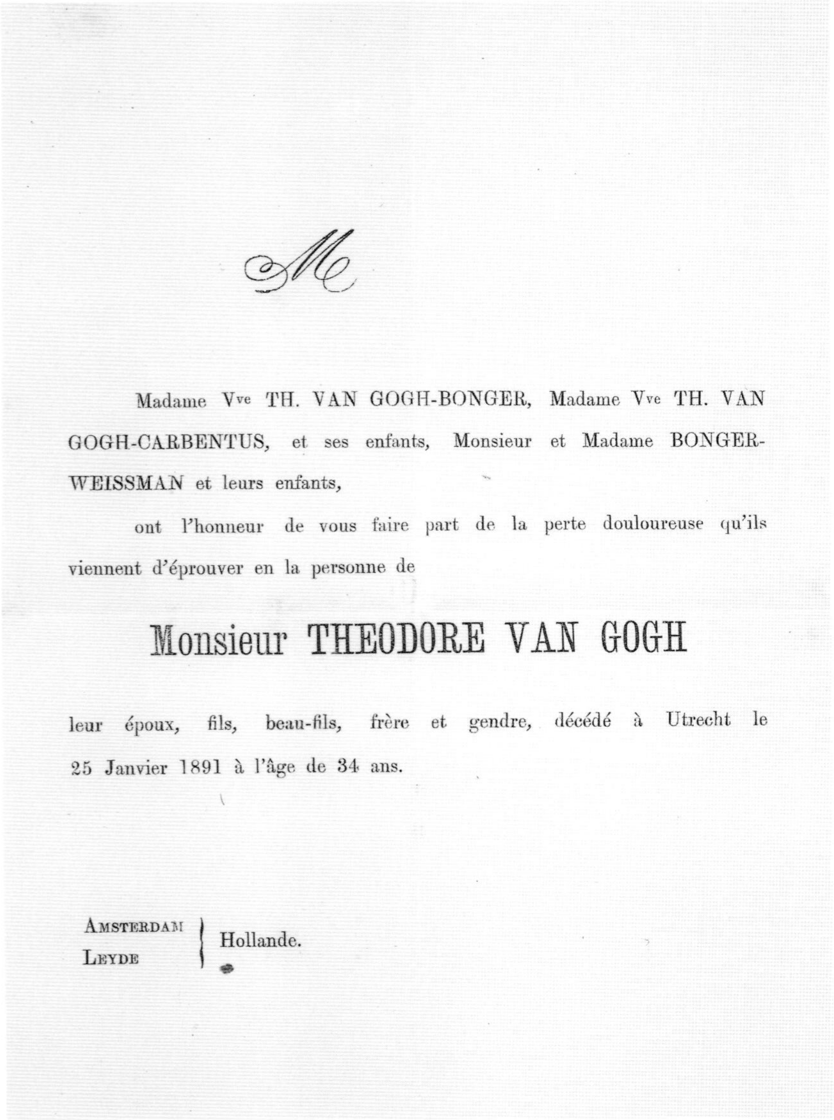

M

Madame Vve TH. VAN GOGH-BONGER, Madame Vve TH. VAN GOGH-CARBENTUS, et ses enfants, Monsieur et Madame BONGER-WEISSMAN et leurs enfants,

ont l'honneur de vous faire part de la perte douloureuse qu'ils viennent d'éprouver en la personne de

Monsieur THEODORE VAN GOGH

leur époux, fils, beau-fils, frère et gendre, décédé à Utrecht le 25 Janvier 1891 à l'âge de 34 ans.

AMSTERDAM
LEYDE } Hollande.

187
Death notice of Theo van Gogh, 25 January 1891

To the reader

In the notes the b-numbers refer to archival *sources (largely family correspondence). These are kept in the Van Gogh Museum, Amsterdam (Vincent van Gogh Foundation).*

Notes

Chris Stolwijk

Theo van Gogh
A life

I would like to dedicate this essay to Jan van Vliet (1929-1998), who gave me the opportunity of spending so many carefree days in the countryside around Teckop.

1 A moving description of this unveiling is to be found in G.J.A. Manders, 'Ten Geleide,' Mark Edo Tralbaut, *De gebroeders Van Gogh*, Zundert 1964, pp. 5-38. See also idem, *Geboorte-akte en doopcel van het Van Gogh-monument te Zundert*, Zundert 1964, pp. 12-13, and Rudi Fuchs, 'Vincent en Theo: reflecties bij Zadkines Van Gogh-monument in Zundert,' *Brabantia* 13 (August 1964), pp. 120-22. Zadkine had already produced *De gebroeders Van Gogh, zittend* in 1956; see Sylvian Lecombre, *Ossip Zadkine: l'oeuvre sculpté*, Paris 1994, no. 497. Models of both sculptures are in the Van Gogh Museum.

2 The history of Van Gogh's reception has been described by Carol M. Zemel, *The formation of a legend: Van Gogh criticism, 1890-1920*, Ann Arbor 1980. For the history of his reception in the Netherlands and the Low Countries see Joop M. Joosten, 'De eerste kennismaking met het werk van Vincent van Gogh in Nederland,' *Museumjournaal* 14 (1969), pp. 154-57, and Fred Leeman, 'Van Goghs posthume roem in de Lage Landen,' exhib. cat. *Vincent van Gogh en de moderne kunst 1890-1914*, Amsterdam (Van Gogh Museum) & Essen (Museum Folkwang) 1990-91, pp. 162-81.

3 In 1892-93 Boele van Hensbroek wrote three articles on Vincent and Theo in *De Nederlandsche Spectator*: Flanor [P.A.M. Boele van Hensbroek], 'Vlugmaeren,' (9 January 1892); 'Vlugmaeren,' (May 1893); and 'De Van Goghs,' (26 August 1893). In May 1892 the critic Loffelt wrote that two tragedies had unfolded around Vincent's work: that of Vincent the sick genius, and that of '[his] loving brother, who had faith in that genius and lapsed into madness himself, dying at an early age'; see E.G.O. [A.C. Loffelt], 'Vincent van Gogh,' *Het Vaderland* (19 May 1892).

4 Jan Veth, 'Th. van Gogh,' *De Amsterdammer* (2 February 1891), p. 3, and J.J. Isaacson, 'Uit de schilderswereld: Theodorus van Gogh,' *De Portefeuille* 12 (7 February 1891), p. 573.

5 See *Vincent van Gogh en de moderne kunst*, cit. (note 2).

6 E.[lisabeth] H.[uberta] du Quesne-Van Gogh, *Vincent van Gogh: persoonlijke herinneringen aangaande een kunstenaar*, Baarn 1910, p. 94.

7 *Vincent van Gogh, brieven aan zijn broeder*, ed. Johanna van Gogh-Bonger, 3 vols., Amsterdam 1914. In 1893-95 and 1897, in the monthly *Mercure de France*, Emile Bernard provided extracts from a selection of letters Vincent had written him during his time in France. In that same year, a number of letters from the Dutch period were published in a special number of the Belgian periodical *Van Nu en Straks* devoted to Van Gogh. The German-speaking regions were introduced to translations of previously published letters in *Kunst und Künstler* in 1904. Two years later Paul Cassirer produced a German translation of the letters from the *Mercure de France*.

8 Julius Meier-Graefe, *Vincent*, 2 vols., Munich 1921. For the 1925 edition Meier-Graefe altered the text in a number of places. In 1919 the author had already published a biographical sketch entitled 'Vincent und Theo' in *Der Neue Mercur* 3 (1919), pp. 36-77. Meier-Graefe's 1921 biography was the starting point for H. Reece's *Vincent: a biographical study*, published in London in 1922. A Dutch translation of parts of Meier-Graefe's 1921 and 1925 editions appeared in 1929, entitled *Het leven van Vincent van Gogh*. In 1929 Just Havelaars's *Vincent van Gogh* was published in Amsterdam.

9 Her brother, Andries Bonger, supported her on this. In reaction to Boele van Hensbroek (op. cit. [note 3]), he had made a case for a more objective approach to the life and work of both brothers. In Bonger's view, transforming him into a legend could only damage Vincent's art. He pointed out that the brothers' relationship had not always been easy, that Theo had in no way overstated Vincent's talent, and that it was Theo rather than Vincent who first became acquainted with the most

recent developments in French contemporary art; see Andries Bonger, 'Letteren en kunst,' *De Nieuwe Rotterdamsche Courant* (5 September 1893). See for Boele van Hensbroek's reply to Bonger's article the same periodical, 7 September 1893.
10 b 2166 VF/1982, Fabian, 25 June 1915 (to Paul Gachet, Jr).
11 See, for example, Evert van Uitert, 'De legendevorming te bevorderen: notities over de Vincent van Gogh mythe,' in exhib. cat. *Rond de roem van Vincent van Gogh*, Amsterdam (Van Gogh Museum) 1977, pp. 15-27, and for a more general approach: Y. Rosenberg and T. Kōdera (eds.), *The mythology of Vincent van Gogh*, Tokyo & Amsterdam 1993.
12 Havelaar, op. cit. (note 8), p. 23.
13 See Jan Hulsker, *Vincent and Theo van Gogh: a dual biography*, Ann Arbor 1990, and John Rewald, 'Theo van Gogh, Goupil and the impressionists,' *Gazette des Beaux-Arts* 81 (January-February 1973), pp. 1-108. This article was also included in his *Studies in post-impressionism*, London 1986, pp. 7-115. Theo van Gogh's business activities are also discussed by Monique Nonne in 'Les marchands de Van Gogh,' exhib. cat. *Van Gogh à Paris*, Paris (Musée d'Orsay) 1988, pp. 336-38, and in Richard Thomson's contribution to this catalogue. Theo's younger years are described in Chris Stolwijk, '"Our crown and our honour and our joy": Theo van Gogh's early years,' *Van Gogh Museum Journal* (1997-98), pp. 42-57. Compare the relationship between Theo and Vincent in, for example, the following studies: W. Jos de Gruyter, 'Theo and Vincent van Gogh,' *Mededelingen van de Dienst van Schone Kunsten der Gemeente 's-Gravenhage* 8 (1953), no. 5/6, pp. 2-5; Charles Mauron, *Vincent et Théo van Gogh: une symbiose*, Amsterdam 1953; Ir. V.W. van Gogh, 'Theo van Gogh without Vincent,' *Art News* 52 (1953), pp. 24-29, 63; G. Kraus, *De verhouding van Theo en Vincent van Gogh*, Amsterdam 1954; Mark Edo Tralbaut, *Vincent, Theo, Johanna*, Amsterdam 1953; L. Roelandt, *Vincent van Gogh et son frère Théo*, Paris 1957; Jan Hulsker, 'What Theo really thought of Vincent,' *Vincent: Bulletin of the Rijksmuseum Vincent van Gogh* 3 (1974), no. 2, and Jean Menaud, *Nous, Théo et Vincent van Gogh*, Paris 1987.
14 The archives of the Vincent van Gogh Foundation – including the surviving correspondence between Theo and Vincent and between Theo and other members of the family – were invaluable to this study. These archives are kept in the Van Gogh Museum.
15 Johanna van Gogh-Bonger, 'Inleiding,' in *Vincent van Gogh*, cit. (note 7), p. xii. See also *De brieven van Vincent van Gogh*, ed. Han van Crimpen and Monique Berends-Albert, 4 vols., The Hague 1990, vol. 1, p. 2.
16 Anna Cornelia Carbentus was born on 10 september 1819, daughter of the bookseller Willem Carbentus (1792-1845) and Anna Cornelia van der Gaag (1792-1835) born in The Hague. She was the older sister of Cornelia Carbentus, who had married Theodorus van Gogh's favourite brother, the art dealer Vincent van Gogh (better known as Uncle Cent) in 1850.
17 Zundert, Gemeentearchief, 'Geboorteakte Theodorus van Gogh,' and b 2745 V/1982, Etten, 30 April 1876 (from Theo's mother to Theo).
18 b 2743 V/1982, Helvoirt, 29 April 1876 (from his father to Theo).
19 b 2742 V/1982.
20 Van Gogh-Bonger, op. cit. (note 15), p. 3.
21 b 900 V/1962, Brussels, 22 April 1885 (from Theo to his mother).
22 For Theodorus van Gogh's salary as a clergyman see Han van Crimpen, 'De familie van Gogh in Brabant,' in exhib. cat. *Van Gogh in Brabant*, 's-Hertogenbosch (Noordbrabants Museum) 1987-88, pp. 80 and 90, note 16. The Van Gogh's had a nurse, a housemaid, a gardener and a governess in service; see Jan Meyers, *De jonge Vincent*, Amsterdam 1989, pp. 41 and 54-55. Compare also a letter from Father Van Gogh to Theo from April 1874: 'Although we weren't rich, we were able to give you a good education'; b 2697 V/1982, Helvoirt, 29 April 1874.
23 b 2600 V/1982, Leeuwarden, 4 February 1873 (from Anna to Theo).
24 b 2 710 V/1982, Helvoirt, 10 July 1874 (from his parents to Theo).
25 b 2 638 V/1982, Helvoirt, 2 July 1873 (from his mother to Theo).
26 b 2595 V/1982, Helvoirt, 24 January 1873, and b 2604 V/1982, Helvoirt, 19 February 1873 (from Theo to his parents).
27 b 2226 V/1982, Tiel, 9 January 1876 (from Lies to Theo).
28 b 2229 V/1982, Tiel, 30 January 1876 (from Lies to Theo). See also her letter dated 27 October, in which she writes that the Van Gogh children had never had such a good time as during 'their pleasant years when [we] were in Zundert'; b 2358 V/1982.
29 Van Gogh-Bonger, op. cit. (note 15), p. 4.
30 b 2404 V/1982, Princenhage, 19 October 1889 (from Wil to Jo Bonger).
31 b 2641 V/1982, Helvoirt, 12 July 1873 (from his mother to Theo).
32 Du Quesne-Van Gogh, op. cit. (note 6), p. 37, and b 2679 V/1982, Leeuwarden, 6 January 1874 (from Anna to Theo).
33 b 1009 V/1962, Leiden, 31 July 1890 (from his mother to Theo).
34 b 2503 V/1982, Tiel, 4 February 1877 (from Lies to Theo).
35 See also Van Gogh-Bonger, op. cit. (note 15), p. 5.
36 b 939 V/1962, undated letter from Theo to his mother. In letter 17/13, from January 1874, Vincent wrote to Theo that these types of walks were necessary to the art lover for various reasons: 'Keep going for walks and loving nature, because this is the only real way to get to understand art. Painters understand nature, they love it and teach us to see.'
37 Vincent did not envy him: he wrote to Theo in his first letter of 29 September 1872: 'What terrible weather, you'll probably feel awful on those walks to Oisterwijk.' See also 2/2, The Hague, 13 December 1872.
38 The cost of educating the other children also posed major financial problems. Father Van Gogh's Helvoirt salary of 880 guilders was not much more than it had been in Zundert. However, there were certain fringe benefits attached to the job; see Van Crimpen, op. cit. (note 22), p. 80. As

far as expenses went, Anna had been at a private school in Leeuwarden since 1872; her parents had to pay about 500 guilders a year for her education. In the near future they would have to find suitable forms of education for Lies and Wil. Van Gogh's parents probably knew that Vincent would have to take part in a lottery in the spring of 1873 to determine whether he would have to do national service or not. Were his number to come up, they would have to find a replacement for him and pay a considerable sum in compensation. It was unthinkable that Vincent should serve in the army, as its soldiers were famous for their rough manners and loose morals. See Meyers, op. cit. (note 22), pp. 58-59.

39 From the late 1830s to 1858 Hendrik Vincent van Gogh (Uncle Hein) had a book and art dealer's business in Rotterdam. In the period 1863-73 he ran the branch of Goupil & Cie. in Brussels. From 1840 Uncle Cent ran a business dealing in artists' materials and art in The Hague. In 1861 he joined forces with Adolphe Goupil, founder of the gallery of the same name in Paris. His shop in The Hague subsequently became a branch of this famous European firm. Cornelis Marinus van Gogh (Uncle Cor) ran a bookshop and art dealership in Amsterdam from 1850; see Van Crimpen, op. cit. (note 22), pp. 75-77, and Chris Stolwijk, *Uit de schilderswereld: Nederlandse kunstschilders in de tweede helft van de negentiende eeuw*, Leiden 1998, pp. 310-13.

40 Hendrik van den Brink was married to Diderika van Binnendijke. On 20 July 1872 they had left Vriezenveen with their children Richard, Hendrik Reinier and Maud and settled in Brussels. Their daughters Catherina Alberta and Gijsberta Diederika were born there. On 23 November the entire family left Brussels for Roulers. The birth of Catherina Alberta on 12 February 1873 and her subsequent illness forced Theo to look for a different house. He moved to 4, Rue St Catherine, where he was registered on 23 March 1873. On 26 June he moved in with his supervisor, Mr Schmidt, at 58, Rue Montagne de la Cour, the address of Goupil & Cie. The house had belonged to his Uncle Hein who, seriously ill, had left for Laeken on 30 April. On 31 October Theo had his name removed from the municipal register. See Brussels, Gemeente Archief, 'Bevolkingregister,' inv. no. Q393 (red) 1866, O14 (red) 1866 and D336 (red) 1866.

41 b 2593 V/1982, Helvoirt, 9 January 1873 (from his mother to Theo).

42 b 2592 V/1982, Breda, 3 January 1873 (from his father to Theo).

43 b 2380 V/1982, Tiel, 13 December 1875 (from Lies to Theo).

44 Father Van Gogh wrote to Theo from Helvoirt on 5 March 1873: 'You have pleased us well with your letters. We need them so much, because life is so difficult apart, and when we are not together such letters are a marvelous elixir'; b 2507 V/1982.

45 b 2601 V/1982, Helvoirt, 10 February 1873 (from his parents to Theo): 'Dear Theo, we are so happy to get such good reports about you, that you are already earning so much money every month and, above all, that Mr Schmidt is pleased with your work and says that you are doing your best, so that you are sure to succeed.'

46 In 1871 his collection was housed in a separate gallery near his house in Princenhage; see Johan Gram, 'De kunstverzameling Vincent van Gogh in Pulchri Studio,' *Haagsche Stemmen* 2 (1889), pp. 371-82, and H. Dirven, 'De kunsthandelaar Vincent van Gogh uit Princenhage,' *Hage* 7 (1977), no. 19, pp. 5-77. The collection was auctioned in April 1889: The Hague (Pulchri Studio/C.M. van Gogh and H.G. Tersteeg), *Collection de feu M. Vincent van Gogh*, 2-3 April 1889.

47 See for example letter 9/9, London, 13 June 1873: 'Write to me above all about the paintings you have seen recently, and the new prints and lithographs. You should keep me up to date.'

48 Saskia de Bodt, *Halverwege Parijs: Willem Roelofs en de Nederlandse schilderskolonie in Brussel 1840-1890* (diss., Universiteit van Amsterdam, 1995), pp. 70-93.

49 b 2638 V/1982, Helvoirt, 2 July 1873 (from his mother to Theo): 'We think it's good, too, that you can go for such nice walks in and around Brussels; we enjoyed our country treks, when you could smell the hay and the potatoes, and saw the wheat which made you think of home.'

50 b 2630 V/1982, Helvoirt, 31 May 1873 (from his father to Theo). Theo also faithfully attended confirmation classes.

51 b 2640 V/1982, Helvoirt, 12 July 1873 (from his mother to Theo).

52 b 1896 V/1982, Brussels, 4 November 1873.

53 b 2673 V/1982, Helvoirt, 15 November 1873 (from his father to Theo).

54 b 2711 V/1982, Helvoirt, 18 July 1874 (from his parents to Theo).

55 After moving to the new premises at Plaats 14 in November 1875, Goupil's had a modern salon at its disposal, where clients were able to select their purchases from a varied, extensive collection of contemporary art in an intimate, homely atmosphere.

56 Having got used to the friendly Mr Schmidt, Theo first found it difficult to get on with his new boss, Tersteeg. He was thought to be too standoffish with his staff: b 2698 V/1982, Leeuwarden 24 February 1874 (from Anna to Theo).

57 b 2225 V/1982, Etten, 4 January 1876 (from his parents to Theo).

58 They also studied works such as Johannes van Vloten's *Nederlandsche schilderkunst van de 14e tot de 18e eeuw* (Amsterdam 1874), and William Bürger's *Les musées de La Hollande* (2 vols., Paris 1858-60).

59 See, for example, letter 17/13, London, January 1874: 'How much I would like to talk about art with you again, but we'll just have to content with writing: *find as much beautiful* as you can, most people *don't find enough beautiful*.'

60 27/20, London 31 July 1874. Vincent was extremely pleased that he could share this book with his brother: 'I'm so happy that you've read Michelet and that you understand it so well. A book like that shows that there is so much more to love than most people think.'

61 b 2696 V/1982, Helvoirt, 21 April 1874 (from his parents to Theo), and 19/14, London, 20 February 1874: 'I completely agree with you about B.H. [Annet

Haanebeek], but watch out for your heart, old fellow.' On Vincent's and Theo's first loves see Elly Cassee, 'In love: Vincent van Gogh's first true love,' *Van Gogh Museum Journal* (1996), pp. 108-17.
62 London, 31 July 1874. Theo's letter has been lost.
63 b 2366 V/1982, Helvoirt, 7 October 1875 (from his father to Theo).
64 b 2346 V/1982, Helvoirt, 8 July 1875 (from his father to Theo).
65 b 2374 V/1982, Tiel, 31 November 1875 (from Lies to Theo): 'Theo! I am so happy that you write me what you are thinking, and it does me such good to hear that there are others besides me who have to struggle to be good.'
66 b 2733 V/1982, Helvoirt, 18 November 1874 (from his parents to Theo). His father also wrote in June 1875 (b 2341 V/1982): 'I'm afraid that something awful will happen, my dear Theo. I say this to you as your confidante – if you run across something that might be useful, let us know. I believe there must be some kind of illness, whether physical or mental. We are worried but believe that God will give us guidance, and this makes us strong, as it should be.'
67 b 2227 V/1982, Helvoirt, 9 January 1876 (from his parents to Theo).
68 b 2463 V/1982, Etten, 27 February 1879 (from his mother to Theo). According to Mother Van Gogh, Uncle Cent also had great expectations of Theo: 'Theo, your uncle loves you so much, I think that after the disappointment with Vincent the thought that you, too, like the work he so loved gives him much-needed hope'; b 980 V/1982, Etten, 7 June 1878.
69 b 2513 V/1982, Etten, 14 March 1877 (from his parents to Theo). See also Hulsker, *Vincent and Theo van Gogh*, cit. (note 13), pp. 67-70, and Stolwijk, op. cit. (note 13), pp. 51-53. In May 1882 Vincent referred back to this episode in letter 227/198, [14 May 1882].
70 b 2520 V/1982, Etten, 18 April 1877 (from his father to Theo). In May 1877 Theo met the woman once again. His father responded to this immediately and wrote on 21 May that this new rendezvous had hurt them. Nevertheless he blamed the woman. In his view she had shown 'a lack of delicacy,' as she should have realised that it was impossible for her to associate with Theo; b 2532 V/1982.
71 b 2537 V/1982, Etten, 18 June 1877 (from his father to Theo).
72 b 964 V/1962, Etten, 26 January 1878 (from his parents to Theo).
73 The offer was a 'a great honour, a spur to your ambition and a reward for your efforts to do your work well and distinguish yourself'; b 971 V/1962, Etten, 16 March 1878 (from his father to Theo).
74 See, for example, 144/123, Etten, 22 July 1878: 'I think about you often and am happy that you are doing well and that you are finding things that stimulate you, things that are nourishment for real life.'
75 b 5342 V/1982, Princenhage, 7 October 1878 (from Uncle Cent to Theo).
76 b 2462 V/1982, Dordrecht, 21 February 1879 (from Lies to Theo): 'I well understand that you aren't having a good time.' Theo made a financial arrangement with Tersteeg in January, so that in future he would receive a bonus if they made a profit. In the spring he made his traditional tour to promote the firm's new wares.
77 Vincent wrote of their meeting from Laeken on 15 November 1878 (147/126): 'I am writing to you on the evening of the day we were together, which for me went by in the wink of an eye. It was a great joy for me to see you again and to talk things over, and it is fortunate that such a day, which goes by in a flash and brings pleasure that is only short-lived, nonetheless stays in our memories, and that our memories of it are lasting.'
78 b 2454 V/1982, Etten, 8 January 1879 (from his mother to Theo): 'Have you written to the poor fellow yet? If not, please do; I can already hear you saying "mother, you musn't say that, it's his choice after all."'
79 See also 92/76, Isleworth 7 October 1876: 'I need so much to see you again, sometimes I feel it so terribly. Write to me so and tell me how you are.' Or 110/90: 'The love between brothers is a great source of strength in life; the living fire that is between us cannot be extinguished; rather, let our experiences strengthen our bond, let us be honest and open with one another, let there be no secrets, as there are now.'
80 Theo was kept informed of Vincent's worrying situation: b 2496 V/1982, Nuenen, 11 March 1881 (from his father to Theo).
81 It is not certain whether Theo went to work at the branch at 19, Boulevard Montmartre immediately upon his arrival in Paris, but it seems likely. On 10 June 1880 Anton Mauve sent Theo a postcard at this address: b 1188 V/1962.
82 See for the Salon, among others: Patricia Mainardi, *The end of the Salon: art and the state in the early Third Republic*, Cambridge, MA 1993; Andrée Sfeir-Semmler, *Die Maler am Pariser Salon 1791-1880*, Frankfurt, New York & Paris 1992; and Harrison C. White and Cynthia A. White, *Canvases and careers: institutional change in the French painting world*, Chicago 1993 [New York 1965].
83 See Richard Thomson's contribution to this catalogue.
84 b 2494 V/1982, Etten, 5 July 1880 (from his father to Theo).
85 b 2495 V/1982, Etten, 5 July 1880 (from his mother to Theo).
86 b 2235 V/1982, Etten, 14 February 1881 (from his father to Theo). See also 161/140, [January 1881]: 'You spoke about changes in the staff at Goupil & Cie., and also of changes to your own position.'
87 On Vincent's opting for a career as an artist and Theo's alleged role in this decision see 213/184, [early April 1882], and Sjraar van Heugten, *Vincent van Gogh: drawings. The early years, 1880-1883*, Bussum 1996, p. 12.
88 Vincent wrote on 19 November 1881 (185/160) in reference to Theo's remarks about three of his drawings: 'You write practical things, I have to learn to be practical from you; you are going to have to preach to me often; I am not resistant to changing, I need to change so much!'
89 On 1 January Vincent moved into a studio on the Schenkweg 138. For Vincent's Hague period(s) in particular see Michiel van der Mast and Charles Dumas, *Van Gogh en Den Haag*, Zwolle 1990.
90 Vincent wrote: 'Oh Theo, why don't

you just throw everything overboard and become a painter, man – you could do it if you wanted to. I think there is a wonderful landscape painter inside you whom you are hiding from yourself.' Vincent returned to this subject on a number of occasions.

91 From 1 January 1882 Theo earned the annual sum of 4,000 francs, which was given to him in twelve monthly payments. In addition he received an annual bonus of 7,5% of the gross profits of the branch on the Boulevard Montmartre. This profit was determined after the annual inventory had been taken; see b 4601 V/1982, 'Contract Boussod, Valadon & Cie. met Théodore van Gogh,' Paris, 22 August 1890.

92 For example in letters 226/198, 227/199, 233/204 and 234/201, with the famous profile of the way Vincent thought the Van Gogh family tackled conflicts.

93 See also Hulsker, *Vincent and Theo van Gogh*, cit. (note 13), pp. 126-29.

94 See for Vincent's reaction to his parents' refusal letters 350/288, 3 June 1883, and 351/290, 3 June 1883.

95 301/259, [c. 11 January 1883].

96 The sales figures of the Boulevard Montmartre branch dropped dramatically during these months. Theo only sold one work in August, and did not make a single purchase; see Los Angeles, The Getty Research Institute for the History of Art and the Humanities, Special Collections, 'Dieterle family collection of 19th century French gallery records,' acc. no. 900239, Series II. Galerie Boussod Valadon, 1879-1919.

97 b 2250 V/1982, Nuenen, 20 December 1883 (from his father to Theo).

98 b 2266 V/1982, Nuenen, 24 January 1885 (from his father to Theo).

99 The annual exhibits provided by Boussod, Valadon & Cie. for the Salon also kept him busy. In addition, this gave him the opportunity to establish new business relations and to see new work.

100 Frans Braat, the son of Vincent's former employer in Dordrecht and a colleague of Theo's, was probably an exception. In the spring of 1884 Theo nursed Braat when he was ill. On 14 April 1884 Braat's father thanked Theo for 'all the love and friendship you have shown to our boy'; b 2962 V/1982, Dordrecht, 13 April 1884 (from P.K. Braat to Theo).

101 For Andries Bonger see, among others, exhib. cat. *André Bonger en zijn kunstenaarsvrienden: Redon – Bernard – Van Gogh*, Amsterdam (Rijksmuseum) 1972; H. Bonger, 'Un Amstellodamois à Paris: extraits des lettres écrites à Paris entre 1880 et 1890 par Andries Bonger à ses parents à Amsterdam,' in *Liber amicorum Karel G. Boon*, Amsterdam 1974, pp. 60-70; F.W.M. Bonger-Baronesse van der Borch van Verwolde, 'Andries Bonger (Amsterdam 20 May 1861-Amsterdam 20 Jan. 1936),' *Jaarboek van de Maatschappij voor Nederlandsche Letterkunde te Leiden*, Leiden 1936-37, pp. 112-22; and Jan Hulsker, 'De Van Goghs en de Bongers,' *Jong Holland* 12 (1996), no. 2, pp. 44-53.

102 Theodorus van Gogh collapsed and died on his doorstep after returning home from a walk; see b 2742 V/1982, *Kerkelijke Courant van Nuenen* (4 April 1885).

103 b 1811 V/1970, Paris, 31 March 1885 (from Dries Bonger to his parents). On 27 March Theo received a telegram with the news 'Father has suffered an attack, come, but it's too late – Vangogh'; see also letters 490/- and 491/-. Theodorus van Gogh was buried on 30 March in Nuenen.

104 On 5 April (493/398) Vincent wrote that he was still 'very much under the impression of all that has happened – nonetheless, I painted all day these last two Sundays.'

105 See also 505/408, [c. 11 May 1885]: 'I understand that you are doing your best to reconcile us but, my dear fellow, I don't wish them any harm and I don't do them any harm.'

106 b 901 V/1962, Paris, 19 May 1885 (from Theo to his mother).

107 On 7 April Theo purchased Monet's *Church at Véthieul* (Southampton City Art Gallery). For the business relations, between Theo and Monet see Ronald Pickvance, 'Monet en Theo van Gogh,' in exhib. cat. *Monet in Holland*, Amsterdam (Van Gogh Museum) 1986, pp. 83-96. See for Besnard and Raffaëlli: 503/406, [4 or 5 May 1885] and 522/418, [July 1885]. See also Richard Thomson's contribution to this catalogue.

108 b 889 V/1975, Nuenen, 6 August 1885 (from Theo to Dries Bonger).

109 b 1820 V/1970, Paris, 25 August 1885 (from Dries Bonger to his parents).

110 b 1821 V/970, Paris, 7 September 1885 (from Dries Bonger to his parents).

111 b 904 V/1962, Paris, 28 December 1885 (from Theo to Lies): 'The streets are full of people and still I feel more lonely than in a village. I have around me every day people with whom I am very friendly and many whose company I value and still it there is nothing like the intimacy we have in Holland.' See also b 905 V/1962, Paris, 12 January 1886 (from Theo to his mother): 'It's so very different here than at home, and our Dutch cosiness is nowhere to be found. The streets are full of people and the shops are open late, even on Sunday. It's kind of like St Nicholas, but without all the fun in the evening.'

112 b 903 V/1962, Paris, 13 October 1885 (from Theo to Lies).

113 See also letter 558/447, [c. 28 January 1886].

114 b 1841 V/1970, Paris, [March] 1886 (from Dries Bonger to his parents).

115 b 1843 V/1970, Paris, 22 June 1886 (from Dries Bonger to his parents).

116 b 942 V/1962, Paris, [July] 1886 (from Theo to his mother).

117 Here Vincent suggested that it might solve all their problems if he were to marry 'S' himself.

118 b 4284 V/1984, Breda, 26 July 1887 (from Theo to Jo): 'André was no more successful in his efforts to obtain funds.'

119 b 1867 V/1970, Paris, 31 December 1886, and b 1846 V/1970, Paris, 18 February 1887 (from Dries Bonger to his parents).

120 b 910 V/1982, Paris, 19 April 1887 (from Theo to Lies). Theo had been seriously ill, 'vooral van geest' (mostly mentally), and he had wrestled with his feelings; see b 912 V/1982, Paris, 15 May 1887. See for Theo's illness: P.H.A. Voskuil, 'Het medisch dossier van Theo van Gogh, '*Nederlands Tijdschrift voor Geneeskunde* 136 (1990), pp. 1777-79.

121 b 907 V/1962, Paris, 11 March 1887 (from Theo to Cor).

122 b 908 V/1962, Paris, 14 March 1887 (from Theo to Wil).
123 b 911 V/1962, Paris, 25 April 1887 (from Theo to Wil).
124 Theo found a supporter in Alexander Reid, an assistant at the Boulevard Montmartre gallery. In October 1886 he, Theo and Vincent joined forces in promoting Adolphe Monticelli's work. Around this time Reid is said to have lived with the brothers for a few months; see Frances Fowle, *Alexander Reid in context*, 2 vols. (diss., University of Edinburgh, 1993), vol. 1, p. 30.
125 He wrote to Lies on 19 April 1887 that he was about to have a change of fortune, which he hoped would be settled by the following summer; see b 910 V/1962. For the history of Boussod, Valadon & Cie. see Richard Thomson's contribution to this catalogue. In May 1887 the firm's old stock was auctioned; see *Catalogue des tableaux, aquarelles, dessins de l'école moderne composant le fonds de l'ancienne Maison Goupil & Cie. Vente par suite de renouvellement de société*, Paris (Hôtel Drouot) 25-27 May 1887.
126 b 910 V/1982, Paris, 19 April 1887 (from Theo to Lies).
127 b 912 V/1982, Paris, 15 May 1887 (from Theo to Lies).
128 b 4550 V/1986, diary of Johanna van Gogh-Bonger, 25 July 1887.
129 b 4284 V/1984, Breda, 26 July 1887 (from Theo to Jo).
130 See *Van Gogh à Paris*, cit. (note 13), p. 33, and exhib. cat. *Georges Seurat 1859-1891*, Paris (Grand Palais) & New York (The Metropolitan Museum of Art) 1991-92, p. 407.
131 See *Félix Fénéon: oeuvres plus que complètes*, ed. Joan U. Halperin, Geneva 1970, p. 90.
132 Ibid., pp. 95-96.
133 Van Gogh-Bonger, op. cit. (note 128), 20 January 1888.
134 On Van Gogh in Arles see Ronald Pickvance, exhib. cat. *Van Gogh in Arles*, New York (The Metropolitan Museum of Art) 1984.
135 b 914 V/1962, Paris, 24 and 26 February 1888 (from Theo to Wil).
136 See also letters 686/538, [c. 17 September 1888]; 698/544, [3 October 1888]; and 726/563, [c. 23 November 1888].
137 In the spring of 1888 Vincent wanted to persuade Tersteeg, *gérant* at the Hague branch, to work with him and Theo to make the work of the impressionists better known. At the end of February 1888 he wrote (581/465): 'You know that Tersteeg knows his way around the English market, and it's possible he will see what's going to happen with the new painting there. Maybe Tersteeg and the manager in London will do a permanent exhibtion of the impressionists there, you'll do one in Paris, and I'll start off in Marseilles, but first Tersteeg has to see a lot of work with his own eyes, and that's why I think he should go around with you to the studios, and while you're together you can explain to him how important this whole thing is.'
138 On 1 May 1888 (604/480) Vincent suggested working together with Gauguin in Arles. See also letters 623/500, [c. 5 June 1888]; 624/494, [c. 5 June 1888]; 632/535a, [21 June 1888]; and 638/507, [29 June 1888]. In June Theo offered Gauguin a monthly allowance of 150 francs in exchange for paintings. Gauguin agreed. For Vincent, Gauguin's arrival in the south was just the beginning, as we see in letter 638/507, [29 June 1888]: 'Everything is going well, and Gauguin has agreed to join us; then we can get down to serious business and suggest that he add his paintings to my own stock so that we can share our profits and losses.'
139 b 916 V/1962, Paris, 6 December 1888 (from Theo to Wil).
140 Koning stayed from March to June 1888 with Theo, Mourier-Petersen in June 1888 and Meijer de Haan from October 1888 to the beginning of March 1889. Jozef Isaacson, a friend of Meijer de Haan's, could be found in the apartment almost every evening.
141 b 917 V/1962, Paris 21 December 1888 (from Theo to his mother). His mother wrote back emotionally by return post: her prayers had been answered at last.
142 b 2 018 VF/1982, Paris, [25] December 1888 (from Theo to Jo).
143 b 2020 VF/1984, Paris, 28 December 1888 (from Theo to Jo).
144 b 2022 VF/1982, Paris, 31 December 1888 (from Theo to Jo). According to Theo, in 1887 Vincent had often encouraged him to ask for Jo's hand in marriage. In this letter Theo also wrote that of the whole Van Gogh family only Wil cared about Vincent's fate. The other members of the family had long since written him off as mad.
145 See also 742/572, [19 January 1889]: 'I have always thought that, because of your social position and your position within our family, you were obliged to marry. It has also long been mother's wish. And by doing what you must do you will – even if there are 1001 problems – have more peace than before. But life isn't easy, for myself either...'
146 b 2024 VF/1982, Paris, 14 January 1889, and b 2036 VF/1982, Paris, 16-17 February 1889 (from Theo to Jo).
147 b 2026 VF/1982, Paris, 19 January 1889 (from Theo to Jo).
148 b 2009 V/1982, Paris, 9-10 February 1889 (from Theo to Jo).
149 b 2050 VF/1982, Paris, 16 March 1889 (from Theo to Jo).
150 Jo was very pleased with the apartment. The Cité might not have been very up-market, but as far as she was concerned, it was an area with a very special character.
151 On 3 April Theo confided in his former employer, Tersteeg, about the discord. He responded on 7 April: 'It is a splendid thing that it has come to a head with the "gentlemen" and I congratulate you on having told them what you think straight out. [...] "Stick with it" I say, but be careful not to do anything Valadon might eventually use against you. When in doubt it is always better to keep quiet. [...] You have to learn not to be so affected by all the questions and discussions, and just go on doing business as you see fit, with all you experience and knowledge'; b 1368 V/1962, The Hague 7 April 1890.
152 See for Vincent van Gogh in St Rémy and Auvers-sur-Oise: Ronald Pickvance, exhib. cat. *Van Gogh in Saint-Rémy and Auvers*, New York (The Metropolitan

Museum of Art) 1987-88.
153 Van Gogh-Bonger, op. cit. (note 15), p. 35.
154 Ibid., p. 37.
155 See also b 4306 V/1984, Paris, 9 June 1890 (from Jo to her sister Mien).
156 b 1855 V/1970, Paris, 30 June 1890 (from Annie Bonger-Van der Linden to her mother- and father-in-law).
157 See also b 1856 V/1970, Paris, 4 July 1890 (from Dries Bonger to his parents).
158 On 14 July Theo wrote to Vincent [905/T41]: 'Although the eight days are over, I've heard nothing from the "gentlemen" about what they are going to do about me.'
159 Theo blamed 'mesjogge' (hare-brained) Annie for Dries's cowardice; see 905/T41, 14 July 1890.
160 b 2057 VF/1982, Paris, 29 July 1890 (from Theo to Jo).
161 On 22 July he wrote to his mother and Wil about his decision to stay with the firm and his talks with the 'gentlemen' (b 933 V/1962): 'On my way back and having arrived here once again I saw only too clearly how reckless it was of me to even contemplate something so uncertain, for although there was a good chance of finding the money for my own business, there was no guarantee. I thought about it like this and very nearly became desperate at having let things go this far, with the possibility that I might have suddenly been without an income. So I went yesterday to speak with the "gentlemen" and found that they were not against me. I said that when I had first spoken to them I had relied simply on my good luck, and hadn't given enough thought to how powerful the firm was, but now, having examined things more closely, I had come to the conclusion that it was wiser for me to stay on, and that even if they decided I didn't deserve a raise, I would bow to my fate and find a way to make ends meet. Etienne B[oussod] was very friendly and said that nothing had been decided and that they would see if they could make things easier for me. I hope now that I can do some business which will hep them make up their minds, but things have been rather slow lately.' See also Theo's letter to Jo of 21 July, b 2061 VF/1982.
162 b 2065 V/1982, Paris, 26 July 1890 (from Theo to Jo).
163 b 2066 V/1982, Auvers, 28 July 1890 (from Theo to Jo).
164 b 2067 V/1982, Paris, 1 August 1890 (from Theo to Jo). Jo was not told about Vincent's death until 1 August when Theo's mother informed her.
165 Ibid.
166 b 934 V/1962, Paris, 1 August 1890 (from Theo to his mother).
167 b 2015 V/1982, Paris, 12 September 1890 (from Theo to Paul-Ferdinand Gachet).
168 For details of the move see b 938 V/1962, Paris, 16 September 1890 (from Theo to his mother). Theo and Emile Bernard arranged the exhibition in the new apartment. See, among others, Hulsker, *Vincent and Theo van Gogh*, cit. (note 13), pp. 450-51.
169 b 947 V/1962, Paris, 27 September 1890 (from Theo to Wil). The business Theo was referring to was the sale of Constant Troyon's *Descente de vaches* (Boussod 20337) to Dowdeswell & Dowdeswell for 45,000 francs on 27 September. Boussod, Valadon & Cie. earned 10,000 francs with this sale 'with the promise of more busines to come.' See also Richard Thomson's contribution to this catalogue.
170 b 2013 VF/1982, Paris, 10 October 1890 (from Dries Bonger to Paul-Ferdinand Gachet), and b 1860 V/1970, Paris, 16 October 1890 (from Dries Bonger to his parents). Tersteeg had meanwhile arrived in Paris and had talked with Theo's employers about his situation. According to Dries, Tersteeg reported that 'there was naturally no question of their accepting Theo's resignation and that, in any case, he would remain their *gérant* until the end of the year. They were certainly not upset with Theo; they had seen clearly that he was unwell and had left him alone as much as possible.'
171 See, for example, b 1431 V/1962, Bussum, 20 October 1890 (from Anna Veth-Dirks to Jo), and b 1140 V/1962, The Hague, 23 October 1890 (from Caroline van Stockum-Haanebeek to Jo).
172 b 1860 V/1970, Paris, 16 October 1890 (from Dries Bonger to his parents).
173 Voskuil, op. cit. (note 120), p. 1777.
174 The pages describing Theo's last four days are missing from the medical report. It is therefore far from certain that Theo committed suicide, as Vincent had done, and as has often been maintained. In March 1891 the critic Octave Mirbeau wrote in 'Vincent van Gogh,' *L'Echo de Paris* (31 March 1891) that Theo had died the same kind of death as his brother – 'mort aussi de la même mort que lui.' By this he probably meant that they had died *for* the same cause, rather than *of* the same cause.
175 In April 1914 Jo had Theo's remains transported to Auvers. The brothers were then reunited in the cemetery.
176 Van Gogh-Bonger, op. cit. (note 128), 28 January 1892.

Richard Thomson

Theo van Gogh
An honest broker

1 G.-A.[lbert]. A.[urier], 'Choses d'art,' *Mercure de France* (March 1891), p. 189.
2 Jan Veth, 'Th. van Gogh,' *De Amsterdammer* (2 February 1891), p. 3.
3 *Correspondance de Camille Pissarro*, ed. Janine Bailly-Herzberg, 5 vols., Paris 1988, vol. 3, p. 46, letter 645, 19 March 1891 (to Mette Gauguin).
4 John Rewald, 'Theo van Gogh, Goupil and the impressionists,' *Gazette des Beaux-Arts* 81 (January-February 1973), pp. 1-108. Reprinted as 'Theo van Gogh as art dealer' in John Rewald, *Studies in post-impressionism*, London 1986, pp. 7-115. References in this article are to the 1986 text. The present essay is intended as a contrast and supplement to Rewald's. Rewald follows a chronological path; this essay has a thematic structure, with a broader view of the art world in which Theo worked. However, full use has been made of his pioneering text, in particular of the tabulated stockbook data on pp. 89-97, which is not repeated here. In addition, Chris Stolwijk has provided a wealth of new information crucial to my understanding of Theo's dealings, gleaned from a thorough study of the firm's ledgers at the Getty Research Institute for the History of Art and the Humanities in Los Angeles, which he generously shared with me.
5 Ibid., p. 9.
6 Our suspicion of Rewald's handling of the evidence is raised already by ibid., op. cit. (note 4), p. 32 (also no. 63, p. 109). Here, in his section on the year 1888, he cites a Dutch acquaintance of Theo's on the latter's bitterness at having to sell Meissoniers and Bouguereaus for such high prices when Pissarros went for so little. The Dutchman was Boele van Hensbroek, and his observations were published not only some time after the dealer's death, in 'De Van Goghs,' *De Nederlandsche Spectator* (26 August 1893), but at a time when this 'traditionally conservative' paper had recently changed its policy to actively support modern art. See Carel Blotkamp, 'Painters as critics: art criticism in the Netherlands, 1880-1895,' exhib. cat. *Dutch painting: the age of Van Gogh, 1880-1895*, Glasgow (The Burrell Collection) & Amsterdam (Van Gogh Museum) 1990-91, pp. 88-89. Van Hensbroek had an axe to grind, and was not necessarily passing on Theo's exact views. In fact, according to the stockbooks, the Boulevard Montmartre branch did not handle a Meissonier after 1886 or a Bouguereau after 1884, and did not handle Pissarro actively until 1887.
7 See Nicholas Green, 'Circuits of production, circuits of consumption: the case of mid-nineteenth century French art dealing,' *Art Journal* 48 (Spring 1989), pp. 29-34.
8 Théodore Rousseau, for example, held them in 1850, 1861 and 1863; see ibid., p. 32.
9 Martinet for one staged them at his premises in the Boulevard des Italiens for painters as different as Ingres – in 1861 and 1862 – and Manet (the following year); see ibid., pp. 31-32.
10 Patricia Mainardi, *The end of the Salon: art and the state in the early Third Republic*, Cambridge, MA 1993, p. 47.
11 Ibid., p. 136; [Anon.], 'Causerie artistique. Le Cercle de l'Union Artistique,' *La Paix* (16 February 1883).
12 Constance Cain Hungerford, 'Meissonier and the founding of the Société Nationale des Beaux-Arts,' *Art Journal* 48 (Spring 1989), pp. 71-77.
13 See Auguste Dalligny, 'Société Nationale des Beaux-Arts. L'exposition du Champ de Mars,' *Le Journal des Arts* 12 (16 May 1890), p. 1.
14 Monique Nonne, 'Les marchands de van Gogh,' exhib. cat. *Van Gogh à Paris*, Paris (Musée d'Orsay) 1988, pp. 338-43.
15 For Durand-Ruel see *inter alia* 'Mémoires de Paul Durand-Ruel,' in Lionello Venturi (ed.), *Les archives de l'impressionnisme*, 2 vols., New York & Paris 1939, vol. 1, pp. 143-220, and Linda Whiteley, 'Accounting for tastes,' *Oxford Art Journal* 2 (1979), pp. 25-28.
16 See Arthur Baignères, 'Société d'Aquarellistes Français (quatrième exposition),' *Gazette des Beaux-Arts* 25 (April 1882), pp. 433-34; see also Martha Ward, 'Impressionist installations and private exhibitions,' *Art Bulletin* 73 (December 1991), pp. 615-16.
17 For Petit and the Expositions Internationales see Robert Jensen, *Marketing modernism in fin-de-siècle Europe*, Princeton 1994, pp. 63-65.
18 Ward, op. cit. (note 16), pp. 599, 605.
19 See Arthur Baignères, 'Société d'Aquarellistes Français (première exposition),' *Gazette des Beaux-Arts* 2 (May 1879), pp. 491-92; idem, *Société d'Aquarellistes Français: ouvrage d'art*, 2 vols., Paris 1883, vol. 1, p. 91; Richard Thomson, 'Impressionism and drawing in the 1880s,' exhib. cat. *Impressionist drawings in British collections*, Oxford (Ashmolean Museum), Manchester (City Art Gallery) & Glasgow (The Burrell Collection) 1986, p. 26.
20 Ward, op. cit. (note 16), pp. 599, 605.
21 See, for example [Anon.], 'Exposition des lauréats de France, Londres 1888,' *Le Journal des Arts* 10 (3 February 1888), p. 4, and Rewald, op. cit. (note 4), pp. 45, 51.
22 Armand Silvestre, 'Le monde des arts. Exposition du Cercle de l'Union Artistique,' *La Vie Moderne* 5 (17 February 1883), p. 107.
23 *Le Temps* (22 March 1880), quoted from Jules Claretie, *La vie à Paris: 1880*, Paris 1881, p. 27.
24 Octave Mirbeau, 'Aquarellistes Français,' *La France* (7 February 1885), quoted from Octave Mirbeau, *Des artistes*, 2 vols., Paris 1922, vol. 1, p. 6.
25 Letter to Theo van Gogh, 9 September 1890, printed in Ronald Pickvance (ed.), *'A great artist is dead': letters of condolence on Vincent van Gogh's death*, Zwolle 1992, p. 153.
26 Letter to Ludovic Halévy, September 1880, printed in exhib. cat. *Degas*, Paris (Grand Palais), Ottawa (National Gallery of Canada) & New York (The Metropolitan Museum of Art) 1988-89, p. 219.
27 Rémy G. Saisselin, *Bricobracomania: the bourgeois and the bibelot*, London 1985, pp. 21, 73.
28 *The correspondence of Berthe Morisot*,

ed. Denis Rouart, London 1986, p. 136, letter of January 1884 (to Edna Poutillon).
29 *Cassatt and her circle: selected letters*, ed. Nancy Mowll Mathews, New York 1984, p. 173, letter of 14 October 1883 (to Alexander Cassatt).
30 Ibid., p. 200, letter of 30 June 1886 (to Louis Cassatt).
31 *Correspondance de Paul Gauguin. I, 1873-1888*, ed. Victor Merlhès, Paris 1984, p. 181, letter 147, early June 1888 (to Emile Schuffenecker).
32 For example, the studio sale held following the death in 1888 of Gustave Boulanger, winner of the Prix de Rome in 1849 and Professor at the Ecole des Beaux-Arts, was certainly a disappointment; the *Source of the Tiber*, from the Salon of 1883, realised only 1,050 francs, while reductions of four prestigious panels for the Paris Opéra together sold for 3,380, then the price of a Monet and a trifle in comparison to a good Daubigny; see [Anon.], 'Vente Gustave Boulanger,' *La Chronique des Arts* (6 April 1889), p. 105.
33 See Auguste Dalligny, 'L'Exposition des 33,' *Le Journal des Arts* 11 (4 January 1889), p. 1.
34 *Le Temps* (3 March 1882), quoted from Jules Claretie, *La vie à Paris: 1882*, Paris 1883, p. 110.
35 Letter of 12 May 1887 from Renoir to Durand-Ruel, reprinted in Venturi, op. cit. (note 15), vol. 1, p. 138.
36 For contemporary sales which included impressionist and other 'modern' work see, for example, [Anon.], 'Revue des ventes. Collection Ch. Leroux,' *Le Journal des Arts* 10 (28 February 1888), p. 3; [Anon.], 'Mouvement des arts. Collection de tableaux des M. Charles L.,' *La Chronique des Arts* (3 March 1888), p. 65; P.[ierre]D.[etouche], 'Ventes prochaines. Collection d'un amateur,' *Le Journal des Arts* 12 (9 May 1890), p. 2; P.[ierre] D.[etouche], 'Ventes prochaines. Collection de M. E. May,' *Le Journal des Arts* 12 (27 May 1890), p. 1; [Anon.], 'Revue des ventes. Collection M.E. May,' *Le Journal des Arts* 12 (6 June 1890), p. 3. For Monet and Degas at these sales see Daniel Wildenstein, *Claude Monet: biographie et catalogue raisonné*, 5 vols., Lausanne 1974-91, nos. 189, 229, 402, 539, 643 687, (?)731, 736, (?)738, 741, 798, 975 and 994, and Paul-André Lemoisne, *Degas et son oeuvre*, 5 vols., Paris 1946-49, nos. 498 and 576.
37 See Wildenstein, op. cit. (note 36), vol. 2, p. 270, letter 638, 10 December 1885 (to Durand-Ruel).
38 Quoted from *Archives de Camille Pissarro*, Paris (Hôtel Drouot), 21 November 1975, no. 21.
39 Bailly-Herzberg, op. cit. (note 3), vol. 2, p. 243, letter 496, 12 July 1888 (to Lucien Pissarro).
40 Indeed, in the Leroux sale a print by Waltner after Millet's *Angelus* fetched almost as much as a canvas by Sisley; see *Le Journal des Arts* (28 February 1888), cit. (note 36), p. 3, no. 107.
41 Anne Distel, 'Albert Hecht: collectionneur (1842-1889),' *Bulletin de la Société de l'Histoire de l'Art Français: année 1981*, Paris 1983, pp. 267-79.
42 Anne Distel, 'Charles Deudon (1832-1914): collectionneur,' *Revue de l'Art* 86 (1989), pp. 58-65.
43 See Chris Stolwijk's contribution to this catalogue.
44 See Sabine du Vignau and Pierre-Lin Renié, 'La Maison Goupil: chronologie détaillée,' in Hélène Lafont-Couturier (ed.), *Etat des lieux*, Bordeaux 1994, pp. 144-46.
45 See Hélène Lafont-Couturier, '"Le Bon Livre" ou la portée éducative des images éditées et publiées par la maison Goupil,' in ibid., p. 30, and Pierre-Lin Renié, 'Goupil et Cie à l'ère industrielle: la photographie appliquée à la reproduction des oeuvres d'art,' in ibid, pp. 93, 96.
46 Nonne, op. cit. (note 14), pp. 330-32.
47 Uncle Cent's taste was eclectic and geared to market success: he admired eminent academic artists of different generations, as well as the landscapists of the Ecole de 1830, and he did much to introduce Dutch painters like Anton Mauve, Johannes Bosboom and Jacob Maris to the international scene. See the sale of his personal collection: *Collection de feu M. Vincent van Gogh*, The Hague (Pulchri Studio/C.M. van Gogh en H.G. Tersteeg), 2-3 April 1889.
48 In 1869 this work was moved from workshops in the central Rue Chaptal to a custom-built factory in the western suburb of Asnières, complete with steam-engines and, from 1874, thermo-electric equipment; by 1879 the Asnières operation was employing a workforce of 100, which produced 48,000 square metres of photographic plates annually; see Nonne, op. cit. (note 14), p. 332, and Renié, op. cit. (note 45), pp. 102, 108.
49 Nonne, op. cit. (note 14), p. 333, and Gilles Cugnier, 'Notice biographique,' exhib. cat. *Jean-Léon Gérôme, 1824-1904*, Vesoul (Musée de Vesoul) 1981, p. 23.
50 Nonne, op. cit. (note 14), p. 333.
51 Rewald, op. cit. (note 4), p. 9; Nonne, op. cit. (note 14), p. 334; and Sabine du Vignau, 'Biographies,' in *Etat des lieux*, cit. (note 44), pp. 148-53.
52 Lafont-Couturier, op. cit. (note 45), p. 96.
53 These were *Cours de dessin exécuté avec le concours de J.J. [sic] Gérôme. Vol. 1: 1ère partie – modèles d'après la bosse*, followed by *2ème partie – modèles d'après les maîtres de toutes les époques et toutes les écoles* and, in 1871, *Vol. 2: excercices au fusain pour préparer à l'étude de l'académie d'après nature*; see Gerald M. Ackerman, *The life and work of Jean-Léon Gérôme*, London 1986, p. 170.
54 See Sabine du Vignau, 'Michel Manzi et Goupil & Cie: 1882-1915,' in *Etat des lieux*, cit. (note 44), pp. 129-32.
55 Ibid., p. 128. See also Edmond and Jules de Goncourt, *Journal: mémoires de la vie littéraire*, 3 vols., Paris 1989, vol. 3, p. 11 (2 February 1887) for Edmond's dismissal of Boussod, Valadon & Cie.'s publications, which he referred to as 'honest and *chic*.'
56 One of the most successful of these was *L'armée française: types et uniformes*, with illustrations by Edouard Detaille, which appeared in instalments from November 1885 and was published in book form in 1889, when a special edition of *Paris Illustré* puffed it (see Francis Roze, 'Edouard Detaille et l'armée française,' *Paris Illustré* 91 [28 September 1888], pp. 686-97). There were several editions, including a two-volume deluxe one retail-

ing at 2,400 francs: about the price of a canvas by Monet.

57 See Madeleine Fidell Beaufort and Jeanne K. Welcher, 'Some views of art buying in New York in the 1870s and 1880s,' *Oxford Art Journal* 5 (1982), p. 54, letter of 31 July 1872 (to John Taylor Johnston).

58 See Lee Johnson, *The paintings of Eugène Delacroix: a critical catalogue*, 2 vols., Oxford 1981, vol. 1, p. 78, no. 101.

59 Fortuny's relations with Goupil were not always easy, and he called in his father-in-law, Director of the Prado, to renegotiate his contract in 1867; this gave him the same terms as Gérôme, which is an indication of his importance to Goupil's market strategy. Fortuny died young in 1874, but his place was quickly taken by two young Italians painting in the same vein: Giuseppe de Nittis, who had opened dealings with Goupil in 1867, and Giovanni Boldini who did so in 1871. See Carlos Gonzales, 'Marià Fortuny i Marsal: biographical notes,' exhib. cat. *Marià Fortuny, 1838-1874*, Madrid (Fundación Caja de Pensiones) 1989, pp. 38-39, 41, 47, and Dario Durbé, 'Introduction,' exhib. cat. *Three Italian friends of the impressionists: Boldini, De Nittis, Zandomeneghi*, New York (Stair Sainty Matthiessen), 1984, pp. 9-10.

60 See Miriam Levin, *Republican art and ideology in late-19th century France*, Ann Arbor 1986, passim.

61 See Rachel Esner, '"Gloria victis": Französische Malerei des Deutsch-Französichen Krieges,' in Stefan Germer and Michael F. Zimmermann (eds.), *Bilder der Macht - Macht der Bilder: Zeitgeschichte in Darstellungen des 19. Jahrhunderts*, Munich 1997, pp. 390-402.

62 *Catalogue des tableaux, aquarelles et dessins de l'école moderne composant le fonds de l'ancienne Maison Goupil & Cie. Vente par suite de renouvellement de la société*, Paris (Hôtel Drouot) 25-27 May 1887.

63 *The letters of Lucien to Camille Pissarro, 1883-1903*, ed. Anne Thorold, Cambridge 1993, p. 89, letter of 25 May 1887.

64 See *Catalogue des tableaux*, cit. (note 62). There was Delacroix's *Natchez*; paintings by old Goupil academic stalwarts like Gérôme and Boulanger; variants of or studies for famous pictures of different generations, from Couture's *Enrolment of the volunteers* to Dagnan-Bouveret's *Accident*; landscapes by Corot, Daubigny and Diaz; Dutch pictures by Josef Israëls, Mesdag and Mauve; animal subjects by Jacque, de Penne and Barye; illustrations which had featured in *Les Lettres et les Arts* by artists as diverse as Cormon, Grasset and the young Bourdelle; modern urban scenes by Raffaëlli and Béraud; and so on. (There were no impressionists included.)

65 See [Anon.], 'Mouvement des arts. Tableaux et aquarelles formant le fond de l'ancienne maison Goupil et Cie,' *La Chronique des Arts* (4 June 1887), p. 177.

66 Fronia E. Wissman, *Bouguereau*, San Francisco 1996, pp. 13, 104.

67 Monique Le Pelley Fonteny, *Léon Augustin Lhermitte (1844-1925): catalogue raisonné*, Paris 1991, p. 39. The contract continued until 1914.

68 See Chris Stolwijk's contribution to this catalogue. On Theo's career before he arrived in Paris see idem, '"Our crown and our honour and our joy": Theo van Gogh's early years,' *Van Gogh Museum Journal* (1997-98), pp. 42-57.

69 Paul Durand-Ruel, 'Mémoires,' in Venturi, op. cit. (note 15), vol. 2, pp. 173-74.

70 See exhib. cat. *De la Place des Victoires à la Place de l'Opéra*, Paris (Musée Carnavalet) 1979, no. 61.

71 The street frontage was about 10 metres, with the ground floor gallery some six metres deep, though the contemporary ground plan reveals that the space was divided into two. A spiral stair led to the *entresol*, where there were again two spaces, but with a low ceiling – roughly 2.5 metres compared to the more generous 4 metres below. For the ground plan see *Van Gogh à Paris*, cit. (note 14), p. 337, fig. 12.

72 Gustave Geffroy, 'Chronique: dix tableaux de Cl. Monet,' *La Justice* (17 June 1888).

73 Their columns list stock numbers, titles of works, dimensions, the names of artists, dates purchased, names of sellers or sources, names of purchaser, and the dates of purchase.

74 For instance, we know from the art press that Boussod, Valadon & Cie. purchased two Millet pastels from the Goldschmidt sale held at Petit's in May 1888: *Return from the fields* (4,100 francs) and *Entry to the forest at Barbizon* (12,500 francs), but they were not recorded in the stockbooks, despite being of value. Thus we do not know which of the galleries handled them, to whom they were sold, when, and for what profit; see G. Pelea, 'Chronique de l'Hôtel Drouot,' *Le Courrier de l'Art* 8 (25 May 1888), p. 168.

75 Rewald, op. cit. (note 4), p. 64.

76 *The diary of George A. Lucas: an American art agent in Paris, 1857-1909*, ed. Lilian M.C. Randall, 2 vols., Princeton 1979, vol. 2, p. 538.

77 Ibid., p. 543.

78 See Karl Baedeker, *Paris and its environs: handbook for travellers*, Leipzig & London, 1881, p. 41, and August Dalligny, *Agenda de la curiosité des artistes et des amateurs, année 1889*, Paris 1889, p. 199.

79 Gustave Geffroy, 'Raffaëlli: peintre-sculpteur,' exhib. cat. *Catalogue de quelques peintures, sculptures et dessins de J.-F. Raffaëlli*, Paris (Boussod, Valadon & Cie.) 1890, p. 5.

80 See Randall, op. cit. (note 76), vol. 2, pp. 656, 664-65, and for Reid, p. 660.

81 Ibid., pp. 606-608, 618, 663-67, 677, 679-81.

82 See Rewald, op. cit. (note 4), pp. 95, 99 (for Desfossés).

83 13 pictures by the Norwegain Hans Olaf Heijerdahl are listed, four by Alfred Wahlberg, and two by Hugo Salmson, while the Danes Ernst Josephson and Peter-Severin Krøyer appear in Theo's address-book, though he does not seem to have purchased their work; see Ronald de Leeuw and Fieke Pabst, 'Le carnet d'adresses de Theo van Gogh,' *Van Gogh à Paris*, cit. (note 14), p. 361.

84 All three were sold to London buyers, which suggests that – in contrast to the Scandinavians – British art had little following in Paris; see Rewald, op. cit. (note 4), pp. 40, 38, 42.

85 *Evening*, by Corot, was puchased from Christie's on 24 April 1882, and found a buyer in Paris within two months, for a mark-up of over 25 percent. It was Christie's again that provided two works by Degas from the sale of the late Captain Henry Hill, of Brighton: the *The dance school* and *Ballet girls*; see ibid., p. 48. See also Ronald Pickvance, 'Henry Hill: an untypical Victorian collector,'*Apollo* 76 (December 1962), pp. 789-91.
86 On 15 October 1889 he purchased five paintings by Hervier from Houbrin and sold them the next day to Dowdeswell & Dowdeswell, while a Manet *Marine* he bought at the Hôtel Drouot on 26 June 1890 was passed on immediately to the same gallery. See Rewald, op. cit. (note 4), p. 91.
87 Ibid., p. 10.
88 b 1177 V/1962.
89 See Chris Stolwijk's contribution to this catalogue.
90 See Nonne, op. cit. (note 14), p. 338 and fig. 13. The paintings (with their original titles) and their prices were: Degas, *Femme aux fleurs*, 4,000 francs (L 125); Van Gogh, *Pont de Clichy*, 150 francs (F 303 JH 1323); Gauguin, *Marine, Dieppe*, 300 francs (W 169); Guillaumin, *Route à Charenton*, 300 francs; Toulouse-Lautrec, *Etude de femme*, 200 francs; C. Monet, *Belle Isle*, 1200 francs; Monticelli, *Le menuet*, 100 francs; *Femmes au bijoux*, illeg.; Pissarro, *Paysage, plein soleil*, 300 francs (P&V 709); Sisley, *Plateau de Roche Contart*, 500 francs. The pictures aroused little interest, with only one of the Monticellis selling to the dealer E.J. van Wisselingh.
91 The reviews are reprinted in *Félix Fénéon: oeuvres plus que complètes*, ed. Joan U. Halperin, 2 vols., Geneva 1970, vol. 1., pp. 90-91, 95-96, 102-03, 111, 118-19.
92 Rewald, op. cit. (note 4), p. 27.
93 Wissman, op. cit. (note 66), p. 105.
94 Thorold, op. cit. (note 63), p. 105, letter of 12 March 1888.
95 Bailly-Herzberg, op. cit. (note 3), vol. 2, p. 231, letter 483, 10 May 1888 (to Lucien Pissarro).
96 For example, the note from Lhermittte thanking Theo for selling him the Degas drawing he coveted (b 1341 V/1962, 23 May 1887), or the message from the writer Gustave Kahn asking for delivery of a gouache Pissarro has given him (b 1175 V/1962). In at least one instance, Theo's reliability seems to have led to a mysteriously intimate request. An undated letter from Besnard (b 1168 V/1962) asks for an urgent loan of 200 francs 'to avert a big, big problem [...] No one at my house must know.' The artist, apparently in deep personal or amorous trouble, evidently regarded Theo as a man of discretion, someone to whom he could turn in an emergency.
97 I am grateful to Frances Fowle for this observation.
98 In 1888 the *Chronique des Arts*, an off-shoot of the establishment *Gazette des Beaux-Arts* and a key listing of art world events, itemised even *faits divers* about independent painting: Sisley's one-man show at Petit's and Dubois-Pillet's at the *Revue Indépendante*, Pissarro, Seurat and Luce's invitation to the 1889 Les XX exhibition in Brussels ([Anon.], *La Chronique des Arts* 29 [8 September 1888], p. 226; and ibid., [8 December 1888], p. 298). Monet's Antibes show, however, was neither trailed nor reviewed. In 1890, the *Journal des Arts*, another art world argus, while listing Boussod, Valadon & Cie.'s Mauve exhibition at its London gallery, did not mention either the Boulevard Montmartre's Pissarro or Raffaëlli exhibitions ([Anon.], *Le Journal des Arts* 12 [22 April 1890], p. 2). The following year, however, with 19, Boulevard Montmartre under a new *gérant*, the *Journal des Arts* both announced the opening of the gallery's Carrière show and reviewed it (ibid., [14 April 1890], p. 2, and [24 April 1890], p. 1).
99 For Geffroy, see JoAnne Paradise, *Gustave Geffroy and the criticism of painting*, New York 1985, and for Geffroy and the 1890 Pissarro one-man show Martha Ward, *Pissarro, neo-impressionism and the spaces of the avant-garde*, Chicago & London 1995, pp. 161-68.
100 A.[lfred] de L.[ostalot], 'Exposition des Aquarellistes Français,' *La Chronique des Arts* (8 February 1890), p. 44.
101 Rewald, op. cit. (note 4), p. 30.
102 See exhib. cat. *Monet in Holland*, Amsterdam (Van Gogh Museum) 1986-87, p. 183, letter 2, 29 December 1888, and b 1152 V/1962, undated letter [March 1890] (from Degas to Theo van Gogh).
103 *Monet in Holland*, cit. (note 102), p. 183, letter 3, 5 March 1889.
104 Rewald, op. cit. (note 4), pp. 63-64.
105 *Monet in Holland*, cit. (note 102), pp. 183-84, letter 6, 10 July 1890.
106 See Rewald, op. cit. (note 4), introduction, fn. 5.
107 [Anon.], 'Mouvement des arts. Collection John Saulnier,' *La Chronique des Arts* (19 June 1886), p. 185.
108 Pictures he purchased but were not not sold tended to be sent on to branches in The Hague or London rather than to the other Paris outlets, and an important figure painting such as 'the marvel entitled *La toilette*,' bought in London in April 1886 for 18,750 francs, was sent to 19, Boulevard Montmartre for sale, where within a week it had fetched 37,000 francs; see Charles Bigot, *Peintres français contemporains*, Paris 1888, p. 64.
109 This included early work from Italy representing Civita Castellana or the cascade at Terni, French sites from Chartres Cathedral to his own locality at Ville d'Avray, rural scenes with or without peasant figures, and his later figure subjects from studio interiors to large compositions.
110 See Vincent Pomarède, 'La collection des peintures,' exhib. cat. *De Corot aux impressionnistes: donations Moreau-Nélaton*, Paris (Grand Palais) 1991, p. 92.
111 Possibly Courbet's political reputation, besmirched by his alleged involvement in the Paris Commune of 1871, continued to deter buyers. It was also public knowledge that his work was being forged, and headlines in the art press such as 'A factory of fake Courbets' would have done little for market confidence!; see [Anon.], 'Une usine de faux Courbet,' *La Chronique des Arts* (30 August 1890), p. 228. See also Linda Nochlin, 'The depoliticization of Gustave Courbet: transformation and rehabilitation under the Third Republic,' *October* 22 (1982), pp. 65-78.
112 These two were bought in London on

12 April 1886. *At sea* was immediately sold to Desfossés, its price increasing from 3,000 to 5,000 francs. The *Shearing sheep* went to Henri Poidatz the following month, the price hiked almost a 100 percent from 6,250 to 12,000 francs. Poidatz sold it back to Theo in December 1888 for 18,000 francs, making himself a fifty 50 percent profit on the picture in a year-and-a-half. Within three months the picture had been purchased, via the New York branch, by Bertha Potter Palmer, the collector-dealer. Within three years, then, the price of this Millet had increased twelve-fold.

113 Michel Melot, 'Daumier and art history: aesthetic judgement/political judgement,' *Oxford Art Journal* 11 (1988), pp. 4-8.

114 Jules Antoine, 'Beaux-arts. Exposition rétrospective de l'art français. Peinture,' *Art et Critique* 17 (22 September 1889), p. 268.

115 On 27 September 1887 he bought from Charles Leroux Cazin's *Starry night* – which, interestingly enough, Vincent might have seen – and sold it the same day, suggesting a prearranged deal. If this was a business triumph, costing 1,900 but selling for 8,300 francs, the next most successful Cazin, *Landscape with a rainbow*, more than doubled its value from 3,000 to 6,500 francs, but only after three years in Theo's stock.

116 He had been instrumental in getting Kaemmerer placed in Gérôme's studio at the Ecole; see Nonne, op. cit. (note 14), p. 351.

117 Shown at the Salon of 1881 and bought from the artist in March that year, *The balloon* was sold the same day to the American multi-millionaire Vanderbilt for a 50 percent profit.

118 Denis Rouart and Daniel Wildenstein, *Edouard Manet: catalogue raisonné*, 2 vols., Lausanne & Paris 1975, vol. 1, no. 28.

119 Besnard wrote to Theo that 'The pink sky is very particular to England and one must have seen further than the end of a Parisian's nose to have discovered that,' thus flattering Theo's cosmopolitanism; see b 1166 V/1962.

120 These were for the Ecole de Pharmacie (1883-86) and the 'salle des mariages' of the Mairie of the 1st *arrondissement* (1887-89); see Camille Mauclair, *Albert Besnard: l'homme et l'oeuvre*, Paris 1914, p. 183.

121 In a letter of early 1888 (b 1167 V/1962) Besnard asked Theo to enquire whether the collector who had purchased 'my big back' would lend it to the forthcoming Pastellistes show. The collector was Antonin Personnaz. The 'big back' was not entered in the stockbooks, though *Eve*, which may have been a pastel, was.

122 See Pickvance, op. cit. (note 25), p. 111.

123 Carrière was well acquainted with Manzi, the chief technician at the Asnières printing works, dedicating a self-portrait to him in 1889 (Lyon, Musée des Beaux-Arts). Two of the pictures Theo purchased the same year came from the magazine *Paris Illustré*, which shortly before had featured one of his paintings as its colour cover; see [Anon.], *Paris Illustré* 39 (29 September 1888), p. 613. Such exposure made his work more marketable, but Carrière was not an altogether unknown quantity: his *Sick child* had been bought by the State from the Salon of 1885 and deposited in the Musée de Montargis; it is now in the Musée d'Orsay. For Manzi, see exhib. cat. *Degas, Boldini, Toulouse-Lautrec: portraits inédits par Michel Manzi*, Bordeaux (Musée Goupil) & Albi (Musée Toulouse-Lautrec) 1997.

124 Wolff's Salon review in 1886 hailed him as the leading painter of everyday life on show, although the State's purchase of his *Portrait of Edmond de Goncourt* for the Musée de Nancy three years later was bitterly opposed in sections of the press; see Albert Wolff, *1886: Figaro-Salon*, Paris 1886, p. 58, and [Anon.], 'Le portrait de M. Edmond de Goncourt,' *Le Courrier de l'Art* 9 (18 January 1889), pp. 19-20.

125 He bought directly from the artist: five works on 30 November and four more on 26 December. He also bought two more from Wolff who, having promoted Raffaëlli, now seemed happy to have profited – unless the Wolff named in the stockbooks was a collector or dealer rather than the art critic. Six more works were purchased in 1890, five from the artist on 21 June.

126 [Anon.], 'Echos,' *Le Figaro* (28 May 1890).

127 See A.[lfred] de L.[ostalot], 'Concours et expositions,' *La Chronique des Arts* (31 May 1890), p. 170, and G.-Albert Aurier, 'Raffaëlli,' *Mercure de France* (September 1890), pp. 424-29.

128 Geoffroy, op. cit. (note 79), nos. 1, 2, 7, 20; see also *Collection Jules Claretie*, Paris (Hôtel Drouot) 8 May 1914, lot 46.

129 Richard Thomson, 'Degas's nudes at the 1886 impressionist exhibition,' *Gazette des Beaux-Arts* 108 (November 1986), p. 190 and fn. 7.

130 Octave Mirbeau, 'Notes sur l'art: Degas,' *La France* (15 November 1884); see also Gary Tinterow, 'Mirbeau on Degas: a little-known article of 1884,' *The Burlington Magazine* 130 (March 1988), p. 230.

131 Richard Kendall, exhib. cat. *Degas: beyond impressionism*, London (National Gallery) 1996, p. 41.

132 Emile Zola, 'Le naturalisme au Salon,' *Le Voltaire* (18-22 June 1880), reprinted in *Emile Zola. Le bon combat: de Courbet aux impressionnistes*, ed. Jean-Paul Bouillon, Paris 1974, p. 211.

133 Letter from Vincent van Gogh to Angrand, postmarked 25 October 1886, printed in Bogomila Welsh-Ovcharov, *The early work of Charles Angrand and his contact with Vincent van Gogh*, Utrecht & The Hague 1971, p. 60; see also Rewald, op. cit. (note 4), p. 13.

134 See b 1145 V/1962.

135 See b 1145-52 V/1962.

136 The *Woman seated beside a vase of flowers*, the first listed purchase (July 1887), sold in February 1889 for 5,500 francs, making a profit of 1,500. The ballet pictures did even better. The *Dance class*, bought for 5,220 francs from Petit in October 1888, was sold the next month to the painter Jacques-Emile Blanche for 8,000; while the *Dance school*, bought at Christie's in May 1889 for a mere 1,417 francs, went immediately into Manzi's collection for 4,000. None of these were new works, the portrait dating from 1865 and the two ballet scenes from the mid-1870s;

two of the other portraits were also quarter of a century old (Lemoisne, op. cit. [note 36], nos. 102 and 133); see Rewald, op. cit. (note 4), pp. 89-90.

137 See b 1151 V/1962.

138 Theo sold *Before the race* on 5 August 1888 to Gallimard for 2,400 francs; see Rewald, op. cit. (note 4), p. 89.

139 By 1890 he had a substantial collection, including Ingres, Menzel, Manet and Pissarro, and it was rapidly expanding; see Ann Dumas, 'Degas and his collection,' exhib. cat. *The private collection of Edgar Degas*, New York (The Metropolitan Museum of Art) 1997, pp. 11-12.

140 Halperin, op. cit. (note 91), vol. 1, pp. 95-96; see also Richard Thomson, *Degas: the nudes*, London 1988, p. 132, where they are identified as Lemoisne, op. cit. (note 36), nos. 1089, ?876, 1010, 1008 and 891. These works formed a slightly curious grouping: although all of nude women, they exhibited a variety of pastel techniques, dates and levels of finish. The nude was certainly a common enough subject, but by the 1880s there were questions about its marketability; this does not, however, appear to have deterred Boussod, Valadon & Cie. from exhibiting and selling the occasional erotic subject. That Degas's pastels did not sit easily with all members of the public can be gleaned from Berthe Morisot's comments on the show: she referred to the works rather cryptically as 'extraordinary'; see Rouart, op. cit. (note 28), p. 152, letter of 14 March 1888 (to Claude Monet).

141 The one-man show organised by Durand-Ruel in 1883 had been much admired in the press. It had merited high praise from the conservative *Journal des Arts* and a complete article in the *Gazette des Beaux-Arts*, although others – like Albert Wolff – continued to snipe at the artist's contributions to Petit's Expositions Internationales; see H. Marriott, 'Exposition de Claude Monet,' *Le Journal des Arts* 5 (6 March 1883), p. 2; Alfred de Lostalot, 'Exposition des oeuvres de M. Claude Monet,' *Gazette des Beaux-Arts* 2 (27 April 1883), pp. 342-48; and Albert Wolff, 'Exposition Internationale,' *Le Figaro* (19 June 1886).

142 Rewald, op. cit. (note 4), p. 15.

143 In short, while Monet's long-standing dealer, the financially pressed Durand, was relieved to sell old stock, Theo the newcomer was confident enough in Monet's marketability to widen the range of his holdings.

144 Petit was unable to show his work until November, and Monet distrusted Cazin's influence. Durand-Ruel wanted to put his work in a paying exhibition, to which Monet objected; he also felt Durand was lowering his profile in France by exporting too many pictures to America and was hurt by the manners of his son Charles; see Wildenstein, op. cit. (note 36), vol. 2, p. 229, letter 833, 10 February 1888 (to Alice Hoschedé); p. 230, letter 843, 26 February 1888 (same); and p. 237, letter 888, 15 May 1888 (to Whistler); and Venturi, op. cit. (note 15), vol. 1, p. 82. For Monet at Antibes see, most recently, Joachim Pissarro, exhib. cat. *Monet and the Mediterranean*, Fort Worth (Kimbell Art Museum) & Brooklyn (The Brooklyn Museum of Art) 1997-98, pp. 41-46, 113-44.

145 Rouart, op. cit. (note 28), p. 154, letter of early June 1888.

146 Eaque, 'Claude Monet,' *Le Journal des Arts* 10 (6 July 1888), p. 3.

147 Halperin, op. cit. (note 91), vol. 1, p. 113.

148 Bailly-Herzberg, op. cit. (note 3), vol. 2, p. 239, letter 492, 8 July 1888 (to Lucien Pissarro).

149 Ibid., pp. 241-42, letter 495, 10 July 1888 (to Lucien Pissarro).

150 Rewald, op. cit. (note 4), p. 27.

151 Wildenstein, op. cit. (note 36), nos. 1170 (Johnson), 1175, 1102, 1204 (Sargent) and 1215 (Pope).

152 Rewald, op. cit. (note 4), p. 46.

153 Exhib. cat. *Claude Monet – Auguste Rodin: centenaire de l'Exposition de 1889*, Paris (Musée Rodin) 1989-90.

154 Rewald, op. cit. (note 4), p. 49.

155 In the early 1880s the dealer had tried to discourage Pissarro's penchant for rural figure subjects, preferring his more marketable landscapes, and reacted strongly against Pissarro's adoption of the neo-impressionist technique pioneered by Seurat and Signac, with whom the artist grouped his work at the 1886 impressionist exhibition. This change of style positioned his closer to the avant-garde and distanced him from former colleagues like Degas and Monet, whose work was primed to make significant market progress. By 'rebranding' himself rather than consolidating his market identity Pissarro drastically and knowingly set back his commercial viability; see Ward, op. cit. (note 99).

156 For detailed studies of Pissarro circa 1886-90 and his relations with Theo van Gogh, see Lili Jampoller, 'Theo van Gogh and Camille Pissarro: correspondence and an exhibition,' *Simiolus* 16 (1986), pp. 50-61; see also Ward, op. cit. (note 99).

157 Bailly-Herzberg, op. cit. (note 3), vol. 2, p. 19, letter 309, 23 January 1886 (to Lucien Pissarro).

158 His friend, the critic and collector Théodore Duret, counselled concessions for the Petit show, at which Pissarro saw one of his recent, luminous paintings replaced by a dark Monet at the behest of a foreign participant, and found other aspects of the Internationale's hang not to his taste: see ibid., p. 144, letter 406, 17 March 1887 (to Lucien Pissarro); p. 161, letter 421, 8 May 1887 (to Lucien Pissarro); pp. 166-67, letter 423, 15 May 1887 (to Lucien Pissarro). With some poor reviews – the *Courrier de l'Art* curtly dismissed his contribution as 'bad' – Pissarro's position was frangible; see G. Dargenty, 'Chronique des expositions. Exposition Internationale de peinture et de la sculpture. Galerie Georges Petit,' *Le Courrier de l'Art* 7 (27 May 1887), pp. 163-64.

159 Bailly-Herzberg, op. cit. (note 3), vol. 2, p. 149, letter 411, 7 April 1887 (to Achille Heymann). The paintings are reproduced in Ludovic Rodo Pissarro and Lionello Venturi, *Camille Pissarro: son art et son oeuvre*, 2 vols., San Francisco 1989 [Paris 1939], vol. 2, nos. 713 and 576.

160 Bailly-Herzberg, op. cit. (note 3), vol. 2, p. 186, letter 439, 10 June 1887 (to Lucien Pissarro).

161 Halperin, op. cit. (note 91), vol. 1, p. 90.

162 Pissarro and Venturi, op. cit. (note 159), vol. 2, nos. 709 and 710.

163 Ibid., no. 1640; see also Rewald, op. cit. (note 4), p. 22.
164 Rewald, op. cit. (note 4), pp. 9, 72, 76-77, with a tabulation of Dupuis's purchases from Theo. Tragically, in December 1890, Dupuis, mistakenly believing himself to be bankrupt, committed suicide, and the impressive collection he had built up with the Dutchman's advice was dispersed.
165 Ward, op. cit. (note 99), p. 87.
166 Bouglé lent *The gleaners*, an important picture on which Pissarro had worked for a couple of years, and Dupuis both his cottage and Rouen paintings. For more on *The gleaners* (Pissarro and Venturi, op. cit. [note 159], vol. 2, no. 730), see Richard Thomson, *Camille Pissarro: impressionism, landscape and rural labour*, London 1990, pp. 59-65.
167 See Gustave Geffroy, 'Camille Pissarro,' exhib. cat. *Exposition d'oeuvres récentes de Camille Pissarro*, Paris (Boussod, Valadon & Cie.) February 1890. See also Ward, op. cit. (note 99), pp. 162-63.
168 Geffroy, op. cit. (note 167), p. 10.
169 Avant-garde periodicals even squabbled over who had been the first to acclaim Pissarro, and if the review in the *Courrier de l'Art* was sarcastic, it still gave his exhibition more space than the Cercle Volney's; see [Anon.], 'Notes et notules,' *Entretiens Politiques et Littéraires* 2 (1 May 1890), p. 61, and G. Dargenty, 'Chronique des expositions. M. Pissaro [sic],' *Le Courrier de l'Art* 10 (7 March 1890), p. 75.
170 b 1171 V/1962.
171 See Geffroy, op. cit. (note 79), no. 51, 'Suite de quinze dessins à la plume sur l'Hôtel Drouot'; see also Theodore Child, 'The Hôtel Drouot,' *Harper's New Monthly Magazine* 78 (February 1889), pp.331-47.
172 See Colin B. Bailey, *Renoir's portraits: impressions of an age*, New Haven & London, 1997, p. 178.
173 See Edmond and Jules de Goncourt, op. cit. (note 55), vol. 3, pp. 278-79 (8 June 1889) for Edmond's views of Millet as a draughtsman.
174 See G. Dargenty, 'Les Pastellistes,' *Le Courrier de l'Art* 8 (27 April 1888), p. 130, and Halperin, op. cit. (note 91), vol. 1, p. 106.
175 *Monet in Holland*, cit. (note 102), p.183, letter 1, 21 April 1887 (Monet to Theo van Gogh).
176 *Archives*, cit. (note 38), no. 189, 16 February 1889 (from Theo van Gogh); Bailly-Herzberg, op. cit. (note 3), vol. 2, p. 289, letter 538, 2 September 1889 (to Theo van Gogh).
177 Randall, op. cit. (note 76), vol. 2, pp. 578-81, 584, 590, 593, 596-97.
178 Ibid, p. 578.
179 [Anon.], 'Mouvement des arts. Collection Léon Gaucherel,' *La Chronique des Arts* (19 June 1886), p. 186.
180 See Gary Tinterow, 'III. 1881-1890,' *Degas*, cit. (note 26), p. 389, and Bailly-Herzberg, op. cit. (note 3), vol. 2, p. 249, letter 504, 4 September 1888 (to Lucien Pissarro). It is possible that these prints were from Theo's own collection. (I am grateful to Chris Stolwijk for this suggestion.) If so, they would still have served the company's purpose of introducing a Dutch public to the modern artists Theo was trying to promote.
181 Manzi is likely to have had a hand in this, together with Henri Rouart, from whose Degas collection 11 of the works were copied; but Theo must also have been closely involved, having included at least one of the originals in his show of nudes earlier in the year; see Halperin, op. cit. (note 91), vol. 1, p. 111; Douglas Druick and Peter Zegers, 'Degas and the printed image, 1856-1914,' in Sue Welsh Reed and Barbara Stern Shapiro, exhib. cat. *Edgar Degas: the painter as printmaker*, Boston (Museum of Fine Arts) & London (Hayward Gallery) 1984-85, pp. lxii-lxiii.
182 Rewald, op. cit. (note 4), p. 44; see also *Paul Gauguin: 45 lettres à Vincent, Theo et Jo van Gogh*, ed. Douglas Cooper, The Hague & Lausanne, 1983, p. 261, letter 35, c. 20 January 1889 (to Vincent van Gogh).
183 Thorold, op. cit. (note 63), pp. 110-13 (and pp.119-20), letter of February 1889.
184 Halperin, op. cit. (note 91), vol. 1, p. 111; see also Maurice Joyant, *Henri de Toulouse-Lautrec, 1864-1901: peintre*, Paris 1926, p. 119.
185 Randall, op. cit. (note 76), vol. 2, pp. 664-66, 679-81.
186 In 1889 alone a retrospective was held at the Ecole des Beaux-Arts, a monograph by Alexandre published, and a monument raised on the Ile St Louis, for which Lucas approached Theo for a contribution from Boussod, Valadon & Cie. (ibid, p. 688); see also [Anon.], 'Concours et expositions,' *La Chronique des Arts* (6 April 1889), p. 105.
187 The highest price paid at the 1886 Auguste Sichel sale was 9,400 francs, considerably more than Theo ever got for a Degas painting; see [Anon.] 'Revue des ventes. Bronzes de Barye,' *Le Journal des Arts* 8 (2 March 1886), p. 3.
188 See Halperin, op. cit. (note 91), p. 111, and b 1339 V/1962.
189 Geffroy, op. cit. (note 79), pp. 8-11; Lostalot, op. cit. (note 127), p. 170; Aurier, op. cit. (note 127), p. 329.
190 *Catalogue des ouvrages de peinture, sculpture, dessins, gravures et objets d'art exposés au Champ-de-Mars*, Paris 1891, no. 1356.
191 Halperin, op. cit. (note 91), p. 91.
192 This transaction, mentioned in Gauguin's correspondence, was not listed in the stockbooks – possibly because it was a maverick move, although other sculpture purchases do not seen to have been noted either; see Rewald, op. cit. (note 4), p. 35.
193 *Lettres de Gauguin à sa femme et à ses amis*, ed. Maurice Malingue, Paris 1946, pp. 181-82, letter 29, February-March 1891 (to Mette Gauguin).
194 *Charles Angrand: correspondances, 1883-1926*, ed. François Lespinasse, Rouen 1988, p. 32, letter to Charles Frechon, early April 1889; see also Malingue, op. cit. (note 193), p. 174, letter 41, November 1889 (to Emile Bernard).
195 See also Rouart and Wildenstein, op. cit. (note 118), no. 155.
196 'Lettres de Theo van Rysselberghe à Octave Maus (ed. M.-J. Chartrain-Hebbelinck and Ph. Mertens),' *Bulletin des Musées Royaux des Beaux-Arts de Belgique* 1-2 (1966), p. 70, letter 11, c. 20 October 1889.
197 *The letters of Henri de Toulouse-Lautrec*, ed. Herbert Schimmel, Oxford

1991, p. 111, letter 139, early 1887 (to Theo van Gogh); see also Julia Frey, *Toulouse-Lautrec: a life*, London 1994, p. 231, 1 September 1887 (from Odon de Toulouse-Lautrec to Gabrielle de Toulouse-Lautrec).

198 Schimmel, op. cit. (note 197), p. 124, letter 160, 12 January 1888 (to Theo van Gogh), and p. 123, letter 158, 9 January 1888 (to his mother, Adèle de Toulouse-Lautrec). Manzi owned two paintings of this period and may have purchased both, although Lautrec was only expecting to sell one: M.-G. Dortu, *Toulouse-Lautrec et son oeuvre*, New York 1971, nos. 285 and 288.

199 See Richard Thomson, 'Illustration, caricature and the type,' exhib. cat. *Toulouse-Lautrec*, London (Hayward Gallery) & Paris (Grand Palais) 1991-92, pp. 196-201.

200 Merlhès, op. cit. (note 31), vol. 1, p. 166, letter 137, 6 December 1887 (to Mette Gauguin); see also Rewald, op. cit. (note 4), p. 24.

201 Georges Wildenstein, *Gauguin*, Paris 1964, nos. 201, 266, 265, ?195 and 262.

202 One was sold to the poster artist Chéret, another to Léon Clapisson, an established impressionist buyer, and three to Dupuis, who seems to have decided that, with canvases at about 500 francs, Gauguin made a good investment. For Clapisson, see Anne Distel, *Impressionism: the first collectors*, New York 1990, p.167; Richard Thomson, *Edgar Degas: Waiting*, Malibu 1995, pp. 43, 46-48; and Anne Distel, 'Léon Clapisson: patron and collector,' in Bailey, op. cit. (note 172), pp. 76-86.

203 Rewald, op. cit. (note 4), p. 32.

204 Ibid., p. 44.

205 Merlhès, op. cit. (note 31), vol. 1, pp. 280-81, letter 43, 13 November 1888 (from Theo van Gogh).

206 Wildenstein, op. cit. (note 201), nos. 250 and 227. The Belgian Anna Boch, sister of a friend of Vincent's, and Henri Lerolle, a Degas intimate, bought the Breton and Martinique subjects, respectively.

207 Malingue, op. cit. (note 193), p. 178, letter 95, late November 1889 (to Emile Bernard).

208 Rewald, op. cit. (note 4), p. 51, and Alec Wildenstein, *Odilon Redon: catalogue raisonné de l'oeuvre peint et dessiné*, Paris 1992, no. 404.

209 Rewald, op. cit. (note 4), p. 89 lists a Cézanne; it is no. 180 in his *Paintings of Paul Cézanne: a catalogue raisonné*, New York 1996. However, Dr Walter Feilchenfeldt, who completed the catalogue, has informed me verbally (15 May 1998) that he does not consider this painting to be by Cézanne.

210 Ward, op. cit. (note 99), p. 85. Lucien Pissarro began to work with Manzi in June 1887. His aunt, a dressmaker, had made clothes for some of the Goupil children, and he was relieved that he did not have to use this connection to get the job; see Thorold, op. cit. (note 63), p. 96, letter of 4 June 1887.

211 Martin Bailey, 'Van Gogh's first sale: a self-portrait in London,' *Apollo* 143 (March 1996), pp. 20-21.

212 *J-F. Raffaëlli – Octave Mirbeau: correspondance*, ed. Pierre Michel, Tusson 1993, pp. 66-67, letter 31, 27 October 1890.

213 *Lettres de Gauguin, Gide, Huysmans, Jammes, Mallarmé, Verhaeren à Odilon Redon*, ed. Rosaline Bacou, Paris 1960, p. 194, October 1890.

214 *Archives*, cit. (note 38), no. 21, late 1890 (from Durand-Ruel).

215 Neither of its main broadsheets, the *Journal des Arts* and the *Chronique des Arts*, which customarily ran obituaries of artists, collectors, administrators and other figures in the arts, mentioned his death. Early 1891 saw the death of several distinguished people – the painters Meissonier, Jongkind, Achille Benouville and Charles Chaplin, and the critic/collector Philippe Burty – and the obituary columns apparently had no space for a Dutch gallery manager, just ten years in Paris.

216 Joyant, op. cit. (note 184), pp. 117-22.

217 Joyant's new developments included a show of drawings by the caricaturist Jean-Louis Forain in May, and over the course of 1891 critics in avant-garde periodicals noted not only work by artists Theo had introduced – Monet, Raffaëlli, Pissarro, Zandomeneghi, Lautrec – but also new additions: violent subjects by the Belgian Henry de Groux, pastels by Forain, Chéret and Whistler; see A.[lfred] de L.[ostalot], 'Concours et expositions,' *La Chronique des Arts* (30 May 1891), p. 170; G.-A.[lbert] A.[urier], 'Choses d'art,' *Mercure de France* (June 1891), p. 374;
C. M.[auclair], 'Beaux-arts,' *Revue Indépendante* (December 1891), p. 429. However, if these were new names, or in the case of Chéret an excursion into a new medium, they were all artists Theo might well have taken up.

218 *Correspondance Mallarmé-Whistler*, ed. Carl Paul Barbier, Paris 1964, pp. 98-99, 13 October 1891 (letter from Joyant to Goupil and Co., London).

219 Rewald, op. cit. (note 4), p. 98.

220 Bailly-Herzberg, op. cit. (note 3), vol. 2, p. 198, letter 450, 28 August 1887 (to Lucien Pissarro), and p. 243, letter 496, 12 July 1888 (to Lucien Pissarro).

221 Cooper, op. cit. (note 182), p. 153, letter 22, 21 or 22 November 1889 (to Theo van Gogh).

222 Bailly-Herzberg, op. cit. (note 3), vol. 2, p. 20, letter 309, 23 January 1886 (to Lucien Pissarro).

Sjraar van Heugten and
Chris Stolwijk

Theo van Gogh
The collector

1 b 2047 VF/1982, Paris, 14 March 1889 (from Theo to Jo).
2 On Theo's collecting activities see also Lilli Jampoller, 'Theo and Vincent as art collectors,' in Evert van Uitert and Michael Hoyle (eds.), *The Rijksmuseum Vincent van Gogh*, Amsterdam 1987, pp. 30-37; Chris Stolwijk, '"Our crown and our honour and our joy": Theo van Gogh's early years,' *Van Gogh Museum Journal* (1997-98), pp. 42-57; and the exhibition of Theo van Gogh's collection compiled by his son V.W. van Gogh in 1953 (and in 1960): exhib. cat. *De verzameling Theo van Gogh, met uitzondering van de werken van zijn broer Vincent*, Amsterdam, (Stedelijk Museum) 1953, and exhib. cat. *Collectie Theo van Gogh*, Amsterdam (Stedelijk Museum) & Otterlo (Kröller-Müller Museum) 1960.
3 See, for example, the entry: 'Received Fr. Uiterwijk f. 3 paintings 1450 guilders.' The accounts are currently being deciphered.
4 The inventories (b 2214 VF/1982; b 2215 VF/1982; b 4553 V/1982; and b 4557 V/1982) always list *four* paintings by Guillaumin while the current collection contains only two. It is possible that the artist's large and remarkably colourful pastel *Farms at Janville* was counted as a painting.
5 b 4284 V/1984, Paris, 26 July 1887 (from Theo to Jo).
6 For Vincent's collection see Louis van Tilborgh, '"A kind of Bible": the collection of prints and illustrations,' in Uitert and Hoyle, op. cit. (note 2), pp. 38-44.
7 The Van Gogh Museum has two albums with prints, one of which – a scrapbook – can be attributed to Vincent on the evidence of the inscriptions; the other album may have been Theo's: t 1488 V/1962.
8 Pierre-Lin Renié, 'Goupil & Cie. à l'ère industrielle: la photographie appliqué à la reproduction des oeuvres d'art,' in Hélène Lafont-Couturier (ed.), *Etat des lieux* Bordeaux 1994, pp. 89-114.
9 In October 1877, for example, Vincent congratulated Theo on what he described as the 'good' acquisition of 'that life of Frederik the Great, illustrated by Menzel' [132/112]. The reference is to Franz Kugler's *Geschichte Friedrichs des Grossen*, with illustrations by Adolph Menzel, Leipzig 1840.
10 On Vincent and Theo van Gogh's collection of Japanese prints see Charlotte van Rappard-Boon, Willem van Gullik and Keiko van Bremen-Ito, *Catalogue of the Van Gogh Museum's collection of Japanese prints*, Amsterdam & Zwolle 1991.
11 See also Chris Stolwijk's contribution to this catalogue. Theo's income can be calculated from the notes in his accounts, a settlement of accounts between Boussod, Valadon & Cie. and their employee (b 2119 VF/1982), and other notes written by Theo (b 2206 VF/1982).
12 Chris Stolwijk, *Uit de schilderswereld: Nederlandse kunstschilders in de tweede helft van de negentiende eeuw*, Leiden 1998, pp. 212-13.
13 Various old inventories in the Van Gogh Museum list five Monticellis. Today there are six: inv. nos. s 249 V/1962; s 250 V/1962; s 251 V/1962; s 252 V/1962; s 253 V/1962; and s 254 V/1962. Which of these were the original five from Theo's collection is unclear. Four of the Monticellis owned by Vincent and Theo were acquired from the Parisian dealer Delarebeyrette, who specialised in his work. Boussod, Valadon & Cie. gave another canvas, *Italian girl*, to their branch manager on 20 November 1886 (BV 18126, 20 November 1886). With thanks to Monique Nonne.
14 See also letter 479/391. In 1947 V.W. van Gogh presented this work to the Nationalmuseum in Stockholm. The completed painting, *The water nymph,* is currently in the Göteborgs Kunstmuseum.
15 See also Chris Stolwijk's contribution to this catalogue.
16 The other works Koning gave to Theo were probably inv. nos. s 281 v/1963; s 264 V/1962; s 266 V/1962; s 267 V/1962; s 268 V/1962; and s 269 V/1962.
17 Theo sent the portrait to Jo, who hung it in the bedroom 'above the bed so I can always see you first thing in the morning': b 4256 V/1984, Amsterdam 25 January 1889 (from Jo to Theo).
18 b 1042 V/1962, Le Pouldu, 22 October 1889 (from Meijer de Haan to Theo). After staying with Theo in Paris De Haan went to Brittany where he worked in Le Pouldu under Gauguin's guidance.
19 In 1884 Vittorio Corcos dedicated his *Portrait of a young woman* to Theo with the words: 'A m. Th. van Gogh / souvenir de Corcos.' Theo traded the work of this Italian figure painter from 1881 until his death. He must have been delighted to have work by Corcos in his collection.
20 On this painting see 'Catalogue of acquisitions: paintings and drawings, July 1994 – December 1996,' *Van Gogh Museum Journal* (1996), p. 203.
21 b 2023 VF/1982, Paris, 3 January 1889 (from Theo to Jo).
22 b 942 V/1962, Paris, [c. July 1886] (from Theo to his mother).
23 *Paul Gauguin: 45 lettres à Vincent, Theo et Jo van Gogh*, ed. Douglas Cooper, The Hague & Lausanne 1983, p. 33.
24 See letters 591/471; 600/477a; 604/480 (which shows that Russell was willing to exchange works); 626/496; 629/501a; 636/B9; and 642/506.
25 b 1117 V/1962. See also Richard Thomson's contribution to this catalogue.
26 b 4302 V/1984, Paris, 5 April 1890 (from Jo to her parents).
27 See for the correspondence between Theo and Jo in the years 1888-90: *Kort geluk: de briefwisseling van Theo van Gogh en Jo van Gogh-Bonger*, ed. Han van Crimpen, Zwolle 1999.
28 b 2034 VF/1982, Paris, 1 February 1889 (from Theo to Jo).
29 b 2050 VF/1982, Paris, 16 March 1889 (from Theo to Jo).
30 b 926 V/1962, Paris, 27 November 1889 (from Theo to Wil van Gogh).
31 b 2009 V/1982, Paris, 9-10 February 1889 (from Theo to Jo).
32 See also Richard Thomson's contribution to this catalogue. Quoted in

Jampoller, op. cit. (note 2), p. 57.

33 According to Jo, when Vincent Willem saw this work he exclaimed: 'Oh, mama, look, what a beautiful sun!' See *Correspondance de Camille Pissarro*, ed. Janine Bailly-Herzberg, 5 vols., Paris 1988, vol. 3, p. 272, fn. 1, 3 December 1892 (from Jo to Pissarro). Presumably this was a landscape with a sunlight effect in no. 10 format (38 x 55 cm).

34 On this date Pissarro wrote to Jo that he had had a no. 10 canvas ready for some time, in exchange for the work that Jo had given him; see b 825 V/1962. On 19 November Pissarro announced that the painting was on its way; see: b 1372 V/1962, 23 November 1896; b 1309 V/1962, 30 November 1896; 1373 V/1962, 3 February 1897; b 1374 V/1962, 16 February 1897; and b 1376 V/1962, 23 March 1897 (from Vollard to Jo).

35 b 916 V/1962, Paris, 6 December 1888 (from Theo to Wil van Gogh).

36 b 876 V/1962. Also published in Cooper, op. cit. (note 25), p. 33. Cooper states that the sale is also mentioned in the notebook which Gauguin kept during 1888 and 1889. See also letters 723/561 and 656/W5.

37 In February 1889 this work was on view at Les XX in Brussels and in June in the Café Volpini; see exhib. cat. *The art of Paul Gauguin*, Washington, DC (The National Gallery of Art), Chicago (The Art Institute of Chicago) & Paris (Grand Palais) 1988-89, p. 47. For the 'place of honour': b 923 V/1962, Paris, 26 April 1889 (from Jo to her 'sisters').

38 Georges Wildenstein, *Gauguin*, Paris 1964, no. 300 and *The art of Paul Gauguin*, cit. (note 37), p. 117.

39 b 1156 V/1962, Paris, 12 January 1888 (receipt from Toulouse-Lautrec to Theo).

Lenders

Belgium
Koninklijke Musea voor Schone Kunsten van België, Brussels

Germany
Wallraf-Richartz Museum, Cologne

France
Musée Goupil, Bordeaux
Musée des Beaux-Arts, Lyon
Musée Carnavalet, Paris
Musée du Louvre, Paris
Musée d'Orsay, Paris
Musée Rodin, Paris

Great Britian
Fitzwilliam Museum, Cambridge
Private collection, London
The National Gallery, London
Manchester City Art Galleries
Southampton City Art Gallery
Private collection

Japan
Private collection

Mexico
Private collection

The Netherlands
Rijksmuseum, Amsterdam
Dordrechts Museum, Dordrecht
Kröller-Müller Museum, Otterlo
Museum Boijmans Van Beuningen, Rotterdam

Norway
Nasjonalgalleriet, Oslo

Taiwan
Chi-Mei Fine Art Museum, Jen-te-Village

United States
Museum of Fine Arts, Boston
The Art Institute of Chicago
Collection Miranda and Robert Donneley, Chicago
The Columbus Museum of Art
The Dallas Museum of Art
Collection Dr and Mrs Michael Schlossberg, Eastpoint
Gerhard Wurzer Gallery/Christopher Drake, Houston
Private collection, New York
The Forbes Magazine Collection, New York
The Metropolitan Museum of Art, New York
The Chrysler Museum of Art, Norfolk
Philadelphia Museum of Art
The Carnegie Museum of Art, Pittsburgh
Collection of Meadow Brook Hall, Oakland University, Rochester
National Gallery of Art, Washington, DC
Norton Museum of Art, West Palm Beach
The Mr and Mrs C. Foundation
The John M. and Sally B. Thornton Trust

Switzerland
Stiftung Langmatt Sidney und Jenny Brown, Baden
Fondation Rau pour le Tiers-Monde, Embraport

Catalogue

This catalogue lists – in alphabetical order – all works loaned to the exhibition *Theo van Gogh (1857–1891): art dealer, collector and brother of Vincent*. Most of these pictures were handled by Theo van Gogh between 1873 and 1890. Information on the provenances is drawn from the stockbooks of Boussod, Valadon & Cie. (formerly Goupil & Cie.), now in the Getty Research Institute for the History of Art and the Humanities in Los Angeles.

Purchases [+] list: gallery where purchased, date, original title, 'Goupil number,' source – if none the work was purchased directly from the artist – and the purchase price in francs (FF).
Sales [–] list: gallery where sold, date, buyer, and the sale price in francs (FF).

94
Sir Lawrence Alma-Tadema 1836–1912
A harvest festival. Opus CCXX 1880
Oil on panel, 30.5 x 23.5 cm
The Forbes Magazine Collection, New York
+ Boulevard Montmartre (Theo van Gogh), 17 March 1881, *Fête céréale*, G 15234, C.M. van Gogh, FF 17,500
– Goupil & Cie. (London), 11 June 1881, Barrow, FF 25,000
Literature V.G. Swanson, *Lawrence-Alma Tadema: the biography and catalogue raisonné of the paintings of Sir Lawrence Alma-Tadema*, London 1990, no. 263.

62
Charles Bargue c. 1825–1883
A bashi-bazouk c. 1875
Oil on canvas, 47.6 x 33.3 cm
The Metropolitan Museum of Art, New York, Catharine Lorillard Wolfe Collection
+ Boulevard Montmartre (Theo van Gogh), 1 June 1883, *Bachi Bougouch*, G 16637, auction (Bargue studio), FF 50
– Boulevard Montmartre (Theo van Gogh), 16 October 1883, Desfossés, FF 600
Literature *French paintings: a catalogue of the collection of the Metropolitan Museum of Art*, New York 1966, p. 176.

98
Albert Besnard 1849–1934
Naked woman warming herself 1886
Pastel on paper, 90 x 72 cm
Musée d'Orsay, Paris
+? Boulevard Montmartre (Theo van Gogh), early 1888 [?], Personnaz
Not mentioned in the stockbooks of Boussod, Valadon & Cie.
Literature G. Monnier, *Musée du Louvre, Cabinet des dessins Musée d'Orsay. Pastels du XIXe siècle*, Paris 1985, no. 17.
[Paris only]

100
Eugène Carrière 1849–1906
Mother and child c. 1889
Oil on canvas, 50.2 x 61 cm
Philadelphia Museum of Art, The John G. Johnson Collection
+ Boulevard Montmartre (Theo van Gogh), 5 October 1889, *Mère et enfant (Sommeil)*, BV 20082, FF 1,200
– Boussod, Valadon & Cie., 29 October 1889, John G. Johnson, FF 2,600
Literature *Paintings from Europe and the Americas in the Philadelphia Museum of Art: a concise catalogue*, Philadelphia 1994, p. 112.

99
Eugène Carrière 1849–1906
The favorite toy c. 1887
Oil on canvas, 65.4 x 52 cm
Norton Museum of Art, West Palm Beach
+ Boulevard Montmartre (Theo van Gogh), 4 July 1890, *Enfant à jouyou*, BV 20893, Paris Illustré, FF 1,275
– Boulevard Montmartre (Theo van Gogh), 21 July 1890, Bowman-Lotti, FF 1,500
Literature *Catalogue of the collection – Norton Gallery of Art*, West Palm Beach 1979, no. 236.

82
Camille Corot 1796–1875
Corot's studio n.d.
Oil on canvas, 63 x 42 cm
Musée du Louvre, Paris
+ Boussod, Valadon & Cie., 20 November 1886, *Atelier de l'amateur (Femme dis'-chevalet)*, BV 18155, Guillot, FF 6,000
– Boulevard Montmartre (Theo van Gogh), 7 July 1887, Desfossés, FF 7,000
Literature A. Robaut, *L'oeuvre de Corot*, 5 vols., Paris 1904-06, no. 1559; I. Compin and A. Roquebert, *Catalogue sommaire illustré des peintures du Musée du Louvre et du Musée d'Orsay*, 5 vols., Paris 1986, vol. 3, p. 154.

83
Camille Corot 1796–1875
A young woman near a well c. 1865-70
Oil on canvas, 65 x 42 cm
Kröller-Müller Museum, Otterlo
+ Boussod, Valadon & Cie., 24 May 1888, *La femme au puits (no. 6 du catalogue)*, BV 19278, Chevalier, FF 4,250
– Boulevard Montmartre (Theo van Gogh), 3 December 1889, Bechuus, FF 10,000
Literature A. Robaut, *L'oeuvre de Corot*, 5 vols., Paris 1904–06, no. 1343; *Schilderijen van het Rijksmuseum Kröller-Müller*, Otterlo 1970, no. 57.
[Amsterdam only]

84
Camille Corot 1796–1875
St Sebastian c. 1874
Oil on canvas, 130 x 88 cm
National Gallery of Art, Washington, DC, Timken Collection
+ Boussod, Valadon & Cie., 13 November 1889, *St. Sebastien (01023) Vente Gallimard*, BV 20139, Ladmiral, FF 17,500
– Boulevard Montmartre (Theo van Gogh), 4 November 1889, Desfossés, FF 20,500
Literature A. Robaut, *L'oeuvre de Corot*, 5 vols., Paris 1904-06, no. 2316.
[Amsterdam only]

no ill.
Camille Corot 1796–1875
Souvenir of Nemi: rocks and shrubs c. 1844-45
Oil on canvas, 102.4 x 86.1 cm
Museum Mesdag, The Hague
+ Boulevard Montmartre (Theo van Gogh), 5 April 1890, *Paysage montaigneux et arbres*, BV 20439, Doria, FF 3,000
– Boussod, Valadon & Cie. (The Hague), 23 June 1890, Hendrik Willem Mesdag, FF 8,064
Literature A. Robaut, *L'oeuvre de Corot*, 5 vols., Paris 1904-06, no. 637; Fred Leeman and Hanna Pennock, *Museum Mesdag: catalogue of paintings and drawings*, Amsterdam & Zwolle 1996, no. 65.

87
Charles-François Daubigny 1817–1878
The house of Mère Bazot 1874
Oil on canvas, 92.5 x 185.4 cm
The Art Institute of Chicago, Mr and Mrs Potter Palmer Collection
+ Goupil & Cie., 3 July 1880, *La maison de la mère Bazot à Valmondois (Seine & Oise). Salon 1874*, G 14729, Karl Daubigny, FF 10,000
– Boulevard Montmartre (Theo van Gogh), 2 May 1882, Desfossés, FF 14,000
+ Boulevard Montmartre (Theo van Gogh), 7 July 1887, *La maison de la Mère Bazot à Valmondois (s&o) (Salon 1874) anc. 14729*, BV 18703, Desfossés, FF 11,000
– Boussod, Valadon & Cie., 30 March 1889, Potter Palmer
Literature Robert Hellebranth, *Charles-François Daubigny, 1817–1878*, Monges 1976, no. 191.

79
Charles-François Daubigny 1817–1878
Sunset near Villerville 1874
Oil on canvas, 84 x 147 cm
Museum Mesdag, The Hague
+ Boulevard Montmartre (Theo van Gogh), 2 August 1888, *Villerville, soleil couchant*, BV 19407, Georges Petit, FF 8,000
– Boussod, Valadon & Cie. (The Hague), 27 September 1888, Mesdag, FF 18,144
Literature Robert Hellebranth, *Charles-François Daubigny, 1817–1878*, Monges 1976, no. 622; Fred Leeman and Hanna Pennock, *Museum Mesdag: catalogue of paintings and drawings*, Amsterdam & Zwolle 1996, no. 91.
[Amsterdam only]

72
Charles-François Daubigny 1817–1878
Beach at low tide 1876
Oil on panel, 34.5 x 55.5 cm
Rijksmuseum, Amsterdam
+ Boulevard Montmartre (Theo van Gogh), 19 June 1889, *Plage de Villerville*, BV 19913, Desfossés, FF 1,400
– Boussod, Valadon & Cie. (The Hague), 24 September 1889, Van Lynden, FF 2,000
Literature Robert Hellebranth, *Charles-François Daubigny, 1817–1878*, Monges 1976, no. 653; P.J.J. van Thiel, *et al.*, *All the paintings of the Rijksmuseum*, Amsterdam 1976, p. 188.
[Amsterdam only]

91
Honoré Daumier 1810–1879
A street scene c. 1852
Oil on panel, 27 x 21.3 cm
Museum Boijmans Van Beuningen, Rotterdam
+ Boulevard Montmartre (Theo van Gogh), 6 November 1888, *Femme et enfant*, BV 19535, Valcourt, FF 600
– Boulevard Montmartre (Theo van Gogh), 20 February 1889, Desfossés, FF 800
Literature K.E. Maison, *Honoré Daumier: catalogue raisonné of the paintings, watercolours and drawings*, San Francisco 1996 [London 1967], no. I-44.

105
Edgar Degas 1834–1911
Mr Ruelle c. 1862
Oil on canvas, 44 x 36 cm
Musée des Beaux-Arts, Lyon
+ Boulevard Montmartre (Theo van Gogh), 9 May 1890, *Ancien portrait d'homme assis tenant son chapeau*, BV 20702, FF 2,000
– Boulevard Montmartre (Theo van Gogh), 31 July 1890, Dupuis, FF 2,500
Literature Paul-André Lemoisne, *Degas et son oeuvre*, 5 vols., Paris 1946-49, no. 102.

104
Edgar Degas 1834–1911
Woman seated beside a vase of flowers (Madame Paul Valpiçon?) 1865
Oil on canvas, 73.7 x 92.7 cm
The Metropolitan Museum of Art, New York, H.O. Havemeyer Collection
+ Boulevard Montmartre (Theo van Gogh), 22 July 1887, *Femme accoudée*, BV 18719, FF 4,000
– Boulevard Montmartre (Theo van Gogh), 28 February 1889, Boivin, FF 5,500
Literature Paul-André Lemoisne, *Degas et son oeuvre*, 5 vols., Paris 1946-49, no. 125; exhib. cat. *Degas*, Paris (Grand Palais), Ottawa (National Gallery of Canada) & New York (The Metropolitan Museum of Art) 1988-89, no. 60.

53
Edgar Degas 1834–1911
The dance school 1873–76
Oil on canvas, 85 x 75 cm
Musée d'Orsay, Paris
+ Boussod, Valadon & Cie., 25 May 1889, *Maître de ballet*, BV 19884, Christie's (London), FF 1,417
– Boulevard Montmartre (Theo van Gogh), 3 June 1889, Manzi, FF 4,000
Literature Paul-André Lemoisne, *Degas et son oeuvre*, Paris 1946-49, no. 341; exhib. cat. *Degas*, Paris (Grand Palais), Ottawa (National Gallery of Canada) & New York (The Metropolitan Museum of Art) 1988-89, no. 129.

68
Edouard Detaille 1848–1912
Attacking the convoy 1880
Oil on canvas, 81 x 131.5 cm
The Forbes Magazine Collection, New York
+ Goupil & Cie., 19 April 1880, *Attaquant un convoi*, G 14416, FF 20,000
– Boulevard Montmartre, 19 April 1880, Sloane, FF 50,000.
Literature Rachel Esner, '"Gloria victis": Französische Malerei des Deutsch-Französichen Krieges,' in Stefan Germer and Michael F. Zimmermann (eds.), *Bilder der Macht – Macht der Bilder: Zeitgeschichte in Darstellungen des 19. Jahrhunderts*, Munich 1997, pp. 390-402.

77
Narcisse Diaz de la Peña 1807–1876
The magician n.d.
Oil on canvas, 33.5 x 23.5 cm
Paris, Musée d'Orsay
+ Boulevard Montmartre (Theo van Gogh), 26 April 1890, *La chance*, BV 20635, Bonjean, FF 6,000
– Boussod, Valadon & Cie., 1 May 1890, Chauchard, FF 15,000
Literature I. Compin and A. Roquebert *Catalogue sommaire illustré des peintures du Musée du Louvre et du Musée d'Orsay*, 5 vols., Paris 1986, vol. 3, p. 226.

78
Narcisse Diaz de la Peña 1807–1876
At the well 1850
Oil on canvas, 35 x 24.5 cm
Musée d'Orsay, Paris
+ Boulevard Montmartre (Theo van Gogh), 18 June 1890, *La verité sortant du puits*, BV 20777, Clarembaux, FF 13,500
– Boussod, Valadon & Cie., 18 June 1890, Chauchard, FF 17,000
Literature I. Compin and A. Roquebert, *Catalogue sommaire illustré des peintures du Musée du Louvre et du Musée d'Orsay*, 5 vols., Paris 1986, vol. 3, p. 226.

65
Julien Dupré 1851–1910
Feeding time c. 1881
Oil on canvas, 65.4 x 81.3 cm
Chi-Mei Fine Art Museum, Jen-te-Village, Taiwan
+ Goupil & Cie., 4 June 1881, *Femme donnant à manger à des poules*, G 15444, FF 1,500
– Boulevard Montmartre (Theo van Gogh), 6 September 1881, Crocker, FF 2,350
Literature New York (Christie's), 15 February 1995, lot 85.
[Amsterdam only]

75
Paul Gauguin 1848–1903
The harbour at Dieppe 1885
Oil on canvas, 58 x 71 cm
Manchester City Art Galleries
Sent by Theo van Gogh in March 1888 to the branch of Boussod, Valadon & Cie. in The Hague. Deposited at Boussod, Valadon & Cie. (Boulevard Montmartre)
Literature Georges Wildenstein, *Gauguin*, Paris 1964, no. 169.

141
Paul Gauguin 1848–1903
Conversation: Bretagne 1888
Oil on canvas, 92.7 x 73 cm
Koninklijke Musea voor Schone Kunsten van België, Brussels
+ Boulevard Montmartre (Theo van Gogh), 21 March 1889, *Berger & bergère*, BV 19746, FF 360
– Boulevard Montmartre (Theo van Gogh), 21 March 1889, Anna Boch, FF 400
Literature Georges Wildenstein, *Gauguin*, Paris 1964, no. 250.

76
Paul Gauguin 1848–1903
La belle Angèle 1889
Oil on canvas, 92 x 73 cm
Musée d'Orsay, Paris
Deposited at Boussod, Valadon & Cie. (Boulevard Montmartre) since early September 1889
Literature Georges Wildenstein, *Gauguin*, Paris 1964, nr. 315; I. Compin and A. Roquebert, *Catalogue sommaire illustré des peintures du musée du Louvre et du Musée d'Orsay*, 5 vols., Paris 1986, vol. 3, p. 267; exhib. cat. *The art of Paul Gauguin*, Washington, DC (The National Gallery of Art), Chicago (The Art Institute of Chicago) & Paris (Grand Palais), 1988–89, no. 89.
[Paris only]

142
Paul Gauguin 1848–1903
Les dindons 1888
Oil on canvas, 92 x 73 cm
The Mr and Mrs C. Foundation
Deposited at Boussod, Valadon & Cie. (Theo van Gogh)
+ Boussod, Valadon & Cie. (Boulevard Montmartre), 19 May 1891, *Les dindons*, BV 21450, FF 360
– Boussod, Valadon & Cie. (Boulevard Montmartre), 19 May 1891, Chavasse, FF 450
Literature Georges Wildenstein, *Gauguin*, Paris 1964, no. 276; John Rewald, 'Theo van Gogh, Goupil and the impressionists,' *Studies in post-impressionism*, London 1986, p. 90; London (Sotheby's), 5 May 1998, lot 29.
[Amsterdam only]

143
Paul Gauguin 1848–1903
Naked Breton boy 1889
Oil on canvas, 93 x 74 cm
Wallraf-Richartz Museum, Cologne
Deposited at Boussod, Valadon & Cie. (Boulevard Montmartre) c. 20 October 1889
Literature Georges Wildenstein, *Gauguin*, Paris 1964, no. 367; exhib. cat. *The art of Paul Gauguin*, Washington, DC (The National Gallery of Art), Chicago (The Art Institute of Chicago) & Paris (Grand Palais) 1988-89, no. 84.
[Amsterdam only]

138
Paul Gauguin 1848–1903
Soyez mysterieuses 1890
Limewood (polychromed), 73 x 95 cm
Musée d'Orsay, Paris
Deposited at Boussod, Valadon & Cie. (Boulevard Montmartre)
Literature Christopher Gray, *Sculpture and ceramics of Paul Gauguin*, Baltimore 1963, no. 89; exhib. cat. *The art of Paul Gauguin*, Washington, DC (The National Gallery of Art), Chicago (The Art Institute of Chicago) & Paris (Grand Palais) 1988-89, no. 110.

no ill.
Paul Gauguin 1848–1903
Still life with oranges and lemons, with a view of Pont-Aven 1890
Oil on canvas, 50 x 61 cm
Stiftung Langmatt Sidney und Jenny Brown, Baden
+ Boulevard Montmartre (Theo van Gogh), 30 April 1890, *Oranges dans une vase*, BV 20648, FF 225
– Boulevard Montmartre (Theo van Gogh), 30 April 1890, Chausson, FF 300
Literature Georges Wildenstein, *Gauguin*, Paris 1964, no. 401.
[Paris only]

no ill.
Paul Gauguin 1848–1903
Set of 10 zincographes 1889
The Metropolitan Museum of Art, New York, Rogers Fund
Executed by Gauguin in January 1889 under Theo van Gogh's initiative and supervision
Literature Elizabeth Mongan, Eberhard W. Kornfeld and Harold Joachim, *Paul Gauguin: catalogue raisonné of his prints*, Bern 1988, nos. 1–11.
[Amsterdam only]

61
Jean-Léon Gérôme 1824–1904
The excursion of the harem 1869
Oil on canvas, 120.6 x 177.8 cm
The Chrysler Museum of Art, Norfolk, VA, Gift of Walter P. Chrysler
+ Boussod, Valadon & Cie., 10 May 1882, *Barrage du Nil (anc. 11730)*, BV 16805, auction, FF 4,725.10
– Boulevard Montmartre (Theo van Gogh), 4 August 1885, Haseltine, FF 5,000
Literature Gerald M. Ackerman, *The life and work of Jean-Léon Gérôme*, London 1986, no. 188.

73
Eugène Isabey 1803–1886
The fish market, Dieppe 1845
Oil on canvas, 35.5 x 52 cm
The National Gallery, London
+ Boulevard Montmartre (Theo van Gogh), 29 June 1883, *Coin de halle*, G 16689, Deschamps, FF 2,020
– Goupil & Cie., 28 March 1884, Bowman, FF 2,500
Literature Pierre Miquel, *Eugène Isabey, 1803–1886: la marine au XIX-siècle*, Maurs-la-Jolie 1980, no. 591.

96
Johan Barthold Jongkind 1819–1891
Canal 1869
Oil on canvas, 41.1 x 65.2 cm
Philadelphia Museum of Art, The John G. Johnson Collection
+ Boulevard Montmartre (Theo van Gogh), 14 June 1889, *Chantiers de bateaux, canal du Hollande*, BV 19907, Chevalier, FF 1,312.60
– Boussod, Valadon & Cie. (New York), 29 October 1889, John G. Johnson, FF 3,224
Literature *Paintings from Europe and the Americas in the Philadelphia Museum of Art: a concise catalogue*, Philadelphia 1994, p. 66.

124
Stanislas Lépine 1835–1892
Place de la Concorde c. 1877-82
Oil on panel, 16.5 x 24 cm
Musée Carnavalet, Paris
+? Boulevard Montmartre (Theo van Gogh), 31 December 1886, *Place de la Concorde*, BV 18262, FF 150
–? Boulevard Montmartre (Theo van Gogh), 29 December 1886, Goupy, FF 700
Literature Robert Schmit and M. Schmit, *Stanislas Lépine, 1835–1892: catalogue raisonné de l'oeuvre peint*, Paris 1993, no. 154.

97
Edouard Manet 1832–1883
The students of Salamanca 1860
Oil on canvas, 79 x 92
Private collection, Japan
+ Boulevard Montmartre (Theo van Gogh), 1 March 1890, *Les étudiants*, BV 20343, Gatti, FF 1,200
– Boulevard Montmartre (Theo van Gogh), 1 March 1890, Manzi, FF 1,380
Literature Denis Rouart and Daniel Wildenstein, *Eduard Manet: catalogue raisonné*, 2 vols., Lausanne & Paris 1975, no. 28.
[Amsterdam only]

22
Jacob Maris 1837–1899
The mill 1879
Oil on canvas, 126 x 94 cm
Museum Mesdag, The Hague
Traded during Theo van Gogh's employment at Goupil & Cie. in The Hague
+ Goupil & Cie. (The Hague), 1 August 1879, *Moulin*, G 13777, 375 guilders
– Goupil & Cie. (The Hague), 1 August 1879, Hendrik Willem Mesdag, 500 guilders
Literature Fred Leeman and Hanna Pennock, *Museum Mesdag: catalogue of paintings and drawings*, Amsterdam & Zwolle 1996, no. 190.

23
Matthijs Maris 1839–1917
The kitchen princess 1872
Oil on canvas, 66.5 x 50 cm
Museum Mesdag, The Hague
Traded during Theo van Gogh's employment at Goupil & Cie. in The Hague
+ Goupil & Cie. (The Hague), 9 November 1875, *La cuisine*, G 10791, Vincent van Gogh, FF 2,000
– Goupil & Cie. (The Hague), 9 November 1875, Hendrik Willem Mesdag, 1,150 guilders
Literature Fred Leeman and Hanna Pennock, *Museum Mesdag: catalogue of paintings and drawings*, Amsterdam & Zwolle 1996, no. 198.

85
Georges Michel 1763–1843
Three windmills n.d.
Oil on paper on canvas, 50.3 x 69.4 cm
Museum Mesdag, The Hague
+ Boulevard Montmartre (Theo van Gogh), 9 January 1888, *Moulins à vent*, BV 19165, Durand-Ruel, FF 2,000
– Boussod, Valadon & Cie. (The Hague), 1 May 1897, Hendrik Willem Mesdag, FF 3,024
Literature Fred Leeman and Hanna Pennock, *Museum Mesdag: catalogue of paintings and drawings*, Amsterdam & Zwolle 1996, no. 260.
[Amsterdam only]

89
Jean-François Millet 1814–1875
Shearing sheep c. 1857-61
Oil on canvas, 40.8 x 32.5 cm
The Art Institute of Chicago, Mr and Mrs Potter Palmer Collection
+ Boussod, Valadon & Cie., 12 April 1886, *Tondeuse des moutons*, BV 17777, Duncan, FF 6,250
– Boulevard Montmartre (Theo van Gogh), 22 May 1886, Poidatz, FF 12,000.
Literature Robert L. Herbert, 'Millet reconsidered,' *Museum Studies. The Art Institute of Chicago* 1 (1966), p. 59.

107
Claude Monet 1840–1926
The church at Vétheuil 1880
Oil on canvas, 50 x 62 cm
Southampton City Art Gallery
+ Boulevard Montmartre (Theo van Gogh), 7 April 1885, *Vernon*, BV 17401, Bernheim-Jeune, FF 680
– Boulevard Montmartre (Theo van Gogh), 7 April 1885, Desfossés, FF 800
Literature Daniel Wildenstein, *Claude Monet: biographie et catalogue raisonné*, 5 vols., Lausanne 1974-91, no. 531; John Rewald, *Studies in post-impressionism*, London 1986, p. 91.

117
Claude Monet 1840–1926
Still life with a honeydew melon 1879
Oil on canvas 90 x 68 cm
Private collection
+ Boulevard Montmartre (Theo van Gogh), 13 August 1889, *Fruits*, BV 20023, Marsault, FF 500
– Boulevard Montmartre (Theo van Gogh), 13 August 1889, Manzi, FF 800
Literature Daniel Wildenstein, *Claude Monet: biographie et catalogue raisonné*, 5 vols., Lausanne 1974-91, no. 544; John Rewald, *Studies in post-impressionism*, London 1986, p. 93.

118
Claude Monet 1840–1926
Cliffs near Dieppe 1882
Oil on canvas, 60 x 81 cm
Carnegie Museum of Art, Pittsburgh, Acquired through the generosity of the Sarah Mellon Scaife family
+ Boulevard Montmartre (Theo van Gogh), 31 December 1889, *Falaise de Pourville (anc. 19488)*, BV 20569, Nunes, FF 1,200
– Boussod, Valadon & Cie., 30 March 1891, Eastman Chase, FF 4,446
Literature Daniel Wildenstein, *Claude Monet: biographie et catalogue raisonné*, 5 vols., Lausanne 1974-91, no. 719; John Rewald, *Studies in post-impressionism*, London 1986, p. 94.
[Amsterdam only]

116
Claude Monet 1840–1926
Rain, Etratat 1886
Oil on canvas, 60.5 x 73.5 cm
Nasjonalgalleriet, Oslo
+ Boulevard Montmartre (Theo van Gogh), 25 January 1889, *Marine, temps de pluie*, BV 19653, Comtesse de Noé, FF 1,000
– Boussod, Valadon & Cie. (Boulevard Montmartre), 3 December 1890, Museum Christiana, FF 1,600
Literature Daniel Wildenstein, *Claude Monet: biographie et catalogue raisonné*, 5 vols., Lausanne 1974-91, no. 1044; John Rewald, *Studies in post-impressionism*, London 1986, p. 93.
[Amsterdam only]

109
Claude Monet 1840–1926
Rocks near Port-Coton 1886
Oil on canvas, 65.5 x 65.5 cm
Fondation Rau pour le Tiers-Monde, Embraport, Switzerland
+ Boulevard Montmartre (Theo van Gogh), 10 May 1887, *Pyramide à Port Coton*, BV 18541, FF 1,616.66
– Boulevard Montmartre (Theo van Gogh), 21 October 1887, Dupuis, FF 2,400
+ Boulevard Montmartre (Theo van Gogh), 14 September 1888, *Pyramide à Port Coton (anc. 18451)*, BV 19467, Dupuis, FF 1,500
– Boulevard Montmartre (Theo van Gogh), 5 August 1889, Gallimard, FF 1,850
Literature Daniel Wildenstein, *Claude Monet: biographie et catalogue raisonné*, 5 vols., Lausanne 1974-91, no. 1087; John Rewald, *Studies in post-impressionism*, London 1986, p. 91.

108
Claude Monet 1840–1926
Rocks near Port-Coton, Le Lion 1886
Oil on canvas, 65 x 81 cm
Fitzwilliam Museum, Cambridge
+ Boulevard Montmartre (Theo van Gogh), 7 April 1887, *Pointes de Port Coton à Belle Isle*, BV 18448, FF 1,100
– Boulevard Montmartre (Theo van Gogh), 20 April 1887, Poidatz, FF 2,200
Literature Daniel Wildenstein, *Claude Monet: biographie et catalogue raisonné*, 5 vols., Lausanne 1974-91, no. 1091; John Rewald, *Studies in post-impressionism*, London 1986, p. 91.
[Amsterdam only]

110
Claude Monet 1840–1926
Trees in winter: view of Bennecourt 1887
Oil on canvas, 81 x 81 cm
The Columbus Museum of Art, OH
+ Boulevard Montmartre (Theo van Gogh), 21 April 1888, *Village de Bennecourt*, BV 19194, FF 1,500
– Boulevard Montmartre (Theo van Gogh), 21 April 1888, Richardson, FF 2,200
Literature Daniel Wildenstein, *Claude Monet: biographie et catalogue raisonné*, 5 vols., Lausanne 1974-91, no. 1125; John Rewald, *Studies in post-impressionism*, London 1986, p. 92.

no ill.
Claude Monet 1840–1926
Antibes, afternoon effect 1888
Oil on canvas, 65 x 81 cm
Museum of Fine Arts, Boston
+ Boulevard Montmartre (Theo van Gogh), 4 June 1888, *Antibes*, BV 19300, FF 1,000
– Boulevard Montmartre (Theo van Gogh), 27 June 1888, Ellissen, FF 3,500
Literature Daniel Wildenstein, *Claude Monet: biographie et catalogue raisonné*, 5 vols., Lausanne 1974-91, no. 1158; John Rewald, *Studies in post-impressionism*, London 1986, p. 93; Joachim Pissarro, exhib. cat. *Monet and the Mediterranean*, Forth Worth (Kimbell Art Museum) & Brooklyn (The Brooklyn Museum of Art) 1997-98, pp. 120-21, no. 48.

111
Claude Monet 1840–1926
Antibes in the morning 1888
Oil on canvas, 65 x 81 cm
Philadelphia Museum of Art, The John G. Johnson Collection
+ Boulevard Montmartre (Theo van Gogh), 11 October 1888, *Antibes. Vue de la Salis, lever de soleil*, BV 19495, FF 1,000
– Boussod, Valadon & Cie. (New York), 29 August 1889, John G. Johnson, FF 3,640
Literature Daniel Wildenstein, *Claude Monet: biographie et catalogue raisonné*, 5 vols., Lausanne 1974-91, no. 1170; John Rewald, *Studies in post-impressionism*, London 1986, p. 93; Joachim Pissarro, exhib. cat. *Monet and the Mediterranean*, Forth Worth (Kimbell Art Museum) & Brroklyn (The Brooklyn Museum of Art) 1997-98, pp. 126 and 129, no. 57.
[Amsterdam only]

113
Claude Monet 1840–1926
Under the pine trees at the end of the day
1888
Oil on canvas, 73 x 92 cm
Philadelphia Museum of Art, Philadelphia, Gift of Otto F. Haas
+ Boulevard Montmartre (Theo van Gogh), 4 June 1888, *Sous les pins, fin du jour*, BV 19308, FF 1,300
– Boulevard Montmartre (Theo van Gogh), 29 June 1888, Aubry, FF 2,800
Literature Daniel Wildenstein, *Claude Monet: biographie et catalogue raisonné*, 5 vols., Lausanne 1974-91, no. 1191; John Rewald, *Studies in post-impressionism*, London 1986, p. 92; Joachim Pissarro, exhib. cat. *Monet and the Mediterranean*, Forth Worth (Kimbell Art Museum) & Brooklyn (The Brooklyn Museum of Art) 1997-98, p. 143, no. 70.

115
Claude Monet 1840–1926
Landscape with figures, Giverny 1888
Oil on canvas, 80 x 80 cm
The Art Institute of Chicago
+ Boulevard Montmartre (Theo van Gogh), 31 December 1888, *Prairie avec figures*, BV 19624, FF 1,300
– Boulevard Montmartre (Theo van Gogh), 20 September 1889, John Singer Sargent, FF 3,000
Literature Daniel Wildenstein, *Claude Monet: biographie et catalogue raisonné*, 5 vols., Lausanne 1974-91, no. 1204; John Rewald, *Studies in post-impressionism*, London 1986, p. 93.

155
Adolphe Monticelli 1824–1886
Italian girl c. 1879
Oil on canvas, 68 x 39 cm
Van Gogh Museum, Amsterdam (Vincent van Gogh Foundation)
+ Boulevard Montmartre (Theo van Gogh), 6 November 1886, *Italienne*, BV 18126, Boyer
– Boulevard Montmartre (Theo van Gogh), 20 November 1886, Theo van Gogh
Literature Evert van Uitert and Michael Hoyle (eds.), *The Rijksmuseum Vincent van Gogh*, Amsterdam 1987, p. 358.

no ill.
Camille Pissarro 1830–1903
A street in Auvers 1880
Oil on canvas, 60 x 73 cm
The John M. and Sally B. Thornton Trust
+ Boulevard Montmartre (Theo van Gogh), 26 July 1889, *Paysage Auvers*, BV 20005, FF 300
– Boulevard Montmartre (Theo van Gogh), 3 January 1890, Oppenheim, FF 600
Literature John Rewald, *Studies in post-impressionism*, London 1986, p. 96; Lodovic Rodo Pissarro and Lionello Venturi, *Camille Pissarro: son art et son oeuvre*, 2 vols., San Francisco 1989 [Paris 1939], no. 512.

120
Camille Pissarro 1830–1903
Woman in a garden, Eragny 1887
Oil on canvas, 54.5 x 65 cm
Musée d'Orsay, Paris
+ Boulevard Montmartre (Theo van Gogh), 17 March 1888, *Paysage, plein soleil*, BV 19099, FF 300
– Boulevard Montmartre (Theo van Gogh), 22 November 1888, Bouglé, FF 600
Literature Isabelle Compin, Geneviève Lacambre and Anne Roquebert (eds.), *Catalogue sommaire illustré des peintures. Musée d'Orsay*, 2 vols., Paris 1986, vol. 2, no. RF 1937-47; John Rewald, *Studies in post-impressionism*, London 1986, p. 95; Lodovic Rodo Pissarro and Lionello Venturi, *Camille Pissarro: son art et son oeuvre*, 2 vols., San Francisco 1989 [Paris 1939], no. 709.
[Paris only]

119
Camille Pissarro 1830–1903
The hay harvest, Eragny 1887
Oil on canvas, 50 x 66 cm
Private collection
Not mentioned in the stockbooks of Boussod, Valadon & Cie.
+ Theo van Gogh, 8 August 1887
– Theo van Gogh, 8 August 1888, Aubry
Literature Exhib. cat. *Van Gogh à Paris*, Paris (Musée d'Orsay) 1988, pp. 33 and 374; Lodovic Rodo Pissarro and Lionello Venturi, *Camille Pissarro: son art et son oeuvre*, 2 vols., San Francisco 1989 [Paris 1939], no. 713.

121
Camille Pissarro 1830–1903
L'Ile Lacroix, Rouen: effect of fog 1888
Oil on canvas, 44 x 55 cm
Philadelphia Museum of Art, The John G. Johnson Collection
Not mentioned in the stockbooks of Boussod, Valadon & Cie.
+ Theo van Gogh, 22 November 1888, FF 300
– Theo van Gogh 29 June 1889, Dupuis, FF 400
Literature Exhib. cat., *Exposition d'oeuvres récentes de Camille Pissarro*, Paris (Boussod, Valadon & Cie.) 1890, no. 14; exhib. cat., *Pissarro*, London (Hayward Gallery), Paris (Grand Palais) & Boston (Museum of Fine Arts) 1980-81, no. 66; Lodovic Rodo Pissarro and Lionello Venturi, *Camille Pissarro: son art et son oeuvre*, 2 vols., San Francisco 1989 [Paris 1939], no. 719.

74
Camille Pissarro 1830–1903
Apple picking, Eragny 1888
Oil on canvas, 60 x 73 cm
Museum of Fine Arts, Dallas, Munger Fund
+ Boulevard Montmartre (Theo van Gogh), 18 March 1888, *Cueillette des pommes*, BV 19082, FF 300
– Boulevard Montmartre (Theo van Gogh), 26 July 1889, Desfossés, FF 400
Literature *Collection de M. Victor Desfossés*, Paris (Haro), 26 April 1899, lot 50; John Rewald, *Studies in post-impressionism*, London 1986, p. 95; Lodovic Rodo Pissarro and Lionello Venturi, *Camille Pissarro: son art et son oeuvre*, 2 vols., San Francisco 1989 [Paris 1939], no. 726.
[Amsterdam only]

no ill.
Camille Pissarro 1830–1903
A flock of sheep 1890
Fan, 28 x 55 cm
Private collection
Exhibited by Theo van Gogh in 1890.
Literature Exhib. cat. *Exposition d'oeuvres récentes de Camille Pissarro*, Paris (Boussod, Valadon & Cie.), no. 23; Lodovic Rodo Pissarro and Lionello Venturi, *Camille Pissarro: son art et son oeuvre*, 2 vols., San Francisco 1989 [Paris 1939], no. 1643.

127
Jean-François Raffaëlli 1850–1924
Brokers in the Mazas, Hôtel Drouot c. 1888
Ink and watercolour on paper on board, 23 x 25.4 cm
Collection of Dr and Mrs Michael Schlossberg, Eastpoint, GA
Exhibited by Theo van Gogh in 1890.
Literature Theodore Child, 'The Hôtel Drouot,' *Harper's New Monthly Magazine* 78 (February 1889), p. 346; exhib. cat. *Catalogue de quelques peintures, sculptures et dessins de J.-F. Raffaëlli*, Paris (Boussod, Valadon & Cie.) 1890, no. 51; exhib. cat. *19th- and 20th-century European drawings and sculpture from the Schlossberg collection*, Atlanta (High Museum of Art) 1994, no. 67.

126
Jean-François Raffaëlli 1850–1924
Seedy lilies and shabby wall-flowers c. 1888
Ink on paper, 21.5 x 32.5 cm
Collection of Dr and Mrs Michael Schlossberg, Eastpoint, GA
Exhibited by Theo van Gogh in 1890
Literature Theodore Child, 'The Hôtel Drouot,' *Harper's New Monthly Magazine* 78 (February 1889), p. 339; exhib. cat. *Catalogue de quelques peintures, sculptures et dessins de J.-F. Raffaëlli*, Paris (Boussod, Valadon & Cie.) 1890, no. 51.

136
Jean-François Raffaëlli 1850–1924
The young housemaid c. 1890
Bronze, 53 x 37 cm
Gerhard Wurzer Gallery/Christopher Drake, Houston
Exhibited by Theo van Gogh in 1890.
Literature Exhib. cat. *Catalogue de quelques peintures, sculptures et dessins de J.-F. Raffaëlli*, Paris (Boussod, Valadon & Cie.) 1890, no. 56 [?]; Arsène Alexandre, *Jean-François Raffaëlli: peintre, graveur et sculptuer*, Paris 1909, p. 169. [Amsterdam only]

102
Jean-François Raffaëlli 1850–1924
Fisherman on the banks of the Seine n.d.
Oil on canvas, 25.7 x 35.6 cm
Private collection, London
+ Boulevard Montmartre (Theo van Gogh), 30 November 1889, *Bords de Seine (pêcheurs-rivière)*, BV 20128, FF 500
+ Boulevard Montmartre (Theo van Gogh), 27 November 1889, Leclanché, FF 700
Literature London (Christie's), 20 February 1990, lot 5.

101
Jean-François Raffaëlli 1850–1924
The woodcutter 1888
Oil on panel, 81.3 x 66 cm
Collection of Meadow Brook Hall, Oakland University, Rochester, MI
+ Boulevard Montmartre (Theo van Gogh), 21 June 1890, *Vieillard venant abattre arbres*, BV 20794, FF 1,650
– Boulevard Montmartre (Theo van Gogh), 21 June 1890, Boivin, FF 2,200
Literature Exhib. cat. *Catalogue de quelques peintures, sculptures et dessins de J.-F. Raffaëlli*, Paris (Boussod, Valadon & Cie.) 1890, no. 2; Barbara Schinman Fields, *Jean-François Raffaëlli (1850–1924): the naturalist artist*, Ann Arbor 1984, no. 328.

144
Odilon Redon 1840–1916
Virgin of the dawn 1890
Oil on canvas, 53,5 x 37 cm
Collection of Miranda and Robert Donneley, Chicago
+ Boulevard Montmartre (Theo van Gogh), 2 May 1890, *Vierge d'aurore*, BV 20671, FF 300
– Boulevard Montmartre (Theo van Gogh), 2 May 1890, Chausson, FF 400
Literature Exhib. cat., *Odilon Redon 1840–1916*, Chicago (The Art Institute of Chicago), Amsterdam (Van Gogh Museum) & London (Royal Academy of Arts) 1994-95, no. 101; Alec Wildenstein, *Odilon Redon: catalogue raisonné de l'oeuvre peint et dessiné*, 3 vols., Paris 1992-96, no. 480.

125
Pierre Auguste Renoir 1841–1919
Lunch at the Restaurant Fournaise c. 1879
Oil on canvas, 54 x 65 cm
The Art Institute of Chicago, Mr and Mrs Potter Palmer Collection
+ Boulevard Montmartre (Theo van Gogh), 21 November 1887, *Canotiers*, BV 18877, Legrand, FF 200
– Boulevard Montmartre (Theo van Gogh), 21 November 1887, Guyotin, FF 350
Literature François Daulte, *Auguste Renoir: catalogue raisonné de l'oeuvre peint*, Lausanne 1971, no. 305.

no ill.
Pierre Auguste Renoir 1841–1919
The bay of Naples 1881
Oil on canvas, 60 x 81 cm
The Metropolitan Museum of Art, New York, Bequest of Julia W. Emmons, 1956
+ Boulevard Montmartre (Theo van Gogh), 18 July 1888, *Vue de Naples*, BV 19390, Inglis, FF 275
– Boussod, Valadon & Cie., 24 December 1891, Paul Durand-Ruel, FF 2,600
Literature Charles Sterling and Magaretta M. Salinger, *French paintings: a catalogue of the collection of The Metropolitan Museum of Art*, 3 vols., New York 1967, vol. 3, pp. 154-55.

135
Auguste Rodin 1840–1917
Victor Hugo 1883
Bronze, 39 x 18, 17.7 cm
Musée Rodin, Paris
Not listed in the stockbooks of Boussod, Valadon & Cie. Probably sent by Rodin to Theo van Gogh in 1889.
Literature Cécile Goldscheider, *Auguste Rodin: catalogue raisonné de l'oeuvre sculpté*, Paris 1989, no. 132 C.

46
Auguste Rodin 1840–1917
Head of St John the Baptist 1887
Bronze, 21 x 41 x 27 cm
Musée Rodin, Paris
Not listed in the stockbooks of Boussod, Valadon & Cie. Marble version exhibited by Theo van Gogh.
Literature Exhib. cat., *From Courbet to Cézanne: a new 19th century*, Brooklyn (The Brooklyn Museum of Art) & Dallas (Dallas Museum of Art) 1986, no. 55.

24
Ary Scheffer 1795–1858
Christ in Gethsemane 1839
Oil on canvas, 140 x 98 cm
Dordrechts Museum, Dordrecht
Literature *De brieven van Vincent van Gogh*, ed. Han van Crimpen and Monique Berends-Albert, The Hague 1990, letter 101/84; Leo Ewals, *Ary Scheffer 1795–1858: gevierd romanticus*, Zwolle 1995, no. 57.

145
Emile Schuffenecker 1851–1934
Still life with a bowl of fruit 1886
Oil on canvas, 65 x 54 cm
Kröller-Müller Museum, Otterlo
Probably exhibited by Theo van Gogh in May 1888.
Literature *Schilderijen van het Rijksmuseum Kröller-Müller*, Otterlo 1970, no. 610.

123
Alfred Sisley 1839–1899
La maison abandonnée c. 1886
Oil on canvas, 36 x 54.5 cm
Private collection
+ Boulevard Montmartre (Theo van Gogh), 22 June 1887, *La maison anbandonnée*, BV 18675, FF 614
– Boussod, Valadon & Cie., 21 February 1891, Widener, FF 2,000
Literature François Daulte, *Alfred Sisley: catalogue raisonné de l'oeuvre peint*, Lausanne 1959, no. 652; John Rewald, *Studies in post-impressionism*, London 1986, p. 97.

86
Constant Troyon 1810–1865
Sheep n.d.
Oil on canvas, 60 x 73.5 cm
Museum Mesdag, The Hague
+ Boulevard Montmartre (Theo van Gogh), 21 January 1881, *Troupeau de moutons*, BV 15085, De Gheus d'Elzenwalle, FF 6,550
– Boulevard Montmartre (Theo van Gogh), 20 January 1881, Mesdag, FF 7,700
Literature Fred Leeman and Hanna Pennock, *Museum Mesdag: catalogue of paintings and drawings*, Amsterdam & Zwolle 1996, no. 319.

Bibliography

A

[Anon.], *Galérie Durand-Ruel, specimens les plus brilliants de l'école moderne*, 2 vols., Paris 1845.

[Anon.], 'Causerie artistique. Le Cercle de l'Union Artistique,' *La Paix* (16 February 1883).

[Anon.], 'Revue des ventes. Bronzes de Barye,' *Le Journal des Arts* 8 (2 March 1886), p. 3.

[Anon.], 'Concours et expositions,' *La Chronique des Arts* (27 March 1886), p. 98.

[Anon.], 'Mouvement des arts. Collection John Saulnier,' *La Chronique des Arts* (19 June 1886), p. 185.

[Anon.], 'Mouvement des arts. Collection Léon Gaucherel,' *La Chronique des Arts* (19 June 1886), p. 186.

[Anon.], 'Mouvement des arts. Tableaux et aquarelles formant le fond de l'ancienne maison Goupil et Cie,' *La Chronique des Arts* (4 June 1887), p. 177.

[Anon.], 'Exposition des lauréats de France, Londres 1888,' *Le Journal des Arts* 10 (3 February 1888), pp. 3-4.

[Anon.], 'Revue des ventes. Collection Ch. Leroux,' *Le Journal des Arts* 10 (28 February 1888), p. 3.

[Anon.], 'Mouvement des arts. Collection des tableaux de M. Charles L.,' *La Chronique des Arts* (3 March 1888), p. 65.

[Anon.], 'Mouvement des Arts. Collection Poidatz,' *La Chronique des Arts* (24 March 1888), p. 89.

[Anon.], *La Chronique des Arts* (8 September 1888), p. 226.

[Anon.], *Paris Illustré* 39 (29 September 1888), p. 613.

[Anon.], *La Chronique des Arts* (8 December 1888), p. 298.

[Anon.], 'Le portrait de M. Edmond de Goncourt,' *Le Courrier de l'Art* 9 (18 January 1889), pp. 19-20.

[Anon.], 'Vente Gustave Boulanger,' *La Chronique des Arts* (6 April 1889), p. 105.

[Anon.], 'Concours et expositions,' *La Chronique des Arts* (6 April 1889), p. 105.

[Anon.], *Le Journal des Arts* 12 (14 April 1890), p. 2.

[Anon.], *Le Journal des Arts* 12 (22 April 1890), p. 2.

[Anon.], *Le Journal des Arts* 12 (24 April 1890), p. 1.

[Anon.], 'Note et notules,' *Entretiens politiques et littéraires* 2 (1 May 1890), p. 61.

[Anon.], 'Echos,' *Le Figaro* (28 May 1890).

[Anon.], 'Revue des ventes. Collection M.E. May,' *Le Journal des Arts* 12 (6 June 1890), p. 3.

[Anon.], 'Une usine de faux Courbet,' *La Chronique des Arts* (30 August 1890), p. 228.

[Anon.], 'Informations,' *Le Journal des Arts* 13 (27 January 1891), p. 2.

Gerald M. Ackerman, *The life and work of Jean-Léon Gérôme*, London 1986.

Paul Adam, 'Le printemps sacré,' *La Vie Moderne* 10 (17 June 1888), pp. 373-74.

Arsène Alexandre, *Jean-François Raffaëlli: peintre, graveur et sculpteur*, Paris 1909.

Charles Angrand: correspondance, 1883–1926, ed. François Lespinasse, Rouen 1988.

Jules Antoine, 'Beaux-arts. Exposition rétrospective de l'art français. Peinture,' *Art et Critique* 17 (22 September 1889), pp. 268-69.

Archives de Camille Pissarro, Paris (Hôtel Drouot), 21 November 1975.

G. Albert Aurier, 'Raffaëlli,' *Mercure de France* (September 1890), pp. 424-29.

G.-A.[lbert] A.[urier], 'Choses d'art,' *Mercure de France* (March 1891), p. 189.

G.-A.[lbert] A.[urier], 'Choses d'art,' *Mercure de France* (June 1891), p. 374.

B

Karl Baedeker, *Paris and its environs: handbook for travellers*, Leipzig & London 1881.

Arthur Bagnières, 'Société d'Aquarellistes Français (première exposition),' *Gazette des Beaux-Arts* 2 (May 1879), pp. 491-501.

Arthur Bagnières, 'Société d'Aquarellistes Français (quatrième exposition),' *Gazette des Beaux-Arts* 25 (April 1882), pp. 433-39.

Arthur Bagnières, *Société d'Aquarellistes Français: ouvrage d'art*, 2 vols., Paris 1883.

Colin B. Bailey, *Renoir's portraits: impressions of an age*, New Haven & London 1997.

Martin Bailey, 'Van Gogh's first sale: a self-portrait in London,' *Apollo* 143 (March 1996), pp. 20-21.

Madeleine Fidell Beaufort and Jeanne K. Welcher, 'Some views of art buying in New York in the 1870s and 1880s,' *Oxford Art Journal* 5 (1982), pp. 48-55.

Charles Bigot, *Peintres français contemporains*, Paris 1888.

Merete Bodelsen, *Gauguin's ceramics: a study in the development of his art*, London 1964.

Saskia de Bodt, *Halverwege Parijs: Willem Roelofs en de Nederlandse schilderskolonie in Brussel 1840–1920* (diss., Universiteit van Amsterdam, 1995).

P.A.M. Boele van Hensbroek, 'Vlugmaeren,' *De Nederlandsche Spectator* (9 January 1892).

P.A.M. Boele van Hensbroek, 'Vlugmaeren,' *De Nederlandsche Spectator* (May 1893).

P.A.M. Boele van Hensbroek, 'De Van Goghs,' *De Nederlandsche Spectator* (26 August 1893).

P.A.M. Boele van Hensbroek, 'De Van Goghs,' *De Nieuwe Rotterdamsche Courant* (7 September 1893).

Andries Bonger, 'Letteren en kunst,' *De Nieuwe Rotterdamsche Courant* (5 September 1893).

F.W.M. Bonger-Baronesse Van der Borch van Verwolde, 'Andries Bonger (Amsterdam 20 May 1861-Amsterdam 20 Jan. 1936),' *Jaarboek van de Maatschappij voor Nederlandsche Letterkunde te Leiden*, Leiden 1936-37, pp. 112-22.

H. Bonger, 'Un Amstellodamois à Paris: extraits des lettres écrites à Paris entre 1880 et 1890 par Andries Bonger à ses parents à Amsterdam,' in *Liber Amicorum Karel G. Boon*, Amsterdam 1974, pp. 60-70.

C

Cassatt and her circle: selected letters, ed. Nancy Mowll Mathews, New York 1984.

Elly Cassee, 'In love: Vincent van Gogh's first true love,' *Van Gogh Museum Journal* (1996), pp. 109–18.

Theodore Child, 'The Hôtel Drouot,' *Harper's New Monthly Magazine* 78 (February 1889), pp. 331-47.

Jules Claretie, *La vie à Paris: 1880*, Paris 1881.

Jules Claretie, *La vie à Paris: 1882*, Paris 1883.

I. Compin and A. Roquebert, *Catalogue sommaire illustré des peintures du Musée du Louvre et du Musée d'Orsay*, 5 vols., Paris 1986.

Han van Crimpen, 'De familie Van Gogh in Brabant,' exhib. cat. *Van Gogh in Brabant*, 's-Hertogenbosch (Noordbrabants Museum) 1987-88, pp. 72-91.

Gilles Cugnier, 'Notice biographique,' exhib. cat. *Jean-Léon Gérôme, 1824–1904*, Vesoul (Musée de Vesoul) 1981, pp. 15-27.

D

August Dalligny, *Agenda de la curiosité des artistes et des amateurs, année 1889*, Paris 1889.

Arthur Dalligny, 'L'exposition des 33,' *Le Journal des Arts* 11 (4 January 1889), p. 1.

Arthur Dalligny, 'Société Nationale des Beaux-Arts. L'exposition du Champs de Mars,' *Le Journal des Arts* 12 (16 May 1890), p. 1.

G. Dargenty, 'Chronique des expositions. Exposition Internationale de peinture et de la sculpture. Galerie George Petit,' *Le Courrier de l'Art* 7 (27 May 1887), pp. 163-64.

G. Dargenty, 'Les Pastellistes,' *Le Courrier de l'Art* 8 (27 April 1888), pp. 130-31.

G. Dargenty, 'Chronique des expositions. Exposition des Trente-Trois à la Galérie Petit,' *Le Courrier de l'Art* 9 (25 January 1889), pp. 26-27.

G. Dargenty, 'Chronique des expositions. M. Pissaro [sic],' *Le Courrier de l'Art* 10 (7 March 1890), p. 75.

François Daulte, *Alfred Sisley: catalogue raisonné de l'oeuvre peint*, Lausanne 1959.

François Daulte, *Auguste Renoir: catalogue raisonné de l'oeuvre peint*, Lausanne 1971.

P.[ierre]D.[etouche], 'Ventes prochaines. Collection d'un amateur,' *Le Journal des Arts* 12 (9 May 1890), p. 2.

P.[ierre]D.[etouche], 'Ventes prochaines. Collection de M.E. May,' *Journal des Arts* 12 (27 May 1890), p. 1.

Pierre Detouche, 'L'Hôtel des Ventes,' *L'Echo de Paris* (3 June 1890).

H. Dirven, 'De kunsthandelaar Vincent van Gogh uit Princenhage,' *Hage* 7 (1977), no. 19, pp. 5-77.

Anne Distel, 'Albert Hecht: collectionneur (1842–1889),' *Bulletin de la Société de l'Histoire de l'Art Français: année 1981*, Paris 1983, pp. 267-79.

Anne Distel, 'Charles Deudon (1832–1914): collectionneur,' *Revue de l'Art* 86 (1989), pp. 58-65.

Anne Distel, *Impressionism: the first collectors*, New York 1990.

Anne Distel, 'Léon Clapisson: patron and collector,' in Colin B. Bailey, *Renoir's portraits: impressions of an age*, New Haven & London 1997, pp. 77-86.

Jean Dolent, *Amoreux d'art*, Paris 1888.

M.-G. Dortu, *Toulouse-Lautrec et son oeuvre*, New York 1971.

Douglas Druick and Peter Zegers, 'Degas and the printed image, 1856–1914,' in Sue Welsh Reed and Barbara Stern Shapiro, exhib. cat. *Edgar Degas: the painter as printmaker*, Boston (Museum of Fine Arts) & London (Hayward Gallery) 1984-85, pp. xv-lv.

Ann Dumas, 'Degas and his collection,' exhib. cat. *The private collection of Edgar Degas*, New York (The Metropolitan Museum of Art) 1997, pp. 3-73.

E

Eaque, 'Claude Monet,' *Le Journal des Arts* 10 (6 July 1888), pp. 2-3.

E.G.O. [A.C. Loffelt], 'Vincent van Gogh,' *Het Vaderland* (19 May 1892).

Rachel Esner, '"Gloria victis": Französische Malerei des Deutsch-Französichen Krieges,' in Stefan Germer and Michael F. Zimmermann (eds.), *Bilder der Macht – Macht der Bilder: Zeitgeschichte in Darstellungen des 19. Jahrhunderts*, Munich 1997, pp. 390-402.

Leo Ewals, *Ary Scheffer 1795–1858: gevierd romanticus*, Zwolle 1995.

Exhib. cat. *Catalogue de quelques peintures, sculptures et dessins de J.-F. Raffaëlli*, Paris (Boussod, Valadon & Cie.) 1890.

Exhib. cat. *Exposition d'oeuvres récentes de Camille Pissarro*, Paris (Boussod, Valadon & Cie.) 1890.

Exhib. cat. *Catalogue des ouvrages de peinture, sculpture, dessins, garvures et objets d'art exposé au Champ-de-Mars*, Paris 1891.

Exhib. cat. *De verzameling van Theo van Gogh, met uitzondering van de werken van zijn broer Vincent*, Amsterdam (Stedelijk Museum) 1953

Exhib. cat. *Collectie Theo van Gogh*, Amsterdam (Stedelijk Museum) & Otterlo (Kröller-Müller Museum) 1960.

Exhib. cat. *André Bonger en zijn kunstenaarsvrienden: Redon – Bernard – Van Gogh*, Amsterdam (Rijksmuseum) 1972.

Exhib. cat. *Rond de roem van Vincent van Gogh*, Amsterdam (Van Gogh Museum) 1977.

Exhib. cat. *De la Place des Victoires à la Place de l'Opéra*, Paris (Musée Carnavalet) 1979.

Exhib. cat. *Pissarro*, London (Hayward Gallery), Paris (Grand Palais) & Boston (Museum of Fine Arts) 1980-81.

Exhib. cat. *Jean-Léon Gérôme, 1824–1904*, Vesoul (Musée de Vesoul) 1981

Exhib. cat. *Three Italian friends of the impressionists: Boldini, De Nittis, Zandomeneghi*, New York (Stair Sainty Matthiessen) 1984.

Exhib. cat. *William Bouguereau 1825–1905*, Paris (Petit Palais), Montreal (Musée des Beaux-Arts) & Hartford (Wadsworth Atheneum) 1984-85.

Exhib. cat. *From Courbet to Cézanne: a new 19th century*, New York (The Brooklyn Museum of Art) & Dallas (Dallas Museum of Art) 1986.

Exhib. cat. *Impressionist drawings in British collections*, Oxford (Ashmolean Museum), Manchester (City Art Gallery) & Glasgow (The Burrell Collection) 1986.

Exhib. cat. *Monet in Holland*, Amsterdam (Van Gogh Museum) 1986-87.

Exhib. cat. *Van Gogh in Brabant*, 's-Hertogenbosch (Noordbrabants Museum) 1987-88.

Exhib. cat. *Van Gogh à Paris*, Paris (Musée d'Orsay) 1988.

Exhib. cat. *Degas*, Paris (Grand Palais), Ottawa (National Gallery of Canada) & New York (The Metropolitan Museum of Art) 1988-89.

Exhib. cat. *The art of Paul Gauguin*, Washington, DC (The National Gallery of Art), Chicago (The Art Institute of Chicago) & Paris (Grand Palais) 1988-89.

Exhib. cat. *Marià Fortuny, 1838–1874*, Madrid (Fundación Caja de Pensiones) 1989.

Exhib. cat. *Claude Monet – Auguste Rodin: centenaire de l'Exposition de 1889*, Paris (Musée Rodin) 1989-90.

Exhib. cat. *Dutch painting: the age of Van Gogh*, Amsterdam (Van Gogh Museum) & Glasgow (The Burrell Collection) 1990-91.

Exhib. cat. *Vincent van Gogh en de moderne kunst 1890–1914*, Amsterdam (Van Gogh Museum) & Essen (Museum Folkwang) 1990-91.

Exhib. cat. *De Corot aux impressionistes: donations Moreau-Nélaton*, Paris (Grand Palais) 1991.

Exhib. cat. *Georges Seurat (1859–1891)*, Paris (Grand Palais) & New York (The Metropolitan Museum of Art) 1991-92.

Exhib. cat. *Toulouse-Lautrec*, London (Hayward Gallery) & Paris (Grand Palais) 1991-92

Exhib. cat. *19th- and 20th-century European drawings and sculpture from the Schlossberg collection*, Atlanta (High Museum of Art) 1994.

Exhib. cat., *Odilon Redon 1840–1916*, Chicago (The Art Institute of Chicago), Amsterdam (Van Gogh Museum) & London (Royal Academy of Arts) 1994-95.

Exhib. cat. *The private collection of Edgar Degas*, New York (The Metropolitan Museum of Art) 1997.

Exhib. cat. *Degas, Boldini, Toulouse-Lautrec: portraits inédits par Michel Manzi*, Bordeaux (Musée Goupil) & Albi (Musée Toulouse-Lautrec) 1997.

F

Felix Fénéon: oeuvres plus que complètes, ed. Joan U. Halperin, Geneva 1970.

Frances Fowle, *Alexander Reid in context*, 2 vols. (diss., University of Edinburgh, 1993).

Julia Frey, *Toulouse-Lautrec: a life*, London 1994.

Rudi Fuchs, 'Vincent en Theo: reflecties bij Zadkines Van Gogh-monument in Zundert,' *Brabantia* 13 (August 1964), pp. 120-22.

G

Lettres de Gauguin à sa femme et à ses amis, ed. Maurice Malingue, Paris 1946.

Lettres de Gauguin, Gide, Huysmans, Jammes, Mallarmé, Verhaeren à Odilon Redon, ed. Rosaline Bacou, Paris 1960.

Paul Gauguin: 45 lettres à Vincent, Theo et Jo van Gogh, ed. Douglas Cooper, The Hague & Lausanne 1983.

Correspondance de Paul Gauguin. I, 1873-1888, ed. Victor Merlhès, Paris 1984.

Gustave Geffroy, 'Chronique: dix tableaux de Cl. Monet,' *La Justice* (17 June 1888).

Gustave Geffroy, 'Camille Pissarro,' exhib. cat. *Exposition d'oeuvres récentes de Camille Pissarro*, Paris (Boussod, Valadon & Cie.) 1890, pp. 5–12.

Gustave Geffroy, 'Raffaëlli: peintre-sculpteur,' exhib. cat. *Catalogue des quelques peintures, sculptures et dessins de J.-F. Raffaëlli*, Paris (Boussod, Valadon & Cie.) 1890, pp. 5–11.

Johanna van Gogh-Bonger, 'Inleiding,' in *De brieven van Vincent van Gogh*, ed. Han van Crimpen and Monique Berends-Albert, 4 vols., The Hague 1990, vol. 1, pp. 1-42.

Kort geluk: de briefwisseling van Theo van Gogh en Jo van Gogh-Bonger, ed. Han van Crimpen, Zwolle 1999.

Vincent van Gogh, brieven aan zijn broeder, ed. Johanna van Gogh-Bonger, 3 vols., Amsterdam 1914.

De brieven van Vincent van Gogh, ed. Han van Crimpen and Monique Berends-Albert, 4 vols., The Hague 1990.

V.W. van Gogh, 'Theo van Gogh without Vincent,' *Art News* 52 (1953), pp. 24-29 and 63.

Cécile Goldscheider, *Auguste Rodin:*

catalogue raisonné de l'oeuvre sculpté, Paris 1989.
Edmond and Jules de Goncourt, *Journal: mémoires de la vie littéraire*, 3 vols., Paris 1989.
Carlos Gonzales, 'Marià Fortuny i Marsal: biographical notes,' exhib. cat. *Marià Fortuny, 1838–1874*, Madrid (Fundación Caja de Pensiones) 1989, pp. 31-51.
Johan Gram, 'De kunstverzameling Vincent van Gogh in Pulchri Studio,' *Haagsche Stemmen* 2 (1989), pp. 371-82.
Christopher Gray, *Sculpture and ceramics of Paul Gauguin*, Baltimore 1963.
Nicolas Green, 'Circuits of production, circuits of consumption: the case of mid-nineteenth century French art dealing,' *Art Journal* 48 (Spring 1989), pp. 29-34.
W. Jos de Gruyter, 'Theo and Vincent van Gogh,' *Mededelingen van de Dienst van Schone Kunsten der Gemeente 's-Gravenhage* 8 (1953), pp. 2-5.

H

Just Havelaar, *Vincent van Gogh*, Amsterdam 1929.
Robert Hellebranth, *Charles-François Daubigny, 1817–1878*, Monges 1976.
Robert L. Herbert, 'Millet reconsidered,' *Museum Studies. The Art Institute of Chicago* 1 (1966), p. 59.
Sjraar van Heugten, *Vincent van Gogh: drawings. The early years, 1880–1883*, Bussum 1996.
Jan Hulsker, 'What Theo really thought of Vincent,' *Vincent: Bulletin of the Rijksmuseum Vincent van Gogh* 3 (1974), no. 2, pp. 2-28.
Jan Hulsker, *Vincent and Theo van Gogh: a dual biography*, Ann Arbor 1990.
Jan Hulsker, 'De Van Goghs en de Bongers,' *Jong Holland* 12 (1996), no. 2, pp. 44-53.
Jan Hulsker, *The new complete Van Gogh: paintings, drawings, sketches*, Amsterdam & Philadelphia 1996.
Constance Cain Hungerford, 'Meissonier and the founding of the Société Nationale des Beaux-Arts,' *Art Journal* 48 (Spring 1989), pp. 71-77.

I

J.J. Isaacson, 'Uit de schilderswereld: Theodorus van Gogh,' *De Portefeuille* 12 (7 February 1891), p. 573.

J

Lilli Jampoller, 'Theo van Gogh and Camille Pissarro: correspondence and an exhibition,' *Simiolus* 16 (1986), pp. 50-61.
Lilli Jampoller, 'Theo and Vincent as art collectors,' in Evert van Uitert and Michael Hoyle (eds.), *The Rijksmuseum Vincent van Gogh*, Amsterdam 1987, pp. 30-37.
Robert Jensen, *Marketing modernism in fin-de-siècle Europe*, Princeton 1994.
Lee Johnson, *The paintings of Eugène Delacroix: a critical catalogue*, 2 vols., Oxford 1981.
Joop M. Joosten, 'De eerste kennismaking met het werk van Vincent van Gogh in Nederland,' *Museumjournaal* 14 (1969), pp. 154-57.
Maurice Joyant, *Henri de Toulouse-Lautrec, 1864–1901: peintre*, Paris 1926.

K

Richard Kendall, exhib. cat. *Degas: beyond impressionism*, London (National Gallery) 1996.
G. Kraus, *De verhouding van Theo en Vincent van Gogh*, Amsterdam 1954.

L

Hélène Lafont-Couturier (ed.), *Etat des lieux*, Bordeaux 1994.
Sylvian Lecombre, *Ossip Zadkine: l'oeuvre sculpté*, Paris 1994.
Fred Leeman, 'Van Goghs posthume roem in de Lage Landen,' exhib. cat. *Vincent van Gogh en de moderne kunst 1890–1914*, Amsterdam (Van Gogh Museum) & Essen (Museum Folkwang) 1990-91, pp. 162-81.
Fred Leeman and Hanna Pennock, *Museum Mesdag: catalogue of paintings and drawings*, Amsterdam & Zwolle 1996.
Ronald de Leeuw and Fieke Pabst, 'Le carnet d'adresses de Theo van Gogh,' exhib. cat. *Van Gogh à Paris*, Paris (Musée d'Orsay) 1988, pp. 348-69.
Paul-André Lemoisne, *Degas et son oeuvre*, 5 vols., Paris 1946-49.
Miriam Levin, *Republican art and ideology in late–19th century France*, Ann Arbor 1986.
Alfred de Lostalot, 'Exposition des oeuvres de M. Claude Monet,' *Gazette des Beaux-Arts* 2 (27 April 1883), pp. 342-48.
A.[lfred] de L.[ostalot], 'Exposition des Aquarellistes Français,' *La Chronique des Arts* (8 February 1890), p. 44.
A.[lfred] de L.[ostalot], 'Concours et expositions,' *La Chronique des Arts* (30 May 1891), p. 170.
The diary of George A. Lucas: an American art agent in Paris, 1857–1909, ed. Lillian M.C. Randall, 2 vols., Princeton 1979.

M

Patricia Mainardi, *The end of the Salon: art and the state in the early Third Republic*, Cambridge, MA 1993.
K.E. Maison, *Honoré Daumier: catalogue raisonné of the paintings, watercolours and drawings*, San Francisco 1996.
Correspondance Mallarmé-Whistler, ed. Carl Paul Barbier, Paris 1964.
G.J.A. Manders, *Geboorte-akte en doopcel van het Van Gogh-monument te Zundert*, Zundert 1964.
G.J.A. Manders, 'Ten Geleide,' in Mark Edo Tralbaut, *De gebroeders Van Gogh*, Zundert 1964, pp. 5-38.
H. Marriott, 'Exposition de Claude Monet,' *Le Journal des Arts* 5 (6 March 1883), p. 2.
Alexis Martin, *Paris: promenades dans les vingt arrondissements*, Paris 1889.
Masque de Satin, 'Petits échos,' *La Vie Moderne* 10 (10 June 1888), p. 367.
Michiel van der Mast and Charles Dumas, exhib. cat. *Van Gogh en Den Haag*, Zwolle 1990.
C.M.[auclair], 'Beaux-arts,' *La Revue Indépendante* (December 1891), p. 429.
Camille Mauclair, *Albert Besnard: l'homme et l'oeuvre*, Paris 1914.
Charles Mauron, *Vincent et Théo van Gogh: une symbiose*, Amsterdam 1953.
Julius Meier-Graefe, 'Vincent und Theo,' *Der Neue Mercur* 3 (1919), pp. 36-77.

Julius Meier-Graefe, *Het leven van Vincent van Gogh*, Amsterdam 1921.

Julius Meier-Graefe, *Vincent*, 2 vols., Munich 1921.

Michel Melot, 'Daumier and art history: aesthetic judgement/political judgement,' *Oxford Art Journal* 11 (1988), pp. 3-24.

Jean Menaud, *Nous, Théo et Vincent van Gogh*, Paris 1987.

Jan Meyers, *De jonge Vincent*, Amsterdam 1989.

Pierre Miquel, *Eugène Isabey, 1803–1886: la marine au XIX-siècle*, Maurs-la-Jolie 1980.

Octave Mirbeau, 'Notes sur l'art: Degas,' *La France* (15 November 1884).

Octave Mirbeau, 'Vincent van Gogh,' *L'Echo de Paris* (31 March 1891).

Octave Mirbeau, *Des artistes*, 2 vols., Paris 1922.

Elizabeth Mongan, Eberhard W. Kornfeld and Harold Joachim, *Paul Gauguin: catalogue raisonné of his prints*, Berne 1988.

G. Monnier, *Musée du Louvre, Cabinet des dessins Musée d'Orsay. Pastels du XIXe siècle*, Paris 1985.

The correspondance of Berthe Morisot, ed. Denis Rouart, London 1986.

N

Linda Nochlin, 'The de-politicization of Gustave Courbet: transformation and rehabilitation under the Third Republic,' *October* 22 (1982), pp. 65-78.

Monique Nonne, 'Les marchands de van Gogh,' exhib. cat. *Van Gogh à Paris*, Paris (Musée d'Orsay) 1988, pp. 330-47.

P

JoAnne Paradise, *Gustave Geoffroy and the criticism of painting*, New York 1985.

G. Pelea, 'Chronique de l'Hôtel Drouot,' *Le Courrier de l'Art* 8 (25 May 1888), p. 168.

Monique Le Pelley Fonteney, *Léon Augustin Lhermitte (1844–1925): catalogue raisonné*, Paris 1991.

Ronald Pickvance, 'Henry Hill: an untypical Victorian collector,' *Apollo* 76 (December 1962), pp. 789-91.

Ronald Pickvance, exhib. cat. *Van Gogh in Arles*, New York (The Metropolitan Museum of Art) 1984.

Ronald Pickvance, exhib. cat. *Van Gogh in Saint-Rémy and Auvers*, New York (The Metropolitan Museum of Art) 1986-87.

Ronald Pickvance (ed.), *'A great artist is dead': letters of condolence on Vincent van Gogh's death*, Zwolle 1992.

Correspondance de Camille Pissarro, ed. Janine Bailly-Herzberg, 5 vols., Paris 1988.

Joachim Pissarro, exhib. cat. *Monet and the Mediterranean*, Forth Worth (Kimbell Art Museum) & Brooklyn (The Brooklyn Museum of Art) 1997-98.

The letters of Lucien to Camille Pissarro, 1883–1903, ed. Anne Thorold, Cambridge 1993.

Ludovic Rodo Pissarro and Lionello Venturi, *Camille Pissarro: son art et son oeuvre*, 2 vols., San Francisco 1989 [Paris 1939].

Vincent Pomarède, 'La collection des peintures,' exhib. cat. *De Corot aux impressionistes: donations Moreau-Nélaton*, Paris (Grand Palais) 1991, pp. 41–134.

Q

E.[lisabeth] H.[uberta] du Quesne-Van Gogh, *Vincent van Gogh: persoonlijke herinneringen aangaande een kunstenaar*, Baarn 1910.

R

J-F.Raffaëlli – Octave Mirbeau: correspondance, ed. Pierre Michel, Tusson 1993.

Charlotte van Rappard-Boon, Willem van Gullik and Keiko van Bremen-Ito, *Catalogue of the Van Gogh Museum's collection of Japanese prints*, Amsterdam & Zwolle 1991.

H. Reece, *Vincent: a biographical study*, London 1922.

Pierre-Lin Renié, 'Goupil et Cie à l'ère industrielle. La photographie appliquée à la reproduction des oeuvres d'art,' in Hélène Lafont-Couturier (ed.), *Etat des lieux*, Bordeaux 1994, pp. 89–114.

John Rewald, 'Theo van Gogh, Goupil and the impressionists,' *Gazette des Beaux-Arts* 81 (January-February 1973), pp. 1–108.

John Rewald, *Studies in post-impressionism*, London 1986.

John Rewald, *The paintings of Paul Cézanne: a catalogue raisonné*, New York 1996.

A. Robaut, *L'oeuvre de Corot*, 5 vols., Paris 1904-06

L. Roelandt, *Vincent van Gogh et son frère Théo*, Paris 1957.

Y. Rosenberg and T. Kōdera (eds.), *The mythology of Vincent van Gogh*, Tokyo & Amsterdam 1993.

Denis Rouart and Daniel Wildenstein, *Edouard Manet: catalogue raisonné*, 2 vols., Lausanne & Paris 1975.

Francis Roze, 'Edouard Detaille et l'Armée française,' *Paris Illustrée* 91 (28 September 1888), pp. 686-97.

'Lettres de Theo van Rysselberghe à Octave Maus (ed. M.-J. Chartrain-Hebbelinck and Ph. Mertens),' *Bulletin des Musées Royaux des Beaux-Arts de Belgique* 1-2 (1966), pp. 59–112.

S

Rémy G. Saisselin, *Bricobracomania: the bourgeois and the bibelot*, London 1985.

Barbara Schinman Fields, *Jean-François Raffaëlli (1850–1924): the naturalist artist*, Ann Arbor 1984.

Robert Schmit and M. Schmit, *Stanislas Lépine, 1835–1892: catalogue raisonné de l'oeuvre peint*, Paris 1993.

Andrée Sfeir-Semmler, *Die Maler am Pariser Salon 1791–1880*, Frankfurt, New York & Paris 1992.

Armand Silvestre, 'Le monde des Arts. Exposition du Cercle de l'Union Artistique,' *La Vie Moderne* 5 (17 February 1883), pp. 107 and 110.

Charles Sterling and Margaretta M. Salinger, *French paintings: a catalogue of the collection of the Metropolitan Museum of Art*, 3 vols., New York 1967.

Chris Stolwijk, *Uit de schilderswereld: Nederlandse kunstschilders in de tweede helft van de negentiende eeuw*, Leiden 1998.

Chris Stolwijk, '"Our crown and our

honour and our joy": Theo van Gogh's early years,' *Van Gogh Museum Journal* (1997-98), pp. 42-57.

V.G. Swanson, *Lawrence Alma-Tadema: the biography and catalogue raisonné of the paintings of Sir Lawrence Alma-Tadema*, London 1990.

T

P.J.J. van Thiel, *et al.*, *All the paintings of the Rijksmuseum*, Amsterdam 1976.

Richard Thomson, 'Degas's nudes at the 1886 impressionist exhibition,' *Gazette des Beaux-Arts* 108 (November 1986), pp. 187-90.

Richard Thomson, 'Impressionism and drawing in the 1880s,' exhib. cat. *Impressionist drawings in British collections*, Oxford (Ashmolean Museum), Manchester (City Art Gallery) & Glasgow (The Burrell Collection) 1986, pp. 23-51.

Richard Thomson, *Degas: the nudes*, London 1988.

Richard Thomson, *Camille Pissarro: impressionism, landscape and rural labour*, London 1990.

Richard Thomson, 'Illustration, caricature and the type,' exhib. cat. *Toulouse-Lautrec*, London (Hayward Gallery) & Paris (Grand Palais) 1991-92, pp. 174-222.

Richard Thomson, *Edgar Degas: Waiting*, Malibu 1995.

Louis van Tilborgh, '"A kind of Bible": the collection of prints and illustrations,' in Evert van Uitert and Michael Hoyle (eds.), *The Rijksmuseum Vincent van Gogh*, Amsterdam 1987, pp. 38-44.

Gary Tinterow, 'Mirbeau on Degas: a little known article of 1884,' *The Burlington Magazine* 130 (March 1988), pp. 229-30.

Gary Tinterow, 'III. 1881-1890,' exhib. cat. *Degas*, Paris (Grand Palais), Ottawa (National Gallery of Canada) & New York (The Metropolitan Museum of Art) 1988-89, pp. 363-480.

The letters of Henri de Toulouse-Lautrec, ed. Herbert Schimmel, Oxford 1991.

Mark Edo Tralbaut, *Vincent, Theo, Johanna*, Amsterdam 1953.

Mark Edo Tralbaut, *De gebroeders Van Gogh*, Zundert 1964.

U

Evert van Uitert, 'De legendevorming te bevorderen: notities over de Vincent van Gogh mythe,' exhib. cat. *Rond de roem van Vincent van Gogh*, Amsterdam (Van Gogh Museum) 1977, pp. 15-27.

Evert van Uitert and Michael Hoyle (eds.), *The Rijksmuseum Vincent van Gogh*, Amsterdam 1987.

V

Lionel Venturi (ed.), *Les archives de l'impressionisme*, 2 vols., New York & Paris 1939.

Jan Veth, 'Th. van Gogh,' *De Amsterdammer* (2 February 1891), p. 3.

P.H.A. Voskuil, 'Het medisch dossier van Theo van Gogh,' *Nederlands Tijdschrift voor Geneeskunde* 136 (1990), pp. 1777-79.

W

Martha Ward, 'Impressionist installations and private exhibitions,' *Art Bulletin* 73 (December 1991), pp. 599-622.

Martha Ward, *Pissarro, neo-impressionism and the spaces of the avant-garde*, Chicago & London 1995.

Bogomila Welsh-Ovcharov, *The early work of Charles Angrand and his contact with Vincent van Gogh*, Utrecht & The Hague 1971.

Bogomila Welsh-Ovcharov, *Vincent van Gogh: his Paris period, 1886–1888*, Utrecht & The Hague 1976.

Harrison C. White and Cynthia A. White, *Canvases and careers: institutional change in the French painting world*, Chicago 1993 [New York 1965].

Linda Whiteley, 'Accounting for tastes,' *Oxford Art Journal* 2 (1979), pp. 25-28.

Alec Wildenstein, *Odilon Redon: catalogue raisonné de l'oeuvre peint et dessiné*, 3 vols., Paris 1992-96.

Daniel Wildenstein, *Claude Monet: biographie et catalogue raisonné*, 5 vols., Lausanne 1974-91.

Georges Wildenstein, *Gauguin*, Paris 1964.

Fronia E. Wissman, *Bouguereau*, San Francisco 1996.

Albert Wolff, *1886: Figaro-Salon*, Paris 1886.

Albert Wolff, 'Exposition Internationale,' *Le Figaro* (19 June 1886).

Z

Carol M. Zemel, *The formation of a legend: Van Gogh criticism, 1890–1920*, Ann Arbor 1980.

Emile Zola. Le bon combat: de Courbet aux impressionistes, ed. Jean-Paul Bouillon, Paris 1974.

Index

Colophon

This book is published in conjunction with the exhibition *Theo van Gogh (1857–1891): art dealer, collector and brother of Vincent*, organised by the Van Gogh Museum, Amsterdam (24 June - 5 September 1999) and the Réunion des Musées Nationaux/ Musée d'Orsay, Paris (27 September 1999 – 9 January 2000).

NUGI 921,642

ISBN ENG HB 90 400 9363 6
(hardcover)

ISBN NL PB 90 400 9359 8
(paperback)

The exhibition at the Van Gogh Museum, Amsterdam, is sponsored by:

TPG
TNT POST GROUP

Scholarly committee
Andreas Blühm, John Leighton, Henri Loyrette, Monique Nonne, Chris Stolwijk, Richard Thomson

Research coordinator
Chris Stolwijk

Registration
Martine Kilburn, Aly Noordermeer (Amsterdam), Anne Fréling (Paris)

Authors
Sjraar van Heugten, Chris Stolwijk, Richard Thomson

Editor
Rachel Esner

Translators
Michelle Hendriks, Wendie Shaffer, Kate Williams

Secretaries
Sandra Sihan, Sara Verboven, Roelie Zwikker

Design
Studio Roozen, Amsterdam

Publisher
Waanders Publishers, Zwolle

Printer
Waanders Printers, Zwolle

Insurance
AON Artscope Nederland, Amsterdam, fine art insurance

Photo credits
Photographs were supplied by the owners.
With special thanks to:
Christie's, London **57**
The Getty Research Institute for the History of Art and the Humanities **59**
Thijs Quispel **1**, **14**, **27**, **39**, **40**, **71**, **122**, **123**, **144**, **147**, **179**
Réunion des Musées Nationaux **81**
Rijksmuseum, Amsterdam **187**
Sotheby's, London **106**

Front cover
Theo van Gogh, Van Gogh Museum, Amsterdam [Vincent van Gogh Foundation]
Back cover
Edgar Degas, *Woman seated beside a vase of flowers (Madame Paul Valpiçon?)*, The Metropolitan Museum of Art, New York, H.O. Havemeyer Collection
Frontispiece
Meijer de Haan, *Theo van Gogh*, 1889, Van Gogh Museum, Amsterdam [Vincent van Gogh Foundation]
Chapter dividers
Vincent van Gogh, *Branches of an almond tree in blossom*, 1890, Van Gogh Museum, Amsterdam [Vincent van Gogh Foundation], pp. 12-13 (detail)
Edgar Degas, *Woman seated beside a vase of flowers (Madame Paul Valpiçon?)*, The Metropolitan Museum of Art, New York, H.O. Havemeyer Collection, pp. 58-59 (detail)
Ernest Quost, *Garden with hollyhock*, c. 1881–90, Van Gogh Museum, Amsterdam [Vincent van Gogh Foundation], pp. 150-51 (detail)
Claude Monet, *Rain, Etretat*, 1886, Nasjonalgalleriet, Oslo, pp. 180-81 (detail)